Reincarnation
The Phoenix Fire Mystery

"Though all dies, and even gods die, yet all death is but a phoenix fire death, and new birth into the Greater and Better."

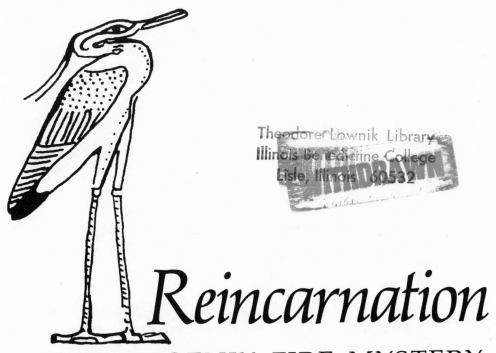

Reincarnation

THE PHOENIX FIRE MYSTERY

*An East-West Dialogue on Death
and Rebirth from the Worlds of
Religion, Science, Psychology,
Philosophy, Art, and Literature,
and from Great Thinkers of the
Past and Present*

*Compiled and Edited by
Joseph Head and S. L. Cranston*

JULIAN PRESS/CROWN PUBLISHERS, INC.
NEW YORK

Printed in the United States of America
Published simultaneously in Canada by General Publishing Company Limited

Library of Congress Cataloging in Publication Data
Main entry under title:

Reincarnation: the phoenix fire mystery.

 Includes bibliographical references and index.
 1. Reincarnation—Addresses, essays, lectures.
I. Head, Joseph. II. Cranston, S. L.
BL515.R43   133.9'013   76-30439
ISBN 0-517-52893-2

Acknowledgment is gratefully made as follows for permission to reprint copyrighted material. Other acknowledgments may be found at the back of the book.

Basic Books, New York, and Herbert Fingarette. *The Self in Transformation* by Herbert Fingarette, © 1963 by Basic Books, Inc.

Thomas Y. Crowell Co., New York. *The Living Reed* by Pearl Buck, copyright © 1963 by Pearl S. Buck, with permission of John Day Company, publisher.

Doubleday & Co., Inc., New York. *The Summing Up* by W. Somerset Maugham, copyright, 1938, by W. Somerset Maugham; *The Sufis* by Idries Shah, © 1964 by Idries Shah; "The Gods of the Copybook Headings," from *Rudyard Kipling's Verse* (confirmed by Hodder & Stoughton Ltd., London).

Farrar, Straus & Giroux, New York. *Poems by Herman Hesse,* translator James Wright, copyright © 1970 by James Wright. German text copyright 1953 by Suhrkamp Verlag, Berlin.

Grosset & Dunlap, Inc., New York. *Marilyn* by Norman Mailer, copyright © by Alskog, Inc., and Norman Mailer.

Harper & Row, New York. *Gandhi's Letters to a Disciple* by Mohandas K. Gandhi, copyright, 1950, by Harper & Brothers; *Blake's Humanism* by John Beer, © John Beer 1968, published by Barnes & Noble, New York; *From the Unconscious to the Conscious* by Gustave Geley; *The Magic of Findhorn* by Paul Hawken, copyright 1975 by Paul Hawken; *The Perennial Philosophy* by Aldous Huxley; *The Imprisoned Splendor* by Raynor C. Johnson; *Sweet Rocket* by Mary Johnston; *Born Twice* by Edward Ryall, copyright © 1974 by Edward Ryall, introduction and appendix copyright © 1974 by Ian Stevenson; *The Religions of Man* by Huston Smith; *Zen Buddhism and Psychoanalysis* by Suzuki, Fromm, and de Martino.

J. B. Lippincott Company, Philadelphia. *Meditation, The Inward Art,* by Bradford Smith, copyright © 1963, 1962 by Bradford Smith.

The Macmillan Company, New York. *Jonathan Livingston Seagull* by Richard Bach, copyright © 1970 by Richard D. Bach; *The Story of the Faith* by W. A. Gifford, copyright, 1946, by The Macmillan Company; "A Creed" from *Collected Poems* by John Masefield, copyright, 1912, by The Macmillan Company, renewed 1940 by John Masefield; "A Prelude and a Song" from

CONTENTS

PREFACE

Brooding over the pain of his life and the inevitability of death, Job cried out, "If a man die, shall he live again?"

This question, recurring today with fresh insistence, has not been taken seriously for generations, even centuries, in the Western world. Whatever Job meant by it, the query was demoted to the status of religious rhetoric belonging to the prescientific age, having only literary or antiquarian interest. Not a fancied life after death, but life here and now has been the area of both practical and intellectual concern. For historical reasons whose validity is only now being questioned, the most influential thinkers of the nineteenth and twentieth centuries adopted skepticism and denial as the foundation of their philosophic outlook, which they regarded as soundly based on an impartial, scientific view, free, at last, from the seductions of sentiment and the deceptions of priestly authority. Modern ideas about life and death were shaped much as Bertrand Russell said some fifty years ago (in his introduction to Lange's *History of Materialism*): "As a rule, the materialistic dogma has not been set up by men who loved dogma, but by men who felt that nothing less definite would enable them to fight the dogmas they disliked."

Until recently the problem of man and the cosmos has been rigidly regarded in terms of two options, two alternatives. Biologist Jacques Monod, the famed author of *Chance and Necessity,* makes this plain in an interview.[1] He was asked: "You write that man was the product of pure chance. How do you come to that conclusion?" He replied: "Well, it's relatively simple in principle, unless we accept the pure creationist view of the origins of the universe. Unless we do that, we have to find some natural interpretation."

The creationist view poses insuperable difficulties for most scientists. Monod admits, however, that the "naturalistic" concept of blind matter as the only reality has its problems too. The core problem of biology, he says, is how to account for a biosphere full of systems that behave as if they had a project and a purpose, existing in a world devoid of a project and a purpose. His own answer and that of the school he represents is "a pure postulate," he acknowledges, "because you can't prove that this is right." Simply put, it regards the origin of life as an "improbable chemical accident," which perpetuated itself in more and more complex organisms through a series of additional accidents. Viewing all this objectively, Joseph Wood Krutch once asked: "But is not the assumption of an 'improbable chemical accident' which results ultimately in something capable of discussing the nature of 'improbable chemical accidents' a staggering one? Is it not indeed preposterous?''[2]

Today the scientific—or scientistic—claim that "matter is all" is being bombarded from all sides. The scientists, people say to themselves, have been wrong in so many ways: They were wrong in making the Bomb, wrong in making technology and industry irresponsibly powerful, they are wrong in wanting to tinker with man's biological endowment, and perhaps they are wrong, too, in insisting that what cultural historians call "mechanism" and "reductionism" provide the only basis for understanding both nature and human life. So speculation and deep wondering about alternative philosophies are going on at a furious rate. Books and magazines are filled with these forays into ancient ideas and old religious beliefs, as well as with modern guesses about outer space and what may be going on there. Notably, some of these inquiries and reflections about other sources of meaning are pursued by distinguished researchers—thoughtful individuals and pioneers in both the hard and the social sciences.

We may not know all there is to know about what really prompts great changes in the outlook of human beings, considered as whole societies, but there can be little doubt that the present is a time of rapid and far-reaching change in the feelings, assumptions, and thinking of men and women everywhere. Job's question now has a living currency.

"If a man die, shall he live again?"

The impetus of unbelief has worn itself out after three hundred years. The signs of this change make an embarrassment of riches.

Among eminent scientists who have expressed themselves, giving voice to the new spirit, Dr. Lewis Thomas, a physician and medical researcher, writes in *The Lives of a Cell:* "Death on a grand scale does not bother us . . . We can sit around a dinner table and discuss war, involving 60 million volatilized human deaths, as though we were talking about bad weather; we can watch abrupt bloody death every day, in color, on films and television, without blinking back a tear. It is when the numbers of dead are very small, and very close, that we begin to think in scurrying circles. At the very center of the problem is the naked cold deadness of one's own self, the only reality in nature of which we can have absolute certainty, and it is unmentionable, unthinkable.'' Dr. Thomas, however, expresses surprise at his own feeling that "dying is an all-right thing to do.'' The dying, he learned from experience, accept death serenely, without fear. Most of his patients "appeared to be preparing themselves with equanimity for death, as though intuitively familiar with the business.'' Death, he concluded, is not evil but *natural*. And now, for him, there comes a logical question:

> But even so, if the transformation is a coordinated, integrated physiologic process in its initial, local stages, there is still that permanent vanishing of

consciousness to be accounted for. Are we to be stuck forever with this problem? Where on earth does it go? Is it simply stopped dead in its tracks, lost in humus, wasted? Considering the tendency in nature to find uses for complex and intricate mechanisms, this seems to me unnatural. I prefer to think of it as somehow separated off at the filaments of its attachment, and then drawn like an easy breath back into the membrane of its origin, a fresh memory for a biospherical nervous system, but I have no data on the matter.[3]

Are there, indeed, "data" on such matters? What is the evidence bearing on the question of a life after death?

This anthology on reincarnation gives access to one sort of data concerned with transcendental questions or mysteries. First, it presents an extraordinary weight of testimony on the subject, showing what distinguished thinkers of the past have thought and said. And second, it illustrates—space allowing— *how* they thought about immortality, and why they chose rebirth as the mode of human experience of eternity.

Our book does not seek to encourage believers. Emulating its contributors, however imperfectly, it invites consideration of an idea—of ideas—that have found hospitality in the greatest minds, the most powerful and influential philosophers of history. These thinkers did not want believers, but listeners who might be drawn to undertake independent journeys of thought similar to their own. There is much evidence in this book of the fact that rebirth or reincarnation is an intuitive feeling as much as an idea, known by countless peoples living often in remote quarters of the globe, far removed from their more "civilized" brothers. And also much evidence that this conception, as Schopenhauer said, "presents itself as the natural conviction of man whenever he reflects at all in an unprejudiced manner." The themes of this volume are virtually timeless—they flow through all history, now on the surface, now submerged and almost forgotten, but constant in meaning, eternal in relevance, with endlessly repeated questions and answers. Read and reflected upon, they seem a great dialogue between Nature and Man, a Cosmic Catechism.

There may still be those—a diminishing group of objectors—who will say that reincarnation is a "romantic" notion, although in the later chapters a surprising number of noted scientists and psychologists will be found to view it in quite another light. Romanticism may have its excesses, but hardly anyone who reads the selections from the romantic poets would want to be without them. Is it conceivable that romantic writers have nothing to say on the side of truth? They may not tell the whole truth, but then, who does? And what intelligent reader would be foolish enough to require it? In matters of this sort, if the reader contributes nothing himself, he can find nothing out. Such, it begins to appear, is the nature of transcendental and subjective inquiry.

Would there be proper hardheadedness in such a science? Again, a sufficiency among our contributors gives answer to this question. Many of them are disciplined thinkers; indeed, they are among the thinkers from whom we have learned the very meaning of logic, of intellectual discipline, and to whom we may with profit return to school.

There are right and wrong ways to be hardheaded, just as there are right and wrong ways to be tender-minded. Our rich inheritance of plays on words makes this clear. If doubt, as someone has said, is the beginning of wisdom, skepticism, Emerson declared, is slow suicide. And who is wise enough to give specific advice on how to aim either doubt or acceptance and affirmation? It is enough to point out that such decisions must always be made, and that wisdom is the art of choosing between faculties of mind that come in ambiguous pairs.

Our book, however, is obviously on the side of affirmation, although the voice of the dissenter will also be heard. It explores a treasury of thought declaring that we live in a universe of hope and promise. Most of its contributors are on the side of life. And surely the time has come for us to learn—once again, and in our own language—how to take the side of life. Too long has man been the producer of deserts, depressions, and downright destruction. Too long has he worshiped at the exclusive shrine of the second law of thermodynamics. There are better litanies, stronger credos, more generous philosophies than the polemics of theology-hating materialists who thought they must choose between a tyrannical Jehovah, and Lucretius's atoms and the void. The harvest of negation is in, and it does not nourish either our bodies or our souls.

All this has been said—and said with reach of vision, depth of feeling, and measured reason—by scores of writers in our time. It is the common understanding, now, of the meaning of the age, and has been well and briefly put by a Catalan writer in an essay that calls the turn and invites to such considerations as are presented here. Luis Racionero might sound oracular, save for the fact that he has the support—the worldwide support—of a new generation of authors and thinkers:

> The Renaissance was aborted by Descartes, the egghead, and by a cold museum science that analyzes, reasons, kills and dissects. It will go on and on, this abortion and defeat, if we listen only to Sartre, to Monod or Ionesco. They are making the end; and in order to make it they had to be heard. So they have helped us, these elder brothers; but they help no longer, for the time has come to empower a fresh imagination. . . .
>
> In the beginning is vision—the shimmering formative power which shapes images within the clay of the brain, where, finding multiple mirrors, we contemplate and understand. Then comes the act—the unexpected power of inspiration which realizes vision by transforming it into action. So history is written, materializing visionary states of mind, forging the still uncreated conscience of the race.

> The vision must be our own, or we shall remain slaves to the dreams of other men. So we shall set aside logic-chopping, undertaking to create. . . . Out of the end of a time we must make a new path to the hidden meaning of things, and choose a new name for the mystery—letting go the dead letter. . . . Once again there must be Apocalypsis and Palingenesis—death and rebirth.[4]

It is even likely that the reader, brought to care about such matters by this appeal to the human spirit, and after investigating the lines of thought unfolded in the present volume, will find himself agreeing with Macneile Dixon (our most quoted contributor), who, in reply to skeptics who thought reincarnation incredible or irrational, wrote in 1937: "Rational? What could be less rational than that the pen and paper should be more enduring than the saint, that we should have Shakespeare's handwriting but not himself? Raphael's pictures but not the mind that conceived them?"

"Many things are hard to believe," says Dixon, "and a future life, some say, is quite incredible, and the mere thought of it a sort of madness. But what hinders if we have already found a present? Well, I should myself put the matter rather differently. The present life is incredible, a future credible. 'Not to be twice-born, but once-born is wonderful.' To be alive, actually existing, to have emerged from darkness and silence, to be here today is certainly incredible."

> A future life would be a miracle, and you find it difficult to believe in miracles? I, on the contrary, find it easy. They are to be expected. The starry worlds in time and space, the pageant of life, the processes of growth and reproduction, the instincts of animals, the inventiveness of nature, they are all utterly unbelievable, miracles piled upon miracles. If there be a skeptical star I was born under it, yet I have lived all my days in complete astonishment.

Today another cause for puzzled wonderment exists. We refer to the experiments in the realm of parapsychology and extrasensory perception conducted by many scientific institutions. One of the renowned workers in this field, Dr. J. B. Rhine, longtime director of the Parapsychology Laboratory at Duke University, has on occasion applied the results of years of exacting research to the problem of survival after death. Writing in the *Journal of Parapsychology,* he remarked that "a type of lawfulness peculiar to mind and contrary to physics is increasingly evident in the extra-sensory perception and psycho-kinetic researches."

> Without these researches and with only the facts of the biological sciences to go on, it is hard to see how any kind of immortality would be possible. The brain-dominating, or cerebro-centric view of personality, would not allow it. In that view the brain is primarily and completely the center of man. But if the psyche is a force and a factor in its own right, with laws and ways peculiarly non-physical, the survival hypothesis has at least a logical chance.

If the mind is different from the physical brain system, it would have a different destiny, could perhaps be independent, separable, unique. This degree of simple possibility must not, of course, be mistaken for probability; but the mere logical possibility is itself very important.

Dr. Rhine adds: "Is it not then provocative, to say the least, to discover certain capacities of mind that appear to operate beyond the boundaries of space and time within which our sensorial, bodily system has to live and move? Here, surely, if ever, 'hope sees a star' and the urge toward an inquiry into the question of survival receives valuable impetus and encouragement."[5]

Jung spoke of Rhine's noted work *The Reach of the Mind* as "one of the greatest contributions to the knowledge of the unconscious processes."[6] "Parapsychology" is referred to in the volume as that "heretical, controversial, pioneering branch of research that is still clamoring for due recognition at the gates of conservative, official, circumspect science."[7] It took ninety years of such research for the gates to finally open. In 1969 the American Association for the Advancement of Science decided to recognize parapsychology as a science in its own right. It was anthropologist Margaret Mead's passionate speech to the A.A.A.S. that prompted a 6 to 1 vote in favor of admitting the Parapsychological Association to membership. "The whole history of scientific advance," she said, "is full of scientists investigating phenomena that the Establishment did not believe were there. I submit that we vote in favor of this association's work."[8]

As to the phenomena of life and death, we need no assurance that *they* are "really there." The question that begs answer, and to which we now turn in the pages of this book, is: Can we have any assurance that *after* life and death, something is "really there," something that in due time will again be "here"?

And so we are brought face to face with Job's searing question, raised by *Reincarnation: The Phoenix Fire Mystery* in the beginning: "If a man die, shall he live again?"

EDITORS' NOTE

Surfacely viewed, this volume may appear to be a reference book, or an encyclopedia, containing a great mass of opinions on reincarnation. This "scholarly" approach may be useful in pursuing a cold, intellectual analysis of the subject, but it is hardly that of the editors. While technically the volume is called an *anthology*—a beautiful word from the Greek, meaning a gathering of flowers, or a choice selection of writings—it is more a symphony of ideas. When the editors first began their researches they took the eclectic approach, to be sure, but what developed was quite surprising. Instead of a dissonance of conflicting and confusing opinions, undertones and overtones of harmony seemed to pervade and unify much of the material. Perhaps the reader will hear this too.

The volume could also be called a journey, or even a pilgrimage. Outwardly, it is a historical passage in time and space through the cultures of antiquity up to the present, but inwardly it may become a journey toward self-discovery. An old Buddhist proverb tells the pilgrim: "Thou canst not travel on the Path before thou hast become that Path itself." Such a Path is mentioned in all mystic works. As Krishna says in the *Dnyaneshvari:* "When this Path is beheld . . . whether one sets out to the bloom of the east, or the chambers of the west, without moving, O holder of the bow, is the traveling in this road. In this Path to whatever place one would go, that place one's own self becomes."

The present work is a successor to two volumes compiled by the same editors: *Reincarnation: An East-West Anthology* (1961) and *Reincarnation in World Thought* (1967). While most people think of reincarnation as an Eastern idea, the greater portion of these volumes was devoted to revealing its long history in Western culture, religion, and civilization. This latest effort, while retaining the best of the earlier books, is a fruitage of extensive additional investigation, particularly in the field of Oriental thought, the sections on Eastern religions having been considerably expanded. Other areas have been appreciably revised and extended, and more attention has been paid to the dynamic flow of ideas and movements from era to era. In the decade since the last volume appeared, the interest in reincarnation has grown tremendously. Consequently, there is much new material to draw on. A new section has been added at the end of chapter 5, "Stories of 'Remembrances' of Past Lives."

A primary task has been to avoid the dry duplication of ideas. Thus the reader will not be listening to "more and more of the same." And even where important themes are now and then re-sounded, the contributors will usually be varying their approach. This policy has had the further advantage of keeping the work in a one-volume edition. Despite its seeming length, it is a short presentation when one considers the vast periods of time and the many civilizations traversed.

Some of the synonyms used for reincarnation may sound unfamiliar to modern ears. In Western tradition, metempsychosis, palingenesis, preexistence, transmigration, and rebirth are terms that have been used. The word "reincarnation" did not come into vogue until the French introduced it in the middle of the last century. As to "transmigration," the word has been so frequently misused to suggest the rebirth of humans into animal forms—a complete reversal of the natural evolutionary processes—that it is hardly satisfactory for general use. In the Orient the popular expressions for reincarnation are *punar-janman*, again birth, and *samsara*, the round of births and deaths.

Where the editors find it necessary to introduce selections or chapters, or survey whole areas of thought, their remarks will be enclosed in brackets. However, as these bracketed parts are often suffused with quotations on rebirth, they are to that extent very much part of the main anthological material.

To preserve the continuity of the Western half of the story, authors are presented in birth-year sequence and not according to nationality as was done in *Reincarnation: An East-West Anthology*. If there is an interest in national classifications, one need but check in the Index under such headings as American, British, Dutch, French, German, Irish, Italian, Russian, the various Scandinavian nationalities, and so on. An exception to the birth-year sequence occurs where the American transcendentalists are presented as a whole. Another occurs in the section on Ireland's literary renaissance.

Subject headings are also extensively used in the Index so that ready access may be had to material on important topics intimately related in the text to reincarnation. (See the special list at the end of the Index.) Thus, to ascertain what contributors have said on karma—a large subject in itself—check under "karma." Similarly, with such diverse topics as after-death states, art and artists, brotherhood, education, evolution, heredity, memory of past lives, music and composers, population, purpose of rebirth, suicide, wishful thinking, worlds reborn, and so forth. The references under the rather ponderous heading "Procrastination, Does Rebirth Encourage" consider the favorite objection raised by Christians to reincarnation: Will not the prospect of many lives invite individuals to postpone perpetually their salvation? Those who find difficulty in considering any religious or philosophical idea until available scientific evidence is first examined may wish to check the Index under "Scientific Research on Reincarnation."

When one looks into the many references under "Fire Symbol"—another of the Index headings—it will become apparent why the editors chose as the book's title *Reincarnation: The Phoenix Fire Mystery.* This universal myth opens the chapter "Language of Myth and Symbol," but it also appears in transfigured forms in much of the imagery used elsewhere in the selections. Incidentally, the pictured bird used in this volume is the Egyptian phoenix, known as the Benu bird, and appears in the Egyptian Book of the Dead both as a vignette and in hieroglyphic form.

Under the entry "Cycles" are indexed periodic phenomena that the authors have mentioned in connection with rebirth. Reincarnationists tend to underline the argument that if the soul exists, it is only natural for it to return because everything in nature comes and goes and comes again. So they point to the vast variety of periodicities scientists have observed and recorded, and to the poets who ever sing of life's ceaseless pulsations; of the in-breathings and out-breathings of worlds; the ebb and flow of the seas; water rising as vapor to the heavens and descending again as rain; the perpetual alternations of day and night, sleeping and waking; winter's death eternally followed by spring. How strange, they say, if man in his life processes should prove an exception!

If the presently unpopular word "man" appears rather often in the pages ahead, the editors—one of whom is a woman—feel no real need to apologize. The great classical writers did not use the expression in a narrow, masculine sense. It is a powerful term, having its origin in the root of the Sanskrit *Manas,* the Indian word for Mind or the Eternal Thinker, and it is not likely to vanish from our vocabulary. Those who find "person" a good substitute may be embarrassed to learn of its weak heritage from *persona,* the Latin word for the mask an actor wears. Another Latin-derived term, "individual," rooted in *individuus,* meaning indivisible, seems a wiser choice. But who can improve on the ringing challenge of the Delphic oracle that has resounded through the centuries: MAN, KNOW THYSELF!

A reader of our previous compilation recently wrote that "it is a book for slow reading and discussion." And we can assure the bright young person, fresh from a rapid reading course, that he will hardly get through *Reincarnation: The Phoenix Fire Mystery* in one short evening! A professor of physics, referring to our earlier work now out of print, but largely reembodied with many additions in the present, writes that he will be reading it for quite a few years to come. "I like books where you can read half a page or so and have enough material to think about for a whole day while even doing manual tasks like mowing a field or building a wall." Such books "are extremely rare," he adds.

If the compilers were the authors of the selections presented, they would be accused of self-flattery in repeating such stories. But they are only anthologists, and in their years of labor—assisted by many friends and associates—have sought to emulate the Buddhist devotees, those who "in humbleness have garnered, low confess: 'Thus have I heard.' "

The Mystery Unfolded

1 CENTRAL CHOICE BEFORE MODERN MAN

[The nineteenth-century historian H. T. Buckle declared: "If immortality be untrue, it matters little whether anything else be true or not." A century later Edmund Wilson said in skeptical counterpoint: "The knowledge that death is not so far away, that my mind and emotions and vitality will soon disappear like a puff of smoke, has the effect of making earthly affairs seem unimportant and human beings more and more ignoble. It is harder to take human life seriously, including one's own efforts and achievements."[1]

Our introductory selections from *The Human Situation*[2] by W. Macneile Dixon deal with these fundamental issues. Dixon has been named a Confucius of the West, uniting its philosophical and scientific thinking. A *New York Times* reviewer called this remarkable volume—composed of Dixon's Gifford lectures—"perhaps the most important book of its kind which the twentieth century has yet produced."]

The modern and shortest way with the soul or self is to deny it outright. Can we suppose "that a ship might be constructed of such a kind that entirely by itself, without captain or crew, it could sail from place to place for years on end, accommodating itself to varying winds, avoiding shoals, seeking a haven when necessary, and doing all that a normal ship can?" Yes, we are told, in the human body we have precisely such a ship, which handles itself admirably without captain or navigator.

You have heard of this curious doctrine, of this psychology which rejects the psyche and retains only the "ology," the science of the self without the self. Thus, in summary fashion, the great authorities deny and dispose of us, and incidentally of themselves. Where we imagined the "I" or self to be, there is only, they tell us, a series of fleeting impressions, sensations, fancies, pains and pleasures, which succeed each other with amazing rapidity, but without any entity over and above them that, as center, thinks, feels or desires. It is then a mirage or hallucination, this notion of the self. And an interesting and peculiar illusion, which till yesterday successfully played the impostor's part upon the whole human race, philosophers included. And not only so, but after this prodigious feat of deception, it laid a snare for itself and caught itself out. This illusion, the most extraordinary that ever was, discovered itself to be an illusion.

I read some time ago of a Spanish girl in England for the first time. Approaching London in the train she looked out on the sea of houses, factories and chimneys. "These people have no view," she cried, and burst into tears. To have no view, how sad a lot. A grey mist descends upon the world. Tolstoy said:

> One can go on living when one is intoxicated by life; as soon as one is sober it is impossible not to see that it is all a mere fraud. Is there any meaning in my life which will not be destroyed by the inevitable death awaiting me? I now see that if I did not kill myself it was due to some dim consciousness of the invalidity of my thoughts. I, my reason, has acknowledged life to be unreasonable. There is something wrong here.

Where lies the flaw? Not in his logic, but in his unstated premises, the assumption that we are in possession of all the relevant facts to form the judgment, that we know all we need to know to estimate the value of life.

And how grotesquely wide of the mark are they who indulge in childish chatter, babbling of the hope for a future existence as a petty, personal desire, born of selfishness. For what, to put no gloss on things, are the implications of its rejection? The story of humanity becomes the story of a long procession of sufferers, for whose suffering no justification is offered, of poor souls intellectually and morally confounded, who entered existence blind to any reason for their coming and will leave it blind, who cannot so much as conjecture their origin, or the meaning of their lives, whose elevation above the lower creatures has been their direct misfortune, their ideals an accentuation of their griefs. To live is by universal consent to travel a rough road. And how can a rough road which leads nowhere be worth the travelling? Mere living, what a profitless performance; mere painful living, what an absurd! There is then, nothing to be hoped for, nothing to be expected and nothing to be done save to await our turn to mount the scaffold and bid farewell to that colossal blunder, the much-ado-about-nothing world. And the revolt of reason against this happy consummation is labeled selfishness. What kind of selfishness is that which asks no more for oneself than for all men and creatures ever born? Let us have no more of this.

Immortality is a word which stands for the stability or permanence of that unique and precious quality we discern in the soul, which, if lost, leaves nothing worth preservation in the world. Give assurance that what death appears to proclaim is not so, and the scene is changed. The sky brightens, the door is left open for unimagined possibilities, things begin to fall into an intelligible pattern. If you have not here among men who reflect, however unwilling they are to acknowledge it, the pivot of the human situation, the question upon the answer to which all turns, I know not where to look for it.

What kind of immortality is at all conceivable? Of all doctrines of a future life, palingenesis or rebirth, which carries with it the idea of pre-existence, is by far the most ancient and most widely held, "the only system to which," as said Hume, "philosophy can hearken."

Our interest in the future, how strange it is if we can never hope to see the future. That interest rarely seems to desert us, and in itself appears inexplicable were we not possessed of an intuition which tells us that we shall have a part in it, that in some sense it already belongs to us, that we should bear it continually in mind, since it will be ours. So closely are all human ideals associated with futurity that, in the absence of the faith that man is an immortal being, it seems doubtful whether they could ever have come to birth. "In the further depths of our being we are secretly conscious of our share in the inexhaustible spring of eternity, so that we can always hope to find life in it again."

If things as they are have not a feature in common with things as they will be, we have no basis for thought at all regarding that future. As Leibniz said, "a leap from one state to another infinitely different state could not be natural." The experiences of time and of our present condition could, one feels, only be valuable in an existence not wholly unlike it; and any doctrine which insists upon a totally dissimilar existence, an indescribable spiritual life as a sequel to the present, makes of the present an insoluble enigma. [Although the idea that man returns to earth life] has for European thought a strangeness, it is in fact the most natural and easily imagined, since what has been can be again. This belief seems, indeed, to be in accordance with nature's own favorite way of thought, of which she so insistently reminds us, in her rhythms and recurrences, her cycles and revolving seasons.

According to Plato's theory of reminiscence, our present knowledge is a recollection of what was learnt or known by the soul in a previous state. You will say, it has no knowledge of its previous lives. But what man remembers every day of this life? And lost memories, as the psychologists will tell you, are recoverable. For the memory appears to be a palimpsest, from which

nothing is ever obliterated. If we have forgotten most days and incidents of
our present lives it is natural that memories of previous lives should fail us.
Yet from infancy every forgotten day and hour has added to our experiences,
to our growth and capacity, made its contribution to the mind and soul. So it
may be with former lives, each of them but a day in our past history.

It is Plato's doctrine, and none more defensible, that the soul before it
entered the realm of Becoming existed in the universe of Being. Released [at
death] from the region of time and space, it returns to its former abode into
communion with itself. After a season of quiet "alone with the Alone," of
assimilation of its earthly experiences and memories, refreshed and invigo-
rated, it is seized again by the desire for further trials of its strength, further
knowledge of the universe, the companionship of former friends, by the
desire to keep in step and on the march with the moving world. There it seeks
out and once more animates a body, the medium of communication with its
fellow travellers, and sails forth in that vessel upon a new venture in the
ocean of Becoming.

Whatever the soul may be, it is never found apart from a self. Apart from
the self, the center of everything, there is neither consciousness nor thinking.
The attempt to derive the self from atoms and the void, from space and time,
to deny it any constructive role in the system of nature, has not failed for lack
of unceasing and desperate effort. It has failed because you cannot explain
the self in terms of the not-self. The philosophies of the future will, I think,
take another and more promising way. They will allow to the self its unique
status, its standing as a factor, a primary factor and an organising factor in
the universal whole. Man may be more interesting and important than our
modern teachers suppose, possibly even a star of some magnitude in the
celestial universe.

W. MACNEILE DIXON

RATIONAL IMMORTALITY

[Tough-minded thinkers are apt to maintain that *all* theories of immortality
should be dismissed as comforting illusions projected by wishful thinking.
Obviously, where reincarnation is concerned, if someone believes in it simply
because he or she wants to come back, that does not make it true. However,
if another, weary and bitterly disillusioned with life, says "What, one more
round? never!" that does not make it false. Furthermore, the latter person
may understandably resent the thought that the vicissitudes presently experienced result from his own actions in a prior existence, and that the misdeeds
of this life must be paid for in lives to come. The Christian fundamentalist has
his bias too: He prefers an everlasting stay in heaven to the painstaking work

of going on with the evolutionary processes. And what about a scientist or psychologist of materialistic inclination? He may instinctively discount the concept because its truth could disqualify the evidence or conclusions of a lifetime of research. Thus, the argument that the rebirth hypothesis stems from pleasant fantasies could cut both ways!

J. Paul Williams in the opening paragraph of our selections from his essay "Belief in a Future Life"[3] has a rather unusual thought on all this. Although Dr. Williams's field is religion, having headed that department at Mount Holyoke College for many years, his thoughts on an afterlife and his conclusions concerning reincarnation are apparently also rooted in philosophy and science.]

One's emotional orientation to the problem of the future life is materially advanced when one realizes that the two great religions of the East—Hinduism and Buddhism—assume that the future life is a fact. They teach that man is reborn into the world over and over again, and they view the prospect with much anxiety. Thus one major function of these religions is to teach men how to avoid being reborn.[4] It is not "wishful thinking" from the Hindu or Buddhist point of view to expect to live again; rather it is stark realism. But it would be "wishful thinking" from their point of view really to believe that religion has found a way to get man off of the "wheel of life."

The argument for the future life which logically precedes all others is the simple one that if man is a soul it is not unreasonable to suppose that he survives death. If man is simply a body, a physio-chemical reaction, and nothing more, it is obvious that he does not live again as such a body. If, however, man is a soul, the door is left open to the possibility that the soul persists after death. Is man just a body, as some of our contemporaries believe? Or is he a body that has a soul? Or (and this is a different proposition) is he a soul that has a body?

There are two ways to prove a thing. One is to show how it follows logically from other things that [are true]. The other is just to point and say, "There it is." I am among those who feel that they must believe in souls simply because they experience them. It may be that my family, the students I meet on the campus, are just bodies, machines, not essentially different from the images I see on a movie screen. But I find that a very hard position to accept. It is much easier to account for one's experience of people and for one's knowledge of himself on the assumption that the essential human being is more than just a physio-chemical reaction. Is man a living soul? For answer observe people: watch a group of boys playing football; read Shakespeare; look into the eyes of one beloved.

The idea that human beings are just bodies is one phase of the notion that nothing exists but matter, that spirit is nonexistent, that mind is but matter in motion. This position is one that some scientists have expounded dogmatically. Because of the prestige of these men, many people have jumped to the conclusion that anyone who is thoroughly abreast of modern thought will discard faith in a soul. Yet there are other scientists, men of equal prestige, who do not accept the faith that the universe is composed exclusively of matter and assert their belief that faith in a future life is rational. But as a matter of fact scientists are in no better position than are the rest of us to decide whether matter and mind are both real. That is a question for philosophy. And we must all, consciously or unconsciously, be philosophers.

Accept if you can the belief that we are souls; that still does not mean that a future life is proved. Do these souls survive death? Our only experience of life is in connection with the body. Some people would contend that we must deduce from this simple fact the conclusion that where there is no body there is no life. But this is not a necessary conclusion. William James pointed out that we can take two positions concerning the relation between the body and life: one is that the body *produces* life; the other that the body *reflects* life. Light is produced by a candle; if the candle is put out its light disappears. Light is reflected by a mirror; if the mirror is taken away the light still continues. Now is it not at least as easy to suppose that the body reflects the soul as it is to suppose that it produces the soul? It may be that this human carcass, full of aches and diseases, produces things like ''Hamlet,'' the theory of evolution, psychoanalysis, and the fortieth chapter of Isaiah, but it is a great deal easier for me to believe that these things are the work of living souls who used bodies as instruments.

If we assume that the soul is reflected rather than is produced by the body, then it is rational to believe that the soul can exist apart from the body. The fact that we have no direct experience of souls which do exist apart from matter is a serious weakness in the argument,[5] but it need not force us to the conclusion that they cannot so exist. The typical reaction of the materialists to this kind of reasoning is an appeal to stick to the known facts. But the materialistic scientist certainly does not limit himself to immediately experienced data. The limits of our experience are so narrow that if we did not permit our thinking to go beyond them, human thought would be puny indeed. Who ever experienced an atom or an electron? The whole conception of the atomic structure is an inference; it is believed because it is consistent with the way in which the elements combine, because it explains why under certain conditions peculiar markings appear on photographic plates. Yet we do not accuse the physicist of irrationality when he says that the solid matter of a rock is really composed of tiny solar systems in which electrons revolve at incredible speed around protons. Let no one think that he has reached perfection in his habits of thought if he accepts inferential logic in physics but rejects it in theology.

Another argument in favor of a future life is the simple fact that we are alive now. Here we are, set in the midst of an infinity of time. It is impossible for us to imagine a limit to time. If that is true, then the chances are infinitely against us that we should be alive at any specific time. But here we are. The only way to get rid of the infinity of chances which are against us is to assume that we are like time; that is, that we too are infinite. Usually thinking about personal immortality takes this form—a human being is created somewhere near the time of his birth, finally he dies, and then he becomes immortal. The conception I am suggesting, however, is that in addition to living after this life is ended we have lived before it began. This is a logically necessary assumption, if one accepts the force of the argument in any measure. But, it may be said, we have no memory of any former existence. True, and therefore, if one accepts the argument, one is forced into the conclusion that some means has operated to prevent memory of previous existences.

One of the fundamental assumptions of modern thought is that the universe is consistent, that it conforms to certain laws and resists caprice. One of the important conclusions of science is that the sum total of matter and energy in the universe is a constant. Would not a consistent universe preserve its highest manifestation, even as it preserves its lowest manifestation, matter? George Herbert Palmer wrote of the death of his wife, "Though no regrets are proper for the manner of her death, who can contemplate the fact of it, and not call the world irrational, if out of deference to a few particles of disordered matter, it excludes so fair a spirit?"

J. PAUL WILLIAMS

OBJECTIONS TO REINCARNATION CONSIDERED

[Our next author is the philosopher C. J. Ducasse. Widely recognized in his field, he was president of the American Philosophical Association and for three decades was chairman of the philosophy department at Brown University. His interests were particularly wide-ranging: He wrote on art, was president of the American Society of Aesthetics, vice-president of the American Society for Psychical Research, and at one time taught psychology.

In two of Ducasse's books he treats of the philosophical and scientific evidence for reincarnation: *A Critical Examination of the Belief in a Life After Death*[6] and *Nature, Mind, and Death,* from which our main selections will come. His 1960 Garvin lecture, "Life After Death Conceived as Reincarnation," is entirely on the subject. (Previous Garvin lecturers have been such distinguished scholars as Paul Tillich, Margaret Mead, and Sidney Hook.) While this lecture deals mainly with empirical evidence, Ducasse mentions in opening that belief that there is for man a life subsequent to the death of his body has always been very widespread. The reason for this becomes evident when one considers the psychological origin of the belief, as compared with, for example, that of the belief in the existence of a God. As the late Professor J. B. Pratt pointed out,[7] "We begin believing in God because we are taught to do so"; but the belief in the continuity of life originates altogether spontaneously. The child, having been alive as far back as he can remember, "takes the continuity of life for granted. It is the fact of death that has to be taught. . . . Hence the explicit idea of a future life comes to him as the most natural thing in the world."

As to reincarnation, Ducasse says in the lecture that the idea "appears fantastic today to most adherents of the Judaeo-Christian religion; but this is only because it diverges from the ideas of life and death to which they have been habituated from childhood. For when these are viewed objectively, they are seen to be more paradoxical than that of reincarnation. An example is the idea of the 'resurrection of the flesh' notwithstanding the dispersion of the dead body's material by cremation or by incorporation of its particles into the living bodies of worms, sharks or vultures."[8]

Now for the selections from *Nature, Mind, and Death*.[9] Reincarnation is introduced in the book to explore the merits of the charge that there is no concept of life after death that "would be both theoretically possible and significant enough to be worth our caring now whether it is a fact or not." The last part of the charge is dealt with first.]

The hypothesis of survival as rebirth in a material world is of course not novel. As [the Reverend] W. R. Alger declares, "No other doctrine has exerted so extensive, controlling, and permanent an influence upon mankind as that of the metempsychosis—the notion that when the soul leaves the body it is born anew in another body, its rank, character, circumstances, and experience in each successive existence depending on its qualities, deeds, and attainments in its preceding lives."[10] Although [this latter idea of Karma] is logically distinct from that of rebirth, it has in fact been virtually always conjoined with rebirth—probably because the transmigration hypothesis then is, as Alger further says:

> marvelously adapted to explain the seeming chaos of moral inequality, injustice, and manifold evil presented in the world of human life. Once admit the theory to be true, and all difficulties in regard to moral justice vanish, the principal physical and moral phenomena of life are strikingly explained; and, as we gaze around the world, its material conditions and spiritual elements combine in one vast scheme of unrivalled order, and the total experience of humanity forms a magnificent picture of perfect poetic justice.

It will be worthwhile now to inquire in some detail whether transmigration really is theoretically tenable, or on the contrary faces insuperable difficulties.

Survival as rebirth at once raises the question whether one's present life is not itself a rebirth. [This] immediately brings up the objection that we have no recollection of having lived before. But if absence of memory of having existed at a certain time proved that we did not exist at that time, it would then prove far too much; for it would prove that we did not exist during the first few years of the life of our present body, nor on most of the days since. Moreover, there is occasional testimony of recollection of a previous life. One such case may be cited here without any claim that it establishes pre-existence. If pre-existence should happen to be a fact, it is obvious that the only possible empirical evidence of it would consist of verifiable recollections such as testified to in the case about to be described.

It is that of "The Rebirth of Katsugoro," recorded in detail and with many affidavits respecting the facts, in an old Japanese document translated by Lafcadio Hearn.[11] The story is, in brief, that a young boy called Katsugoro, son of a man called Genzo in the village of Nakanomura, declared that in his preceding life a few years before he had been called Tozo; that he was then the son of a farmer called Kyubei and his wife Shidzu in a village called Hodokubo; that his father had died and had been replaced in the household by a man called Hanshiro; and that he himself, Tozo, had died of smallpox at the age of six, a year after his father. He described his burial, the appearance of his former parents, and their house. He eventually was taken to their village, where such persons were found. He himself led the way to their house and recognized them; and they confirmed the facts he had related. Further, he pointed to a shop and a tree, saying that they had not been there before; and this was true.

Testimony of this kind is directly relevant to the question of rebirth. The recollections related in this case are much too circumstantial to be dismissed as instances of the familiar and psychologically well-understood illusion of déjà vu, and although the testimony that they were verified is not proof that they were, it cannot be rejected a priori. Its reliability has to be evaluated in terms of the same standards by which the validity of testimonial evidence concerning anything else is appraised.

A second objection to the transmigration hypothesis is that the native peculiarities of a person's mind as well as the characteristics of his body appear to be derived from his forebears in accordance with the laws of heredity. McTaggart makes clear that "there is no impossibility in supposing that the characteristics in which we resemble the ancestors of our bodies may be to some degree characteristics due to our previous lives." [Likening the inherited body and tendencies to a hat, and the wearer thereof to the reincarnating soul] he points out that "hats in general fit their wearers with far greater accuracy than they would if each man's hat were assigned to him by lot. The adaptation comes about by each man selecting, from hats made without any special reference to his particular head, the hat which will suit his particular head best.'' And, McTaggart goes on to say: ''This may help us to see that it would be possible to hold that a man whose nature had certain characteristics when he was about to be reborn, would be reborn in a body descended from ancestors of a similar character. It would be the character of the ancestors of the new body, and its similarity to his character, which determined the fact that he was reborn in that body rather than another.''[12]

McTaggart's use of the analogy of the head and the hats if taken literally would mean, as a correspondent of mine suggests, that, like a man looking for a hat to wear, a temporarily bodiless soul would shop around, trying on one human foetus after another until it finds one which in some unexplained manner it discovers will develop into an appropriate body. McTaggart, however, has in mind nothing so far-fetched, but rather an entirely automatic process. He refers to the analogy of chemical affinities.

But although McTaggart's supposition is adequate to dispose of the difficulty which the facts of heredity otherwise constitute, the rebirth his supposition allows is nevertheless not personal rebirth if, by a man's personality, one means the habits, skills, knowledge, character, and memories, which he gradually acquires during life on earth. If our present birth is indeed a rebirth, they certainly are not brought to a new earth life; for we know very well that we are not born with the knowledge, habits, and memories we now have, but gained them little by little as a result of the experiences and efforts of our present lifetime.

But this brings up another difficulty, namely, what then is there left which could be supposed to be reborn? A possible solution of it is definable in terms of the difference familiar in psychology between, on the one hand, *acquired* skills, habits, and memories, and on the other, *native* aptitudes, instincts, and proclivities; that is, in what a human being is at a given time we may distinguish two parts, one deeper and more permanent, and another more superficial and transient. The latter is his personality. The other we may here agree to call his individuality.

There can be no doubt that each of us, on the basis of his same individuality, would have developed a more or less different mind and personality if, for instance, he had been put at birth in a different family, or had later been thrust into a radically different sort of environment, or had had a different kind of education, or had met and married a very different type of person. Reflection on this fact should cause one to take his present personality with a large grain of salt, viewing it no longer humorlessly as his absolute self, but rather, in imaginative perspective, as but one of the various personalities which his individuality was equally capable of generating had it happened to enter phenomenal history through birth in a different environment. And the fact might further be that, perhaps as a result of persistent striving to acquire a skill or trait for which he now has little gift, aptitude for it in future births would be generated and incorporated into his individuality.

Another objection which has been advanced against the transmigration hypothesis is that without the awareness of identity which memory provides, rebirth would not be discernibly different from the death of one person followed by the birth of another. In this connection, Lamont quotes Leibniz's question: "Of what use would it be to you, sir, to become king of China, on condition that you forgot what you have been? Would it not be the same as if God, at the same time he destroyed you, created a king in China?"[13]

But continuousness of memory, rather than preservation of a comprehensive span of memories, is what is significant for consciousness of one's identity. Thus, for example, none of us finds his sense of identity impaired by the fact that he has no memories of the earliest years of his present life. That the sense of identity depends on *gradualness of change* in ourselves, strikes one forcibly when he chances to find letters which he wrote thirty or forty years before. Many of them may awaken no recollections whatever, even of the existence of the persons to whom they were addressed or whom they mentioned, and it sometimes seems incredible also that the person who wrote the things they contain should be the same as his present self. In truth, it is not the same in any strict sense, but only continuous with the former person.

One more difficulty remains to be examined. It concerns not so much the theoretical possibility of transmigration as its capacity to satisfy certain demands which death appears to thwart—such capacity being what alone gives to a conception of survival practical importance and interest for us in this life.

One of these demands, as we have seen, is that the injustices of this life should somehow be eventually redressed; hence, conceptions of survival have generally included the idea of such redress as effected in the life after death. And, when survival has been thought of as later lives on earth, the redress has been conceived to consist in this—that the good and evil deeds, the strivings, the experiences, and the merits and faults of one life, all would have their just fruits in subsequent lives.

Now, however, it may be objected that, without memory of what one is being rewarded or punished for, one learns nothing from the retribution, which is then ethically useless. But the eye-for-eye and tooth-for-tooth mode of moral education is not the only one there is, nor necessarily always the most effective. If, for example, impatience caused Tom to do Dick an injury, the morally important thing as regards Tom is that he should acquire the patience he lacks; but the undergoing by him of a similar injury at the hand of Dick is not the only possible way in which he could come to do so. Other ways in which Tom might learn patience are conceivable. He might, for example, eventually find himself in a situation psychologically conducive to the development of patience—one, where his love for someone would cause him to endure year after year without resentment the vagaries or follies of the loved person—or, more generally, some situation which for one reason or another he would be powerless to alter or to escape and in which only patient resignation would avail to bring him any peace.

It is further conceivable that Tom's eventual landing into a situation forcing him to practice patience should be a perfectly natural consequence of his vice of impatience. Each of us that is old and mature enough to view the course of his life in perspective can see that again and again his aptitudes, his habits, his tastes or interests, his virtues or his vices, brought about, not by plan but automatically, changes in his material or social circumstances, in his associates, in his opportunities and so on; and that these changes in turn, quite as much as those due to purely external causes, contributed to shape for the better or the worse what he then became. This, which is observable within one life, could occur equally naturally as between the present and the subsequent lives of a continuous self.

We have now considered the chief of the difficulties in the way of the transmigration form of the survival hypothesis. In attempting to meet them we have gradually defined a form of survival which appears possible and which, if it should be a fact, would have significance for the living.

C. J. DUCASSE

KARMA, REBIRTH, AND FREE WILL

[Since its appearance in 1958, Huston Smith's *The Religions of Man*—from which we now quote—has been exercising friendly persuasion and strengthening the current dialogue between Eastern and Western thought. Born in China of American parents, Dr. Smith has for some years been professor of philosophy at Massachusetts Institute of Technology, and now teaches religion at Syracuse University.

In the material that follows from *The Religions of Man*,[14] Dr. Smith discusses reincarnation in relation to karmic law. Although karma—defined as the moral law of cause and effect—is often viewed as a form of cosmic accountancy, of fixed debits and credits, the author suggests that it is better to think of it organically in terms of cosmic harmony which, when disturbed, must be restored. Westerners are apt to fear karma as a punitive, harshly retributive law. However, Buddha explained that "the heart of it is Love, the end of it is Peace and Consummation sweet." The implication here may be that the effects produced by our actions eventually teach us how to bring harmony into our lives. In theory, it is just as "simple" as a violinist learning from his dissonant, spine-chilling sounds what movements of bow and fingers to avoid, and discovering at last how to play beautiful, soulful music. How long this will take depends on his effort and talent. According to karmic doctrine the same is true in mastering the human instrument.

Objectors to reincarnation nevertheless often ask: If all of us have lived thousands of lives why are we not much further advanced? Such questioners usually equate reincarnation with progress, whereas it only provides the *opportunity* for progress. Consider the daily ''reincarnation'' cycle: If mere multiplication of days made one automatically wise, then all octogenarians would be sages! The Buddha well appreciated that the vast majority advance quite slowly. He likened man's pilgrimage to climbing a mountain. ''By steep or gentle slopes the climber comes where breaks that other world. Strong limbs may dare the rugged road. . . . The weaker must wind from slower ledge to ledge with many a place of rest. . . . The firm soul hastes, the feeble tarries. All will reach the sunlit snows.''[15]

Let us see how a contemporary philosopher presents these ideas to the modern mind.]

Science has alerted the Western world to the importance of causal relationships in the physical world. Every physical event has its cause, and every cause will have its determinate effects. India extends this concept of universal causation to include man's moral and spiritual life as well. To some extent the West has also. ''As a man sows, so shall he reap''; or again, ''Sow a thought to reap an act, sow an act and reap a habit, sow a habit and reap a character, sow a character and reap a destiny''—these are ways the West has put the point. The difference is that India tightens up and extends its concept of moral law to see it as absolutely binding and brooking no exceptions. The present condition of each individual's interior life—how happy he is, how confused or serene, how much he can see—is an exact product of what he has wanted and got in the past; and equally, his present thoughts and decisions are determining his future states. Each act he directs upon the world has its equal and opposite reaction on himself. Each thought and deed delivers an unseen chisel blow toward the sculpturing of his destiny.

This idea of *karma* and the completely moral universe it implies, commits the Hindu who understands it to complete personal responsibility. Most persons are unwilling to admit this. They prefer, as the psychologists would say, to project—to locate the source of their difficulties outside themselves. This, say the Hindus, is simply immature.

Because *karma* implies a lawful world, it has often been interpreted as fatalism. However often Hindus may have succumbed to this interpretation, it is untrue to the doctrine itself. *Karma* decrees that every decision must have its determinate consequences, but the decisions themselves are, in the last analysis, freely arrived at. Or, to approach the matter from the other direction, the consequences of a man's past decisions condition his present lot, as a card player finds himself dealt a particular hand, but is left free to play that hand in a number of ways. This means that the career of a soul as it threads its course through innumerable human bodies is guided by its choices.

In the Hindu view, spirit no more depends on the body it inhabits than body depends on the clothes it wears or the house it lives in. When we outgrow a suit or find our house too cramped we exchange these for roomier ones that offer our bodies freer play. Souls do the same. [To approach such an awareness, the individual should] examine the language he uses every day and ponder its implications. The word "my" always implies a distinction between the possessor and what is possessed. When I speak of my coat [or my house], there is no thought that I am these things. But I also speak of my body, my mind, or my personality, giving evidence that in some sense I think of myself as standing apart from these also. What is this "I" that is the possessor of my body and mind but cannot be equated with them?

Science tells me there is nothing in my body that was with me seven years ago. In the course of my lifetime my mind and personality have undergone changes that are equally radical. Yet through all these revisions I have remained on some level the same person. What is this something in our make-up deeper than either body or personality that provides this continuity in the midst of incessant change?

Our word "personality" comes from the Latin *persona* which originally meant the mask an actor donned as he stepped onto the stage to play his role. The mask carried the make-up of the role, while the actor behind it remained hidden and anonymous. This mask is precisely what our personalities are—the roles into which we have been cast for the moment in this greatest drama of all, life itself.

The disturbing fact, however, is that we have lost sight of the distinction between our true self and the veil of personality that is its present costume, but which will be laid aside when the play is over. We have come completely under the fascination of our present lines, unable to remember previous roles or to anticipate future ones. The task is to correct this false identification. Turning his awareness inward [man] must pierce and dissolve the innumerable layers of the manifest personality until, all strata of the mask at length cut through, he arrives finally at the anonymous actor who stands beneath.

Never during its pilgrimage is the spirit of man completely adrift and alone. From start to finish its nucleus is the *Atman*—the self-luminous abiding point, "boundless as the sky, indivisible, absolute," the only reality.

HUSTON SMITH

2

Language of Myth and Symbol

The dreams of ancient and modern man are written in the same language as the myths whose authors lived in the dawn of history. . . . Yet this language has been forgotten by modern man. Not when he is asleep, but when he is awake. Is it important to understand this language also in our waking state? . . . I believe that symbolic language is the one foreign language that each of us must learn. Its understanding brings us in touch with one of the most significant sources of wisdom, that of the myth, and it brings us in touch with the deeper layers of our own personalities. . . . Indeed, both dreams and myths are important communications from ourselves to ourselves. If we do not understand the language in which they are written, we miss a great deal of what we know and tell ourselves in those hours when we are not busy manipulating the outside world.

ERICH FROMM
The Forgotten Language

Myth is the secret opening through which the inexhaustible energies of the cosmos pour into human cultural manifestations. Religions, philosophies, arts, the social forms of primitive and historic man, prime discoveries in science and technology, the very dreams that blister sleep, boil up from the basic, magic ring of myth. . . . The symbols of mythology are not manufactured; they cannot be ordered, invented, or permanently suppressed. They are spontaneous productions of the psyche, and each bears within it, undamaged, the germ power of its source.

JOSEPH CAMPBELL
The Hero with a Thousand Faces

𝕴 "FRAGMENTS OF A LOST WHOLE"

["The cycle of birth, death, and rebirth is about the most basic theme of myth and religion," writes Alan Watts in his introduction to *The Wisdom of the Serpent—The Myths of Death, Rebirth, and Resurrection*. "Nothing is more provocative than the idea of death," he continues. "It is because men know that they will die that they have created the arts and sciences, the philosophies and religions. For nothing is more thought-provoking than the thought which seems to put an end to thought: 'What will it be like to go to sleep and never wake up?' Irresistibly this seems to suggest a corollary: 'Where and who was I before my father and mother conceived me?' For the unthinkable-after-death appears to be the same as the unthinkable-before-birth, so that if once I came out of nothing, the odds are that I can come again and again."[1]

Although some of the myths and symbols considered in this section appear in later forms of Christianity to teach a once-for-all resurrection, originally they were nurtured by peoples who believed in a process of continuous rebirth for both man and the universe, and as we shall see, most obviously reflected that outlook.

In the nineteenth century, scholars inclined to the theory that mythmaking was a disease that sprang up at an early stage of human culture, and had no deeper basis than primitive man's observation of the movements of heavenly bodies, or his supposed preoccupation with fertility cycles. Today, more mature evaluations of myth are becoming current. William Irwin Thompson writes in his widely appreciated volume *At the Edge of History:*

> There may indeed be a "mythopoeic mentality," but it is not restricted to precivilized man, but is to be found in geniuses as different as Boehme, Kepler, Blake, Yeats, Wagner, Heisenberg, and that student of Boehme's theory of action and reaction, Isaac Newton. Myth is not an early level of human development, but an imaginative description of reality in which the known is related to the unknown through a system of correspondences in which mind and matter, self, society, and cosmos are integrally expressed in an esoteric language of poetry and number. . . .[2]

In this chapter the myths and symbols described have an evident relationship to our subject. As to those which in more subtle fashion may teach reincarnation, we leave the task of analysis to the specialist. Later under "The Greek Mysteries," several other reincarnation myths will be reviewed.

Giorgio de Santillana in his volume *Hamlet's Mill* speaks of a "great world-wide archaic construction" of thought that existed before the Greeks and that survives to this day in myths and fairy tales that are no longer understood. But, says this modern scholar, who teaches the history and philosophy of science at Massachusetts Institute of Technology, the original themes of the ancient thought construction were preserved by the Pythagoreans and Plato as "tantalizing fragments of a lost whole." Plato, de Santillana declares, understood "the language of archaic myth" and gave to the West the foundations of all modern philosophy, based on this "imposing body of doctrine" commonly attributed to Pythagoras. He observes that most Platonic myths "act like a floodlight that throws bright beams upon the whole of 'high mythology.' "[3] Plato's writings will be considered in chapter 5.

Bruno Bettelheim, a world figure in child psychology, writes in *The Uses of Enchantment—The Meaning and Importance of Fairy Tales* that "in most cultures, there is no clear line separating myth from folk or fairy tale . . ."

> The Nordic languages have only one word for both: *saga*. . . . Some fairy and folk stories evolved out of myths; others were incorporated into them. Both forms embodied the cumulative experience of a society, as men wished to recall past wisdom for themselves and transmit it to future generations. These tales are the purveyors of deep insights that have sustained mankind through the long vicissitudes of its existence. . . . The myth presents its theme in a majestic way; it carries spiritual force; and the divine is present and is experienced in the form of superhuman heroes who make constant demands on mere mortals. . . . The fairy tale is presented in a simple, homely way; no demands are made on the listener. [It] reassures, gives hope for the future, and holds out the promise of a happy ending.[4]

We will not be considering fairy tales in the present work, but Dr. Bettelheim remarks that in those stories of heroism so lavish with deaths, the "predecessors of the hero who die are nothing but the hero's earlier immature incarnations."[5]]

THE IMMORTAL PHOENIX

[For millennia the symbol of symbols for rebirth has been the phoenix, "a mythical bird of great beauty, the only one of its kind, fabled to live 500 or 600 years in the Arabian wilderness, to burn itself on a funeral pile and rise from the ashes in the freshness of youth and live through another cycle of years.''[6] When reduced to ashes, one glowing spark, signifying the immortal being, is supposed to remain, and from this the new life is evolved.

Another familiar form of the legend is found in the *Physiologus,* a collection of some fifty Christian allegories relating to the animal world. Though banned by the Church, they were avidly read during the Middle Ages. The phoenix is there described as an Indian bird that subsists on air for five hundred years. Then, laden with spices, he flies to Egypt, enters the temple at Heliopolis, and is burned to ashes on the altar. Next day the young phoenix is already feathered; on the third day his pinions are full grown, he salutes the priest and flies away.[7]

E. V. H. Kenealy, a writer of the last century, remarked that ''it is a curious circumstance that we find nations the most remote from each other well acquainted with this symbol. The ancient Irish ascribed a longevity of six centuries to their Phoenix. . . . By the Japanese [it] is called *Kirin,* and by the Turks *Kerkes.* According to the latter it lives a thousand years.''[8]

While the allegory taken as a whole obviously suggests immortality and cyclic rebirth, each of its facets and variations seems to bear on sacred matters pertaining to the soul's life, history, and immense age. Even the idea that the bird is ''only one of its kind,'' and consequently has no mate, has significance if applied to the spiritual and sexless character of the reincarnating entity.

Kenealy considers some of the larger meanings of the myth:

> The Phoenix is also very plainly the same as the *Simorgh* of Persian romance; and the account which is given of this last bird yet more decisively establishes the opinion that the death and revival of the Phoenix exhibit the successive destruction and reproduction of the world, which many believed to be effected by the agency of a fiery deluge.
>
> [The rabbis speak of] an enormous bird, sometimes standing on the earth, and sometimes walking in the ocean . . . while its head props the sky; and with the symbol, they have also adopted the doctrine to which it relates. They teach that there are to be seven successive renewals of the globe. . . . This opinion, which involves the doctrine of the pre-existence of each renewed creature, they may either have learned during their Babylonian captivity, or it may have been part of the primeval religion which their priests preserved from remote times.[9]

The prince of Persian Sufi poets, Hafiz, applying the myth to man, movingly depicts the phoenix as the human soul alighting on Tuba—the tree of spiritual life—and then descending into material existence again and again:

> My phoenix long ago secured
> His nest in the sky-vault's cope;
> In the body's cage immured
> He was weary of life's hope.

> Round and round this heap of ashes
> Now flies the bird amain,
> But in that odorous niche of heaven
> Nestles the bird again.
>
> Once flies he upward he will perch
> On Tuba's golden bough;
> His home is on that fruited arch
> Which cools the blest below. . . .
>
> Either world inhabits he,
> Sees oft below him planets roll;
> His body is all of air compact,
> Of Allah's love, his soul.[10]

Kenealy informs us that "Herodotus mentions that the Phoenix was one of the sacred birds, or hieroglyphics of the Egyptians." It appears frequently in the Book of the Dead and is called the Benu bird. As we mentioned earlier, the title of our present work suggested the use of a reproduction of the Benu bird as a key symbol for this volume. The translator of the Book of the Dead remarks that this bird, "probably the original of the phoenix of the Greeks," was self-begotten, deathless, and apparently symbolized the Spirit-soul.[11] In the text proper the deceased is shown undergoing numerous transformations in the heavenly world. Finally having achieved the highest afterdeath state, he exultingly declares: "I am the Benu bird, the Heart-soul of Ra" and "upon earth . . . shall come forth" again. The Heart-souls of the gods, or great beings, are also said to come forth on earth as they may wish.[12]

In a beautiful passage in his *Philosophy of History,* Hegel remarks that metempsychosis as taught by the Orientals is perhaps the highest idea in their metaphysics, and adds: "But a myth more generally known is that of the phoenix. . . . Spirit—consuming the envelope of its existence—does not merely pass into another envelope, nor rise rejuvenescent from the ashes of its previous form; it comes forth exalted, glorified, a purer spirit. It certainly makes war upon itself—consumes its own existence; but in this very destruction it works up that existence into a new form, and each successive phase becomes in its turn a material, working on which it exalts itself to a new grade."[13]

This recalls a passage in *The Voice of the Silence,* of Tibetan Buddhist origin: "Out of the furnace of man's life and its black smoke, winged flames arise, flames purified, that weave in the end the fabric glorified of the . . . vestures of the Path."

In the chapters ahead we will discover a number of parallels to the phoenix myth, particularly where the soul is depicted as a perpetual fire that periodically "dies down" and then reemerges with fresh vigor. The Buddha compared rebirth to the lighting of a new candle from the flame of a dying one. The flame goes on, he said, but the candle or body is consumed. How interesting that two hundred years ago the Irish poet Thomas Moore independently used somewhat similar imagery in *Lalla Rookh,* when he gave these lines to a Persian prophet: "Though new the frame thy soul inhabits now, I've tracked its flame for many an age, in every chance and change . . . as through a torch-race, where, from hand to hand, the flying youths transmit their shiny brand. From frame to frame the unextinguished soul rapidly passes, till it reach the goal!"[14]]

𝕴 THE WHEEL OF REBIRTH

[In *From Religion to Philosophy,* the Cambridge philosopher F. M. Cornford speaks of reincarnation or palingenesis as among "the cardinal doctrines of mysticism." "This life, which is perpetually renewed, is reborn out of that opposite state, called 'death,' in which, at the other end of its arc, it passes again." "In this idea of reincarnation," he says, "we have the first conception of a cycle of existence, a Wheel of Life, divided into two hemicycles of light and darkness, through which the one life, or soul, continuously revolves. . . . Caught in the wheel of Time, the soul, preserving its individual identity, passes through all shapes of life. This implies that man's soul is not 'human'; human life is only one of the shapes it passes through. Its substance is divine and immutable, and it is the same substance as all other souls in the world. In this sense, the unity of all life is maintained; but, on the other hand, each soul is an atomic individual, which persists throughout its . . . cycle of reincarnations."[15]

In Buddhist art, sculpture, and architecture, the wheel is widely used to symbolize karma and rebirth, and also appears on the Buddhist flag. Buddha's first sermon after attaining enlightenment was called "Turning the Wheel of the Law." Later in Buddhist philosophy the ceaselessly revolving wheel, which involves the unwary soul in the *obligatory* round of rebirth—as distinguished from *will-chosen* ones—signified the Twelve Nidanas, or Wheel of Causation. These twelve causes of repeated existence, each dependent on its predecessor, belong to the most abstruse doctrines of the Buddhist metaphysical system.

The wheel of rebirth is also found in Greece and Italy, as A. C. Pearson of Cambridge relates. Speaking of transmigration, he says that "the prevalence of this mystical belief and its religious potency are illustrated with remarkable clearness in certain inscriptions on golden tablets found in south Italy, near Rome, and in Crete, which are chiefly attributed to the 4th and 5th centuries B.C. . . . One of these contains some words which form part of the appeal of the purified soul:

"I have flown out of the sorrowful weary Wheel; I have passed with eager feet to the Circle desired." This refers to the mystical Wheel of Fortune which in its revolutions symbolizes the cycle of successive lives necessary to be traversed by the harassed soul before its final release. This specific cycle of progress, as well as the more general conception of a *Kuklos* in human affairs, is traditionally attributed to the Orphic-Pythagorean sphere of thought.[16]

W. R. Inge, for many years dean of Saint Paul's in London and a scholar of note, writes that "even in the most Judaic of the epistles, that attributed to St. James, we are almost startled to find the Orphic phrase 'the wheel of birth.' "[17]

The later Greeks continued the analogy, as G. R. S. Mead states in *Orpheus:* "The wheel of life referred to by Pythagoras, is called by Proclus the 'cycle of generation.' " According to Simplicius, Mead continues, "it was symbolized by the wheel of Ixion," who had been "bound by God to the wheel of fate and of generation."[18] Ixion was punished by Zeus for his love for Hera by being bound on an eternally revolving wheel in Tartarus.

Regarding humanity as a whole, Burne-Jones has painted a marvelous picture of a wheel on which the rich and the poor, the great and the small, are bound. Each has his moment of good fortune when the wheel brings him uppermost. Each in his turn is crushed as the wheel turns on. "Only while turns this wheel invisible, no pause, no peace, no staying-place can be; who mounts will fall, who falls may mount; the spokes go round unceasingly!" Thus once spoke the Buddha, as told in Sir Edwin Arnold's *The Light of Asia.* But the Buddha added in tones of powerful affirmation:

> If ye lay bound upon the wheel of change,
> And no way were of breaking from the chain,
> The Heart of boundless Being is a curse,
> The Soul of Things fell Pain.
> Ye are not bound! the Soul of Things is sweet,
> The Heart of Being is celestial rest;
> Stronger than woe is will: that which was Good
> Doth pass to Better—Best.

Philosophically viewed, the whirling wheel and its ever motionless center can be a potent symbol of the human struggle toward insight and harmony. Identification of consciousness with the rising and falling rim—or the body and personality—inevitably leads to an unbalanced outlook. Only in the still center of the imperishable Self is true perspective apparently achieved. Then the ups and downs of rebirth, even while experienced, cause no loss of spiritual equilibrium. As Krishna asserts in the *Bhagavad-Gita:* ''There dwelleth in the heart of every creature the Master—Ishwara—who by his magic power causeth all things and creatures to revolve mounted upon the universal wheel of time. Take sanctuary with him with all thy soul.''[19] Ishwara is viewed as the impersonal, sexless spirit within all beings. The heart mentioned could be what Browning called that ''inmost center in us all, where truth abides in fulness; and around, wall upon wall, the gross flesh hems it in.'' Thus, ''to know,'' he said, ''rather consists in opening out a way whence the imprisoned splendor may escape, than in effecting entry for a light supposed to be without.''[20]

Joseph Campbell observes that ''those who have identified themselves with the mortal body and its affections will necessarily find that all is painful, since everything—for them—must end,'' even if subsequently reembodied. ''But for those who have found the still point of eternity, around which all—including themselves—revolves, everything is acceptable as it is; indeed, can even be experienced as glorious and wonderful.'' The West's ''concept of the hero,'' he says, ''is of the actual, particular individual, who indeed is mortal and so doomed.'' ''Whereas in the Orient the true hero of all mythology is not the vainly striving, empirical personality, but that reincarnating one and only transmigrant, which''—to quote a celebrated verse from the Gita—'' 'is never born; nor does it die; nor, having once been, does it ever cease to be. Unborn, eternal, changeless and of great age, it is not slain when the body is slain.' ''[21] In one passage from an Oriental text, the hero himself is likened to a wheel: ''And when the Great King of Glory saw the Heavenly Treasure of the Wheel, he sprinkled it with water and said: 'Roll onward, O my Lord, the Wheel! O my Lord, go forth and overcome.' ''[22]]

PSYCHE AND THE BUTTERFLY

[The goddess Psyche, to whom we are indebted for the root of our word psychology, was one of the names given by the Greeks to the soul. It was also their designation for the butterfly. In fact, in early Greek art this goddess, as the soul, was represented as a butterfly or tiny winged creature.[23] The symbology involved here is well known. However, while everyone is familiar with the amazing metamorphic change from caterpillar to butterfly, few are aware that while in the caterpillar stage, the larva undergoes three or four complete sheddings of the skin, a characteristic that can be related to the serpent symbol next to be considered. The newly clothed caterpillar is so different in marking from its ''predecessor'' that only a trained observer appreciates that the same species is involved in all these transformations. Then after the "sleep of death" in the tomblike chrysalis, form, function, and habit are all so changed that nothing but the evidence of direct testimony would convince us that the beautiful butterfly was the "reembodiment" of the crawling, earthbound caterpillar.

Of course, metamorphosis and reincarnation are not identical processes, for metamorphosis usually means the transformation of the *same* form while rebirth involves the use of *new* forms. Yet Leibniz had grounds for believing that metempsychosis was actually a form of metamorphosis.[24] However, as symbols, both ideas have ever been inseparable. Ovid's celebrated volume, the *Metamorphoses*—from which poets and scholars have recounted the myths of Greece and Rome—reveals that all these stories signify eternal transformation and reembodiment. "My design leads me to speak of forms changed into new bodies." The reincarnation teaching of Pythagoras formed part of Ovid's design. These verses, in John Dryden's translation, will be quoted later.

The Psyche myth itself has undergone radical metamorphosis in modern times. Western psychology, denying an eternal Self in man, was obliged to identify Psyche with the mind and mental processes alone. "Psychology," as Erich Fromm remarks, "became a science lacking its main subject matter, the soul."[25] But some psychologists, as we shall see, are fast extending their horizons to include the insights of Eastern psychology, and if this trend continues, perhaps the goddess Psyche, as originally conceived, may incarnate again on earth.]

THE SERPENT REBORN

["The snake as a symbol of rebirth following death," writes Joseph Henderson in *The Wisdom of the Serpent,* "is an ancient, yet ever-present conception which can be traced through endless patterns of sculpture, painting, verse, and the myths of gods, demi-gods, or heroic mortals. This is so because during its yearly period of hibernation the snake sheds its skin and reappears as if renewed."[26] This periodic renewal has made the reptile a graphic symbol for both reincarnation and psychological rebirth. Furthermore, to free itself from the constricting, seamless, outgrown encasement, the snake must verily undergo the throes of "death." These regenerative aspects of the symbol are to be found in the Caduceus, the serpent staff of Hermes and Mercury, adopted as the emblem of the healing profession.

The serpent's eggs also symbolize rebirth and self-regeneration. The famous seven-hundred-foot Serpent Mound in Ohio bears an egg in its opened

mouth, while in other representations the serpent is swallowing its tail, indicating the Circle of Eternity, or beginningless and endless life.

"The wisdom of the serpent," Henderson remarks, "is suggested by its
watchful lidless eye," and "lies essentially in mankind's having projected
into this lowly creature his own secret wish to obtain from the earth a
knowledge he cannot find in waking daylight consciousness alone. This is the
knowledge of death and rebirth forever withheld except at those times when
some transcendent principle, emerging from the depths, makes it available to
consciousness."[27]

The mythical dragon was a serpent, too. In the East the expression "dragons of wisdom" refers to wise beings who have reached heights of wisdom
and power, having shed all constricting ideas and attitudes. One word for
these dragons and serpents in Sanskrit is Naga. The Greek teacher, Apollonius of Tyana, told of having been instructed by the Nagas of Kashmir.
Among the Chinese—as evidenced by their universal use of the dragon
motif—the honoring of the Nagas was widespread, one reason being that
Nagarjuna, the great Indian sage and fourteenth Buddhist patriarch, visited
China. Buddha had serpent lineage through the Naga race of kings that
reigned at Magadha, and half around the world in Mexico ancient medicine
men, called Nagals, were associated with the serpent. The great teacher of
the Toltecs and the Aztecs was Quetzalcoatl, "Feathered Serpent." He, like
many of the others, tradition predicts, will be reborn on earth. Those who feel
repugnance for the serpent symbol because of the Garden of Eden story
might recall the words of Jesus: "Be ye . . . wise as serpents, and harmless
as doves."[28] The Eastern dragon, while awe-inspiring, was held to be *both*
harmless and wise.]

TRANSFORMATIONS OF PROTEUS

[In classical mythology, Proteus, the god of the sea, could change his form at
will, and when pursued would escape by transforming himself into perhaps a
dreadful beast, or into fire or flood. Our word "protean" has this derivative
heritage. One day a man decided to catch Proteus to find out what he really
was. The god at the time was sleeping heavily as a stone, but woke when
touched and turned himself into a plant. The man was about to pull up the
plant, when, lo! a serpent coiled at his feet, and when he sought to kill the
snake, a man stood laughing in his face. The man melted into thin air, a
lightning flash disclosing the outline of a wondrous spirit mounting ever
higher until it was lost in the starry heavens. Here, it may be, we have a tale
of the universal Proteus—Life—in its transmigratory journey through the

kingdoms. A Kabalistic aphorism tells the same story: "A stone becomes a plant, a plant an animal, an animal a man, and man a god."

Various gods, of whom Proteus was one, were amphibious. Here the symbol suggests repeated alternating existences of waking and sleeping, of life and after death. For the Greeks, amphibious meant "life on two planes," from *amphi*, "on both sides," and *bios*, life. "Souls are necessarily of an amphibious nature," said Plotinus, "and alternately experience a superior and inferior condition."

Proteus had the gift of prophecy, but exercised it reluctantly. When human beings wished to consult him he would change his form with bewildering rapidity, and unless they clung to him through all the changes would give no answer to their questions. Old philosophy suggests that the changing forms in which life is embodied are illusory, never for an instant the same, and only he who clings to the Real within the form becomes the true seer and sage.]

MYTH OF THE ETERNAL RETURN

[Joseph Campbell explains that this myth "displays an order of fixed forms that appear and reappear through all time." "The daily round of the sun, the waning and waxing moon, the cycle of the year, and the rhythm of organic birth, death, and new birth, represent a miracle of continuous arising that is fundamental to the nature of the universe." The world "will disintegrate presently in chaos, only to burst forth again, fresh as a flower, to recommence spontaneously the inevitable course. . . . The dreamlike spell of this contemplative, metaphysically oriented tradition, where light and darkness dance together in a world-creating cosmic shadow play, carries into modern times an image that is of incalculable age."[29]

Regarding the lunar cycle, Mircea Eliade writes in his much translated work *The Myth of the Eternal Return:*

> The phases of moon—appearance, increase, wane, disappearance, followed by reappearance after three nights of darkness—have played an immense part in the elaboration of cyclical concepts. We find analogous concepts especially in the archaic apocalypses and anthropogenies; deluge or flood puts an end to an exhausted and sinful humanity, and a new regenerated humanity is born, usually from a mythical "ancestor" who escaped the catastrophe. . . .
>
> In the "lunar perspective," the death of the individual and the *periodic* death of humanity are necessary, even as the three days of darkness preceding the "rebirth" of the moon are necessary. The death of the individual and the death of humanity are alike necessary for their regeneration. Any form whatever, by the mere fact that it exists as such and endures, necessarily loses vigor and

becomes worn; to recover vigor, it must be reabsorbed into the formless if only
for an instant; it must be restored to the primordial unity from which it issued.
. . . What predominates in all these cosmico-mythological lunar conceptions is
the cyclical recurrence of what has been before, in a word, eternal return . . .
the motif of the repetition of an archetypal gesture, projected upon all
planes—cosmic, biological, historical, human.[30]

Eliade finds this idea in Western tradition as well as in the East. In the third
century B.C., he says, "Berosus popularized the Chaldean doctrine of the
'Great Year' in a form that spread through the entire Hellenic world (whence
it later passed to the Romans and the Byzantines). According to this doctrine, the universe is eternal but it is periodically destroyed and reconstituted
every Great Year. . . . This doctrine of periodic universal conflagration . . .
dominates the thought of Zeno and the entire Stoic cosmology."

The myth of universal combustion was decidedly in fashion throughout the
Romano-Oriental world from the first century B.C. to the third century of our
era; it successively found a place in a considerable number of gnostic systems.
. . . Similar ideas . . . are found in India and Iran, as they are among the
Mayas of Yucatan and the Aztecs of Mexico. . . . We are in a position to
emphasize [now] the optimistic character of these ideas. In fact, this optimism
can be reduced to a consciousness of the normality of the cyclical catastrophe,
to the certainty that it has a meaning, and above all, that it is never final.[31]

Better than the Stoic conception of a rigid, unaltered repetition of cycles is
the idea that cycles—human and cosmic—are always spirals, similar but not
the same, never returning to a former level. The earth in yearly orbit around
the sun cannot repeat paths already traversed because the sun in its tremendous journey around its own moving center in the Milky Way galaxy is
ceaselessly drawing the planets into new regions of space.
Respecting the idea that the cyclical catastrophe has a meaning, Eliade
explains that "nowhere—within the frame of the archaic civilizations—are
suffering and pain regarded as 'blind' and without meaning." "Thus the
Indians quite early elaborated a conception of universal causality, the karma
concept, which accounts for the actual events and sufferings of the individual's life and at the same time explains the necessity for transmigrations."
"In the light of the law of karma," he continues, "sufferings not only find a
meaning but also acquire a positive value. The sufferings of one's present life
are not only deserved—since they are in fact the fatal effect of crimes and
faults committed in previous lives—they are also welcome, for it is only in
this way that it is possible to absorb and liquidate part of the karmic debt that
burdens the individual and determines the cycle of his future existences."[32]
Thus man is not a victim of cyclic and karmic law, but has the power to

change its course, and use it to reach the heights of perfection. What applies
to the individual may also apply to larger cycles, even worlds.]

☥ THE DANCE OF SHIVA

[In Hinduism the theme of eternal recurrence finds illustration in the stories
centering around the god Shiva, the destroyer and regenerator. The myth
that follows, sensitively repeated in Hermann Hesse's *Magister Ludi,* embraces cosmic cycles, as well as lesser yugas involving the death and rebirth
of races and civilizations:

> The world as [the Hindu] myths portray it was in the beginning divine,
> radiant and happy, beautiful as spring—a golden age. But suddenly it grows
> sick and begins to degenerate, becomes more and more coarsened and
> wretched, until finally, at the end of four ever declining aeons, it is ripe to be
> stamped underfoot and destroyed by the dancing feet of Shiva. That is not the
> end of the world, however. It begins anew with the smile of the dreaming
> Vishnu. . . .

Hesse comments: "It is truly marvelous: these people discerning and capable of suffering as hardly any other, looked upon the gruesome game of
world history with horror and shame. . . . They saw and understood the
decay of creation, the lust and devilry of man and simultaneously his deep
longing for purity and harmony, and discovered this glorious allegory for the
whole beauty and tragedy of creation. . . . the powerful Shiva who tramples
the putrefying world to pulp and the laughing Vishnu who lies in slumber and
allows a new world to be born of his divine golden dreams."[33] The aid of
Shiva, however, is needed in the realization of these dreams, Dr. Henderson
shows in *The Wisdom of the Serpent:*

> Amongst the greatest of the names of Shiva is Nataraja, Lord of Dancers, or
> King of Actors. The cosmos is His theatre, there are many different steps in His
> repertory. He Himself is actor and audience. . . . In the night of Brahmâ,
> nature is inert, and cannot dance till Shiva wills it; He rises from His rapture,
> and dancing sends through inert matter pulsing waves of awakening sounds,
> and lo! matter also dances appearing as a glory round about Him. Dancing, He
> sustains its manifold phenomena. In the fulness of time, still dancing, he de-
> stroys all forms and names by fire and gives new rest. This is poetry; but none
> the less, science. . . . And there is no end to this cycle which will be repeated
> throughout eternity in the dance of death and rebirth.
>
> The Western world has also had its myths of destruction and an equivalent
> myth of recreation, expressed either as rebirth or resurrection, or as the return

of the dead to life, providing an echo of the Eastern belief in transmigration or reincarnation. But nothing we have in our cultural tradition seems quite to equal the overwhelming power of the destructive and its inevitable and unending power of rebirth as do the Eastern mythical systems.[34]

The words "This is poetry; but none the less, science" make it appropriate to mention that astronomers now consider it likely that the universe is reborn numerous times. *The New Yorker* reports that "scientists are coming around to the view that the universe has a heart-beat. . . . The cosmos expands and contracts much as a heart does, pumping once every eighty-two billion years, and destroying and bringing to life a succession of universes with each lub-dup. . . ." The magazine comments: "We congratulate science on finally beginning to discover its true identity, as an agency for corroborating ancient wisdom. Long before our century, before the Christian era, and even before Homer, the people of India had arrived at [such a] cosmogony."[35] The Buddhists apparently have a similar teaching.[36]]

THE EVER-RESURRECTING SUN

[In the daily appearance of the sun, in its annual "rebirth" at the winter solstice, and in its "resurrection" at the vernal equinox, we have a "reincarnation" symbol that has had universal appeal. Does this appeal persist today? In answer we turn to the volume *Man and His Symbols,* edited by C. G. Jung. At eighty-three Jung worked out the plan for this book, including the sections he wished his four closest associates to write. The closing months of his life were devoted to its editing and to writing the introduction. We quote from the opening section, "Ancient Myths and Modern Man," by Joseph Henderson:

We read the myths of the ancient Greeks or the folk stories of American Indians, but we fail to see any connection between them and our attitudes to the "heroes" or dramatic events of today. Yet the connections are there. And the symbols that represent them have not lost their relevance for mankind. [A] striking example should be familiar to anyone who has grown up in a Christian society. At Christmas we may express our inner feeling for the mythological birth of a semidivine child, even though we may not believe in the doctrine of the virgin birth of Christ or have any kind of conscious religious faith. Unknowingly, we have fallen in with the symbolism of rebirth. This is a relic of an immensely older solstice festival, which carries the hope that the fading winter landscape of the northern hemisphere will be renewed. For all our sophistication we find satisfaction in this symbolic festival, just as we join with our children at Easter in the pleasant ritual of Easter eggs and Easter rabbits.

But do we understand what we do, or see the connection between the story of Christ's birth, death, and resurrection and the folk symbolism of Easter? Usually we do not even care to consider such things intellectually. Yet they complement each other. Christ's crucifixion on Good Friday seems at first sight to belong to the same . . . symbolism that one finds in the rituals of such other "saviors" as Osiris, Tammuz, Orpheus, and Balder. They, too, were of divine or semidivine birth, they flourished, were killed, and were reborn. They belonged, in fact, to cyclic religions in which the death and rebirth of the god-king was an eternally recurring myth.[37]

Commenting, in effect, on fabricated church doctrines rather than original Christianity, which included gnostic ideas, Dr. Henderson continues: "But the resurrection of Christ on Easter Sunday is much less satisfying from a ritual point of view than is the symbolism of the cyclic religions. For Christ ascends to sit at the right hand of God the Father: His resurrection occurs once and for all. It is this finality of the Christian concept of the resurrection (the Christian idea of the Last Judgment has a similar 'closed' theme) that distinguishes Christianity from other god-king myths. It happened once, and the ritual merely commemorates it." This sense of finality, Dr. Henderson suggests, may have led to the blending of pagan and Christian customs. "The recurring promise of rebirth" was needed, "and that is what is symbolized by the egg and the rabbit of Easter." The pagan Easter was a sun reincarnating festival, coinciding with the vernal equinox when nature gloriously reawakens; the word Easter itself being derived from Ostara, the Scandinavian goddess of spring. Easter eggs were called eggs of Ostara.

Was it for a similar reason that the Church of the fifth century settled on the anciently honored solstice cycle for the birth of Jesus—when most of the sun gods were believed to be reborn? Jesus now shares his birth time with the Persian Mithra, Egyptian Osiris, Greek Bacchus, the Roman and Greek Apollo, and the Phoenician Adonis. Previous to the fifth century a wide variety of dates had been used for "Christmas."[38]]

THE RETURN OF THE GODS

[Archaeologists are infinitely perplexed to explain the marvelous structures of ancient man. How could an infant or adolescent humanity build such enduring monuments? How were enormous blocks of stone weighing many tons quarried, transported long distances, and fitted with unerring precision into some grand design? How did the men of old arrive at advanced astronomical knowledge? How explain their inventive genius, and exquisite artistic talents? The legends of the people concerned often tell of a golden age when the gods incarnated among men and taught them the arts and sciences, that in the course of time these teachers went away, promising to return at times of special need. During the golden age everyone lived as brothers; all knew the same truth and spoke the same language. But the time came when men and women had to put their knowledge to the test, when the gods departed and left them to work out their destiny, as parents do when their children come of age. It was then that many forgot the Real and began to think that forms and appearances were real instead.

Scientists tend to dismiss such stories as childish imaginings, and yet the celebrated Darwinist Thomas Huxley voiced his conviction—now echoed by many astronomers—that in an infinite universe there must be beings as much beyond man as man is beyond the beetle, and who may take an active part in the government of the natural order of things.[39] Reincarnationists would think of such entities as products of evolutionary growth through countless lives in many worlds.

Erich von Däniken has popularized the theory that the gods descended from outer space as astronauts riding in rocket ships.[40] But why should they take so much trouble, requiring extreme measures to permit their superior organisms to survive in our atmosphere, when all such difficulties could be avoided simply by incarnating here? Of Jesus it has been said, ''He became in all things like unto us.'' If he had appeared in his glorified body, how could he have communicated with ordinary mortals?

Turning now to ages subsequent to the legendary golden age, we shall find in chapter 4 that Hiawatha promised to return to his people, as did Viracocha of the Incas, Quetzalcoatl of the Aztecs, and across the seas there was the prophecy that King Arthur would come back. In the East the doctrine of avatars is taught, an avatar being the incarnation of a god or some exalted being who has progressed beyond the necessity of rebirths for his own individual progress. Krishna, Buddha, Lao Tze, and other sages are believed to be such incarnations. The Hindus speak of the Kalki Avatar to come, the Buddhists of Maitreya Buddha, the Zoroastrians of Sosiosh, while in Islam it is foretold that one of the Imam or great spiritual leaders will reappear. The Jews still expect their Messiah, who, we will see, some think had been Adam and later David. And do not Christians anticipate Christ's second advent? A few noted church fathers believed such help would be given many times, and so we find Synesius, Bishop of Ptolemais, in his *Treatise on Providence,* quoting approvingly this teaching received by Osiris, the great teacher of the Egyptians:

> You must not think that the gods are without employment, or that their descent to this earth is perpetual. For they descend according to orderly periods of time, for the purpose of imparting a beneficent impulse in the republics of

mankind. . . . But this happens when they harmonize a kingdom and send to this earth for that purpose souls who are allied to themselves. For this providence is divine and most ample, which frequently through one man pays attention to countless multitudes of men. . ·. . For there is indeed in this terrestrial abode the sacred tribe of heroes who pay attention to mankind, and who are able to give them assistance even in the smallest concerns. . . . This heroic tribe is, as it were, a colony [from the gods] established here in order that this terrene abode may not be left destitute of a better nature.

But when matter excites her [progeny] to war against the soul, the resistance made by these heroic tribes is small when the gods are absent; for everything is strong only in its appropriate place and time. . . . But when the harmony adapted in the beginning by the gods to all terrene things becomes old, they descend again to earth that they may call the harmony forth, energize and resuscitate it when it is as it were expiring.[41]

Synesius adds the further instruction received by Osiris that there is another compelling reason that will also bring the gods back: "When, however, the whole order of mundane things, greatest and least, is corrupted, then it is necessary that the gods should descend for the purpose of imparting another orderly distribution of things." In other words, "a new order of ages" must be commenced—something that many contemporary observers think our sick, war-torn, exhausted world, with its dying political, economic, and social systems, desperately needs today! As Krishna, the great teacher of the Hindus, says in the *Bhagavad-Gita:* "I produce myself among creatures whenever there is a decline of virtue and an insurrection of vice and injustice in the world; and thus I incarnate from age to age, for the preservation of the just, the destruction of the wicked, and the establishment of righteousness." A comparable idea may be found in the New Testament where Christ tells of his next coming. In Matthew 24:7–8, as translated in the New English Bible, published jointly by Oxford and Cambridge universities, he says: "The time is coming when . . . nation will make war upon nation, kingdom upon kingdom; there will be famines and earthquakes in many places. With all these things the birth-pangs of the *new age* begin." Please note that he says a "*new* age," not the end of the world, as the old translators of the Bible usually imply.

It is of interest to observe that the legends of the "return of the gods" are not to be found exclusively in the older mythologies and religions. Parallel ideas exist today. For example, "the sacred tribe of heroes," as just described, corresponds very closely to the view held by many people—and taught in modern theosophy—that connected with our globe is a fraternity of adepts and masters of wisdom who after death choose to return to earth life to help on the evolution of the human race to the degree its karma permits. With the theosophists, the gods of higher stature mentioned by Synesius would signify the saviors and avatars who at important cyclic intervals are believed to reincarnate here. It is held, however, that in the intervening times between their appearances, they never really depart from our universe, and never cease working for the human race. On the planes of mind and heart there are said to be no barriers to their help save those that individuals impose upon themselves.

Speaking generally of these various orders and degrees of advanced beings, William Q. Judge wrote in *The Ocean of Theosophy:* ''Man has never, then, been without a friend, but has a line of elder brothers who continually watch over the progress of the less progressed, preserve the knowledge gained through aeons of trial and experience, and continually seek for opportunities of drawing the developing intelligence of the race on this or other globes to consider the great truths concerning the destiny of the soul.''

The Elder Brothers of Humanity are men who were perfected in former periods of evolution. . . . In some periods they are well known to the people and move among ordinary men whenever the social organization, the virtue, and the development of the nations permit it. For if they were to come out openly and be heard of everywhere, they would be worshipped as gods by some and hunted as devils by others. In those periods when they do come out some of their number are rulers of men, some teachers, a few great philosophers, while others remain still unknown except to the most advanced of the body. . . .

The older mysteries continually refer to them. Ancient Egypt had them in her great king-initiates. . . . The story of Apollonius of Tyana is about a member of one of the same ancient orders. . . . Abraham and Moses of the Jews are two other Initiates, adepts who had their work to do with a certain people. . . . A mighty Triad acting on and through ethics is that composed of Buddha, Confucius, and Jesus. . . . All these great names represent members of the one single brotherhood, who all have a single doctrine. . . .

In the Sanskrit language there is a word which, being applied to them, at once thoroughly identifies them with humanity. It is Mahatma. This is composed of *Maha* great and *Atma* soul; so it means great soul, and as all men are souls, the distinction of the Mahatma lies in greatness. . . . All along the stream of Indian literature we can find the names by scores of great adepts who were well known to the people and who all taught the same story—the great epic of the human soul. . . . Still more, in the quiet unmovable East there are today, by the hundred, persons who know of their own knowledge that the Great Lodge still exists and has its Mahatmas, Adepts, Initiates, Brothers. . . . But in the West a materialistic civilization having arisen through a denial of the soul life and nature consequent upon a reaction from illogical dogmatism, there has not been any investigation of such subjects and, until lately, the general public has not believed in the possibility of anyone save a supposed God having such power . . . as I have ascribed to the Initiates.[42]

''The myth of the Mahatmas,'' incredible as it must seem to many, can probably receive its ultimate justification only if and when reincarnation is found to be a law in nature. On a one-life basis, perfection is an obvious impossibility. But given sufficient experience over vast periods of time, it is conceivable that any man can become a ''god.'' Of the Buddha it has been said, ''This is that Blossom on our human tree, which opens once in many myriad years—but opened, fills the world with Wisdom's scent.''[43]

In concluding our discussion we turn briefly to one area yet to be considered, but first mention that for those interested in a comparative study of world views on the ''return of the gods'' idea, the references in the Index under ''Reincarnation of Great Beings'' may prove helpful. The area now to be touched upon concerns the Scandinavian and Germanic myths relating to the twilight and death of the gods, which ends in a general conflagration. This theme is prominently featured in the *Ring* operas of Wagner. However, Carlyle, in *Heroes and Hero-Worship*, tells of the promised sequel, which calls to mind ''the new order of ages''[44] prophecies already discussed. He writes:

> The Gods and Jötuns, the divine powers and chaotic brute ones, after long contest and partial victory by the former, meet at last in universal world-embracing wrestle and duel; World-serpent against Thor, strength against strength; mutually extinctive; and ruin, ''twilight,'' sinking into darkness, swallows the created Universe. The Old Universe with its God is sunk; but it is not final death: there is to be a new Heaven and a new Earth.

Carlyle comments: ''Curious, this law of mutation, which also is a law written in man's inmost thought, had been deciphered by these old earnest Thinkers in their rude style; and how, though all dies, and even gods die, yet all death is but a phoenix fire-death, and new-birth into the Greater and the Better! It is the fundamental Law of Being for a creature made of Time, living in this Place of Hope. All earnest men have seen into it; may still see into it.''[45]]

In this chapter on myths and symbols an attempt has been made to correlate and synthesize ideas from many of the religions of the past and present. In chapter 3 the major religions will be taken up individually. Then tribal faiths and beliefs will be examined. This will complete the sections on religion, before proceeding in subsequent chapters to other departments of human search, learning, and living.

The Religious View–East and West

HINDU

["In the East the life of man is held to be a pilgrimage, not only from the cradle to the grave, but also through that vast period of time, embracing millions upon millions of years, stretching from the beginning to the end of a Manvantara, or period of evolution, and as he is held to be a spiritual being, the continuity of his existence is unbroken. Nations and civilizations rise, grow old, decline and disappear; but the being lives on, spectator of all the innumerable changes of environment. Starting from the great All, radiating like a spark from the central fire, he gathers experience in all ages, under all rulers, civilizations and customs, ever engaged in a pilgrimage to the shrine from which he came. He is now the ruler and now the slave; today at the pinnacle of wealth and power, tomorrow at the bottom of the ladder, perhaps in abject misery, but ever the same being. To symbolize this, the whole of India is dotted with sacred shrines, to which pilgrimages are made."[1]

The acceptance of rebirth has been practically universal in the Orient. Consequently, its philosophers and religious teachers felt no need to prove the doctrine, any more than an instructor in Western society would spend time demonstrating that day follows night, and night, day. Thus, the selections in the sections ahead will reflect the chief concern in the East: What kind of life releases one from unnecessary misery-causing involvement in the round of rebirths and leads to spiritual illumination, freedom, and ultimately Nirvana?

In the West there is considerable puzzlement about the latter concept, although the notion that Easterners equate Nirvana with annihilation has generally been abandoned. The original Hindu and Buddhist texts appear to support the view that it is essential to distinguish between the actual teachings of the great sages of the East and the later conventional emphasis on the attainment of the bliss and quietude of Nirvana as the supreme aim of man's incarnations on earth. If any religion promises a selfish, everlasting absorption in Nirvana, the philosophy of rebirth obviously fails to communicate its central message of eternal growth. In an infinite universe there should be infinite possibilities for growth in wisdom, self-realization, and expansion of consciousness, and for the development of compassion and the power to sacrifice—provided, of course, one is around to develop all these precious powers!]

The Vedas

What extracts from the Vedas *I have read fall on me like the light of a higher and purer luminary, which describes a loftier course through a purer stratum—free from particulars, simple, universal.*

HENRY DAVID THOREAU[2]

"If we wish to learn to understand the beginning of our own culture," writes Moriz Winternitz, "if we wish to understand the oldest Indo-European culture, we must go to India, where the oldest literature of an Indo-European people is preserved. For whatever view we may adopt on the problem of the antiquity of Indian literature, we can safely say that the oldest monument of the literature of the Indians is at the same time the oldest monument of Indo-European literature which we possess."[3] This is the generally accepted view of the Western Oriental scholars.

What is this oldest monument? Of the thousands of volumes of Indian literature that have thus far come to light, the Vedas are the most ancient. According to all traditions, they were first written down by the shores of Lake Manasarovara in Tibet before the Hindus or Aryas—the noble ones— descended into the Indian peninsula from their original home in central Asia. This scripture, says Nicol Macnicol, is, of course, "earlier than that of either Greece or Israel and reveals a high level of civilization among those who found in it the expression of their worship."[4] It should then be of significance to learn what the Vedas contain concerning reincarnation. Save for a few exceptions, Western orientalists deny outright that the Vedas teach reincarnation, and state that only in the Brahmanas and Upanishads the doctrine appears. Albert Schweitzer wrote: "The hymns of the Rig-Veda knew nothing as yet of a cycle of rebirths."[5]

However, the eminent philosopher and scholar Radhakrishnan, former president of India, in the introduction to his translation of *The Principal Upanishads,*[6] observes that the elements of reincarnation are to be found even in the earliest of the Vedas, the Rig: "The passage of the soul from the body, its dwelling in other forms of existence, its return to human form, the determination of future existence by the principle of Karma are all mentioned." "Mitra is born again.[7] The Dawn (Usas) is born again and again (I.92.10). 'I seek neither release nor return.'[8] 'The immortal self will be reborn in a new body due to its meritorious deeds.' "[9]

In *The Indian Heritage,* an anthology published on behalf of Unesco, Dr. V. Raghavan, head of the department of Sanskrit at the University of Madras, translates from the Rig Veda (X.16.3) "an important part of the prayers addressed to a dead person as his body is being cremated": "Let your eye go to the Sun; your life to the Wind; by the meritorious acts that you have done, go to heaven, and then (for rebirth) to the earth again. . . ."[10] Another writer, S. E. Gopala Charlu, in an article entitled "The Indian Doctrine of Reincarnation," comments favorably on Max Müller's translation from the 32nd Rik of the Rig Veda, I, 164: "Taking many births he has entered upon misery."[11]

If such references seem scant, we are reminded by Max Müller that a comprehensive evaluation of early Aryan thought is not possible. "We have no right to suppose," he says, "that we have even a hundredth part of the religious and popular poetry that existed during the Vedic age."[12] Furthermore, Dayanand Saraswati, the greatest Sanskritist of his day in India, declared in an interview that the most important of the ancient Hindu scriptures are preserved in places inaccessible to European scholars!

> When told that Professor Max Müller had declared to the audiences of his "Lectures" that the theory "that there was a primeval preternatural revelation granted to the fathers of the human race, finds but few supporters at present,"—the holy and learned [Dayanand Saraswati] laughed. His answer was suggestive: "If Mr. Moksh Mooler," as he pronounced the name, "were a Brahmin, and came with me, I might take him to a *gupta* cave (a secret crypt) near Okhee Math, in the Himalayas, where he would soon find out that what crossed the *Kalapani* (the black waters of the ocean) from India to Europe were only the *bits of rejected copies of some passages from our sacred books.* There *was* a 'primeval revelation,' and it still exists; nor will it ever be lost to the world, but will reappear; though the Mlechchhas [Western outcasts] will of course have to wait." Questioned further on this point, he would say no more. This was at Meerut, in 1880.[13]

The Vedas and later Hindu classical scriptures were composed in Sanskrit, described by its rediscoverer in the West, Sir William Jones, as "more perfect than the Greek, more copious than the Latin, and more exquisitely refined that either."[14] "Since the Renaissance," says Macdonell of Oxford, "there has been no event of such world-wide significance in the history of culture as [this] discovery of Sanskrit literature in the latter part of the eighteenth century."[15] It led directly, he says, to the formulation of four branches of comparative scientific study: comparative religion, mythology, literature, and philology, and had important effects in other fields as we shall see.

While Max Müller at one time believed the Vedas to be the lispings of infant humanity, the passages given here concerning the periodic sleep of the universe indicate a maturity of thought few people today can approach. The selections are from the Hymn of Prajapati in the Rig-Veda:

> Nor Aught nor Nought existed; yon bright sky
> Was not, nor heaven's broad roof outstretched above.
> What covered all? what sheltered? what concealed?
> Was it the water's fathomless abyss?
> There was not death—yet there was nought immortal,
> There was no confine betwixt day and night;
> The only One breathed breathless by itself,
> Other than It there nothing since has been.

The hymn tells later of the time when the universe reawakens, when "the germ that still lay covered in the husk burst forth, one nature, from the fervent heat." Then follow these tremendous questions:

> Who knows the secret? who proclaimed it here?
> Whence, whence this manifold creation sprang?
> The Gods themselves came later into being—
> Who knows from whence this great creation sprang?
> THAT, whence all this great creation came,
> Whether Its will created or was mute,
> The Most High Seer that is in highest heaven,
> He knows it—or perchance even He knows not.[16]

One should appreciate that the Sanskrit classics to which we now turn belong to the India of long-gone ages when her civilization attained prodigious heights in learning, art, medicine, and trade—quite a contrast to the squalor, disease, and poverty of modern India, only now struggling to recover from centuries of foreign domination, internal strife, and decline.

The Upanishads

[The Upanishads present the intimate yet profoundly impersonal instructions of master to disciple. They are viewed as philosophic interpretations of the

Vedas, and are a portion thereof, although composed much later. Together with the *Bhagavad-Gita,* next to be considered, they have over the centuries achieved such importance and stature in India as to be regarded as the Hindu bible. Dr. Radhakrishnan remarks that these sacred texts "are respected not because they are a part of *sruti* or revealed literature and so hold a reserved position but because they have inspired generations of Indians with vision and strength by their inexhaustible significance and spiritual power. . . . The fire still burns bright on their altars."[17]

Max Müller, who edited the fifty volumes of the *Sacred Books of the East* series, devotes the first volume to the Upanishads. In the introduction he writes: "My real love for Sanskrit literature was first kindled by the Upanishads. It was in the year 1844, when attending Schelling's lectures at Berlin, that my attention was drawn to those ancient theosophic treatises. . . . The earliest . . . will always, I believe, maintain a place in the literature of the world, among the most astounding productions of the human mind in any age or in any country."[18] Schopenhauer was quite rhapsodic about the Upanishads: "From every sentence deep, original, sublime thoughts arise. . . . In the whole world there is no study . . . so beneficial and so elevating. . . . It has been the solace of my life, it will be the solace of my death!"[19]

Our selections are from the translation of Charles Johnston, published in *Selections from the Upanishads and the Tao Te King.*[20] Johnston was a theosophist and a Sanskrit scholar who taught at Columbia University. The first extracts come from the Brihad Aranyaka Upanishad, the portion that deals with the states of sleep and dreams. Then this daily "reincarnation" cycle of sleeping and waking leads to a consideration of the alternations of death and rebirth.

The Brihad Aranyaka Upanishad tells of the visit of the sage Yajnavalkya to the kindgom of King Janaka. The sage avoids discussion with the king but eventually allows him to ask questions. "What is the light of the Spirit of man?" asks the king. Yajnavalkya tests both the persistence of the king and the depth of his question by responding with evasive answers. First the king is told that the sun is the light of the Spirit of man; next that the moon is the light; then fire; then voice. Each reply leads the king to question more deeply until he finally asks:]

But when the sun is set, Yajnavalkya, and the moon is also set, and the fire sinks down, and the voice is stilled, what is then the light of the Spirit of man?

The Soul then becomes his light; he answered. . . . What is the Soul? It is the Consciousness in the life-powers. It is the Light within the heart. . . .

The Spirit of man has two dwelling-places: both this world and the other world. The borderland between them is the third, the land of dreams. . . . This Spirit of man wanders through both worlds, yet remains unchanged.

Leaving the bodily world through the door of dream, the sleepless Spirit views the sleeping powers. . . . Soaring upward and downward in dreamland, the god makes manifold forms; now laughing and rejoicing with fair beauties, now beholding terrible things. . . . Then clothed in radiance, returns to his own home, [he] the gold-gleaming Genius, swan of everlasting. . . . [From this state, called *Sushupti,* when the body is in deepest slumber and the soul is said to be completely free] the Spirit of man returns again by the same path hurrying back to his former dwelling-place in the world of waking. . . .

Then as a wagon heavy-laden might go halting and creaking, so the embodied soul goes halting . . . when it has gone so far that a man is giving up the ghost. When he falls into weakness, then like as a mango or the fruit of the holy fig-tree is loosened from its stem, so the Spirit of man is loosed from these bodily members. . . . When he falls into a swoon, as though he had lost his senses, the life-powers are gathered in round the soul; and the soul, taking them up together in their radiant substance, enters with them into the inner heart. . . . Then the point of the heart grows luminous. . . . The soul becomes conscious and enters into Consciousness. . . .

And like as the [skin] of a snake lies lifeless, cast forth upon an ant-hill, so lies his body, when the Spirit of man rises up bodiless and immortal, as the Life, as the Eternal, as the Radiance. . . . As a worker in gold, taking an ornament, moulds it to another form newer and fairer; so in truth the soul, leaving the body here, and putting off unwisdom, makes for itself [in the heavenly state] another form newer and fairer: a form like the forms of departed souls, or of the seraphs, or of the gods. . . .

Through his past works he shall return once more to birth, entering whatever form his heart is set on. When he has received full measure of reward in paradise for the works he did, from that world he returns again to this, the world of works. . . . According as were his works and walks in [another] life, so he becomes. He that does righteously becomes righteous. He that does evil becomes evil. He becomes holy through holy works and evil through evil. As they said of old: Man verily is formed of desire; as his desire is, so is his will; as his will is, so he works; and whatever work he does, in the likeness of it he grows. . . .

Who knows the Soul, and sees himself as it—what should he long for, or desiring what should he fret for the fever of life? By whom the awakened Soul is known while he dwells in the wilderness of the world, he is creator of all and maker of all; his is the world, for he is the world. . . . This mighty Soul unborn grows not old, nor dies, for the Soul is immortal and fearless. The Soul is the fearless Eternal. He grows one with the Eternal, the fearless Eternal, who knows this. . . .

This is to be understood by the heart: there is no separateness at all. He goes from death to death who beholds separateness.

[The next extracts are from the Katha Upanishad. A young man, Nachiketas, has gone to the House of Death, and Yama, the god of death, grants him three wishes. It is interesting that later in the dialogue the name Nachiketas is used to designate the spiritual fire hidden deep within all beings. When lit up in the individual it is believed capable of transmuting the "mortal" into the immortal.]

NACHIKETAS SPEAKS   This doubt there is of a man that has [died]: "He exists," say some; and "He exists not," others say. A knowledge of this, taught by thee, this of my wishes is the third wish.

DEATH SPEAKS   . . . not easily knowable, and subtle is this law. Choose, Nachiketas, another wish; hold me not to it; but spare me this. . . . Choose sons and grandsons of a hundred years, and much cattle, and elephants and gold and horses. . . . Choose wealth and length of days. . . . These beauties, with their chariots and lutes . . . be waited on by them. . . . Ask me not of death, Nachiketas.

NACHIKETAS SPEAKS   Tomorrow these fleeting things wear out the vigour of a mortal's powers. Even the whole of life is short. . . . Not by wealth can a man be satisfied. Shall we choose wealth if we have seen thee? Shall we desire life while thou art master?. . . . This that they doubt about, O Death, what is in the great Beyond, tell me of that. This wish that draws near to the mystery, Nachiketas chooses no other wish than that. . . .

DEATH SPEAKS   Thou indeed, pondering on dear and dearly-loved desires, O Nachiketas, hast passed them by. Not this way of wealth hast thou chosen, in which many men sink. . . . The great Beyond gleams not for the child led away by the delusion of possessions. "This is the world, there is no other," he thinks, and so falls again and again under my dominion. . . . Thou art steadfast in the truth; may a questioner like thee, Nachiketas, come to us. . . .

   The knower is never born nor dies, nor is it from anywhere, nor did it become anything. Unborn, eternal, immemorial, this ancient is not slain when the body is slain. . . . Smaller than small, greater than great, this Self is hidden in the heart of man. . . . In all beings it shines not forth; but is perceived by the piercing subtle soul of the subtle-sighted. . . . Understanding this great lord the Self, bodiless in bodies, stable among unstable, the wise man cannot grieve. . . . He is released from the mouth of Death, having gained the lasting thing which is above the great, which has neither sound nor touch nor form nor change nor taste nor smell, but is eternal, beginningless, endless.

This is the immemorial teaching of Nachiketas, declared by Death. Speaking it and hearing it the sage is mighty in the eternal world. Whosoever, being pure, shall cause this supreme secret to be heard in the assembly of those who seek the Eternal . . . he indeed builds for endlessness, he builds for endlessness. . . .

DEATH SPEAKS   As fire, being one, on entering the world, is assimilated to form after form; so the inner Self of all being is assimilated to form after form, and yet remains outside them. As the air, being one, on entering the world, is assimilated to form after form; so the inner Self of all being is assimilated to form after form, and yet remains outside them. . . .

Know that the Self is the lord of the chariot, the body verily is the chariot; know that the soul is the charioteer, and emotion the reins. They say that the bodily powers are the horses, and that the external world is their field. When the Self, the bodily powers and emotion are joined together, this is the right enjoyer; thus say the wise. But for the unwise, with emotion ever unrestrained, his bodily powers run away with him, like the unruly horses of the charioteer. . . . He who is unwise, restrains not emotion, and is ever impure . . . returns to the world of birth and death. . . . He whose charioteer is wisdom, who grasps the reins—emotion—firmly, he indeed gains the end of the path, the supreme resting-place of the emanating Power.

The impulses are higher than the bodily powers; emotion is higher than the impulses; soul is higher than emotion; higher than soul is the Self, the great one.[21] Higher than this great one is the unmanifest; higher than the unmanifest is spirit. Than spirit nothing is higher. . . . In it all the worlds rest. . . .

He who perceives the living Self . . . close at hand, the lord of what has been and what shall be, he is no longer seeking for refuge. . . . This is the ineffable supreme joy. . . . This is . . . the undying Eternal . . . the harbor of those who would cross over—may we master the fire of Nachiketas. . . . When all the desires that dwell in his heart are let go, the mortal becomes immortal, and reaches the Eternal. When all the knots of his heart are untied here, the mortal becomes immortal. . . .

NACHIKETAS SPEAKS   I know that what [people] call treasure is unenduring; and by unlasting things what is lasting cannot be obtained. Therefore the Nachiketas fire was kindled by me, and for these unenduring things I have gained that which endures. . . .

Nachiketas thus having received the knowledge declared by Death, and the whole law of union, became a passionless dweller in the Eternal, and Deathless; and so may another who thus knows the union with the Self.

※ ※ ※

The Bhagavad-Gita

[The theme of reincarnation pervades much of the celebrated scripture, *The Bhagavad-Gita*. The important second chapter is largely devoted to rebirth. It has been known and admired in the West for some two hundred years, and in the last century the interest in reincarnation of various American and European transcendentalists can be traced to the study of this poem.

The *Gita* has appealed to minds of diverse character. The atomic scientist Robert Oppenheimer not only studied the *Gita* but learned Sanskrit in order to read it and other works in the original.[22] A century earlier, a very different sort of man, Henry David Thoreau, had this to say in *Walden* (chapter 16):

> In the morning I bathe my intellect in the stupendous and cosmogonal philosophy of the *Bhagvat Geeta*, since whose composition years of the gods have elapsed, and in comparison with which our modern world and its literature seem puny and trivial; and I doubt if that philosophy is not to be referred to a previous state of existence, so remote is its sublimity from our conceptions. I lay down the book and go to my well for water, and lo! there I meet the servant of the Brahmin . . . come to draw water for his master, and our buckets as it were grate together in the same well. Thé pure Walden water is mingled with the sacred water of the Ganges.

In Emerson's *Journal* (1848) there is this entry: "I owed—my friend and I owed—a magnificent day to the *Bhagavat Geeta*. It was the first books; it was as if an empire spake to us, nothing small or unworthy, but large, serene, consistent . . ."[23] Arthur Christy writes that "no one oriental volume that ever came to Concord was more influential than the *Bhagavadgita*." "This is evident from the manner and frequency in which the Concordians spoke of it." "Sanborn says[24] that for years Emerson was one of the very few Americans who owned a copy, and that his was even more widely used than that in the Harvard College Library."[25]

Emerson used the translation of Sir Charles Wilkins, which when it appeared in Europe in 1785 was received with astonishment. Three years later a Russian translation was published at the Moscow University Press through the agency of Nikolai Novikov, the eminent Russian journalist and writer.[26] The first German rendition is dated 1802, and August von Schlegel, who studied Sanskrit, edited the work in 1823. Schlegel's glowing tribute will be quoted later.

The preface to the Wilkins *Gita* was penned by Warren Hastings, the first British governor-general of India. Emerson in his essay "English Traits" made this comment: "I am not surprised . . . to find an Englishman like Warren Hastings, who had been struck with the grand style of thinking in the Indian writings" offering his countrymen a translation of the *Gita*. "For a self-conceited modish life, made up of trifles, clinging to a corporeal civilization, hating ideas, there is no remedy like the Oriental largeness. That astonishes and disconcerts English decorum. For once, there is thunder it never heard, light it never saw, and power which trifles with time and space."[27]

In India the *Gita* has always been held in highest esteem, and numerous commentaries have been made. "When disappointments stare me in the face," wrote Gandhi, "and when I see not one ray of light . . . I turn to the *Bhagavad-Gita* . . . and I immediately begin to smile in the midst of overwhelming sorrow. My life has been full of external tragedies and if they have not left any visible and indelible effect on me, I owe it to the teaching of *The Bhagavad-Gita*."[28]

In the *Gita,* the Upanishads, and earlier texts, hard-and-fast class distinctions were not made, and untouchability as later enforced was unheard of. Only in subsequent ages did cruel caste practices arise. In fact, much of the irrational belief of rebirth into subhuman forms arose because orthodox Brahmins, preserving power through rigid caste rules, threatened that violation could mean incarnation as an animal or insect! As to the outcasts, or untouchables—whom Gandhi renamed Harijans—the great reformer wrote that "it is a misuse of the doctrine of previous births to argue that these people will require generations before they can come up to the level of the so-called higher castes. The *Gita* teaches us that it is as open to an untouchable as to a learned pundit to attain salvation in the existing birth."[29] If the high castes are really higher, he said, they should have no fear of associating with the lower.

The *Gita* forms a small but all-important part of the longest and perhaps greatest epic ever written, the *Mahabharata*. Elizabeth Seeger, in her young people's version of this classic, says that it "is three times as long as the Bible and eight times as long as the *Iliad* and the *Odyssey* put together" and contains "the storehouse of genealogy, mythology, and antiquity" of the Hindus.[30]

The *Bhagavad-Gita* is referred to as the heart and soul of the *Mahabharata*. *Gita* means song, and *Bhagavad* is one of the titles of Krishna, the great spiritual teacher of the Hindus whose instruction is recorded in the poem. He is regarded as an avatar who descended among men at a crucial cycle in humanity's history, the eve of what the Indians call the Kali Yuga, or spiritually dark age, the first five thousand years of which ended in 1897, according to the Brahmanical calendar. Krishna is said to have incarnated in order to strike the keynote of those moral and philosophical ideas that should resound in people's minds and hearts throughout the revolution of the entire age, at the end of which a new golden age is to begin.

The *Gita* is in the form of a dialogue between Krishna and Arjuna, a prince who is waging war to regain his kingdom usurped by a hundred wicked cousins. Those unaware of the Hindu psychological system might view this only in a literal sense as an actual armed conflict. In reality the war theme may enhance the story rather than, as some think, disfigure it, because a battle demands supreme effort and commitment. Did not Jesus say that the Kingdom of Heaven is to be taken by violence[31] and not by weakness of attack? "Know'st thou not," writes Walt Whitman, that "there is but one theme for ever enduring bards? And that is the theme of War, the fortune of battles, the making of perfect soldiers."[32] Gandhi viewed the *Gita* in this light, as the noted Hindu writer Ved Mehta makes plain in a three-issue series in *The New Yorker* on the life of Gandhi. Mehta speaks of Gandhi's first acquaintance with the poem when the latter went to London to study law, and was introduced to that scripture by some theosophists, at the same time making his first acquaintance with the Bible:

> The humanitarian spirit of the Theosophists and the moral lessons of the Sermon on the Mount made a lasting impression on him. . . . It was actually thanks to his Theosophist friends that Gandhi started learning about his own religion, by reading the *Bhagavad Gita,* which he was ashamed of never having read, either in the original Sanskrit or in a Gujarati translation, and which he now tackled eagerly in Sir Edwin Arnold's popular English translation. In time, the *Bhagavad Gita* became the most important book in his life. . . .
>   "Even in 1888–89, when I first became acquainted with the Gita," Gandhi writes, "I felt that it was not a historical work, but that, under the guise of physical warfare, it described the duel that perpetually went on in the hearts of mankind, and that physical warfare was brought in merely to make the description of the internal duel more alluring." For Gandhi, the two armies were the forces of good and evil—the higher and baser impulses—and the battlefield of Kurukshetra was the atman. For him, the forces of good and evil were constantly at war in the atman, and every action, however insignificant or inconsequential, was a cause for battle.[33]

Elsewhere Gandhi says: "I regard Duryodhana and his party as the lower impulses. . . . Krishna is the Dweller within,[34] ever whispering to a pure heart. . . . An eternal battle is going on between the two camps, and the Poet-seer vividly describes it."[35] These interpretative clues will deepen our understanding of Arjuna's harrowing description (in the first chapter) of his confused mental and emotional state at the prospect of slaying his "kindred." Once any Arjuna—the hero in each human—has resolved to live a higher life, his old selfish tendencies or "relatives," fighting for their very existence, throw up clouds of doubt, fear, and despondency to attempt to deter him from proceeding further.

The translation we use is a composite one and is largely from the Wilkins edition, but where there are obvious obscurities or blind renderings in this latter edition, they have been corrected back to the original by the compiler. The most authoritative of the scholarly translations is probably that of Radhakrishnan.[36] This is necessarily a literal reading, and while excellent, hardly does justice to the poetic beauty and power of the Sanskrit original. The Wilkins edition may prove of special interest to our readers. This was the *Gita* of Emerson and Thoreau, and of all the others in England and America who first read the poem in English. We add at the end a brief excerpt from the Prabhavananda-Isherwood translation.]

ARJUNA Now, O Krishna, that I have beheld my kindred thus standing anxious for the fight, my members fail me, my countenance withereth, the hair standeth on end upon my body, and all my frame trembleth with horror! Even Gandiva, my bow, slips from my hand, and my skin is parched and dried up. I am not able to stand; for my mind as it were, whirleth round, and I behold on all sides adverse omens. When I shall have destroyed my kindred, shall I longer look for happiness? . . . I would rather patiently suffer that the sons of Dhritarashtra . . . kill me unresisting in the field. . . . I shall not fight, O Govinda. . . .

KRISHNA Whence, O Arjuna, cometh upon thee this dejection in matters of difficulty, so unworthy of the honorable, and leading neither to heaven nor to glory? . . . Abandon this despicable weakness of thy heart, and stand up. . . . Thou grievest for those who may not be lamented. . . . I myself never was not, nor thou, nor all the princes of the earth; nor shall we ever hereafter cease to be. As the Lord of this mortal frame experienceth therein infancy, youth, and old age, so in future incarnations will it meet the same. One who is confirmed in this belief is not disturbed by anything that may come to pass. . . . As a man throweth away old garments and putteth on new, even so the dweller in the body, having quitted its old mortal frames, entereth into others which are new. . . .[37]

The man who believeth that it is this Spirit which killeth, and he who thinketh that it may be destroyed, are both alike deceived; for it neither killeth nor is it killed. It is not a thing of which a man may say, "It hath been, it is about to be, or is to be hereafter"; for it is without birth and meeteth not death; it is ancient, constant, and eternal, and is not slain when this its mortal frame is destroyed. . . . The weapon divideth it not, the fire burneth it not, the water corrupteth it not, the wind drieth it not away; for it is indivisible, inconsumable, incorruptible, and is not to be dried away; it is eternal, universal, permanent, immovable; it is invisible, inconceivable, and unalterable; therefore, knowing it to be thus, thou shouldst not grieve. . . .

This perishable body, O son of Kunti, is known as Kshetra; those who are acquainted with the true nature of things call the soul who knows it, the Kshetrajna. . . . That knowledge which through the soul is a realization of both the known and the knower is alone esteemed by me as wisdom. . . . Know, O chief of the Bharatas, that whenever anything, whether animate or inanimate, is produced, it is due to the union of the Kshetra and Kshetrajna—body and the soul[38]. . . . The deluded do not see the spirit when it quitteth or remains in the body, nor when, moved by the qualities, it has experience in the world. But those who have the eye of wisdom perceive it, and devotees who industriously strive to do so see it dwelling in their own hearts.

KRISHNA   This exhaustless doctrine of Yoga[39] I formerly taught unto Vivaswat; Vivaswat communicated it to Manu and Manu made it known unto Ikshwaku; and being thus transmitted from one unto another it was studied by the Rajarshees (Royal Sages), until at length in the course of time the mighty art was lost. . . . It is even the same exhaustless, secret, eternal doctrine I have this day communicated unto thee because thou art my devotee and my friend.

ARJUNA   Seeing that thy birth is posterior to the life of Ikshwaku, how am I to understand that thou wert in the beginning the teacher of this doctrine?

KRISHNA   Both I and thou have passed through many births! Mine are known unto me, but thou knowest not of thine. . . . I produce myself among creatures, O son of Bharata, whenever there is a decline of virtue and an insurrection of vice and injustice in the world; and thus I incarnate from age to age for the preservation of the just, the destruction of the wicked, and the establishment of righteousness. . . .

ARJUNA   On account of the restlessness of the mind, I do not perceive any possibility of steady continuance in this yoga of equanimity which thou hast declared. For indeed, O Krishna, the mind is full of agitation, turbulent, strong, and obstinate. I believe the restraint of it to be as difficult as that of the wind.

KRISHNA   Without doubt, O thou of mighty arms, the mind is restless and hard to restrain; but it may be restrained by practice and absence of desire. . . . To whatsoever object the inconstant mind goeth out [one] should subdue it, bring it back, and place it upon the Spirit. Supreme bliss surely cometh to the sage whose mind is thus at peace. . . .

ARJUNA   What end, O Krishna, doth that man attain who, although having faith, hath not attained to perfection in his devotion because his unsubdued mind wandered from the discipline? Doth he . . . become destroyed, being deluded in the path of the Supreme Spirit? . . .

KRISHNA   Such a man doth not perish here or hereafter. For never to an evil place goeth one who doeth good. The man whose devotion has been broken off by death goeth to the regions of the righteous, where he dwells for an immensity of years and is then born again on earth in a pure and fortunate family; or even in a family of those who are spiritually illuminated. But such a rebirth into this life as this last is more difficult to obtain. Being thus born again he comes in contact with the knowledge which belonged to him in his former body, and from that time he struggles more diligently towards perfection, O son of Kuru. For even unwittingly, by reason of that past practice, he is led and works on. Even if only a mere enquirer, he reaches beyond the word of the Vedas. But the devotee, who, striving with all his might, obtaineth perfection because of efforts continued through many births, goeth to the supreme goal. . . .

ARJUNA   If according to thy opinion, O giver of all that men ask, knowledge is superior to the practice of deeds, why then dost thou urge me to engage in an undertaking so dreadful as this? Thou, as it were with doubtful speech, confusest my reason. . . .

KRISHNA   A man enjoyeth not freedom from action from the non-commencement of that which he hath to do; nor doth he obtain happiness from a total abandonment of action. . . . He who remains inert, restraining the senses and organs, yet pondering with his heart upon objects of sense, is called a false pietist of bewildered soul. But he who having subdued all his passions performeth with his active faculties all the duties of life, unconcerned as to their result, is to be esteemed. . . . The man of purified heart, having his body fully controlled, his senses restrained, and for whom the only self is the Self of all creatures, is not tainted although performing actions. . . . Whoever in acting dedicates his actions to the Supreme Spirit and puts aside all selfish interest in their result is untouched by sin, even as the leaf of the lotus is unaffected by the waters. . . .

The action which is right to be done, performed without attachment to results, free from pride and selfishness, is of the *sattva* quality [of goodness]. That one is of the *rajas* quality [of passionate action] which is done with a view to its consequences, or with great exertion, or with egotism. And that which is undertaken without regard to its consequences, or the power to carry it out, or the harm it may cause, is of the quality of darkness—*tamas*. . . . When the embodied self surpasseth these three qualities of goodness, action, and indifference . . . it is released from rebirth and death, old age and pain, and drinketh of the water of immortality. . . . [He] who is of equal mind in pain and pleasure, self-centered, to whom a lump of earth, a stone, or gold is as one; who is of equal mind with those who love or dislike; constant, the same whether blamed or praised; equally minded in honor and disgrace, and the same towards friendly or unfriendly side, engaging only in necessary actions, such an one hath surmounted the qualities. . . .

Those who thus preserve an equal mind gain heaven even in this life. Such illuminated sages whose sins are exhausted, who are free from delusion . . . and devoted to the good of all creatures, obtain assimilation with the Supreme Spirit. Assimilation with the Supreme Spirit is on both sides of death for those who are free from desire and anger, temperate, of thoughts restrained; and who are acquainted with the true Self. [They are] emancipated from birth and death even in this life. . . . He who seeth the Supreme Being existing alike imperishable in all perishable things, sees indeed. Perceiving the same Lord present in everything and everywhere, he does not by the lower self destroy his own soul, but goeth to the supreme end. . . . As a single sun illuminateth the whole world, even so doth the One Spirit illumine every body. . . .

Hast thou heard all this, O son of Pritha, with mind one-pointed? Has the delusion of thought which arose from ignorance been removed, O Dhanajaya? . . . I [have] made known unto thee this knowledge which is a mystery more secret than secrecy itself; ponder it fully in thy mind; act as seemeth best unto thee. . . .

ARJUNA   By thy divine power, O thou who fallest not, my delusion is destroyed, I am collected once more; I am free from doubt, firm, and will act
according to thy bidding.[40]

[The *Gita* has sections on cosmogony as well as human psychology, and these teach of reincarnation on a universal scale. In Hindu cosmogenesis the periodic rebirth of the universe is referred to in the doctrine of the days and nights of Brahmâ. Each day of activity, or Manvantara, is supposed to last several billions of years, and the night of sleep and rest has equal length. Of this cosmic law the *Gita* says:]

All the worlds, and even the heavenly realm of Brahmâ, are subject to the laws of rebirth. . . . [When a new world is born] day dawns, and all those lives that lay hidden asleep come forth and show themselves, mortally man-ifest. Night falls, and all are dissolved into the sleeping germ of life. Thus they are seen, O Prince, and appear unceasingly, dissolving with the dark, and with day returning back to the new birth, new death. . . .[41] But behind the manifest . . . there is another Existence, which is eternal and changeless. This is not dissolved in the general cosmic dissolution. It has been called the unmanifest, the imperishable. To reach it is said to be the greatest of all achievements.[42]

The Anugita

[The dialogue in the *Anugita* forms part of the *Mahabharata* and takes place after Arjuna has regained his kingdom. The hero is walking with Krishna in the palace of Maya, and confesses that he has forgotten much that the sage had taught him on the field of battle. Krishna replies: "From me you heard a mystery, and learnt about the eternal (principle), about piety in (its true form), and about the everlasting worlds. . . . That doctrine was perfectly adequate . . . It is not possible for me to state it again in full in that way. . . . But I shall relate an ancient story upon that subject, so that adhering to this knowledge, you may attain the highest goal." Krishna then says that he lived on earth in those early days when a visitor from the heavenly world of Brahmâ descended among men and originally told the story. The first episode selected is from a dialogue between the senses and the mind as to which of them is most powerful. The mind that incarnates from life to life is obviously more powerful, but, as the senses point out, it is dependent upon the bodily senses to manifest in this world.]

The mind said: The nose smells not without me, the tongue does not perceive taste, the eye does not take in color, the skin does not become aware of any object of touch. Without me, the ear does not in any way hear sound. I am the eternal chief among all elements. Without me, the senses never shine, like an empty dwelling, or like fires the flames of which are extinct. Without me, all beings . . . fail to apprehend qualities or objects, even with the senses exerting themselves.

[Experiments in somnambulism would appear to support what the mind has just declared. When an object, for example, is waved before the sleep-walker's opened eyes, the retina, as usual, mechanically picks up the light vibrations reflected from the object, transmits them via the optic nerve to the brain, but nothing is perceived because the mind has been withdrawn from waking life and is conscious in another state. The next selections consider the subject of the incarnation of the mind-soul in a new body, and then how emancipation may be obtained.]

There is no destruction here of actions good or not good. Coming to one body after another they become ripened in their respective ways. As a fruitful (tree) producing fruit may yield much fruit, so does merit performed with a pure mind become expanded. For the self engages in action, putting forward this mind.

And now further, hear how a man, overwhelmed with action . . . enters a womb. Within the womb of a woman he obtains as the result of action a body good or bad. . . . [The soul] is the seed of all beings; by that all creatures exist. That soul, entering all the limbs of the foetus, part by part, and dwelling in the seat of the life-wind (the heart), supports them with the mind. Then the foetus, becoming possessed of consciousness, moves about its limbs. . . . And as a blazing lamp shines in a house, even so does consciousness light up bodies. And whatever action he performs, whether good or bad, everything done in a former body must necessarily be enjoyed or suffered. . . .

I shall explain the science of concentration of mind, than which there is nothing higher, (and which teaches) how devotees concentrating (their minds) perceive the perfect self. . . . Learn from me the paths by which one directing the self within the self perceives the eternal (principle). Restraining the senses, one should fix the mind on the self. . . . And as one may show the soft fibres, after extracting them from the mango fruit, so does a devotee see the self extracted from the body. The body is called the mango; the soft fibres[43] stand for the self. This is the excellent illustration propounded by those who understand concentration of mind. When an embodied (self) properly perceives the self concentrated, then there is no ruler over him, since he is the lord of the triple world. He obtains various bodies as he pleases; and casting aside old age and death, he grieves not and exults not. . . . [The Self] is not to be grasped by the eye, nor by any of the senses. Only by the mind used as a lamp is the great Self perceived. . . .

Two syllables are death; three syllables the eternal Brahma. "Mine" (mama) is death, and "not mine" (na mama) is the eternal. . . . Therefore those who are farsighted have no attachment to actions. . . . The self-restrained man who thus understands the immortal, changeless, incomprehensible, and ever indestructible, unattached (principle), he dies not. He who thus understands the self to which there is nothing prior, which is uncreated . . . he certainly becomes immortal. . . .

I have now declared everything to you . . . Act thus forthwith; then you will acquire perfection.[44]

[This instruction concludes the ancient story, covering many chapters, related by Krishna, and Arjuna asks: Who, indeed, was that Teacher O Krishna, and who the pupil? Krishna answers: "I am the preceptor and know the mind to be my pupil." So here, again, as indicated when introducing the Bhagavad-Gita, Krishna appears to be a symbol for the Higher Self in all beings, while the pupil is the awakened mind, or the Arjuna in each of us.]

✳ ✳ ✳
The Puranas

[The *Puranas,* which literally mean "ancient," are a collection of symbolical and allegorical writings, eighteen in number, supposed to have been composed by Vyasa, the author of the *Mahabharata.* The most perfectly preserved is held to be the *Vishnu Purana,* while the most popular is the *Bhagavata Purana,* which deals at length with the incarnations of Vishnu and particularly with his embodiment as Krishna.

The writings are divided into three groups in each of which one of the three chief gods of the Hindu pantheon holds preeminence. Philosophically viewed, Brahmâ, Vishnu, and Shiva, the Hindu trimurti—or the Creator, Preserver, and the Destroyer—are not anthropomorphic deities dwelling in their respective heavens, but beneficent, universal, impersonal powers at the root of all life, and which all beings are using all the time. Shiva, the Destroyer, is held to be higher than Vishnu because in phoenix-fire manner he destroys only to regenerate on a higher plane. All centers of life, from atoms up to worlds and galaxies, are therefore said to go through these cyclic periods of creation, preservation, and destruction, followed by regeneration or rebirth. Reincarnation is thus regarded as a universal law applicable at all times and at all levels of being.

The *Kurma Purana,* from which the following allegory is taken, relates to the god Shiva, the patron of Yogis, one of his many titles being Maha-Yogi, the great ascetic. He is the patron of the true Yogi, probably because the latter has undertaken the difficult task of destroying, or rather transforming, all the lower elements of his nature. This is the daily job of every man, according to Goethe: "As long as you are not aware of the continual law of Die and Be Again, you are merely a vague guest on a dark earth" ("Selige Schnucht").]

There was a great god-sage called Narada. . . . He traveled everywhere, and one day he was passing through a forest, and he saw a man who had been meditating until the white ants had built a huge mound round his body, so long had he been sitting in that position. He said to Narada, "Where are you going?" Narada replied, "I am going to heaven." "Then ask [Shiva] when He will be merciful to me, when I shall attain freedom." Further on Narada saw another man. He was jumping about, singing and dancing, and he said, "O Narada, where are you going?" Narada said, "I am going to heaven." "Then ask when I shall attain freedom."

So Narada went on. In the course of time he came again by the same road, and there was the man who had been meditating till the ant-hills had grown

round him. He said, "O Narada, did you ask the Lord about me?" "O yes."
"What did He say?" "The Lord told me that you would attain freedom in
four more births." Then the man began to weep and wail, and said, "I have
meditated until an ant-hill has been raised around me, and I have to endure
four more births yet!" Narada went on to the other man. "Did you ask about
me?" "O yes. Do you see this tamarind tree? I have to tell you that as many
leaves as there are on that tree, so many times you will be born, and then you
will attain freedom." Then the man began to dance for joy, and said, "After
so short a time I shall be free!" A voice came, "My child, you shall have
freedom this instant."[45]

The Laws of Manu

[The *Code of Manu,* a metrical work of some twenty-six hundred verses,
dealing with religion, law, custom, and politics, has exercised immeasurable
influence on the Hindus over the centuries. Manu gave support to custom
and convention at a time when they were apparently being seriously under-
mined. A number of changes have probably been made in the original code to
serve the special interests of the higher castes in keeping the other castes "in
line." A few of the "laws" are designed to inculcate fear of regression into
lower castes or into subhuman forms. Although women are to be highly
honored, they are not allowed independence at any stage of their life. However, many noble ethical precepts still remain in the code. The parenthetical
additions are by the translator.]

With whatever disposition of mind (a man) performs any act, he reaps its
result in a (future) body endowed with the same quality. . . .

Giving no pain to any creature, let him slowly accumulate spiritual
merit. . . . For in the next world neither father, nor mother, nor wife, nor
sons, nor relations stay to be his companions; spiritual merit alone remains
(with him). Single is each being born; single it dies; single it enjoys (the reward
of its) virtue; single (it suffers the punishment of its) sin. . . .

By deep meditation let him recognize the subtle nature of the supreme
Self, and its presence in all organisms. . . . Let him recognize by the practice of meditation the progress of the individual soul through beings of various kinds, (a progress) hard to understand for unregenerate men. He who
possesses the true insight (into the nature of the world), is not fettered by his
deeds; but he who is destitute of that insight is drawn into the circle of births
and deaths. . . .

(If you ask) whether among all these virtuous actions, (performed) here below, (there be) one which has been declared more efficacious (than the rest) for securing supreme happiness to man, (the answer is that) the knowledge of the Self is stated to be the most excellent among all of them; for that is the first of all sciences, because immortality is gained through that.[46]

[The idea that immortality is to be "gained" relates to the teaching that *conscious* immortality must be earned or won. While all beings are held to be essentially immortal, few have acquired the power to maintain continuity of consciousness through any and every state. The perfected soul can apparently rise or descend at will from state to state in full awareness, preserving in one state the knowledge gained in previous conditions. Consequently, such beings possess actual knowledge of the states after death and before birth. A practical and indispensable means for attaining conscious immortality is said to be through what the Hindus call *ekagrata,* or one-pointedness, and a ceaseless dwelling on that which is real in all things and beings. Buddha frequently spoke of the need to cultivate the ability to preserve spiritual wakefulness from moment to moment. One who gains this capacity may remain fully conscious of the inner transitions that come after death.

Another perhaps unfamiliar idea included in the extracts quoted is that the soul experiences the afterdeath states "singly." The Hindus teach that such states are subjective, similar to dreams. The people and scenes there encountered are self-created, having as their basis the thoughts and acts of waking life. The lower thoughts and feelings are accumulated and disposed of in a kind of purgatorial condition, leaving intact the noble qualities and tendencies deserving survival as part of the immortal soul. The latter then form the basis for a blissful, heavenly state that endures until the individual's unfulfilled aspirations are fully assimilated into the character through a process of visionary realization. He is then irresistibly and magnetically drawn back to earth life by the force of his unexpended karma. It is here, in this objective sphere, the Hindus say, we meet again our friends and companions. In the afterworld they will be deeply felt as ever present, but objective communication is no more likely there than in a nightly dream. This may be fortunate, for in all verbal exchanges the possibility of friction exists, and then peace and tranquillity would be at an end!]

The Hitopadesa

[The *Hitopadesa* is composed of a collection of ethical precepts, allegories, and other tales from an old scripture, *The Panchatantra.* The word

Hitopadesa means "good advice." The parable as here retold is called "The Tale of the Banana Peel."]

A laughing child running after a butterfly saw a banana peel lying in the path. He kicked it aside and ran on. Soon, a bent and blind old man came that way. He would have slipped and fallen into the ditch but for the impulsive act of the good-natured little boy. For this unconscious deed, the Karma of his next life saved the boy from being struck by a great tumbling stone on that very path. . . .

Once again the banana peel is found lying in a path. Wandering wearily and hungrily along, a beggar saw the peel and picked it up, hoping to find a morsel of food. But no; it was only a peel; so he threw it away, saying to himself, "This is my Karma." Then along came a fat merchant, whose unfaithful servant the beggar had been in a former life. Not watching the path, the merchant would have had a bad fall, but for the beggar's care to throw aside the banana peel. This action, and the beggar's acceptance of his own lot, made him a respected master of caravans in his next incarnation.

Again the picture changes, this time showing a desert warrior mounted on a dromedary, a "flying camel," as the Arabs say. All day he had been pursuing a fleeing enemy. Now, at last, he was gaining in the chase, even though his hungry dromedary was stumbling from exhaustion. Seeing the banana peel in the track, the warrior bethought him of his faithful mount. He stopped that it might eat this delicious tidbit—delicious, that is, for a camel! Meanwhile, the enemy escaped; but in the next life, for his kindness this warrior was reborn as a beneficent teacher of gods, men, and beasts.

Next, a "true believer," a Sudra or servant, walking humbly, as befits all men, whatever their caste, stepped on a banana peel. "Ah," he thought, "but for my good Karma, I might have fallen. Perchance another would not be so blessed." So he tossed the peel into a little stream to feed the fishes in the river below. For his humbleness and for his brotherhood, this Sudra was reborn as a Hotri, or Family Priest.

Then a proud Brahmin—one noble in name—came upon the banana peel in his path. He communed with himself, saying "Every man reaps in the future the fruits of all his acts. If, therefore, I take this peel from the pathway, I shall have done a deed of merit, and be rewarded by Karma in my next life." So mused the Brahmin, and he carefully removed the peel. For this crafty thought of self, the proud Brahmin was born in a lower caste in his next life.

Finally. . . . along comes a true Yogi, one who has risen above all rules of caste and custom. In him, Soul, and Mind, and Body have each found their rightful sphere of Karma. As he walks, the Yogi is meditating in his heart gentle service to all that lives. In his mind, he is pondering the words that he will say at the next village. In his body, all the senses are alert in their sentinel duties. His eyes catch sight of the banana peel. His arm reaches, his fingers grasp the peel, putting it to one side, and the senses then resume their watchfulness, without troubling either the mind or the heart of the Yogi. Thenceforth, all that are touched by the Yogi, in this or any future life, will be blessed by the contact, and themselves be led to find and follow the path of service.[47]

Kapila

*Founder of
the School of Sankhya Philosophy*

[Tradition ascribes the authorship of the Sankhya system to the great sage Kapila, an almost legendary figure in Indian history. There apparently was a line of Kapilas. The Sankhya philosophy may have been taught originally by the first and written down by the last. The aphorisms here given are taken from *The Sankhya Philosophy of Kapila,* translated by Jag Mohan Lawl.[48] Of this form of instruction George Russell writes:

> It is the traditional way of the East to concentrate its wisdom in aphorisms just as it is our European sin to expand an aphorism into a volume. Kapila, Lao-Tse, Patanjali, Sankara and many another sage left us concentrated brevities. The Eastern sage gives his pupils a few aphorisms to meditate over and when they have fathomed the profundity of one, the pupil is almost able to create philosophies for himself. When we meet this concentration at first it repels us, for it implies a conviction that the pupil must think at least as hard as the sage, and the European writer explains so much and is so clear that the reader has not to think at all. All he gets is ready-made opinions, whereas the brooding on the aphorisms of any of the great Eastern sages creates another with an original mind.[49]

The aphorisms that follow consider the question of what causes the soul to be bound. It is interesting that Kapila did not teach—as is now frequently taught in the East—that emancipation comes from becoming free of earthly conditions and the wheel of rebirth.]

Because the Soul exists in all times, therefore time is not the cause of the bondage [of the Soul]. Because the Soul can exist in any country or anywhere, therefore locality cannot be the cause of the bondage. Because age is the property of the body, and not of the Soul, therefore age cannot be the cause of the bondage. . . . Because the Soul is independent of matter, therefore matter cannot be the cause of bondage. . . . Because the Soul which is by nature free is subject to so many desires, even that is not the cause of bondage. . . . The transmigration of Souls is not the cause of bondage. . . . Bondage is not caused even by the conjunction of the body and the Soul, but by the wrong knowledge as to the nature of their conjunction and the proper functions of body and Soul. . . . The real cause of bondage is non-discrimination or misunderstanding the nature of the Soul and the body, and not finding the true purpose of life. Just as darkness is removed by its natural opposite, light, so non-discrimination is removed by true discrimination. . . . The seat of bondage is in the mind; it is [only] by way of expression we call it the bondage of the Soul. . . .

Emancipation [does not] consist in going to a special spot, for the soul is motionless and all-pervading. . . . Nor does it consist in destroying everything, for that cannot be the soul's aim. . . . The soul's aim cannot be to destroy its own creation. Emancipation does not consist in the acquisition of property and wealth, for they are all perishable and non-eternal. Emancipation does not imply the absorption of the part in the whole. . . . Emancipation does not consist in getting superhuman powers. . . . The destruction of non-discrimination and its effects is emancipation. . . . It is only by discrimination and self-knowledge that emancipation is obtained.

Sankaracharya

Founder of

the Adwaita School of Vedanta Philosophy

[In his *Three Lectures on the Vedanta Philosophy,* addressed to a British public in the 1890s, Max Müller introduced the then novel idea of reincarnation in a practical light. Remarking that in Vedanta and Hindu teachings generally "the previous existence, nay the eternal existence of individual souls is taken for granted, as it seems to be likewise in certain passages in the New Testament (St. John ix)," he added that "whatever we may think of the premises on which this theory rests, its influence on human character has been marvelous."

> If a man feels that what, without any fault of his own, he suffers in this life can only be the result of some of his former acts, he will bear his sufferings with more resignation, like a debtor who is paying off an old debt. And if he knows besides that in this life he may actually lay by moral capital for the future, he has a motive for goodness, which is not more selfish than it ought to be. The belief that no act, whether good or bad, can be lost, is only the same belief in the moral world which our belief in the preservation of force is in the physical world. Nothing can be lost.[50]

The Vedanta philosophy as taught by Sankaracharya, its greatest exponent, does not encourage escape from rebirth because, as the *Vedanta Dic-*

tionary states, "a series of improving lives provides for an increase in the capacity to be aware of one's essential freedom in all circumstances. Indeed, the realization of one's freedom has to be gained in those circumstances, not by any escape or release, in which there would be no overcoming."[51]

Sankara was India's most celebrated teacher after the Buddha left the scene and is regarded as one of the greatest minds the world has known. There is some controversy as to when he lived. The Hindus took it for granted that he lived within a century after Buddha, and Ernest Wood suggests in the *Vedanta Dictionary* that the conclusion of Western orientalists that Sankara lived around the eighth century A.D. was due to a series of scholarly mistakes, which he enumerates.[52]

The title of honor, *acharya,* added to Sankara's name means "he who causes others to go forward." Various commentaries on the Upanishads, the *Bhagavad-Gita,* and the *Brahma Sutras* are attributed to him. The following is taken from his incomparable work, *The Crest Jewel of Wisdom,* or the *Vivekachundamani:*]

Fear not, wise one! Thou art not in danger; there is a way to cross the ocean of this life beset by death, whereby the saints have gained the other shore. That way I shall reveal to thee. . . .

Not by Yoga nor by Sankhya, not by works nor by knowledge, but only through awaking to the oneness of one's true Self with the Eternal, does liberation come. . . . Sons and kindred may free a father from his debts; but other than a man's self, none can free him from bondage. . . .

The food-formed vesture is this body, which comes into being through food, which lives by food, which perishes without food. It is formed of cuticle, skin, flesh, blood, bone, water; this is not worthy to be the Self, eternally pure. The Self was before birth or death, and now is; how can it be born for the moment, fleeting, unstable of nature, not unified, inert, beheld like a jar? For the Self is the witness of all changes of form. The body has hands and feet, not the Self; though bodiless, yet because it is the Life, because its power is indestructible, it is controller, not controlled. Since the Self is witness of the body, its character, its acts, its states, therefore the Self must be of other nature than the body. . . . Of this compound of skin, flesh, fat, bone and water, the man of deluded mind thinks, "This is I"; but he who is possessed of judgment knows that his true Self is of other character, is nature transcendental.

The mind of the dullard thinks of the body, "This is I"; he who is more learned thinks, "This is I," of the body and the separate self; but he who has attained discernment and is wise knows the true Self, saying, "I am the Eternal." Therefore, O thou of mind deluded, put away the thought that this body is the Self . . . discern the universal Self, the Eternal, changeless, and enjoy supreme peace. . . .

In whom this wisdom is well established . . . he is said to be free even in life. . . . In whom the circle of birth and death has come to rest, who is individual though without separateness, whose imagination is free from imaginings, he is said to be free even in life. Even though the body remains, he regards it as a shadow; he is without the thought of "I" and "my": this is the hallmark of him who is free even in life. . . . Whether good or evil fortune come, he regards it as equal in the Self, remaining unchanged by either: this is the hallmark of him who is free even in life. . . .

How indeed can that which is not atman, unreal and insignificant, illumine him (atman) by whose radiance, like that of the sun this whole universe shines?[53] They indeed possess soul vision who have dissolved outer things, the allurements of sense, imagination and the "I," in pure consciousness . . . not they who merely repeat tales about the mystery. . . . Attached to the Real, the man goes to the Real, through steadfastness in the one; so the larva, meditating on the bee, is transformed into the nature of the bee, enters into the being of the bee; so the seeker for union, meditating on the reality of the supreme Self, enters therein through steadfastness in the one. . . .

To those who are wandering in the desert of the world, athirst, on the path of circling birth and death, weary, oppressed and worn by sorrow . . . may this teaching reveal the secondless Eternal, bringing joy, like an ocean of nectar near at hand.[54]

✳ ✳ ✳

Hinduism in Recent Times

[Thus far our study of India has been concerned with the golden age of her religious and cultural life before various foreign powers invaded the land and internal dissensions, accompanied by pernicious caste practices, obscured her glorious past. In recent centuries dire economic conditions, the demoralizing effect of conquest and of the missionaries, plus the seductive influences of Western materialism have brought further deterioration. It is natural to ask, then, how the doctrines of karma and reincarnation have fared during this difficult period. Writing on India in his *Travel Diary of a Philosopher*, Count Hermann Keyserling notes the tenacity of ancient philosophy and belief:

> Benares is overflowing with the diseased and the infirm. No wonder: a great number of the pilgrims come here in order to die on the shores of the Ganges. . . . yet I have never felt less compassion. These sufferers suffer so little; they have, above all, no fear whatever of death. Most of them are superlatively happy . . . ; and as to their infirmity—well, that must be endured; it will not take very long anyhow. And some old sin is no doubt scored off in the process. The faith of the Indians is said to be pessimistic. I know of none which is less so. . . .

The Indian does not know the feeling of sinfulness. The word "sin" appears often enough in their religious literature, if one can believe the translations, but the meaning to which it corresponds is a different one [from ours]. . . . Every action entails, according to the law of Karma, its natural and inevitable consequence; every one must bear those for himself, no merciful Providence can remove them. . . . The Christian consciousness of sin depends . . . upon the commandment to bear it in mind constantly, and this is what the Indian doctrine of salvation forbids. It teaches: as man thinks, so will he become. If he thinks of himself constantly as bad and low, he will become bad. . . . The man who does not believe in himself is considered to be an atheist in the real sense of the word. The highest ideal would be if a man could think of himself continuously, not as the most sinful of sinners . . . but as perfect; such a man would no doubt attain perfection even in this life.[55]

Keyserling wrote and traveled during the World War I period. What about modern India? A probing study of the prevailing trends in Hinduism appeared in the *Illustrated Weekly of India* for September 26, 1971, under the title "Will Hinduism Survive?" The survey revealed that many Hindus are ignorant of their religion and indifferent to their basic scriptures. They practice rites without knowing their meaning, yet unconsciously they are influenced by certain persisting conceptions. Despite the confusion of the present, a substratum of timeless philosophy has recognizably survived:

Hinduism has grown like a vast forest over the centuries and one gets lost in it. The scriptures are so many and the commentaries, and the commentaries on the commentaries, are so numerous that a lifetime is not enough to be acquainted with them. Moreover Hinduism embraces everything from animism to monism and a Hindu does not care where he stands in all this. He has many alternatives before him, but surprisingly he does not exercise his choice—maybe because the alternatives are too bewildering for him to make up his mind. . . .

Apparently Hindus are no more "spiritual" than Westerners . . . But paradoxically, despite the degeneration and hypocrisy, there still remains a substratum of spirituality in India. For Hindus cannot erase what is deeply imprinted in the Racial Unconsciousness. . . . It exists like a lotus in the mire. . . . And it is conveyed by Hindus in numerous subtle, indescribable ways. Karma and reincarnation are to them more than a dogma: they are like the air that they breathe. And Hindus cannot help themselves feeling that they are part of a cosmic scheme that is perpetually in a whirl.

The possibility of a new rising cycle in India is envisaged: "There is a growing awareness of the challenges faced by Hinduism today. Many people want a break with the iniquities of the past and feel the need to accentuate the higher aspects of the religion. . . . This new awakening has touched even those who have been trained in modern science . . . A new Hinduism may emerge in the days to come—that is, a Hinduism with all its lofty ideals of the past translated to the needs of modern man. Hinduism will survive as long as the *Bhagavad-Gita* is understood by people. The *Gita* has integrated a life of action with a life of renunciation. It has accomplished the impossible. And that is what life demands of us . . . .''']

BUDDHIST

What Buddha Taught

[''After 2500 years, the teachings of Gotama Buddha are being regarded as 'really quite modern.' . . . This Indian sage, perhaps more than any other who has ever lived, provided a meeting-ground for all extremes of persuasion—gnosticism and agnosticism, belief and the skepticism of caution, appreciation of intuition, and devotion to logic. While the world of the mind is still quivering from abrupt change—transition from too much other-worldly religion to too much physical science—a man who recognized, as parts of a larger whole, the valid emphases of each, is a man whose thoughts are worth knowing today.''[1]

In the 1890s Lafcadio Hearn wrote in *Gleanings in Buddha-Fields:* ''I remember that when I first attempted, years ago, to learn the outlines of Buddhist philosophy, one fact which particularly impressed me was the vastness of the Buddhist concept of the universe. Buddhism, as I read it, had not offered itself to humanity as a saving creed for one inhabited world, but as the religion of 'innumerable hundreds of thousands of myriads of *kotis* of worlds.' And the modern scientific revelation of stellar evolution and dissolution then seemed to me, and still seems, like a prodigious confirmation of certain Buddhist theories of cosmical law. . . . By its creed the Oriental intellect has been better prepared than the Occidental to accept this tremendous [astronomical] revelation. . . . And I cannot but think that out of the certain future union of Western knowledge with Eastern thought there must eventually proceed a Neo-Buddhism inheriting all the strength of Science, yet spiritually able to recompense the seeker after truth . . . .''[2]

It seems important to realize that most Buddhists do not regard Buddha or his teachings as unique. The noted Buddhist scholar Edward Conze remarks that while ''it is easy to see that we could not have any 'Buddhism' unless a

Buddha had revealed it . . . we must, however, bear in mind that 'Buddha' is not the name of a person, but designates a type. 'Buddha' is Sanskrit for someone who is 'fully enlightened' about the nature and meaning of life.''

> Numerous ''Buddhas'' appear successively at suitable intervals. Buddhism sees itself not as the record of the sayings of one man who lived in Northern India about 500 B.C. His teachings are represented as the uniform result of an often repeated irruption of spiritual reality into this world. . . . The state of a Buddha is one of the highest possible perfection. It seems self-evident to Buddhists that an enormous amount of preparation over many lives is needed to reach it.[3]

''Preparation over many lives''? Would this not suggest an immortal soul or self undergoing such preparation? Yet Buddha is accused by the missionaries of teaching there is no soul, and many Buddhists themselves believe there is no soul. ''This *anatta* (no soul) doctrine,'' says Huston Smith, ''has . . . caused Buddhism to look like a peculiar religion, if indeed deserving of the name at all.'' ''But . . . the word in question must be used with the greatest possible care. What was the *atta* (Pali for the Sanskrit *atman*) or soul that Buddha denied? In Buddha's day it had come to signify (1) a spiritual substance which . . . (2) retained its separateness throughout eternity. Buddha denied both elements in his concept of soul.'' Dr. Smith states that ''Buddha's denial of soul as a spiritual substance—a sort of miniature self in the head [or heart]—appears to have been the chief point that distinguished his concept of transmigration from prevailing Hindu interpretations. Authentic child of India, he never doubted that reincarnation in some sense was a fact, but he was openly uncomfortable over the way his Brahmanic contemporaries were interpreting the concept.''[4]

The mission of this latest Buddha was evidently not to teach metaphysical truths to the people at large; hence his frequent silence when asked about such concepts as the soul. Again and again he turns attention to the individual, his suffering, and his search for spiritual freedom. In the Pali text of the *Majjhima-Nikaya,* the Buddha speaks in typical fashion:

> Malunkyaputta, bear always in mind what it is that I have not elucidated and what it is that I have elucidated. . . . I have not elucidated that the world is eternal, I have not elucidated that the world is not eternal. . . . I have not elucidated that the saint exists after death, I have not elucidated that the saint does not exist after death. I have not elucidated that the saint both exists and does not exist after death. . . . And what, Malunkyaputta, have I elucidated? Misery . . . the origin of misery . . . the cessation of misery . . . the path leading to the cessation of misery.[5]

These words recall another statement attributed to Gotama, quoted in Max Hoppe's preface to George Grimm's *The Doctrine of the Buddha.* In the preface and elsewhere in the volume, evidence is presented to show that Buddha did not deny an enduring self in man.

> In one of the discourses in which [Buddha] has shown again in the usual way that the five groups [of Skandhas[6]] are not the I or self, he breaks out in the following words: "And I, O monks, who speak thus and teach thus, am accused wrongly, vainly, falsely, and inappropriately by some ascetics and Brahmans: 'A denier is the ascetic Gotama, he teaches the destruction, annihilation, and perishing of the being that now exists (satah *sattvasya*).' These ascetics . . . accuse me of being what I am not, O monks, and of saying what I do not say. . . . Only one thing, monks, do I teach, now as before, namely suffering and the abolition of suffering."[7]

Max Müller makes this interesting observation: "Buddha might have taught whatever philosophy he pleased, and we should hardly have heard his name. The people would not have minded him, and his system would only have been a drop in the ocean of philosophical speculation, by which India was deluged at all times. . . . The most important element of the Buddhist reform has always been its social and moral code, not its metaphysical theories. That moral code, taken by itself, is one of the most perfect which the world has ever known."[8] Although the ethical aspects of karma and rebirth are the foundation of that code, Buddha apparently did not discuss their metaphysical and scientific foundation with either the unlearned monks or the laity.

Is it possible, then, that the great saviors of mankind have two teachings? "Unto you it is given to know the mystery of the kingdom of God," said Jesus to his disciples, "but unto them that are without, all these things are done in parables."[9] Did Buddha do likewise? Christmas Humphreys, president-founder of the Buddhist Society in London and author of numerous works on Buddhism, says: "The Buddha gave his deeper teaching to the Arhats; to the people he gave a limited yet magnificent way of life, which, at first transmitted orally, was written down as remembered in the first century B.C. [400 years after Buddha's death], and is now available to all as the Pali Canon of the Theravada school"—the Buddhism of Ceylon, Burma, Thailand, Cambodia, and parts of Vietnam. When the Indian Mahayana school arose, later to be transformed into the Buddhism of China, Tibet, Korea, and Japan, "it was a blend of the esoteric tradition," says Humphreys, "and of doctrines developed from the earlier teaching by minds which, if not of the Buddha's calibre, were some of the greatest yet to appear in the history of mankind. Within a thousand years the various forms of the teaching had spread over a large part of the earth."[10]

In an article entitled "Buddhism Teaches Rebirth," Humphreys relates that Mrs. Rhys Davids, in her day the leading Pali scholar in the West, once made a list of "ten things which Gotama the Buddha will *not* have taught." The first is "that the man, the very man: self, spirit, soul, *purusa* is not real."[11] Mrs. Rhys Davids, a life student of Theravada Buddhism—the very school that lays so much stress on the no-soul idea—adds that in reality Buddha "began his mission by advising men to seek thoroughly for the Atma, and ended by bidding men live as having Atma for their lamp and refuge." The Buddha's concern, she said, was with a Wayfarer upon a Way. "How to wayfare from this to That: here was life's problem." And this was a long journey. Mr. Humphreys asks:

> Are there, then, two types of self in the Pali Canon? Miss I. B. Horner, a pupil of Mrs. Rhys Davids and the present President of the Pali Text Society, shows that this is so. In a famous article reprinted in *The Middle Way* (Vol. 27, p. 76) she lists some seventeen passages from the Pali Canon which make this clear. The "lesser self" and the "greater self" are clearly distinguished, and the "great self" is described as "a dweller in the immeasurable." But the *Dhammapada*, the most famous text in the Canon, will itself suffice. "Self is the lord of self. What other lord could there be?" And again, "Self is the lord of self, and self's bourn," i.e. the very goal of all endeavour.[12] If it is possible to lift the Buddhist teaching nearer still to the Hindu original, look at: "The Self in thee knows what is true and what is false." Every mystic since the world began would agree.

"If," Humphreys continues, "the Buddha, then, taught Atta, as his brilliant predecessors in the field of Indian thought, what did he say was Notself, *an-atta?* He is quite specific. It is the five skandhas, the constituents of personality in which there is no permanent Self to be found. . . . But the monks would not leave this statement alone. Attacking the concept of the Atman as degraded in the Buddha's day to a thing, the size of a thumb, in the human heart, they swung too far. 'No self, no self' they cried, and in time produced the joyless, cramping doctrine as drearily proclaimed today," especially in Theravada Buddhism.[13]

Elsewhere Humphreys concedes that the attack of the Theravada monks, or Bhikkhus, is legitimately "directed against the concept of an unchanging individuality, a separate Self, distinct from the vast totality of Life and its illimitable forms." However, he adds, "the Bhikkhus ignore the 'Unborn, Unoriginated, Unformed' of their own Scriptures,[14] as inherent in every manifested thing." "Clearly the phenomenal self, whether called ego, shadow, or the evolving soul, is changing all the time," but this does not mean "no soul, no soul, no self at all."[15]

One might wonder how it is possible to believe simultaneously in no-self and in rebirth. Francis Story gives the Theravadin answer:

Anatta [the] state of soullessness is capable of producing birth. How can this be so, if there is no transmigrating entity . . . to reincarnate? . . . The act of willing is a creative force, which produces effects in and through the conditions of the physical world. The thought-force of a sentient being, generated by the will-to-live, the desire to enjoy sensory experiences, produces after death another being who is the causal resultant of the preceding one. . . . [When birth occurs] it is not a question of a "soul" entering the embryo, but of the natural formation of the foetus being moulded by an energy from without, supplied by the causative creative impulse from some being that lived before. . . .

The general characteristics of personality are maintained, but only in the same way that a river maintains the same course until something diverts it or it dries up. Thus there is no "immortal soul" that transmigrates, just as there is no river, but only the passage of particles of water flowing in the same direction. . . . Rebirth in conditioned existences is not to be regarded as a blessing, but rather as a curse which man pronounces upon himself.[16]

It seems useful to analyze the implications of some of the expressions just used. There is an "act of willing," there is "the will-to-live," but no real entity that wills. There is a "thought-force" that obviously has great power and creates tremendous effects, but no real entity who thinks. Rebirth is a "curse which man pronounces upon himself," but there is no real man and there is no self. Incidentally, if rebirth is a curse, life itself must be a curse. How and why, then, did the universe produce such a sorry scheme of things, with no possibility of relief save by escaping to Nirvana?

Now it is important to appreciate that the kind of rebirth this noted Buddhist is talking about is immediate rebirth, with no time for rest and assimilation between lives, for there is no soul-entity to do either. "From tomb to womb" is the doleful refrain of the Theravadists. However, Story himself states that it is "another being" that is produced at birth, and as that being is not an "I," why concern oneself about the whole matter? The new being that is "my" offspring, or who is continuous with "me," is not any more real and enduring than I am, and cannot truly suffer because there is no self to experience suffering. "Particles of water flowing in the same direction" can hardly feel pain. And yet the first of the four truths of Buddha is the fact of suffering. The second is sorrow's cause: "Ye suffer from yourselves." The third is sorrow's ceasing. The fourth is the noble eightfold path. But who or what treads that path?

Forests of paper and rivers of ink have been used to answer these and similar questions, but it is of interest to learn that the sad views of the Theravadin scholars leave the masses largely untouched. Alan Watts remarks that "the vast majority of Asian Buddhists continue to believe that reincarnation is a fact" in the sense that a real being is reborn.[17] Furthermore, karma, a key teaching in Buddhism, would appear senseless to them when divorced from a self that sets up causes, stores them, and experiences their results. Von Hartmann points out in his book on Buddhism that "the practical power of the transmigration theory as *motive* stands or falls with the belief in the essential identity of the person of my successor with me, and is not preserved by the mere continuance of the hypostasized sum of merit."[18]

H. Fielding Hall's beautiful book about the Burmese, *The Soul of a People,* confirms what Alan Watts has said. Despite the teaching of their monks "that when life goes out, this thing which we call 'I' goes out with it," the laymen insist:

> When a man dies his soul remains, his "I" has only changed its habitation. . . . It is reborn among us, and it may even be recognized very often in its new abode. And that we should never forget this [they say], that we should never doubt that this is true, it has been so ordered that many can remember something of these former lives of theirs. This belief is not to a Burman a mere theory, but is as true as anything he can see. For does he not daily see people who know of their former lives? Nay, does he not himself, often vaguely, have glimpses of that former life of his? No man seems to be quite without it, but of course it is clearer to some than others. Just as we tell stories in the dusk of ghosts and second sight, so do they, when the day's work is over, gossip of stories of second birth; only that they believe in them far more than we do in ghosts. . . . Many children, the Burmese will tell you, remember their former lives. As they grow older the memories die away and they forget, but to the young children they are very clear. I have seen many such. . . .
>
> This [then] is the common belief of the people. . . . A man has a soul, and it passes from life to life, as a traveller from inn to inn, till at length it is ended in heaven. But not till he has attained heaven in his heart will he attain heaven in reality.[19]

It should be mentioned that some Buddhists—Coomaraswamy, for one—attempt to get around the *anatta* problem by introducing the idea that what reincarnates could be called character. In this connection H. S. Olcott writes in his *Buddhist Catechism,* a small volume that has been widely circulated over the years in the East and West, and translated into many languages: "Mr. Rhys Davids calls that which passes from personality to personality along the individual chain [of rebirths], 'character' or 'doing.' " But "since 'character' is not a mere metaphysical abstraction, but the sum of one's mental qualities and moral propensities, would it not help to dispel what Mr. Rhys Davids called 'the desperate expedient of a mystery' (see *Buddhism,* p. 101), if we regarded [the chain of] life-undulation as individuality, and each of its series of natal manifestations as a separate personality?"

> The perfected individual, Buddhistically speaking, is a Buddha. . . . And as countless generations . . . are required to develop a man into a Buddha, and *the iron will to become one* runs throughout all the successive births, what shall

we call that which thus wills and perseveres? Character? [Or rather] one's individuality? . . . Karma, the DEUS EX MACHINA, masks (or shall we say reflects?) itself now in the personality of a sage, again as an artisan, and so on throughout the string of births. But though personalities ever shift, the one line of life along which they are strung, like beads, runs unbroken; it is ever that particular line, never any other. It is therefore individual, an individual vital undulation, which began in Nirvana, or the subjective side of nature . . . and leads through many cyclic changes back to Nirvana.[20]

We turn now to a representative of the Mahayana school of Buddhism, the Japanese teacher and scholar D. T. Suzuki who writes: 'We can conceive of the soul as not entering into a body . . . ready to receive the soul, but as creating a body suitable for its habitation . . . the soul comes first and the body is constructed by it. This is really the Buddhist conception of transmigration. . . . We can think of the soul not as an entity, but as a principle.'[21] This soul-principle, of course, is not the personalized being of which Western religions usually speak. "Mr. John Smith, turned immortal, would not recognize himself at all," states Conze. He could be transformed "only if he has learned to deny all that constitutes his dear little self." "Buddhist training consists, indeed, in systematically weakening our hold on those things in us which keep us from regaining the immortality we lost when we were born."[22]

Particularly helpful are these additional remarks of Dr. Suzuki:

> Without self there will be no individual; without an individual there will be no responsibility. Without the idea of responsibility morality ceases to exist . . . human community becomes impossible. We must in some way have a self.[23]
>
> We can never get rid of a self—we somehow always stumble over it. . . . Can this ego be really such a ghostly existence, an empty nothing . . . ? If it is really such a non-existent existence, how does it ever get into our consciousness or imagination?
>
> The Self then is not a thing or an emptiness and something incapable of producing work. It is much alive in our innate feeling of freedom and authenticity. When it is stripped of all its trappings, moral and psychological, and when we imagine it to be a void, it is not really so. . . .[24]

"When the self thus stands in its native nakedness," Suzuki continues, "it beggars all description. . . . The emptied self is no other than the psychological self cleansed of its ego-centric imagination. It is just as rich in its contents as before; indeed it is richer than before because it now contains the whole world in itself instead of having the latter stand against it. Not only that, it enjoys itself being true to itself. It is free in the real sense of the word because it is the master of itself, absolutely independent, self-relying, authentic, and autonomous. . . . It is not really the ears or eyes that hear or see. . . . The sense-organs are instruments the Self uses for Itself. . . . The Self . . . is here right before us in full revelation."[25]

"This," he says, "is the great affirmation, the ultimate affirmation." "To say there is no ego, there is no Atman—that is not enough. We must go one step beyond and say that there *is* Atman, but this Atman is not on the plane of the relative but on the plane of the absolute."[26] "The denial of Atman maintained by the earlier Buddhists refers to Atman as the relative ego, and not the absolute ego, the ego after enlightened experience. . . . Enlightenment is seeing the absolute ego reflected in the relative ego and acting through it."[27] "Each religion has its own method of realisation whereby the ultimate reality, the final self, the integrating principle is reached."[28]

Two very important questions now enter our discussion: Does the Buddha of Compassion presently exist? Will he ever reincarnate again? Suzuki relates that as the decades and centuries passed after his departure, "Nirvana as the ideal of Buddhist life engaged the serious attention of Buddhist philosophers. . . . [They asked:] Did the Buddha really enter into a state of utter extinction leaving all sentient beings to their own fate? Did the love he showed to his followers vanish with his passing? Would he not come back among them in order to guide them, to enlighten them, to listen to their spiritual anguish? The value of such a grand personality as the Buddha could not perish with his physical existence, it ought to remain with us forever as a thing of eternal validity."[29]

The Theravada school holds that he exists not; the goal of Nirvanic absorption has been reached. The Mahayana school affirms, to use the words of Radhakrishnan, "that Buddha standing on the threshold of Nirvana took the vow never to make the irrevocable crossing so long as there was a single undelivered being on earth."[30] A similar pledge is traditionally ascribed to the Chinese Buddhist goddess Kwan-Yin, called Kannon in Japan: "Never will I seek nor receive private, individual salvation; never will I enter into final peace alone; but forever, and everywhere, will I live and strive for the redemption of every creature throughout the world." All earnest students of the Mahayana make such a vow.]

※ ※ ※

"The Light of Asia"

[Before drawing on the classical scriptures of the various Buddhist schools, we use as our text Sir Edwin Arnold's *The Light of Asia* and consider two momentous events in the Buddha's life: the night under the Bo tree when enlightenment came, and the day he returned to his father's kingdom after years of self-imposed exile. During his youth and early manhood, Buddha was surrounded by loving-kindness and luxury. His possessive father, resisting the prophecy that his son, instead of inheriting the throne, would become a great and holy Buddha, took fantastic measures to isolate him from the world and all knowledge of sorrow, sickness, and death. How this plan became thwarted is told in *The Light of Asia,* published in 1879 and in print ever since. Prior to the large-scale Buddhist revival of recent years, the popularity Buddhism enjoyed in the West was due more to this memorable poem than to anything written before or since. Scholars may question its correctness in places, but as a whole it admirably portrays the main events in Gotama's life and his message to humanity. As karma and reincarnation pervade much of the poem, the work must have contributed to the growing Western interest in these conceptions. The very first line of the poem—after a stanza of introduction—reads: "Then came he to be born again for men."

The American transcendentalist Bronson Alcott zealously promoted the volume in the United States at the prompting of the Boston clergyman William Henry Channing, whose daughter married Sir Edwin Arnold. According to the British *Dictionary of National Biography,* "The poem aroused the animosity of many pulpits, but there were sixty editions in England and eighty in America, and translations were numerous."[31] In a twenty-six-page review, Oliver Wendell Holmes[32] wrote: "Its tone is so lofty there is nothing with which to compare it but the New Testament."[33] It was not Buddha's ethical teachings that astounded Arnold's readers—the Sermon on the Mount teaches these—but the fact that five hundred years before Jesus another savior had gloriously lived and taught the Christ life.

Arnold, who was knighted by Queen Victoria, also rendered the *Bhagavad-Gita* into English verse under the title *The Song Celestial.* When Britain's poet laureate Tennyson died in 1892, the queen favored Sir Edwin as his successor, but because Prime Minister Gladstone wanted a fundamentalist, the coveted office remained vacant for several years.[34] Conze identifies Arnold as a theosophist.[35]

Quoting from the preface to *The Light of Asia:*

In the following Poem I have sought, by the medium of an imaginary Buddhist votary, to depict the life and character and indicate the philosophy of that noble hero and reformer, Prince Gautama of India, the founder of Buddhism. A generation ago little or nothing was known in Europe of this great faith of Asia, which had nevertheless existed during twenty-four centuries, and at this day surpasses, in the number of its followers and the area of its prevalence, any other form of creed. Four hundred and seventy millions of our race live and die in the tenets of Gautama; and the spiritual dominions of this ancient teacher extend, at the present time, from Nepal and Ceylon, over the whole Eastern Peninsula, to China, Japan, Tibet, Central Asia, Siberia, and even Swedish Lapland. India itself might fairly be included in this magnificent Empire of Belief; for though the profession of Buddhism has for the most part passed away from the land of its birth, the mark of Gautama's sublime teaching is stamped ineffaceably upon modern Brahmanism, and the most characteristic habits and convictions of the Hindus are clearly due to the benign influence of Buddha's precepts.

This concluding idea appears also in the poem, in a line declaring that Buddha's wisdom "hath made our Asia mild." The reader who wonders at the recent tragic violence in Asian countries might reflect that when Gotama's teaching of compassionate love and harmlessness took root in India after his death, wars were unknown in that country for a long period. And even a hundred years ago the "benign influence" of Buddha's teaching was still reflected in the statistics of crime in India. The British census of 1881 gives the record of convictions:

Europeans	1 in 274
Eurasians	1 in 509
Native Christians	1 in 799
Mahommedans	1 in 856
Hindus	1 in 1,361
Buddhists	1 in 3,787

These statistics were reprinted in the leading Catholic organ in Britain, *The Tablet,* with the comments: "The last item is a magnificent tribute to the exalted purity of Buddhism. . . . It appears from these figures that while we effect a very marked moral deterioration in the natives by converting them to our creed, their natural standard of morality is so high that, however much we Christianize them, we cannot succeed in making them altogether as bad as ourselves."[36] These Indian converts, of course, had given up their conviction in reincarnation and karma in exchange for the church doctrine of forgiveness of sins.

The sixth book of *The Light of Asia* tells of that night of nights when Buddha conquered the tempter "Mara and his furious hosts," and achieved vision after vision of life's workings.]

In the third watch . . . our Lord attained *Samma-sambuddh;* he saw
By light which shines beyond our mortal ken
The line of all his lives in all the worlds,
Far back and farther back and farthest yet,
Five hundred lives and fifty. Even as one,
At rest upon a mountain-summit, marks
His path wind up by precipice and crag . . . through bogs
Glittering false-green; down hollows where he toiled
Breathless; on dizzy ridges where his feet
Had well-nigh slipped . . . thus Buddha did behold
Life's upward steps long-linked, from levels low
Where breath is base, to higher slopes and higher

Whereon the ten great Virtues wait to lead
The climber skyward. Also, Buddha saw
How new life reaps what the old life did sow;
How where its march breaks off its march begins;
Holding the gain and answering for the loss;
And how in each life good begets more good,
Evil fresh evil; Death but casting up
Debit or credit, whereupon th' account
In merits or demerits stamps itself
By sure arithmic . . . on some new-springing life;
Wherein are packed and scored past thoughts and deeds,
Strivings and triumphs, memories and marks
Of Lives foregone;

And in the middle watch,
Our Lord attained *Abhijna*—insight vast
Ranging beyond this sphere to spheres unnamed,
System on system, countless worlds and suns
Moving in splendid measures. . . . cycle on epicycle. . . .
A Power which builds, upbuilds, and builds again. . . .

[Many more visions did the Buddha behold that night, and when dawn came:]

He arose—radiant, rejoicing, strong—
Beneath the Tree, and lifting high his voice
Spake thus, in hearing of all Times and Worlds:

MANY A HOUSE OF LIFE
HATH HELD ME—SEEKING EVER HIM WHO WROUGHT
THESE PRISONS OF THE SENSES, SORROW-FRAUGHT:
SORE WAS MY CEASELESS STRIFE!
BUT NOW,
THOU BUILDER OF THIS TABERNACLE—THOU!
I KNOW THEE! NEVER SHALL THOU BUILD AGAIN
THESE WALLS OF PAIN,
NOR RAISE THE ROOF-TREE OF DECEITS, NOR LAY
FRESH RAFTERS ON THE CLAY;
BROKEN THY HOUSE IS, AND THE RIDGE-POLE SPLIT!
DELUSION FASHIONED IT!
SAFE PASS I THENCE—DELIVERANCE TO OBTAIN.

[The foregoing is the famous Hymn of Victory, to be found in *The Dham-mapada*. Dr. Suzuki believes it has been gravely misunderstood in the East. He analyzes the key terms in an article "The Seer and the Seen," and shows that the Buddha has *seen,* not destroyed, Tanha, the house-builder and his house. It is not a victory of one side over the other but the healing vision that "the builder and the seer and the author are one and the same personality, and that tanha is nirvana and nirvana tanha!"[37]]

[The verses now presented are from book eighth of *The Light of Asia,* and tell of the joyous day when Buddha after years of absence returned to visit his father's kingdom. Regretfully only a sampling of the teachings spoken to the assembled multitude can be offered. The Four Truths and the Noble Eightfold Path must be omitted. However, other verses from Arnold's poem will be found quoted elsewhere in this anthology.

As a prologue to what follows, it should be mentioned that after his enlightenment Buddha had deep misgivings as to whether his fellow humans could appreciate his message. "How shall men—Buddha mused—who love their sins . . . and drink of error from a thousand springs—having no mind to see, nor strength to break the fleshly snare which binds them—how should such receive the Twelve Nidanas and the Law redeeming all . . . ?" Does not "the caged bird oft shun its open door?" The narrator comments that all men would miss their redemption if Buddha having won the way "deemed it all too hard for mortal feet, and passed, none following him." As the Buddha in compassion pondered, he heard the piercing moan of the earth: "Surely I am lost, I and my creatures." Another voice, borne on the wind, pleads: "Oh Supreme, let thy great Law be uttered!" "Whereupon the Master cast his vision forth on flesh, saw who should hear and who must wait to hear, as the keen Sun gilding the lotus-lakes seeth which buds will open to his beams and which are not yet risen from their roots." "Yea, I preach!" he said. "Whoso will listen let him learn the Law" (book seventh).]

> At sinking sun Lord Buddha set himself
> To teach the Law in hearing of his own. . . .
> All the earnest throng catching the opening of his lips to learn
> That wisdom which hath made our Asia mild. . . .
> Nay, outside those who crowded by the river, great and small,
> The birds and beasts and creeping things—'tis writ—
> Had sense of Buddha's vast embracing love. . . .
> And in mute gladness knew their bondage broke
> Whilst Buddha spake these things before the King:
>
> Behold, I show you Truth! Lower than hell,
> Higher than heaven, outside the utmost stars,
> Farther than Brahm doth dwell,
> Before beginning, and without an end,

As space eternal and as surety sure,
Is fixed a Power divine which moves to good. . . .

I, Buddha, who wept with all my brothers' tears,
Whose heart was broken by a whole world's woe,
Laugh and am glad, for there is Liberty!
Ho! ye who suffer! know
Ye suffer from yourselves. None else compels
None other holds you that ye live and die,
And whirl upon the wheel, and hug and kiss
Its spokes of agony. . . .

Seek nought from the helpless gods by gift and hymn,
Nor bribe with blood, nor feed with fruit and cakes;
Within yourselves deliverance must be sought;
Each man his prison makes.
Each hath such lordship as the loftiest ones. . . .

The Books say well, my Brothers! each man's life
The outcome of his former living is;
The bygone wrongs bring forth sorrows and woes
The bygone right breeds bliss.
That which ye sow ye reap. See yonder fields!
The sesamum was sesamum, the corn
Was corn. The Silence and the Darkness knew!
So is a man's fate born.

He cometh, reaper of the things he sowed,
Sesamum, corn, so much cast in past birth;
And so much weed and poison-stuff, which mar
Him and the aching earth.
If he shall labour rightly, rooting these,
And planting wholesome seedlings where they grew,
Fruitful and fair and clean the ground shall be,
And rich the harvest due. . . .

[The Law] knows not wrath nor pardon; utter-true
Its measures mete, its faultless balance weighs;
Times are as nought, tomorrow it will judge,
Or after many days.
By this the slayer's knife did stab himself;
The unjust judge hath lost his own defender;
The false tongue dooms its lie; the creeping thief
And spoiler rob, to render.

Such is the Law which moves to righteousness,
Which none at last can turn aside or stay;

The heart of it is Love, the end of it
Is Peace and Consummation sweet. Obey! . . .

So merit won winneth the happier age
Which by demerit halteth short of end;
Yet must this Law of Love reign King of all
Before the Kalpas end. . . .

Enter the Path! There is no grief like Hate!
No pains like passions, no deceit like sense!
Enter the Path! far hath he gone whose foot
Treads down one fond offence. . . .

So all that night he spake, teaching the Law;
And on no eyes fell sleep—for they who heard
Rejoiced with tireless joy. Also the King,
When this was finished, rose upon his throne
And with bared feet bowed low before his Son
Kissing his hem; and said, ''Take me, O Son!
Lowest and least of all thy Company.[38]

Indian Buddhism

[Buddhism spread mainly in northern India, where Buddha was born, until King Asoka became ruler of the Indian empire in 270 B.C. The king's grandfather, Chandragupta, had founded the empire upon defeating the Greek forces in India after the death of Alexander the Great, and Asoka continued to expand these conquests until, repelled by the horrors of war, he embraced Buddhism. The effect of the conversion on this greatest of India's rulers was tremendous, and his dynamic mind and compassionate heart were soon felt in every corner of the land. During Asoka's forty-year reign, Buddhism became the established religion, and wars were abolished. Everywhere, in caves, on rocks, and glorious pillars, Asoka's famous edicts were engraved, setting forth the moral precepts of Buddhism.

An ardent propagandist,[39] Asoka sent numerous missionaries to Syria, Egypt, Judea, and Greece, and it appears that communal groups like the Pythagoreans in Greece and the Essenes in Judea welcomed the new-old faith. Jesus, we know, was closely associated with the Essenes, and scholars now wonder about a possible Buddhist influence in the Sermon on the Mount, especially its love-thy-enemy theme so contrary to the eye-for-an-eye code of retaliation prevalent in his day.

To honor Buddha and his predecessors, Asoka "stimulated India to produce an art unsurpassed in her history."[40] However, some Buddhists believe that because of the seductive aspects of art, the All Enlightened One
would frown on such achievements as possibly leading to entanglements in
this and future incarnations. Yet, it is recorded in the *Samyutta Nikaya* that
when the elder Ananda said to Buddha "half of the holy life, Lord, is the
friendship with what is lovely," the teacher replied: "Say not so, Ananda,
say not so! It is the whole, not the half of the holy life."[41]

After Asoka's death the Brahmins again gained supremacy and despite
periodic Buddhist revivals and royal patronage, the religion was slowly
forced out of most of India, only to spread prolifically in China, Tibet,
Mongolia, Korea, Japan, and all the Southeast Asian countries, including
Ceylon, whose ancient name of Lanka has now been restored. Thus, for
more than a thousand years Buddhism became the largest religious body in
the world, bringing in its wake fuel to reinforce reincarnation teachings
wherever the embers burnt low.

While for four hundred years the Buddha's teachings were transmitted
orally, many were recorded in writing prior to the large-scale exodus from
India of Buddhist arhats and monks. To some of these writings we now turn.
The total dialogues and sermons are said to number over ten thousand, only a
small portion having been translated into Western tongues, although the
complete Pali Canon of the Theravada school is now in English. It is the
Mahayana scriptures, originally in Sanskrit and later in Tibetan and Chinese,
of which the West as yet knows little. We begin with the Pali Suttas and
conclude with the Sutras of the Indian Mahayanists. Then there will be
sections on Chinese, Japanese, and Tibetan Buddhism.

The term Sutta, or Sutra, means a thread on which jewels are strung, a
beautiful symbol for the teaching of any sage! The Hindus make another use
of the word; they speak of the Sutratma, the luminous thread of immortality
upon which are "strung" our many lives, each worthy incarnation adding its
"pearl of great price."]

THE DHAMMAPADA

[*The Dhammapada* is the most popular and influential of the Suttas of the
Buddha. The verses quoted here are from the Cunningham Press edition,
which sought to select the best renditions from scores of translations.[42] The
foreword states that a student under Freud's personal tutelage related that
his teacher called Buddha the greatest psychologist of all time. Some of the
slokas included here are not directly on death or rebirth, yet suggest a higher,
controlling Self in man. The implications of this in relation to reincarnation
have just been discussed under "What Buddha Taught."]

All that we are is the result of what we have thought; all that we are is founded on our thoughts and formed of our thoughts . . . (1)

Vigilance is the path to Life Eternal. Thoughtlessness is the path to death. The reflecting vigilant die not. The heedless are already dead. . . . By vigilance did Indra rise to the lordship of the gods. Vigilance is always praised, heedlessness ever deprecated. (21 and 30)

The craving of a thoughtless man grows like Maluva creeper that eats up the tree on which it fastens. From life to life he is like a monkey seeking fruits in a forest. (334)

Who shall overcome this earth? And who the sphere of Yama, the god of death? And who the world of the happy gods? And who shall choose the steps on the Path of Law even as the gardener culls the choicest blooms? The disciple will overcome this earth. Also Yamaloka. Also the sphere of the gods. The disciple chooses to take steps on the Path of Law. He is the expert gardener who culls the choicest blooms. (44 and 45)

Knowing that this body is like froth, knowing that its nature is that of a mirage, and breaking the flowery shafts of Mara, the disciple passes untouched by death. Death bears off the man whose mind is intent on plucking the flowers of sense, as a flood sweeps away a sleeping hamlet. (46 and 47)

Better than the life of a hundred years of the man who perceiveth not the deathless state is the short life of a single day of the man who senses that deathless state. (114)

Lo! you are now like a withered leaf. The messengers of Yama (Death) are fast approaching you. You stand on the threshold of departure. And you have made no provisions for the journey. Be wise, make for yourself an island. Strive quickly. Purged of stains and sinless you will be ready for heaven, the world of the elect. (235 and 236)

You yourself must strive; Buddhas are but signposts . . . "Impermanent are all conditioned beings." He who knows this ceases to be in the thrall of grief. This is the Path of Purity. (276 and 277)

The SELF is the Lord of self; what higher Lord could there be? When a man subdues well his self, he will find a Lord very difficult to find. . . . Let one sit alone, sleep alone, act alone, and unwearied subdue the self by the Self; he finds delight being out of the forest of desires. (160 and 305)

He indeed is a Bhikku [a monk] who does not identify his soul with his name and form, his mind and body, and who grieves not for what he does not possess. (367)

Rouse your self by your Self, examine your self by your Self. Thus self-guarded and mindful you will live happily, O Bhikku. For Self is the lord of self; Self is the refuge of self; therefore curb yourself, even as a merchant curbs a fine horse. (379 and 380)

O Brahamana,[43] be energetic; dam the stream; cut away desires. When you understand how things get disintegrated you will also realize the Uncreate, O Brahamana. (383)

Him I call a Brahamana, who has no desires, who has destroyed his doubts by knowledge and has plumbed the depth of the Eternal. (411)

Him I call a Brahamana who knows the mystery of death and rebirth of all beings, who is free from attachment, who is happy within himself and enlightened. . . . Him I call a Brahamana who knows his former lives, who knows heaven and hell, who has reached the end of births, who is a sage of perfect knowledge and who has accomplished all that has to be accomplished. (419 and 423)

SANGITI SUTTA

[According to Buddha there are four modes of birth, each apparently the result of the degree of awareness achieved in previous lives:]

Brethren, in this world, one comes into existence in the mother's womb without knowing, stays in it without knowing, and comes out from the mother's womb without knowing; this is the first.

Brethren, one comes into existence in the mother's womb knowingly, stays in it without knowing, and comes out from it without knowing; this is the second.

Brethren, one comes into existence in the mother's womb knowingly, stays in it knowingly, and comes out from it without knowing; this is the third.

Brethren, in this world, one comes into existence in the mother's womb knowingly, stays in it knowingly, and comes out from it knowingly; this is the fourth.[44]

JATAKA TALES

[The *Jataka Tales,* often allegorical in character, appear in the Pali Canon. The King Kalinga incident to be mentioned in the selection from *The Diamond Sutra* is from this source. Limitations of space permit here only a summary of their contents, using the words of the introduction to the tales published in the Wisdom of the East Series.]

The Jataka Tales (Birth-Stories)—of which there are 547—are tales told by the Buddha of his previous births. . . . It is not a new idea that some people can recall their past lives on earth (though much so-called memory is wishful thinking or imagination) for Pythagoras, whom no one could accuse of wishful thinking or embroidery, gave instances of a few of his own past lives. And since the main teaching of the Buddha was that actions bring their due effects under immutable law, against which all prayers are unavailing, and that each life is the outcome of previous lives, it is not surprising that part of his method of impressing this on his listeners was by means of the descriptions of the past lives of himself and of others. . . . The stories were told around some incident then happening, and it is in their relationship with that incident that we find their true lesson. At the close of the story the Buddha always identified the birth so that lines of action and character stand out clearly from the past to the present. . . .

Throughout the stories we see the line of life possessing those spiritual qualities which blossom in Buddhahood acting in and through various types of bodies, always helping, always reasoning, acting after forethought, full of effort and animated by love, finally developing the power to sacrifice life itself.[45]

SAMANNAPHALA SUTTA

[The Buddha did not encourage his disciples to develop psychic powers. In the course of disciplined spiritual development these powers unfolded naturally and then became valuable aids in detecting the needs of the human heart and giving wise instruction. In this selection Buddha indicates the qualities a monk should possess when he consciously views his own previous lives. How different a method from the hypnotic age-regression experiments so popular today! Premature, indiscriminate attempts to break the silence of the past has had serious psychological consequences in some cases.]

With his heart thus serene, made pure, translucent, cultured, devoid of evil, supple, ready to act, firm and imperturbable, he bends down his mind to the knowledge of the memory of his previous temporary states. He recalls to mind . . . one birth, or two or three . . . or ten or twenty . . . or fifty or a hundred or a thousand or a hundred thousand births, through many an aeon of dissolution, many an aeon of evolution, many an aeon of both dissolution and evolution.[46] . . . thus does he call to mind his temporary states in days gone by in all their details, and in all their modes.[47]

THE DHAMMAPADA COMMENTARY

[The *Dhammapada Commentary* is composed of legendary stories, recorded in Pali, illustrating incidents in Buddha's life.]

Although the Master was preaching, yet, of five laymen who sat there in his presence, one, being drowsy, fell asleep; another sat grubbing in the ground with his finger; the third idly shook a tree to and fro; the fourth sat gazing at the sky and paid no heed to what was said; while the fifth was the only one of them who gave heed to the teaching. So the Elder Ananda, who stood there fanning the Master, observing the behavior of these men, said to him: "Lord, thou art teaching the Truth to these men even as the voice of the thunder when the heavy rains are falling. Yet, behold! they sit doing this and that. . . . Thy teaching cleaveth even through the skin and reacheth unto bones and marrow. How can it be that when thou preachest the Law these men pay no heed thereto?

"Ananda, such things as The Buddha, or The Law, or The Order of Brethren, through countless hundred thousand cycles of time have never been heard of by these beings. Therefore they cannot listen to this Law. In this round of births and deaths, whose beginning is incalculable, these beings have come to birth hearing only the talk of divers animals. They spend their time in song and dance, in places where men drink and gamble and the like. Thus they cannot listen to the Law."

"But what, Lord, is the actual reason, the immediate cause why they cannot?"

The Master replied: "Ananda, owing to hatred, owing to delusion, owing to lust, they cannot do so. . . . But this one, who, sitting, hears the Law attentively, for many, many times successively was a master of the Vedas three, a brahmana who could repeat the Sacred Texts. So now also he pays good heed unto my words."[48]

THE PATH OF PURITY

[The Path of Purity is the *Visuddhimagga,* the famous Pali work of Buddhaghosa, believed to have been written in the fifth century A.D. and, of course, is not one of the Suttas. However, the italicized portion is from one of the Buddha's short Suttas and is used here by Buddhaghosa to recommend a meditation suitable for overcoming hostility.]

If, in spite of . . . reflections on the qualities of the [Buddha's] conduct, [one's] hatred does not subside . . . he should then consider the Suttas on the repeated round of births, wherein it is said: *"It is not easy, monks, to find a being who has not in the past been one's mother, or one's father, brother, sister, son or daughter."*[49] Therefore the person should be considered thus: "This, they say, was formerly my mother, who for ten months carried me in her womb, removed my urine, excrement, saliva, snot and so on without loathing, as if they were yellow sandal-wood, hid me in her bosom, carried me on her hip and brought me up. He who was my father went to trade by goat-tracks, by paths rough with stakes, and for my sake risked his life; who went to war where the battle was in array on both sides; who went out in his boat on the high sea, and did other difficult deeds; who amassed wealth in various ways with the object of bringing up children, and so brought me up. And those also who were my brother, sister, son, daughter, did such and such service to me. Therefore it does not behoove me to bear ill feelings against them."[50]

THE DIAMOND SUTRA

[The *Diamond Sutra*, a Mahayanist Sutra, addressed by the Buddha to a large assembly of monks, has enjoyed immense popularity in China, Japan, Tibet, and Mongolia, but according to Conze, whose translation is used, "it would be difficult to find anything as remote from the interests of the present day. . . . This in itself may recommend it to some of those for whom it is intended."

The sermon stresses the nonreality of the personal soul or self, indicating that behind this separative, fleeting appearance is the real "I," impersonal, formless, undivided, everlasting. In a Buddha this universal power is focused through what is called in the Sutra the Dharmabodies—perfected, ethereal, invisible bodies, "robes sublime." When not incarnated on earth, the Buddhas are said to remain in these vehicles, radiating help to all that lives. Such transcendent bodies could, of course, not be evolved if they were not already latent in every being. Certain Hindus teach that the highest of these *koshas* is immortal throughout the evolutionary period unless Nirvana puts an end to it before. It is this radiant vehicle, they intimate, that assimilates the essence of each life on earth, and gives to man his feeling of a permanent individuality within the ever-changing personality.

The opening paragraph refers to a past life of the Buddha when he was born a king's son and his raging father cut the infant to pieces.]

When the king of Kalinga cut my flesh from every limb, at that time I had no perception of a self, of a being, of a soul, or a person. And why? If at that time I had had a perception of self, I would also have had a perception of ill-will. . . . With my superknowledge I recall that in the past I have for five hundred births led the life of a sage devoted to patience. Then also have I had no perception of a self, a being, a soul, or a person. Therefore then, the Bodhi-being, the great being, after he has got rid of all perceptions, should raise his thought to the utmost, right and perfect enlightenment. He should produce a thought which is unsupported by forms, sounds, smells, tastes, touchables, or mind-objects. . . .

Does it occur to a Tathagata, "by me have beings been set free"? Not thus should you see it! And why? There is not any being whom the Tathagata has set free. Again, if there had been any being whom the Tathagata had set free, then surely there would have been on the part of the Tathagata a seizing of a self, of a being, of a soul, of a person. . . . And yet the foolish common people have seized upon it. . . .

> Those who by my form did see me,
> And those who followed me by voice
> Wrong the efforts they engaged in,
> Me those people will not see. . . .

That spot of earth where one has taken from this discourse . . . but one stanza of four lines, taught or illumined it, that spot of earth will be like a shrine for the whole world. . . . What then should we say of those who will bear in mind this discourse . . . in its entirety, who will recite, study, and illuminate it in full detail for others! Most wonderfully blest, they will be! And on that spot of earth either the Teacher dwells, or a sage representing him.[51]

THE LOTUS SUTRA

[In *The Lotus of the Wonderful Law* the Buddha—called Shakyamuni in China—instructs: "The world thinks that Lord Shakyamuni after going out from the home of the Shakyas arrived at the highest perfect enlightenment. But the truth is that many hundred myriads of *kotis* of aeons ago I arrived at supreme perfect enlightenment. . . . The Tathagata who was perfectly enlightened so long ago has no limit to the duration of his life, being everlasting. Never extinct, he makes a show of extinction for the sake of those he leads to salvation."[52]

In the *Lotus Sutra* the Buddha publicly reveals the teaching of the Mahayana, a term meaning Great Vehicle. What he had taught earlier and is now recorded in the Pali Canon is called Hinayana, or the Small Vehicle. The Small Vehicle is so named because like a bicycle it accommodates only oneself on the path to Nirvana, while the Great Vehicle like a large train compassionately takes on many as well. As Edwin Burtt observes in *The Teachings of the Compassionate Buddha,* the Mahayanist "wants to overcome craving and obstructions . . . not to achieve his own perfection but for the sake of a deeper oneness with others, and for the greater power to serve them."[53] And this he does from life to life, and between lives, refusing Nirvana for himself alone. This is called the Bodhisattva ideal, a Bodhisattva being one step away from Buddhahood.

In this celebrated Sutra, Buddha indicates by parables that although he had a far more wonderful truth to give to those who could understand it, he was not deceiving the minds of beginners by teaching them Theravada ideas. This was because such were all they could grasp, and although limited would lead them in the right direction. Buddha is speaking in the verses that follow; then the hearers add their comments.]

> The dull, who delight in petty rules,
> Who are greedily attached to mortality,
> Who have not, under countless Buddhas,
> Walked the profound and mystic Way,
> Who are harassed by all the sufferings—
> To these I (at first) preach Nirvana.

Such is the expedient I employ
To lead them to Buddha-wisdom.

Not yet could I say to them,
"You all shall attain to Buddhahood,"
For the time had not yet arrived.
But now the very time has come
And I must preach the Great Vehicle. . . .
My final Seal of the Law . . . is now announced. . . .
If there be any who receive
This Sutra-law in faith,
These people must already
Have seen Buddhas of past times . . .
And listened to this Law. . . .
Men shallow of knowledge hearing it,
Go astray, not understanding.

The World-honoured One, knowing beforehand that our minds were attached to low desires and took delight in inferior things, let us go our own way. . . . In his tactfulness [he] told of the Tathagata-wisdom; but we, though following the Buddha and receiving a day's wage of Nirvana, deemed this a sufficient gain, never having a mind to seek after the Great Vehicle. . . . The Buddha . . . taught according to our capacity, but still we did not perceive that we were really Buddha-sons.

Now we have just realized that the World-honoured One does not grudge even the Buddha-wisdom. Wherefore? From of old we are really sons of Buddha, but have only taken pleasure in minor matters . . . At length, in this Sutra, he preaches only the One Vehicle. . . . Now the Great Treasure of the King of the Law has of itself come to us, and such things as Buddha-sons should obtain, we have all obtained.[54]

Chinese Buddhism

[In the Western Hills near Peking, in the Temple of the Clouds, there stood, and perhaps still stands, the majestic Hall of Five Hundred Lohans, depicting Buddhist arhats who over the centuries came from India and Tibet to promulgate Buddhism in China. In commemoration of their advent, the statues in the tiers of ascending galleries were arranged, the early comers first, and the last, just under the roof. The periodic arrival of these wise men naturally increased the interest in China in such teachings as reincarnation and karma, for, as we shall see, Confucianism had virtually nothing to say on these subjects. With the resulting inflow of Indian thought in China, many people added Buddhist teachings to the moral code and practices established by Confucius.

However, time and human imagination apparently reduced the purity and philosophy of the Buddhist ideas when transplanted into soil less prepared for metaphysical conceptions than India, and a number of sects arose in China. In *The Chinese Mind,* Wing-tsit Chan tells of the popular Pure Land School founded in the fourth century, which stressed the great attraction of rebirth in paradise, the chief means being "to repeat the name of the Buddha and to express faith by making offerings, reciting scripture, etc. The Buddhist said, 'Take refuge in the Buddha.'" "In the seventh century a revolt arose and demanded the shift to self-effort, and that was the realization of one's own nature. The movement was led, or probably started by Hui Neng. . . . In his famous Platform Scripture [next to be considered], he emphatically urged his followers to take refuge in the nature within oneself instead of taking refuge in the buddhas outside."[55]

Hui Neng is ranked as the sixth Zen patriarch, the first was the great Indian sage Bodhidharma who brought Ch'an to China in the sixth century A.D. In India, called Dhyana Buddhism, in China, Ch'an, this teaching became known as Japanese Zen when many Ch'an masters escaped to Japan during the strenuous years of the Mongol invasions in the twelfth and thirteenth centuries.

Bodhidharma and Hui Neng adapted Indian Buddhism to the Chinese mind. "Their message," says Christmas Humphreys, "was largely a repudiation of the written word in favour of 'direct seeing into the heart of man.' What irony, that [the Zen literature] without which it is difficult to understand the Masters and their remembered words, is one of the largest and most exalted . . . yet produced by man!"[56]]

HUI NENG (638–713)

[*The Sutra of Hui Neng,* called the Platform Scripture—the basic text of Zen Buddhism—includes sermons and discussions spanning the thirty-seven-year ministry of this most renowned Zen master of the T'ang Dynasty (618–907). Wing-tsit Chan states that "it was inevitable that a vigorous movement such as this should have exercised a tremendous influence." "Within Buddhism itself, Zen dominated the scene [in China] from the tenth through the fourteenth century," exerting "a strong influence on Chinese philosophy and art." The Platform Scripture, Dr. Chan says, is unique as the only Chinese produced work honored as a scripture or Sutra. "For 750 years, the version edited by Tsung-pao (1291) has been revered and recited by millions of Buddhists, whether they are special followers of Zen or not."[57]

Wong Moul-Lam, the translator here selected, says the book may be particularly "useful to those who cannot read the original, but who had mastered it so well in their previous lives that they only need a paragraph or two . . . to refresh their memory in order to bring back the valuable knowledge they have now forgotten." Hui Neng mentions having had such an experience in his own life. His mind was instantly illuminated when as a poor, illiterate seller of firewood he listened to a few lines from the *Diamond Sutra.* "It must be due to my good karma in past lives that I heard about this," and later came "into possesson of the esoteric teaching of the Dhyana School,"[58] called the Heart-Seal in the Sutra.

His school was called the Sudden School, but as Dwight Goddard remarks: "It is not a question of quickness or slowness in arriving at [Satori or enlightenment]; 'gradual attainment' may arrive sooner than 'sudden enlightenment.' It is the question whether enlightenment comes as the culmination of a gradual process of mental growth, or whether it is a 'sudden turning at the seat of consciousness' from an habitual reliance on the thinking faculty (a looking outward) to a new use of a higher intuitive faculty (a looking inward)."[59] Basically there may be no conflict, for as one Zen teacher says: Heated water *gradually* approaches the boiling point; it *suddenly* boils. Dr. Suzuki observes that "the coming of enlightenment is instantaneous but the process of arriving at enlightenment is naturally gradual, requiring much time and concentration."[60]]

Learned Audience, the Wisdom of Enlightenment (Bodhi-prajna) is inherent in every one of us. It is because of the delusion under which our mind works that we fail to realise it ourselves, and that we have to seek the advice and the guidance of enlightened ones before we can know our own Essence of Mind. . . . Those who recite the word "Prajna" the whole day long do not seem to know that Prajna is inherent in their own nature. But mere talking on food will not appease hunger, and this is exactly the case with these people. We might talk on Sunyata (the Void) for myriads of *kalpas*[61] but talking alone will not enable us to realize the Essence of Mind, and it serves no purpose in the end. . . .

Our Essence of Mind (literally, self-nature) which is the seed or kernel of enlightenment is pure by nature, and by making use of this mind alone we can reach Buddhahood directly. . . . To attain supreme enlightenment, one must be able to know spontaneously one's own nature or Essence of Mind, which is neither created nor can it be annihilated. From *ksana* to *ksana* (thought-moment to thought-moment), one should be able to realise the Essence of Mind all the time. . . . All things are the manifestation of the Essence of Mind. . . .

He who believes in the reality of outward objects tries to seek the form (from without) by practicing a certain system of doctrine. He may furnish spacious lecture-halls for the discussion of Realism or Nihilism, but such a man will not for numerous *kalpas* realise the Essence of Mind. . . .

The Kingdom of Buddha is in this world, within which enlightenment is to be sought. To seek enlightenment by separating from this world, is as absurd as to search for a rabbit's horn. . . . *Kalpa* after *kalpa* a man may be under delusion, but once enlightened it takes him only a moment to attain Buddhahood. . . .

Ordinary men and heretics believe in "heretical eternalism." The victims of ignorance . . . identify the union of five *skandhas* as the "self," and regard all other things as "not-self". . . . [They] drift about in the whirlpool of life and death without realising the hollowness of mundane existence . . . commit themselves to unnecessary suffering by binding themselves to the wheel of rebirth. . . . [In his dying instruction] Lord Buddha preached in the *Maha Parinirvana Sutra* the "Ultimate Doctrine" of Buddhist teaching, i.e., true eternity, true happiness, true self, and true purity. . . .

Since the scope of the mind is for great objects, we should not practice such trivial acts (as sitting quietly with a blank mind). . . . There is a class of foolish people who sit quietly and try to keep their mind blank.[62] They refrain from thinking of anything and call themselves "great". . . . Sentient beings are mobile. Inanimate objects are stationary. He who trains himself by [meditation] exercise to be motionless (gets no benefit) other than making himself as still as an inanimate object. Should you find true Immobility there is Immobility within activity. . . . Treaders of the Path, exert yourselves and take heed that as followers of the Mahayana School you do not embrace that sort of knowledge which binds you to the wheel of birth and death. . . . Those who have realised the Essence of Mind . . . they are at liberty to "come" or to "go" (i.e., they may remain in or leave this world at their own free will). . . .

Learned Audience, all of us have declared that we vow to deliver an infinite number of sentient beings; but what does that mean? It does not mean that I, Hui Neng, am going to deliver them. And who are these sentient beings within our [own] mind? They are the delusive mind, the deceitful mind, the evil mind, and such like minds—all these are sentient beings. Each . . . has to deliver himself by means of his own Essence of Mind. Then the deliverance is genuine. . . . Enlightened by Right Views, we call forth the Buddha within us. . . . Know your own mind and realize your own Buddha-nature, which neither rests nor moves, neither becomes nor ceases to be. . . . Your time will have been badly wasted if you neglect to put this teaching into practice.[63]

※ ※ ※
Japanese Buddhism

[Zen has been described as the revolt of the Chinese mind against the contemplative, metaphysically oriented Buddhism of India. The Chinese wished above all to apply Buddhism to everyday life, asserting that Enlightenment could be found as much by working in the world as in withdrawing from it as many Indian holy men do. Zen and other forms of Chinese and Japanese Buddhism have therefore had profound influence on Far Eastern culture, especially in the arts, and this is particularly true of Japan. Lafcadio Hearn says that "architecture, painting, sculpture, engraving, printing, gardening—in short, every art and industry that helped to make life beautiful—developed first in Japan under Buddhist teaching."[64]

As art and industry reflect the ideas of a people, one may probably rightly assume that Far Eastern views of reincarnation were spontaneously reflected in this area of their culture. Hargrave Jennings, whose specialty was deciphering the symbols of the past, speaks of the design of Chinese pagodas, widely adapted by the Japanese for their sacred buildings:

> In the very form of the Chinese pagodas, the fundamental article of the Chinese religion—transmigration, through stages of being, out into nothingness of this world—has been architecturally emblemned in the diminishing stories, carried upwards, and fining away into the series of unaccountable discs struck through a vertical rod, until all culminates, and the last *achievement* is blazoned in the gilded ball, which means the final, or Buddhist, glorifying absorption. Buildings have always telegraphed the insignia of the mythologies; and, in China, the fantastic speaks the sublime.[65]

Although Zen in Japan has been closely linked with the arts, Ruth Sazaki makes clear that it is basically a religion.[66] In one of her lectures, "Zen: A Method for Religious Awakening," she declares that "the aim of Zen is first of all awakening, awakening to our true self. With this awakening to our true self comes emancipation from our small self or personal ego. . . . The True Self, which from the beginning we have always been, has at last become the master."[67]

There are, of course, other forms of Japanese Buddhism. The Shin School, which presently shares predominance with Zen, corresponds to the simple faith of the Jodo, or Pure Land School of China, already mentioned. Then, among others, there is the learned Tendai School—the Japanese counterpart of the renowned Chinese T'ient'ai and the Indian Yogacharya. It emphasizes that the life in everything—animals, plants, even drops of water and specks of dust—is ceaselessly reembodied and will one day reach Buddhahood, the Buddha nature being Potential in all. Thus is taught an all-embracing compassion that should bind man and everything in the universe which, like him, is pressing toward the Light.

Some consideration is now given to Japanese daily life as it existed in the early decades of this century and the seven centuries preceding. Selections from one of the many noted Japanese Zen masters follow, concluding with material on D. T. Suzuki, generally regarded as the first to popularize Zen in the West.]

REBIRTH AND KARMA IN JAPANESE LIFE

[From Lafcadio Hearn's *Kokoro: Hints and Echoes of Japanese Inner Life,* published in 1896.]

Were I to ask any reflecting Occidental, who has passed some years in the real living atmosphere of Buddhism, what fundamental idea especially differentiates Oriental modes of thinking from our own, I am sure he would answer: "The Idea of Pre-existence." It is this idea, more than any other, which permeates the whole mental being of the Far East. It is universal as the wash of air: it colors every emotion; it influences, directly or indirectly, almost every act . . . The utterances of the people—their household sayings, their proverbs, their pious or profane exclamations, their confessions of sorrow, hope, joy, or despair—are all informed with it. . . .

The term "ingwa," or "innen," meaning karma. . . . comes naturally to every lip as an interpretation, as a consolation or as a reproach. The peasant toiling up some steep road, and feeling the weight of his handcart straining every muscle, murmurs patiently: "Since this is ingwa, it must be suffered." Servants disputing, ask each other, "By reason of what ingwa must I now dwell with such a one as you?" . . . The lawbreaker confesses his crime, saying: "That which I did I knew to be wicked when doing; but my ingwa was stronger than my heart." . . . So likewise even the commonest references to a spiritual future imply the general creed of a spiritual past. The mother warns her little ones at play about the effect of wrong-doing upon their future births, as the children of other parents. The pilgrim or the streetbeggar accepts your alms with the prayer that your next birth may be fortunate. The aged inkyo, whose sight and hearing begin to fail, talks cheerily of the impending change that is to provide him with a fresh young body.[68]

[To understand how this state of mind became so natural, we must go back to the twelfth century when Buddhism arrived in Japan and was confronted by the prevailing beliefs of Shintoism. Hearn writes in his best-known work, *Japan—An Attempt at Interpretation:*]

In Shinto there was no doctrine of metempsychosis. . . . The spirits of the dead . . . continued to exist in the world: they mingled somehow with the viewless forces of nature, and acted through them. . . . Those who had been wicked in life remained wicked after death; those who had been good in life became good gods after death; but all were to be propitiated. . . . With these ancient beliefs Buddhism attempted to interfere only by expanding and expounding them—by interpreting them in a totally new light. . . . In most Japanese houses . . . the "god-shelf" and the Buddhist shrine can both be found; both [religions] being maintained under the same roof. . . .

One particular attraction of Buddhist teaching was its simple and ingenious interpretation of nature. Countless matters which Shinto had never attempted to explain . . . Buddhism expounded in detail. . . . Its explanations of the mysteries of birth, life, and death were at once consoling to pure minds, and wholesomely discomforting to bad consciences. It taught that the dead were happy or unhappy not directly because of the attention or the neglect shown them by the living, but because of their past conduct while in the body. . . . To die was not to melt back into nature, but to be reincarnated. . . .

A man . . . was now sickly and poor, because in some previous existence he had been sensual and selfish. This woman was happy in her husband and her children, because in the time of a former birth she had proved herself a loving daughter and a faithful spouse; this other was wretched and childless, because in some anterior existence she had been a jealous wife and a cruel mother. . . . The girl whom you hoped to marry has been refused you by her parents—given away to another. But once, in another existence, she was yours by promise; and you broke the pledge then given. Painful indeed the loss of your child; but this loss is the consequence of having, in some former life, refused affection where affection was due. Maimed by mishap, you can no longer earn your living as before. Yet this mishap is really due to the fact that in some previous existence you wantonly inflicted bodily injury. . . .

Life was expounded as representing but one stage of a measureless journey, whose way stretched back through all the night of the past, and forward through all the mystery of the future—out of eternities forgotten into the eternities to be. . . . Even the Shinto doctrine of conscience—the god-given sense of right and wrong—was not denied by Buddhism. But this conscience was interpreted as the essential wisdom of the Buddha dormant in every human creature—wisdom darkened by ignorance, clogged by desire, fettered by Karma, but destined sooner or later to fully awaken, and to flood the mind with light.[69]

[An illuminating view of Japanese religious culture from a more general philosophical perspective, and in contrast with life in the West, is given in *The Japanese Cult of Tranquillity*, by Professor Karlfried von Durckheim:]

Against a background of Western culture we can clearly appreciate the very different approach to life and death among the peoples of the East. The concept "life" has a completely different implication; so, too, has death. The prevailing Western concept of death is opposed to that of life, whereas the Eastern concept of life embraces both simultaneously.

The meaning of this may be grasped in the image of the relation between the leaf and the tree. If the little leaf on the big tree were conscious of its own individuality, and limited its vital consciousness to being nothing but a leaf, it would feel its life limited to its own life span. Death in autumn would mean the destroying of its life and would be antagonistic to its consciousness of life. It would be therefore hardly surprising if this leaf should attempt to enjoy its short life as a leaf to the utmost, to protect itself against autumn and winter, and forget its fear of death in a dream world of unending leaf-images.

Would it not, however, be possible for the little leaf to experience its existence as a leaf in deepened self-consciousness as a mode of the tree's realizing its being as a tree? Would it not be nearer its own "reality" too, if it identified its own self-consciousness with that of the tree, that is, if it should feel its individual existence to be the form of the tree, whose greater life gives birth to the lesser life of the leaf, surviving it and embracing its death in itself? [In great nature this kind of dying actually happens, for, as autumn approaches, the vital elements in the leaves are withdrawn into the parent tree. Only then does the foliage fall off.]

The image should not be exaggerated but . . . it may indicate what we are referring to here—that the prevalent concept of life for the Eastern person is that of the "Greater Life" which transcends all "Lesser Life". . . . Culture consists in revealing the Greater Life in the Lesser . . . and overcoming all natural inclination on the part of the Lesser Life to assert itself absolutely and thus to become opposed to death and the transitory world. To accept this task as a matter of course and to attempt it again and again is only possible for men whose concept of the Greater Life is the result of a constant reunion with the latter and which does not proceed from some edifice in the mind or some metaphysical speculation. Seen against this background, Western culture appears to be the product of fear of death. . . . There can be no doubt that the vital instinct of self-preservation dominates man's consciousness in the West, despite all other forces of Christian origin urging a different way. . . .

Where man loses touch with the kernel of his essential being, he identifies himself exclusively with his outer shell. When his sense of inner achievement becomes muted, he turns to the clamour of the world without and, losing all sense of the living center, is caught in the bondage of a hardened periphery. Alienated from his spiritual powers, man tries to find fulfilment in protecting and indulging his own ego, in the excitement of cheap stimuli, or the satisfaction of his instinctive desires, or even in the sensations of a disproportionate mind, whose very roots are withered. Man becomes a refuge from himself. He takes flight from life's calm rhythm to find refuge in the measured beat of organized existence, relinquishing his contact with the indestructible within himself for security in the transitory world, and drowning the quiet voices of being, in the clamour of worthless illusion. . . .

The Japanese is as fond of life as we are, cherishing power and property, suffering sickness and death, and possessing a positive appreciation of all life's joys. However, to cling to material possessions, complain over losses, to be distracted at suffering, or become bitter in old age, or to overlook death . . . and to oppose the law of change, is for the Japanese the mark of great immaturity and therefore of a want of culture. . . .

The Zen monk who has reached the final stage can determine the moment of his own death. He knows when his hour has come . . . and the soul prepares to continue its journey in another form. Having invited his friends, he seats himself in his accustomed place to write his last poem and then simply does not return from his contemplation, which he performs just as he has done every day of his life.[70]

BASSUI TOKUSHO (1327–1387)

[Certain events in Bassui Tokusho's early life provide significant clues to his later development. When only seven he questioned the priest officiating at a memorial service for his late father as to who was to receive the offerings of rice, cakes, and fruits, inasmuch as the cremated remains of his father could not eat them. Upon hearing that the soul was the recipient, the boy exclaimed: "If there is such a thing as a soul, I must have one in my body. What is it like?" Throughout his remaining childhood, youth, and early manhood, uncertainties as to the soul's existence tormented him. For hours on end he pondered the problem, always ending with the thought: "But if there is no soul, what is it within me which this very moment is seeing and hearing?" The first selections quoted here are from Bassui's "Sermon on One-Mind"; the remainder are from his letters. Both are highly prized volumes in Japan.]

If you would free yourself of the sufferings of samsara [rebirth], you must learn the direct way to become a Buddha. This way is no other than the realization of your own Mind. Now what is this Mind? It is the true nature of all sentient beings, that which existed before our parents were born and hence before our own birth, and which presently exists, unchangeable and eternal. So it is called one's Face before one's parents were born. . . . When we are born it is not newly created, and when we die it does not perish. It has no distinction of male or female, nor has it any coloration of good or bad. It cannot be compared with anything, so it is called Buddha-nature. . . .

If you want to realize your own Mind, you must first of all look into the source from which thoughts flow. Sleeping and working, standing and sitting, profoundly ask yourself, "What is my own Mind?" with an intense yearning to resolve this question. . . . Repeatedly cast off what has been realized, turning back to the subject that realizes, that is, to the root bottom, and resolutely go on. Your Self-nature will then grow brighter and more transparent as your delusive feelings perish, like a gem gaining luster under repeated polishing, until at last it positively illumines the entire universe. Don't doubt this! Should your yearning be too weak to lead you to this state in your present lifetime, you will undoubtedly gain Self-realization easily in the next, provided you are still engaged in this questioning at death, just as yesterday's work half done was finished easily today. . . .

Keep asking with all your strength, "What *is* it that hears?" Only when you have completely exhausted the questioning will the question burst; now you will feel like a man come back from the dead. This is true realization. You will see the Buddhas of all the universes face to face and the Patriarchs past and present.

[Letter to a man from Kumasaka.] You ask me to write you how to practice Zen on your sickbed. Who is he that is sick? Who is he that is practicing Zen? Do you know who you are? One's whole being is Buddha-nature. One's whole being is the Great Way. The substance of this Way is inherently immaculate and transcends all forms. Is there any sickness in it? Man's own Mind is the essential substance of all Buddhas, his Face before his parent's birth. It is the master of seeing and hearing, of all the senses. One who fully realizes this is a Buddha, one who does not is an ordinary human being. Hence all Buddhas and Patriarchs point directly to the human mind so man can see his own Self-nature and thereby attain Buddhahood. . . .

[Letter to the governor of Aki Province.] Go back to questioning, "What is hearing now?" Find out this very moment! The problem of birth-and-death is momentous, and the world moves fast. Make the most of time, for it waits for no one. . . .

[Letter to the layman Ippo.] However much you try to know . . . one's Face before birth or one's Original Home . . . through logical reasoning or to name or call it, you are doomed to failure. And even though all of you becomes one mass of questioning as you turn inward and intently search the very core of your being, you will find nothing that can be termed [a personal] Mind or Essence. Yet should someone call your name, something from within will hear and respond. Find out this instance who *it* is!

If you push forward with your last ounce of strength at the very point where the path of your thinking has been blocked, and then, completely stymied, leap with hands high in the air into the tremendous abyss of fire confronting you—into the ever-burning flame of your primordial nature—all ego-consciousness, all delusive feelings and thoughts and perceptions will perish with your ego-root and the true source of your Self-nature will appear. You will feel resurrected, all sickness having completely vanished, and will experience genuine peace and joy.[71]

DAISETZ TEITARO SUZUKI (1870–1966)

[At the time of Dr. Daisetz Teitaro Suzuki's death at the age of ninety-five, the *London Times* carried this summary of his career: "Dr. Suzuki was a remarkable figure in the field of Oriental philosophy, for he was at the same time a scholar of international rank, a spiritual teacher who had himself attained the enlightenment he strove to hand on, and a writer who in some twenty volumes taught the West the nature and purpose of Zen Buddhism. As a scholar he was a master of Sanskrit and Chinese Buddhist texts, with an up-to-date knowledge of European thought in several languages."[72]

Up until 1927 the only Buddhism the West really knew was Theravada, says Christmas Humphreys, but in that year "there was published the first of [Suzuki's] *Essays in Zen Buddhism,* and a new world was opened. For the first time we began to study the complementary principles of the Mahayana, particularly as found in Zen."[73] The historian Lynn White says that the publication of these essays in 1927 "will seem in future generations as great an intellectual event as William of Moerbeke's Latin translations of Aristotle in the thirteenth century or Marsiglio Ficino's of Plato in the fifteenth."[74] "Speaking for myself," writes Father Thomas Merton, "I can venture to say that in Dr. Suzuki, Buddhism finally became for me completely comprehensible, whereas before it had been a very mysterious and confusing jumble of words, images, doctrines, legends, rituals, buildings, and so forth."[75] Conze states that "as a direct result of Suzuki's books on Zen there is now a flourishing Zen movement all over the world, and this movement has caused an immense interest in those aspects of Zen not covered by Suzuki."[76] Wherever Zen goes some idea of reincarnation usually accompanies it, and thus the movement is contributing to the revival of reincarnation in the West.

In a featured survey of Buddhism in the United States, with particular emphasis on Zen, the *New York Times* (February 4, 1976) reports that Buddhism "is rapidly becoming a distinctive form of American religion." "Buddhism has existed here among Asian-Americans for decades. . . . But only in the last few years has American Buddhism evolved as a solid religion. In the view of observers Buddhism has gone beyond faddishness and has acquired traits of an indigenous religious form with staying power, to the extent that world Buddhism is taking it very seriously. 'The spirit of Buddhism is in

America now'. . . . . The surge of interest in Buddhism here could rejuvenate
the tradition in large areas of Asia, including Japan, where it has been in
decline.''

In the summer of 1957 some fifty psychiatrists and psychologists met for a
week with Dr. Suzuki under the auspices of the medical school of the National University of Mexico in Cuernavaca. An outgrowth of the conference
was the book *Psychoanalysis and Zen Buddhism* by Erich Fromm, Suzuki,
and DeMartino. Dr. Fromm writes:

> There is an unmistakable and increasing interest in Zen Buddhism among
> psychoanalysts. . . . [As to] the conference held in Cuernavaca. . . . any
> psychologist, even twenty years ago, would have been greatly surprised—or
> shocked—to find his colleagues interested in a "mystical" religious system
> such as Zen Buddhism. He would have been even more surprised to find that
> most of the people present were not just "interested" but deeply concerned,
> and that they discovered that the week spent with Dr. Suzuki and his ideas had
> a most stimulating and refreshing influence on them, to say the least. . . .
>
> The study of Zen Buddhism has been of vital significance to me and, as I
> believe—is significant for all students of psychoanalysis. . . . [It] helps man to
> find an answer to the question of his existence, an answer which is essentially
> the same as that given in the Judaeo-Christian tradition, and yet which does not
> contradict the rationality, realism, and independence which are modern man's
> precious achievements. Paradoxically, Eastern religious thought turns out to be
> more congenial to Western rational thought than does Western religious thought
> itself.[77]

Dr. Suzuki's views on reincarnation and a permanent Self in man have
been given in the section "What Buddha Taught." A few additional selections now follow. The first is from *The Essence of Buddhism,* originally two
lectures delivered at the Imperial Palace in Japan by command of the Shinto
emperor Hirohito, eight months after the bombing of Hiroshima. During the
war Suzuki lived in seclusion in his Japanese home, suspect for his Western
sympathies.]

When the Master Daito saw the Emperor Godaigo (reigned 1318–1338)
who was another student of Zen, the Master said, "We were parted many
thousands of Kalpas ago, yet we have not been separated for a moment. We
are facing each other all day long, yet we have never met."

Here we have the same idea as expressed by [Buddha] himself in the
Saddharma-Pundarika [the Lotus Sutra]. . . . In spite of the historical fact
that he attained Enlightenment near Buddhagaya at a definite moment of
time, he says that he was fully enlightened even before the world was
created. The historical fact of his Englightenment is a record which we
time-minded make with the intellect, because the intellect likes to divide,
and cuts time into years and days and hours, and constructs history, whereas

time itself underlying history knows no such human artificial cuttings. We are living partly in this time-space-conscious history but essentially in history-transcending time-space. Most of us would recognise the first, but not the second phase of our life. Daito the Master here wishes to remind the Emperor of this most fundamental experience. . . .

Human suffering is due to our being bound in Karma, for all of us, as soon as we are born, carry a heavy burden of past Karma. . . . In this sense, human beings are the only beings which have their Karma. All others move in accordance with the laws of their being, but it is human beings alone that can design and calculate and are conscious of themselves and of their doings. . . . From thinking, from thinking consciously, we develop the faculty of seeing, designing, and planning beforehand, which demonstrates that we are free, and not always bound by the ''inevitable laws'' of Nature. . . .

Not only are we wrapped up in our Karma but we know the fact that we are so wrapped up. . . . This very fact of our being aware of the Karma-bondage is the spiritual privilege of humanity. For this privilege, implying freedom, means our being able to transcend Karma. . . . We must make full use of it, and, accepting the Karma-bondage as far as it extends, resolutely face all forms of suffering and thereby qualify ourselves for transcending them.[78]

[The final selection offers wholesome counseling to those who would selfishly strive for instant Satori, instant enlightenment:]

Enlightenment is not a mere personal affair which does not concern the community at large; its background is laid in the universe itself. . . . That I have been able to conceive a great longing for enlightenment means that the entire world wishes to be liberated from ignorance and evil passions. . . . It requires a long preparation, not of one life but of many lives. . . . The great ocean of transmigration drowns everybody that goes into it. Especially the philosophers, who are satisfied with interpretations and not with facts themselves, are utterly unable to extricate themselves from the bondage of birth and death, because they never cut asunder the invisible tie of karma and knowledge that securely keeps them down to the earth of dualities because of their intellectualism. Therefore the awakening . . . which takes place in the depths of one's being is a great religious event.[79]

✳ ✳ ✳

Tibetan Buddhism

[For ages Tibet has been regarded as a land of mystery, towering beyond the Himalayas in a colossal natural fortress in the very heart of Asia. The climate and high, lonely mountains, the rarefied air and profound silences, foster introspective tendencies. Prior to 1951 when Chinese troops invaded the Tibetan capital of Lhasa—the seat of the Dalai Lama—Tibet undoubtedly led the world in the number of priests in proportion to population. Yet, visitors say there was more practical freedom for the individual, more well-being for the family, less poverty and squalor than in any other country. By all accounts the people were charming, lovable, and deeply artistic.[80]

Before embracing Buddhism, Tibet had a long history as an important seat of mysticism and occult learning in central Asia. The Brahmins, it will be remembered, originally came from the far north, and the *Vedas,* agreeably to all traditions, were written on the shores of Lake Manasarovara in Tibet. Buddha himself was born in Nepal, a kingdom bordering ''the roof of the world,'' as Tibet has been called.

Tibet, or Ti-Boutta, yields etymologically the words Ti—equivalent for deity in Chinese—and Buddha or Wisdom, and thus means the Land of the Wisdom-Deity or of the Incarnations of Wisdom. This relates, perhaps, to a prominent feature of Tibetan Buddhism, belief in the successive incarnations of the two highest Lamas, the Dalai and the Panchen, and some others, into the same high role or office as previously held. Westerners are accustomed to thinking of all Tibetan monks as Lamas. This title, however, is formally allowed only to these high-ranking ''Incarnations,'' and to monks who have lived unusually saintly lives. In *Seven Years in Tibet,* Heinrich Harrer, once tutor to the present Dalai Lama, intimates that because of the eternal continuity of soul, ''Birthdays are unimportant dates in Tibet . . . are generally not known and never celebrated.''

> For the people the date of their King's birth [the Dalai Lama] is quite without interest. He represents in his person the return to earth of Chenrezi, the God of Grace, one of the thousand Living Buddhas who have renounced Nirvana in order to help mankind. . . . With us it is generally, but mistakenly, believed that each rebirth takes place at the moment of the predecessor's death. This does not accord with Buddhist doctrine, which declares that years may pass before the god once more leaves the fields of Heaven and resumes the form of man.[81]

The office and line of incarnations of the Dalai Lama were established soon after the death of the great Tibetan religious reformer Tsong-kha-pa (1355–1417). Viewed as an avatar of Buddha, and called the Second Buddha, Tsong-kha-pa introduced a purified form of Buddhism into Tibet and founded the Gelukpa or Yellow Cap order that prevailed for centuries in eastern Tibet and to which the Dalai and Panchen Lamas belong, the latter Lama being considered an avatar of Tsong-kha-pa himself. Tsong-kha-pa, being unable to endure any longer the desecration of Buddhist philosophy by the false priests who had made it a marketable commodity—mixing it with base forms of

Hindu tantra and the old Bhon sorcery rites of some of Tibet's aborigines—
exiled thousands of these monks to the southern border and adjoining states,
and to western and Little Tibet. Here their successors continued to live and
convey much misinformation about Tibetan Buddhism to Western scholars
who never penetrated to Lhasa and Shigatse. For example, in the *Information
Please Almanac,* under "Tibet," we read that "the religion and predominant
factor in Tibet's social system is Lamaism, a late form of Buddhism modified
by animism and primitive magic." To correct such misconceptions the Dalai
Lama wrote in his book *The Opening of the Wisdom-Eye:*

> Some persons have the idea that the religion of Tibet is that of the "lamas"
> who have fabricated a system called "lamaism." They say, too, that this is
> very far from the true teachings of Lord Buddha. Such ideas are very misin-
> formed since there is no separate "ism" of the lamas apart from Lord Buddha's
> teachings. . . . Tibetan scholars suffering many and various hardships on the
> way to Nepal and India, traveled there many times to get the correct manu-
> scripts and traditions, and their comings and goings could be compared to a
> river always flowing between two countries. They studied and practiced
> Dharma under the guidance of the great and learned teachers whose scholarship
> was beyond question. . . . *Apart from this authentic Dharma there is no arbi-
> trary teaching begun by lamas in Tibet.*[82]

Beginning in the seventh century, the Sutras and other Mahayana Buddhist works were translated into Tibetan, the language of scholars in both
China and Mongolia. This literature is embodied in the Tibetan *Kanjur,* comprising 108 volumes, and the *Tanjur,* 225 volumes. Thus, Sanskrit Buddhist
texts, lost during the persecutions that drove Buddhism out of all but south-
ernmost India, were saved, at least in translated form. The Tibetans also
study and prize the Theravada scriptures and thus regard themselves as non-
sectarian Buddhists.

All this, of course, has an intimate bearing on the Tibetan view of reincarnation, a teaching that permeates their entire culture and is applied to the
most varying circumstances. A minor example is afforded by Sir Charles Bell
who lived in Lhasa for many years and whose books on Tibet have recently
been republished:

> Not once or twice, but frequently and from all classes, I heard that I was
> generally believed to have been in my last life on earth a Tibetan, a high lama
> who prayed on his deathbed that he might be reborn in a powerful country so as
> to be able to help Tibet. Thus they explained why I had been engaged for so
> long and so profitably on Tibetan affairs; why, though of delicate constitution, I
> had been able to come to Lhasa in winter without injury to my health, and had
> stayed in Lhasa longer than any Englishman had done before. . . . My prayer
> having been granted, this, according to the Buddhist creed, became for me a
> destined work, left over from my last life, and therefore bound to be carried
> through in this one.][83]

MILAREPA (1038–1122)

[Milarepa, born three hundred years before Tsong-kha-pa, is apparently held in great reverence by all schools of Tibetan Buddhism. He was one of the founders of the Kargyupta school, which subsequently underwent various deteriorations, and became partially reformed at the time of Tsong-kha-pa. He has been called the Saint Francis of Buddhism, and the love that he felt for animals, plants, and all living things is honored by the devotion Tibetans have shown ever since to this poet and saint. He had a fine singing voice, and the classic *Hundred Thousand Songs of Milarepa,* from which we quote, is familiar to all his countrymen. Herdsmen sang them in the high pastures of the Himalayas until silenced by the Chinese.]

However beautiful a song's words may be, it is but a tune to those who grasp not the words of Truth. . . . Much talking is of no avail. Follow what I sing, and practice Dharma! . . .

How stupid it is to sin with recklessness while the pure Dharma spreads all about you. How foolish to spend your lifetime without meaning, when a precious human body is so rare a gift. . . . From beginningless time in the past until now, we all have taken myriads of bodily forms in our past incarnations, comparable only to the total sum of grains of sand in the great Universe. Nevertheless, we have seldom utilized those bodies for a worthwhile purpose. Instead, we have wasted them by doing meaningless things, thus accumulating more and more Skandhas and pains. . . . So from all bindings [the wise man] gains freedom. Like the immaculate lotus growing out of mud, he attains the conviction of Practice. . . .

The omnipresent mind resembles Space: It never separates from the Realm of the Unborn. It cuts the path of the Three Worlds of Samsara [or Rebirth]. This is the conviction of Enlightenment. If a yogi realizes this, when he leaves his mortal body and enters into the Bardo,[84] he may then perfect all merits. . . .

The nature of mind is the Illuminating Essence. . . . It is never born and it never dies. Even though the myriad armies of the Lord of Death encircle it, and rain weapons upon it, they cannot harm, destroy, or sully it. Even though all the Buddhas . . . should gather all their merits, and ray their infinite beams of light upon it, they could not make it better; nor could they color it or form it into substance. It will remain as it is, and can never be destroyed. . . .

> There is no Nirvana to attain beyond;
> There is no Samsara here to renounce;
> Truly to know the Self-mind
> It is to be the Buddha Himself.
> These are the Key-points of Accomplishment.[85]

TSONG-KHA-PA (1355–1417)

[The veneration in which *Tsong-Kha-Pa,* the great Buddhist reformer, has been held over the centuries, and the appreciation accorded his mission and work, may be gathered from the fact that his remains were later preserved in a solid gold coffin in the Ganden monastery that he founded. This monastery, close to Lhasa, was ravaged by the Chinese Communists and the casket confiscated, an incredibly cruel blow to the Tibetans!

The selections are from Tsong-Kha-Pa's renowned work *Lam-Rim-Chen-Mo,* the Great Road to Perfection. In the appended notes to this translation, the word *samsara* is defined in a pessimistic light as "the vicious circle of continued rebirth. The nature of *Samsara* is that it is fraught with endless sufferings, such as from sickness, old age, impermanence and death." However, it is instructive to learn from the text itself that the rebirth process when intelligently and compassionately used becomes the very means of reaching enlightenment and true happiness, and affords the opportunity of contacting suffering mankind in order to redeem it.]

All activities of the *samsaric* world are like threshed husks of grain in that worldly activities do not employ the human body for its essential value as an instrument for the attainment of enlightenment. . . . The basis most conducive for successful practice of the Mahayana path is an ideal human body totally endowed with the eight favorable qualities, which are the ripened fruits of previously commited virtuous actions. . . . You should practice those virtuous actions which will cause you to be reborn with this ideal form. Likewise, it is very important to make a great effort to remove from the three doors of your body, speech, and mind the karmic obstacles which might prevent such a rebirth. . . . These three doors have become polluted with the foul odor of the unripened consequences of your previously committed non-virtuous actions and of your breaches of vowed moral conduct. . . .

The Discipline of Moral Self-Control is the water to wash away the dirt of non-virtuous actions. . . . Patience is the best adornment for the mighty ones to wear. . . . Generosity . . . is the best weapon for cutting the selfish knot of miserliness. It is the basis of the Enlightened Conduct of the bodhisattvas in that it develops the selflessness and undaunted courage to help all sentient beings toward enlightenment. . . . Knowing this, the wise masters have taught the path of giving away to others your body and wealth and the merit from your virtuous actions. . . .

Meditative Concentration is the king who rules over the dominion of the mind. If you focus it on one point, it stays there like the immovable Mount Meru. If you project it, it can fix on any object of virtuous and religious value you choose. It leads to your attainment of great exhilaration and bliss at being able to have your body and mind always at attention and under your control, [and it] overcomes the enemies of mental-wandering and mental-dullness. . . .

Wisdom . . . is the path by which to cut through Ignorance, the root of *samsara*. It is the treasure of knowledge praised in all the scriptural texts. It is well known as the lamp which eliminates all the darkness of Closed-Mindedness. Knowing this, the masters who have wished to attain liberation have made all efforts to progress along this path. . . . Once you wear the armor of resolute and unfluctuating Enthusiastic Perseverance, its beneficial effects towards your gaining both knowledge of the scriptural texts and insights into their meanings will increase like the waxing moon. All your actions will become effective for your attainment of Buddhahood . . . Knowing this, the bodhisattvas have exerted great waves of Enthusiastic Perseverance, eliminating all laziness.[86]

THE FOURTEENTH DALAI LAMA (1935–   )

[It is common knowledge that each Dalai Lama is supposed to be a reincarnation of his predecessor. As to the present Dalai Lama, it is not easy to obtain a picture of what he is really like. Dr. Raghavan Iyer in "My Talk with the Dalai Lama" says:

> The Dalai Lama is a remarkable man by any standards, rare in any age but perhaps unique in ours. He is five years younger than I am, and yet throughout the interview I knew I was in the august presence of a man who is ageless, who could assume a variety of poses, utterly without affectation. He was wise and benevolent, but also artless and childlike; he was intensely involved, yet deeply detached, in every utterance; he was a most lovable man of a divinely meek disposition but he was also something else . . . an impassive, impersonal presence. . . . a visible holiness that shone out of an inner wholeness. . . . I felt that almost for the first time I was communicating effectively and adequately with another human being.[87]

In the fall of 1973 the Dalai Lama made his historic six weeks' tour of Europe, commencing at the Vatican, and including eleven countries. At the unprecedented meeting with Pope Paul, the latter said: "Your Holiness comes to us from Asia, the cradle of ancient religions and human traditions which are rightly held in deep veneration. . . ." One needs to respect "these ways of conduct and those teachings of other religions which mirror the ray of eternal truth enlightening all men."[88]

The London *Spectator* (October 20, 1973) took advantage of the occasion of the Dalai Lama's visit to England to inform the public how, as a two-year-old child, he was identified as the latest reincarnation in the line of Dalai Lamas. His immediate predecessor had died in 1933. In the extracts that follow, the *Spectator* speaks first of the intimations the Tibetans received as to where the searching party should look to find the new babe:

In the "Wood-Hog" year of 1935 the [acting] Regent saw in a vision three letters of the Tibetan alphabet; a monastery with a roof of jade-green and gold; and a house with turquoise tiles. A detailed description of the vision was written down and kept secret. When Tibet's wise men . . . travelled eastwards in search of their new-born babe they found him in the village of Taktser, in Amdo Province in North-East Tibet, in a turquoise-tiled house next to a green-and-gold-roofed monastery.

But the real test for a reincarnation is whether he can recall men and matters from a previous life, thereby demonstrating the triumphant transmigration of the soul. So the leader of Tibet's wise men disguised himself as a servant, and his servant as the leader, and entered "the house of the turquoise roof." The unsuspecting parents invited the "leader" of the party into their respected altar-room while the "servant" went to the kitchen—where a two-year-old child was playing.

The disguised leader was wearing a rosary round his neck that had belonged to the thirteenth Dalai Lama, and the child asked to be given it. Surprised but alert the leader promised to give it to the boy-child if he could guess who he was. The toddler replied that he was "Seraaga," which, in the local dialect meant a Lama of Sera Monastery in Lhasa. This was correct, and to the mounting excitement of the search party he proceeded to name them all correctly. [Then followed other difficult tests, which the boy easily passed.]

Sir Basil Gould, the former British agent in Lhasa, gave his firsthand account of some aspects of the story in the British *Geographical Magazine* (October 1946) and also in his book *The Jewel in the Lotus*.[89] In the latter work he explains why he was personally convinced of the genuineness of the incarnation.

Bradford Smith of Columbia University has given this thoughtful evaluation of the same events, prompting him to wonder about the uniqueness of what Christians call "the greatest story ever told":

When the previous Dalai Lama died, wise men had gone forth to seek the new holy one, had found a little boy who recognized things that had belonged to his predecessor and could pick them out unerringly from among similar objects. . . . So here is a religion where an infant is born obscurely, recognized by wise men and worshipped; where a holy man prophesies that he will return from the dead. Does this make me suspect Christianity? Good—face the doubt. Virgin birth, infant god, the holy one violently killed, yet resurrected—these are repeated themes in the history of world religions. . . . These repetitions do not palliate or cancel the strength of the Christian story. Rather they are reinforcing examples of the universal religious impulse and of the way man seeks to represent the cycle of death and rebirth that runs through all of nature. In Tibetan Buddhism, with its firm faith in the rebirth of the soul, not only of Dalai Lamas but of all, and of a progress based upon behaviour during past lives, this impulse is dramatically present.[90]

In his memoirs, *My Land and My People,* the Dalai Lama writes: "I must give a brief explanation of our beliefs . . . because these beliefs had a most profound influence on all that I did and all that our people did when our time of trouble came." Among these beliefs, karma and rebirth are, of course, explained, followed by a number of observations. Conviction in rebirth, the Dalai Lama says, "should engender a universal love," because all living beings in the course of their numberless lives and our own, have probably been our friends, or even our beloved parents, children, brothers, or sisters. This should encourage "tolerance, forbearance, charity, compassion." Similarly, one could add, that the making of separative distinctions of race, creed, sex, color, and social condition would cease when it is seriously considered that in prior lives one may have been a member of other races, religions, societies, sometimes a woman, sometimes a man, and that in the future such transformations will continue. The Lama adds:]

If belief in afterlife is accepted, religious practice becomes a necessity, which nothing else can supplant, in the preparation for one's future incarnation. . . . By whatever name religion may be known, its understanding and practice are the essence of a peaceful mind and therefore of a peaceful world. If there is no peace in one's mind, there can be no peace in one's approach to others, and thus no peaceful relations between individuals or between nations. . . .

How do we know that there is an afterlife? According to Buddhism, although the nature of cause and effect may be different, they must have the same essential properties, they must have a definite connection . . . For example, the human body can be perceived—it has form and color—and therefore, its immediate source or cause must also have these qualities. But mind is formless, and hence its immediate source or cause must also be formless. . . . Both mind and body begin in this life as soon as conception occurs. The immediate source of a body is that of its parents. But physical matter cannot produce mind, nor mind matter. The immediate source of a mind must, therefore, be a mind which existed before the conception took place; the mind must have a continuity from a previous mind. This we hold to prove the existence of a past life. It has been demonstrated by the accounts of adults and children who remember their past lives. . . . On this basis, we can conclude that past life existed, and thence that future life will exist also.[91]

[The Dalai Lama provides an illustration of such remembering in the chapter "Rebirth" in *The Opening of the Wisdom-Eye.* Although as now quoted the story does not supply facts sufficient to authenticate the memory, it is interesting to observe that in old India there was not always unanimity of opinion about rebirth, and that proofs were demanded.]

There is the account of a Buddhist scholar in India who had to prove rebirth to an opponent convinced of the truth of Lokayata doctrines (Materialism). In the debate with his opponent which was held before the king, the Buddhist scholar undertook to prove in a practical way that rebirth was a true doctrine. Just there, in the presence of that king, he gave up his life voluntarily, asking the monarch to be the witness of his death and of his promise to be reborn.

The rival Lokayatas after his demise became so strong that no one dared speak against their teachings. The king then published an open invitation to any Buddhist who could prove the truth of rebirth. No one offered any reply except a boy of four or five years old who, to the surprise of his mother, said that he could prove rebirth. Going before the king, he reminded him of the previous events that had occurred and stated that he was formerly the Buddhist scholar. This boy later became very famous as a Buddhist poet, the works of Chandragomin, for that was his name, being well known to scholars for their poetic excellence.

[Turning to modern times and the sad state of affairs in Tibet where great suffering has been inflicted upon the people, and where the Chinese are attempting to stamp out every vestige of Buddhism, one may wonder how the Dalai Lama views all this in the light of karma and reincarnation. An answer is given in an interview with the Lama, as reported in the *New York Times* (November 12, 1967):

> [The Lama's] hope for his country was not that the current instability in China would enable Tibet to shake loose from Peking's domination. Rather, he said, it was a long-range conviction that the next generation of Chinese leaders would be "more reasonable." Then he proceeded to show just how long-range his judgments were. As a Buddhist, he said, he believes that present events are determined by intricate sets of causes stretching back into the previous lives of those who are affected by them. Thus, he said, it was only an "outward appearance" that the Tibetans were suffering today because of the Chinese aggression. "The aggression must have come because we did something bad." Similarly, he went on, it is only an "outward appearance" that Chinese rule in Tibet is now permanent. The chain of causes that will eventually undermine it, must already be lengthening, even if it cannot be seen. "Cause and effect, cause and effect, cause and effect," he said cheerfully in English, his fingers darting in the air to join the links on the imaginary chain. Then his hands dropped to his lap and he said, "There will certainly be change."

In the London *Spectator* article previously quoted, note was taken of an ancient Tibetan prophecy that a fourteenth Dalai Lama would never rule in Tibet. Thus far the prophecy seems accurate for the present Lama came to the throne in 1950 on the eve of the Chinese invasion, and since 1959 he has

been in self-imposed exile. However, his escape from Tibet has left him free
to further the cause of world Buddhism by writing books and by traveling to
Buddhist centers in Japan, Ceylon, and other Asian countries, and now to the
West. In India itself he is contributing in various ways to the current revival
of Buddhism in the land of its origin.]

THE BOOK OF THE GOLDEN PRECEPTS

[Writing of mysticism in *The Varieties of Religious Experience,* William James
quotes several passages from H. P. Blavatsky's *The Voice of the Silence,* a
translation of a portion of "The Book of the Golden Precepts." Commenting,
James says: "There is a verge of the mind which these things haunt; and
whispers therefrom mingle with the operations of our understanding, even as
the waters of the infinite ocean send their waves to break among the pebbles
that lie upon our shores."[92]

Of the same work D. T. Suzuki remarked: "I saw *The Voice of the Silence*
for the first time when at Oxford. I got a copy and sent it to Mrs. Suzuki (then
Miss Beatrice Lane) at Columbia University, writing to her: 'Here is the real
Mahayana Buddhism.'"[93] Later, reviewing William Kingsland's biography,
The Real H. P. Blavatsky,[94] Dr. Suzuki again called *The Voice of the Silence*
"true Mahayana doctrine," and added:

> Undoubtedly Madame Blavatsky had in some way been initiated into the
> deeper side of Mahayana teaching and then gave out what she deemed wise to
> the Western world as Theosophy. . . . There is no doubt whatever that the
> Theosophical Movement made known to the general world the main doctrines
> of Mahayana Buddhism, and the interest now being taken in Mahayana in the
> Western world has most certainly been helped forward by the knowledge of
> Theosophy. . . . As Mr. Kingsland says, "She did more than any other single
> individual to bring to the West a knowledge of Eastern religious philosophy."[95]

The original 1889 edition of the *Voice* was reissued in English in 1927 by the
Chinese Buddhist Research Society in Peking at the personal request of the
then Tibetan Panchen Lama who for some time had been in China on a
mission, and was en route to Inner Mongolia. The Panchen Lama—who with
the Dalai Lama were the crown of the Tibetan hierarchy—was born in 1883
and died in 1937. (While the duties of the Dalai Lama were governmental and
religious, those of the Panchen Lama pertained chiefly to spiritual matters
and extended to China, Mongolia, and other Mahayana Buddhist countries,
where he was highly revered as a unifying power in northern Buddhism.) He
penned in Tibetan calligraphy a short Sutra for the new edition, and his suite
together with several Chinese scholars verified Madame Blavatsky's translations of Tibetan words. The new foreword mentions that this Russian
noblewoman studied for a considerable period at Tashi-lhum-po, the seat of

the Panchen Lama in Shigatse, Tibet, and knew the previous Lama very well. The present Dalai Lama is familiar with the original (1889) edition of the *Voice* and signed Christmas Humphrey's copy in 1956 when they both were in India at the twenty-five-hundredth anniversary of the Buddhist era.[96] When in 1973 the Dalai Lama visited the Buddhist Society in London, he was shown a copy of the Peking edition, and was fascinated by the photograph it contains of the just-mentioned Panchen Lama.[97]

Madame Blavatsky writes in the preface to her rendition:

> The Book of the Golden Precepts . . . contains about ninety distinct little treatises. Of these I learned thirty-nine by heart, years ago. . . . Therefore . . . the work of translating [a few of these] has been relatively an easy task for me. . . . The original Precepts are engraved on thin oblongs; copies very often on discs. These discs, or plates, are generally preserved on the altars of the temples attached to centres where the so-called "contemplative" or Mahayana (Yogacharya) Schools are established.
>
> [These] maxims and ideas, however noble and original, are often found under different forms in Sanskrit works. . . . This is but natural, since most, if not all, of the greatest Arhats, the first followers of Gautama Buddha, were Hindus and Aryans, not Mongolians, especially those who emigrated into Tibet.

The subject matter of this small volume concerns the steps on the path of discipleship and the goal to be achieved. Thus, the selections on karma, rebirth, and an enduring Self in man have an intimate bearing on the journey depicted, although owing to space limitations much that might prove helpful in finding the Way, had to be omitted. The word "Alaya" which appears several times is defined as "the Universal Soul or Atma, each man having a ray of it in him and being supposed to be able to identify himself with and to merge himself into it." The second "a" in Alaya is pronounced "ah".]

All is impermanent in man except the pure bright essence of Alaya. Man is its crystal ray; a beam of light immaculate within, a form of clay material upon the lower surface. That beam is thy life-guide and thy true Self, the Watcher and the silent Thinker, the victim of thy lower Self.

The moth attracted to the dazzling flame of thy night-lamp is doomed to perish in the viscid oil. The unwary Soul that fails to grapple with the mocking demon of illusion, will return to earth the slave of Mara. Behold the Hosts of Souls. Watch how they hover o'er the stormy sea of human life, and how, exhausted, bleeding, broken-winged, they drop one after other on the swelling waves.

Alas, alas, that all men should possess Alaya, be one with the Great Soul, and that possessing it, Alaya should so little avail them! Behold how like the moon, reflected in the tranquil waves, Alaya is reflected by the small and by the great, is mirrored in the tiniest atoms, yet fails to reach the heart of all.

Alas, that so few men should profit by the gift, the priceless boon of learning truth.

Search for the Paths. But before thou takest thy first step, learn to discern the real from the false, the ever-fleeting from the everlasting. Learn above all to separate Head-learning from Soul-wisdom. False learning is rejected by the Wise, and scattered to the Winds by the Good Law. The wheel of the Good Law moves swiftly on. It grinds by night and day. The worthless husks it drives from out the golden grain, the refuse from the flour. True knowledge is the flour, false learning is the husk. But if thou kneadest husks with Maya's dew, thou canst create but food for the black doves of death, the birds of birth, decay and sorrow.

Chafe not at Karma, nor at Nature's changeless laws. But struggle only with the personal, the transitory, the evanescent and the perishable. Thou canst create this "day" thy chances for thy "morrow." [" 'Tomorrow' means the following rebirth or reincarnation." H.P.B.] In the "Great Journey," causes sown each hour bear each its harvest of effects, for rigid Justice rules the World. With mighty sweep of never erring action, it brings to mortals lives of weal or woe, the karmic progeny of all our former thoughts and deeds. Follow the wheel of life; follow the wheel of duty to race and kin, to friend and foe, and close thy mind to pleasures as to pain. Exhaust the law of karmic retribution. Gain Siddhis for thy future birth. ["There are two kinds of Siddhis or psychic faculties. One group embraces the lower, coarse, psychic and mental energies; the other is one which exacts the highest training of Spiritual powers." H.P.B.]

Have perseverance as one who doth forevermore endure. Thy shadows live and vanish, that which in thee shall live forever, that which in thee *knows,* for it is knowledge, is not of fleeting life: it is the Man that was, that is, and will be, for whom the hour shall never strike. Learn to part thy body from thy mind, to dissipate the shadow, and to live in the eternal. Seek in the Impersonal for the "Eternal Man," and having sought him out, look inward: thou art Buddha. [" 'Personalities' or physical bodies called 'shadows' are evanescent. Mind *(Manas)* the thinking principle or Ego in man, is referred to as 'Knowledge' itself, because the human *Egos* are called *Manasa-putras,* the sons of (universal) Mind. The reincarnating Ego is called by the Northern Buddhists the 'true man,' who becomes in union with his Higher Self, a Buddha." H.P.B.]

Thou hast to reach that fixity of mind in which no breeze, however strong, can waft an earthly thought within. Behold it written: "Ere the gold flame can burn with steady light, the lamp must stand well guarded in a spot free from all wind." Exposed to shifting breeze, the jet will flicker and the quivering flame cast shades deceptive, dark and ever-changing, on the Soul's white shrine. And then, O thou pursuer of the truth, thy Mind-Soul will become as a mad elephant, that rages in the jungle. Mistaking forest trees for living foes, he perishes in his attempts to kill the ever-shifting shadows dancing on the wall of sunlit rocks. Beware, lest in the care of Self thy Soul should lose her foothold on the soil of Deva-knowledge. Beware, lest in forgetting SELF, thy Soul lose o'er its trembling mind control.

Give light and comfort to the toiling pilgrim, and seek out him who knows still less than thou; who in his wretched desolation sits starving for the bread of Wisdom and the bread which feeds the shadow, without a Teacher, hope or consolation, and—let him hear the Law. Tell him that he who makes of pride and self-regard bond-maidens to devotion; that he, who cleaving to existence, still lays his patience and submission to the Law, as a sweet flower at the feet of [the Buddha], becomes a Srotapatti in this birth. Tell him that true devotion may bring him back the knowledge, that knowledge which was his in former births. ["Srotapatti means 'he who enters in the stream' of Nirvana. Unless he reaches the goal owing to some exceptional reasons, he can rarely attain Nirvana in one birth. Usually a Chela (a disciple) is said to begin the ascending effort in one life and end or reach it only in his seventh succeeding birth." H.P.B.]

[A new disciple speaks:] "The choice is made, I thirst for Wisdom. Thy servant here is ready for thy guidance."

'Tis well. Prepare thyself, for thou wilt have to travel on alone. The Teacher can but point the way. The Path is one for all, the means to reach the goal must vary with the Pilgrims. Of teachers there are many; the MASTER-SOUL is one, Alaya, the Universal Soul. Live in that MASTER as ITS ray in thee. Live in thy fellows as they live in IT. Disciples may be likened to the strings of the soul-echoing Vina; mankind, unto its sounding board; the hand that sweeps it to the tuneful breath of the GREAT WORLD-SOUL. The string that fails to answer 'neath the Master's touch in dulcet harmony with all the others, breaks—and is cast away. Thus do the "Brothers of the Shadow"— the murderers of their Souls.

Let thy Soul lend its ear to every cry of pain like as the lotus bares its heart to drink the morning sun. Let not the fierce Sun dry one tear of pain before thyself hast wiped it from the sufferer's eye. But let each burning human tear drop on thy heart and there remain; nor ever brush it off, until the pain that caused it is removed. These tears, O thou of heart most merciful, these are the streams that irrigate the fields of charity immortal. 'Tis on such soil that grows the midnight blossom of Buddha. It is the seed of freedom from [compulsory] rebirth.

No Arhan becomes one in that birth when for the first the Soul begins to long for final liberation. Yet, O thou anxious one, no warrior volunteering fight in the fierce strife between the living and the dead ["the immortal Higher Ego, and the lower personal Ego" H.P.B.], not one recruit can ever be refused the right to enter on the Path that leads toward the field of Battle. For, either he shall win, or he shall fail. Yea, if he conquers, Nirvana shall be his. In him will men a great and holy Buddha honor. And if he falls, e'en then he does not fall in vain; the enemies he slew in the last battle will not return to life in the next birth that will be his. Remember, thou that fightest for man's liberation, each failure is success, and each sincere attempt wins its reward in time. The holy germs that sprout and grow unseen in the disciple's soul, their stalks wax strong at each new trial, they bend like reeds but never break, nor can they e'er be lost. But when the hour has struck they blossom forth. ["A reference to human passions and sins which are slaughtered during the trials of the novitiate, and serve as well-fertilized soil in which 'holy germs' or seeds of transcendental virtues may germinate. Pre-existing or innate virtues, talents or gifts are regarded as having been acquired in a previous birth. Genius is without exception a talent or aptitude brought from another birth." H.P.B.]

The PATH is one, Disciple, yet in the end, twofold. At one end—bliss immediate, and at the other—bliss deferred. Both are of merit the reward: the choice is thine. The One becomes the two, the *Open* and the *Secret*. ["The 'Open' and the 'Secret Path'—or the one taught to the layman, the exoteric and the generally accepted, and the other the Secret Path—the nature of which is explained at Initiation." H.P.B.] The *Open Path* leads to the changeless change—Nirvana, the glorious state of Absoluteness, the Bliss past human thought. Thus the first Path is Liberation. But Path the second is Renunciation. That Secret Path leads the Arhan to mental woe unspeakable; woe for the living Dead, and helpless pity for the men of karmic sorrow; the fruit of karma Sages dare not still. For it is written: "Teach to eschew all causes; the ripple of effect, as the great tidal wave, thou shalt let run its course." ["Men ignorant of the Esoteric truths and Wisdom are called 'the living Dead.'" H.P.B.]

The "Secret Way" leads also to Paranirvanic bliss—but at the close of Kalpas without number; Nirvanas gained and lost from boundless pity and compassion for the world of deluded mortals. But it is said "The last shall be the greatest." Samyak Sambuddha, the Teacher of Perfection, gave up his SELF for the salvation of the World, by stopping at the threshold of Nirvana—the pure state.

Now bend thy head and listen well, O Bodhisattva—Compassion speaks and saith: "Can there be bliss when all that lives must suffer? Shalt thou be saved and hear the whole world cry?" If thou would'st be Tathagata [Buddha], follow upon thy predecessors' steps, remain unselfish till the endless end. Thou art enlightened—choose thy way.

He standeth now like a white pillar to the west, upon whose face the rising

Sun of thought eternal poureth forth its first most glorious waves. His mind, like a becalmed and boundless ocean, spreadeth out in shoreless space. He holdeth life and death in his strong hand. Yea, he is mighty. The living power made free in him, that power which is HIMSELF, can raise the tabernacle of illusion high above the Gods, above great Brahm and Indra. *Now* he shall surely reach his great reward! Shall he not use the gifts which it confers for his own rest and bliss, his well-earn'd weal and glory—he, the subduer of the Great Delusion?

Hark! . . . from the deep unfathomable vortex of that golden light in which the Victor bathes, all Nature's wordless voice in thousand tones ariseth to proclaim: Joy unto ye, O Men of [Earth], a Pilgrim hath returned back "from the other shore." A new Arhan is born. Peace to all beings.[98]

 TAOIST

Lao-tze (c. 604 B.C.–?)

[Before the political and social change that recently enveloped China, it could be said that almost every Chinese Buddhist wore "a Confucian cap, a Taoist robe, and Buddhist sandals."[1] A Confucian or a Taoist often embraced the three faiths, thus complicating for statisticians the tabulation of the religious populations of the Oriental world.[2] While Confucius neither taught nor denied immortality and rebirth, a Confucian through his interest in Taoism or Buddhism could be a reincarnationist. Confucius avoided metaphysical inquiry, his mission being clearly that of a teacher of ethics and elaborator of moral codes. He had, however, great respect for Lao-tze, regarded as the founder of Taoism. Attracted by what he had heard of this sage, Confucius at thirty-five sought out and visited Lao-tze, who was then eighty-eight. After the meeting, Confucius said: "Of birds I know that they have wings to fly with, of fish that they have fins to swim with, of wild beasts that they have feet to run with. . . . But who knows how dragons surmount wind and cloud [and rise] into heaven? This day I have seen Lao-tze. Today I have seen a dragon."[3]

Lao-tze appeared in the time of Buddha, Pythagoras, Ezekiel, and Isaiah. He was born in the Chou dynasty, the longest in China's history and a period of momentous change. His story includes the usual legends attached to the lives of humanity's great teachers. Like Jesus and Buddha he was supposed to be of virgin birth. As a token of hoary wisdom, he was said to have emerged from the womb with a white beard. One of his titles was long-eared. Interestingly, most of the images of the Buddha reveal elongated ears, perhaps indicative of the power to listen to the inner Self—to the "Voice of the Silence"—as well as to hear the heartbeat of all that lives and breathes. Lao-tze is known and honored by reason of his small volume *The Tao Te King*.

> [It] was first officially recognized as a "canon" or "classic" under the Emperor Ching Ti (B.C. 156–140) of the Han Dynasty, after which the study of Tao survived many vicissitudes, being now under a cloud, and now again in high favor at Court. . . . The first Emperor of the later Chin dynasty asked if Tao was of any use in government. Chang Ch'ien-ming told him that "with Tao a corpse could govern the Empire." By successive edicts the *Tao Te King* was made obligatory at the examination for graduates of the second degree, every one was required to possess a copy of the work, and it was cut on stone at both capitals.[4]

The Tao Te King, sometimes rendered "Treatise of the Way and of Virtue," relies upon intimation and paradox to convey what Lionel Giles has called a "well-defined though rudimentary outline of a great system of transcendental and ethical philosophy." While the extracts on immortality here presented reveal only hints of man's eternal renewal, and of the periodical return of the cosmos, reincarnation will be found more specifically in the writings of Lao-tze's renowned disciple Chuang Tzu, next to be considered. As to Lao-tze himself, Taoist traditions relate that he practiced Tao in previous incarnations: as Kwang Chang Tze in the era of Hwang-Ti, the Yellow Emperor; also as Po-Chang in the time of Yao; and the stone tablets of Hsieh Tao-Hang add that "from the time of Fu-Hsi down to that of the Chou dynasty, in uninterrupted succession, his person appeared, but with changed names."[5] The following is from the Giles translation of *The Tao Te King:*]

There is something . . . which existed before Heaven and Earth. Oh how still it is, and formless, standing alone without changing, reaching everywhere without harm . . . It appears to be everlasting. Its name I know not. To designate it, I call it Tao. . . . How unfathomable is Tao! . . . All things return to it. . . . Not visible to the sight, not audible to the ear, in its use it is inexhaustible. . . .

Tao produces all things; its Virtue nourishes them; its Nature gives them form; its Force perfects them. . . . [But] the Tao which can be expressed in words is not the eternal Tao. Without a name, it is the beginning of Heaven and Earth; with a name, it is the Mother of all things. . . .

All things in Nature work silently. They come into being and possess nothing. They fulfil their functions and make no claim. When merit has been achieved, do not take it to yourself; for if you do not take it to yourself, it shall never be taken from you. . . . He that humbles himself shall be preserved entire. He that bends himself shall be made straight. He that is empty shall be filled. He that is worn out shall be renewed. . . . He who, conscious of his own light, is content to be obscure,—he shall be the whole world's model . . . His Virtue will never fail. He reverts to the Absolute. . . .

Use the light that is in you to revert to your natural clearness of sight. Then the loss of the body is unattended by calamity. This is called doubly enduring.

The Great Way is very smooth, but the people love the by-paths. . . . The wearing of gay embroidered robes, the carrying of sharp swords, fastidiousness in food and drink, superabundance of property and wealth:—this I call flaunting robbery; most assuredly it is not Tao. . . . He who acts in accordance with Tao, becomes one with Tao. . . . Being akin to Heaven, he possesses Tao. Possessed of Tao, he endures forever. . . . Being great [Tao] passes on; passing on, it becomes remote; having become remote, it returns.[6]

Chuang Tzu (fl. c. 300 B.C.)

[Chuang Tzu has been called the Saint Paul of Taoism. Although Dr. D. T. Suzuki ranked this illustrious disciple of Lao-tze as China's greatest philosopher, perhaps he should have added "in the past two thousand years." Taoism has often been associated with Zen Buddhism. This was because the renowned Zen master Hui-Yuan (A.D. 334–416), as well as other early Buddhist philosophers in China, were well versed in the Taoist writings of Chuang Tzu, and through this influence adapted the Buddhism of India to the ways of the Chinese. Thus, though Chuang Tzu lived some five hundred years before Buddhism reached China, Thomas Merton in his little volume *The Way of Chuang Tzu* reveals that he was largely responsible for turning Indian Buddhist metaphysics into the practical, iconoclastic aspects of Zen.[7] Incidentally, just as Zen eventually migrated from China to Japan, so also at an earlier date Taoism spread to that country. Some of the finest Taoist scholars and mystics lived in Japan.

Suzuki wrote the introduction to the new edition of James Legge's translation of the works of Chuang Tzu—the edition used in our opening selections. The parentheses used in the extracts are those of the translator. Regarding the "faggots and the fire" illustration in the opening paragraph, Dr. Legge explains: "The 'faggots' are understood to represent the body, and the 'fire' the animating spirit. The body perishes at death as the faggots are consumed by the fire. But the fire may be transmitted to other faggots, and so the spirit may migrate, and be existing elsewhere." This is a variation of the candle and flame simile employed by Buddha, and the torch-race imagery of Thomas Moore, both used in the section "The Immortal Phoenix."]

When the Master [Lao-tze] came, it was at the proper time; when he went away, it was the simple sequence (of his coming). Quiet acquiescence in what happens at its proper time, and quietly submitting (to its ceasing) afford no occasion for grief or for joy. The ancients described (death) as the loosening of the cord on which [Tao] suspended (the life). What we can point to are the faggots that have been consumed; but the fire is transmitted (elsewhere), and we know not that it is over and ended. . . .

Heaven, Earth, and I were produced together, and all things and I are one. . . . There was a beginning. There was a beginning before that beginning. There was a beginning previous to that beginning. . . . Death and life are not far apart. . . . When I look for their origin, it goes back into infinity; when I look for their end, it proceeds without termination. . . . Life is the follower of death, and death is the predecessor of life; but who knows the Arranger (of this connection between them)? . . .

Things indeed die and are born, not reaching a perfect state which can be relied on. Now there is emptiness, and now fulness; they do not continue in one form. . . . Man [at birth] again enters into the great Machinery (of Evolution), from which all things come forth. . . . Decay and growth, fulness and emptiness, when they end, begin again. It is thus we describe the method of great righteousness, and discourse about the principle pervading all things. . . . The Yin and Yang, and the four seasons revolve and move by it, each in its proper order. Now it seems to be lost in obscurity, but it continues; now it seems to glide away, and have no form, but it is still spirit-like. All things are nourished by it, without their knowing it. . . .

The True men of old did not dream when they slept, had no anxiety when they awoke, and did not care that their food should be pleasant. . . . Composedly they went and came. They did not forget what their beginning had been, and they did not inquire into what their end would be. They accepted (their life) and rejoiced in it; they forgot (all fear of death), and returned (to their state before life). Thus there was in them what is called the want of any mind to resist the Tao, and of all attempts by means of the Human to assist the Heavenly. Such were they who are called the True men.[8]

[From Joseph Campbell's *The Masks of God: Oriental Mythology:*[9]]

There is an anecdote recounted of the Taoist sage Chuang Tzu; that when his wife died, the logician Hui Tzu came to his house to join in the rites of mourning but found him sitting on the ground with an inverted bowl on his knees, drumming upon it and singing. "After all," said Hui Tzu in amazement, "she lived with you, brought up your children, grew old along with you. That you should not mourn for her is bad enough; but to let your friends find you drumming and singing—that is really going too far!"

"You misjudge me," Chuang Tzu replied. "When she died, I was in despair, as any man well might be. But soon, pondering on what had happened, I told myself that in death no strange new fate befalls us. In the beginning [of the world] we lack not life only, but form; not form only, but spirit. We are blent in the one great featureless, undistinguishable mass [the universal Tao]. Then a time came when the mass evolved spirit, spirit evolved form, form evolved life. And now life in its turn has evolved death. For not nature only but man's being has its seasons, its sequence of spring and autumn, summer and winter. If someone is tired and has gone to lie down, we do not pursue him with shouting and bawling. She whom I have lost has lain down to sleep for a while in the Great Inner Room. To break in upon her rest with the noise of lamentation would be to show I knew nothing of nature's Sovereign Law."

"This attitude toward death," writes Arthur Waley, "exemplified again and again in Chuang Tzu, is but part of a general attitude toward the universal laws of nature, which is one not merely of resignation nor even of acquiescence, but a lyrical, almost ecstatic acceptance, which has inspired some of the most moving passages in Taoist literature."[10]

[In the following excerpt from *The Self in Transformation* by Herbert Fingarette, Chuang Chou is the same as Chuang Tzu (a spelling variation):]

Chuang Tzu tells an anecdote which is often quoted in Western literature—but, no doubt because of our Western bias, almost always with the omission of the crucial last two sentences. I add these, in Giles's translation and italicized, to Waley's text: "Once Chuang Chou dreamt that he was a butterfly. He did not know that he had ever been anything but a butterfly and was content to hover from flower to flower. Suddenly he woke and found to his astonishment that he was Chuang Chou. But it was hard to be sure whether he really was Chou and had only dreamt that he was a butterfly, or he was really a butterfly and was only dreaming that he was Chou. *Between a man and a butterfly there is necessarily a barrier. The transition is called metempsychosis.*"[11]

[In our final selection from Chuang Tzu, taken from *The Musings of a Chinese Mystic,* the Taoist view of reincarnation contrasts sharply with the doleful picture of some other schools of Oriental thought. Conceivably both views are true, depending on the mood, temperament, or philosophy of the observer.]

To have attained to the human form must be always a source of joy. And then, to undergo countless transitions, with only the infinite to look forward to—what incomparable bliss is that! Therefore it is that the truly wise rejoice in that which can never be lost, but endures always.[12]

✳ ✳ ✳

Po Chu-I (A.D. 772–846)

TAOIST POET

[From "Peaceful Old Age," translated by Lionel Giles:]

> If I depart, I cast no look behind
> Still wed to life, I still am free from care.
> Since life and death in cycles come and go,
> Of little moment are the days to spare.
> Thus strong in faith I wait, and long to be
> One with the pulsings of Eternity.[13]

EGYPTIAN

[From our travels in Asiatic lands, we now turn westward to ancient Egypt, and then to other Middle East countries. Egypt has a fascination for many people. They are set aglow by pictures of her royal palms, the gigantic columns of temples, the judgment scenes from Budge's Book of the Dead, and all manner of Egyptian antiquities. Edna Ferber in her autobiography, *A Peculiar Treasure*, recalls that as a child the sound of circus wagon wheels evoked vague and terrible sensations of "something that went back, back, perhaps to Egyptian days and the heavy wheels of chariots." Prompted by great expectations, she later visited Egypt only to experience intense dislike for everything connected with her ancient past. "I can only venture to say, at the risk of being hooted, that somewhere in Egypt a couple of thousand years ago I probably had a very tough time of it." When writing *Show Boat* she says the very thought of the mystery and terror of the Mississippi caused a surging up from some hidden treasure-trove a flood of visualized pictures, people, and incidents. "I don't to this day know where that river knowledge came from." (When *Show Boat* became a musical, Jerome Kern apparently caught some of this imagery in his powerful song "Old Man River.") Miss Ferber writes: "Perhaps, centuries and centuries ago, I was a little Jewish slave girl on the Nile."[1] The Egypt of biblical times, of course, was already a declining nation.

Our present chapter would have little to offer directly from Egyptian sources were it not for the pioneer work of Champollion, the father of Egyptology. As a child, feeling a passionate interest in hieroglyphics, he became determined to devote his life to deciphering the hitherto sealed book of the Egyptian writings. At sixteen he astonished scholars of the academy at Grenoble with his paper on the Coptic language and was given a teaching post. In 1821 his famous paper was issued, revealing the alphabetical character of the hieroglyphs and the true key to their decipherment.[2]

Herodotus, Plato, Plutarch, and other ancient writers spoke of reincarnation as the general belief of the Egyptians.[3] "The Greek testimony is so strong that it seems unlikely to have all been derived from the metamorphoses" section of the Book of the Dead. Thus writes one of the great Egyptologists, Sir Flinders Petrie. He adds, however, that Greek authors are post-Persian and therefore it is possible that the idea of reincarnation "really did blend with Egyptian belief during the Persian occupation, when other Indian ideas came into Egypt, such as asceticism."

> Transmigration is plainly stated in the Koré Kosmou, of the Persian period, probably about 500 B.C.[4] After that it is natural that the Greek writers, Herodotus, Plato, Theophrastus, Plutarch [De Iside 31, 72], and others, should ascribe the belief to the Egyptians of their times, unconscious that it was a new importation.[5]

However, Dr. Margaret Murray, a distinguished Egyptologist who worked with Petrie for many years, points to evidences of reincarnation belief far anterior to the Persian invasion. She writes in The Splendour That Was Egypt that one theory of the hereafter held by the Egyptians, "which has received little attention from Egyptologists, is the theory of reincarnation. . . . The ka-names of the first two kings of the xx-th dynasty [a remote period in Egyptian history] show this belief clearly: Amonemhat I's name was 'He who repeats births,' and Sensusert I's name was 'He whose births live.' In the xix-th dynasty the ka-name of Setekhy I was 'Repeater of births,' and it was by this epithet that he was addressed by the god Amon at Karnak. . . . Pythagoras is usually credited with having invented the theory of reincarnation, but it was already hoary with age before the Greeks had emerged from barbarism."[6]

In his volume Oldest Books in the World, Isaac Myer states that "life on this earth, to the ancient people of Egypt, certainly under the Theban dynasty, and most likely long before, was only a to become (Khopir or kheper) in the content of many to becomes (khopriu) which had preceded and would follow it. It had an infinity of duration, a pre-existence before birth in this world, it would have an infinity of duration after such birth, and the soul would pass through all this content, guarding its own identity. Before its birth in this world it had been born and died in many other worlds."[7]

It may be significant that the word "kheper," which Pierret says in his Livres des Morts means "to be, to become, to build again," was the name given by the Egyptians to the sacred beetle, the scarabaeus. The prayer so often found in the tumular inscriptions, "the wish for the resurrection of one's living soul," includes the image of a scarabaeus. This winged insect was the most frequent and highly honored of all Egyptian symbols, no mummy being without several of them, and it was the favorite ornament on household furniture and utensils. Dévéria mentions later that The Book of the Dead "shows us clearly that resurrection was in reality but a renovation, leading to a new existence, a new infancy, a new youth."

The mummification of the dead has been a great puzzle to Western investigators. Those who have read Sax Rohmer's short story "The Mysterious Mummy," or have seen the screen version with Boris Karloff, may imagine that the Egyptians were naïve enough to believe that the embalmed body could be revived and used again when the soul returned. The theosophical writer William Q. Judge remarks that "it has been suggested very justly that the practice [of mummification] began with their Adept kings for reasons of their own, and that it came to be imitated afterwards." "If this is so, then it would be natural for the kings to permit it among the people so as to create a greater security for their own mummies; for if there be mummies for all, no one will bother to look for any particular mummy for some special reason, whereas if only kings were known to be mummied, then later people might want to exhume and inspect them . . ."[8] If credence can be given to the many stories of dire misfortune attending those who against all warnings opened up the tombs of the later pharaohs, one may wonder whether some occult force was resident in these places.

H. P. Blavatsky in her *Theosophical Glossary* under "Reincarnation" speaks of the general significance of the mummy as a symbol:

> All the Egyptian converts to Christianity . . . believed in [reincarnation], as shown by the writings of several. In the still existing symbols, the human-headed bird flying towards a mummy, a body, or "the soul uniting itself with its *sahou*" (glorified body of the Ego . . .) proves this belief. "The song of the Resurrection" chanted by Isis to recall her dead husband [Osiris] to life, might be translated "Song of Rebirth," as Osiris is [in this case] collective Humanity. . . . The funeral prayer of the priest over the deceased [was:] "Oh! Osiris (here follows the name of the Osirified mummy, or the departed), rise again in holy earth (matter), august mummy in the coffin, under thy corporeal substances." . . . "Resurrection" with the Egyptians never meant the resurrection of the mutilated mummy, but of the *Soul* that informed it, the Ego in a new body.[9]]

The Book of the Dead

[The most celebrated scripture of the Egyptians is the Book of the Dead. Maspero ascribes the earliest discovered copies to the eleventh and twelfth dynasties, but believes the originals trace back to the first dynasties, and the historian Bunsen points out that extracts are found on monuments of the very first kings. The book was usually placed in tombs of important personages, and bears their individual names because it had been especially copied for them during life. Thoth-Hermes is the supposed author of the Book of the Dead. C. C. J. Bunsen revered it as "that precious and mysterious book," but it is more the Book of Immortal Life than a funereal volume. The scenes describe the journey of the soul through the states following death. When the higher levels are reached the defunct is "Osirified," and exclaims: "I am Osiris, the Lord of Eternity!" In the chapter "Reincarnation or Transmigration of Souls," in *Egyptian Belief and Modern Thought,* James Bonwick says regarding the Book of the Dead:

> The Ritual is full of allusions to the doctrine. Chapters 26 to 30 relate to the preservation of the heart or life for this purpose. . . . [Dévéria, the French Egyptologist] shows how this esoteric doctrine was revealed in that portion of Egyptian sacred Scripture, known as the "Book of that which is in the Lower Hemisphere." He admits that "the funeral books show us clearly that resurrection was, in reality, but a renovation, leading to a new existence, a new infancy, and a new youth." He says further, "The *sahou* was not [merely] the mortal body. It was a *new* being [or personality] formed by the re-union of corporeal elements elaborated by nature, and in which the soul was reborn in order to accomplish a new terrestrial existence under many forms."[10]

The passages from the Book of the Dead that follow are from the Papyrus of Ani, scribe and treasurer of the temples of Egypt about 1450 B.C. We have quoted another passage in chapter 2 under "The Immortal Phoenix." There the human soul, having reached in the afterdeath world the peak state, is shown declaring: "I am the Benu Bird, the Heart-soul of Ra," and "upon earth . . . shall come forth." As previously mentioned, the pictured symbol in our present work is the Benu bird, or Egyptian phoenix.

The opening extract is from a hymn to Ra, who has been defined as "the divine Universal Soul in its manifested aspect—the ever-burning light; also the personified Sun." While most people think of the ancients as sun worshipers, it was not the physical sun they apparently honored but the universal spirit and the divine powers within and behind this heart of the solar system.[11]]

Thou king of Right and Truth, thou lord of eternity, thou prince of everlastingness, thou sovereign of all the gods, thou god of life. . . . The company of the gods rejoice at thy rising, the earth is glad when it beholdeth thy rays; the peoples *that have been long dead* come forth with cries of joy to see thy beauties every day. . . .

I am the Benu, the soul of Ra, and the guide of the gods in the Tuat (underworld). Their divine souls come forth upon earth to do the will of their kas, let therefore the soul of Osiris Ani come forth to do the will of his ka. . . .

Homage to thee Osiris, O Governor of those who are in Amenti [heaven], who maketh mortals to be born again, who renewest thy youth. . . .

Nebensi, the lord of reverence, saith: "I am Yesterday, Today, and To-morrow, [and I have] the power to be born a second time; [I am] the divine hidden Soul who createth the gods. . . ."

[Osiris in his character as a great king among men asks:]

How long . . . have I to live? [Answer:] It is decreed that thou shalt live for millions of millions of years. [Osiris:] May it be granted unto me that I pass on unto the holy princes, for indeed, I am doing away with all the wrong which I did, from the time when this earth came into being.[12]

[Commenting on the last selection, J. B. Priestley remarks: "I agree that it could be argued . . . that what the god Thoth was offering his questioner was not the false eternity of popular Christianity but the innumerable incarnations . . . accepted by the Buddhists. This Egyptian, it could be said, would live for millions of years because he would return again and again and again to Time, in one shape and personality after another, until finally purged of all desire for any further existence on this earth."[13]]

The Hermetic Works

[At the beginning of the Christian era the chief religious movements rivaling with Christianity for the mastery of the Middle East and Western world were Persian Mithraism, the Egyptian Mysteries, and Alexandrian Neoplatonic theology.[14] As we shall see later, all these movements taught that man lives numerous times on earth. Included in the Egyptian mysteries was the great Hermetic tradition, the word Hermetic in this connection referring to any doctrine or writing associated with the teachings of Thoth-Hermes. The books of Hermes, renowned throughout antiquity, have been lost in their Egyptian form for at least two millennia. The Neoplatonist Iamblichus relates in his book *The Egyptian Mysteries* (Part VIII) that Manetho, an Egyptian priest, attributed to Hermes 36,525 treatises. As already mentioned, Hermes is the reputed author of the Book of the Dead. It appears likely that a line of teachers assumed this name. The Egyptians called Hermes by the name Tahuti, "thrice great," the Greek equivalent being Trismegistus. Hermes Trismegistus was also a generic name used by various Greek writers on philosophy and alchemy.

The selections that follow are from the Egyptian Hermetic Fragments that have come down through the Greeks and Romans and were in some degree altered by them, particularly by Christian writers who interpolated anthropomorphic ideas of God. In his French translation of the Fragments, Dr. Louis Ménard says that in the early days of Christianity the Hermetic writings enjoyed a high repute among the most eminent church fathers, such as Augustine, Clement, and Origen, who invoked their testimony in support of the Christian mysteries, and considered them as genuine monuments to that ancient Egyptian theology in which Moses had been instructed. Lost to Europe during the Dark Ages, the Hermetic teachings reappeared prior to the Renaissance, having meanwhile been preserved and studied by the Arabians and the Moors. (The Hermetic revival of the Renaissance will be considered in chapter 5.) However, in the 1600s a controversy arose that raged for several centuries concerning the authenticity of the Fragments. Religious writers began labeling them as plagiarisms from Christian teachings, dating the works as among the later productions of Greek philosophy. G. R. S. Mead in his three-volume history and translation *The Thrice-Greatest Hermes* analyzes the falseness of these charges and concludes with this summary:

> Why did the early Church Fathers accept the Trismegistic writings as exceedingly ancient and authoritative, and in their apologetic writing quote them in support of the main impersonal dogmas of Christianity? . . . Why during the last two centuries and a half has a body of opinion been gradually evolved, infinitesimal in its beginnings, but well-nigh shutting out every other view, that these writings are Neoplatonic forgeries?
>
> The answers to these questions are simple:—The Church Fathers appealed to the authority of antiquity . . . in order to show that they taught nothing fundamentally new. . . . [15] They lived in days too proximate to that tradition to have [themselves] ventured bringing any charge of plagiarism and forgery against it without exposing themselves to a crushing rejoinder from men who were still the hearers of its "living voice" and possessors of its "written word." . . . [Toward the close of the Renaissance] it was perceived that, if the old tradition were accepted, the fundamental originality of general Christian doctrines . . . could no longer be maintained. It, therefore, became imperatively necessary to discredit the ancient tradition by every possible means. With what success this policy has been attended we have already seen; we have also reviewed . . . its baseless character and the straits to which its defenders have been put.
>
> From the clouds of this obscurantism the sun of Thrice-Greatest Hermes and the radiance of his Gnosis have once more shone forth in the skies of humanistic enquiry and unprejudiced research. He is no longer to be called bastard, and plagiarist, and thief of other people's property, but must be regarded as a genuine teacher of men, handing on his own and giving freely of his substance to all who will receive the gift. [16]

Mead states, however, that the old unsubstantiated theories still persist as facts in current encyclopedias and are "trotted out with complacency and with the impressive air of official knowledge . . . Unfortunately these *ex cathedra* encyclopaedic pronouncements are all the general reader will ever hear.''[17]

In the opening selection from Hermes, it appears that the Egyptians taught a spiritual evolution through the lower kingdoms, to man and beyond.]

From one Soul of the Universe are all Souls derived. . . . Of these Souls there are many changes, some into a more fortunate estate, and some quite contrary. And they which are of creeping things are changed into those of watery things, and those of things living in the water to those of things living on the land; and airy ones into men. Human souls that lay hold of immortality are changed into holy powers. And so they go on into the sphere of the Gods. . . . And this is the most perfect glory of the soul. . . .

Not all human souls but only the pious ones are divine. Once separated from the body, and after the struggle to acquire piety, which consists in knowing God and injuring none, such a soul becomes all intelligence. The impious soul, however, punishes itself by seeking a human body to enter into, for no other body can receive a human soul; it cannot enter the body of an animal devoid of reason. Divine law preserves the human soul from such infamy.

The Key[18]

HORUS   How are souls born male or female?

ISIS   Souls, my son Horus, are all equal in nature. . . . There are not among them either males or females; this distinction exists only between bodies, and not between incorporeal beings. . . . (Part II)

HORUS   Thou hast given me admirable instruction, O my most powerful Mother Isis . . . but thou hast not yet shown me whither souls depart when set free from bodies. . . .

ISIS   O great and marvellous scion of the illustrious Osiris, think not that souls on quitting the body mix themselves confusedly in the vague immensity and become dispersed in the universal and infinite spirit, without power to return into bodies, to preserve their identity, or to seek again their primeval abode. Water spilt from a vase returns no more to its place therein, it has no proper locality, it mingles itself with the mass of waters; but it is not thus with souls, O most wise Horus. I am initiated into the mysteries of the immortal nature; I walk in the ways of the truth, and I will reveal all to thee without the least omission. . . .

Souls do not, then, return confusedly [to the afterdeath states], nor by chance, into one and the same place, but each is despatched into the condition which belongs to her. And this is determined by that which the soul experiences while yet she is in the tenement of the body, loaded with a burden contrary to her nature. . . . The law of equity presides over the changes which take place above, even as upon earth also it moulds and constructs the vessels in which the souls are immured. (Part III)

The Virgin of the World[19]

PERSIAN

[If the Christian legends are based on facts, then the first men to be aware of Christ's birth were heathens—the three wise men from the East called the Magi. "They saw his star," says the gospel of Matthew. They also were likely to have been reincarnationists, according to the Neoplatonist Porphyry:

> Among the Persians those who are wise in divine concerns, and worship divinity, are called Magi. . . . But so great and so venerable are these men thought to be by the Persians, that Darius [558?–486 B.C.], the son of Hystaspes, had among other things this engraved on his tomb, that he had been the master of the Magi. They are divided into three genera, as we are informed by Eubulus, who wrote the history of Mithra, in a treatise consisting of many books. In this work he says . . . the dogma with all of them which ranks as the first is this, that there is a transmigration of souls; and this they also appear to indicate in the mysteries of Mithra.[1]

Is it not probable, then, that the three Magi would have honored Jesus as the return to earth life of some great teacher or prophet of the past?

The Magi were disciples of Zarathustra (Zoroaster in Greek) who founded the religion variously called Magianism, Mazdaism, Parseeism, and Zoroastrianism. Like Hermes in Egypt, Zarathustra appears to have been a generic name for great Iranian teachers and reformers.[2] The hierarchy may have begun with the divine Zarathustra of the *Zend-Avesta,* and ended with the latest one, who is conceded to have lived about eight thousand years ago. Bunsen describes him as "one of the mightiest intellects and one of the greatest men of all time."[3] Only fragments of the immense body of Zoroastrian literature remain. More would exist if Alexander the Great had not destroyed so many sacred and precious works.

Under Islamic rule many of the Zoroastrians fled from Iran in the seventh century and their modern successors are the Parsis of India, a highly respected community living chiefly in Bombay. In a 1964 radio broadcast from Karachi on the occasion of Zarathustra's birthday, Gool K. Minwalla stated:

There is much confusion and error in the minds of people of other faiths regarding the pure monotheism of Zarathustra, because the Prophet also expounded the Doctrine of Dualism. This however is different from the doctrine of duality which speaks of two mighty Beings distinct from and always opposed to each other. . . . Because man is free to exercise his will for good or evil, he often oscillates between the two during his lifetime, not being wholly good nor wholly evil. Zarathustra has not conceived of evil as something permanent in man's constitution; he does not believe . . . in an original sin which cannot be conquered by man by his own exertions. On the contrary, he affirms over and over again the triumph of the good and the possibility of perfectibility. . . .

The outer symbol that represents the living spirit of this great religion is fire. Here again those who seek to belittle the religion designate the Parsis as "Fire-Worshippers," as against the worshippers of the true God. Not the fire but the Immortal Holy Spirit symbolised by the fire is worshipped. As the fragrant sandalwood is offered to the fire so man is reminded to offer to the highest the fragrance of his pure and sacrificial life.

In Zarathustra's teachings the expression Fire-Soul is used for the eternal self in man. As an ever-living flame, it has over the years been beautifully and impressively symbolized in certain sacred temples as a perpetual fire that must never be allowed to go out. Although the Magi held that this Fire-Soul returned to earth life again and again, the present-day Parsi priests do not accept reincarnation. A few Parsi scholars do, and point to confirmation of the idea in ancient works.[4]

In the earliest Zoroastrian scriptures, known under the general heading of the *Zend-Avesta,* we gain a glimpse in the *Vendidad* of a teaching of animal evolution through rebirth. Zarathustra asks Ahura-Mazda what happens when a male or female dog dies. "Where does its consciousness *(baodhangh)* go?" The reply is that it is reborn as "the Udra that resides in the waters."[5] Among the Iranians the Udra, or water dog—probably the seal or walrus— was highly valued.

In the *Zend-Avesta,* the Gathas, or hymns (together with the *Vendidad*), are regarded as direct utterances of Zarathustra. Here is one stanza:

> Souls whose Inner Light continues dim,
> Who have not yet beheld the Light of Truth,
> Unto this Home of Falsehood shall return,
> Surrounded by false Leaders, Egos false,
> By those who think and speak and act untrue.[6]

Although this leaves the impression that only sinners return to earth, another Gatha affirms that in each succeeding birth good deeds bring greater self-knowledge and self-control, while evil deeds beget a dire fate.[7]

Reincarnation is explicitly taught in *The Desatir.* This old mystical work was a literary relic in 500 B.C. and is the sole surviving example of the lost

Mahabhadian language. Mulla Furuz, who rendered *The Desatir* into English in 1818, used the only copy known to exist—unintelligible without the ancient Persian commentary found with it. Each book of *The Desatir* is by a different prophet, Zoroaster being the thirteenth and last. "The Book of the Prophet, the Great Abad" has this passage:

> Mezdam separated man from the other animals by the distinction of a soul, which is a free and independent substance, without a body or anything material, indivisible and without position, by which he attaineth to the glory of the Angels. . . .
> And everyone who wisheth to return to the lower world [the earth] and is a doer of good shall, according to his knowledge and conversation and actions, receive something, either as a King or a Prime Minister, or some high office or wealth, until he meeteth with a reward suited to his deeds. . . . Those who, in the season of prosperity, experience pain and grief, suffer them on account of their words or deeds in a former body, for which the Most Just now punisheth them.[8]

In the introduction to their translation (1843) of *The Dabistan* (a compendium of the teachings of Persian schools and sects), Shea and Troyer summarize their understanding of the views of the ancient Iranians on man's destiny:

> Human souls are eternal and infinite; they come from above, and are spirits of the upper spheres. If distinguished for knowledge and sanctity while on earth, they return above, are united with the sun, and become empyreal sovereigns; but if the proportion of their good works bore a closer affinity to any other star, they become lords of the place assigned to that star; their stations are in conformity with the degrees of their virtue; perfect men attain the beatific vision of the light of lights. . . . Vice and depravity, on the contrary, separate souls from the primitive source of light, and chain them to the abode of the elements: they become evil spirits. The imperfectly good migrate from one body to another, until, by the efficacy of good words and actions, they are finally emancipated from matter, and gain a higher rank.[9]]

Mithraism

[The excavation in this century of the ruins of a Mithraic temple in the city of London revived an age-old mystery concerning the disappearance of a religion that during the first three centuries A.D. was adopted by Roman emperors and legions alike.[10] Radhakrishnan remarks that the emperor Julian "was an ardent votary of Mithra" and that Mithraism "proved the most dangerous rival to the Christian Church before its alliance with Constantine." No wonder Ernest Renan observed that "if Christianity had been stopped in its growth by some deadly disease, the world would have been Mithraist."[11]

The Belgian historian Franz Cumont indicates that reincarnation was "accepted by the mysteries of Mithras"[12] as does Eubulus in the volume just mentioned by Porphyry. In *The Gnostics and Their Remains,* C. W. King explains that Mithraism "was the theology of Zoroaster in its origin, but greatly simplified so as to assimilate it to the previously existing systems of the West. . . . Under this form it took its name from Mithras, who in the Zoroastrian creed is not the Supreme Being (Ormuzd) but the chief of the subordinate Powers, the seven Amshaspends. Mithras is the Zend name for the sun."[13]

Franz Cumont, the foremost authority in this field, gives some very interesting information in his work *The Mysteries of Mithra.* He shows that while the civilizations of the Greeks and Romans were unsuccessful in establishing themselves among the Persians, the religion of the Magi exercised a deep influence on Occidental culture at three different periods. It made a very distinct impression on Judaism in its formative stage. Later the influence of Mazdaism on European thought was still more direct when Asia Minor was conquered by the Romans. But at the beginning of the Christian era, this religion, as Mithraism, suddenly emerged and pressed forward rapidly and simultaneously into the valleys of the Danube and the Rhine, and into the heart of Italy itself. Remains of its temples are to be found in Germany, France, Switzerland, as well as in Britain. The Mithraists admitted members of all religions to their meetings.[14] Cumont adds:

> In the heyday of its vigor, it exercised [a] remarkable influence on the society and government of Rome. Never perhaps, not even in the epoch of the Mussulman invasion, was Europe in greater [likelihood of becoming] Asiaticized than in the third century of our era. . . . When the flood subsided it left behind in the conscience of the people a deep sediment of oriental beliefs which have never been completely obliterated. . . . The defeat of Mithraism did not utterly annihilate its power. It had prepared the minds of the Occident for the reception of a new faith, which like itself, came also from the banks of the Euphrates. . . . Manicheism appeared as its successor and continuator. This was the final assault made by Persia on the Occident.[15]]

Manicheism

[Manicheism, which taught reincarnation and eventually comprised as many as seventy sects, was founded by a Babylonian, a half-Christian mystic, named Manes, born about A.D. 215. His seat of proselytizing was in Persia, but he journeyed into China and India, and westward into Christian lands. He called himself the expected "Comforter," the Messiah and Christ, and taught that there were two eternal principles of good and evil; the former furnishing mankind with souls and the latter with bodies. Manes opposed Catholic Christianity but was influenced by the Christian Gnostics. He borrowed from older Oriental faiths, especially from Babylonian and Zoroastrian sources, and even Buddhist ethics. Branded as the greatest heretic of his day by the Church, he was flayed alive around the year 276 by the Persian king at the instance of the Magi who had become powerful and corrupt.

Beausobré reports the beliefs of the Manichees concerning reincarnation.[16] He quotes Augustine's reproach to these "heretics": "You do not promise Resurrection to your Disciples, but a return to a mortal body; in order that born again, they will live the life of the Elect."[17] While in Christian accounts the Manichees are shown embracing ridiculous notions on reincarnation, Edward Tylor says: "These details come to us from the accounts of bitter theological adversaries, and the question is, how much of them did the Manichaeans really and soberly believe?"[18]

The rapid growth of this movement made it "one of the great religions," having "secret support even among the clergy." After A.D. 330 Manicheism spread rapidly throughout the Roman Empire, its adherents being recruited from the Gnostics and from "the large number of the 'cultured' who were striving after a 'rational' and yet in some manner Christian religion."[19]

In the latter part of the fourth century the Christian Byzantine and Roman emperors enacted strict laws against Manicheism, and Justinian decreed punishment of death for being a member. "But it still continued to exist elsewhere, both in the Byzantine Empire and in the West, and in the earlier part of the Middle Ages it gave an impulse to the formation of new sects, which remained related to it." Among these sects there were "the Paulicians and Bogomils, as well as the Catharists and the Albigenses," who are "traced back to Manichaeism (and [Gnostic] Marcionitism)." The conquests of Islam could not erase Manichaean influence: "It seems to have become still more widely diffused by the victorious campaigns of the Mohammedans, and it frequently gained secret adherents among the latter themselves."[20]

The Gnostic teaching of reincarnation and the conceptions of the Catharists and Albigenses are still to be considered. Eventually, at the close of the Middle Ages, these Christian reincarnationists grew so numerous and influential that they almost unseated ecclesiastical Christianity itself.

JEWISH

[In her study of ancient and modern religions and sciences, *Isis Unveiled,* H. P. Blavatsky says of the Israelites that "the present remains of a once-glorious people bear witness [to] how faithfully and nobly they have stood by their ancestral faith under the most diabolical persecutions. . . . The Christian world has been in a state of convulsion from the first to the present century; it has been cleft into thousands of sects; but the Jews remain substantially united. Even their differences of opinion do not destroy their unity."[1]

One difference of opinion concerns reincarnation. The strictly orthodox tend to reject it, and deny it a place in early Jewish philosophy. Others, including some orthodox rabbis, accept rebirth as an integral part of Judaism, as does Sholem Asch in the opening of *The Nazarene:*

> Not the power to remember, but its very opposite, the power to forget, is a necessary condition of our existence. If the lore of the transmigration of souls is a true one, then these, between their exchange of bodies, must pass through the sea of forgetfulness. According to the Jewish view we make the transition under the overlordship of the Angel of Forgetfulness. But it sometimes happens that the Angel of Forgetfulness himself forgets to remove from our memories the records of the former world; and then our senses are haunted by fragmentary recollections of another life. They drift like torn clouds above the hills and valleys of the mind, and weave themselves into the incidents of our current existence. They assert themselves, clothed with reality, in the form of nightmares which visit our beds. Then the effect is exactly the same as when, listening to a concert broadcast through the air, we suddenly hear a strange voice break in, carried from afar on another ether-wave and charged with another melody.[2]

In the first century the Jewish historian Flavius Josephus matter-of-factly speaks of reincarnation in his famed work *The Jewish War.* As a general in the campaign against the Roman commander Vespasian, he had been one of the few survivors of a bloody siege. Addressing some Jewish soldiers who were about to commit suicide rather than be captured by the Romans, he said: "The bodies of all men are, indeed mortal, and are created out of corruptible matter; but the soul is ever immortal, and is a portion of the divinity that inhabits our bodies. . . . Do not you know, that those who depart out of this life according to the law of nature . . . enjoy eternal fame: that their houses and their posterity are sure; that their souls are pure and obedient, and obtain a most holy place in heaven, from whence, in the revolution of ages, they are again sent into pure bodies; while the souls of those whose hands have acted madly against themselves are received by the darkest place in Hades?''[3]

Josephus also tells how the three chief schools of Jewish philosophy, the Pharisees, the Sadducees, and the Essenes, regarded immortality. The Sadducees apparently believed that the soul dies with the body. The Pharisees ''say that all the souls are incorruptible, but the souls of good men only, are removed into other bodies, but the souls of bad men are subject to eternal punishment.''[4] (With the Jews, ''eternal'' did not mean everlasting, but a very long time.) In *The Antiquities of the Jews,* Josephus repeats that the Pharisees ''believe that souls have an immortal vigor,'' and that the virtuous ''shall have power to revive and live again'' on earth, ''on account of which doctrines they are able greatly to persuade the body of the people.''[5]

Josephus gives a fascinating picture of the communal life of the Essenes of Dead Sea Scrolls' fame, recounting their religious beliefs too. A passage from *The Jewish War* shows that the Essenes taught the soul's pre-existence—the foundation for all reincarnation teaching—but it is not clear whether rebirth is implied by the words ''expecting to receive their souls again.'' However, in *Die Christliche Mystik,* J. V. Görres says that ''the Kabala was held in high esteem particularly by the Essenes,''[6] and reincarnation is basic in kabalistic thinking. Other scholars show that the Essenes came under the influence of Buddhist monks who crowded into the Middle East in the centuries preceding the Christian era. In addition, they had affinities with other reincarnationists, namely the Pythagoreans, whose doctrines and communal practices were fitted into the Essenes' scheme of living. Quoting from *The Jewish War:*

> [The Essenes] condemn the miseries of life, and are above pain, by the generosity of their mind. And as for death . . . our war with the Romans gave abundant evidence what great souls they had in their trails. . . . They smiled in their very pains and laughed to scorn those who inflicted torments upon them, and resigned up their souls with great alacrity, as expecting to receive them again. For their doctrine is this, that bodies are corruptible, and that the matter they are made of is not permanent; but that the souls are immortal, and continue forever; and that they come out of the most subtile air, and are united to their bodies as to prisons, into which they are drawn by a certain natural enticement; but that when they are set free from the bonds of flesh, they then, as released from a long bondage, rejoice and mount upward. . . . These are the divine doctrines of the Essenes about the soul, which lay an unavoidable bait for such as have once had a taste of their philosophy.[7]

Another witness to this period is the Alexandrian philosopher Philo Judaeus. He penetrated into the esotericism of the oldest Judaic teachings and made correlations with the Platonic philosophy. In his *De Somniis* (I:22) he said that "the air is full of souls; those who are nearest to earth descending to be tied to mortal bodies, return to other bodies, desiring to live in them." In *De Gigantes* (2 et seq.) he wrote that "the company of disembodied souls is distributed in various orders. The law of some is to enter mortal bodies and after certain prescribed periods to be again set free. But those possessed of a diviner structure are absolved from all local bonds of earth. Some souls choose confinement in mortal bodies because they are corporeally inclined. . . . Yet those who are wise, like Moses, are also living abroad from home because they chose this expatriation from heaven in order to acquire knowledge and so came to dwell in earthly nature. While here they urge men to return to their original source."

Rabbi Moses Gaster considers Judaic reincarnation beliefs in his article "Transmigration" in the *Encyclopaedia of Religion and Ethics*. Although he takes the orthodox position that the doctrine was borrowed from other systems, he makes some significant admissions:

> There cannot be any doubt that these views are extremely old [in Judaism]. Simon Magus raises the claim of former existences, his soul passing through many bodies before it reaches that known as Simon. The Samaritan doctrine of the *taheb* teaches the same doctrine of a pre-existing soul which was given to Adam, but which, through successive 'incarnations' in Seth, Noah, and Abraham, reached Moses, for whom it was originally formed and for whose sake the world had been created. . . . This doctrine of migration is nowhere to be found systematically developed [in Jewish writings]. Wherever it occurs, it is tacitly assumed as well known, and no explanation is given in detail. It has, therefore, been pieced together and reconstructed by the present writer mostly from the Zoharistic literature. . . . While these are by far the most complete writings, they are by no means the oldest.
>
> This brings us to the question of the date and probable origin of this doctrine among the Jews. All the beginnings of esoteric teachings are lost in the mist of antiquity, and, when such doctrines finally see the light of day, they have, as a rule, a long history behind them. It is, therefore, a fallacy to date the origin of metempsychosis among the Jews from the time when it becomes known publicly in the 9th or 10th century. The [Hebrew] masters of the occult science never doubted its Jewish character or its old origin. [They asked:] Was it not part of that heavenly mystery handed down from Adam on through all the great men of the past?[28]

The Old Testament

[After retiring as director of the Harvard College Observatory, the astronomer Harlow Shapley wrote *Beyond the Observatory*. In the chapter "Out of the Whirlwind," he suggests that "those who are thoughtful about the history of science should read Job. . . . They would learn thereby how poetic the sciences can be, and how science-touched is some poetry. . . . My favorite chapter is number 38. It contains, in the midst of fine imagery, a revealing survey of the knowledge and manners of Job by no less a surveyor than the Lord himself. This is no elementary quiz. I would call it a swift-moving doctoral oral. Witness the grand opening of the examination: '*Then the Lord answered Job out of the whirlwind, and said, Who is this that darkeneth counsel by words without knowledge?*' No answer."

Dr. Shapley warns us to prepare ourselves "for here comes the most profound question known to doctoral examination committees. . . . '*Where wast thou when I laid the foundations of the earth? declare, if thou hast understanding.*' Again no answer. When that question is put to our current graduate students, they, too, are silent. Silent at best; and on the average, dazed, for they cannot successfully reply, with or without a whirlwind. Some might venture: 'I was not anywhere.' But that is clearly wrong, for practically every atom of Job's body . . . was in or on the surface of the earth when the foundations were laid . . . some five or six billion years ago."[9]

In the Book of Proverbs, King Solomon appears to make quite a different reply:

> The Lord possessed me in the beginning of his way, before his works of old. I was set up from everlasting, from the beginning, or ever the earth was. When there were no depths, I was brought forth; when there were no fountains abounding with water. Before the mountains were settled, before the hills was I brought forth: While as yet he had not made the earth, nor the fields, nor the highest part of the dust of the world. When he prepared the heavens, I was there. . . . When he established the clouds above . . . when he appointed the foundations of the earth: Then I was by him as one brought up with him: and I was daily his delight, rejoicing always before him; Rejoicing in the habitable part of his earth; and my delights were with the sons of men. (Proverbs 8:22–31)

Incidentally, *The Scofield Reference Bible,* which is authoritative in many Christian circles, links the entire passage from Proverbs to the preexistence of Christ, and concludes: "Prov. 8.22–36, with John 1.1–3; Col. 1.17, can refer to nothing less than the Eternal Son of God."[10]

Another biblical reference possibly suggesting reincarnation may be found in Psalms 90:3–6 at the beginning of a prayer of Moses. Plato, and Vergil, we shall see later, spoke of a thousand-year cycle between incarnations. Could Moses have had something like this in mind when he uses the words quoted below? If he did, the analogies used seem particularly appropriate.

> Thou turnest man to destruction (dust[11]); and sayest, Return, ye children of men. For a thousand years in thy sight are but as yesterday when it is past, and as a watch in the night. Thou carriest them away as with a flood, they are as

asleep; in the morning they are like grass which groweth up. In the morning it flourisheth, and groweth up, in the evening it is cut down, and withereth.

It has already been mentioned that the Jews expected the return of their great prophets. And in the extract from Rabbi Gaster's article, it was stated that the Samaritans believed Adam returned as Seth, then as Noah, Abraham, and Moses. The Kabalists affirm that Adam was reincarnated as David and is still to return as the Messiah. (See next section.) These traditions may have a bearing on interpreting the following verse from Jeremiah 1:4–5, in which it is said that this prophet existed before his birth: "Then the word of the Lord came unto me [Jeremiah] saying, Before I formed thee in the belly I knew thee; and before thou camest forth out of the womb I sanctified thee, and I ordained thee a prophet unto the nations."

When we come to selections from the New Testament, strong additional evidence is furnished as to how general was the expectation among the Jews that the prophets would return. In Matthew 16:13–14, for example, Jesus asks his disciples: "Who do men say that I the Son of man am? And they said, Some say that thou art John the Baptist [who had already been beheaded]; some, Elijah; and others, Jeremiah, or one of the prophets." In Chapter 17:9–13, the disciples remind Jesus that the scribes have prophesied that before the Messiah appears, Elijah, who lived centuries before, would come again and restore all things. Jesus replies that Elijah has already come. The disciples understood that he spoke of John the Baptist.

It is of some importance to note that this prophecy by the scribes is based on the last verses of the Old Testament: "Saith the Lord of hosts: . . . the Son of righteousness [shall] arise with healing in his wings. . . . Behold, I will [first] send you Elijah the prophet before the coming of the great and dreadful day of the Lord" (Malachi 4:2–6). According to Jewish belief, this prophecy remains unfulfilled—Elijah and the Messiah have yet to reappear.

✺ ✺ ✺
The Kabala and the Kabalists

["In the Jewish Kabala . . . metempsychosis is an essential part of the system," states G. F. Moore in his Harvard Ingersoll Lecture on reincarnation.[12] The Kabala is said to represent the hidden wisdom behind the Old Testament, derived by the rabbis of the Middle Ages from still older secret doctrines. The first Jews to call themselves Kabalists were the Tanaiim who lived in Jerusalem about the beginning of the third century B.C. Two centuries later three important Kabalists appeared: Jehoshuah ben Pandira; Hillel, the great Chaldean teacher; and Philo Judaeus, the Alexandrian Platonist.

In *A Talmudic Miscellany,* Paul Isaac Hershon explains that the word Kabala means "a thing received," or traditional law. This, he says, together with the written law, was received by Moses on Mount Sinai, "and we are distinctly told in The Talmud *(Rosh Hashanah* fol. 19, col. I) 'the words of the Kabbalah are just *the same* as the words of the law.'" Hershon states that in another part of The Talmud "we find the Rabbis declare the Kabbalah to be *above* the law."[13]

The renowned Italian Renaissance Humanist, Kabalist, and Neoplatonist Pico della Mirandola explained in his *Conclusiones and Apologia* that the great teachers such as Moses transmitted many of their ideas orally through the seventy wise men in unbroken tradition until they had been embodied in the written Kabala.[14]

During medieval times there were many celebrated Kabalists. Rabbi Isaac Luria—who will be considered separately—founded a Kabalistic school in Galilee, and Rabbi Chaim Vital, the great exponent of Luria's teachings, wrote a widely circulated work, *The Tree of Life,* which the Christian Kabalist Baron von Rosenroth (1636–1679) used as the basis of his *Book on the Rashith ha Gilgalim,* revolutions of souls or scheme of reincarnations. The literature on "this subject of transmigration is an exceedingly rich one," says J. Abelson in *Jewish Mysticism.*[15]

As shall be illustrated later, Kabalists played a part in bringing to birth the Italian Renaissance and the German Reformation. Among Western authors who made abundant use of the Kabala were Milton and Blake.[16] Isaac Myer's noted work on the Kabala provides a long list of other Europeans who came under the same influence. They included Paracelsus, Jacob Boehme, Ficino, Pico, Pope Sixtus IV, Raymond Lully, Cornelius Agrippa, John Reuchlin, Spinoza, Leibniz, Ralph Cudworth, Henry More, Francis Bacon, Isaac Newton, and the later German philosophers Schopenhauer, Hegel, and Schelling.[17]

In attempting to answer the intriguing question as to where the ancient Jews originally obtained these teachings, Myer writes:

> The Qabbalah most likely, originally came from Aryan sources, through Central Asia, Persia, India and Mesopotamia, for from Ur and Haran came Abraham and many others, into Palestine. We know that the Hebrew Genesis and many parts of the Old Testament, are tinctured with Aryan, Akkadian, Chaldean and Babylonian thought, and that Isaiah, Daniel, Ezra, Jeremiah, Ezekiel and other learned Israelites were under the influence of Persian and Chaldean learning. We find several references to the wisdom of "the Sons of the East," in the Hebrew Sacred Writings. (Comp. Kitto's Bib. Cyclop., Ed. 1876, Vol. i, p. 336 *sq.*) Communication between the ancient nations of Asia, was much more general than has been usually thought by the learned of our day.[18]

But there was another strong influence exercised on Judaism. Moses was educated in Egypt and Midian, and it is believed received much occult knowledge there.

The following selections from the Kabala are from Hershon's *Talmudic Miscellany*[19]:]

Most souls being at present in a state of transmigrations, God requites a man now for what his soul merited in a bypast time in another body, by having broken some of the 613 precepts. . . . Thus we have the rule:—No one is perfect unless he has thoroughy observed all the 613 precepts. If this be so, who is he and where is he that has observed all the 613 precepts? For even the lord of the prophets, Moses our Rabbi—peace be on him!—had not observed them all. . . . He who neglects to observe any of the 613 precepts, such as were possible for him to observe, is doomed to undergo transmigration (once or more than once) till he has actually observed all he had neglected to do in a former state of being.

Kitzur Sh'lu, p. 6, col. I and II

The sages of truth (the Kabbalists) remark that Adam, contains the initial letters of Adam, David, and Messiah; for after Adam sinned his soul passed into David, and the latter having also sinned, it passed into the Messiah.

Nishmath Chaim, fol. 152, col. 2

Know thou that Cain's essential soul passed into Jethro, but his spirit into Korah, and his animal soul into the Egyptian. This is what Scripture saith. "Cain . . . shall be avenged sevenfold" (Gen. iv. 24) . . . i.e. the initial letters of the Hebrew word rendered "shall be avenged," form the initials of Jethro, Korah, and Egyptian. . . . Samson the hero was possessed by the soul of Japhet, and Job by that of Terah.

Yalkut Reubeni, Nos. 9, 18, 24

Cain had robbed the twin sister of Abel, and therefore his soul passed into Jethro. Moses was possessed by the soul of Abel, and therefore Jethro gave his daughter to Moses.

Yalkut Chadash, fol. 127, col. 3

If a man be niggardly either in a financial or a spiritual regard, giving nothing of his money to the poor or not imparting of his knowledge to the ignorant, he shall be punished by transmigration into a woman.[20] . . . Know thou that Sarah, Hannah, the Shunammite (2 Kings iv. 8), and the widow of Zarepta were each in turn possessed by the soul of Eve. . . . The soul of Rahab transmigrated into Heber the Kenite, and afterwards into Hannah; and this is the mystery of her words, "I am a woman of a sorrowful spirit" (I Sam. i. 15), for there still lingered in her soul a sorrowful sense of inherited

defilement. . . . Eli possessed the soul of Jael, the wife of Heber the Kenite.
. . . Sometimes the souls of pious Jews pass by metempsychosis into Gentiles, in order that they may plead on behalf of Israel and treat them kindly.

Yalkut Reubeni, Nos. 1, 8, 61, 63

The Zohar

[Tradition assigns the authorship of this Kabalistic classic to Rabbi Simeon
ben Jochai. During the siege of Jerusalem in A.D. 80 he escaped from the city
and hid in a cave for twelve years. After his death two disciples, Rabbi
Eliezar and Rabbi Abba, collected some of the manuscripts he left, compil-
ing them into a book. This was the original *Zohar*—The Book of Splendor.
For the next thousand years the Kabala in its various forms was studied in
secrecy and silence. But in the eleventh century the renowned Rabbi Ibn
Gebirol, also known as Avicebron, produced two important Kabalistic
works, the *Fons Vitae* and the *Kether Malchuth*. In 1280 the *Zohar* reappeared, this time compiled and edited in Spain by Rabbi Moses de Leon. It
was after the appearance of this work that the Kabalistic teachings were
taken up by the Christians; the first to call himself a Kabalist was the Spanish
mystic Raymond Lully. The *Zohar* is in five sections, the last being "the
Book of the Revolutions of Souls." Quoting from the work:]

All souls are subject to the trials of transmigration; and men do not know
the designs of the Most High with regard to them; they know not how they
are being at all times judged, both before coming into this world and when
they leave it. They do not know how many transformations and mysterious
trials they must undergo; how many souls and spirits come to this world
without returning to the palace of the divine king.

The souls must re-enter the absolute substance whence they have
emerged. But to accomplish this end they must develop all the perfections,
the germ of which is planted in them; and if they have not fulfilled this
condition during one life, they must commence another, a third, and so forth,
until they have acquired the condition which fits them for reunion with God.[21]

Rabbi Isaac Luria (1534–1572)

[In an article "The Lion of the Cabbalah,"[22] Cecil Roth gives a vivid picture
of Rabbi Isaac Luria and his times. The author, a distinguished historian, was
former president of the Jewish Historical Society of England. He writes:]

It was the darkest hour in Jewish history. The crowning tragedy of the expulsion from Spain had just taken place, in 1492, turning tens of thousands of homeless wanderers into an unfriendly world. As today, many of the exiles directed their footsteps towards Palestine, the Holy Land, there reëstablishing the settlement which had been all but extinct since the period of the Crusades. From the crushing vicissitudes of this world, they sought refuge in the contemplation of the mysteries of the next.

With greater singleness of purpose than ever before, they turned their attention to the study of the Zohar and the kindred esoteric literature. Gradually, the choicer spirits became concentrated in the "Holy City" of Safed in Upper Galilee—the scene of the terrestrial activity, fourteen centuries before, of Rabbi Simeon ben Jochai, reputed author of the Zohar, "The Book of Splendour." Here there grew up the strangest, strictest, maddest, most amazing community in Jewish history: a veritable Congregation of the Saints, recruited by eager mystics from every corner of Asia and Europe, passing twenty-four hours of every day in the study of the Holy Cabbalah, and maintaining in perpetuity the spirit of a revivalist camp. This was the scene of the activity of the Lion of the Cabbalah . . . Rabbi Isaac Luria. . . .

The new teacher's fame rapidly spread. Pupils came from as far afield as Italy or Bohemia, and filled the courts of Safed with their mystical chants. . . . The Master [Luria] differentiated between the five different aspects of the human soul, and taught not only metempsychosis, or the migration of souls, but also the "impregnation" of two souls, under certain circumstances, in one body. . . .

[His teaching] speedily permeated the Jewish world through and through, giving fresh life to old observances. . . . It was the most vital movement that had come from Palestine since the days of the Second Temple. The modern rationalists who sneer at the tendency do not realize what comfort it brought to their fathers in the long nightmare of the Ghetto, how it consoled them for the vicissitudes of daily life, how it made mechanical observances instinct with beauty, with hope, even with divinity.

Rabbi Manasseh Ben Israel (1604–1657)

THEOLOGIAN AND STATESMAN

[Owing to the efforts of Rabbi Manasseh Ben Israel, Oliver Cromwell removed the legal prohibition of Jews from England that had existed for three hundred and fifty years since the reign of Edward I. In his book *Nishmath Hayem,* this revered son of Israel writes:]

The belief or the doctrine of the transmigration of souls is a firm and infallible dogma accepted by the whole assemblage of our church with one accord, so that there is none to be found who would dare to deny it. . . . Indeed, there are a great number of sages in Israel who hold firm to this doctrine so that they made it a dogma, a fundamental point of our religion. We are therefore in duty bound to obey and to accept this dogma with acclamation . . . as the truth of it has been incontestably demonstrated by the Zohar, and all books of the Kabalists.[23]

Hasidism

[According to the *Universal Jewish Encyclopedia,*[24] reincarnation is a universal belief in Hasidism (or Chassidism). This influential movement began in the eighteenth century among Polish Jews. Martin Buber devoted much of his life to spreading its teachings and way of life. Irving Spiegel reports in the *New York Times* (October 16, 1966):

> A group of Jewish scholars, working in cooperation with the Harvard University Press, will undertake the publication of a comprehensive 10-volume work embracing 37 Hasidic texts that reflect the thinking, sermons, commentaries and exegesis of Hasidism—the colorful Jewish religious movement. It will be the first English translation of this rich literature of Hasidism. . . .
>
> Hasidism exerted marked influence for roughly two centuries as a major force in Judaism. The Nazis destroyed its great centers of learning during World War II. But there still exist Hasidic sects in this country, particularly in Brooklyn [New York], and throughout the free world.

The selections that follow are from the Hasidic play *The Dybbuk.* The author, Solomon Judah Rapoport, who wrote under the name S. Ansky, is identified in the *Univeral Jewish Encyclopedia* as a "unique figure in Yiddish literature . . . his masterpiece . . . known as *The Dybbuk* . . . is mystical and symbolical, yet taken from actual Hasidic life."]

[If a man dies prematurely] what becomes of the life he has not lived . . .? What becomes of his joys and sorrows, and all the thoughts he had no time to think, and all the things he hadn't time to do . . .? No human life goes to waste. If one of us dies before his time, his soul returns to earth to complete its span, to do the things left undone and experience the happiness and griefs he would have known. . . .

It's not only the poor it pays to be careful with. You can't say for a certainty, who any man might have been in his last existence, nor what he is doing on earth. . . . Through many transmigrations, the human soul is drawn by pain and grief, as the child to its mother's breast, to the source of its being, the Exalted Throne above. But it sometimes happens that a soul which has attained to the final state of purification suddenly [through pride?] becomes the prey of evil forces which cause it to slip and fall. And the higher it has soared, the deeper it falls. . . . [Such] vagrant souls which, finding neither rest nor harbor, pass into the bodies of the living, in the form of a Dybbuk, until they have attained purity. . . .

The souls of the dead *do* return to earth, but not as disembodied spirits. Some must pass through many forms before they achieve purification.[25]

EARLY CHRISTIAN

That which is called the Christian religion existed among the ancients, and never did not exist, from the beginning of the human race until Christ came in the flesh, at which time the true religion which already existed began to be called Christianity.

Saint Augustine[1]

[The mission of Jesus was apparently a very important one for the West, for the ethics and path to liberation he taught have remained as a beacon of light throughout the intervening centuries. It has been said that Jesus came as "a witness on the scene" to the reality of spiritual knowledge, power, and compassion during the periods of ignorance and superstition, of material advancement and spiritual darkness, which were to come. The question before us is whether reincarnation was part of his message.

Two main sources of information are available: the New Testament together with the writings of the Church Fathers; and the teachings of the Christian Gnostics. The New Testament was not recorded until long after Jesus died, and its books subsequently passed through the censoring hands of church councils. At the Council of Nicea in A.D. 325, when the present bible was decided on, a number of differing gospels existed. Those deemed unacceptable were destroyed. By this time there was a strong antireincarnationist sentiment in the Church and it would be surprising if anything on reincarnation managed to survive. Nevertheless, let us see what the record reveals and whether the reincarnationist is justified in claiming that the New Testament teaches a plurality of lives.

But first a preview is offered as to what this "Early Christian" chapter contains. After a consideration of the New Testament and some of the so-called apocryphal texts, there will be a section on the Church Fathers and their views on rebirth. Thus far, we will have considered the path taken by Christian orthodoxy and will then take up a parallel Christian movement that also claimed a close connection with primitive Christianity. We refer to what is known in history as the widespread Gnostic movement, which among modern scholars today is receiving some extra attention as a result of new archaeological discoveries and the unearthing of lost Gnostic texts. It may be that in the light of these findings the story of the early beginnings of Christianity may have to be substantially rewritten. Reincarnation was a universal teaching among the Gnostics, as we shall learn.

Following the Gnostics, the line of orthodoxy will be resumed, and consideration will be given to "The Anathemas against Preexistence." Here will be told what occurred at the important church council of A.D. 553. The chapter will conclude with "Reincarnation in the Dark Ages," which deals with the widescale rebirth in western Europe and Asia Minor of numerous Gnostic sects, generally known as the Cathari. By the thirteenth century they had grown to such proportions that ecclesiastical Christianity was in danger of becoming permanently eclipsed. Few today are aware that it was to stamp out the Gnostic Cathari that the first of the Holy Inquisitions was set up by the Church.

We will start by focusing on the great source book of Christianity, and see what clues it may offer on the subject of rebirth.]

The New Testament

[In the ninth century B.C. the Hebrew prophet Elijah is supposed to have lived. Four centuries later, Malachi recorded this prophecy in the closing lines of the Old Testament: "Behold, I will send you Elijah the prophet before the coming of the great and dreadful day of the Lord." The first book of the New Testament, Matthew, refers to this prophecy on three occasions, and the remaining gospels speak of it seven times. In the verses that follow from the King James Bible, the Greek form of the prophet's name is used. It will be noted from the remarks of the disciples of Jesus that there was much speculation among the Jews concerning not only the return of Elijah, but of other ancient Hebrew prophets.

> When Jesus came into the coasts of Caesarea Philippi, he asked his disciples, saying, Who do men say that I the Son of man am? And they said, Some say that thou art John the Baptist; some, Elias; and others, Jeremias, or one of the prophets.
>
> *Matthew 16:13–14*
>
> And as they came down from the mountain, Jesus charged them saying, Tell the vision to no man, until the Son of man be risen again[2] from the dead. And his

disciples asked him, saying, Why then say the scribes that Elias must first come? And Jesus answered them, Elias truly shall first come, and restore all things. But I say unto you, That Elias is come already, and they knew him not, but have done unto him whatsoever they listed. Likewise shall also the Son of man suffer of them. Then the disciples understood that he spake unto them of John the Baptist [who had already been beheaded by Herod].

Matthew 17:9–13

Jesus began to say unto the multitudes concerning John . . . this is he, of whom it is written, Behold, I send my messenger before thy face, which shall prepare thy way before thee. Verily I say unto you, Among them that are born of women there hath not risen a greater than John the Baptist. . . . And if ye will receive it, this is Elias, which was for to come.[3] He that hath ears to hear, let him hear.

Matthew 11:7, 10–11, 14–15

The foregoing statement from Matthew 16 is repeated almost verbatim in Mark 8:27–28 and Luke 9:18–19. The statement from Matthew 17 is also made in Mark 9:9–13, but the name of John is omitted.

In John 1:19–23, John the Baptist is approached by priests and others from Jerusalem. "And they asked him . . . Art thou Elias? And he saith, I am not. Art thou that Prophet? and he answered, No. Then said they unto him, Who art thou? that we may give an answer to them that sent us." John replied in the words of Isaiah (Isaiah 40:3): "I am the voice of one crying in the wilderness, Make straight the way of the Lord." Does this imply that John did not know (as Jesus supposedly did) that he was a reappearance of Elias? That John had limitations seems evident from Jesus's remark: "He that is the least in the kingdom of heaven is greater than he" (Matthew 11:11). Whatever the truth of all this, it is obvious from the questions asked of John and later of Jesus that the Jews of this period were expecting the rebirth not only of Elias but of other of their prophets.

Another reference is to be found in Luke 9:7–9: "Now Herod the tetrarch heard of all that was done by [Jesus], and he was perplexed, because that it was said of some, that John was risen from the dead; and of some, that Elias had appeared; and of others, that one of the old prophets was risen again. And Herod said, John have I beheaded; but who is this of whom I hear such things?" The same incident is related in Mark 6:14–16.

Tertullian (see the section on "Church Fathers") gives the view that some orthodox people take concerning all these verses from the New Testament. In brief, Tertullian's reasoning is that Elias never died in the first place. God translated him directly to heaven. Thus, his subsequent re-descent was not a rebirth, but merely a return visit. Tertullian probably bases this on the statement in II Kings 2:11: "Behold there appeared a chariot of fire, and horses of fire . . . and Elijah went up by a whirlwind into heaven" and was seen no more. However, if this church father's reasoning is to be logically sustained, Elijah's return to earth as John the Baptist should have been in the same miraculous way he left: He should have been precipitated on earth as a mature man. Yet, the Scriptures indicate that John was born in the ordinary way. In Luke 1:13–17 an angel makes this prophecy to Zacharias: "And thy wife Elizabeth shall bear thee a son, and thou shalt call his name John . . . and he shall go before him in the spirit and power of Elias."

Incidentally, this last clause is made much of to show that John was merely overshadowed by Elias. Yet, as translated in the New English Bible, published jointly in 1961 by Oxford and Cambridge universities, this part now reads: "*possessed* by the spirit and power of Elijah." At any rate, Christ, as just quoted, states without qualification: "THIS IS ELIAS, which was for to come. *He that hath ears to hear, let him hear.*"

Scholar and poet Robert Graves in an article, "Reincarnation," in *Playboy* (December 1967), makes some comments on why Jesus repeats the Malachi prophecy in Matthew 11:10 and there identifies Elijah with John the Baptist:

> The crucial importance of this point has seldom been stressed. When Jesus was asked by the captain of the temple guard, shortly before the crucifixion (Mark 11:28), "By what authority doest thou these things?" he replied with a counter question: "The baptism of John, was it from heaven or of men?" He meant: "Was my installation by John as the Messiah, in a lustral ceremony at which the traditional coronation psalm was recited, divinely inspired or not?"
>
> Had the captain denied John's inspiration, he would have infuriated the pilgrim crowds who identified this martyred hero with Elijah. They knew that none but a prophet was entitled to perform the coronation ceremony; they also knew that the acceptance of any new prophet, apart from Elijah's reappearance in the last days, had been banned by an edict of the Sanhedrin some 200 years previously. Jesus was now claiming a right to purge the temple courts in accordance with Zechariah's Messianic prophecy; but the genuineness of his Messiahship depended on Elijah's reincarnation as John the Baptist—another lonely and persecuted prophet. No honest theologian can therefore deny that his acceptance of Jesus as Christ logically binds every Christian to a belief in reincarnation—in Elijah's case, at least.

The nineteenth-century American philosopher Francis Bowen of Harvard, after citing a number of the Gospel passages already quoted, remarks in his article, "Christian Metempsychosis":[4] "That the commentators have not been willing to receive, in their obvious and literal meaning, assertions so direct and so frequently repeated as these, but have attempted to explain them away in a non-natural and metaphorical sense, is a fact that proves nothing but the existence of an invincible prejudice against the doctrine of the transmigration of souls."

Christ, himself, often spoke of his own previous eternal existence. "Ye shall see the Son of man ascend up where he was before" (John 6:62). "I am the living bread which came down from Heaven'' (John 6:51). But did he ever exist previously on earth, not only in heaven? Consider the implications of these passages in which Jesus is taunted by the Israelites for setting himself up as greater than Abraham. He replied: ''Your father Abraham rejoiced to see my day; and he saw it, and was glad.'' ''Then said the Jews unto him: Thou art not yet fifty years old, and hast thou seen Abraham? Jesus said unto them, Verily, verily, I say unto you, Before Abraham was, I am'' (John 8:56–59). John the Baptist said of Jesus: ''This was he of whom I spake, He that cometh after me is preferred before me: for he was before me'' (John 1:14–15). The Church Father Origen put it this way: ''When God sent Jesus to the human race, it was not as though He had just awakened from a long sleep. Jesus has at all times been doing good to the human race.''[5]

Saint Paul in Ephesians 1:4 appears to include mankind (or at least Christians) as having preexisted with Christ. God ''hath chosen us in him [Christ] before the foundation of the world, that we should be holy and without blame before him in love.'' If this seems like a very strange statement to those who have imagined that at the birth of every child, a new soul, fresh from the hands of God, has been created, then listen to these words of Jesus: ''Glorify thou me with thine own self with the glory which I had with thee before the world was'' (John 17:5). (The subject of preexistence will receive special attention later.[6])

We have talked about the eternal past of Christ, what about the eternal future? In John 14:3 he tells of his coming reappearance on earth: ''I will come again, and receive you unto myself; that where I am, there ye may be also.'' In Revelation 22:12 he predicts: ''Very soon now, I shall be with you again, bringing the reward to be given to every man according to what he deserves.'' For almost two millennia this so-called second coming was imminently expected and associated with the end of the world, but since the revised translation of the New Testament in 1881, scholars became aware that Jesus was referring only to the consummation of an age and the beginning of a new one. We quote from Matthew 24:1–8, using the New English Bible:

> Jesus was leaving the temple when his disciples came and pointed to the temple buildings. He answered, ''Yes, look at it all. I tell you this: not one stone will be left upon another; all will be thrown down.''
>
> When the disciples were sitting on the Mount of Olives the disciples came to speak to him privately. ''Tell us,'' they said, ''when will this happen? And what will be the signal for your coming AND THE END OF THE AGE?'' Jesus replied: ''Take care that no one mislead you. For many will come claiming my name and saying, 'I am the Messiah'; and many will be misled by them. The time is coming when . . . nation will make war upon nation, kingdom upon kingdom; there will be famines and earthquakes in many places. With all these things THE BIRTH-PANGS OF THE NEW AGE BEGIN.''

Saint Paul in Galatians 4:19 likewise seems to speak of his own return to earth life until mankind is redeemed: "My little children, of whom I travail in birth again until Christ be formed in you, I desire to be present with you now, and to change my voice; for I stand in doubt of you."

The rebirth of saviors and prophets is clear enough in Christian teaching, but what about ordinary men? Do they return? That the disciples of Jesus thought of this possibility is evident from their question concerning the man who had been born blind. They asked: "Who did sin, this man, or his parents?" (John 9:1–3). The apostles must have had the idea of reincarnation in mind for obviously if the man had been born blind his sin could not have been committed in this life. Jesus had a good opportunity to crush the whole idea but he did not. He merely replied that the man was afflicted because he was destined through Christ to have his sight restored so that "the works of God should be made manifest in him." It is not known how he would explain the cause of blindness in other cases where no healing is involved.

That it may be legitimate to look to a previous life for the source of individual goodness or badness seems plain from Saint Paul's comments on Jacob and Esau. He says that the Lord loved the one and hated the other before they were born (Romans 9:10–13; Malachi 1:2–3). How could a nonexistent being be loved or hated?

Another illustration of what the East calls karmic law is the one in which Christ warns that those who live by the sword shall die by the sword (Matthew 26:52). This could only be universally true if there is more than one life in which to experience the reaction, for many professional combat soldiers die quietly in their own beds.

A similar reference is found in Mark 10:28–31, where rewards are listed that could hardly be fulfilled in one life. Peter said unto Jesus: "Lo, we have left all, and have followed thee." And Jesus answered and said: "Verily I say unto you, There is no man that hath left house, or brethren, or sisters, or father, or mother, or wife, or children, or lands, for my sake, and the gospel's, But he shall receivė an hundredfold now in this time [in this age[7]] houses, and brethren, and sisters, and mothers, and children, and lands, with persecutions; and in the world to come eternal life. But many that are first shall be last; and the last first." Certainly the enumerated rewards could not possibly be fulfilled in one incarnation. The age mentioned could be a long cycle of time. History speaks of the Bronze Age, the Iron Age, the Age of Dinosaurs, and so forth—periods that last hundreds of thousands of years.

Reincarnationists translate the last quoted verse this way: "But many that are first in this incarnation, shall be last or in lowly positions in the next rebirth; while the last or least esteemed may be first in their future life." "Who toiled a slave," said Buddha, "may come anew a prince, for gentle worthiness and merit won. Who ruled a king may wander earth in rags, for things done, and undone."[8]

Saint John states in Revelation 3:12: "Him that overcometh will I make a pillar in the temple of my God, *and he shall go no more out.*" Possibly he had gone out into incarnation before, otherwise the words "no more" could have no place or meaning. It may have been the old idea of the exile of the soul and the need for it to be purified by long wandering before it could be admitted as a "pillar in the temple of my God." In Luke 20:35–36, a similar idea occurs. Jesus says: "They who are accounted worthy to obtain that world . . . neither marry . . . *neither can they die any more.*"

It could be assumed from both these verses that the goal to be achieved is of such a transcendent nature, one short life would be insufficient to reach it. Thus in Professor Bowen's essay, "Christian Metempsychosis," previously cited, he wonders whether in addition to the obvious spiritual meaning, there may be "a literal meaning in the solemn words of the Saviour 'Except a man be born again, he cannot see the kingdom of God.' " "An eternity either of reward or punishment," says Bowen, "would seem to be inadequately earned by one brief period of probation" on earth.]

The Apocrypha

[Seven of the fourteen books of the Apocrypha are considered canonical by the Roman Catholics and form part of their Old Testament. The extracts below are from two of these canonical books. While no apocryphal books are regarded as canonical by most Protestants, they were considered of sufficient importance to be put into English during the reign of King James. The brief verses here given are from the King James translation:]

[King Solomon speaks:] Now I was a child good by nature, and a good soul fell to my lot. Nay, rather, being good, I came into a body undefiled.
The Wisdom of Solomon 8:19–20

Woe be unto you, ungodly men, which have forsaken the law of the most high God! for if ye increase, it shall be to your destruction; *and if ye be born, ye shall be born to a curse;* and if ye die, a curse shall be your portion.
Ecclesiasticus 41:11–12

The Church Fathers

[The Church Fathers were not of one mind concerning the soul's origin and destiny. Jerome (A.D. 304–420) here summarizes what various Fathers and "heretical" groups taught. It will be observed that all the theories save the one that became orthodox involve some form of the soul's preexistence.

"As to the origin of the soul, I remember the question of the whole church: whether it be fallen from heaven, as Pythagoras and the Platonists and Origen believe; or be of the proper substance of God, as the Stoics, Manicheans and Priscillian heretics of Spain believe; or whether they are kept in a repository formerly built by God, as some ecclesiastics foolishly believe; or whether they are daily made by God and sent into bodies according to that which is written in the Gospel: 'My Father worketh hitherto and I work'; or whether by traduction, as Tertullian, Apollinarius, and the greater part of the Westerns believe, i.e., that as body from body so the soul is derived from the soul."[9]

Our task is to evaluate what the fathers specifically say for or against reincarnation. Regarding those who speak up for the idea, Beausobré comments in his famous history of the Manicheans: "Thus, it was not only the . . . Gnostics who accepted the error of Metempsychosis; it was the Christian Philosophers of high merit, or great virtue—the error being very attractive because of its antiquity, its universality, and its Principles, of which they believed it was a consequence."[10]]

JUSTIN MARTYR (A.D. 100?–C.165)

[Justin Martyr, a Church Father, was a student of philosophy and a teacher of Platonic doctrines. He founded the first Christian School in Rome, and was supposedly scourged and martyred there. Under "Pre-Existence" in the *Britannica,* it is stated that in the Christian era supporters of this doctrine, who called themselves "the Pre-existants or Pre-existiani," "are found as early as the 2nd century, among them being Justin Martyr and Origen."[11] In his "Dialogue with Trypho," Justin speaks of the soul's inhabiting more than once a human body, but that it cannot remember previous experiences. Souls who have become unworthy to see God, he says, are joined to the bodies of wild beasts. Thus, he defends the grosser conception of transmigration. Trypho a Hebrew whom he meets in his travels, opposes Justin's views. At this point the translation into English seems quite obscure, and Justin's reactions to Trypho's arguments are not clear.[12]]

CLEMENT OF ALEXANDRIA (A.D. 150?–220?)

Greek Theologian

[In his "Exhortation to the Heathen," Saint Clement of Alexandria wrote: "Before the foundation of the world were we, who, because destined to be in Him, pre-existed in the eye of God before—we the rational creatures of the Word of God, on whose account we date from the beginning; for 'in the beginning was the Word.' . . . The Saviour, who existed before, has in recent days appeared. . . . He did not now for the first time pity us for our error; but He pitied us from the first, from the beginning."[13]

In the foregoing, Clement appears to posit the preexistence of both Christ and man, but in his *Eclogae ex Scripturis Propheticis* he states: "God created us when we did not exist before. For if we had existed before, we would know where we had been, and we would know in what way and for what reason we had come into this world."[14] In *Stromata* (IV, p. 12), Clement postpones discussion as to whether "the soul is changed to another body." A contemporary says that this Church Father wrote "wonderful stories about metempsychosis and many worlds before Adam."[15] These stories have not survived.

Clement was a Platonist and headed the famous catechetical school in Alexandria (A.D. 190–203). W. R. Inge says that Clement "admits frankly that he does not write down all that he thinks; there is an esoteric Christianity which is not for everybody. But it is plain that he leans towards the doctrines which [his pupil] Origen develops more boldly."[16] Origen's views on preexistence and reincarnation will shortly be considered. Clement was deposed as head of the catechetical school because of his eclecticism, and Origen, although only eighteen, took his place.]

TERTULLIAN (A.D. 160?–230)

[Tertullian, a Latin Father of the early church, was converted to Christianity about 190, and wrote many works in its defense. Around the year 207 he became a "heretic" and headed a small Montanist group in Carthage. In *De Anima,* Chapters 28 through 35, he devotes a number of pages to refuting reincarnation. The familiar objections raised today were current then: If previous lives are not remembered, they might as well not have been lived; human transmigration into animal forms is a ridiculous notion. Tertullian regarded Pythagoras as a deceitful fabricator of stories when he claimed to remember former lives. As to the Elias-John the Baptist "reincarnation," Tertullian wrote in *De Anima:*]

I apprehend that heretics . . . seize with especial avidity the example of Elias, whom they assume to have been so reproduced in John [the Baptist] as to make our Lord's statement sponsor for their theory of transmigration, when He said, "Elias is come already, and they knew him not;" and again, in another passage, "And if ye will receive it, this is Elias, which was for to come." Well, then, was it really in a Pythagorean sense that the Jews approached John with the inquiry, "Art thou Elias?" and not rather in the sense of the divine prediction, "Behold, I will send you Elijah" the Tisbite? The fact, however, is, that their metempsychosis, or transmigration theory, signifies the recall of the soul which had died long before, and its return to some other body. But Elias is to come again, not after quitting life [in the way of dying], but after his translation [or removal without dying];[17] not for the purpose of being restored to the body, from which he had not departed, but for the purpose of revisiting the world from which he was translated; not by way of resuming a life which he had laid aside, but of fulfilling prophecy,— really and truly the same man, both in respect of his name and designation, as well as of his unchanged humanity.[18]

[Tertullian objected to reincarnation also because he said it was inconsistent with the increase in the world's population. (The Romans had population worries too!)

The reincarnationists point out that those who raise the objection usually assume that the proportion of beings out of incarnation to those in incarnation is about one to one. If this is not a fact, the picture materially changes. Plato indicates in the *Phaedo* that save for certain exceptions "many revolutions of ages" ensue between lives.[19] In *The Republic,* he mentions a thousand-year cycle of rebirth.[20] Vergil does likewise in the *Aeneid.*[21] The *Bhagavad-Gita* also speaks of an "immensity of years" between lives.[22] Such statistics are, of course, beyond our power to prove. But if the average time out of incarnation should possibly be much longer than the average life-span, then obviously the number of beings out of incarnation would be much greater than those on earth. If then for some reason the period out of incarnation should be shortened for an appreciable number of souls, or if people on earth should live longer than prior generations, as is the fact today in the West, a population boom would be inevitable. One explanation offered for the lengthy stay in the afterdeath condition is that it is an assimilative state. Using the analogy of food: A meal may be eaten quickly, but hours are required to digest and assimilate it.

One writer on reincarnation compared the total number of souls connected with our earth—whether they be in incarnation or not—to the population of a town, while those in incarnation at a particular time were likened to people attending a meeting in that town. The hall might be half empty or crowded without any change in the town's total population. So our little earth could be thinly or thickly populated, and the vast number of beings on which it can draw to replenish its stock remains practically inexhaustible.[23]

Many Christians, of course, think in terms of an everlasting stay in heaven, and if they are right, then, according to some sects, for thousands of generations souls have been pouring into paradise, with no end in sight. According to other sects, the dead sleep in their graves until judgment day, at which time the elect will rise en masse to heaven in their resurrected physical bodies. Considering that billions of souls are newly created each century, according to the orthodox scheme, is there, or will there be, an overpopulation problem in heaven?

We will later quote Bernard Bosanquet on this dilemma. But Bob Ripley in his famous "Believe-It-or-Not" column once portrayed the difficulty most

graphically. Those who believe in an objective heaven, he said, expect ultimately, of course, to be with their parents after death, and their parents will
have expected to be with their parents, and so on down the line. Now each of
us has two parents, four grandparents, eight great-grandparents, sixteen
great-great-grandparents, the number doubling each generation. In twenty
generations we have the astounding figure of 1,048,576 in the parental clan,
all presumably hoping to be together after death. However, in actual life the
figure is reduced owing to the intermarrying, at times, of various branches of
the maternal and paternal lines; and then, too, one must take into account
those who never made it to heaven. Nevertheless, when in addition to parents, we add to the heavenly conclave, husbands and wives, brothers, sisters,
and children, the most densely populated area in a large city is a paradise of
spaciousness and quiet compared to the fundamentalist's heaven!

It seems undeniable that in recent years there has been a population explosion, particularly in Eastern countries. However, we have no means of proving that this exceeds peak periods of ancient times. Vast civilizations have
disappeared from Central Asia, Egypt, Chaldea, and other Middle East
areas, to say nothing of ancient America, and possible former continents. In
its article on population, the *Britannica* states that "few reliable population
figures exist for any period before the eighteenth century."[24] This pertains to
individual countries; as to ancient world-population statistics they are
nonexistent. Population growth, like everything else in the universe, appears
subject to cyclic rises and falls. Tertullian was concerned about Rome's
mounting population, yet soon thereafter in the Middle Ages, the inhabitants
of Europe dwindled alarmingly. In the long run there appear to be some
balancing forces at work, inexplicable at present to biologists. It has been
noted, for instance, that after a destructive war, there is usually a large
inrush of new arrivals, particularly male babies!

But now let us return to early Christian times.]

ORIGEN (A.D. C. 185–C. 254)

Greek Theologian

[Origen was "the most distinguished and most influential of all the theologians of the ancient church, with the possible exception of Augustine,"
writes the noted German theologian Adolf Harnack in his article on Origen in
the *Britannica*. "He is the father of the church's science; he is the founder of a
theology which was brought to perfection in the fourth and fifth centuries,
and which still retained the stamp of his genius when in the sixth century [the
church] disowned its author."[25] At one time Saint Jerome considered Origen
"the greatest teacher of the Church after the apostles," while Saint Gregory
of Nyssa called him "the prince of Christian learning in the third century."

An illuminating summary of Origen's philosophy on preexistence and rebirth is to be found in the Gifford Lectures of the Reverend William R. Inge, dean of Saint Paul's Cathedral in London and a scholar of distinction. He states:

> Origen takes the step which to every Greek seemed the logical corollary of belief in immortality—he taught the pre-existence of Souls. The Soul is immaterial, and *therefore* has neither beginning of days nor end of life. . . . So convincing is this Platonic faith to him, that he cannot restrain his impatience at the crude beliefs of traditionalists about the last day and resurrection of the dead. The predictions in the Gospels cannot have been intended literally. How can material bodies be recompounded, every particle of which has passed into many other bodies? To which body do these molecules belong? So, he says scornfully, men fall into the lowest depths of absurdity, and take refuge in the pious assurance that "everything is possible with God." . . .
>
> As for the "conflagration" [at the end of the world], Origen, as is well known, follows the Stoics in teaching . . . that there will be a series of world-orders. But whereas Greek [Stoic] philosophy could admit no prospect except a perpetual repetition of the same alternate evolution and involution, a never-ending systole and diastole of the cosmic life, Origen holds that there is a constant upward progress. Each world-order is better than the last. . . . The conflagration is really a purifying fire. . . . All Spirits were created blameless, all must at last return to their original perfection. *The education of Souls is continued in successive worlds.*[26]

It is interesting to observe how Saint Jerome viewed these articles of Origen's creed after Pope Theophilus's crusade against Origen. In A.D. 402, Jerome wrote in his "Apology against Rufinus":

> Now I find among many bad things written by Origen the following most distinctly heretical: . . . that there are innumerable worlds, succeeding one another in eternal ages; that angels have been turned into human souls; that the soul of the Saviour existed before it was born of Mary; . . . that in the restitution . . . Archangels and Angels, the devil, the demons and the souls of men whether Christians, Jews or Heathen, will be of one condition and degree [i.e., they too will be saved]; and when they have come to their true form . . . and the new army of the whole race returning from the exile of the world presents a mass of rational creatures with all their dregs left behind, then will begin a new world from a new origin . . . so that we may have to fear that we who are now men may afterwards be born women, and one who is now a virgin may chance then to be a prostitute. These things I point out as heresies in the books of Origen.[27]

That Origen taught the preexistence of the soul in past world orders of this earth and its reincarnation in future worlds is beyond question. An occasional dispute has arisen as to whether he taught preexistence and reincarnation on this earth as presently constituted. According to *The Catholic Encyclopedia*[28] he did so teach. Beausobré writes that "it is certain that Origen believed that souls animate several bodies successively, and that these transmigrations are regulated according to the souls' merit or demerits."[29] G. F. Moore mentions that "Origen is accused by Theophilus of teaching that the soul was frequently re-embodied and repeatedly experienced death (See Jerome, Ep. 98, 10 f.)."[30] It is not strange, of course, that as a Platonist, Origen should teach reincarnation. He also had strong Gnostic tendencies. As Dr. Harnack remarks:

> The science of faith, as expounded by him bears unmistakably the stamp both of Neo-Platonism and of Gnosticism. . . . He regularly attended the lectures of [the great Neoplatonist] Ammonius Saccas, and made a thorough study of the books of Plato and Numenius, of the Stoics and the Pythagoreans. . . . As a philosophical idealist, however, he transmutes the whole contents of the faith of the church into ideas which bear the mark of Neo-Platonism, and were accordingly recognized by the later Neo-Platonists as Hellenic.[31]

Clement and Augustine were also Platonists.[32] Reverend William Fairweather states that half a century after Origen's death, Neoplatonism "became the prevailing philosophy in Christian as well as in pagan circles."[33] Neoplatonism will receive special treatment in chapter 5.

The supposed condemnation of Origen by the Fifth Ecumenical Council of A.D. 553 will be reviewed shortly under "The Anathemas against Preexistence." It will be shown why theologians today are loath to believe he was ever officially condemned. However, in the fourteen centuries following this council, churchmen were taught he had been banned, and consequently dared not raise their voice for him, although during the Renaissance for a brief time Origen "rose from the dead." After reading a great part of his extant works, Erasmus wrote to Colet: "Origen opens the fountains of theology."[34]

The scant references that follow from Origen's writings hardly do justice to his convictions. Many of his works have perished. Dr. Harnack states: "Origen was probably the most prolific author of the ancient church. 'Which of us,' asks Jerome, 'can read all that he has written.' " The number of his works was estimated at six thousand, but that is certainly an exaggeration. Owing to the increasing unpopularity of Origen in the church, a comparatively small portion of these works have come down to us in the original. We have more in the Latin translation of Rufinus; but this translation is by no means trustworthy, since Rufinus, assuming that Origen's writing had been tampered with by the heretics, considered himself at liberty to omit or amend heterodox statements.[35]

The first selection is from Origen's *Contra Celsum,* the second from his *De Principiis,* or *The First Principles,* called by Robert Payne "the most important and the most wide-reaching of Origen's works. . . . What survives is the wreck of an original text, in which we can discern the true voice of Origen at intervals, when Rufinus was either too lazy or too engrossed in the task of translation to alter Origen's theology."[36]]

Is it not more in conformity with reason, that every soul, for certain mysterious reasons (I speak now according to the opinion of Pythagoras, and Plato, and Empedocles, whom Celsus frequently names), is introduced into a body, and introduced according to its deserts and former actions? It is probable, therefore, that the soul which conferred more benefit by its [former] residence in the flesh than that of many men (to avoid prejudice, I do not say "all"), stood in need of a body not only superior to others, but invested with all excellent qualities.

Contra Celsum (Book I, Chapter 32)[37]

I am, indeed, of opinion that, as the end and consummation of the saints will be in those [ages] which are not seen, and are eternal, we must conclude . . . from a contemplation of that very end, that rational creatures had also a similar beginning. And if they had a beginning such as the end for which they hope, they existed undoubtedly from the very beginning in those [ages] which are not seen, and are eternal.

And if this is so, then there had been a descent from a higher to a lower condition, on the part not only of those souls who have deserved the change by the variety of their movements, but also on that of those who, in order to serve the whole world, were brought down from those higher and invisible spheres to these lower and visible ones . . . [As] to those souls which, on account of their excessive mental defects, stood in need of bodies of a grosser and more solid nature . . . this visible world was also called into being. . . . The hope indeed of freedom is entertained by the whole of creation—of being liberated from the corruption of slavery—when the sons of God, who either fell away or were scattered abroad, shall be gathered together into one, or when they shall have fulfilled their other duties in this world.

De Principiis[38]

[During Jerome's life the Greek *De Principiis* was still extant and we have a translation therefrom on reincarnation made by him for his friend Avitus who, appreciating that Rufinus's translation was unreliable, desired to know what Origen really taught. The extract here is from Jerome's "Epistle to Avitus" written around A.D. 410.]

The following passage is a convincing proof that [Origen] holds the transmigration of souls and annihilation of bodies. "If it can be shown that an incorporeal and reasonable being has life in itself independently of the body and that it is worse off in the body than out of it; then beyond a doubt bodies are only of secondary importance and arise from time to time to meet the varying conditions of reasonable creatures. Those who require bodies are clothed with them, and contrariwise, when fallen souls have lifted themselves up to better things, their bodies are once more annihilated. They are thus ever vanishing and ever reappearing."[39]

SAINT GREGORY OF NAZIANZUS (A.D. 329–389)
Bishop of Constantinople

[At the conclusion of this selection from "On the Soul and Resurrection," Saint Gregory of Nazianzus indicates the central issue between the orthodox and reincarnationist points of view.]

[Some hold] that the soul exchanges one man for another man, so that the life of humanity is continued always by means of the same souls. . . . As for ourselves, we take our stand upon the tenets of the Church, and assert that it will be well to accept only so much of these speculations as is sufficient to show that those who indulge in them are to a certain extent in accord with the doctrine of the Resurrection. Their statement, for instance, that the soul after its release from this body insinuates itself into certain other bodies is not absolutely out of harmony with the revival which we hope for. For our view, which maintains that the body, both now, and again in the future, is composed of the atoms of the universe, is held equally by these heathens. In fact, you cannot imagine any constitution of the body independent of a concourse of these atoms. But the divergence lies in this: we assert that the same body again as before, composed of the same atoms, is compacted around the soul; they suppose that the soul alights on other bodies.[40]

SAINT AUGUSTINE (354–430)
Bishop of Hippo

[Saint Augustine was a "strangely divided genius," remarks Dean Inge.[41] Reverend William Alva Gifford's *The Story of the Faith* supplies some interesting facts regarding his career:

> Unable to rest in Catholicism [in which he was raised] Augustine [became] a Manichaean for nine years. . . . Still restless and falling into skepticism, Augustine removed to Rome. . . . Very fortunately [he] now came upon the writings of [the Neoplatonist] Plotinus. . . . They were medicine for his skepticism. . . . Augustine never . . . ceased to be a Neoplatonist; but his early confidence in the power of reason steadily gave way to reliance on divine revelation. . . . In the authoritative Church and its authoritative Scriptures . . . he found certitude. . . .
>
> Augustine's system, in fact is a curious combination of mystical piety, Neo-

platonic philosophy, allegorical interpretation of the Scriptures, and Catholic tradition, all handled with rigorous logic, but often inconsistent with each other. . . . Augustine's logic led him [to] the doctrine of predestination [which] was as yet no part of the Catholic tradition. . . . [He] is as vivid as Tertullian when he pictures the joys of eternal life and the torments of the damned. . . . He was to become the most influential theologian of the West, and the father of much that is characteristic of both medieval Catholicism and Protestantism.[42]

J. W. Draper in his *History of the Conflict Between Religion and Science* states that "no one did more than this Father to bring science and religion into antagonism." Among Draper's examples of this is Augustine's refutation of the heretic's claim that the earth was globular and not flat.[43] In the following excerpts from Augustine's writings we find an open-minded consideration of the possibility of reincarnation gradually turn into a definite rejection of the idea.]

Say, Lord, to me . . . say, did my infancy succeed another age of mine that died before it? Was it that which I spent within my mother's womb? . . . and what before that life again, O God my joy, was I anywhere or in any body? For this I have none to tell me, neither father nor mother, nor experience of others, nor mine own memory.

The Confessions of Saint Augustine[44]

The message of Plato, the purest and most luminous in all philosophy, has at last scattered the darkness of error, and now shines forth mainly in Plotinus, a Platonist so like his master that one would think they lived together, or rather—since so long a period of time separates them—that Plato is born again in Plotinus.

Contra Academicos[45]

That noble philosopher Plato endeavored to persuade us that the souls of men lived even before they bore these bodies; and that hence those things which are learnt are rather remembered, as having been known already, than taken into knowledge as things new. . . . But we ought rather to believe, that the intellectual mind is so formed in its nature as to see those things, which by the disposition of the Creator are subjoined to things intelligible in a natural order, by a sort of incorporeal light of a unique kind; as the eye of the flesh sees things adjacent to itself.

On the Trinity[46]

[The Neoplatonist, Porphyry] was of opinion that human souls return indeed into human bodies [and not into animal bodies]. He shrank from the other opinion, lest a woman who had returned into a mule might possibly carry her own son on her back. He did not shrink, however, from a theory which admitted the possibility of a mother coming back into a girl and marry-

ing her own son.[47] How much more honorable a creed is that which was
taught by the holy and truthful angels, uttered by the prophets who were
moved by God's Spirit, preached by Him who was foretold as the coming
Saviour by His forerunning heralds, and by the apostles whom He sent forth,
and who filled the whole world with the gospel,—how much more honorable,
I say, is the belief that souls return once for all to their own bodies [at the
resurrection], than that they return again and again to divers bodies?

The City of God[48]

SYNESIUS (C. 370–430)
Bishop of Ptolemais

[The Neoplatonic Church Father Synesius was reluctant to accept from the
citizens of Ptolemais the invitation to be their bishop, because of certain
opinions he thought they might not approve, but which after mature reflection
had become deeply rooted in his mind. Foremost among these was the doctrine of preexistence.[49] Beausobré writes that "Nicephorus Gregoras was
right in attributing [metempsychosis] to Synesius. It is to be found in several
passages of the works of this Father, and especially in the following prayer
. . . 'grant that my soul, mingling in the Light, may no more be plunged in
the delusion of Earth.'"[50] His thoughts on the periodical incarnation of wise
benefactors and heroes were given earlier. Here we quote from his *Treatise
on Dreams:*]

> Philosophy speaks of souls being prepared by a course of transmigrations.
> . . . When first [the soul] comes down to earth, it embarks on this animal spirit
> as on a boat, and through it is brought into contact with matter. The soul's
> object is to take this spirit back with her; for if she were to abandon it and leave
> it behind on earth . . . the manner of her return would bring disgrace on her.
> . . . The soul which did not quickly return to the heavenly region from which it
> was sent down to earth had to go through many lives of wandering.[51]

OTHER CHURCH FATHERS

[Quoting Beausobré again: "Let us add to Synesius another Christian philosopher Chalcidius of an earlier date who gives his unqualified consent to
the same error [of rebirth], when writing: 'Souls who have failed to unite
themselves with God, are compelled by the law of destiny to begin a new
kind of life, entirely different from their former, until they repent of their
sins.'"[52]

In the *Library of Christian Classics* is included *De Natura Hominis,* a work
of the fourth-century philosopher Nemesius, Bishop of Emesa, who writes:
"Moses does not say that the soul was created at that moment at which it
was put into the body, nor would it be reasonable to suppose it. . . . That the

soul is not thus mortal and that man's destiny is not bounded by his present life is shown by the fact that the wisest of the Greeks believe in the transmigration of souls and that souls attain different grades according to the life they have lived.'' Nemesius concurs with Iamblichus who, he says,

> . . . declares that there is a form of soul appropriate to each form of living creature, and that these forms differ from one another. He accordingly wrote a monograph in which he argued that there is no transmigration of souls from men into irrational beasts, nor from beasts into men, but only from one beast into another, and from one human being into another. And it seems to me that, for this reason, Iamblichus, more than all the others, both hit upon Plato's meaning and lighted on the truth itself. This stands to be established by many and different proofs [which Nemesius then sets forth at length.][53]

Irenaeus in his *Against Heresies* discounts rebirth because the individual does not remember previous existences.[54] The question of memory also seems important to Lactantius, tutor of the son of Constantine the Great. He says in *The Divine Institutes* that ignorance has caused some to say that we are born to suffer punishment for former crimes.

> . . . but I do not see what can be more senseless than this. For where or what crimes could we have committed when we did not even exist? Unless we shall happen to believe that foolish old man [Pythagoras], who falsely said that in his former life he had been Euphorbus. He, I believe, because he was born of an ignoble race, chose for himself a family from the poems of Homer. O wonderful and remarkable memory of Pythagoras! O miserable forgetfulness on the part of us all, since we know not who we were in our former life! But perhaps it was caused by some error, or favor, that he alone did not touch the abyss of Lethe, or taste the water of oblivion; doubtless the trifling old man (as is wont to be the case with old women who are free from occupation) invented fables as it were for credulous infants.[55]

The *Octavius* by Minucius Felix is the earliest known work of Latin Christian literature and is in the form of a dialogue between a Christian and a pagan in which the Christian refutes all the charges brought by people against the new religion. He states: ''Your most famous philosophers, Pythagoras first and especially Plato, have handed down an account of the dogma of resurrection in a corrupt and mutilated form; according to them after the dissolution of the body only the soul abides forever and often passes into fresh bodies. A further distortion of the truth is that the souls of men return to the bodies of cattle, birds, and beasts: such an idea rather deserves the ridicule of a buffoon than the serious consideration of a philosopher.''[56] The last charge is repeated by several saints of the fourth century, Ambrose, Basil the Great, Gregory of Nyssa, and John Chrysostom, all of whom apparently confine their remarks on reincarnation to this one point.[57] There will be ample opportunity when we come to the Greek philosophers to see what Plato and Pythagoras really taught.

The slurs against the Greek philosophers became more and more typical of the times. The decline of the Roman Empire, the infiltration of hordes of barbarians from the north, and the escape of persecuted scholars and philosophers to the Middle East caused the love of learning to grow dim for a while, and many ignorant men flocked to the priesthood.]

The Christian Gnostics

[The Christian Gnostics were all reincarnationists. They included the followers of Basilides, Valentinus, and Marcion; the Simonists, disciples of that much maligned personage Simon Magus;[58] the Priscillians of Spain; the half-Gnostic Manicheans; and many lesser known groups. The word Gnostic comes from the Greek "gnose," meaning knowledge, which may relate to the fact, as stated by Gibbon, that the Gnostics were "the most learned of the Christian name,"[59] and thus were not content to be mere believers. Nor were they content with mere learning, but sought direct, personal experience of the Gnosis.

According to Radhakrishnan, "Gnosticism was one of the most powerful currents of thought which influenced Christian doctrine and practice." It "remained a power down to the fifth century through its alliance with Neoplatonism."[60] However, in orthodox circles, Gnosticism has been regarded as a pseudo-Christian religious philosophy running parallel to the mainstream of Christianity, but for some years now scholars have been re-forming their views. In the introduction to his translation of the Gnostic work *Codex Brucianus,* published in 1918 as *The Gnosis of the Light,* the Reverend A. A. F. Lamplugh states: "Recent investigations have challenged . . . the traditional 'facts.' With some today, and with many more tomorrow, the burning question is, or will be—not how did a peculiarly silly and licentious heresy rise within the Church—but how did the Church rise out of the Great Gnostic Movement, how did the dynamic ideas of the Gnosis become crystallized into Dogmas?"[61]

Jung was convinced that "the central ideas of Christianity are rooted in Gnostic philosophy . . ."[62] Those acquainted with his writings know how deeply he studied Gnostic teachings and symbols. At a critical turning point in his life, he wrote, in Gnostic fashion, a tiny volume called *Seven Sermons to the Dead,* imagining the sermons to have been penned by Basilides himself.[63] In the chapter "Gnostic Symbols of the Self" in his volume *Aion,* Jung remarks that "the idea of an unconscious was not unknown" to the Gnostics. "It is clear beyond a doubt that many of the Gnostics were nothing more than psychologists." They "have a vast number of symbols for the source or origin—the centre of being . . .''[64] Jung's views on reincarnation will be found in chapter 6.

Some scholars believe that the Gnostics may have been the descendants of the original Christians and the inheritors of the esoteric teachings of Christ. That Jesus had a secret doctrine is manifest from the Gospels themselves. He said to his disciples: ''Unto you it is given to know the mystery of the Kingdom of God; but unto them that are without, all these things are done in parables'' (Mark 4:11). ''And when they were alone'' Jesus ''expounded all things to his disciples, but without a parable spoke he not'' to the others (Mark: 4:33–34). In the New Testament we have the parables, but what happened to the inner teaching?[65] In this connection we quote from Smith and Wace's *Dictionary of Christian Biography:*

> We have no reason to think that the earliest Gnostics intended to found sects separated from the Church and called after their own names. Their disciples were to be Christians, elevated above the rest as acquainted with deeper mysteries, and called *Gnostikoi* because possessed of a Gnosis superior to the simple faith of the multitude. . . .''[66] They also boasted to be in possession of genuine apostolical traditions, deriving their doctrines, some from St. Paul, others from St. Peter, and others again from Judas, Thomas, Philip, and Matthew. In addition moreover, to [this] secret doctrine which they professed to have received by oral tradition, they appealed also to alleged writings of the apostles themselves or their disciples.[67]

Basilides, who taught in Alexandria about A.D. 125, and around whom the founders of the various Gnostic schools grouped themselves, maintained that he had all his doctrines from the Apostle Matthew and from Peter, through Glaucus, his disciple. The orthodox Eusebius reports that Basilides published twenty-four volumes of *Interpretations of the Gospels,* which were later burned by the Church.[68] Such a loss seems incalculable in the light it would throw upon Christian beginnings and original Christian doctrine. ''Of the actual writings of the Gnostics, which were extraordinarily numerous, very little has survived. They were sacrificed to the destructive zeal of their ecclesiastical opponents.''[69]

Now, on the basis of what has survived, let us consider reincarnation in Gnosticism.

In 1900 G. R. S. Mead's volume *Fragments of a Faith Forgotten* appeared. Kenneth Rexroth states in his introduction to the 1960 reprint: ''After sixty years Mead is still the most reliable guide to the corpus of Gnosticism that we have.'' Mead makes this summary of Gnostic teaching:

> The whole of [Gnosticism] revolved round the conception of cyclic law for both the universal and individual soul. Thus we find the Gnostics invariably teaching the doctrine not only of the pre-existence but also of the rebirth of

human souls. . . . They held rigidly to the infallible working out of the great law of cause and effect. It is somewhat curious that these two main doctrines [of reincarnation and karma] which explain so much in Gnosticism and throw light on so many dark places, have been either entirely overlooked or, when not unintelligently slurred over, despatched with a few hurried remarks in which the critic is more at pains to apologise for touching on such ridiculous superstitions as "metempsychosis" and "fate," than to elucidate tenets which are a key to the whole position.[70]

Mead also translated the important Gnostic scripture the *Pistis Sóphia,* a name that means "knowledge-wisdom." In the introduction, Mead writes:

Our Gnostics . . . found no difficulty in fitting [transcorporation or reincarnation] into their plan of salvation, which shows no sign of the expectation of an immediate end of all things—that prime article of faith [of the orthodox Christian] of the earliest days. So far from thinking that reincarnation is alien to gospel-teaching, they elaborately interpret certain of the most striking sayings in this sense, and give graphic details of how Jesus, as the First Mystery, brought to rebirth the souls of John the Baptizer and of the disciples, and supervised the economy of his own incarnation. In this respect the *Pistis Sophia* offers richer material for those interested in this ancient and widespread doctrine than can be found in any other old-world document in the West.[71]

In the first extracts from this translation the Saviour is relating what chastisements will befall various souls when they enter upon a new incarnation:

[THE SAVIOUR:]   This is the chastisement of the curser . . . Yaluham . . . bringeth a cup filled with the water of forgetfulness and handeth it to the soul, and it drinketh it and forgetteth . . . all the regions to which it hath gone. And they cast it down into a body which will spend its time continually troubled in its heart. . . .

    This is the chastisement of the arrogant and overweening man. . . . Yaluham . . . cometh and bringeth the cup with the water of forgetfulness and handeth it to the soul; and it drinketh and forgetteth all things and all the regions to which it hath gone. And they cast it up into a lame and deformed body, so that all despise it persistently. . . .

[JOHN SAID:]   A man who hath committed no sin, but done good persistently, but hath not found the mysteries . . . what will happen unto him? . . .

[THE SAVIOUR:]   Thereafter there cometh a receiver of the little Sabaoth, the Good, him of the Midst. He himself bringeth a cup filled with thoughts and wisdom, and soberness is in it; he handeth it to the soul. And they cast it into a body which can neither sleep nor forget because of the cup of soberness which hath been handed unto it; but it will whip its heart persistently to question about the mysteries of the Light until it finds them, through the decision of the Virgin of Light, and inherit the Light for ever. . . .

> I have turned Elias and sent him into the body of John the Baptizer, and
> the rest [of the prophets] also I turned into righteous bodies, which will find
> the mysteries of the Light, go on high and inherit the Light-kingdom.[72]

The purpose and goal of incarnations on earth is intimated in the foregoing.
It is also implied in the way the Gnostics viewed the names Christ and Jesus.
To the orthodox they are usually synonymous terms, but not so with the
Gnostics. To them Jesus represented the personal name of their Teacher,
while Christ is the divine spirit in every being. In a divine incarnation like
Jesus the spirit was fully manifest. Therefore, it was proper to add to his
personal name a title expressive of this fact, and thus call him Jesus, the
Christ. To the Gnostic, the words in Matthew 14:6, "I am the way and the
truth and the life: no one cometh unto the Father, but by me"—words that
have prevented so many Christians from impartially investigating other
religions—would refer not to Jesus, the man, but to the Christ-Self, which is
of the nature of "the kingdom of Heaven within you," of which Jesus spoke.
Saint Paul appears to use the word Christ in the Gnostic sense when he says,
"I travail in birth again until Christ be formed in you" (Galatians 4:19). To
the Gnostics this grand consummation would take many lives of patient,
persistent, selfless effort. An advanced disciple was called a *Chrestos;* when
fully illuminated, a *Christos.*

Such an idea may be viewed with dismay by the orthodox. It seems to take
away the glory and uniqueness of the Saviour. To the Gnostic, on the contrary,
it added to his luster, stature, and greatness. To be created perfect, what
merit is there in that! But to have become such through ages of compassionate striving, that is worthy of one's deepest admiration and reverence. Jesus
did not take the position of uniqueness. He continually referred to himself as
the Son of Man, not the Son of God. When the Jews accused him of setting
himself up as God, he replied: "Is it not written in your law . . . YE ARE
GODS?" (John 10:34). (So Jesus did not think of us as miserable sinners!) And
when the disciples marveled at his so-called miracles, what did he tell them?
"Even greater things than these can ye do also."

In the quarterly *Diogenes* (Spring 1959) an article appeared by Eva
Meyerovitch, "The Gnostic Manuscripts of Upper Egypt." Translated from
the French, it tells of a new path of exploration that is being opened in the
study of Gnosticism:

> Our epoch . . . has in recent years seen several discoveries which hold
> extraordinary interest for history in general and for the history of religions in
> particular. Around 1930 seven volumes of Manichean writings were discovered
> at Fayum; in 1941, a few miles outside Cairo, near Tura, unpublished works of
> Origen and his disciple Didymus the Blind were found; the discovery of the

Dead Sea Scrolls occurred around 1945; and in Egypt, at roughly this same time, an equally fortuitous find was made of a considerable body of Coptic manuscripts dating perhaps from the third century A.D. Although these last have not been entirely deciphered, they are considered by specialists to be prodigiously rich; such a find, says one, "does not merely enrich or renew our previous knowledge of the literature, the genealogy, or the history of Gnosticism: it revolutionizes this knowledge, and opens to research in the field a path absolutely distinct from all those which criticism has previously followed."[73]

In the Acts and in the Epistles we find traces of the struggle that primitive Christianity had to wage against Gnostic tendencies, a struggle that became more and more intensified and no doubt reached its apogee in the second century. The works of Christian writers of that time bear witness to the bitterness of the struggle. However, they all look upon the Gnose . . . as a phenomenon to be considered uniquely *in relation* to Christianity, as a heresy within the church. We cannot view it in this light today. The comparative history of religions shows us that the term must be given a much wider meaning; it is essentially concerned, as a matter of fact, with a specific religious attitude in regard to the problem of salvation. . . . There exist pagan Gnoses, such as Hermetism; extra-Christian Gnoses such as Mandeism,[74] oriental Gnoses like Ishmaelism.[75]

All outward manifestations of Christian Gnosticism and Gnostic Manicheism were eventually suppressed by emperors and popes alike, the death penalty often being inflicted for belief. Yet these movements long maintained an underground existence even in the West. In the Byzantine empire where the Eastern half of the Church prevailed, they withdrew ostensibly to the boundaries of the empire, but still maintained secret relations with kindred groups scattered throughout the provinces and even in Constantinople. The subsequent large-scale medieval revival of Gnostic ideas will be considered in the section "Reincarnation in the Dark Ages."]

The Anathemas against Preexistence

[For fourteen centuries the dialogue on reincarnation was silenced in orthodox Christendom because it was generally believed that in the year 553 an important church council anathematized (cursed) the doctrine of the preexistence of the soul. While reincarnation and preexistence (in the limited sense the latter term is used by some churchmen) are not synonymous terms, obviously if preexistence is false, previous lives on earth are impossible, and by inference future lives also. Recently disclosed evidence advanced by Catholic scholars—who now have access to the original records—throws an entirely new light on what actually occurred at this council, as shall be seen shortly. The story surrounding the anathemas is an engrossing one, and as these curses brought in their wake serious consequences affecting for many centuries the life and thoughts of millions in the West, the whole matter seems worth exploring somewhat at length.

In the early centuries of Christian history, many battles were waged over issues of doctrine, church councils being convened to settle disputes. In the sixth century, Emperor Justinian, the head of the whole Eastern empire, declared war against the followers of Origen. At Justinian's instigation it appears that a local synod, which convened in Constantinople in 543, condemned the teachings of Origen, and ten years later, in 553, Justinian issued his anathemas against Origen, possibly submitting them for final ratification at an extra-conciliary or unofficial session of the Fifth Ecumenical Council, also called the Second Council of Constantinople. The anathemas cursed, among other teachings of Origen, the doctrine of the preexistence of the soul.

The *Catholic Encyclopedia*[76] gives some rather astonishing information concerning this Fifth Ecumenical Council, permitting the conclusion, on at least technical grounds, that there is no barrier to belief in reincarnation for Catholic Christians.[77] With the exception of six Western bishops from Africa, the council was attended entirely by Eastern bishops; no representative from Rome was present. Although Pope Vigilius was in Constantinople at the time, he refused to attend. The president of the council was Eutychius, Patriarch of Constantinople and head of the Eastern church. However, "from the time of Justinian the emperor controlled the patriarch absolutely."[78]

There apparently had been intense conflict between Justinian and Pope Vigilius for several years. Violating previous agreements, Justinian in 551 issued an edict against what was known as "The Three Chapters," the teachings of three supposed heretics, none of whom were Origen or his followers. "For his dignified protest Vigilius thereupon suffered various personal indignities at the hands of the civil authority [Justinian] and nearly lost his life."[79] In fact, for eight years the Pope had been Justinian's prisoner, having been kidnapped from Rome in November of 545.[80] To bring peace between the Eastern and Western branches of the church, this Fifth Ecumenical Council was called. Justinian, however refused Pope Vigilius's request for equal representation of bishops from East and West, and summarily convened the council on his own terms; hence the Pope's refusal to attend. When we learn that of the 165 bishops at the final meeting, 159 were from the Eastern church, it can safely be concluded that the voting during all the sessions was very much in Justinian's hands.

Quoting directly from *The Catholic Encyclopedia,* regarding the Fifth Ecumenical Council:[81]

Were Origen and Origenism anathematized? Many learned writers believe so; an equal number deny that they were condemned; most modern authorities are either undecided or reply with reservations. Relying on the most recent studies on the question it may be held that:

   1. It is certain that the fifth general council was convoked exclusively to deal with the affair of the Three Chapters, and *that neither Origen nor Origenism* was the cause of it.
   2. It is certain that the council opened on 5, May, 553, in spite of the protestations of Pope Vigilius, who though at Constantinople refused to attend it, and that in the eight conciliary sessions (from 5 May to 2 June), the Acts of which we possess, *only the question of the Three Chapters is treated.*
   3. Finally it is certain that *only the Acts concerning the affair of the Three Chapters were submitted to the pope* for his approval, which was given on 8 December, 553, and 23 February, 554.
   4. It is a fact that Popes Vigilius, Pelagius I (556–61), Pelagius II (579–90), Gregory the Great (590–604), in treating of the fifth council deal only with the Three Chapters, *make no mention of Origenism, and speak as if they did not know of its condemnation.*
   5. It must be admitted that *before the opening of the council,* which had been delayed by the resistance of the pope, the bishops already assembled at Constantinople had to consider, by order of the emperor, *a form of Origenism that had practically nothing in common with Origen,* but which was held by one of the Origenist parties in Palestine. . . .
   6. The bishops [at this extra-conciliary session referred to in No. 5 above] certainly subscribed to the fifteen anathemas proposed by the emperor [against Origen]; an admitted Origenist, Theodore of Scythopolin, was forced to retract; *but there is no proof that the approbation of the pope, who was at that time protesting against the convocation of the council, was asked.*
   7. It is easy to understand how this extra-conciliary sentence *was mistaken at a later period* for a decree of the actual ecumenical council. (Italics added.)

However, one far-reaching result of the mistake still persists, namely, the exclusion from consideration by orthodox Christianity of the teaching of the preexistence of the soul and, by implication, reincarnation. Probably many a good Christian would have another look at the whole subject if he were only aware of the foregoing facts.

Of this period the Reverend William Alva Gifford wrote in *The Story of the Faith:* "Justinian assumed the headship of the Church. Imperial edicts regulated public worship, directed ecclesiastical discipline, and even dictated theological doctrines. The Church had to submit for a time to 'Caesaro-papism,' a papacy of the Emperor." Gifford adds that in 529 Justininan closed the University of Athens, the last stronghold of Neoplatonism. "As for the scholars of Athens, they fled to Persia, where their descendants became leaders of the literary and scientific life of Islam, at Bagdad and other centres."[82]

As to the Fifth Ecumenical Council, some further significant details are furnished by Joseph Campbell in *The Masks of God: Occidental Mythology.*

Although refusing to attend the council, the pope produced his own document, the *Constitutum ad Imperatoreum,* in which he condemned only sixty passages of one of the three "heretics," and not the author himself, on the ground that it was not customary to condemn the dead. Nor would he condemn the works of the other two. The ecumenical council thereupon condemned not only the works and authors in question *but the captive Pope himself;* and, thoroughly undone, the poor man finally joined his name to theirs and, permitted to return to his see, died in Syracuse on the way.[83] But, as we have already seen, all this had nothing to do with Origen. Even if it had, for him to be condemned through such despotic acts would nullify the whole proceedings in the sight of every fair-minded individual.

The council's "decrees were received in the East," but were "long contested in the Western Church, where a schism arose that lasted for seventy years."[84]

For centuries the so-called anathemas against Origen have been part of the published proceedings of the Fifth Ecumenical Council. Four of the fifteen anathemas are aimed at preexistence, but also include subtle references to reincarnation. It seems likely that these doctrines must have been widely held, else why go to the trouble of condemning them?

> 1. If anyone assert the fabulous pre-existence of souls, and shall assert the monstrous restoration which follows from it: let him be anathema.
>
> 7. If anyone shall say that Christ . . . had different bodies and different names, became all to all, an Angel among Angels, a Power among Powers, had clothed himself in the different classes of reasonable beings with a form corresponding to that class, and finally has taken flesh and blood like ours and is become man for man; [if anyone says all this] and does not profess that God the Word humbled himself and became man: let him be anathema.
>
> 13. If anyone shall say that Christ is in no wise different from other reasonable beings, neither substantially nor by wisdom nor by his power and might over all things but that all will be placed at the right hand of God, as well as he that is called by them Christ, as also they were in the feigned pre-existence of all things: let him be anathema.
>
> 15. If anyone shall say that the life of the spirits shall be like to the life which was in the beginning while as yet the spirits had not come down or fallen, so that the end and the beginning shall be alike, and that the end shall be the true measure of the beginning: let him be anathema.[85]

Since an anathema is "a formal ecclesiastical curse involving excommunication," the concluding paragraph was obviously intended to threaten damnation to any inquiring mind venturing to embrace the forbidden ideas:

> If anyone does not anathematize Arius, Eunomius, Macedonius, Apollinaris, Nestorius, Eutyches and Origen, as well as their impious writings, as also all other heretics already condemned and anathematized by the Holy Catholic and

Apostolic Church, and by the aforesaid four Holy Synods and (if anyone does not equally anathematize) all those who have held and hold or who in their impiety persist in holding to the end the same opinion as those heretics just mentioned: let him be anathema.

To curse! To commit to eternal hellfire all who disagree with a particular interpretation of sacred writ! How unlike the spirit and example of the Prince of Peace.

As to later church councils, *The Oxford Dictionary of the Christian Church* states that metempsychosis "Was implicitly condemned by the Council of Lyons (1274) and Florence (1439), which affirmed that the souls go immediately to heaven, purgatory, or hell."[86] This does not nullify rebirth, for most reincarnationists teach that after death the soul undergoes a purgatorial condition before it is pure enough to experience heaven. They merely deny that these states of consciousness last forever. Commenting on the *Oxford Dictionary* statement, the Reverend Patrick Blakiston, rector of the Episcopal Church in Alvechurch, Worcester, England, wrote in his monthly letter to parishioners (May 1963): "The Church of England is not bound by the decisions of the mediaeval Roman Catholic Councils and, even if it could be shown that the undivided ancient Church officially forbade belief in reincarnation the 21st of our Articles of Religion says 'General Councils may err and sometimes have erred, even in things pertaining unto God.'"

Our next section answers the question: Did the anathemas against preexistence entirely erase the idea of reincarnation from European awareness during the ensuing centuries?]

※ ※ ※

Reincarnation in the Dark Ages

[In the light of modern scholarship, searching out and identifying the believers in reincarnation during the centuries of European history that came after the suppression of Neoplatonic philosophy and Gnostic teaching is not too difficult a task. This period is justly called the Dark Age, since it was characterized by ignorance, superstition, and almost unrelieved barbarism and cruelty. Within the past fifty years or so, cultural historians have begun to give unprejudiced attention to themes of belief that survived in underground channels, often emerging to provoke the reaction of persecution and ruthless slaughter. Such tragic events are often obscure in background, since writers attempting to provide an impartial record have been obliged to construct their accounts of the teachings of "heretical" groups from the testimony of their bitterest enemies, the champions of Christian orthodoxy. However, the bias of these authorities is now generally admitted, and a new sort of scholarship is slowly revising our understanding of the origins of Western religion, sometimes suggesting that feared and hated gnostic beliefs were indeed central to early Christianity. Reincarnation was a cardinal doctrine of the Gnostics, and their various successors in the period under consideration carried forward this same teaching, as will be illustrated later.

Supporting the change in scholarly attitudes have come new archaeological discoveries, such as the Nag Hammadi Gnostic texts, unearthed in an ancient Egyptian cemetery in 1946. These manuscripts—some fifty in all—are being translated, and one conclusion of the scholars involved is that the writers of the New Testament, such as the author of the Gospel of John or of the epistle of Colossians, "drew their thought patterns" from a "gnosticising milieu."[87] All Christianity may require reinterpretation in the light of such discoveries.

Despite the ruthless policies of both the Eastern and Western churches, the ideas of the Gnostic sects proved almost irrepressible. On several occasions, both the reasonableness of these teachings and the personal qualities of their followers made them a serious threat to the orthodox religion, and their suppression, as known under various names, was accomplished only by mass execution, torture, and the dreaded methods of the Holy Inquisition, an institution that had its beginnings in the thirteenth century as a weapon devised to seek out Gnosticizing heretics and punish or destroy them. During the latter part of the Middle Ages, the various Gnostic groups "spread so rapidly and resisted so stubbornly the sternest efforts of suppression that at one time it may be fairly said to have threatened the permanent existence of Christianity itself." This statement by Henry Lea appears in his monumental three-volume *History of the Inquisition of the Middle Ages.*[88]

Tracing how these groups gained such prominence, we must first go to Asia Minor during the fifth century where the Gnostic Paulicians in Syrian Armenia were growing in numbers. Their doctrines are said to have included "a theory of metempsychosis."[89] This movement gradually spread throughout Asia Minor, and in the eighth century, by order of the Byzantine Emperor Constantine Copronymus, a number of its followers were transplanted to Thrace (later known as Bulgaria). From Bulgaria the movement spread among the Slavs, and followed the routes of commerce into central Europe. The earliest record of their presence there is the condemnation of ten canons of Orleans (in northern France) as Manichees in 1022, and soon after this are found complaints of the prevalence of heresy in northern Italy and in Germany.[90] Some scholars, however, say that even before the year 1000, they had reached Italy gaining many followers, especially in Milan.[91]

It appears that this focus of Gnostic influence became the fertile source of ethical and metaphysical teachings that spread to many parts of Europe and eventually contributed to the great ferment of religious ideas that brought on the Reformation. These European bearers of Gnostic teachings are known to history as the Cathars and the Albigenses (the latter being no more than a geographic designation that obtained wide use). In *The Holy Heretics,* Edmond Holmes said that "Catharism overran southern and western Europe from Constantinople to the Pyrenees and from the Mediterranean to the North Sea."[92] In all there were about seventy-two groups.[93]

"In Italy," Holmes writes, "Catharism found a soil prepared for its reception." "There the Manichaean heresy had maintained itself for many centuries in spite of all the efforts of Popes and Emperors to extirpate it. . . . And, with the awakening of the humanistic spirit in Italy at the end of the eleventh century, came a readiness to welcome and propagate ideas which had the charm of novelty, besides being free from the odious associations which orthodox Catholicism had contracted. . . . The ignorance, the avarice, and the immorality of the Italian clergy exposed them to the contempt of the laity and inclined the latter to lend willing ears to antiorthodox doctrine. . . . Catharism [was] the religion of *catharsis,* or purification. . . . Membership of the Church was confined to those who had received the Holy Spirit and were leading pure and sinless lives."[94] Lea remarks that "the highest authorities in the church admitted that its scandals were the cause, if not the justification of heresy. . . . No more unexceptionable witness as to the Church of the twelfth century can be had than St. Bernard, and he is never weary of denouncing the pride, the wickedness, the ambition, and the lust that reigned everywhere."[95] F. C. Conybeare writes that "the influence of Catharism on the Catholic Church was enormous. To counteract it celibacy was finally imposed on the clergy, and the great mendicant orders evolved . . . The sacrament of 'extreme unction' was also evolved by way of competing with the death-bed *consolamentum* of the Catharists."[96]

Holmes summarizes the basic teachings of the Catharists in this way: "The Catharists claimed that their Church was carrying on the work of Christ," and that by joining it, human beings could enter "the path of penitential purification, and so shorten their stay on earth. . . . But how about the souls of those who died before Christ came?"—which the Orthodox Church, until fairly recently, taught were irretrievably damned.

> The Catharists met this difficulty by teaching, what in any case they were bound to teach, the doctrine of rebirth. If there was an original Fall, as the result of which a definite number of souls fell from heaven to earth, and if there has since been no addition to that number, it is only by the action of the law of rebirth that the earth has continued to be inhabited by mankind. The departed soul is reborn in another body, reborn again and again, until the time comes for its final deliverance from earth.[97]

In his *History of the Inquisition,* Lea speaks of this teaching as belonging to "all the sects of Cathari, leading to a theory of transmigration very similar to that of Buddhism,"[98] and Zoé Oldenbourg, in her history of the crusade against the Albigenses, remarks that their doctrine of metempsychosis was like that of the Hindus, including the "same precise calculations governing posthumous retribution for the individual." The just man "would be reincarnated in a body better suited for his further spiritual development; whereas the criminal was liable, after his death, to be reborn in a body full of flaws and hereditary vices."[99]

Professor Lynn White writing in *Science* (March 10, 1967) discusses a possible connection between the Cathari and the teachings of Saint Francis of Assisi, whom he calls "the greatest radical in Christian history since Christ." Saint Francis, he shows, opposed the arrogance of man as king of creation and sought to establish a democracy of all creatures. In his eyes all living things had souls. "What Sir Steven Runciman calls 'the Franciscan doctrine of the animal soul' was quickly stamped out," says White. "Quite possibly it was in part inspired, consciously or unconsciously, by the belief in reincarnation held by the Cathar heretics who at that time teemed in Italy and southern France."

Industry, art, and science, says Lea, were far in advance of the age in twelfth-century southern France—the home of the Albigenses. The cities had won virtual self-government, and citizens, both men and women, boasted a degree of education and enlightenment unknown elsewhere.[100] The ghastly story of the slaughter of the Albigenses has been told by Lea, Edmond Holmes, and other historians. Here we record some notes from Holmes concerning their beliefs, which were simple and persuasive. In their teaching, Christ came, not to die for men, but to help them to save themselves "by unfolding to them their origin and their destiny, and showing them how best to accomplish their work of penitential purgation." This was to be accomplished through purifying cycles of metempsychosis such as were taught in the Orphic mysteries.

The moral code of the Albigenses involved the renunciation of property, truth-telling, vegetarianism, and chastity. Most important were nonresistance, harmlessness, and respect for all living things, so that the taking of life in war was anathema to them. Depending on their degree of practice, the Albigenses were divided into grades, the highest of which was the *perfecti*, who were "initiates" and teachers. "The leaders of the heretics," Dana Monro says in his *Middle Ages*, "were admired for their virtuous lives and asceticism." Men sought the company of the *perfecti* to benefit from the association, and Monro states that even Catholics sometimes asked to be buried in the Albigensian cemeteries, "in order that they might be among the good people," seeking, it seems, a curious sort of salvation by association!

Commenting on the crusade against these wholesome, virtuous, intelligent people, Arthur Guirdham remarks that Catharism was "a resurgence of primitive Christianity, and was stamped out for the very reason that it was primitive Christianity. It was a mystical, real, living experience of Christianity as opposed to an avidly theological concept."[101] In his book *The Cathars and Reincarnation,* Dr. Guirdham points out that it was because of their belief in reincarnation, along with other things, that the Albigenses were "completely massacred, very, very completely."[102]

Why was the belief in reincarnation so offensive to the Defenders of the Faith? Various reasons may be given, but the implicit psychology of reincarnation may be the best explanation. The believer in this teaching tends to hold himself responsible for his own progress and salvation. Such a person has no need of priests and little regard for external dead-letter observance, rite, or conformity. The devices (such as the confessional) of a redemption conferred by institutional authority were to believers in evolution through rebirth transparently fraudulent or false. Hence their persecution over the many centuries while dogmatic religion remained in power.[103]

During the period 1209 and 1226 when the Albigenses were being exterminated, their provinces devastated, and their language (the *langue d'oc*) proscribed, small bands of troubadours and artisans escaped to various parts of Europe and there continued their work of humanistic and mystical education. Embers of reincarnation teaching were also kept alive by the Knights Templar, some of the Hermetic philosophers, alchemists, Rosicrucians, and leading lights of the Renaissance. (See chapter 5.) To the list of the reincarnationists must, of course, be added the Hebrew and Christian Kabalists, and also the Taborites,[104] a branch of the Hussites. In his *History of the Hussite Revolution* of Bohemia and its instigator John Huss, Howard Kaminsky indicates that only in the Taborite communities was the full promise of the original Hussite aspirations fulfilled.[105]

After the Renaissance, the iron hand of the "Holy" Inquisition descended over most of Europe, and for several centuries heretic-hunting on the part of the masses and clergy alike raged with an unparalleled fury, sending to the stake, as sons of Satan, hundreds of thousands of brave, freethinking Christians. Gradually the night of enslavement over the human mind came to an end. But as to reincarnation, the supposed curse against preexistence of A.D. 553, followed later by the indefatigable work of the Inquisitors, proved exceedingly effective. Reincarnation was now dead to the masses of people in the West. Henceforth, and until the latter half of the nineteenth century, only among philosophers, writers, and a few daring theologians was the doctrine to be quietly welcomed.

The Christian story will continue after the next section. Meanwhile if we are to follow the rising tide of civilization, we must go to the Middle East where some of the persecuted Neoplatonists, Gnostics, Kabalists, and Hermetists fled, bringing with them the philosophy of rebirth.

A final thought seems appropriate concerning the term "heretic"—a fearful, detestable word to those of pious faith. By derivation it simply means one who is "able to choose." Thus, all who choose to think for themselves rather

than blindly believe are heretics, and they have a noble predecessor in Saint Paul, who, in his first epistle to the Thessalonians (5:21), counseled:
"Prove all things: hold fast that which is good."]

ISLAMIC

Early Islam

[The persecution of scholars by the medieval church had gradually driven most students of science and philosophy out of Europe. Some found refuge in Persia, others in Arabia, the land of liberty in those days. The Christian Gnostics gave the Arabs a knowledge of Greek philosophy and Gnosticism; the Nestorians acquainted them with the Neoplatonic philosophers; and the exiled Jews instructed them in the Kabala. Fragments of the teachings of Hermes found their way into the Middle East. Alberuni, a Moslem scholar, accompanied into India Sultan Mahmud of Ghazni and acquired a knowledge of Hindu religious classics; a number were translated into Arabic. All these influences combined to make Islamic thinkers natural heirs to the philosophy of rebirth.

The reincarnation views of the Kabalists and the Gnostics have already been discussed. The Platonists and Neo-Platonists will be discussed later. As to the Nestorians they too accepted reincarnation according to the thirteenth-century Franciscan missionary Rubruquis, also known as William of Ruysbroeck.[1] Nestorius, the founder, was the Alexandrian Christian bishop and Neoplatonist who in the fifth century refused to accept the Virgin Mary as the Mother of God, was excommunicated and exiled to an African oasis where he died of thirst. After his death his followers emigrated to Asia Minor, China, Tartary, and India, and soon outnumbered all the Christians of the Greek and Roman churches combined. Many of the Nestorians were students of the Hermetic philosophy and the Kabala. Many, like Nestorius, were Neoplatonists, while others followed the Gnostic teachings. Mohammed when a boy came in contact with a Nestorian monastery in Busra and grew deeply interested in the religious and philosophical views of the monks. On reaching manhood, some say he came more and more under Nestorian influence.

In the eighth century Neoplatonic thought gained new life from the great

Arabian philosopher Al-Kindi, and in the ninth century from Al-Ferabi, who in turn taught the Persian-born physician and philosopher Avicenna. Spain had been conquered by the Muslims in the eighth century, and under Islamic influence the Iberian Peninsula became a great center of civilization and enlightenment. An important link in the Neoplatonic succession was the Kabalist Ibn Gebirol, a Spanish Jew, known to medieval scholastics as Avicebron (1021?–1058). It was through him that the long-exiled teachings of Plato returned to Europe via Spain, where during the Dark Ages adventurous Christian scholars and monks traveled in search for knowledge. However, the real revival of Neoplatonism did not take place in Europe until the Renaissance.

Dr. W. Y. Evans-Wentz of Oxford, well known for his works on Eastern religion, stated in his lecture "The Christian Doctrine of Rebirth": "During the Dark Ages of Europe, when the Moors of Spain almost alone in the Western world kept alight the sacred Torch of Learning. . . . the doctrine of rebirth was being taught by the great Saracenic philosophers—Al Ghazali and Al Batagni—in the Schools of Bagdad in the East and of Cordova [Spain] in the West. And in Europe, the disciples of these great teachers were Paracelsus and the martyred Bruno. It was due chiefly to Moslem scholars of those days that to Europe was restored the classical culture of Greece, and the Light from the Orient was re-lit in the Occident."[2] (Paracelsus and Giordano Bruno will be quoted on reincarnation in chapter 5.)

In a series of articles, "Reincarnation—Islamic Conceptions," M. H. Abdi, a Moslem scholar, expresses some interesting thoughts on how rebirth gradually lost popularity in Islam:

> The position adopted by the successive luminaries who followed [Mohammed] was to affirm the belief in reincarnation but not to propagate it as a teaching for the masses. This attitude was due to psychological reasons. The emphasis in Islamic teachings has throughout been on the purity of action.
>
> Another factor to remember is that the defensive wars, which have been described as Jehad or holy wars, which the Muslims fought in the early days and the wars of conquests (therefore not holy) which the Muslims fought in later days . . . gave a different shift to Islamic teachings. Philosophical, mystical and ethical teachings received an impetus in the first phase but they had subdued existence in the later phase. During this phase the republican character of the State was changed into monarchy and the supremacy no more belonged to the saints and philosophers. A subject like reincarnation demands a subtle mental attitude. It entails understanding of the higher planes of consciousness, the laws of cause and effect and the working of the laws of evolution. The monarchs had no interest in such subjects. Like so many other teachings, reincarnation was confined to the study and attention of the outer and inner students of Sufism . . . [However,] there is no danger for a Muslim being called a heretic if he believes and expresses himself in favour of reincarnation.[3]

But it was not only through Sufism—which will be separately considered—that the fire of rebirth was transmitted. G. F. Moore states in his Ingersoll lecture on metempsychosis that "among Mohammedans the difficulty of reconciling the sufferings of innocent children . . . with the goodness or even the justice of God led some of the liberal theologians (Mu'tazilites) to seek a solution in sins committed in a former existence. . . . Reincarnation is fundamental to the doctrine of the Imam[4] as held by the [Shiites]; it was developed in a characteristic form by the Ism'ilis, and is a cardinal doctrine of Babism."[5] The Shiites are one of the two great religious divisions of Islam; these two having branched into some seventy sub-sects.

E. G. Browne confirms all this in his three-volume work, *The Literary History of Persia,* particularly the chapters on the Ismailis and the many other esoteric schools of Islam.[6] Three aspects of rebirth were accepted, he says:

Hulul   The periodical incarnation of the Perfect Man or Deity.
Rij'at   The return of the Imam or spiritual leader after death.
Tanasukh   Reincarnation of the souls of ordinary men.

According to N. K. Mirza, the Ismailis go so far as to say that the Hindu Krishna incarnated as the Buddha and then as Mohammed; while one of the Rafziah sects believes "that at no time is the world left without a Teacher as a guide, that in some person or another . . . this great soul, is manifesting all the time." Mirza states that "the Behais of Iran believe that . . . Christ reincarnated in their leader Abdul Beha, while in [Pakistan] the Kadyanis claim the same distinction for their head, Mirza Ahmed."[7]]

The Koran

[The Koran, the bible of Islam, is supposed to have been revealed to Mohammed by Allah. It is largely ethical in character. Honor is paid therein to Issa Ben Yussuf, or Jesus, son of Joseph, as also to the Hebrew prophets such as Moses. Mohammed affirmed that the Koran has an esoteric foundation: It was "sent in seven dialects; and in every one of its sentences there is an external and an internal meaning. . . . I received from the messenger of God two kinds of knowledge: One of these I taught . . . [but] if I had taught them the other it would have broken their throats."[8]

The renowned Lebanese mystic Mikhail Naimy, biographer of Kahlil Gibran, wrote to Joseph Head (October 8, 1963): "In Al Koran clear hints [on rebirth] are found which orthodox Islam brushes aside as meaning something else than reincarnation. . . . In Al Koran occurs the following verse which I give in my own translation: 'And you were dead, and He brought you back to life. And He shall cause you to die, and shall bring you back to life, and in the end shall gather you unto Himself' [Sura 2:28]. The words 'you were dead' mean that they had lived before becoming dead. That is the clear implication of the phrase. Then the whole sentence would clearly indicate that it had reference to more than one life and one death.'' Quoting now from other parts of the Koran, using the translation of Dr. Abdi:

> As the rains turn the dry earth into green thereby yielding fruits, similarly God brings the dead into life so that thou mayest learn. (Chapter 8—Sura Iraf—Meccan Verses 6–6–13.)

> And He sent down rains from above in proper quantity and He brings back to life the dead earth, similarly ye shall be reborn. (Chapter 25—Sura Zakhraf—Meccan Verses 5–10–6.)

> [Those who doubt immortality] are dead and they do not know when they will be born again. Your God is peerless and those who have no faith in the ultimate have perverse hearts and they want to pose as great men. (Chapter 14—Sura Nahel—Verses 2–12–8.)

> Dr. Abdi remarks that ''commentator Ayashi on the authority of Imam Baqer says that the ultimate referred to in the foregoing verse really means Rajat [reincarnation], or going up and down, and . . . that Rajat means rebirth in this world of great Holy Beings as well as of well known kafirs before Qiyamat (resurrection). . . . Kafir means the perverse.'' In this relation Abdi again quotes from the Koran: The Kafirs ''have sworn by the strongest oath that one who dies shall not be reborn. Surely they will be reborn and this law is perfect but people who do not possess wisdom do not comprehend it.'' (Chapter 14—Sura Nahel Verses 4–0–10.) ''Commentator Qummi quoting Imam Jafer, the well-known authority in the Islamic world, says that [this] means rebirth to be undergone before entering the Heaven world.''[9]]

The Sufis

[''It is a well known historical fact,'' states Abdi, ''that Muslims were divided on the question of succession of the Prophet, which ultimately resulted in the establishment of the two main sects of the Sunnis and the Shias'' or Shiites. ''The significant fact has however been that there has always existed a cementing class that brought the two sects and their sub-sects together and that was the class known as Sufis. . . . The soul of Islam always yearned after them. . . . Even now Rumi, Hafiz, Jami, Ibne Sina and a host of other Sufis command universal respect.''[10]

It was among the Sufis—from Sophia, wisdom—that the teaching of reincarnation was especially preserved. The Sufis claimed to possess the esoteric
philosophy of Islam and to have preceded Mohammed by several thousand
years. Saadi, Rumi, Hafiz, and other celebrated Sufi poets apparently concealed many of their ideas behind the symbolism of "the Beloved," a practice later adopted by the Troubadours, and by Dante and Raymond Lully.
"The Sufi doctrine," says C. W. King, "involved the grand idea of one
universal creed which could be secretly held under any profession of outward
faith . . ."[11]

The enormous though largely unacknowledged impact of Sufism on Western as well as Middle Eastern thought is disclosed in Idries Shah's book *The
Sufis* and in the introduction by Robert Graves. Mr. Shah, who indicates that
the Sufis believe in conscious evolution and the limitless perfectibility of
man, states:

> The Eastern impact in the dark ages [of Europe] was absorbed on several
> levels. Of these the most important are the theological and the occultist. Lully,
> Assisi, Scot [Duns Scotus] and dozens of others passed on the theological
> version. But we have only to glance at the list of the famous names of occult
> illuminati of Europe to see what was the nature of the secret doctrine which
> they were passing down, in however garbled a form.
> Raymond Lully, according to the occultists, was an alchemist and illuminate.
> According to the devout, he was a Christian missionary. According to his own
> writings, he was an adapter of Sufi books and exercises. Roger Bacon, another
> hierophant of occultism, wrote on Sufi illuminism. Paracelsus, who tried to
> reform Western medicine, presents Sufi ideas. . . . Geber the alchemist was
> one of the best-known Sufis of Iraq. He is known as a master of occultism [and
> the father of chemistry]. Also in the occult tradition is Albertus Magnus, both
> scholastic and magician, who studied in Arab schools and inspired St. Thomas
> Aquinas. Numerous Popes supposed to be magicians or transmitters of a secret
> doctrine . . . were graduates of Arab schools—such as Gerbert, Pope Silvester
> II. . . . In organizations it is the same story. If the Franciscan Order bears the
> stamp of Sufi origins, so do the Rosicrucians and the Masons.[12]

The seventeenth-century Oriental treasure-house *The Dabistan* states that
the eastern school of Sufis was derived from certain ancient Zoroastrian
mystics. These Sufis taught: "When the souls not yet come forth from the pit
of the natural darkness of bodily matter, are nevertheless in a state of increasing improvement, then, in an ascending way, they migrate from body to
body, each purer than the former one, until the time of climbing up to the
steps of the wished-for perfection of mankind . . . after which, purified of the
defilement of the body, they join the world of sanctity . . ."[13] In the chapter
"Religion of the Sufis," the master Sáid Muhammed Nurbakhsh is shown
distinguishing between *tanasukh,* or ordinary reincarnation, and *buruz,* the
reincarnation of a perfect soul "for the sake of perfecting mankind."

Selections from two Sufi poets follow. The lovely poem of Hafiz on the soul's cyclic journey has been given in chapter 2 under "The Immortal Phoenix."]

MANSUR AL-HALLAJ (TENTH CENTURY)

[Mansur Al-Hallaj was executed on the cross because of his claim of *Inal Haq*, or being one with deity. He is called "the Prince of Sufi Masters," in Browne's *Literary History of Persia*. There the author says that Mansur held to all the cardinal teachings of reincarnation.[14] One of his couplets, as translated by Nadarbeg K. Mirza, a Moslem lawyer, in his little volume *Reincarnation and Islam*, reads:]

Like the herbage I have sprung up many a time on the banks of flowing rivers. For a hundred thousand years I have lived and worked and tried in every sort of body.[15]

JALALU' L-DIN RUMI (1207–1273)

[Rumi was the greatest of the Persian Sufi mystical poets. His *Mathnawi* comprises six books of about 25,000 couplets. It is considered next in rank to the Koran, and in fact is called "the Koran in Persian" because the views therein are based on the writings and sayings of the Prophet. Idries Shah writes in *The Sufis:*

The extent of Rumi's influence can hardly be calculated; though it can be glimpsed occasionally in the literature and thought of many schools. Even Doctor Johnson, best known for his unfavorable pronouncements, says of Rumi, "He makes plain to the Pilgrim the secrets of the Way of Unity, and unveils the Mysteries of the Path of Eternal Truth." His work was well enough known within less than a hundred years of his death in 1273 for Chaucer to use references to it in some of his works, together with material from the teachings of Rumi's spiritual precursor, Attar the Chemist (1150–1229/30). From the numerous references to Arabian material which can be found in Chaucer, even a cursory examination shows a Sufi impact of the Rumi school of literature.[16]

From *The Mathnawi:*]

> I died as mineral and became a plant,
> I died as plant and rose to animal,
> I died as animal and I was Man.
> Why should I fear? When was I less by dying?
> Yet once more I shall die as Man, to soar
> With angels blest; but even from angelhood
> I must pass on . . .[17]

If one who has lived many years in a city, goes to sleep and beholds [in his dream] another city full of good and evil, his own city vanishes from his mind. He does not say to himself, "This is a new city: I am a stranger here." Nay, he thinks he has always lived in this city and was born and bred in it. What wonder, then, if the soul does not remember her ancient abode and birthplace, since she is wrapt in the slumber of this world, like a star covered by clouds; especially as she has trodden so many cities and the dust that darkens her vision is not yet swept away.[18]

For a million years I floated in ether, even as the atom floats uncontrolled. If I do not actually remember that state of mine, I often dream of my atomic travels. I am but one soul but I have a hundred thousand bodies. Yet I am helpless, since Shariat (exoteric religion) holds my lips sealed. Two thousand men have I seen who were I; but none as good as I am now.[19]

There have been thousands of changes in form . . . Look always to the form in the present; for, if you think of the forms in the past, you will separate yourself from your true Self. These are all states of the permanent which you have seen by dying. Why then do you turn your face from death? As the second stage has always been better than the first, then die happily and look forward to taking up a new and better form. Remember, and haste not. You must die before you improve. Like the sun, only when you set in the West can you rise again with brilliance in the East.[20]

THE SUFIS OF SYRIA

[The Sufis of Syria, popularly known as the Druses of Mount Lebanon, came to prominence in the eleventh century. They exist today mainly in Syria, Lebanon, and Jordan. Many theories of their origin have been suggested, and their religion is described as a blending of Islamism, Judaism, and Christianity, strongly tinged with Gnosticism, Tibetan Lamaism, and the Magian system of Persia. They are thought to be the descendants of the persecuted mystics of all nations who found refuge in the mountains of Syria during the early years of the Christian era. Some of them trace their order back to Hemsa, the uncle of Mohammed, who in 625 went to Tibet in search of secret wisdom. He is said to have incarnated again as H'amsa, the founder of the Order. From that time he is supposed to have reincarnated successively in the body of the chief Hierophant (or Okhal) in the same way that some of the Buddhas are said to incarnate in the Tibetan Lamas. Alexander Lawrie in his *History of Freemasonry* claims that the original Knights Templar, founded in

1118, inherited their knowledge from the Druses. Reincarnation is one of their fundamental teachings. In a documented study, "Belief in Rebirth of the Druses and other Syrian Sects," Theodore Besterman writes:

> The individual, according to Druse philosophy, is made up of soul, spirit, and body, the last being usually referred to as *kamis,* shirt, to indicate its transitory and unessential nature. The union of these three elements forms a person. The soul passes successively into various bodies, thus forming a series of otherwise independent persons. . . .
>
> The strength of the belief is shown by the fact that in the form of the Druse oath, the swearer, amongst many other things, declares that if the oath is false he will be a "denier of the appearance of the Highest, who has appeared ten times in the form of mankind, and also a denier of the transmigration and transfer of the spirits. . . ."

Theodore Besterman remarks that the Druses even employed a reincarnation formula to enable them to recognize each other among strangers: "In a Druse catechism dating from A.D. 1012, in answer to the question how a brother is to be distinguished, the answer is given, 'By saying—"Man: do they grow the Thlilij (myrobalan tree) in your country?" If his answer be, "Yes, it is planted in the hearts of the believers," he is therefore one of us. Then we are to present to him two earthen water bottles, the one full and the other empty. If he pours the water from the full one into the empty bottle then he is certainly one of us, because by this he acknowledges the transmigration of souls, as the water is poured out from one vessel into another.' . . . . Today the doctrine is held as strongly as ever, and with little change."[21]]

LATER CHRISTIAN

The Rebirth of Preexistence and Reincarnation

[The door that was shut by the anathemas against preexistence in A.D. 553, and later by the extermination of the Cathars and Albigenses, was reopened prior to the Renaissance when Platonic philosophy was reborn. (That story will be saved for chapter 5.[1]) Here we will discuss only certain subsequent religious aspects.

"The pre-existence of the soul, whether taught by Pythagoras, sung by Empedocles, dreamed by Fludd, or contended for by Beecher is the principal foundation of the belief in metempsychosis." Thus writes the Reverend William R. Alger in *A Critical History of the Doctrine of a Future Life*.[2] From the seventeenth century onward, many ministers and religious writers taught preexistence. However, they usually confined the soul's incarnation to one earthly visit, to be followed by an eternal stay in heaven. In *Reincarnation, An East-West Anthology* a number of these writers were quoted,[3] but in the present work Chevalier Ramsay and Sir Thomas Browne are the sole representatives of this school of thought.

As applied to men generally, two reasons made the teaching of preexistence popular: first, as David Hume and many philosophers before and after him have pointed out, only the beginningless can be endless; a soul created in time must end in time. The *Britannica* therefore calls preexistence "the natural correlative of a belief in immortality."[4] Second, preexistence explains "original sin," and thus exonerates deity of the crime of supposedly cursing all the generations after Adam simply because Adam ate of the forbidden fruit.

However, a little thought will reveal that those who believe in immortality but deny a special creation of souls at birth come very close to reincarnation thinking. Wherever the soul existed previously it must have had some vesture through which to manifest its powers and communicate with others. On earth it acquires a body of flesh. In the afterlife it must there, too, have its appropriate vehicle. Therefore, as McTaggart states, "A belief in preexistence and post-existence is itself a belief in a plurality of lives, since it is a belief in three at least."[5]

The question at issue then becomes: "*Where* is the soul to be reborn?" A farmer reaps his harvest in the field where he casts the seed. It is natural for souls to do likewise, says the reincarnationist. Saint Paul's words "As ye sow so shall ye reap" would then connote: "Where you sow and with whom you sow, there too shall you reap."

The reincarnationist further suggests that to allow human beings but one sojourn on an earth that has been evolving for millions of years and that affords almost illimitable opportunities for growth of intelligence, talents, and moral powers would be an inconceivable waste of valuable resources. Benjamin Franklin adds a significant point, using as his premise the idea of a personal creator as generally accepted in his day: "When I see nothing annihilated and not a drop of water wasted, I cannot suspect the annihilation of souls, or believe that [God] will suffer the daily waste of millions of minds ready made that now exist, and put himself to the continual trouble of making new ones. Thus, finding myself to exist in the world, I believe I shall, in some shape or other, always exist; and, with all the inconveniences human life is liable to, I shall not object to a new edition of mine, hoping, however, that the *errata* of the last may be corrected."[6] Kipling once wrote: "They will come back, come back again, as long as the red Earth rolls. He never wasted a leaf or a tree. Do you think He would squander souls?"[7]

Ministers and religious writers rarely consider such points because one very large objection to reincarnation obscures further thinking on the subject. Here is how a Christian writer explained the problem in *Teenage Religion* when replying to young people who expressed their conviction that we live many lives: "Reincarnation cannot be disproved; but it is open to the objection that it makes *this* life of less importance because it gives us further chances. We do not need to listen to a history lesson if we know we shall get the same thing tomorrow. And our conviction is that this life does matter, in a once-for-all kind of way."[8] How emotionally charged such discussions sometimes become is evident from this diary entry of a writer:

> Had a rather irritable telephone conversation with my parsonical friend. I said that Buddhism was more christian than Christianity; that in the end it promised salvation to all—it did not look on the multitudes as chaff to be burned eternally. He said that there had to be a certain urgency; that with endless lives in prospect, one would always put off making the effort until the next. I said that to hinge eternal salvation on one single, confused and handicapped lifetime seemed to me a diabolical idea. He didn't agree; he said that everyone had their chance in this life, and if they wouldn't take it, "well, you've had it." If this is orthodoxy, then may God save me from it.[9]

The parson's argument is an excellent one—but only when reincarnation is divorced from the law of retribution, or karma. The wages of procrastination are heavy enough within one life, and if human beings have future lives, the karma of postponing obligations is likely to be increasingly painful. Who would wish to start his next life plagued with unnecessary handicaps?

Speaking of reincarnation, C. S. Lewis says: "I believe that if a million chances were likely to do good, they would be given."[10] But what of cases in which they are not likely to do good? Some reincarnationists say that if despite the ever-increasing Karmic penalties an individual inflicts upon himself, he persists life after life in the path of either inertia or active evil he becomes a dropout, a failure in the school of earth life. The evolutionary ascent must some day recommence in a new world, reborn from the old, but at a low stage of human development. Out of such or similar considerations, Eastern thought joins Western religious teaching in placing supreme importance upon the NOW. NOW is the hour for decision. Deluded is he who is always thinking "tomorrow I will do better."

Buddha once handled the problem of procrastination in a rather startling fashion. It is told that upon meeting King Pasenadi of Kosali, the Buddha asked him this seemingly casual question: "What have you been doing recently?" The king replied: "Lord, I'm afraid I have been very busy lately.

My days have been filled with all kinds of things—none of them very serious or actually important, but I have been busy.'' The Buddha, however, seeing that ''busyness'' tends to serve as an excuse for inaction in important matters, told King Pasenadi the story of the moving mountain.

> ''Supposing,'' said the Buddha, ''that an overwhelming catastrophe were to strike the country, perhaps a violent break up of the earth's crust, causing mighty earthquakes and shifting the dominant mountain range slowly yet inevitably down to the sea, covering the plains and bringing death and destruction to all in its path. Faced with this total, terrible and inescapable disaster, what would you do?
> The King's reply was that he would accept the inevitable, have faith, make amends where he could for his past misdeeds and embrace death with a good heart while living righteously in the time he had left.
> ''And yet,'' said the Buddha, ''surely all reliable messengers carry the news that such a mountain is rolling remorselessly towards us for is not old-age and death approaching, and are not all barriers ineffective?''
> Wide-awake now, to the reality of life and death, King Pasenadi realized fully the fleeting nature of his existence, and saw just how important it was that time should not be wasted in trivial pursuits. . . . Posed with such a stark dilemma and seeing no possibility of escape, King Pasenadi dedicated himself once more to the wholehearted practice of the Dharma, certain that joy and peace could be obtained only by the development of wisdom and compassion.[11]

Thus, against the background of numerous incarnations, Buddha viewed each life as a precious opportunity, one that could never be duplicated, and depending upon how it is lived, shifted the future up or down, for good or ill. The proverb ''opportunity knocks but once'' could apply here. It never knocks again in exactly the same way; in the same psychological setting; in the same combination of circumstances and people.

Returning to the idea of preexistence in Christianity, some good cross-references are the verses previously quoted from the New Testament, wherein were demonstrated how often Christ spoke of having lived before. In the gospel of John (8:56–59), for example, the Hebrews were shown accusing Jesus of setting himself above Abraham. He replied: ''Your father Abraham rejoiced to see my day; and he saw it, and was glad.'' ''Then said the Jews unto him: Thou art not yet fifty years old, and hast thou seen Abraham? Jesus said unto them, verily, verily, I say unto you, Before Abraham was, I am.'' It was also shown that Saint Paul included ordinary humans as having preexisted with Christ. If Paul was right, then each individual could also say: ''Before Abraham was, I am.'' And does not Christ imply the same thing when in John 17:5 he is quoted as saying: ''Glorify thou me with thine own self with the glory which I had with thee before the world was.'']

※ ※ ※
Churchmen and Religious Writers

JOSEPH GLANVILL (1636–1680)
British Divine

[Joseph Glanvill, chaplain to King Charles II, was one of the leading lights of the movement known as "The Cambridge Platonists" (see chapter 5), although Glanvill himself was from Oxford. The extracts are from his *Lux Orientalis,* which bears the subtitle "An Inquiry into the Opinions of the Eastern Sages concerning the Praeexistence of Souls. Being a Key to Unlock the Grand Mysteries of Providence in Relation to Man's Sin and Misery."[12] Glanvill argues for rebirth as well as preexistence.]

Christ and His Apostles spoke and writ as the condition of the persons, with whom they dealt, administered occasion. . . . Therefore doubtless there were many noble theories which they could have made the world acquainted with. . . . Few speculative truths are delivered in Scripture but such as were called forth by the controversies of those times; and Pre-existence was none of them, it being the constant opinion of the Jews. . . .

Every soul brings a kind of sense with it into the world, whereby it tastes and relisheth what is suitable to its peculiar temper. . . . What can we conclude but that the soul itself is the immediate subject of all this variety and that it came prejudiced and prepossessed into this body with some implicit notions that it had learnt in another? To say that all this variety proceeds primarily from the mere temper of our bodies is methinks a very poor and unsatisfying account. For those that are the most like in the temper, air, and complexion of their bodies, are yet of a vastly differing genius. . . . What then can we conjecture is the cause of all this diversity, but that we had taken a great delight and pleasure in some things like and analogous unto these in a former condition?

CHEVALIER RAMSAY (1686–1743)
Scottish Author

[Coleridge's interest in reincarnation has been thought to stem, in part, from reading Chevalier Ramsay's *Philosophical Principles,* from which the selection below is taken. (See Index under "Coleridge.") The edition used is the 1748, Edinburgh one (II, pp. 236–46).]

The holy oracles always represent Paradise as our native country, and our present life as an exile. How can we be said to have been banished from a place in which we never were? This argument alone would suffice to convince us of pre-existence, if the prejudice of infancy inspired by the schoolmen had not accustomed us to look upon these expressions as metaphorical, and to believe, contrary to Scripture and to reason, that we were exiled from a happy state, only for the fault of our first parents. . . .

St. Paul seems to confirm this when he says: For the children being not yet born, having neither done good nor evil, it was said unto Rebecca, "Jacob have I loved, but Esau have I hated." [Romans 9:13.] God's love and hatred depend upon the moral dispositions of the creature. Since God says that he loved Jacob and hated Esau ere they were born, and before they had done good or evil in this mortal life, it follows clearly that they must have pre-existed in another state.

If it be said that these texts are obscure; that pre-existence is only drawn from them by induction, and that this opinion is not revealed in Scripture by express words, I answer, that the doctrines of the immortality of the soul are nowhere revealed expressly in the sacred oracles of the Old or New Testament, but because all their morals and doctrines are founded upon these great truths. We may say the same of pre-existence. The doctrine is nowhere expressly revealed, but it is evidently supposed, as without it original sin becomes not only inexplicable, but absurd, repugnant, and impossible.

JOHANN PETER HEBEL (1760–1826)
Swiss-born German Poet and Prelate

[From notes for a sermon at Karlsruhe where Johann Peter Hebel was prelate (published in Volume II of Hebel's works), the theme being "Have We Lived Before?":]

(a) Yes, it is possible; here or elsewhere. . . . We drank from Lethe's sweet bowl and a sweeter one, Mneme's [Memory's] is awaiting us. How much we forget in this life!

(b) Multiplicity of experience; wisdom is the fruit of experience; but how little one life has to offer!

(c) And have we really no memories at all? Do we not observe: easy developments, certain talents. What if we had possessed those once before? . . . Inexplicable sympathy. Preference for the history of special periods, men, countrysides. Have we been there before . . .?

(d) How attractive the thought: I have lived in the period of the mammoths, the patriarchs, have been an Arcadian herdsman, a Greek adventurer, partaken in Hermann's battle. . . .

Some day, having drunk from the golden cup of Mneme, having finished with many wanderings, preserved my "I" through so many forms and conditions, become acquainted with joys and sorrows, and purified through both; what memories, what bliss, what gain!

FRIEDRICH SCHLEIERMACHER (1768–1834)
German Theologian and Philosopher

[Of his *Reden über Die Religion* ("Talks on Religion"), published in 1799, it is said the whole Western world sat up and took notice, although Friedrich Schleiermacher was then a relatively unknown chaplain. He became a major reformer of Protestant theology, and eventually one of the greatest theologians of the Evangelical Church. His *Talks on Religion* are classics of theological as well as German literature. Quoting from the Second Talk:]

History, in its essential meaning, is the highest aspect of religion. . . . For here you observe the return of Spirits and Souls ordinarily regarded as mere tender, poetic imaginings. In more than one sense we have [in this conception of metempsychosis] a wonderful arrangement of the universe, enabling us to compare the different periods of mankind on the basis of a reliable measure. For after a long interval, during which nature could not produce anything comparable, an excellent individual will return, recognized only by the Seers, and from the effect this individual produces they alone can judge the signs of the different cycles. A single moment of mankind's history will return, and from the various causes leading thereto, you shall discern the course of the universe and the formula of its laws. A genius . . . will awaken from his slumber, appearing on a new scene. His speedier growth, his broader exertions, his more beautiful and powerful body, shall then indicate by how much the climate of mankind has improved, and is better adapted to the nourishing of noble growths.

CYRUS AUGUSTUS BARTOL (1813–1900)
Unitarian Minister and American Transcendentalist

[From Reverend Cyrus Augustus Bartol's *The Rising Faith:*]

In some sense, I was born and must die. In some sense, my dwelling holds me; your babe is in the crib, and your sires in the tomb. But there is an I, by which all these contents and consignments are disallowed. Before Abraham was, I am [John 8:58]; *I have power to lay down my life and power to take it up again.* I am conscious of Eternal Generation, that I am what never lay in the cradle and no coffin can hold, but sits behind smiling at what was brought forth and expires.[13]

ARCHBISHOP PASSAVALLI (1820–1897)

Italian Prelate

[Wincenty Lutoslawski, a noted Platonic scholar and former professor of philosophy at the University of Wilno, Poland, wrote in *Pre-Existence and Reincarnation:*]

For those who are interested in the relation of the Church to the dogma of palingenesis, an Italian book, published in 1911, is of the greatest importance: *Monsignor Arcivescovo L. Puecher Passavalli,* [by] Attilio Begey e Allessandro Favero.[14] Here we find the life and letters of a pious and learned Roman Catholic archbishop who at the age of sixty-four accepted the truth of pre-existence and reincarnation from two disciples of the Polish seer Towianski, namely Stanislaw Falkowski and Tancredi Canonico. Archbishop Passavalli admitted that reincarnation is not condemned by the Church, and that it is not at all in conflict with any Catholic dogma. . . . He lived up to the age of seventy-seven, unshaken in his conviction that he had already lived many times on earth and that he was likely to return.[15] [He remained archbishop until his death.]

Another Catholic priest, who also after long discussion gave up the prejudice against reincarnation . . . was Edward Dunski, whose *Letters,* edited by Attilio Begey and Jozef Komenda, were published by Bona in Torino in 1915. Many other priests in Poland and Italy believe in reincarnation, being influenced by the great mystic Andrzej Towianski (1799–1878) whose works were printed privately in three large volumes at Torino in 1882.[16]

WILLIAM R. ALGER (1822–1905)

American Minister and Scholar

[To appreciate William R. Alger's remarks on reincarnation, the following background information from E. D. Walker's *Reincarnation, A Study of Forgotten Truth* (p. 100) is of particular importance:

> The noblest work of modern times, and probably of all time, upon immortality, is a large volume by the Rev. William R. Alger, entitled ''A Critical History of the Doctrine of a Future Life.''[17] It was published in 1860 and still remains [1888] the standard authority upon that topic throughout Christendom. . . . The author is a Unitarian minister, who devoted half his lifetime to the work, undermining his health thereby. In the first edition (1860) the writer characterizes reincarnation as a plausible delusion, unworthy of credence. For fifteen years more he continued studying the subject, and the latest edition (1878) gives the final result of his ripest investigations in heartily endorsing and advocating reincarnation. . . . That a Christian clergyman, making the problem of the

soul's destiny his life's study, should become so overpowered by the force of this pagan idea as to adopt it for the climax of his scholarship is extremely significant.

A few extracts will suffice here; others may be found elsewhere in our book.]

The argument [for reincarnation] from analogy is especially strong. It is natural to argue from the universal spectacle of incarnated life that this is the eternal scheme everywhere, the variety of souls finding in the variety of worlds an everlasting series of adventures in appropriate organisms.

It must be confessed that of all the thoughtful and refined forms of the belief in a future life none has had so extensive and prolonged prevalence as this. It has the vote of the majority, having for ages on ages been held by half the human race with an intensity of conviction almost without a parallel. Indeed, the most striking fact at first sight about the doctrine of the repeated incarnations of the soul . . . is the constant reappearance of the faith in all parts of the world, and its permanent hold on certain great nations. . . .

It is not propounded with the slightest dogmatic animus. It is advanced solely as an illustraton of what may possibly be true, as suggested by the general evidence of the phenomena of history and the facts of experience. The thoughts embodied in it are so wonderful, the method of it so rational, the region of contemplation into which it lifts the mind is so grand, the prospects it opens are of such universal reach and import, that the study of it brings us into full sympathy with the sublime scope of the idea of immortality, and of a cosmopolitan vindication of providence uncovered to every eye. It takes us out of the littleness of petty themes and selfish affairs, and makes it easier for us to believe in the vastest hopes mankind has ever known.[18]

WILLIAM J. POTTER (1830–1893)
Unitarian Minister

[From Reverend William J. Potter's article in *The Radical* for April 1868 entitled "The Doctrine of Pre-Existence and the Fourth Gospel":]

It is possible, perhaps probable, that the soul will always have some form of body and some material limitation . . . now taking this form, now that—yet always ascending in form as giving larger freedom of nature . . . as the scale of being ascends. But over and above all change, independent of all limitations of time and matter, beyond the reach of the accidental and fluctuating relations of individual existence, there enters into human nature another factor by which it lays hold of a substance that is Infinite and Everlasting, and draws its being therefrom. There is somewhat of the absolute and eternal in every human soul . . . something that transcends time and space and organic form, and makes eternity for the soul to be the continuous unfolding of a perpetual and indestructible principle of life rather than the infinite multiplications of days and years.

CARDINAL MERCIER (1851–1926)

Belgian Cardinal and Scholastic Philosopher

[From Cardinal Mercier's *Psychologie:*]

Under the term *Wiedermenschwerdung,* metempsychosis, or the transmigration of souls, a great variety of ideas may be understood: either a series of repetitions of existence under the twofold condition that the soul maintains consciousness of its personality and that there is a final unit in the series of transmigrations; or a series of repetitions of existence without any final unit, and yet with the presupposition that the soul maintains consciousness of its personality; or, finally, an endless series of repetitions of existence with the loss of consciousness of personal identity. . . . So far as concerns the first assumption, we do not see that reason, if left to itself, would declare this to be impossible or certainly false.[19]

RICHARD WILHELM (1873–1930)

German Theologian

[From an article entitled "Reincarnation," by Richard Wilhelm, who became a missionary, an orientalist, and later collaborated with C. G. Jung:]

Let us consider what attitude to take toward this idea. In the first place we must insist that, from the viewpoint of Christianity, it is absolutely feasible. Christianity, it is true, lays stress only on the law of Karma, though it remains silent as to the working of its operations; looking only to its ultimate consummation, it does not touch upon the intervening stages. . . .

Unprejudiced observation and reasonable reflection lead us to the conviction that this law [of Karma] actually exists. However, in one life, bounded by birth and death, we can only experience a part of the whole of existence. We live through certain occurrences in which one tangled skein of Karmic effects is unraveled, while at the same time new threads of Karma are spun that cannot be worked out in this life, because their disentanglement is cut short by death. On the other hand we see results come to fruition, the causes of which are not to be found in this life. These are the great problems with which a Job battles, and to which—in spite of all faith in a hereafter—only the words "and yet?" of the Psalmist must be uttered, if the Wisdom of the East is not called to our aid. And so it is easy to understand that many of our deepest and clearest thinkers, as for instance Lessing and Goethe, look upon reincarnation as a theory well worthy of consideration. . . . .

The following is an important point: heredity evidently plays a part in the life of man, but does not adequately account for every phase of the question. Children of the same parents, in spite of family likenesses, show entirely different traits of character that cannot be accounted for by heredity alone. Indeed, the fact is irrefutable that in one and the same family more and less advanced souls are born. It is Karmic law undoubtedly that plays the most decisive part.[20]

NICOLAS BERDYAEV (1874–1948)

Russian Christian Philosopher

[The translated selection that follows is from an essay of Nicolas Berdyaev's that appeared in *Pereselienye Doosh* (Transmigration of Souls).[21] The volume bears the subtitle, "The Problem of Immortality in Occultism and Christianity." It contains the usual pro and con reincarnation arguments, presented by such well-known Russian writers as Father O. Boulgakov, B. Vysheslavtshev, B. B. Zenkovsky, O. G. Florovsky, and S. Frank. Berdyaev's essay is "The Teaching of Reincarnation and the Problem of Man."]

The popularity of Theosophy and Anthroposophy is due precisely to the teaching of reincarnation. And the weakness and unreasonableness of theologic teachings concerning the genesis of the soul and its final destiny are responsible for this popularity. It is difficult to reconcile oneself to the traditional teaching according to which the soul is created at the moment of conception and at this moment the primordial sin is communicated as if it were a communicable disease. Also it is difficult to accept the other teaching, according to which the soul is a product of a hereditary process and receives the primordial sin as it would receive an hereditary disease. Neither of these teachings . . . supply any justification whatsoever for human sufferings and the injustices of individual destiny. But most intolerable is the teaching of eternal suffering in Hell. . . . Any attempt to construct a sensible teaching about Hell awakens moral protest. . . .

The teaching of reincarnation is simple. It makes rational the mystery of human destiny and . . . reconciles man to the [apparent] unjust and incomprehensible sufferings of life . . . man stops comparing his destiny with the happier destiny of other people and accepts it.

ALBERT SCHWEITZER (1875–1965)

Physician, Clergyman, Musician

[From Albert Schweitzer's *Indian Thought and Its Development:*]

The idea of reincarnation contains a most comforting explanation of reality by means of which Indian thought surmounts difficulties which baffle the thinkers of Europe. . . . By reason of the idea of reincarnation Indian thought can be reconciled to the fact that so many people in their minds and actions are still so engrossed in the world. If we assume that we have but one existence, there arises the insoluble problem of what becomes of the spiritual ego which has lost all contact with the Eternal. Those who hold the doctrine of reincarnation are faced by no such problem. For them that non-spiritual attitude only means that those men and women have not yet attained to the purified form of existence in which they are capable of knowing the truth and translating it into action.[22]

[Schweitzer says that in India "the fear of reincarnation no longer plays the part it did in the Buddha's time." "Union with God is again striven after for its own sake" and thus the importance "of the doctrine of reincarnation is shaken." Up to the modern era "ethics were only considered in relation to reincarnation. By right action one could only attain to a better reincarnation, not to union with God." Schweitzer's acquaintance with the basic scriptures of Hinduism may have been rather limited. The great sages of the Orient showed that rebirth was the very *means* of attaining an ever-increasing oneness with Deity, the One Universal SELF. Such self-realization was regarded as a stupendous achievement. Consequently, one brief existence was hardly sufficient to attain it. In the *Bhagavad-Gita,* Krishna declares: "The devotee who, striving with all his might, obtaineth perfection because of efforts continued through many births, goeth to the supreme goal" (chapter 6).

As to the "fear of reincarnation," Schweitzer may have had in mind the distortions the doctrine underwent at the hands of the "higher" castes to keep the "lower" ones in line. As indicated earlier, rigid caste rules become easier to impose when accompanied by threats that violations will be punished by incarnation as an untouchable, an insect, or an animal!]

[In an article appearing in the Schweitzer memorial issue of *The Saturday Review,* Emory Ross wrote:]

In 1959 Robert Hutchins persuaded Albert Schweitzer to come to America. Many had tried previously, with no success. But the Goethe bicentennial commemoration that Hutchins and his colleagues were planning at Aspen, Colorado, won his consent. He and his wife came by ship, and my wife and I went to meet them when they docked. Sixty-five men and women of the American and world press, radio, and television were also there, pencils and cameras poised. The first thing Schweitzer did was to bow deeply and say in French, "Ladies and gentlemen, in my youth I was a stupid young man. I learned German and French, Latin, Greek, Hebrew—but no English. In my next incarnation, English shall be my first language."[23]

ARTHUR P. SHEPHERD (1885–1968)

Canon of Worcester Cathedral, England

[From Dr. Arthur P. Shepherd's lecture "Christ and the Modern Man":]

If we take into our unprejudiced thinking the picture of reincarnation as the process of human evolution, we shall find in it the answer to the problems of the new world situation. . . . So too, the vast picture of the meaningless masses and movements of the [starry] nebulae resolves itself into a universe of spirit beings, in infinite creative relationships to one another and to man. The perplexity of history, with its procession of rising and falling civilizations, is seen as mankind's pilgrimage of spiritual descent and ascent, in which we all have taken part, and in which recurring individual reincarnation is the principle of unification and progress. So too, the apparent inadequacy of a single earth life, or its bondage to physical or mental or moral or circumstantial deficiency, is given new hope and understanding in the realization of the process of reincarnation.

Finally, there is the certainty that in all this man has never been alone. The Christ, whose earthly incarnation the Gospels declare to us, has always shepherded man's path of evolution, and since his descent into our earthly life He is always with us, to be found by those who seek Him.[24]

LESLIE D. WEATHERHEAD (1893–1976)

British Clergyman and Author

[We quote first from an article called "Leslie Weatherhead . . . A Bit of a Saint." Dr. Weatherhead, "a former president of the Methodist Conference of Great Britain, was minister of London's historic City Temple—'the cathedral of nonconformism'—for 28 years until his retirement in 1960. In a country where fewer than 10 percent regularly attend church, it was standing room only at The City Temple during the Weatherhead ministry. . . . He is a genuine intellectual, a Ph.D. in psychology, whose 37 books have sold over a half-million copies. [He] was a pioneer in the area of pastoral psychology. Nearly 30 years ago he set up a religio-psychological clinic which combined the insights of faith and psychiatry to help disturbed people."[25]

The extracts below are from Dr. Weatherhead's lecture "The Case for Reincarnation," delivered at the opening session of the 1957–1958 season of the City Temple Literary Society, of which he was then president. The lecture has been published in pamphlet form, some fifty thousand copies being now in print.[26]]

The intelligent Christian asks not only that life should be just, but that it shall make sense. Does the idea of reincarnation help here? I think it does.

Let us suppose that a very depraved or entirely materialistic person dies. Let us suppose that from a religious point of view he has entirely misused his earth-life. Will his translation to a spiritual plane do all that needs doing? Will it not be like putting a person who has never given himself any chance to understand music, into an everlasting concert . . . ? Can a man who has entirely neglected spiritual things be happy in a spiritual environment? If you say, "Oh well, he can learn in the next phase"—can he? Doesn't such a speculation make the earth-life meaningless? . . . I don't think we shall be able to skip the examinations of life like that. It would be as incongruous and unsound as telling a medical student who failed his qualifying examination, not to bother, but to go on treating people as if he had qualified. If I fail to pass those examinations in life which can only be taken while I dwell in a physical body, shall I not have to come back and take them again? . . .

If every birth in the world is the birth of a new soul, I don't see how progress can ever be consummated. Each has to begin at scratch. . . . How then can there be progress in the innermost things of the heart? We can pass on some wisdom and, in outward circumstance, those who follow us can in some ways go on where we left off. They will not have to re-discover electricity or atomic energy. But they *will* have to discover, for example, each for himself, the vital supremacy of love. Each child is born a selfish little animal . . . not able in character to begin where the most saintly parent left off. . . . How can a world progress in inner things—which are the most important—if the birth of every new generation fills the world with unregenerate souls full of original sin? There can never be a perfect world unless gradually those born into it can take advantage of lessons learned in earlier lives instead of starting at scratch.

[In the chapter "Reincarnation and Renewed Chances" in Dr. Weatherhead's *The Christian Agnostic,* he considers this familiar argument:]

"But," says the objector, "I should lose my identity in a number of incarnations." I don't think you will, any more than you have lost it already half a dozen times. You are William Tompkins, let us suppose. All right. You are the little, runny-nosed Willie Tompkins who got punished for being late at school. Do you want to keep your identity with him? You are the Will Tompkins who wrote those wet verses and slipped them into the hand of that girl of sixteen with blonde plaits. Do you want to assert your identity with him? You are the William Tompkins who got sacked for being unable to account for money received on behalf of the firm. Do you feel robbed if he passes out of your sense of identity? You are W. Tompkins, with rheumatic joints and poor hearing and peering sight, whose body is now a nuisance. Try this experiment: Say "William Tompkins, William Tompkins, William Tompkins" over to yourself aloud a hundred times. Imagine a hundred

thousand angels all round you doing the same thing. . . . Is it really important that the whole personality of Tompkins should go on for a hundred, a
thousand, ten thousand, a hundred thousand years? Still William
Tompkins . . . !

Our true identity will not be lost, the pure gold of the ego will be maintained, purified, and strengthened. But why this emphasis on separateness?
. . . We may lose our separateness in a new context of closer relationship
. . . I don't want to be one note sounding on alone. . . . If I could be one
note in a glorious symphony, would it not be well for separateness to be lost
in symphony?[27]

✳

In our consideration of religion, we have yet to investigate the beliefs in
rebirth of so-called tribal peoples around the world, including the peoples
who lived in Europe prior to the advent of Christianity. This is the subject of
the next chapter.

Reincarnation Among the Early Races

Transmigration, dating back to a remote antiquity, and being spread all over the world, seems to be anthropologically innate, and to be the first form in which the idea of immortality occurred to man.

> M'Clintock and Strong's Cyclopaedia of
> Biblical, Theological and Ecclesiastical Literature

Rebirth [in its various forms of reincarnation, resurrection, and transformation] is an affirmation that must be counted among the primordial affirmations of mankind.

> C. G. JUNG
> *"Concerning Rebirth"*

Fresh Approaches to "Primitive" Man

[A remarkable change has taken place in the study of the myths, religions, and symbolisms of tribal peoples around the world. Gone is the Victorian's simple, nineteenth-century faith in his own racial, moral, and cultural superiority, and in the so-called comparative method that was the application of these standards outside their legitimate context. Limited by this parochial outlook, the renowned author of *The Golden Bough,* Sir James Frazer, "in some 20,000 pages, had discovered how all the thoughts, imaginings and yearnings of archaic man, all his myths and rites, all his gods and religious experiences, are only a monstrous mass of beastliness, cruelty and superstition, happily abolished by scientific human progress." Thus speaks one of

187

the most distinguished contemporary scholars, Professor Mircea Eliade.[1] Another eminent scholar, Lord Raglan, a past president of the Royal Anthropological Institute, adds that "the 'primitive man' of Frazer" was "always asking himself questions and giving himself the wrong answers." The word "primitive," this authority remarks, "has led to more muddled thinking than all the other words in the dictionary put together." It should be banished from our vocabulary.[2]

Whatever the intellectual and cultural confinements of his time, Frazer was inevitably impressed by the prevalence of belief in some form of reincarnation. "However it has been arrived at," he wrote, "this doctrine of the transmigration or reincarnation of the soul is found among many tribes of savages; and from what we know on the subject we seem to be justified in conjecturing that at certain stages of mental and social evolution the belief in metempsychosis has been far commoner and has exercised a far deeper influence on the life and institutions of primitive man than the actual evidence before us at present allows us positively to affirm."[3] Since Frazer's time a great amount of additional evidence has been unearthed to support his conclusion.

Our chapter heading "Reincarnation among the Early Races" should perhaps more accurately read "Reincarnation among the *Remnants* of the Early Races." Owing to new discoveries each year, man's antiquity is being pushed further and further back in time so that what is called the prehistoric period now runs into millions of years. Consequently, our study must concern itself with the thoughts of ancient man as passed on to his descendants.

The following works and others cited in this chapter provide evidence that the peoples listed in the various subsections believe in some form of reincarnation.

Edward Tylor, *Primitive Culture*. London, 1871, II, Chapter 12; 2nd edition, 1873, reprinted as *Religion in Primitive Culture,* Harper Torchbook, 1958.
J. G. Frazer, *The Golden Bough,* unabridged edition; *The Belief in Immortality and the Worship of the Dead,* I, Australia, New Guinea and Melanesia (Gifford Lectures, 1911–1913); II, Polynesians.
Encyclopaedia of Religion and Ethics, editor, James Hastings, article, "Transmigration," XII, pp. 425–529. Original British edition reprinted in 1955 by Scribner's, New York.
Encyclopaedia Britannica, 1959 edition, article, "Metempsychosis."]

Africans

["In tropical Africa, belief in rebirth is deeply enrooted. The studies made by anthropologists and other serious writers in many different parts of Africa, especially in the last forty years, have revealed deep-seated beliefs in reincarnation held by many different African peoples." Thus writes E. G. Parrinder, author of *African Traditional Religion, West African Psychology,* and similar volumes. Dr. Parrinder continues:

> Reincarnation, to most Africans, is a good thing. It is a return to this sunlit world for a further period of invigorating life. There is little idea of an end to the number of incarnations, or a search for that as desirable. . . . On the contrary, it is bad not to be reborn, and childlessness is a great curse because it blocks the channel of rebirth. Hence the great attention devoted to fertility and the continuing popularity of polygamy, for the ancestor is only reincarnated in his own family. . . . It is a common practice for the diviner to be called in at the birth of a child to declare which ancestor is reincarnated, and family resemblances are explained as due to use of the same soul-stuff. . . .
>
> Various phrases are used to describe reincarnation. One West African people calls it "the shooting forth of a branch," and another "a recurring cycle." In the latter case the same word is used to describe a vine which twines round a post, reappearing continually higher up.[4]

Edward Tylor, regarded as the father of anthropology, states in *Primitive Culture* that the Yorubas of West Africa, "greeting a new-born infant with the salutation, 'Thou art come!' look for signs to show what ancestral soul has returned among them." An article by K. Brakatu Ateko, a native of Ghana, outlines four main beliefs:

> I. *God* A maxim says Obi Nkyere abofra Nyame, literally, No one teaches a child God. Over and above the tutelary, tribal and family gods and goddesses is the Supreme Being to whom no sacrifices are made. . . . It is crystal clear that the African conception of the High God is not of recent growth. . . .
>
> II. *Karma* There are proverbs which illustrate this law: (1) When Mr. Lizard eats pepper, it is he who perspires and not Mrs. Lizard. (2) When Akosua commits evil, Akua is not punished.
>
> III. *Reincarnation* The Yoruba and the Edo-speaking tribes, among whom I sojourned as a teacher half a century ago, have a strong belief in reincarnation. At that period the white man's influence had not affected the beliefs and the ways of life of the hinterlands of Nigeria. The Yorubas, for instance, name a boy Babatunde, meaning "Father has returned," and the girl, Yetunde (Iyantude) signifying "Mother has returned." In Ghana, the name Ababio "he has come again," carries the same meaning.
>
> IV. *Death* Our traditional philosophy of death was grander than that acquired in the wake of Christianity. Death was not looked upon as an enemy to be feared and propitiated. If one died, he was believed to have been born on the other side of the veil and vice versa in the case of birth in our world.[5]

Writing of the Ba-ila of Rhodesia, Edwin Smith remarks in *Knowing the African:* "My only friend Mungalo now sitting smoking his pipe with me, or sitting yonder under the eaves of his hut and carving a wooden spoon, is the

Mungalo who lived here a hundred years ago and, furthermore, Mungalo is his musedi, his guardian spirit, shall we say, always accompanying him, guarding him, warning him of danger.''[6]

Interesting tales of rebirth are told by Mrs. D. Amaury Talbot concerning the Ibibios of southern Nigeria.[7] She comments regarding their culture: "Fragments of legend and half-forgotten ritual still survive to tell of times shrouded in the mists of antiquity, when the despised Ibibio of today was a different being, dwelling not amid the fog and swamp of fetishism, but upon the sunlit heights of a religious culture hardly less highly evolved perhaps than that of Ancient Egypt.''[8] ''Africans and their descendants may well be proud of their past,'' adds a writer in the *New Yorker* (August 6, 1963). ''The great empires of Ghana, Mali, and Songhai and the powerful kingdoms of Ashanti, Ife, and Benin all flourished centuries before the Europeans arrived in Africa. Timbuktu, in Mali, formerly the Sudan, was a seat of advanced learning in the fifteenth century; the records of the old university are still there.'' Janheinz Jahn in *Munti—The New African Culture* says that ''the Africans' zeal for learning, which so delights the educators, is not the zeal of an illiterate people, to whom writing comes as a revelation. It is the zeal for learning of a civilized people whose own script has been destroyed and who therefore need a new medium for communicating and preserving information.''[9]

The African groups who believe in many lives are too numerous to list here. Theodore Besterman summarizes the beliefs in rebirth of over one hundred tribes, his survey including all parts of Africa and the island of Madagascar. Thirty-six tribes believe that human beings come back as humans; forty-seven believe human beings come back as animals; twelve accept either possibility. The more civilized cultures tend to fall into the first category. Tylor gives this explanation of the belief in ''transmigration'':[10]

> As it seems that the first conception of souls may have been that of the souls of men, this being afterwards extended by analogy to the souls of animals, plants, etc., so it may seem that the original idea of transmigration was the straightforward and reasonable one of human souls being reborn in new human bodies, where they were recognized by family likenesses in successive generations. This notion may have been afterwards extended to take in rebirth in bodies of animals. . . . The half-human features and actions and characters of animals are watched with wondering sympathy by the savage, as by the child. The beast is the very incarnation of familiar qualities of man; and such names as lion, bear, fox, owl, parrot, viper, worm, when we apply them as epithets to men, condense into a word some leading feature of a human life. Consistently with this, we see in looking over details of savage transmigration that the creatures often have an evident fitness to the character of the human beings whose souls are to pass into them, so that the savage philosopher's fancy of transferred souls offered something like an explanation of the likeness between beast and man.[11]

Radhakrishnan thinks that the Hindu idea of regression into animal forms "may have been derived from the beliefs of the aboriginal tribes," when the ancient Aryans descended into the Indian peninsula from their original home in northern Asia.[12] But another reason for such beliefs may derive from a misunderstanding of ideas concerning the purgatorial state immediately after death. According to Hinduism and other religions, the passionate animal nature is there thrown off, releasing the purified soul to rise to a heavenly condition. Swedenborg and other seers have claimed to see newly departed humans assuming for a time the likeness of animals that corresponded to their earthy nature. In this connection we quote from a remarkable article by Patrick Bowen who lived in Africa for many years:

As a boy, ten or twelve years of age, following my father's wagon through the wild Bushlands of the Northern Transvaal, I gained the friendship of many *Isanusi* (Wise Men) of the Zulus. One of these, Mankanyezi ("the Starry One") said to me, "Within the body is a soul; within the soul is a spark of the *Itongo*, the Universal Spirit. After the death of the body, *Idhlozi* (the soul) hovers for a while near the body, and then departs to *Esil-weni*, the Places of Beasts. This is very different from entering the body of a beast. In *Esilweni*, the soul assumes a shape, part beast and part human. . . . After a period, long or short, according to the strength of the animal nature, the soul throws aside its beast-like shape, and moves onward to—a place of rest. There it sleeps, till a time comes when it *dreams* that something to do and learn awaits it on earth; then it awakes, and returns, through the Place of Beasts, to the earth, and is born again as a child. Again and again does the soul travel thus, till at last the man becomes true Man, and his soul, when the body dies, becomes one with the *Itongo*, whence it came."[13]

When Bowen was older, Mankanyezi told him of a society to which he belonged, "whose members are the guardians of the *Wisdom-which-comes-from-of-old;* they are of many ranks, from learner to Master, and Higher Ones whose names may not be spoken; and there is one member at least in every tribe and nation throughout this great land" of Africa. "The Brotherhood is called, in the ancient Bantu speech, *Bonabakulu abase-Khemu,* i.e., *The Brotherhood of the Higher Ones of Egypt.* (Khem, whence 'Chem-istry,' was an ancient name of Egypt.) It was founded by a Priest of Isis in the reign of the Pharaoh Cheops, to spread *The Wisdom which comes from of Old,* among all races and tribes of Africa . . ." "The grades of the Brotherhood are: (1) the Pupil, (2) the Disciple, (3) the Brother, (4) the Elder, (5) the Master, (6) Those who Know *(Isangoma),* (7) *Abakulu-bantu,* i.e., Perfect Men, for whom rebirth has ceased, who dwell on earth in physical form by their own will, and can retain or relinquish that form as they choose."]

Australians

[Baldwin Spencer and F. J. Gillen affirm in *Northern Tribes of Central Australia:* "In every tribe without exception there exists a firm belief in the reincarnation of ancestors. Emphasis must be laid on the fact that this belief is not confined to tribes such as the Arunta, Warramunga, Binbinga, Anula, and others, amongst whom descent is counted on the male line, but is found just as strongly developed in the Urabunna tribe, in which descent, both of class and totem, is strictly maternal."[14]

Frazer commends the researches of Spencer and Gillen, and remarks: "We naturally ask . . . whether the belief in reincarnation of the dead, which prevails universally among the Central tribes, reappears among the tribes in other parts of the continent. It certainly does so, and although the evidence on this subject is very imperfect it suffices to raise a presumption that a similar belief in the rebirth or reincarnation of the dead was formerly universal among the Australian aborigines."[15] This seems particularly interesting, because scientists have suggested that the Australian native—coexisting as he does with an archaic fauna and flora to be found practically nowhere else on the globe—probably dates back to an enormous antiquity. Commenting on the religion and mythology of the tribes, Gerland writes: "The statement that the Australian civilization indicates a [previous] higher grade, is nowhere more clearly proved than here, where everything resounds like the expiring voices of a previous and richer age."[16]

James Bonwick in *The Wild White Man and the Blacks of Victoria* tells how the life of an escaped white convict "was saved because he was believed to be the embodied spirit of a deceased friend of the tribe. . . . 'They certainly entertain the idea that after death they will again exist in the form of white men.'" Bonwick comments that "it is not without consolation to the savage, for when one was being executed in Melbourne he exclaimed, 'Very good—me jump up Whitefellow.'"[17]]

Pacific Islanders and East Indians

[In the vast area of the Pacific and East Indian islands, many peoples believe in some form of reincarnation. In the South Pacific they include the New Zealand Maoris, the Tasmanians, Tahitians, Fijians, Solomon Islanders, Marquesans, tribes of New Caledonia, and the Melanesians generally. In the East Indies there are the Balinese, the Bakongs and Dyaks of Borneo, the

Papuans of New Guinea, and the Poso-Alfures of Celebes. The Okinawans and perhaps others in that area represent the North Pacific.

During the Second World War, an American soldier interviewed the former chief librarian of the Okinawan Prefecture concerning the religious views of his people. The librarian, Shimabuku Zenpastu, stated that "according to the Okinawan God-idea, Deity is without shape and sexless. . . . The majority of Okinawans believe in Reincarnation, i.e., that the human being has a spirit which leaves his body at death and returns to earth in a new-born babe. This spirit can not occupy an animal body." The soldier reported:

> The original Okinawan belief is this: After a man's death, the spirit stays in his home for 49 days; on the 49th day, when the memorial services are complete, the spirit enters Gusho—"after this present world." The period in the after-death state varies, but the Okinawans believe that the spirit will return within seven generations, producing an individual who strongly resembles its former embodiment. Not all spirits reincarnate. Some remain in *Gusho* indefinitely, and will greet new arrivals in that state. It should be understood that the Okinawan conception of *Gusho* is a spiritual state, where only the spirit of man exists. . . . Not mind, but *spirit,* reincarnates . . . mind being received by the individual through ancestral descent.[18]

Time reports that a United States Navy psychiatrist has discovered that the psychic health of the Okinawans is superior to most other people. Of five hundred natives subjected to terrible bombardment—"a nerve-shattering ordeal that drove many a Jap to suicide and many a G.I. into the mental ward"—only one became mentally unstable. The early training of the Okinawan child, the psychiatrist said, is such that by the time he is five, "he has such a sense of security that his mental foundation is sturdy enough to survive catastrophe."[19]

This bears on the question of whether a person's conviction of reincarnation can contribute to his mental stability. Anthropologist Margaret Mead in *Male and Female* indicates how her own mind works in doing research along these lines:

> If reincarnation seems relevant, I may think over the cultures known to have a belief in reincarnation, and then may add, "Of course it will be interesting to see what is the relationship between who you are when you are born and who you will be when you die." This may lead to comparing Esquimo and Balinese [who both accept reincarnation]; among both peoples infants are treated as having prophetic powers at birth, and in both of them children learn complex skills early. I may add a question here, "Is the relationship between learning and a theory of birth and immortality perhaps a key point?" and then compare the Balinese position—in which the individual is reincarnated over and over in the same family, so that the life-cycle . . . merely completes one of an endless set of circles between this world and the other—and the Manus position, where

human beings are originally built from material from fathers' and mothers' bodies, reach their full powers at maturity, survive a little as strong ghosts immediately after death and then dribble off into lower and lower levels of sea-slugs and slime.

Then I may say: "The Balinese believe you can learn at any age—the very young and the old learn with great relative effortlessness, beauty lasts into old age—while among the Manus, people are finished at forty. Perhaps we may suggest that there is a relationship here which it would be worth while to explore further." From there I may go on to consider whether I know any instances of a group who believe in reincarnation but also have a sharply marked decline in vigor during the life-span—thus looking for negative instances to disprove my developing hypothesis.

"At the same time," Dr. Mead continues, "I will be running over in my mind what we know about learning at different ages in different cultures. . . . Or I may turn back to two ethnological categories, like 'belief in reincarnation' and 'life-cycle,' in which case it would be possible to go up to Yale University and pull out a card catalogue in which material on a great many societies has been arranged in such categories, so that it is possible to see how the two things fit together."[20]

Related to these possibilities is the joyous way in which the happy and friendly Balinese regard death. According to a *New York Times* writer:

"If you are lucky you may also observe a cremation . . ." That's what a guidebook on Bali may say. Westerners may shudder at the thought. But the Balinese—who practice a religion called Bali-Hindu, based on Hinduism, Buddhism and island worship—believe in reincarnation and regard death as passing from this life to a far better one. "It is a most joyous time, colorful, with the body covered by a large paper, a beautifully decorated horse, cow or fish," an islander said. "Then [the body is] consumed by flames, and ashes taken in a long procession to the sea, to be scattered on the waters."[21]]

Tribes of the Americas

AMERICAN INDIANS

[In the final verses of Longfellow's *Song of Hiawatha,* the great teacher of the Indians speaks these words as he departs "to the Islands of the Blessed," the kingdom of death:

I am going, O my people,
On a long and distant journey;
Many moons and many winters
Will have come, and will have vanished,
Ere I come again to see you . . ."

On the shore stood Hiawatha,
Turning and waved his hand at parting;
On the clear and luminous water
Launched his birch canoe for sailing. . . .
Westward, westward Hiawatha
Sailed into the fiery sunset
Sailed into the purple vapors,
Sailed into the dusk of evening. . . .
To the kingdom of Ponemah,
To the land of the Hereafter!

That Hiawatha's promise was more than a poetic device is evident from the writings of Henry Schoolcraft, the main source of Longfellow's story.[22] Schoolcraft wrote in *Algic Researches* that the Indians believed that Hiawatha, also known as Manabhozho, "is again to appear, and to exercise an important power in the final disposition of the human race."[23]

The course of history in some parts of the Americas was radically altered by reason of similar anticipations of the rebirth of great heroes. Daniel Brinton, professor of archaeology and linguistics at the University of Pennsylvania, says in *Myths of the New World:*

> The Maryland Indians said the whites were an ancient generation who had come to life again, and had returned to seize their former land. . . . [That such legends existed] is almost proved by the fact that in Mexico, Bogota, and Peru, the whites were at once called from the proper names of the heroes of the dawn, Suas, Viracochas, and Quetzalcoatls. . . . The dawn heroes were conceived of as of fair complexion, mighty in war, and though absent for a season, destined to return and claim their ancient power. . . . Historians have marveled at the instantaneous collapse of the empires of Mexico, Peru, the Mayas, and the Natches, before a handful of Spanish filibusters. The face was, wherever the whites appeared they were connected with these ancient predictions of the spirit of the dawn returning to claim his own.[24]

When the Central Americans "first beheld the fair complexioned Spaniards," Brinton writes, "they rushed into the water to embrace the prows of their vessels, and despatched messengers throughout the land to proclaim the return of Quetzalcoatl—which means the Feathered Serpent.

The great teacher of the Peruvians, Viracocha, was pictured not only as white but bearded. Thus, when the bearded Spaniards came, riding on horses—unknown animals—the conquerors were mistaken for returning gods. In an article on Viracocha, entitled "Inca's Sun God," H. J. Maidenberg observes that despite centuries of Christianizing, "Today many Christian Indians still look to their holy lake [Lake Titicaca] for the return of the Sun God and the restoration of the highly advanced civilization that was destroyed by Francisco Pizarro's expedition from Spain more than 400 years ago."[25]

Professor Brinton, who wrote at the turn of the century, stated that "this seemingly extraordinary doctrine" of reincarnation, "which some have asserted was entirely unknown and impossible to the American Indians, was in fact one of their most deeply-rooted and widespread convictions, especially among the tribes of the eastern United States. It is indissolubly connected with their highest theories of a future life, their burial ceremonies, and their modes of expression."[26] Anthropologist Paul Radin also speaks of this widespread belief in rebirth.[27] Then there is the testimony of an Indian, Charles Eastman (Ohiyesa), who writes in The Soul of the Indian that "many of the Indians believed that one may be born more than once; and there were some who claimed to have full knowledge of a former incarnation."[28] The Lenape of Delaware and New Jersey held "that the pure in heart might be able to recall their former lives . . . this led to medicine men interpreting dreams."[29]

Ernest Thompson Seton relates in The Gospel of the Redman that "the Pueblos and some other tribes, according to Dr. E. L. Hewett, are strangely indifferent to the body after death. They consider it a mere husk, an empty case, to be disposed of with view only to the comfort of the survivors. The soul that emerged will go on to the next life, and construct for itself a new and better body."[30]

Wesley Bradfield, in charge of archaeological excavations at Otowi, New Mexico, found beneath the hearth of a very ancient house a jar containing the skeleton of a baby. No explanation was forthcoming until an Indian woman from a nearby tribe told Bradfield that "since time immemorial," her people had believed that a babe taken by death would return, and that if the body were buried beneath the ancestral home, the soul would more easily find the family who cherished it before.[31]

Reincarnation was known to the Iroquois, Algonquins, and Creeks in the east; the Dakotas, Hurons, and Winnebagos in the north; the Kiowas of the Plains; and the Hopi and Mohaves of Arizona. In Canada there are the Ahts of Vancouver Island; the Montagnais (an Algonquin tribe of Quebec and Labrador); and five northern tribes: the Tlingits, Haidas, Tsimsyans, Aleuts, and Athapaskans.[32] In Central America: the Mayans and Quiches, as well as the Powhattans and Tiacalans of Mexico. In South America: the Peruvians, the Chiriquanes of Brazil, and a whole string of remote tribes whose names would mean little to recite. The Patagonians of Argentina, the tallest race in the world, are also supposed to believe in rebirth, as did the Caribs who in the fifteenth century overran much of South America.[33]]

ESKIMOS

[Some curious doctrines of the Eskimos are described in *Redbook* by Vilhjalmur Stefansson, a naturalist and explorer. The author, who lived with the Coronation Gulf Eskimos in northern Canada for ten years, discovered among his Eskimo friends "beliefs that resembled, in a way, the reincarnation theories that we associate with India."[34] The excerpt that follows from Stefansson's report justifies the title of his article, "Primitive People Are Far from Simple," and suggests that many so-called primitives may be descendants of once highly civilized races. His theory also bears on the question of the original source of the views on reincarnation of these peoples.

> I know from experience that two men who speak English and Eskimo well are not going to converse in English unless what they are talking about is some particularly English subject, like the dramas of Shakespeare or the cotton-spinning of Lancashire. . . . You can say as much in one hour of Eskimo-speaking as you can in two hours with English, and you will say it more precisely as well as more concisely. . . . In Eskimo a single noun, like "man" or "house," can have more than a thousand forms, each different in meaning from any other, and the difference is so precise that no misunderstanding is possible. . . . If you were to study in succession Latin, Greek, Hebrew and Russian, each till you could think in it and speak in it fluently and correctly, you would find those four languages combined easier to learn than Eskimo alone. . . . The most brilliant conversation I ever listened to has been among Stone Age Eskimos.[35]

"What do we know of savage tribes beyond the latest chapter of their history?" asks Max Müller, speaking of "primitives" in general. "Their language proves indeed that these so-called heathens, with their complicated systems of mythology, their artificial customs [?], . . . are not the creatures of today or yesterday. . . . They may have passed through ever so many vicissitudes, and what we consider as primitive may be, for all we know, a relapse into savagery, or a corruption of something that was more rational and intelligible in former stages."[36]

Max Müller's theory brings to mind a logical question: If reincarnation is supposed to be the process of evolutionary progress, how do you account for the degeneration of once noble races? One reincarnationist answers in this way:

> The persistence of savagery, the rise and decay of nations and civilizations, the total extinction of nations, all demand an explanation . . . Savagery re-

mains because there are still Egos whose experience is so limited that they are still savage; they will come up into higher races when ready. Races die out because the Egos have had enough of the experience that sort of race gives. . . . A time comes when the whole mass of Egos which built up the race leaves it for another physical environment more like themselves. The economy of Nature will not permit the physical race to suddenly fade away, and so in the real order of evolution other and less progressed Egos come in and use the forms . . . These lower Egos are not able to keep up to the limit of the capacity of the congeries of energies left by the other Egos, and so while the new set gains as much experience as is possible the race in time dies out after passing through its decay. . . .

Many savages have good actual brain capacity, but still are savage. This is because the Ego in that body is still savage and undeveloped, for in contrast to the savage there are many civilized men with small actual brain force who are not savage in nature because the indwelling Ego has had long experience in civilization during other lives, and being a more developed soul has power to use the brain instrument to its highest limit.[37]]

Ancient Europeans

[Reincarnation beliefs have been found among the Finns; Lapps; Danes; Norse; Icelandic peoples; Early Saxons; Celts of Gaul, Wales, England, and Ireland; Old Prussians and Early Teutonics; Lithuanians; Letts; and Lombards of Italy.]

TEUTONIC

[The northern European Caucasian stock—tall in stature, with blond hair, blue eyes, and elongated head—from which many of the German, Dutch, Scandinavian, and British peoples are descended are known to ethnologists as the Old Teutons. Bruce Dickins, author of *Runic and Heroic Poems of the Old Teutonic Peoples,* states in his article on transmigration in the *Encyclopaedia of Religion and Ethics:* "It is clear that the doctrine of metempsychosis was held by the early Teutonic peoples. . . . Such evidence as exists is chiefly derived from Scandinavian [prose] records. The only reference in early poetry is to be found in *Siguroarkvipa kinn skamma,* 45, where Hogni refuses to hold Brynhild back from self-destruction: 'Let no man stay her from the long journey, and may she never be born again.'"[38] As we shall see, Wagner preserved this thought in his *Götterdämmerung.*

Dickins's article continues: "More striking evidence for the [reincarnation] belief is furnished by the prose passages contained in *Helgakvipa Hjorvarossonar* and *Helgakvipa Hundingsbana, ii.* At the end of the former it is said that

Helgi and Sváva, the hero and heroine, were born again (*endrborin*); in the latter we are told that the heroine Sigrún was Sváva reincarnate, and later that both she and her husband Helgi Hundingsbani were born again as Kára and Helgi Haddingjaskati."

In *Viking Civilization,* Axel Olrik states: "A special form of family relationship was that in which one newly deceased was reborn in his descendants, and the latter were accordingly given the name of the deceased. This belief appears as late as the period of the Migration, first among the East Goths, from whom it spread far and wide. . . . It continued to exist as a current folk belief for many centuries. 'We shall come again' said the old people in Saetersdal [Norway], when death called them from the ancestral home.'"[39]

Appian's *History of the Romans* describes the Germans who followed Ariovistus as "scorning death because of their hope of rebirth.'"[40]

The transition from pagan to Christian belief is well illustrated in a story from the *Flateyjarbok*. Prior to the birth, around A.D. 995, of King Olaf the Holy to Queen Asta of Norway, a man named Hrani had an unusual dream in which an early Norse king, Olaf Geirstaoaalfr, appeared and begged him to break into the howe or burial mound of this old monarch and remove his gold ring, sword, and belt. These treasures, Hrani was instructed, were to be taken to Queen Asta and the belt placed around her to ease the child-bearing that had long been delayed. According to the dream the child was to be called Olaf and given the ring and sword. All these directions were carried out, and it was natural for the people to believe that the old king had come back. The saga relates that after Olaf the Holy became king and a Christian convert, he

> rode with his bodyguard past the howe of Olaf Geirstaoaalfr. "Tell me, lord" [says one of his men], "were you buried here?" The king replied to him: "My soul has never had two bodies; it cannot have them, either now or on the Resurrection day . . ." Then the man said: "They say that when you came to this place before you spoke so, and said 'We have been here before also.'" "I have never said this," said the king, "and never will I say it." And the king was much moved, and clapped spurs to his horse immediately, and fled from the place as swiftly as he might.

H. R. Ellis, who tells this story, comments: "Here the belief in rebirth seems to be clearly expressed, all the more convincingly because of the Christian king's determined denial of it later on.'"[41]]

CELTIC

[In his *Literary History of Ireland,* Douglas Hyde (former president of Ireland) says that "the idea of rebirth, which forms part of a half-a-dozen existing Irish sagas, was perfectly familiar to the Irish Gael.'"[42] And Evans-Wentz, in *The Fairy-Faith in Celtic Countries*,[43] quotes Alfred Nutt, an authority on the subject: "In Greek Mythology as in Irish, the conception of rebirth proves to be a dominant factor of the same religious system in which Elysium is likewise an essential feature."[44] Chapters 7 and 12 of Evans-Wentz's book treat in detail the Celtic doctrine of reincarnation, and also provide evidence that even to the present day the idea is alive among some of these peoples.

Bryher writes in the foreword to *Ruan:* "We know something of Celtic doctrine from early Welsh poetry and Breton folklore. It seems to have had much in common with some forms of Eastern thought. Life was considered as a time of trial: if its initiation was successfully passed, the spirit rested after death until the moment came for another return to earth. This continued until, after many lives, some attained the state of spiritual perfection that admitted them to Gwenved, the "white" heaven where they became fully conscious of God. They chose, however, to return as teachers to mankind from time to time until that ultimate and future moment should come when all humanity would attain their state."[45]

The ancient Celts are today represented by the Irish Gaels, the Welsh, the Cornish of England, the Scotch of the Hebrides and Highlands, the Manx of the Isle of Man, and the Bretons of northwestern France, or Brittany. In early Roman times, however, their territory included, in addition to Great Britain and Ireland, northern Italy, France, Belgium, western Switzerland, and Germany west of the Rhine.

Whence sprang Celtic beliefs in reincarnation? The source was certainly pre-Roman, considering the statements of Julius Caesar, Valerius Maximus, and Lucan (who are discussed later in this volume). For centuries the world has been intrigued by the "Atlantis theory," a widely held belief that there once existed in the Atlantic Ocean, opposite the mouth of the Mediterranean Sea, a large island, which was but the remnant of a vast Atlantic continent. From the mighty civilization which it is thought developed on that continent, colonizing parties went out to the Americas, Europe, Africa, and Asia. The biblical story of the flood is supposed by some to be a fragmentary record of the sinking of Atlantis. Although the literature on this subject comprises some five thousand works in twenty different languages, the classic work is Ignatius Donnelly's *Atlantis: The Antediluvian World,* published by Harper Brothers in New York in 1882 (revised edition, 1949). No other writing since Plato's story of Atlantis in the *Timaeus* and the *Critias* has stimulated the minds of so many people to give serious consideration to this strange theory, which if proved would radically alter scientific views in anthropology, archaeology and related fields, and push back the origin of civilization perhaps millions of years. Here is Donnelly's idea of how the Celts and their Druidic priests obtained their reincarnation beliefs:

> There are many evidences that the Old World recognized Ireland as possessing a very ancient civilization. In the Sanskrit books it is referred to as Hiranya, the "Island of the Sun," . . . . The Greeks called Ireland the "Sacred Isle" and "Ogygia." "Nor can any one," says Camden, "conceive why they

should call it Ogygia, unless, perhaps, from its antiquity; for the Greeks called nothing Ogygia unless what was extremely ancient." . . .

We would naturally expect, in view of the geographical position of the country, to find Ireland colonized at an early day by the overflowing population of Atlantis. And, in fact, the Irish annals tell us that their island was settled *prior to the Flood*. . . . We have seen their annals laying claim to an immigration from the direction of Atlantis prior to the Deluge. . . . Many analogies have been found to exist between the beliefs and customs of the Druids and the other religions which were drawn from Atlantis. . . . It would appear probable that the religion of the Druids passed from Ireland to England and France. The metempsychosis or transmigration of souls was one of the articles of their belief long before the time of Pythagoras; it had probably been drawn from the storehouse of Atlantis.[46]

M. F. Cusack in *A History of the Irish Nation*[47] also speaks of a high civilization in Innis Fail (the old name for Ireland), long before the Christian missionaries came in the fifth century. The ancient system of education and tradition of learning kept the Irish monastaries from succumbing as early as the monasteries of the Continent to the ignorance of the Middle Ages. In Druidic times the scholars entrusted with the ancient records were called *Ollamhs*. Cusack says their diplomas were obtained after a collegiate course that might deter many a modern aspirant to professional chairs. As prescribed by the Brehon Laws, the course lasted twelve years. The studies included philosophy, law, and knowing and practicing the druidical secrets.

On the arrival of the missionaries, many of the ancient books were burned or rewritten. According to Dudley Firbisse, professor of antiquities, "One hundred and eighty tracts of the doctrine of the Druids or magi were condemned to the flames during the time of St. Patrick." While some of the sagas containing ideas of rebirth were allowed to survive, whatever learned works there may have been on the subject were not.]

From this brief glance at pre-Christian peoples of northern Europe, we turn to southern Europe and a very different scene—ancient Greece and Rome, where Western civilization was born. Then comes the Middle Ages, the Renaissance and Reformation, followed by other eras up to and including modern times. That the chapter on the Western tradition should be one of the longest demonstrates that the idea of many lives was not foreign to thinkers in the Occident. Today the popular view is that illuminating and useful knowledge on our subject can be found only in the Orient. After reading the contributions of the great minds of the West, one is likely to conclude otherwise.

The Western Tradition

🕊 GREEK AND ROMAN HERITAGE

I cannot recite, even rudely, laws of the intellect, without remembering that lofty and sequestered class who have been its prophets and oracles, the high-priesthood of the pure reason, the Trismegisti, the expounders of thought from age to age. When, at long intervals, we turn over their abstruse pages, wonderful seems the calm and grand air of these few, these great spiritual lords, who have walked in the world—these of the old religion. . . . This band of grandees, Hermes, Heraclitus, Empedocles, Plato, Plotinus, Olympiodorus, Proclus, Synesius, and the rest, have somewhat so vast in their logic, so primary in their thinking, that it seems antecedent to all the ordinary distinctions of rhetoric and literature, and to be at once poetry, and music and dancing, and astronomy, and mathematics. I am present at the sowing of the seed of the world. With a geometry of sunbeams the soul lays the foundations of nature.

RALPH WALDO EMERSON
"Intellect"

How can an educated person stay away from the Greeks? I have always been far more interested in them than in science. . . . I maintain that cosmic religious feeling is the strongest and noblest incitement to scientific research.

ALBERT EINSTEIN[1]

[In India, the ancient schools of philosophy were rooted in religion. In Greece, religion and the mystery schools merged into philosophy. We have therefore saved the Greek story to open our consideration of reincarnation in Western thought in all its "secular" aspects—philosophy, art, literature, psychology, and science. Whereas in later centuries these areas became departmentalized, in Grecian times they were at least to some degree blended.

The genuine study of philosophy can evidently provide a meeting ground for both science and religion, for as Bertrand Russell has said, "The greatest men, who have been philosophers, have felt the need both of science and mysticism. The attempt to harmonize the two was what made their life."[2] This goal, however, need not be limited to philosophers—great or otherwise. Today searchers for truth in many fields are becoming convinced that the ideal mentioned is not an impractical dream but worthy of pursuit.]

ORPHEUS

[Thomas Taylor wrote in *Mystical Hymns of Orpheus:* "This alone may be depended upon, from general assent, that there formerly lived a person named Orpheus, who was the founder of theology among the Greeks . . . the first of prophets and the prince of poets . . . who taught the Greeks their sacred rites and mysteries, and from whose wisdom . . . the divine muse of Homer and the sublime theology of Pythagoras and Plato flowed."[3] To use the words of Proclus, "All the theology of the Greeks comes from Orphic mystagogy," that is to say, initiation into the mysteries.[4] And although in modern times there have been disputes as to whether Orpheus ever existed, the great honor in which he was held by so many generations of the highest intellects of antiquity would suggest that the theology attributed to him came from a venerable source.

"The doctrine of metempsychosis," writes Professor Zeller, "seems really to have passed from the theology of the mysteries into Philosophy. . . . In the Orphic theology . . . transmigration is clearly to be found. . . . We have every reason to believe that it was taught in the Orphic mysteries prior to the date of Pythagoras. According to Herodotus, the Orphics obtained it from Egypt. But it is also conceivable that this belief, the affinity of which with Hindu and Egyptian doctrines indicates an Eastern source, may have originally emigrated from the East with the Greeks themselves, and have been at first confined to a narrow circle becoming afterwards more important and more widely diffused."[5]

Alfred Bertholet, professor of theology at the University of Basel, remarks in *The Transmigration of Souls* that the Orphici teach that "the soul is divine, immortal, and aspires to freedom, while the body holds it in fetters as a prisoner. Death dissolves the compact, but only to re-imprison the liberated soul after a short time: for the wheel of birth revolves inexorably. . . . The Orphic belief seems to have been widely current in the Greek colonies in

Southern Italy and Sicily.''[6] The purified soul, of course, could achieve release from the need for periodic return.]

PHERECYDES OF SYROS (6TH CENTURY B.C.)
Greek Philosopher

[Pherecydes has been called one of the Seven Wise Men of Greece. Mead writes of him in *Orpheus:* ''Pherecydes is said to have been the master of Pythagoras, and to have obtained his knowledge from the secret books of the Phœnicians. . . . He is further stated to have been the pupil of the Chaldæans and Egyptians. . . . The most important subject he treated of, was the doctrine of metempsychosis and the immortality of the soul, and this he set forth in his great prose work *Theologia,* generally known as the 'Seven Adyta.' . . . He is said to have been the first who used prose for such a subject.''[7]]

PYTHAGORAS (C. 582–507 B.C.)
Greek Philosopher and Mathematician

[Pythagoras was given the surname Mnesarchides, ''one who remembers his origins.'' Diogenes Laertius wrote in his *Life of Pythagoras* that this Sage of Samos was accustomed to speak of himself in this manner, that he had formerly been Aethalides. At a subsequent period he passed into Euphorbus, and was wounded by Menelaus at the siege of Troy, and so died. In that life he used to say that he had formerly been Aethalides; and that he had received as a gift from Mercury, the god of Wisdom, the memory of his soul's transmigrations, also the gift of recollecting what his own soul and the souls of others had experienced between death and rebirth.[8] ''What Pythagoras wished to indicate by all these particulars,'' said Iamblichus, ''was that he knew the former lives he had lived, and that [thenceforth] he commenced his providential attention to others, reminding them of their former life.''[9]

While it is generally agreed that reincarnation was one of the main teachings of Pythagoras, throughout European literature he is also linked with the idea that human beings can incarnate in animal forms. In *As You Like It* (III, ii) Shakespeare's Rosalind says: ''I was never so be-rhymed since Pythagoras' time, that I was an Irish rat, which I can hardly remember.'' Shakespeare's fellow dramatist Christopher Marlowe uses the idea in *Doctor Faustus.* As in Goethe's and Gounod's *Faust,* this doctor sold his soul to the devil. In the final scene after vainly appealing for God's last-minute pardon—for a shortening of the damnation sentence to say 100,000 years— Faustus wishfully exclaims:

> Ah, Pythagoras' metempsychosis! were that true,
> This soul should fly from me and I be changed
> Into some brutish beast! all beasts are happy,
> For when they die,
> Their souls are soon dissolved in elements;
> But mine must live, still to be plagued in hell.[10]

Pythagoras himself left no writings, but Dacier in his *Life of Pythagoras* points out: "A sure token that Pythagoras never held the opinion attributed to him lies in the fact that there is not the faintest trace of it in the symbols we have left of him, or in the precepts his disciple, Lysis, collected together and handed down as a summary of the Master's teaching." Sir Thomas Browne stated in *Religio Medici:* "I cannot believe the wisdom of Pythagoras did ever positively, and in a literal sense, affirm his Metempsychosis, or impossible transmigration of the Souls of men into beasts."[11] To a similar opinion, the *Britannica* adds that the many allusions to transmigration in the writings of the Greeks are generally of a playful character: "Thus Menander, in the play called *The Inspired Woman,* supposes some god to say to an old man Crato, 'When you die, you will have a second existence; choose what creature you would like to be, dog, sheep, goat, horse, or man.' To which he replies, 'Make me anything rather than a man, for he is the only creature that prospers by injustice.'"[12] The great German humanist and reputed father of the Reformation John Reuchlin remarked concerning the supposed regression belief of Pythagoras: "We cannot imagine this of so knowing a person. This suspicion of this transanimation seems rather to have been raised by such, as were partly ignorant, partly envious, of the Pythagorean mysteries, as Timon, Xenophanes, Cratinus, Aristophon, Hermippus, and others, who have ascribed many things to Pythagoras which he never said nor wrote, and have perverted what he did say."[13]

Hierocles, a Pythagorean, wrote in his *Commentary of the Golden Verses of Pythagoras:* "He who expects that after his death he shall put on the body of a beast, and become an animal without reason, because of his vices, or a plant because of his dullness and stupidity; such a man . . . is infinitely deceived, and absolutely ignorant of the essential form of our soul, which can never change; for being and continuing always man, 'tis only said to become god or beast by virtue or vice, though by its nature it cannot be either the one or the other, but only by its resemblance to the one or the other."[14]

This view was shared by the Neoplatonists regarding Plato's remarks on regression. Proclus, in *Commentaries on the Phaedrus of Plato,* showed by a multitude of arguments why man's soul can never incarnate in an animal, and in *Commentaries on the Timaeus* wrote:

> It is usual to inquire how human souls can descend into brute animals. And
> some, indeed, think that there are certain similitudes of men to brutes, which

they call savage lives: for they by no means think it possible that the rational essence can become the soul of a savage animal. . . . In his "Republic" Plato says, that the soul of Thersites assumed an ape, but not the body of an ape; and in the "Phædrus," the soul descends into savage life, but not into a savage body. For life is conjoined with its proper soul. And in this place he says it is changed into a brutal nature. For a brutal nature is not a brutal body, but a brutal life.[15]

On this very subject Aristotle stated: "For any soul to be clothed with any body is as absurd as to say that the art of carpentry could embody itself in a musician's flutes; each art must use its tools, each soul its body."[16]

Pythagoras traveled widely and some say he visited India. Reuchlin believed he derived the heart of his philosophy from the wise men of the East.]

The Greek Mysteries

In Greece, the doctrine of transmigration . . . appears to have been generally inculcated as one of the deepest doctrines of the mysteries. . . . The Greek mysteries were, in fact, not only a school in which metempsychosis was taught, but an indispensable grade or lodge through which all of the aspirants must pass before they could be purified and go on to higher stages of existence. *M'Clintock and Strong's Cyclopædia of Biblical, Theological and Ecclesiastical Literature*[17]

["In all ages of which we have any literary records," writes William Kingsland, "we find the tradition of a recondite knowledge which could not be disclosed to any save to those who had undergone the severest tests as to their worthiness to receive it. This knowledge was very generally known under the term of the *Mysteries,* and it was concerned with the deepest facts of Man's origin, nature, and connection with supersensual worlds and beings, as well as with the 'natural' laws of the physical world."[18]

The Greek Mystery Schools are believed to be copies of the more ancient Indian and Egyptian Mysteries. Herodotus stated that they were introduced into Greece by Orpheus. "It is only when we come to the first five or six centuries B.C., and to the palmy days of Greece and Alexandria," says Kingsland, "that we obtain a definite knowledge of the existence of the Mystery Schools, and of some of their more detailed teachings. This period is associated with such names as Anaxagoras, Pythagoras, Socrates, Plato, Aristotle, and later on, before the dominance of ecclesiastical Christianity had suppressed the Gnosis . . . we have such names as Philo Judæus, Clement of Alexandria, Valentinus, Origen, Proclus, Basilides, Iamblichus, and Plotinus, all speaking openly of the existence of the *Mysteries* and Mystery Schools, claiming initiation therein, and openly teaching as much of it as it was permitted for them to make public."[19]

The most celebrated, and the last to be destroyed, were the Eleusinian Mysteries, whose center was located in a hamlet not far from Athens. Those initiated bound themselves by this promise: "I swear to give up my life for the salvation of my brothers, who constitute the whole of mankind, and, if called upon, to die in the defense of truth." For two thousand years the Mysteries of Eleusis illuminated Greece, until in the fifth century A.D. the lips of the last Hierophant were sealed by death. One of the foremost archaeologists of our time, George Mylonas, writes in *Eleusis and the Eleusinian Mysteries* that "whatever the substance and meaning of the Mysteries, the fact remains that the cult of Eleusis satisfied the most sincere yearnings and the deepest longings of the human heart." After quoting Sophocles and Pindar on the beneficent influence of the Mystery teaching, Professor Mylonas says:

> When we read these and similar statements written by the great or nearly great of the ancient world . . . we cannot help but believe that the Mysteries of Eleusis were not an empty, childish affair devised by shrewd priests to fool the peasant and the ignorant, but a philosophy of life that possessed substance and meaning and imparted a modicum of truth to the yearning human soul. That belief is strengthened when we read in Cicero that Athens has given nothing to the world more excellent or divine than the Eleusinian Mysteries.[20]

In the mystery dramas enacted in the various Mystery Schools, nature's laws and processes were personified by the priests and neophytes who, assuming the role of various gods and goddesses, repeated scenes from their respective lives. These were explained in their hidden meaning to the candidates for initiation and incorporated into philosophical doctrines. The soul's preexistent condition and lapse into earth life and Hades, its long wanderings through many lives, followed by gradual purification and eventual reunion with spirit, were all symbolized.

At Eleusis the familiar story of Demeter and Persephone was portrayed, signifying, according to Sallust, the periodical descent of souls.[21] Thomas Taylor agrees with this interpretation in his *Eleusinian and Bacchic Mysteries*.[22] The six months of Persephone's stay in the upper world of sunlight midst the beauties and glories of nature depicted the heavenly state of bliss after death, while the equal period in Hades, or the dark region of Pluto, symbolized incarnation on earth. (In Eastern tradition the earth is called Myalba, or Hell—the only hell that mortals have to endure.) In this context, the red pomegranate seeds that Persephone has eaten in the underworld and which condemn her to return periodically to that realm are suggestive of attachment to sensuous existence, making reincarnation obligatory.

In the Orphic Mysteries, Bacchus, torn to pieces by the Titans and then made whole again, was dramatized. Plutarch calls this "a sacred narrative concerning reincarnation."[23]]

HERACLITUS OF EPHESUS (C. 540–480 B.C.)
Greek Philosopher

[The noted thinker Heraclitus of Ephesus, born a hundred years before Plato, wrote that "this world which is the same for all, neither god nor any man made; but was always, is, and ever shall be, an ever-living fire. . . . The quick [or living] and the dead, the wakers and the sleepers, young and old; all are the same. For the last are moved about to be the first, and the first in turn become the last. They rise again and become watchful guardians of the quick and the dead." In quoting these words, the German philosopher George Misch adds some comments in his *Dawn of Philosophy:* "The 'everliving fire' subsists only in its transmigrations, as that which is perpetually changing, since it is not a fixed quantity that 'is,' but 'lives.' " "This dynamic principle," says Misch, "accords very well with the idea of world-cycles of events; indeed periodicity was a self-evident fact to all thinking persons right down to modern times. In connection with these up-down cycles or the 'wheel of births,' to use the Indian term, [Heraclitus] says, 'The way up and the way down are the same.' "[24]]

PINDAR (522?–443 B.C.)
Greek Lyric Poet

[In one of his dirges Pindar writes that "while the body of all men is subject to over-mastering death," the soul "remaineth alive, for it alone cometh from the gods. But it sleepeth, while the limbs are active." Another verse from this poem is used by Plato in his dialogue Meno (81), and tells of what transpires when individuals have paid their karmic debts: "As for those from whom Persephone has exacted the penalty of their ancient sins . . . she once more restoreth their souls to the upper sunlight [of earth life]; and from these come into being august monarchs, and men who are swift in strength and supreme in wisdom; and, for all future time, men call them sainted heroes."[25]]

HERODOTUS (484?–425? B.C.)
Greek Historian

[Herodotus is called the Father of History, and his writings, in nine volumes, are recognized as classics of world literature. Our brief quotation is from

Book II, Euterpe, Section 123. Herodotus mentions here a three-thousand-year period between incarnations, taught by the Egyptians. From our study of Egypt it may be recalled that this time is largely spent in a heavenly condition. As to the strange idea, reported by this historian, that after the heavenly state the soul passes before birth through various lower orders of life, it is interesting that embryologists have for some time observed that the foetus before assuming a human shape in the womb actually "goes through" various animal types—a kind of quick review, perhaps, of early stages of evolution.]

The Egyptians were the first who asserted that the soul of man is immortal, and that when the body perishes it enters into some other animal, constantly springing into existence and when it has passed through the different kinds of terrestrial, marine, and aerial beings, it again enters into the body of a man that is born; and that this revolution is made in three thousand years. Some of the Greeks have adopted this opinion, some earlier, others later, as if it were their own; but although I know their names I do not mention them.[26]

EMPEDOCLES (C. 490–430 B.C.)
Greek Philosopher and Statesman

[Among the Greeks there were various orders of gods, man in his noble state being called a demigod, part divine and part human. Empedocles indicates how this state could be lost, resulting in wandering through many lives estranged from one's real source:]

There is an oracle of Necessity, ancient decree of the gods, eternal and sealed with broad oaths; whenever one of those demigods, whose lot is long-lasting life, has sinfully defiled his dear limbs with bloodshed, or following strife has sworn a false oath, thrice ten thousand seasons does he wander far from the blessed, being born throughout that time in the forms of all manner of mortal things and changing one baleful path of life for another. . . . Of these I too am now one, a fugitive from the gods, who put my trust in raving strife.[27]

[In some verses in *The Purifications,* Empedocles reveals that evolutionary progress through the kingdoms was apparently not a foreign idea to the Greeks:]

> I was once already boy and girl,
> Thicket and bird, and mute fish in the waves.
> All things doth Nature change, enwrapping souls
> In unfamiliar tunics of the flesh.
> The worthiest dwellings for the souls of men.[28]

SOCRATES (469?–399 B.C.)

Greek Philosopher

[What we know of the philosophy of Socrates comes mainly from the dialogues of Plato, but as Plato developed and expanded his teacher's ideas, one can never be sure where Socrates ends and Plato begins. However, it is probably safe to include in the present item selections from the *Phaedo*— Plato's story of Socrates' last day on earth. A. E. Taylor writes in *Socrates, the Man and His Thought,* that the *Phaedo* "is perhaps the greatest thing in the prose literature of Europe." Taylor gives this summary of the dialogue: Socrates "finding that his young friends . . . Cebes and Simmias, were much troubled with 'scientific' doubts that the soul may be no more than a perishable function of the body, devoted his last morning to reasoning with them in his own justification, on the 'real distinction of the soul from the body,' and the grounds for believing that it is neither born with the body nor dies with it. . . . Through the whole discussion he showed himself free alike from depression by the prospect of imminent death, and from over-anxiety to cling to a comforting belief without giving full weight to all there might be to urge against it."[29]

Of the various evidences adduced by Socrates to support immortality, one is here selected bearing particularly on rebirth. The translation is by Benjamin Jowett. In this dialogue Socrates also reviews all the arguments supporting his "favorite doctrine that knowledge is simply recollection," stating that this "implies a previous time in which we have learned that which we now recollect," and that "this is another proof of the soul's immortality" (see sections 73–77).]

Suppose we consider the question whether the souls of men after death are or are not in the [heavenly] world below. There comes into my mind an ancient doctrine which affirms that they go from here into the other world, and returning hither, are born again from the dead. Now if it be true that the living come from the dead, then our souls must exist in the other world, for if not, how could they have been born again? . . .

Let us consider the whole question, not in relation to man only, but in relation to animals generally, and to plants, and to everything of which there is generation, and the proof will be easier. Are not all things which have opposites generated out of their opposites? . . . The state of sleep is opposed to the state of waking, and out of sleeping waking is generated, and out of waking, sleeping. [Other examples are furnished, such as pleasure and pain, heat and cold.] Then here is a new way by which we arrive at the conclusion that the living come from the dead, just as the dead come from the living; and this, if true, affords a most certain proof that the souls of the dead exist in some place out of which they come again. . . .

[For] if generation were in a straight line only, and there were no compensation or circle in nature, no turn or return of elements into their opposites, then all things would at last have the same form and pass into the same state, and there would be no more generation of them. . . . If all things which partook of life were to die, and after they were dead remained in the form of death, and did not come to life again, all would at last die, and nothing would be alive—what other result could there be? . . . Must not all things at last be swallowed up in death? . . . But I am confident that there truly is such a thing as living again, and that the living spring from the dead, and that the souls of the dead are in existence, and that the good souls have a better portion than the evil.

[The sensuous man was believed to return to earth life more quickly than the good, for in the same dialogue—and this time Harry Cary's translation is used—Socrates states:]

The soul of the true philosopher . . . abstains as much as possible from pleasures and desires, griefs and fears . . . because each pleasure and pain, having a nail, as it were, nails the soul to the body, and fastens it to it, and causes it to become corporeal, deeming those things to be true whatever the body asserts to be so. For, in consequence of its forming the same opinions with the body, and delighting in the same things . . . it can never pass into Hades in a pure state, but must ever depart polluted by the body, and so quickly falls into another body . . . and consequently is deprived of all association with that which is divine, and pure, and uniform.

PLATO (427?–347 B.C.)

Greek Philosopher

["Out of Plato come all things that are still written and debated among men of thought," wrote Emerson, adding: "Among secular books, Plato only is entitled to Omar's fanatical compliment to the Koran, when he said, 'Burn the libraries; for their value is in this book.' . . . Plato is philosophy, and philosophy, Plato—at once the glory and the shame of mankind, since neither Saxon nor Roman have availed to add any idea to his categories. No wife, no children had he, [but] the thinkers of all civilized nations are his posterity and are tinged with his mind . . . An Englishman reads and says, 'how English!' a German—'how Teutonic!' an Italian—'how Roman and how Greek!' . . . so Plato seems to a reader in New England an American genius. His broad humanity transcends all sectional lines."[30] Alfred North Whitehead's observation that all subsequent philosophy has been "but footnotes to Plato" seems increasingly expressive of the modern view.

"The real weight and importance of metempsychosis" in the West, remarks Henry Sturt, "is due to its adoption by Plato." "Had he not embodied it in some of his greatest works it would be merely a matter of curious investigation for the anthropologist and student of folklore."[31] We may not entirely agree with this, but nevertheless the degree to which Plato's reincarnation ideas influenced Western literature and philosophy has been considerable. (This may be easily shown by consulting the references under his name in the Index.)

The Platonic schools of Athens formed after the model of Plato's Academy, where he taught for nearly fifty years, flourished almost without a break for nine centuries until abolished by a decree of Justinian.

The first selection is from *Meno,* Jowett's translation:[32]]

SOCRATES   I have heard from certain wise men and women who spoke . . . of a glorious truth, as I conceive.

MENO   What was it? and who were they?

SOCRATES   Some of them were priests and priestesses, who had studied how they might be able to give a reason [for] their profession: there have been poets also, who spoke of these things by inspiration, like Pindar, and many others who were inspired. And they say—mark, now, and see whether their words are true—they say that the soul of man is immortal, and at one time has an end, which is termed dying, and at another time is born again, but is never destroyed. And the moral is, that a man ought to live always in perfect holiness. . . .
The soul, then, as being immortal, and having been born again many times, and having seen all things that exist, whether in this world or in the world below, has knowledge of them all; and it is no wonder that she should be able to call to remembrance all that she ever knew about virtue, and about everything; for as all nature is akin, and the soul has learned all things, there is no difficulty in her eliciting or as men say learning, out of a single recollection all the rest, if a man is strenuous and does not faint; for all enquiry and all learning is but recollection. . . .

MENO   . . . if you can prove to me that what you say is true, I wish that you would.

SOCRATES   It will be no easy matter, but I will try to please you to the utmost of my power. Suppose that you call one of your numerous attendants, that I may demonstrate on him.

[A young boy, a Greek slave, is introduced, from whom answers to certain mathematical problems are elicited by Socrates during a long series of questionings.]

SOCRATES   Now, has any one ever taught him all this? You must know about him, if, as you say, he was born and bred in your house.

MENO   I am certain that no one ever did teach him. . . .

SOCRATES   But if he did not acquire the knowledge in this life, then he must have had and learned it at some other time?

MENO   Clearly he must. . . .

SOCRATES   And if there have been always true thoughts in him . . . which only need to be awakened into knowledge by putting questions to him, his soul must have always possessed this knowledge? . . .

MENO   Obviously.

SOCRATES   And if the truth of all things always existed in the soul, then the soul is immortal. Wherefore be of good cheer, and try to recollect what you do not know, or rather what you do not remember.

MENO   I feel, somehow, that I like what you are saying.

SOCRATES   And I, Meno, like what I am saying. Some things I have said of which I am not altogether confident. But that we shall be better and braver and less helpless if we think that we ought to enquire, than we should have been if we indulged in the idle fancy that there was no knowing and no use in seeking to know what we do not know—that is a theme upon which I am ready to fight, in word and deed, to the utmost of my power.

[The foregoing prompts an obvious question: If the soul is already all-wise on its own plane, what need could there be to descend periodically into matter? Plotinus and Proclus will touch upon this problem later. At this point it can be said that a distinction should probably be drawn between inherent or potential perfection and its actualization in this world. The need for such actualization seems evident in Plato's *Phaedrus.*

Before quoting from the *Phaedrus* itself, some related ideas from an article entitled "The Phaedrus and Reincarnation" in the *American Journal of Philology* may prove helpful. The author, R. S. Bluck, a philologist from the University of London, shows that when in this dialogue Plato speaks of the soul's "fall," he explains it in the light of a difficult incarnation resulting from "bad training" by the inner man of some of his instruments in a prior life. Therefore the "fall" has none of the connotations associated with the doctrine of original sin. As Dr. Bluck states, Plato "may be suggesting, rather, that the human soul," through rebirth, "may aspire to promotion which would enable it to enjoy such happiness as it has never known before. . . . How long it takes to achieve that will depend upon individual effort, and will not be fixed at all."[33] Plato mentions a ten-thousand-year cycle of periodic rebirths, but Dr. Bluck does not believe this was meant to represent the total life history of the soul's peregrinations on earth. Large cycles operate within the sweep of still grander revolutions.

In the context of the extracts that follow from the *Phaedrus,* the soul is compared to a charioteer who drives a pair of winged steeds, one horse being "of noble, generous breed," the other "of opposite descent and character."

Plato explains that the analogy of wings is used because of their unique power to elevate and transport a heavy body, implying that within man a corresponding psychological power must exist. It may be recalled that a favorite Egyptian symbol for the soul was that of a winged disk or globe.]

Every soul is immortal—for whatever is in perpetual motion is immortal. . . . All that is soul presides over all that is without soul and patrols all heaven, now appearing in one form and now in another. When it is perfect and fully feathered, it roams in the upper air and regulates the entire universe. . . . Real existence, colorless, formless and intangible, visible only to the intelligence which sits at the helm of the soul . . . has its abode in [the highest] region. . . . But the soul that has lost its feathers is carried down till it finds some solid resting-place; and when it has settled there [and] has taken to itself an earthly body, which seems capable of self-motion, owing to the power of its new inmate, the name of animal is given to the whole; to this compound, I mean of soul and body. . . .

Now the chariots of the Gods being of equal poise and obedient to the rein, move easily, but all others with difficulty; for they are burdened by the horse of vicious temper, which sways and sinks them towards the earth, if he has received no good training from his charioteer. Whereupon there awaits the soul a crowning pain and agony. . . . [But] every man's soul has by the law of his birth been a spectator of eternal truth, or it would never have passed into this our mortal frame, yet still it is no easy matter for all to be reminded of their past by their present existence.[34]

[From *The Laws*, as translated by Jowett, comes this short extract on karma:]

O youth or young man, who fancy that you are neglected by the Gods, know that if you become worse you shall go to the worse souls, or if better to the better, and in every succession of life and death you will do and suffer what like may fitly suffer at the hands of like. This is the justice of heaven, which neither you nor any other unfortunate will ever glory in escaping. . . . Take heed thereof, for it will be sure to take heed of you. If you say—I am small and will creep into the depths of the earth, or I am high and will fly up to heaven, you are not so small or so high but that you shall pay the fitting penalty. . . . And thinkest thou, bold man . . . that you needest not to know this?—he who knows it not can never form any true idea of the happiness or unhappiness of life or hold any rational discourse respecting either.

[The final selection is from the conclusion of Plato's celebrated work *The Republic*. The translation is by Josiah Wright, save for the last paragraph, which is by Jowett. It may be of some significance that the closing lines of the ten books of *The Republic* end on the note of rebirth. One writer introduces this portion of the dialogue in an illuminating way: "Plato . . . constructed the Myth of Er, in the tenth book of the *Republic,* to provide a scheme which preserved both moral freedom and the rule of Necessity or Law. Before birth, the tale relates, the souls who are to be reborn are brought to a place where they are able to see 'the working of Universal Law' at the very axis of the cosmos, as J. A. Stewart explains in *The Myths of Plato.* They are given opportunity to choose their lives to come, but are informed that this decision will include 'the whole complex of circumstances' which go with the attractions that influence their choice."[35] Stewart observes that

> Plato lays stress, as he does elsewhere, on the unbroken continuity of the responsible Self evolving its character in a series of life-changes. It is the choice made before the Throne of *Ananke* [Necessity] which dominates the behaviour of the Soul in the bodily life on which it is about to enter; but the choice made before the throne of *Ananke* depended itself on a disposition formed in a previous life; the man who chooses the life of a tyrant, and rues his choice as soon as he has made it, but too late, has been virtuous in a previous life, [but] his virtue has been merely "customary," without foundation upon consciously realized principle. . . . To be free is to be a continuously existing, self-affirming, environment-choosing personality, manifesting itself in . . . its own natural environment which is the counterpart of its own character. . . .
>
> It is, in other words, the freedom of the "noumenal," as distinguished from the "phenomenal" Self, which Plato presents as the "prenatal choice of a Life"—mythically; which is, indeed, the only way in which such a transcendental idea can be legitimately presented. . . . The momentary prenatal act of choice . . . is the pattern of like acts which have to be performed in a man's natural life. Great decisions have to be made in life, which, once made, are irrevocable, and dominate the man's whole career and conduct afterwards. The chief use of education is to prepare a man for these crises in his life, so that he may decide rightly.[36]

Now we quote from *The Republic:*]

Well, I will tell you a tale . . . of what once happened to a brave man, Er, who, according to the story, was killed in battle [but his body would not disintegrate]. . . . On the twelfth day after his death, as he lay on the funeral pyre, he came to life again, and then proceeded to describe what he had seen in the other world. . . . Each soul, as it arrived [from the earth], wore a travel-stained appearance . . . and those who had descended from heaven were questioned about heaven by those who had risen out of the earth; while the latter were questioned by the former about the earth. Those who were come from earth told their tale with lamentations and tears, as they bethought them of all the dreadful things they had seen and suffered in their subterranean journey . . . while those who were come from heaven described enjoyments and sights of marvellous beauty.

[The souls about to enter earth life are thus addressed:] "Ye short-lived souls, a new generation of men shall here begin the cycle of its mortal existence. Your destiny shall not be allotted to you, but you shall choose it for yourselves. . . . Virtue owns no master. He who honors her shall have more of her, and he who slights her less. The responsibility lies with the chooser. Heaven is guiltless." . . .

It was a truly wonderful sight, he said, to watch how each soul selected its life—a sight at once melancholy, and ludicrous, and strange. The experience of their former life generally guided the choice. . . . It so happened that the soul of Odysseus had drawn the last lot of all. When he came up to choose, the memory of his former sufferings had so abated his ambition that he went about a long time looking for a quiet retired life, which with great trouble he discovered lying about, and thrown contemptuously aside by the others. As soon as he saw it, he chose it gladly, and said that he would have done the same if he had even drawn the first lot. . . .

Now, when all the souls had chosen their lives . . . they all travelled into the plain of Forgetfulness . . . and took up their quarters by the bank of the river of Indifference. . . . each, as he drinks, forgets everything. When they had gone to rest, and it was now midnight, there was a clap of thunder and an earthquake; and in a moment the souls were carried up to their birth, this way and that, like shooting stars. Er himself was prevented from drinking any of the water; but how, and by what road, he reached his body, he knew not: only he knew that he suddenly opened his eyes at dawn, and found himself laid out upon the funeral pyre.

And thus, Glaucon, the tale has been saved and has not perished, and will save us if we are obedient to the word spoken; and we shall pass safely over the river of Forgetfulness and our soul will not be defiled. Wherefore my counsel is that we hold fast ever to the heavenly way and follow after justice and virtue always, considering that the soul is immortal and able to endure every sort of good and every sort of evil. Thus shall we live dear to one another and to the gods . . . and it shall be well with us both in this Life and in the pilgrimage of a thousand years [between incarnations] which we have been describing.

ARISTOTLE (384–322 B. C.)

Greek Philosopher

[In the volume *Aristotle—Fundamentals of the History of His Development*, one finds that Aristotle accepted preexistence and reincarnation in his early dialogue *Eudemus* or *On the Soul*, but in later works, he largely rejected these ideas. The author, the well-known classical scholar Werner Jaeger

further shows that the historic split between Aristotle and his teacher
Plato—which was to make of the former the father of materialism in philosophy, science, and religion of all subsequent eras of Western thought—
occurred over Plato's teaching of immortality, preexistence, and reincarnation. Jaeger states:]

In the *Eudemus* Aristotle follows the view of [Plato's] *Phædo* even in
holding that "the whole soul" is immortal. This realistic view is the only one
that can give religious comfort to the heart of man, which cares nothing for
the eternity of the impersonal reason, without love and without memory of
this life. But Aristotle has wrestled with doubts, and they have left traces in
his notion of Platonic recollection. We know that in his psychology he rejects
recollection along with the Idea-theory and the survival of "the whole
soul."[37] The *Eudemus,* on the other hand, is still based on this theory. But at
the time of writing it Aristotle had already put to himself, and attempted to
answer by Plato's methods, the psychological question whether consciousness is continuous in the life after death. This is the question on which
immortality in the sense meant in the *Phædo* later seemed to him to founder.
[Aristotle held that] the continuity of consciousness depends on memory.
Whereas he later denies that *Nus* [*Nous* or Spirit] possesses this, in the
Eudemus he tries to save it for the soul that has returned to the other world.
He does this by enlarging Plato's [theory of] recollection into a doctrine of
the continuity of consciousness in all three phases of the soul's existence—its
former existence, its life on this earth, and its life after death. Alongside the
Platonic view that the soul remembers the other world he sets his thesis that
[in the afterlife] it remembers this one.

He supports this by an analogy. When men fall ill they sometimes lose their
memories, even to the extent of forgetting how to read and write; while on
the other hand those who have been restored from illness to health do not
forget what they suffered while they were ill. In the same way the soul that
has descended into a body forgets the impressions received during its former
existence, while the soul which death has restored to its home in the other
world remembers its experiences and sufferings here. Life without a body is
the soul's normal state; its sojourn in the body is a severe illness. Our Lethe
of what we beheld in our previous lives is only a temporary interruption and
obscuration of our memories and of the continuity of our consciousness.
Since nothing of this kind is to be feared when we grow well again, i.e., when
our souls are freed from their bodies, this view appears to guarantee the
immortality of "the whole soul."

The validity of the proof depends on the correctness of its presupposition,
that man's knowledge is a recollection of "the visions there." The personal
immortality that the *Eudemus* teaches necessarily stands or falls along with
this Platonic dogma. Plato had supported his great logical discovery, the *a
priori,* with the myth of recollection. At first the young Aristotle followed

along the lines of this myth, and we should not be justified in regarding this way of thinking . . . as a mere metaphor in the pupil. But the moment that he had clearly grasped the specifically logical nature of pure thought, and realized that memory is a psycho-physical phenomenon, he denied that *Nus* was capable of recollection and dropped preexistence and immortality.[38]

[The objections to rebirth on the basis of memory have been considered at length by C. J. Ducasse in our introduction. In chapter 6 another twentieth-century philosopher, John McTaggart, deals with the problem, as does also Gustave Geley, who speaks from the standpoint of modern psychology.[39]]

[In Aristotle's later dialogues he did not completely abandon the philosophy of preexistence, for as the seventeenth-century Cambridge Platonist Henry More points out in his treatise on the "Immortality of the Soul":]

We shall evince that Aristotle, who has the luck to be believed more than most authors, was of the same opinion [as to the preexistence of the soul], in his treatise "De Anima," where he says . . . "for every art must use its proper instruments, and every soul its body." . . . He speaks something more plainly in his "De Generatione Animae." "There are generated," saith he, "in the earth, and in the moisture thereof, plants and living creatures . . . and in the whole universe an animal warmth or heat; insomuch that in a manner all places are full of souls." . . .

We will add a third place still more clear, out of the same treatise, where he starts this very question of the pre-existency of souls, of the sensitive and rational especially . . . and he concludes thus: . . . It remains that the rational or intellectual soul only enters from without, as being only of a nature purely divine; with whose actions the actions of this gross body have no communication. Concerning which point he concludes like an orthodox scholar of his excellent master Plato; to whose footsteps the closer he keeps, the less he ever wanders from the truth. For in this very place he does plainly profess, what many would not have him so apertly guilty of, that the Soul of man is immortal, and can perform her proper functions without the help of this terrestrial body.[40]

The Roman Renaissance

[Classical Roman history was closely linked with that of her neighbor Greece by both cultural interchange and Greek colonization. Pythagoras settled and taught in southern Italy, founding a religious brotherhood that persisted and ramified over a long period. All the Greek gods were eventually transformed into Roman deities. There was even a supposed linkage through reincarnation. The Calabrian poet Ennius (239?–169 B.C.) relates in his *Annals* that Homer appeared to him in a dream and said that their bodies had been animated by the same soul. The *Annals* have been lost but the dream has survived through repetition by the classical Roman authors. However, the period of greatest interest and importance in our study is the first century B.C. Our chief source is Franz Cumont's *After Life in Roman Paganism,* the Silliman memorial lectures at Yale.[41] This study brings to light facts seldom included in our history books.

Setting the stage, Cumont says that the "rationalistic" era of Greek thought, inaugurated by Aristotle, pervaded the Hellenistic and Roman period for several centuries. By the end of the Roman Republic—signaled by the assassination of Julius Caesar in 44 B.C.—faith in a future life had reached its lowest ebb. The skepticism or indifference of the Greek Alexandrians had infected the Romans, and a vulgarized Epicureanism had become very popular. As Plato deduced the persistence of the soul after death from its supposed previous existence, so Epicurus drew an opposite conclusion from man's ignorance of his earlier life. He glorified death as annihilation and the end of all men's troubles. This doctrine, which the Roman Lucretius preached with the enthusiasm of a neophyte, had a profound reaction in Rome. Its adepts in Cicero's circle were numerous, including Cassius, the chief conspirator against Caesar. The Roman historian Sallust goes so far as to make Caesar himself affirm, in full senate, that death, as rest from torment, dispels the ills that afflict mankind. Epicureanism also spread into the lowest strata of society, as can be proven from numerous epitaphs. One maxim was repeated so often on tombstones that it was sometimes expressed only by initials: "I was not; I was; I am not: I do not care."

The other system that shared the dominance of minds in Rome was Stoicism. The Stoics, Cumont informs us, held man to be a microcosm who reproduces in his being the constitution of the universe, and that he periodically reincarnates. The universe was thought to be governed by cycles, and after the destruction of each world, the individual souls returned to their divine home, the Soul of the World, from which they originally emanated. Cosmic life was conceived as formed of an infinite series of exactly similar cycles, so in a new world the same souls, endowed with the same qualities, found themselves in existence again. The Christian writer Hippolytus (martyred c. A.D. 235), in his chief work *Philosophumena* (a refutation of heresies), says that the Stoics "acknowledge there is a transition of souls from one body to another."[42] It should be noted that the most eminent of the Stoic philosophers, such as Epictetus and Marcus Aurelius, devoted themselves to ethical ideas and did not mention reincarnation. Marcus Aurelius, one historian remarks, "had not the ready solution, of all the East, of Plato, and Pythagoras, in Metempsychosis, in the long training of the soul through different lives and fortunes."[43]

In the first century B.C., which was Rome's darkest spiritual hour, says Cumont, "the birth was seen, or rather the rebirth, of a mystic movement." The teachings of Plato and Pythagoras gained new life in the Roman world. Epicureanism died away, and Stoicism, which had become materialistic, was replaced by Neo-Stoicism. The rebirth of spiritual ideas is described in *After Life in Roman Paganism:*

> The chief preoccupation of philosophers began to be those capital questions as to the origin and end of man which the schools of the earlier [Aristotelian and Epicurean] period had neglected as unanswerable. It was above all the Neo-Pythagoreans who gave up pure rationalism, and thus brought Roman thought to admit new forms of immortality. . . . They claimed that they remained faithful to the wisdom of the sages who, at the dawn of [their] civilization, had received a divine revelation, which had been transmitted first to Pythagoras and then to Plato. . . .
>
> The first to give new life to the Pythagorean school, which had died in Italy centuries before, was, according to Cicero, his friend, the senator Nigidius Figulus . . . a Roman magistrate, a man of singular erudition [who was] bitten with all the occult sciences. . . . This religious philosophy, which, by a symbolism transforming the meaning of the traditional beliefs, reconciled these with men's intelligence, did more than any other to revive faith in immortality. . . .

One of the main causes of skepticism had been that the gods "lost face" with the masses, and the old mythological stories of the afterlife, which had been taken literally, were now regarded as ridiculous fairy tales. The new movement portrayed the myths as grand symbols of cosmic and psychological processes.

The belief in immortality and metempsychosis of the Pythagoreans, says Cumont, found a powerful advocate in Posidonius, a thinker who exercised a predominant influence over his contemporaries and the succeeding generation.

> We know little of his life. Born at Apamea in Syria, about the year 135 [B.C.], he early left his native country . . . and as a young student in Athens he attended the lectures of the older Stoic Panaetius. The universal curiosity which was to make him a scholar of encyclopaedic knowledge soon impelled him to take long journeys. . . . Upon his return he opened a school in the free city of Rhodes and there numbered Cicero among his hearers. When he died at the age of eighty-four the prestige he enjoyed both in the Roman world and among the Greeks was immense.
>
> He owed his intellectual ascendancy as much to the marvellous variety of the knowledge which he displayed, as philosopher, astronomer, historian, geog-

rapher and naturalist, as to his copious, harmonious and highly coloured style [of writing]. . . . He gave the support of his authority and his eloquence to the eclecticism which reconciled the principles of the ancient Greek Schools. Moreover, his Syrian origin led him to combine these doctrines with the religious ideas of the East. . . . Posidonius introduced into Stoicism momentous ideas derived at once from Pythagorism and from Eastern cults, and sought to establish them firmly by connecting them with a system of the world, which his vast intelligence had sought to understand in all its aspects.

Commenting on Posidonius's concept of reincarnation and the afterlife, Cumont says: "This theology attributed to man a power such as to satisfy his proudest feelings. It did not regard him as a tiny animalcule who had appeared on a small planet lost in immensity, nor did it, when he scrutinised the heavens, crush him with a sense of his own pettiness as compared with bodies whose greatness surpassed the limits of his imagination. It made man king of creation." Cumont states further:

[Posidonius] exerted a far-reaching action beyond the narrow circle of the school. . . . Seneca in particular . . . shows the imprint of the philosopher of Apamea. . . . The erudition of the antiquarian Varro, the poems of Vergil and Manilius and the biblical exegesis of Philo the Jew, all drew on [Posidonius] for inspiration. But the author in whom we can best discern his influence is his pupil Cicero, the abundance of whose writings allows us to follow the evolution of his thought, which is characteristic of the whole society of his time. Cicero was an agnostic for the greater part of his life [but] by his study of the writings of his master Posidonius and by his intercourse with the senator Nigidius Figulus, a fervent adept of Pythagorism, [Cicero] had been brought in contact with the stream of mystical ideas which was beginning to flow through the West.

To add to this brief account of Roman ideas on reincarnation, the reader may turn to the sections under Persian religions entitled "Mithraism" and "Manicheism"—two religions that had a powerful effect on Roman thought during the early centuries of our era—and also to the treatment of Neoplatonism to be presented shortly. As Cumont remarks: "The mental evolution of Roman society was complete when Neoplatonism took upon itself the office of directing minds. The powerful mysticism of Plotinus (A.D. 205–262) opened up the path which Greek philosophy was to follow until the world of antiquity reached its end."]

CICERO (106–43 B.C.)

Roman Orator, Statesman, and Philosopher

[Cicero's gradual transition from agnosticism to Platonism is well illustrated in two selections from his writings. The first, taken from his *Hortensio*, evinces a germinal interest in karma and rebirth: "The ancients, whether they were seers, or interpreters of the divine mind in the tradition of the sacred initiations, seem to have known the truth, when they affirmed that we were born into the body to pay the penalty for sins committed in a former life."[44] The second is from his dialogue *On Old Age*. Here Cicero speaks more affirmatively through his leading character:]

The soul is of heavenly origin, forced down from its home in the highest, and, so to speak, buried in earth, a place quite opposed to its divine nature and its immortality. . . . Nor is it only reason and argument that have brought me to this belief, but the great fame and authority of the most distinguished philosophers. I used to be told that Pythagoras and the Pythagoreans—almost natives of our country, who in old times had been called the Italian school of philosophers—never doubted that we had souls drafted from the universal Divine intelligence.

I used besides to have pointed out to me the discourse delivered by Socrates on the last day of his life upon the immortality of the soul—Socrates . . . the wisest of men. I need say no more. I have convinced myself, and I hold—in view of the rapid movement of the soul, its vivid memory of the past and its prophetic knowledge of the future, its many accomplishments, its vast range of knowledge, its numerous discoveries—that a nature embracing such varied gifts cannot itself be mortal. And since the soul is always in motion and yet has no external source of motion, for it is self-moved, I conclude that it will also have no end to its motion, because it is not likely ever to abandon itself. . . .

It is again a strong proof of men knowing most things before birth, that when mere children they grasp innumerable facts with such speed as to show that they are not then taking them in for the first time, but remembering and recalling them. . . .

No one, my dear Scipio, shall ever persuade me that your father, Paulus, and your two grandfathers . . . or the father of Africanus, or his uncle, or many other illustrious men not necessary to mention, would have attempted such lofty deeds as to be remembered by posterity, had they not seen in their minds that future ages concerned them.[45]

JULIUS CAESAR (100–44 B.C.)

Roman General and Statesman

[Julius Caesar found the Celts to be remarkably fearless in battle. He apparently investigated the reason for this and wrote in his volumes on the wars with the Gauls: "They wish to inculcate this as one of their leading tenets, that souls do not become extinct, but pass after death from one body to another, and they think that men by this tenet are in a great degree excited to valor, the fear of death being disregarded."[46]

A number of other Roman authors speak of the reincarnation beliefs of the Celts. The Spanish-born Roman poet Lucan (A.D. 39–65), addressing the Druids, writes: "From you we learn that the destination of man's spirit is not the grave, nor the Kingdom of the Shades. The same spirit in another world animates a body and, if your teaching be true, death is the center, not the finish, of a long life."[47] Valerius Maximus said that he was tempted to call the Druids fools for believing such things, "were not their doctrine the same as that of the mantle-clad Pythagoras."[48]]

LUCRETIUS (96?–55 B.C.)
Roman Poet and Physicist

[Lucretius was an ardent follower of Epicurus. Wade Baskin writes that Lucretius "is now ranked among the outstanding poets of all time. Milton, Tennyson, Shelley and Whitman are numbered among those who have drawn attention to the life and work of the poet whose tense, electric *De Rerum Natura* (On the Nature of Things) is the confession of a mind tormented by violent passions and obsessed by a longing for philosophical calm."[49] The scientific portions, which explain the Epicurean theory of the material origin and workings of life and the cosmos, have excited discussion among thinkers for centuries. Henri Bergson sums up his own sympathetic study of the poem:

> Lucretius tried to show the powerlessness of men and gods in the face of natural laws. . . . He felt compassion for mankind; for man must act and not achieve, struggle and not succeed, and be unwillingly drawn into the vortex of things by rigid natural laws. Why work or take pains to accomplish anything? Why struggle or complain? We are victims of a common law, and nature shows little concern over us.[50]

Lucretius hoped to liberate man from fear, particularly the fear of death, death being regarded as a blessed annihilation. He himself is supposed to have committed suicide in a fit of insanity. His objections to reincarnation are given in these selections from the poem.]

> If soul immortal is, and winds its way
> Into the body at the birth of man,
> Why can we not remember something, then,
> Of life-time spent before? why keep we not
> Some footprints of the things we did of old?
> . . . . Were mind
> Immortal, were it wont to change its bodies,
> How topsy-turvy would earth's creatures act!

The Hyrcan hound would flee the onset oft
Of Antlered stag, the scurrying hawk would quake
Along the winds of air at the coming dove,
And men would dote, and savage beasts be wise. . . .
But should some say that always souls of men
Go into human bodies, I will ask:
How can a wise become a dullard soul?
And why is never a child's a prudent soul?
And at the rites of Love, that souls should stand
Ready hard by seems ludicrous enough—
Immortals waiting for their mortal limbs
In numbers innumerable, contending madly
Which shall be first and chief to enter in!—
Unless perchance among the souls there be
Such treaties stablished that the first to come
Flying along, shall enter in the first,
And that they make no rivalries of strength!
. . . . Death to us
Is nothing, nor concerns us in the least,
Since nature of mind is mortal evermore. . . .
Nor yet if time our scattered dust re-blend,
And after death upbuild the flesh again,
Yea, and our light of life arise re-lit,
Can such new birth concern the self one whit,
When once dark death has severed memory's chain.
Naught heed we, then, our lives lived in the past,
Nor for their sorrows feel one pang of pain.[51]

VERGIL (70–19 B.C.)

Roman Poet

[Albert Einstein in writing to Hermann Broch, thanking him for his book on
Vergil, expressed himself in Faustian terms: "I am fascinated by your
Vergil—and am steadfastly resisting him. The book shows me clearly what I
fled from when I sold myself body and soul to Science—the flight from the I
and WE to the IT."[52]

In Book the Sixth of Vergil's *Aeneid,* the hero Aeneas is shown traveling
through the Valley of Oblivion. Charles Galey summarizes this phase of the
journey in *Classic Myths in English Literature and Art:*]

Aeneas perceived before him a spacious valley, with trees gently waving
to the wind, a tranquil landscape, through which the river Lethe flowed.
Along the banks of the stream wandered a countless multitude, numerous as

insects in the summer air. Aeneas, with surprise, inquired who were these. Anchises answered: "They are souls to which bodies are to be given in due time. Meanwhile they dwell on Lethe's bank and drink oblivion of their former lives."

"O father!" said Aeneas, "is it possible that any can be so in love with life as to wish to leave these tranquil seats for the upper world?" [Anchises replies by explaining the plan of evolution, and how man eventually became impure.] Thus the more earth predominates in the composition the less pure is the individual; and we see that men and women with their full-grown bodies have not the purity of childhood. So in proportion to the time which the union of body and soul has lasted, is the impurity contracted by the spiritual part. This impurity must be purged away after death. . . .

Some few, of whom Anchises intimates that he is one, are admitted at once to Elysium, there to remain. . . . Anchises, having explained so much, proceeded to point out to Aeneas individuals of his race who were hereafter to be born, and to relate to him the exploits they should perform in the world.[53]

OVID (43 B.C.–A.D. 17)

Roman Poet

[We have already discussed the theme of Ovid's *Metamorphoses*. In these verses from Book the Fifteenth, translated by John Dryden, Pythagoras is speaking:]

> Those I would teach; and by right reason bring
> To think of death as but an idle thing.
> Why thus affrightened at an empty name,
> A dream of darkness, and fictitious flame? . . .
> What feels the body when the soul expires,
> By time corrupted, or consumed by fires?
> . . . the spirit, but new life repeats
> In other form, and only changes seats.
> Ev'n I, who these mysterious truths declare,
> Was once Euphorbus in the Trojan war;
> My name and lineage I remember well,
> And how in fight by Sparta's king I fell. . . .
>
> Then death, so call'd, is but old matter dress'd
> In some new figure, and a varied vest:
> Thus all things are but alter'd, nothing dies;
> And here and there the unbodied spirit flies. . . .
> From tenement to tenement though toss'd,
> The soul is still the same, the figure only lost:

And as the soften'd wax new seals receives,
This face assumes, and that impression leaves;
Now call'd by one, now by another name;
The form is only changed, the wax is still the same.
So death, so call'd, can but the form deface,
The immortal soul flies out in empty space;
To seek her fortune in some other place.[54]

APOLLONIUS OF TYANA (FIRST CENTURY A.D.)

Greek Philosopher

[The most renowned philosopher of the first century A.D. was Apollonius of Tyana. Born in the year 1, some biographers state he lived to be one hundred. Marcus Aurelius said: "From him I have learned freedom of will and understanding, steadiness of purpose, and to look to nothing else, not even for a moment, except to reason."[55] Apollonius journeyed extensively through Italy, Greece, Spain, Africa, Asia Minor, Persia, and India, teaching wherever he went. Thirteen years were spent with the sages in Kashmir. He was the author of a voluminous philosophical literature, which was collected and preserved by the Emperor Hadrian. Daniel Tredwell says: "He speaks and acts as a reformer and lover of humanity everywhere. . . . He had no narrow notions of nationality, no local clique to serve: he came to no chosen people, but to all mankind."[56] The record of his life was written by Damis, his constant companion for more than fifty years. This was partially transcribed by the historian Philostratus (170?–245), and published in A.D. 210 at the request of the Neoplatonist Emperor Severus and his wife, Julia Domna, one of the illustrious women of history and a philosopher of note.

Philostratus reports a conversation—which we quote here in part—between Apollonius and Iarchas, a wise man of Kashmir, to whom Apollonius had traveled to be instructed in the higher philosophy. Although Iarchas gives particulars of Apollonius's former life, Apollonius later emphasizes that as far as he is concerned he "never declared to the Greeks either from what body [his] soul has migrated, or into what it is to migrate."[57]]

"And what view do you take of the soul?" [asked Apollonius]. "That which Pythagoras imparted to you, and which we imparted to the Egyptians." "Would you then say," said Apollonius, "that, as Pythagoras declared himself to be Euphorbus, so you yourself, before you entered your present body, were one of the Trojans or Achaeans or someone else?" And the Indian replied: "Those Achaean sailors were the ruin of Troy, and your talking so much about it is the ruin of you Greeks. For you imagine that the campaigners against Troy were the only heroes that ever were, and you forget other heroes both more numerous and more divine, whom your own country and that of the Egyptians and that of the Indians have produced. . . ."

[Iarchas related some incidents of a previous incarnation in India, and then remarked:] "You must not be surprised at my transformation from one Indian to another; for here is one," and he pointed to a stripling of about twenty years of age, "who in natural aptitude for philosophy excels everyone . . . yet in spite of all these advantages he detests philosophy." "What then," said Apollonius, "O Iarchas, is the matter with the youth? For it is a terrible thing you tell me, if one so well adapted by nature to the pursuit refuses to embrace philosophy, and has no love for learning. . . ."

"The truth is this stripling was once Palamedes of Troy, and he found his bitterest enemies in Odysseus and Homer; for the one laid an ambush against him of people by whom he was stoned to death, while the other denied him any place in his Epic; and because neither the wisdom with which he was endowed was of any use to him, nor did he meet with any praise from Homer . . . he has conceived an aversion to philosophy, and deplores his ill-luck. And he is Palamedes, for indeed he can write without having learned his letters." . . .

[Iarchas] asked Apollonius the question: "Will you tell us . . . about your earlier incarnation, and who you were before the present life?" And he replied: "Since it was an ignoble episode, I do not remember much about it." Iarchas therefore took him up and said: "Then you think it ignoble to have been the pilot of an Egyptian vessel, for I perceive that this is what you were?" "What you say," said Apollonius, "is true, Iarchas; for that is really what I was. . . ."

[The two men then proceed to a discussion of philosophical subjects, at the conclusion of which Damis comments that "he was transported with admiration and applauded loudly; for he could never have thought that a native of India could show such mastery of the Greek tongue, nor even that, supposing he understood that language, he could have used it with so much ease and elegance."[58]]

PLUTARCH (A.D. 46?–120?)
Greek Biographer and Philosopher

[The name of Plutarch usually evokes but one thought: Oh, yes, he wrote that huge volume called *Plutarch's Lives*. While it is regarded as a biographical classic, Plutarch was nevertheless much more than a biographer. He was trained in philosophy at Athens, and also initiated into the Mysteries of

Dionysus. When he lived for a while in Rome he taught philosophy there. In *Roman Society from Nero to Marcus Aurelius,* Samuel Dill writes that Plutarch and Maximus as the leaders of the new Platonist school of the first century "were in this age, the great apostles of the hope of immortality. Platonists in their theory of mind and God, Neo-Pythagorean in their faith in the openness of the human spirit at its best to supernatural influences, they felt the doctrine of the coming life to be axiomatic."[59] Radhakrishnan calls Plutarch "a cultivated Gnostic of a tolerant frame of mind. . . . Plutarch believes in the rebirth of souls. . . . In the development of his views he was influenced by Greek thought and Egyptian religion."[60]

In Plutarch's *Moralia* he speaks of the afterdeath condition in which souls are "ordained to wander between incarnations," and that in a higher region dwell advanced beings whom he terms genii. "They are present at, and assist in, the most advanced of the initiatory rites . . . , they act, and shine as saviors in battle and at sea; and whatsoever thing in these capacities they do amiss . . . they are punished for it, for they are driven down again to earth and coupled with human bodies."[61]]

❊ ❊ ❊

The Neoplatonists

["Neoplatonic thought is metaphysically, the maturest thought the European world has seen," writes Thomas Whittaker in *The Neo-Platonists.*[62] Arthur Hillary Armstrong adds that "pagan Greek philosophy was Neoplatonist till it faded out in the sixth century A.D." "Many of the greatest Christian thinkers of this period, the great formative period of Christian theology, were deeply influenced by Neoplatonism, as were later the great Moslem philosophers. The influence of Neoplatonism on the thought of the Middle Ages was thus very great; and it has continued, through very diverse channels, to influence men's minds down to our own day."[63] R. T. Wallis remarks in a recent work that "a survey of Neoplatonism's influence threatens to become little less than a cultural history of Europe and the Near East, down to the Renaissance, and on some points far beyond."[64]

The famous Alexandrian school of Neoplatonism was founded in Egypt by Ammonius Saccas in A.D. 193. Origen and Plotinus were among his immediate disciples. Iamblichus; Porphyry; Proclus; the astronomer Eratosthenes; the Emperor Julian; Hypatia, the virgin philosopher; and numerous stars of second magnitude, all belonged at various times to this school, helping to make Alexandria with its incomparable library one of the finest seats of learning the world has known.

With the revival of the teachings of Plato, the philosophy of reincarnation again came into prominence, as can be seen from the selections from the voluminous works of Ammonius's pupils, although he himself left no written record of his thought. The Neoplatonists, however, did not limit themselves to Plato. Known as the Philalethians, "the lovers of truth," and the eclectic theosophical school, they sought to reconcile all religions and philosophies under one system of truth, and restore to its purity the wisdom of the ancients. This they held to be the real object of Jesus. Ammonius received the cooperation of the two Church Fathers Clement and Athenagoras, the learned rabbis of the synagogues, and the initiates of the various Mystery Schools.

However, "it was Plotinus," says Armstrong, "a philosophical genius of the first order . . . a man of deep contemplative religion and one of the world's greatest mystical writers, who made this new Platonism into one of the great religious philosophies. The success of Neoplatonism was rapid. Soon after Plotinus' death it came to dominate the Greek philosophical world."[65]

The movement reached its height of popularity in the fifth century. The leading Platonist then was Hypatia, the daughter of Theon—himself a celebrated philosopher and mathematician. After contacting the school in Athens, Hypatia went to Alexandria where she held lectures and classes in philosophy and mathematics at the famous museum. Her eloquence, wisdom, youth, and extraordinary beauty soon attracted crowds of students, and among her champions and students were two of the most influential men of the day, Orestes, the Prefect of Alexandria, and the Christian philosopher Synesius, then Bishop of Cyrene.

In 412 Saint Cyril became Bishop of Alexandria, and in 414 under his instigation a group of his monks led by Peter the Reader murdered Hypatia on the altar of a Christian church, dragged her naked body through the streets, later scraping the flesh from the bones. Clergyman-author Charles Kingsley tells the story in his two-volume novel, *Hypatia*. With Hypatia's death the Neoplatonic School came to an end in Alexandria. Some of the philosophers removed to Athens but their school was closed by the Emperor Justinian in 529 and the last seven Neoplatonic philosophers fled to the Middle East. It was not until the Renaissance that Platonism returned to Christian Europe, but Moorish Spain had a Platonic revival earlier. The death of Hypatia has been called the beginning of the Dark Ages for Europe.

Now we take up Plotinus, followed by Porphyry, the Emperor Julian, and several other Neoplatonists, and this will conclude our sojourn in Greece, Rome, and Alexandria.]

PLOTINUS (A.D. 205–270)

Neoplatonic Philosopher

[Father Elmer O'Brien writes in *The Essential Plotinus* that for the student of history of ideas there is to be had at first hand in Plotinus's *Enneads* ideas that played an influential part in molding Western thinking. ''The doctrine of the *Enneads* . . . has always managed to overleap the usual confinement of time and space . . . the most varied minds down the ages have served from time to time as its native land; the most unpropitious of circumstances have seemingly brought about its successive reincarnations in an Augustine, a Hugh of St. Victor, a Meister Eckhart.''[66] Augustine, who attended the lectures of Plotinus, even wondered whether Plotinus may have been Plato reborn![67] George Foot Moore calls Plotinus ''the fountainhead of the higher Christian mysticism,'' and states that ''the bible of the mediaeval mystics, Dionysius Areopagita, is thoroughly Plotinian . . . but the transmigration of souls . . . was tacitly let fall.''[68] Of course, to remove the latter concept from the philosophy of Plotinus would appreciably confine its horizon and undermine its structure.

W. R. Inge in his 1948 Gifford Lectures is especially enthusiastic regarding this pupil of Ammonius:

> The lecturer has found Plotinus a most inspiring and fortifying spiritual guide, as well as a great thinker. In times of trouble like the present he has much to teach us, lifting us up from the miseries of this world to the pure air and sunshine of eternal truth, beauty, and goodness.
>
> On the intellectual side, Neoplatonism sums up the results of 700 years of untrammelled thinking, the longest period of free speculation which the human race has enjoyed. The greater part of it passed over into Christian philosophy, which it shaped for all time. . . . The neglect of Plotinus, alike by students of Greek philosophy and of Christian dogma, is therefore much to be regretted. It makes a gap where no gap exists.[69]

The highlights of Plotinus's career are reviewed by Alice Zimmern in the introduction to her translation of *Porphyry, the Philosopher, to His Wife Marcella.* She writes that after eleven years of instruction by Ammonius, Plotinus ''set out for the East to study the wisdom of Persia and India.'' However, owing to wars in the Middle East, he could not reach India. ''At the age of forty he settled in Rome, and there opened a school of philosophy. . . . In spite of the abstruse nature of his teaching, crowds flocked around Plotinus. Men of science, physicians, senators and lawyers came to hear him; even Roman ladies enrolled themselves among his disciples. . . . This popularity of an abstruse philosopher is a curious and perhaps unique phenomenon; and we can but ask whether Plotinus may not have condescended a little to his audience, and reserved his inner doctrines for a privileged few.''[70]

The translator of the first selections from the *Enneads* is Stephen Mac-Kenna, a member of the Dublin circle of George Russell, Yeats, James Stephens, and others of Ireland's literary renaissance. As we read on, it will become evident that in these opening thoughts Plotinus is indulging in no callous condonement of war and strife.]

The animals devour each other: men attack each other: all is war without rest, without truce: this gives new force to the question how Reason can be author of the plan and how all can be declared well done. . . . What does it matter when [beings] are devoured only to return in some new form? It comes to no more than the murder of one of the personages in a play; the actor alters his make-up and enters in a new role. The actor, of course, was not really killed; but if dying is but changing a body as the actor changes a costume, or even an exit from the body like the exit of the actor from the boards when he has no more to say or do, what is there so very dreadful in this transformation of living beings one into another? . . .

Murders, death in all its guises, the reduction and sacking of cities, all must be to us just such a spectacle as the changing scenes of a play; all is but the varied incident of a plot, costume on and off, acted grief and lament. For on earth, in all the succession of life, it is not the Soul within but the Shadow outside of the authentic man, that grieves and complains and acts out the plot on this world stage which men have dotted with stages of their own constructing. *All this is the doing of man knowing no more than to live the lower and outer life,* and never perceiving that, in his weeping and in his graver doings alike, he is but at play. . . .

Every man has his place, a place that fits the good man, a place that fits the bad: each . . . makes his way, naturally, reasonably, to the place, good or bad, that suits him, and takes the position he has made his own. There he talks and acts, in blasphemy and crime or in all goodness: for the actors bring to this play what they were before it was ever staged. . . .

But these actors, Souls, hold a peculiar dignity; they act in a vaster place than any stage; the Author has made them masters of all this world; they have a wide choice of place; they themselves determine the honor or discredit in which they are agents since their place and part are in keeping with their quality. . . . If a man were . . . nothing more than a made thing, acting and acted upon according to a fixed nature—he could be no more subject to reproach and punishment than the mere animals. But as the scheme holds, man is singled out for condemnation when he does evil; and this with justice. For he is no mere thing made to rigid plan; his nature contains a Principle apart and free.

Translator, Stephen MacKenna[71]

The soul . . . falling from on high, suffers captivity, is loaded with fetters, and employs the energies of sense. . . . She is reported also to be buried and to be concealed in a cave; but when she converts herself to intelligence she then breaks her fetters and ascends on high, receiving first of all from reminiscence the ability of contemplating real beings. . . . Souls therefore are necessarily of an amphibious nature, and alternately experience a superior and inferior condition of being; such as are able to enjoy a more intimate converse with Intellect abiding for a longer period in the higher world, and such to whom the contrary happens, either through nature or fortune, continuing longer connected with these inferior concerns. . . .

Thus the soul, though of divine origin, and proceeding from the regions on high, becomes merged in the dark receptacle of body. . . . By this means it receives a knowledge of evil, unfolds its latent powers, and exhibits a variety of operations peculiar to its nature, which, by perpetually abiding in an incorporeal habit, and never proceeding into energy, would have been bestowed in vain. . . . For the experience of evil produces a clearer knowledge of good. . . . Indeed, if it is proper to speak clearly what appears to me to be the truth . . . the whole of our soul does not enter into body, but something belonging to it always abides in the intelligible . . . world. . . . For every soul possesses something which inclines downwards to body, and something which tends upwards toward intellect . . . but the superior part of the soul is never influenced by fraudulent delights, and lives a life always uniform and divine.

Translator, Thomas Taylor[72]

PORPHYRY (A.D. 233–C. 304)

Greek Scholar and Neoplatonic Philosopher

[Esmé Wynne-Tyson writes that "in the present age Porphyry is renowned chiefly for having been the pupil of the great Neoplatonist, Plotinus . . . and for having edited *The Enneads* of his Master; but in earlier times he was considered to be one of the most erudite philosophers of the West. Augustine refers to him as 'the noble philosopher,' 'the great ethnic philosopher' and ranks him even above Plato. Eusebius, his implacable enemy, speaks of him as 'the wonderful theologian' and 'the great prophet,' while to Simplicius he was 'the most learned of philosophers.' "[73]

Porphyry was a Hellenized Hebrew. Some have thought that his works surpassed those of Plotinus, but there is no way of knowing this as his books were publicly burned by Constantine and Theodosius, and only a few treatises remain. That Porphyry taught reincarnation is, of course, beyond question, but his views have come to us mainly through the reports of adversaries. Augustine has been quoted earlier on Porphyry's supposed ideas. Voltaire wrote of Porphyry's *De Abstinentia:* "One might believe in reading him that this great enemy of the Church is a Father of the Church. He does not speak of the metempsychosis [in this treatise] but he regards other animals as our brothers. . . ."[74] Porphyry does speak of reincarnation in *De Abstinentia;* one selection was included under "Mithraism," another is offered here. The term intellect as used by Porphyry in this excerpt, and by the Platonists generally, is not to be associated with the hard, cold, clever reasoning faculty prized by the materialistic thinker, but relates to the highest intellection and rationality—that illuminated by *Nous,* or spiritual wisdom.]

As long as any one injures another, though he should possess the greatest wealth, and all the acres of land which the earth contains, he is still poor. . . . He is unjust, without God, and impious, and enslaved to every kind of depravity, which is produced by the lapse of the soul into matter. . . . He wanders from the principle of the universe. . . . He likewise yields to the mortal part of his nature, while he remains ignorant of his real self. . . . However, in the choice of lives [that individual] is the more accurate judge who has obtained an experience of both [the better and the worse kind of life], than he who has only experienced one of them. . . . Hence, he who lives according to intellect, will more accurately define what is eligible and what is not, than he who lives under the dominion of irrationality. For the former has passed through the irrational life . . . but the latter, having had no experience of an intellectual life [acts] like a child among children.[75]

IAMBLICHUS (A.D. C. 250–C. 330)

Greek Philosopher

[Iamblichus, the third member of the great Neoplatonic triad, was born in Chalsis in Coele-Syria. From the fragments of his life collected by impartial historians, it is evident that he was a man of great learning, renowned for his charity and self-denial. His mind was deeply impregnated with the Pythagorean doctrines, and in his biography of Pythagoras set forth the philosophical, ethical, and scientific teachings of the Grecian sage.

Iamblichus was a profound student of the Egyptian Mysteries and was determined to make public what hitherto had been taught in secrecy. To accomplish this he founded a school of theurgy among the Neoplatonists. Porphyry at first opposed this project because the knowledge of practical theurgy is dangerous for most men. He therefore addressed a letter to an Egyptian initiate known as Anebo, asking for an explanation of certain points in the Egyptian system. The letter was answered by Iamblichus under the name of his teacher Abammon. The discussion between Porphyry and Iamblichus composes the book known as The Egyptian Mysteries, recorded by Iamblichus himself. The selections below are from the translation of Alexander Wilder. Iamblichus is speaking.]

What shall we say in regard to the question: "Why do the divinities that are invoked require the worshiper to be just, although they themselves when entreated consent to perform unjust acts?" In reply to this I am uncertain in respect to what is meant by "performing unjust acts," as the same definition may not appear right both to us and to the gods. We, on the one hand, looking to that which is least significant, consider the things that are present, the momentary life, what it is and how it originates. The beings superior to us, let me say, know for certain the whole life of the soul and all its former

lives; and if they bring on a retribution from the supplication of those who
invoke them, they do not increase it beyond what is just. On the contrary,
they aim at the sins impressed upon the soul in former lifetimes, which men
do not perceive, and so imagine that it is unjust that they fall into the misfortunes which they suffer.

The many are also generally accustomed to propose the same doubt in
regard to Providence; that certain persons are suffering from wrong-doing,
who had not wronged any one previously. For they are unable here to reason
as to what the soul is, what its entire life has been, the magnitude of its great
errors in former lives, and whether it is now suffering these things for what it
did formerly. . . .

That condition about which thou utterest doubt, does not exist, namely:
*"That all things are bound fast in the indissoluble bonds of Necessity, which
they term Fate"*. . . . All things in the world of Nature are not controlled by
Fate. . . . For the soul has a principle of its own leading to the realm of
Intelligence, and not only standing aloof from things of the world of generated existence, but also joining it to that which IS, even to the divine nature.
. . . [This] principle of the soul . . . is superior to the whole realm of nature
and generated existence. By it we can be united to the gods, rise above the
established order of the world, and likewise participate in the life eternal and
in the energy of the gods of the highest heaven. Through this principle we are
able to set ourselves free. For when the better qualities in us are in activity,
and the soul is exalted to those beings superior to itself, then it becomes
separate altogether from every thing which held it fast in the realm of generated existence, keeps itself aloof from inferior natures, exchanges one life for
the other, and gives itself to a different order, entirely abandoning the
former.[76]

EMPEROR JULIAN (A.D. 331–363)
Roman Neoplatonist

[Julian, the nephew of the first Christian emperor, Constantine, was a pupil
of Aedesius, who had been taught by Iamblichus. He was initiated at
Ephesus, and later into the Eleusinian Mysteries. Succeeding the despotic
Constantine, his reign lasted only eighteen months, but was noted for its
enlightenment and religious tolerance. Exiled Christian bishops were returned to their posts, and pagan subjects were granted complete religious
liberty. Few characters in history have been as unjustly maligned as Julian
"the Apostate." This is mildly implied in Henry Fielding's reincarnation
story of Julian.[77] Incidentally, Julian appears to have had reason to believe
himself the reincarnation of the unenviable Alexander the Great. Ibsen dwelt
on this theme in his play *The Emperor Julian*.[78]

Julian was mortally wounded by an assassin. While dying he said: "I have learned from philosophy how much more excellent the soul is than the body, and that the separation of the nobler substance should be the subject of joy rather than affliction.''[79] Then, emulating Socrates, Julian turned to the two philosophers Priscus and Maximus and entered into a metaphysical discussion as to the nature of the soul.]

SALLUSTIUS (FOURTH CENTURY)
Roman Philosopher

[Julian chose Sallust as his Pretorian Prefect, or chief magistrate. Thomas Whittaker writes that "in setting forth a creed for the reformed paganism" begun under Julian's reign, Sallust "had put only in cryptic language his explanation of the change that had come over the world. The guilt, he says, that is now punished in some by total ignorance of the true divine order may be that of having deified their kings in a former life. Thus it appears that in Julian's circle Christianity was regarded as nemesis for the deification of the Emperors.''[80]

Another author quotes Sallust's views on why atheism exists: "It is not unlikely that the rejection of God is a kind of punishment: we may well believe that those who knew the gods and neglected them in one life may in another be deprived of the knowledge of them altogether.''[81]]

MACROBIUS (FOURTH-FIFTH CENTURY)
Roman Neoplatonist

[In his *Commentary on the Dream of Scipio*, Macrobius offers a very illuminating explanation of Plato's myth of the river Lethe whose waters when imbibed by the incoming soul caused both forgetfulness of prior earthly lives and a form of spiritual amnesia. The extract is to be found as a footnote in Thomas Taylor's *Select Works of Porphyry:*[82]]

As soon as the soul gravitates towards body . . . she begins to experience a material tumult, that is, matter flowing into her essence. And this is what Plato remarks in the *Phædo,* that the soul is drawn into body staggering with recent intoxication; signifying by this, the new drink of matter's impetuous flood, through which the soul, becoming defiled and heavy, is drawn into a terrene situation. . . . Hence oblivion, the companion of intoxication . . . begins silently to creep into the recesses of the soul. For if souls retained in their descent to bodies the memory of divine concerns, of which they were conscious in the heavens, there would be no dissension among men about divinity. But all, indeed, in descending, drink of oblivion; though some more, and others less. On this account, though truth is not apparent to all men on the earth, yet all exercise their opinions about it; because a *defect of memory is the origin of opinion.* But those discover most who have drunk least of oblivion, because they easily remember what they had known before in the heavens. . . .

The soul is drawn down to these terrene bodies, and is on this account said to die when it is enclosed in this fallen region, and the seat of mortality. Nor ought it to cause any disturbance that we have so often mentioned the death of the soul, which we have pronounced to be immortal. For the soul is not extinguished by its own proper death, but is only overwhelmed for a time. Nor does it lose the benefit of perpetuity by its temporal demersion. Since,when it deserves to be purified from the contagion of vice, through its entire refinement from body, it will be restored to the light of perennial life, and will return to its pristine integrity and perfection.

PROCLUS (A.D. 410–485)

Greek Neoplatonic Philosopher

[Proclus is called "the last grand master of Neoplatonism." The material chosen is from his *Elements of Theology,* as translated by E. R. Dodds, the statements being presented as propositions:]

The soul-order, originating from one primal Soul, descends to a manifold of souls and again carries back the manifold to the one. . . .

Every particular soul can descend into temporal process and ascend from process to [spiritual] Being an infinite number of times. For if at certain times it is in the company of gods and at others falls away from its upward tension towards the divine . . . it is plain that by turns it comes to be in the world of process and [then] has true Being among the gods. For it cannot (have been for an infinite time in material bodies and thereafter pass a second infinite time among the gods, neither can it) have spent an infinite time among the gods and again be embodied for the whole time thereafter, since that which has no temporal beginning will never have an end, and what has no end cannot have had a beginning.

It remains, then, that each soul has a periodic alternation of ascents out of process and descents into process, and that this movement is unceasing by reason of the infinitude of time.

Therefore each particular soul can descend and ascend an infinite number of times, and this shall never cease to befall every such soul.[83]

[As mentioned before, Proclus goes into the vital question of what may be the need for repeated incarnations. Professor Dodds in commenting on the selection just given touches upon this whole problem and his interesting summation may fittingly conclude this section on Greek and Roman thinkers:]

The question whether the human soul can attain a final release from the "circle of birth" . . . was one on which the Neoplatonists were not unanimous. . . . , Porphyry . . . seems to have asserted in *de regressu animae* . . . that the soul, at any rate the soul of the philosopher, will eventually be released for ever. Later we find the contrary opinion, that souls cannot "leave the body once for all and remain through all time in idleness," maintained by Sallustius (who is very probably following Iamblichus here): he supports it (a) by the argument from function, that souls have their natural citizenship in the body; and (b) by the consideration that . . . the earth would on the Porphyrian theory eventually be depopulated.

Proclus takes the same view as Sallustius, but relies on the more general argument that an eternal life cannot start from, or finish at, a point in time. He holds with Syrianus that while self-will causes some human souls to descend more often than is necessary, cosmic law requires that each shall descend at least once in every world-period. Consistently with this, he rejects the . . . view that such descent is in itself sinful. . . . *He definitely treats the descent as a necessary part of the soul's education or as a necessary cosmic service.*[84]

THE MIDDLE AGES

Taliesin (sixth century?)

Welsh Bard

[Joseph Campbell writes in *The Hero with a Thousand Faces*: "Taliesin, 'Chief of the Bards of the West,' may have been an actual historical personage of the sixth century A.D., contemporary with the chieftain who became the 'King Arthur' of later romance. The bard's legend and poems survive in a thirteenth-century manuscript, 'The Book of Taliesin,' which is one of the 'Four Ancient Books of Wales'. . . . Gwion Bach, who, having tasted three drops from the poison kettle of inspiration, was eaten by the hag Caridwen, reborn as an infant, and committed to the sea, was found next morning in a fishtrap. . . . When the men took up the leathern bag out of the trap and opened it and saw the forehead of the baby boy, they said . . . 'Behold a

radiant brow (taliesin)!' 'Taliesin be he called.' . . . The larger portion of the
bard's song is devoted to the Imperishable, which lives in him. . . . Those
listening are oriented to the Imperishable in themselves. . . . Though he had
feared the terrible hag, he had been swallowed and reborn. Having died to
his personal ego, he arose again established in the Self."[1] The poems tell of
actual reincarnation as well as psychological rebirth.]

> Knowest thou what thou art in the hour of sleep—
> A mere body, a mere soul—or a secret retreat of light? . . .
> I marvel that in their books they know not with certainty
> The properties of the soul; or what form are its members;
> In what part, and when, it takes up its abode,
> Or by what wind or stream it is supplied.[2]

> I have been in many shapes before I attained a congenial form . . .
> There is nothing in which I have not been. . . .
> I was with my Lord in the highest sphere
> On the fall of Lucifer into the depth of hell;
> I have borne a banner before Alexander. . . .
> I am a wonder whose origin is not known.
> I have been in Asia with Noah in the ark,
> I have seen the destruction of Sodom and Gomorrah.
> I have been in India when Roma was built. . . .
> I shall be until the doom on the face of the earth. . . .
> I was originally little Gwion,
> And at length I am Taliesin.[3]

✳ ✳ ✳

The Grail Epics and a New Light on the Renaissance

[Under "Reincarnation in the Dark Ages," in the chapter on early Christianity, the story of the Cathari, and that branch thereof known as the Albigenses,
was told. We learned how these numerous reincarnationist groups spread all
over Europe, seriously threatening the survival of the Orthodox Church, and
how through peaceful propagation of Christian Gnostic teachings and the
ethics of Jesus, exemplified in the unusual purity of their lives, the Cathari
had weaned many thousands from the Church. Various scholars were cited
attesting to the universal belief in reincarnation among the Cathari. We
learned also how the clerics ruthlessly stamped out the Albigensian civilization in France and set up the first of the Holy Inquisitions, whose sole business was to deal with "heresy," torture and burning at the stake being its
weapons for dissenters. The Cathari that survived were forced underground,

and were obliged to devise secret means to preserve their ideas. It is here that the work of the troubadours and related groups becomes important to consider.

In the south of France where the Albigensian reincarnationists were so deeply rooted, the troubadours, as an integral part of that civilization, had for centuries exercised an enormous influence, and kept aflame the love of art and literature traditional to that region. At a time of almost total illiteracy in Europe and when the printing press was unknown, the troubadours filled the role now occupied by the press, and also embraced the callings of poet, musician, chronicler, *littérateur,* and theologian. When between the years 1209 and 1226 the Church devastated the Albigensian provinces, the home of the troubadours was demolished and its language (the *langue d'oc*) proscribed and extinguished. Finding asylum in all parts of Europe, they continued their work of humanistic and mystical education, adding perpetual fuel to the smoldering fires of heresy and rebellion to Rome. Likewise small bands of Albigensian artisans penetrated to the remotest parts of the continent, some of them emigrating to England where history knows them as the Lollards.

Harold Bayley in his remarkable work *A New Light on the Renaissance*[4] presents evidence that the Grail romances—amounting in bulk to a set of the *Britannica!*—were nothing less than the scriptures of the Albigenses, propagated during the age of chivalry by the troubadour poets of southern France and northern Italy and Spain. These vast cycles of mystic literature, written and declaimed by the troubadours, spread like wildfire over Europe, and were translated into many languages. Later they degenerated into mere tales of romance and adventure.

In reviewing *King Arthur's Avalon* by Geoffrey Ashe, DeLancey Ferguson writes: "The Grail stories mostly grew up outside the Church. . . . Mr. Ashe suggests possible reasons why the Church fought shy of this cult. A wonder-working vessel is a recurrent theme in ancient religions; so is the idea of special knowledge to be achieved by an initiate who performs secret rituals. 'The Grail cult may well have been only the most complex codification of a bold strain of mysticism, persisting through the centuries but never openly unfolded.' To the Church, of course, the hint of spiritual knowledge hidden even from the clergy was flat heresy."[5] One of the King Arthur legends made this prophecy: "He shall come again full twice as fair to rule over his people."[6]

The troubadours were conspicuous as Pilgrims of Love, and Knights Errant in the service of a mysterious lady. (Cervantes followed this traditional pattern in *Don Quixote.*) They viewed their service as both an art and a science, their "gai savoir," their "gai *science,*" and it is believed that under a well-recognized erotic jargon, matters and ideas of great moment were communicated to the scattered *fidèles.* Many of their love poems, which today

are regarded as amatory trifles, may in reality be works of a recondite
character, enshrining doctrines traditionally handed down from past ages.
The troubadours themselves at times made little effort to dissemble the fact.
"Thou can'st go whither thou wilt," says one of them, addressing his own
love poem, "I have dressed thee so well that thou will be understood by
those endowed with intelligence: of others thou need'st not be concerned."[7]

This symbolism of the Beloved was also used by the Sufi poets of Islam;
Dante and the Fideli d'Amore; the Spanish mystics of whom Raymond Lully
was one; and the Minnesingers or Love Singers of Germany who play leading
roles in Wagner's *Tannhäuser* and *Die Meistersinger*. In Act Two of *Tannhäuser*, the Landgrave speaks of the "veiled wisdom" behind the minstrels'
songs. One scholar of this period remarks on "the strange insistent call to
something else, something which awaits us, something which as human beings we have yet to accomplish," which suffused the Provençal and
troubadour singing, and which became an integral part of subsequent Western music.[8]]

Dante and the Fideli d'Amore

[Dante's *Divine Comedy* gives a description in allegorical language of the
drama of afterdeath conditions, of purification in purgatory, of sublimation in
heaven, and at least one hint of the soul's return to earth. In Canto XX of
Paradiso, Dante writes of meeting a Roman emperor in the Heaven of Jupiter
and being told:

> He from Hell came back into his bones, and this was the reward of living
> hope—the living hope which put power into the prayers made to God to raise
> him up, that his will might be moved. The glorious soul returning to flesh where
> it abode awhile, believed in Him who had power to help, the believing, kindled
> into such a flame of Love that at the second death it was worthy to come into
> this Joy.

Dante, who was born in 1265 and was one of the leading forerunners of the
Italian Renaissance, apparently exercised great caution in what he said. It
has been demonstrated by such scholars as Gabriele Rossetti, Luigi Valli,
Francesca Perez, and Giovanni Pascoli that Dante and the group of poets
known as the Fideli d'Amore, or the Faithful in Love, used a secret language
similar to that employed by the troubadours. At least thirty words commonly
used by the group were found to have one and sometimes two hidden meanings. Belonging to the cipher were love, madonna, death, life, women, na-

ture, stone, rose, flower—all of which appear repeatedly, often confusing the surface meaning. Characteristically, the "Beloved," be it Rosa, Beatrice, or Savage, always seems to represent Wisdom. Dante wrote: "I say and affirm that the lady of whom I was enamoured after my first love was the most beautiful and pure daughter of the Emperor of the Universe to whom Pythagoras gave the name Philosophy."[9]

In his two-volume work *Disquisitions on the Anti-Papal Spirit which Produced the Reformation,* Gabriele Rossetti—the father of Christina and Dante Gabriel Rossetti—states that the art of speaking and writing in a language bearing a double interpretation is of great antiquity; it was in practice among the priests of Egypt, brought thence by the Manichees, from whom it passed to the Templars and Albigenses, spread over Europe, and aided in bringing about the Reformation. John Yarker, who mentions this in *Mysteries of Antiquity,* comments that Boccaccio left several works, including parts of *The Decameron,* written in this jargon, which all refer to Dante, as to a great model," and that beyond doubt "Dante borrowed his style of figurative writings from the Templars and Albigenses."[10] In this connection it is worth reporting that in a work on Dante published in Paris in 1854, the Catholic writer Eugene Aroux called him a fountain of heresy and a leader of the Albigensian or Cathari "church" who had conceived the audacious project of employing ecclesiastical symbols to convey his Platonic teaching.

Another author, Maurice Magre, states that "it was after the visit of Nicetas . . . the Bulgarian mystic and great propagator of Catharism . . . that the group of the Faithful in Love was formed, whose doctrine had so much in common with Catharism. It is said that Frederick II, the protector of heretics, was an initiate. One of the masters of this group was Guido Cavalcanti, the friend and initiator of Dante."[11]

There are also strong indications that the Sufi mystics, whose reincarnation ideas we have already considered, had an important influence upon Dante and his fellow poets. The leading work on the subject is *Islam and The Divine Comedy* by Señor Asin y Palacios.[12]]

[From the foregoing chapter on the Middle Ages, one can draw the likely conclusion that after the destruction of the wide-ranging Cathari movement, in which reincarnation had been a universal teaching, the philosophy of rebirth was preserved chiefly in esoteric form in Europe. The flame was hidden, but did not die. How it slowly burst its subterranean prison will be the subject of the next phase of our story.]

RENAISSANCE AND REFORMATION

❋ ❋ ❋
The Italian Renaissance and the Neoplatonic Revival

[In his Hulsean Lectures at Cambridge, W. R. Inge remarked that "the light of the Renaissance dawned gradually upon Europe." "Greek scholars had begun to visit the Latin countries some time before the fall of Constantinople [in 1453]; and there were many other reasons for the great emancipation of the human mind which spread from Italy all over the West. It was like an awakening from a deep sleep. . . . the dropped threads are taken up again; civilization resumes its course with the recovered remains of the Classics in its hand."[1] Or, as the reincarnationist might audaciously suggest, the very souls who lived in ancient Greece and Rome came back to carry on their work. In the Renaissance, says Inge, "new worlds are opened to the seeker after truth, Galileo's new worlds above, the new worlds of the explorers beyond the seas, and the new world of the philosophers within."[2]

The new world within had its source in the rebirth of the philosophy of Plato and the Neoplatonists. Inge states that the Platonic tradition had never really been extinct; "or we may say more truly that the fire which, in the words of Eunapius, 'still burns on the altars of Plotinus,' has a perennial power of rekindling itself when the conditions are favourable."[3] G. F. Moore remarks in his Harvard Ingersoll lecture: "It is not surprising . . . that with the revival of Platonism and Plotinianism at the renaissance, the theory of metempsychosis was revived in European philosophy."[4]

The Neoplatonic revival appeared first in the city of Florence and under the protection of the powerful house of Medici. Cosmo de Medici made the acquaintance of George Gemistus, a venerable Byzantine Platonic philosopher who attended the Council of Florence in 1439 as a deputy of the Greek Church. Gemistus, who lived for a time at Cosmo's court, gave him the idea of founding a Platonic academy. With this in view, Cosmo selected Marsilio Ficino, the son of his chief physician, for a thorough education in Greek language and philosophy. Ficino's natural aptitude was so great that he completed his first work on the Platonic Institutions when only twenty-three years old. At thirty he began his translation of Plato, later making excellent translations of Hermes, Plotinus, Iamblichus, Proclus, and Synesius. He also wrote a treatise on the Platonic doctrine of immortality. Lynn White cites

Ficino's translation of Plato as one of the great intellectual events of Western history.[5]

When Cosmo's grandson Lorenzo was eight years old, Ficino became his tutor, imbuing him with a deep reverence for the Greeks. After Lorenzo (the "Magnificent") became the head of the house he brought his grandfather's plans to completion and, going further, founded a university in Pisa, established public libraries, and became a patron of Michelangelo, Botticelli, and Leonardo da Vinci. Pope Leo X, the second son of Lorenzo, shared his family's love of art and literature and befriended those interested in the extension of knowledge. Pope Nicholas V also had a deep love of the classics and paid highly for translations of Plato into Latin. His collection of manuscripts, numbering from three to five thousand, formed the basis for the Vatican library.

The revival of Neoplatonism made rapid headway when Pico, the brilliant youthful son of the Prince of Mirandola, joined forces with Lorenzo and Ficino. Although only a young man, Pico was deeply versed in the learning of the Chaldeans, Hebrews, and the Arabians. He was a Hermetist as well as a Kabalist, but today he is chiefly known as the author of the humanist classic *An Oration on the Dignity of Man.* Pico taught that "the soul passes out of one body and enters another."[6]

After the death of Ficino and his younger colleagues, the Platonic Academy declined, but not without having made a major contribution to the advancement of philosophy, art, and science, and to the spread of Platonism in France, England, and Germany. The Platonic revival in each of these centers will receive separate treatment.]

GEORGE GEMISTUS (1355–1450)

Byzantine Philosopher

[George Gemistus, called Pletho, after Plato, by Cosmo de Medici, was in effect a founding father of the Italian Renaissance. "He is . . . chiefly memorable for having been the first person who introduced Plato to the Western world . . . Cardinal Bessarion became his disciple; he produced a great impression upon Cosmo de Medici; and . . . effectually shook the exclusive domination which Aristotle had exercised over European thought for eight centuries."[7] Byzantium, or the eastern half of the Roman Empire, survived by a thousand years the fall of the western portion. It may be of more than passing significance that the Platonic ideas on reincarnation were openly restored to the West through a Byzantine philosopher considering that it was the Byzantine Emperor Justinian who in the sixth century closed the door to a free dialogue on the subject. In the following extract Pletho makes an unusual point regarding the need for rebirth:]

As to ourselves, our soul, partaking of the divine nature, remains immortal and eternal in the precincts which are the limit of our world. Attached to a mortal envelope, it is sent by the gods now into one body, now into another, in view of the universal harmony, in order that the union of the mortal and immortal elements in human nature may contribute to the unity of the Whole. . . .

If, in man, the immortal nature is united for an instant to the mortal nature, only to abandon it for the rest of time, no permanent bond would be made between these two mortal and immortal elements, but a temporary union which, the mortal element once removed, would immediately dissolve, and dissolve with it the general harmony. It remains to be said that [upon incarnating] the union of these two natures exists partially, temporarily, and that whenever the body is destroyed each returns [for the time being] to its respective independence, and this process is renewed indefinitely throughout eternity.[8]

The French Renaissance

[The brief and glorious revival of Neoplatonic thought during the Renaissance, which flourished in Italy under the Medicis, was carried from there to the French Court by an enthusiastic François I. In *The Century of the Renaissance in France,* Louis Batiffol remarks that "thanks to the invention of printing, fresh editions of Greek and Latin authors came into existence every day [in France], and interest in the works of the ancients, which had hitherto been practically inaccessible, increased considerably . . . and a large number of people developed a taste for the careful study of Greek and Latin forms. Interested in everything connected with the exercise of the intellect, Francis I was greatly attracted by this movement. . . . The most famous scholars of his reign were gradually introduced into his circle."[9]

Among the most illustrious was Guillaume Postel, the orientalist, one of the first to unravel the tangled skein of Oriental languages. He was sent on a mission to the East to find manuscripts. Jean Pierre Niceron in his noted *Mémoires* speaks of Postel as one of the most learned men of his age, a judgment confirmed by Postel's numerous works. He was the ideal all-round Renaissance man, excelling in philosophy, languages, cosmography, mathematics, and medicine. The king and his learned sister, the Queen of Navarre, regarded him as the marvel of the world. While in Constantinople, Postel embarked on Chaldean and Kabalistic studies under the tuition of a learned Jew, and while in the Levant is said to have been initiated by an Eastern fraternity. His mystical ideas earned him endless abuse from the theologians and he nearly perished at the hands of the Inquisition, which became more active than ever in Europe after the Renaissance. His *Clavis Absconditorum,* a key to things hidden and forgotten, was very celebrated. Postel speaks of reincarnation in his writings as well as various occult doctrines.[10]]

The English Renaissance

[In *The Platonic Tradition in English Religious Thought,* Inge relates that "while the Italian Renaissance issued in a new school of art, in England there was born a new piety, a new poetry, and a new drama. . . . [English] Renaissance poetry is steeped in Platonic thoughts."[11] John Smith Harrison furnishes details in *Platonism in English Poetry of the Sixteenth and Seventeenth Centuries.*[12]

"The Renaissance proper," says Inge, "reached England in the time of Colet and Erasmus. The flame which they kindled . . . was lighted in Italy, where Grocyn and Linacre visited the famous Platonic Academy at Florence. These Oxford Platonists represented a new idea of humane learning in England; at Cambridge the study of Greek was promoted by the teaching of Erasmus in 1512 and 1513."

Erasmus, of course, was a Dutch scholar and some regard him as the greatest humanist of the Renaissance and the most brilliant man of his time. He made his first journey to England in 1499 and there met John Colet, who was later to become the renowned dean of Saint Paul's. Erasmus wrote of Colet: "When I listen to him it seems as if I am listening to Plato himself." This friendship is said to have been a turning point in Erasmus's life, and he soon gave most of his time to the study of Greek and translated a number of Greek classics into Latin.

The British story continues shortly under "The Cambridge Platonists."]

Greek Philosophy and Jewish Mysticism in Germany

[In the Germany of the fifteenth century we find a strong interest in three schools of thought already shown to be fundamentally reincarnationist: Platonism, Pythagoreanism, and Kabalism.

The revival of Platonism was undertaken by Nicolas de Cusa, a Catholic cardinal and noted ecclesiastical and philosophical writer. His efforts to revive Platonic teachings were continued by Trithemius, the abbot of the

Benedictine Monastery of Spanheim, who was a Kabalist as well as
Platonist. It is of significance that Trithemius found need to originate the
modern system of diplomatic cipher writing to convey teachings and messages that dared not be openly disclosed. His fame was perpetuated by his
two distinguished pupils Paracelsus and Cornelius Agrippa.

In the middle of this century appeared John Reuchlin of whom Goethe
wrote: "Reuchlin! who would himself with him compare, in his own time a
sign so rare!"[13] While acting as Imperial Counsellor of Emperor Frederick
III, Reuchlin found time to study Neoplatonism, several Oriental languages,
and to write books on the Kabala. When he denounced the burning of the
Hebrew bibles, the Dominicans caused his expulsion for a time from Germany, and his own works were burned. But later when Erasmus, Martin
Luther, and Melanchthon (the grandson of Reuchlin's sister, and for a long
period under his care) came to him for instruction, Reuchlin set going a
ferment of ideas that caused him to be called "the father of the
Reformation."[14]

In *The Religious Renaissance of the German Humanists,* Lewis Spitz writes
that in Reuchlin's Kabalism man is viewed "as a unique creature, situated at
the center of the great chain of being, able to descend or ascend until united
with the One, as in Neoplatonism," and that "the goal of both the Kabala
and Pythagoras," according to Reuchlin, "is to lead the souls of men back to
the gods, that is, to raise them to perfect beatitude."[15] In *De arte cabalistica,*
Reuchlin remarked that Ficino "produced Plato for Italy. Lefèvre d'Estaples
restored Aristotle to France. I shall complete the number and . . . show to
the Germans, Pythagoras reborn through me."[16]

William Robertson Smith provides some illuminating facts regarding
Reuchlin and his influence on German culture:

> In February 1482 [he] left Stuttgart for Florence and Rome [which] brought
> the German scholar into contact with several learned Italians. . . . Reuchlin's
> life at Stuttgart was often broken by important missions, and in 1490 he was
> again in Italy. Here he saw Pico to whose Cabbalistic doctrines he afterwards
> became heir. . . .
>
> [Later in Heidelberg] Reuchlin's appointed function was to make translations
> from the Greek authors, in which his reading was already extremely wide . . .
> and formed an important element in his efforts to spread a knowledge of Greek.
> For, though Reuchlin had no public office as teacher, and even at Heidelberg
> was prevented from lecturing openly, he was during a great part of his life the
> real centre of all Greek teaching as well as of all Hebrew teaching in Germany.
> . . . His Greek studies had interested him in philosophy, and not least in those
> fantastical and mystical systems of later times with which the Cabbala has no
> small affinity. Following Pico, he seemed to find in the Cabbala a profound
> theosophy which might be of the greatest service for the defence of Christianity
> and the reconciliation of science with the mysteries of faith. . . . The most
> esoteric wisdom of the rabbis was in his eyes of the greatest value.[17]

Reuchlin, however, did not go along with succeeding developments in Protestanism. In many respects, as W. R. Inge points out, the "Reformation checked the progress of the religion of the Spirit. . . . and real Christianity was once more driven underground, poorly represented by the harsh and gloomy asceticism of the Counter-Reformation, and by the *Schwärmerei* of German pietism. The Reformers made no direct return to the Hellenic tradition."[18]]

Other Mystical Movements

[The pages of late medieval history and subsequent eras reveal the existence of secret fraternal orders such as the original Knights Templar, the Freemasons, and the Rosicrucians. John Yarker, a high-ranking Mason, links these orders to reincarnationist groups like the Gnostic Cathari and the Kabalists:

There can be no doubt that the Operative Association of Freemasons and the Chivalric Order of Templars, both included searchers into Kabalism, Alchemy, and the recondite mysteries of nature and Science. We have also arrived at the time when these were known as Rosicrucianism. . . . [In fact, our Masonic rites] were introduced by the Gnostics and Kabalists, and transferred to the Templars, Rosicrucians, and Freemasons. . . . There can be no doubt whatever that the Gnostic [Cathari] associations spread early into England [having emigrated from France]. The Abbé Pluqet, remarking on this says: ". . . They made their way into Germany and England, and everywhere gained many proselytes. The Manichees seduced numbers of people, and their sect was considered by the simple minded to be a society of Christians who made profession of an extraordinary perfection."

Another Gnostic branch, headed by Walter Lollard, and his twelve apostles, united with the followers of John Wycliffe [a leader of the English reformation]. Chaucer was one of their number, and obliged to quit England for a time; whilst in Italy he visited Petrarch[19] . . . ; throughout [Chaucer's] works we find the alchemical and otherwise veiled language and marked resemblance to our secret mysteries. . . .

It is well known that the Templar Order in England was dissolved on the proofs of Gnostic knowledge brought against them. . . . They doubtless acquired their knowledge [during the Crusades] in the East, where remnants of the Essenian and other secret schools existed at the time. . . . In A.D. 1296 Edward I, of England, the son of Henry III, was admitted into the order by Raymond Lully—the great pioneer of the Rosicrucians . . . and the friend of John Cremer, Abbot of Westminster, and the celebrated monkish philosopher and alchemist, Roger Bacon.[20]

Of the Rosicrucian alchemists, "There were two orders," states the *Royal Masonic Cyclopaedia,* "those who laboured at the physical forge and crucible, and those who, by a theosophic process, sought to elevate the mind into a knowledge of its constitution; thus perfecting a much higher series of investigations, and arriving at a mystical gold beyond all price."[21] In other words, they sought to transmute the baser elements in human nature. Jung, convinced of this transcendental side to medieval alchemy, spent years investigating its psychological and symbolical aspects.[22] "I must confess," he wrote, "that it cost me quite a struggle to overcome the prejudice, which I shared with many others, against the seeming absurdity of alchemy. . . . But my patience has been richly rewarded. . . . True alchemy was never a business or a career, but a real *opus* that a man carried on in silent self-sacrificing labour."[23] Doubtless the peculiar jargon and fantastic symbols of the alchemists were a necessity of the times. The dungeon, the rack, and the fagot employed against heretics were ample excuse for esotericism.

This process of self-transmutation was evidently regarded by some Rosicrucians as extending over more than one lifetime, for included in the present work are a number of the noted members or friends of the Order: Thomas Vaughan, Paracelsus, one of the Van Helmonts, Tommaso Campanella, and Jerome Cardan.

An evolutionary palingenesis through the kingdoms was also taught, anticipating a spiritual form of Darwinism centuries before *The Origin of Species*. As Hargrave Jennings writes in his classic work *The Rosicrucians, Their Rites and Mysteries,* the Rosicrucians believed that every form contains an "eager fire" or "jewel of light," the development of which brings about its evolution. "Thus all minerals, in this spark of life, have the rudimentary possibilities of plants and growing organisms . . . thus all plants and all vegetation might pass off into more distinguished highways, as it were, of independent, completer advance, allowing their original spark of light to expand and thrill with higher and more vivid force, and to urge forward with more abounding, informed purpose."[24]

Many Rosicrucians were also Hermetists. In the section "The Hermetic Works," we have seen that the philosophy of reincarnation often appears in the Hermetic Fragments. The allusions to Hermes Trismegistus in late Medieval and Renaissance literature are extensive, and Ficino, Pico, Patricius, and other Renaissance men regarded him as the source of the Orphic initiations and of the philosophy of Pythagoras and Plato. In fact, a strong movement was under way to supplant the Scholastics' model, Aristotle, with Trismegistus. An interesting work which yokes Hermetism to Neoplatonic, Rosicrucian, Kabalistic, and similar movements of this period is *Giordano Bruno and the Hermetic Tradition,* by Frances Yates.[25] She explains how Renaissance Hermetism stimulated new attitudes toward the cosmos and affected the religious issues, leading toward toleration of nonorthodox viewpoints. Bruno's open espousal of reincarnation, which contributed to his being martyred at the stake, will be considered shortly.]

LEONARDO DA VINCI (1452–1519)

Italian Painter, Sculptor, Architect, Musician, Engineer, Inventor, Mathematician, Anatomist, and Scientist

[To this amazing catalogue of Leonardo da Vinci's talents we should add "Writer," as his Notebooks, from which we quote, include over 4,000 pages, although a number contain drawings. In the Notebooks there are several passages that clearly reveal that Leonardo accepted the preexistence of the soul, thus discounting the orthodox view of a special creation of souls at birth. Here is one: "Behold now the hope and desire to go back to our own country, and to return to our former state, how like it is to the moth with the light! . . . this longing is the quintessence and spirit of the elements, which, finding itself imprisoned within the life of the human body, desires continually to return to its source. And I would have you to know that this very same longing is that quintessence inherent in nature, and that man is a type of the world."[26] However, in three other passages, Leonardo seems to appreciate that there is a need for earth life, and in one of these he even intimates that he will return occasionally to this world:]

The soul desires to dwell in the body because without the members of that body it can neither act nor feel. . . .

The soul can never be infected by the corruption of the body, but acts in the body like the wind which causes the sound of the organ, wherein if one of the pipes is spoiled, the wind cannot produce a good result in that pipe. . . .[27]

Read me, O Reader, if you find delight in me, because very seldom shall I come back into this world.[28]

PARACELSUS (1493–1541)

Swiss Physician and Alchemist

[The following excerpts from the writings of Paracelsus are taken from *The Life of Philippus Theophrastus Bombast of Hohenheim* (known by the name of Paracelsus), by Franz Hartmann, M.D.]

Some children are born from heaven, and others are born from hell, because each human being has his inherent tendencies, and these tendencies belong to his spirit, and indicate the state in which he existed before he was born. Witches and sorcerers are not made at once; they are born with powers for evil. ["They are born with the tendencies which they acquired in former lives upon the earth or upon some other planet." (Hartmann)] The body is only an instrument; if you seek for man in his dead body, you are seeking for him in vain. . . . The form may be destroyed; but the spirit remains and is living, for it is the subjective life. . . .

The body which we receive from our parents . . . has no spiritual powers, for wisdom and virtue, faith, hope and charity, do not grow from the earth. These powers are not the products of man's physical organization, but the attributes of another invisible and glorified body, whose germs are laid within man. The physical body changes and dies, the glorified body is eternal. This eternal man is the real man, and is not generated by his earthly parents. He does not draw nutriment from the earth, but from the eternal invisible source from which he originated. . . . The temporal body is the house of the eternal, and we should therefore take care of it, because he who destroys the temporal body destroys the house of the eternal, and although the eternal man is invisible, he exists nevertheless, and will become visible in time.[29]

[The idea of an immortal "glorified body" is a most interesting one. The Gnostics believed in such a form.[30] The Hindus also speak of a highly refined body, the highest sheath of the soul and the storehouse of the essence of experiences garnered from life to life. These are important theories to consider, for the basic argument of the materialist is that consciousness must dissolve with the destruction of the body, as there is then no body and brain to focus it. Saint Paul stated that there is "a natural body, and there is a spiritual body . . . the first man is of the earth, earthy: the second man is the Lord from heaven." He said further that immortality is derived only through the incorruptible body.[31] The ninth-century genius John Scotus Erigena, who appeared in his age as "a meteor, none knew whence," indicated in his celebrated work *The Division of Nature* that the soul and the spiritual body came into existence simultaneously "and the soul therefore precedes the [spiritual] body only in dignity, not in space or in time. . . . But where, then, is that spiritual and incorruptible body . . . ? It is hidden in the secret recesses of our nature, and it will reappear in the future, when this mortal shall put on immortality.[32] The soul will then, he says, "return into a former state which it lost by transgression."[33] Some hold that the real meaning of the bodily resurrection of Jesus and of mankind still to come lies concealed in these ideas.]

GIORDANO BRUNO (1548–1600)

Italian Philosopher, Poet, and Dramatist

[The seventeenth century was darkly ushered in with the burning at the stake on February 17, 1600 of Giordano Bruno. Yet his life and work became a torch to light a long struggle toward freedom in the centuries that followed. Among liberal-minded Italians he is recognized as the greatest and most daring thinker their country has produced. Spinoza and Leibniz are two of the philosophers who were particularly influenced by Bruno.

Born near Naples of a distinguished Italian family, Bruno entered a Dominican monastery at fifteen. Dissatisfied with the dogmas of the Church, he found in the teachings of Pythagoras, Plato, Hermes, and several of the Neoplatonists the philosophy he sought. Later he studied the writings of Nicolas de Cusa and Raymond Lully. Accused of heresy and rebellion at the monastery, he fled to Rome, only to be soon charged with heresy on 130 counts! Then began his life of wandering. He lectured and taught in Germany, Switzerland, Prague, as well as in France and England. After teaching philosophy at the University of Paris under the protection of the king of France, he went to London for two years. In an essay on Bruno to which Walt Whitman wrote the foreword, Daniel Brinton relates that in London at that time

> were such glorious stars as Shakespeare and Spenser, Francis Bacon and Sir Philip Sidney, and the galaxy of the Elizabethan age gathered around the throne of the virgin queen, herself learned and a patron of learning. In this incomparable circle Bruno entered as a welcome guest. He became the friend of Sidney, to whom he dedicated two of his books, and the influence of his teaching has been recognized in the philosophy of Bacon and the reflections of Hamlet.[34]

J. Lewis McIntyre's *Giordano Bruno,* a principal work on Bruno, gives this summary of the philosopher's view on reincarnation:

> Each monad . . . takes on successively all possible forms. . . . The soul of man does not change in itself as it passes through its innumerable forms. . . . The soul is not limited to the earth alone, but has the infinite worlds before it, for its dwelling-place. . . . "By birth and growth the spirit-architect expands into this mass of which we consist, spreading outwards from the heart. Thither again it withdraws, winding up the threads of its web, returning by the same path along which it advanced, passed out by the same gate through which it entered. Birth is expansion of the center . . . death contraction to the center." It is the soul that gathers about it, groups and vivifies the atom-mass.
>   . . . there are, strictly speaking, only two *substances,* matter and spirit: all particular things result from the composition in varying degrees of these two— are therefore mere "accidents," and have no abiding reality. . . . Neither "body nor soul need fear death, for both matter and form are constant abiding principles." This theory of substance and immortality was regarded by Bruno as one of the cardinal points of his philosophy. . . . Its statement . . . occurs again and again throughout his works, and he believed the removal from man of the fear of death to be one of the greatest results of this teaching.[35]

Before quoting directly from Bruno's writings on reincarnation, we will examine the many facets the idea had for him. It received application to the most diverse philosophical and scientific problems.

Brinton states that "the doctrine of Evolution, the progressive development of nature . . . was first propounded in [Bruno's] works, not vaguely or partially, but to the full extent of the most advanced evolutionist of today."[36] Bruno, however, believed that spiritual evolution should unfold concomitantly with the development of form, because "the divine perfection of the individual soul is the aim of all progression."[37] In these connections, he appears to have been the first European to introduce the term Monad, which, as we shall see, Leibniz adopted as the key idea of his philosophy. Leibniz held with Bruno that each monadic center—whether of an atom, a man, or a sun—is a mirror and replica of the entire cosmos, as well as the moving power in evolution.

In *De Rerum Principiis* and *De Monade Numero,* Bruno was the first Westerner to teach the circulation of the blood, later demonstrated by Harvey. Dr. Félix Martí-Ibáñez, former director of the department of the history of medicine at New York Medical College, notes this fact in *Centaur, Essays on the History of Medical Ideas*. This medical historian shows that Bruno's ideas on the circulation of the blood were simply an application of his cosmic views of rebirth, summarized by the doctor in these words: "Every movement that returns to its point of origin must adopt the form of a circle. Only circular movement is continuous and consistent. Every object of nature is, then, a circle, whose function and activity derive from its center point, which is the soul. From the soul the active principle tends, according to Bruno, to go to the periphery, whence it flows back to the center. Harvey's discovery, therefore, is bound to a philosophy of circles, and the circular motion of the blood is a microcosmic example of a macrocosmic pattern, it being the cycle that conducts the process of return to its point of departure."[38] In other words, this is the ancient doctrine of the periodic emanation and return of worlds, atoms, and men, applied to physiology.

At Oxford, Bruno lectured on the leading heresy of his day, the Copernican theory, which aroused the animosity of the Oxford professors, who asked him to leave. The view of the perpetual motion of the planets around the sun—which Copernicus acknowledged he learned from Pythagoras and Hermes—was soon to give rise to an intense yearning to impart movement to everything. The Baroque period, says Dr. Martí-Ibáñez, "was essentially an explosion of movement." Art and music became dynamic. "Spiral columns soared into space, replacing the old classical columns, and the stone of cathedrals and palaces was wrenched from its mystic Gothic placidity and turned into veritable whirlpools."[39] In such an atmosphere it is not strange, perhaps, that the theory of reincarnation, with its perpetually revolving cycles, should have found some ardent champions.

The Brunian system, however, was more theo-centric, than helio-centric, holding with de Cusa and the Kabalists that deity and the cosmos may be likened to a circle or sphere whose circumference is nowhere—hence boundless—but whose center is everywhere. And that each monad is such a divine, immortal, preexistent center. This magnificent thought—reminiscent of Christ's words that the Kingdom of Heaven is *within* you—may explain why each person feels himself to be the center of the universe. It should not lead to egotism when one realizes that every other being is likewise the center.

Bruno applied this conception to worlds as well as to individuals. In an illuminating article on Bruno in the *Scientific American* for April 1973, it is contended that Bruno's espousal of the Copernican system was not merely on behalf of scientific accuracy, but as a metaphor in the construction of a metaphysical system of thought that would heal the religious strife of the sixteenth century. "Bruno's real interest in heliocentrism was that it implies that the earth is not the only center of the universe. The implication allowed him to put forth his own views that the universe is infinite in extent, that it contains an infinite number of worlds, each of which can be considered as much the center of the universe as any other." As Dorothea Waley Singer writes in her biography of Bruno:

> To Bruno and Bruno alone the suggestion of Copernicus entered into the pattern of a completely new cosmological order. In this sense Bruno not only anticipated Galileo and Kepler, but he passed beyond them into an entirely new world which had shed all the dross of tradition. It was a great vision which, from the very nature of the case, could be shared in full neither by his own nor the succeeding generation.
>
> The whole of Bruno's philosophy is based on his view of an infinite universe with an infinity of worlds. . . . Thus the Lucretian universe of innumerable minimal parts or atoms in perpetual concourse and discourse became for Bruno the symbol of the spiritual universe of an infinity of monads . . . each pursuing the development congruent to its inner nature. And to Bruno the universe like all its parts had the quality of life.[40]

Of necessity, then, the endlessly numerous worlds spread out in space were inhabited, and some of these inhabitants, Bruno said, must be superior to the terrestrial race (*De Immenso* I, 9).

The foregoing conceptions, says Mrs. Singer—who is noted for her scholarship in medieval and Renaissance science and literature—were symbolic of Bruno's view of the human soul, "every individual soaring to the uttermost height of thought and spiritual development congruent with his own nature, every individual imbued with the divine spirit whereby the whole infinity of discrete and independent souls is yet fused into a vast Whole . . . within the immensity of the World Soul . . ."[41]

The authors of the *Scientific American* article, Lawrence Lerner and Edward Gosselin, state that Bruno saw Hermetic-Neoplatonism "as a basis for reconciling Catholics and Protestants in an era of violent religious warfare," and also for improving the prevailing corrupt state of moral affairs that appeared to derive from man believing himself "the detestable product of the original sin, destined to fall lower and lower in the absence of some more or less capricious divine intervention in human affairs." "In contrast to the orthodox Christian view that man had fallen from a state of grace, through the original sin, the Hermetists believed man had descended voluntarily from the non-material world of the Divine Mind to earth and continued to partake of the divine nature that had been his before the descent." In conclusion Lerner and Gosselin write:

> we believe that for two reasons [Bruno's] influence on the birth of the scientific revolution was profound. First, Bruno was supremely confident that man was at least in part a divine being. . . . Bruno's advocacy of [this] Neoplatonic view made him a leading figure in the rebirth of man's confidence in himself, the like of which had not existed since classical antiquity. . . . Second, Bruno believed the path to perfection is the path of knowledge.

Two selections follow from Giordano's recorded thought. The first is from *The Expulsion of the Triumphant Beast,* the most popular of his works, and the one that was singled out by the Roman tribunal at his trial. Published in 1584 it was a daring indictment of the corruption of the social and religious institutions of the day. The extracts are mainly on justice or karma, as related to rebirth, and underline the importance of taking full advantage of each incarnation as it arises, for each lifetime is unique and can never be duplicated. "Opportunity knocks only once"—in exactly the same way.]

Come, Diligence, what are you doing? Why do we idle and sleep so much alive, if we so very long must idle and sleep in death? Indeed, although we still await another world or another manner of being ourselves, that life will not be the same as that possessed by us at present; so that this life, without ever expecting to return, passes on forever. . . .

In order not to burden too much the transmigrating souls, [Fate] interposes the drinking from the Lethean river . . . so that through oblivion everyone may be . . . eager to preserve himself in his present state. Therefore, youths do not recall their state of infancy; infants do not long for the state in their mothers' wombs; and none of these longs for the state in that life which he lived before he found himself in such a nature. The pig does not want to die for fear of not being a pig; the horse fears most to lose his equine nature. Jove . . . greatly fears not being Jove. But Fate's mercy and grace will not change his state without having saturated him in the waters of that river. . . .

You see then, dear sister, how treacherous time subdues us, how we are all subject to mutation. And that which most afflicts us . . . is that we have neither certainty nor any hope of at all reassuming that same being in which we once found ourselves. We depart, and do not return the same; and since we have no recollection of what we were before we were in this being, so we cannot have a sample of that which we shall be afterward. . . .

Because some do not see the reward of their virtues in this life, there is therefore promised and presented before their eyes the good and evil of their next life, its rewards and punishments, in accordance with their deeds. . . . It follows that by virtue of the High Justice that presides over all things . . . that [the hero and divinity in man] must not expect the government and administration of a better dwelling when it has badly guided itself in the rule of another. . . . By decree of Eternal Law it is sanctioned that the most powerful be most powerfully compressed and bound, if not under one mantle and inside of one cell, then under another mantle and within another cell, which will be worse. . . .

By the chain of errors we are bound; by the hand of Justice we free ourselves. Where our frivolity has abased us, there it is necessary that our seriousness exalt us. Let us be converted to Justice, because since we have departed from her, we have departed from ourselves; so that we are no longer gods, are no longer ourselves. Let us then return to her, if we wish to return to ourselves.[42]

[The following selection is from what is called Bruno's last testament: his answers at his trial before the Father Inquisitor in Venice in May 1592. Bruno had been cordially invited to Venice by an Italian nobleman, Zuane Mocenigo, who became a tool of the Inquisition. Mocenigo accused Bruno of teaching various heretical ideas, among which were: "souls created by the operation of nature pass from one animal to another"; when the world is destroyed by deluge, souls are again reborn.[43] On these points Bruno replied:]

I have held and hold souls to be immortal. . . . [Catholics teach] they do not pass from body to body, but go to Paradise, Purgatory or Hell. But I have reasoned deeply, and, speaking as a philosopher, since the soul is not found without body and yet is not body, it may be in one body or in another, and pass from body to body. This, if it be not [proved] true, seems at least likely, according to the opinion of Pythagoras. . . .[44]

In the circle, which comprehends in itself the beginning and the end, we have the figure of true being; and circular motion is the only enduring form of motion. From this Spirit, which is called the Life of the Universe, proceed the life and soul of everything which has soul and life,—which life, however, I understand to be immortal, as well in bodies as in their souls, all being immortal, there being no other death than division and congregation; which doctrine seems to be expressed in Ecclesiastes, where it is said nothing is new under the sun.[45]

[Bruno was tortured, then solitarily confined in a tiny, dark dungeon for seven years in the famed Castel Sant' Angelo in Rome, where he was again tortured. At a final trial he refused a last opportunity to recant and his doom was sealed. A German witness reports that Bruno looked his judges in the eye and said: "It is with far greater fear that you pronounce, than I receive, this sentence." After the burning, the tribunal publicly branded Bruno an atheist, decreeing that henceforth his writings be banned and burned. Albert Einstein has written that "it is precisely among the heretics of every age that we find men, who were filled with the highest kind of religious feeling, and were in many cases regarded by their contemporaries as Atheists . . ."[46]

On the spot in the Campo di Fiora in Rome where Giordano perished now stands, close to the Vatican, an imposing statue in his honor. The liberation movement in Italy, inaugurated by the great Italian emancipator Mazzini—another reincarnationist, as we shall see—joined forces in the 1870s and 1880s with Robert Ingersoll, the renowned foe of religious bigotry in America,[47] and aroused world opinion to overcome the fierce opposition of the Church to this mark of belated recognition.]

AGE OF SHAKESPEARE

EDMUND SPENSER (1552–1599)

British Poet

[Spenser's *Faerie Queene,* particularly "The Garden of Adonis" canto, from which the lines that follow are taken, shows a pronounced Neoplatonic influence.[1] The influence of Ficino, Porphyry, and possibly Bruno is considered in the notes covering books 3, 6, and 7 of *The Faerie Queene* in the nine-volume variorum edition of Spenser's works.[2] Like Plato and Vergil he speaks here of a thousand-year cycle between incarnations.]

> [The Garden of Adonis] is the first seminary
> Of all things that are born to live and die . . .
> Double gates it had which opened wide,
> By which both in and out men must pass:
> Th'one fair and fresh, the other old and dried.
> Old Genius the porter of them was. . . .
>
> He letteth in, he letteth out to wend
> All that to come into the world desire:
> A thousand thousand naked babes attend

About him day and night, which do require
That he with fleshly weeds would them attire:
Such . . . he clothes with sinful mire,
And sendeth forth to live in mortal state,
Till they again return back by the hinder gate . . .

They in that Garden planted be again,
And grow afresh, as [if] they had never seen
Fleshly corruption, nor mortal pain.
Some thousand years so do they there remain,
And then [by] him are clad with other hue,[3]
Or sent into the changeful world again,
Till thither they return where first they grew;
So, like a wheel, around they run from old to new.[4]

WILLIAM SHAKESPEARE (1564–1616)

British Dramatist and Poet

[In Shakespeare's Sonnet 59 he ponders the subject of reincarnation from two aspects: First he evinces great puzzlement as to why the same child (or soul) should be born twice to the same parents and each time die. Next he considers the source of present character in a previous life.]

If there be nothing new, but that which is
Hath been before, how are our brains beguiled,
Which labouring for invention, bear amiss
The second burthen [bearing] of a former child!
O, that record could with a backward look,
Even of five hundred courses of the sun,
Show me your image in some antique book,
Since mind at first in character was done!
That I might see what the old world could say
To this composèd wonder of your frame;
Whether we are mended, or whether better they,
Or whether revolution be the same.
   O, sure I am, the wits of former days
   To subjects worse have been given admiring praise.

[In Shakespeare's dramas, thoughts on death and immortality vary in mood and philosophical approach from character to character, although the overall pattern and structure of his plays may teach a larger lesson, as we shall see. Hamlet's mother affirms that "all that lives must die, passing through nature to eternity,"[5] but her son is not so sure of this, for thoughts of suicide soon torture him: "To be, or not to be: that is the question. . . . To die: to sleep . . . and . . . end the heartache . . . To die, to sleep . . . perchance to dream: ay, there's the rub: for in that sleep of death what dreams may come, when we have shuffled off this mortal coil." This, he says, "must give us pause."[6] Then there is the utter desolation of King Lear when viewing the body of Cordelia, his only faithful daughter: "Why should a dog, a horse, a rat have life, and thou no breath at all? Thou'lt come no more, never, never, never, never, never!"[7] Macbeth, on the other hand, sounds a note of bitterest indifference when on the eve of his deserved destruction he learns of the demise of Lady Macbeth: "All our yesterdays have lighted fools the way to dusty death. Out, out, brief candle! Life's but a walking shadow, a poor player that struts and frets his hour upon the stage and then is heard no more: it is a tale told by an idiot, full of sound and fury, signifying nothing."[8]

In vivid contrast are the words of Lord Talbot in *King Henry the Sixth* about a noble Self in Man. Assailed for the murderous strife he has caused, Talbot responds: "No, no, I am but shadow of myself: you are deceiv'd, my substance is not here; for what you see is but the smallest part, and . . . were the whole frame here, it is of such a spacious lofty pitch, your roof were not sufficient to contain it."[9] In similar vein, Hamlet speaks in one scene: "What a piece of work is a man! how noble in reason! how infinite in faculty! in form and moving how express and admirable! in action how like an angel! in apprehension how like a god!"[10]

These elevated views in Shakespeare lead appropriately to some illuminating passages from John Vyvyan's *Shakespeare and Platonic Beauty*. The author provides rich evidence of the bard's use of Platonic and Neoplatonic sources, and reveals that Shakespeare's plays were structured according to Platonic ethical views and Neoplatonic metaphysics, including such ideas as preexistence, postexistence, and karma:

> Shakespeare's ethic rests on his belief in law that *cannot* be circumvented; and the miraculous in his plays is never a suspension of this, but a demonstration of its finer workings. If there are certain ways to calamity and death, there are others, equally reliable, leading to immortal life. . . .
>
> The Neoplatonic pattern . . . found in Ficino, Pico, and the oration of Ulysses is being carefully filled out into a picture of all-embracing order [in *Troilus and Cressida*]. If it were lived, it would be a divine harmony, and the achievement of the heart's most deep desire. Why, then, is it rejected? According to the Shakespearean argument, it is rejected because man is not true to himself; and he is not true to himself because he does not know himself and the secret of his well-being. He mistakes the mask for the face, the false Helen for the true, the shadow for the substance: the metaphors are many. . . . Hector supplies a sad example. Having said so much that is noble, he is yet unable—like Hamlet—to be true to the highest that he knows. . . .

The renouncing of what is, in Shakespeare's conception, the hero's spiritual self for his superficial self is of fundamental importance. By doing this the lordship of the soul is lost. The divine harmony and order within become discord and insurrection, and there is consequential chaos in the outer world. To grasp Shakespeare's meaning here is immeasurably to enhance the dramatic impact of his plays. It is human history, not merely the fortunes of one character, that is being debated in the great soliloquies. But it is not easy for us to feel this, because it is so different from our accepted view of life. It is habitual for most of us to envisage man, like everything else, as the product of environment; but to experience the full power of Shakespeare's drama we must suspend this modern thought and participate . . . in his: *He conceives the soul as antecedent to its environment, determinant and creative.*[11]]

TOMASSO CAMPANELLA (1586–1639)

Italian Poet and Philosopher

[This celebrated Renaissance philosopher and Dominican monk was imprisoned for twenty-seven years, undergoing much torture and misery, though his spirit remained unbroken. Many of his poems and philosophical works were written during this period. In his "Sonnet on Caucasus," which calls up the imagery of Prometheus chained to the rock, he says: "I know not whether strife or peace was with me in some earlier life. Philip in a worse prison has me put these three days past. . . . I fear that by my death the human race would gain no vantage. Thus I do not die."[12]]

JOHN DONNE (1573–1631)

British Poet

[John Donne's "The Progress of the Soul" is a satirical poem directed mainly against the folly of believing in transmigration of human beings into animals. However, the following lines are in another vein:]

> I sing the progress of a deathless soul,
> Whom Fate, which God made, but doth not control,
> Placed in most shapes. . . .
> For though through many straits and lands I roam,
> I launch at paradise, and I sail towards home;
> The course I there began, shall here be stay'd,
> Sails hoisted there, struck here, and anchors laid
> In Thames, which were in Tigris, and Euphrates weigh'd.
> For the great soul which here amongst us now
> Doth dwell, and moves that hand, and tongue, and brow. . . .
> This soul, to whom Luther and Mahomet were

Prisons of flesh; this soul which oft did tear
And mend the wracks of th'Empire, and late Rome,
And lived when every great change did come,
Had first in paradise, a low, but fatal room.[13]

SIR THOMAS BROWNE (1605–1682)
British Physician and Author

[In Sir Thomas Browne's classic work *Religio Medici* he suggests the preexistence of the soul, but his belief in metempsychosis extends only to the rebirth of ideas and types of men.]

We are men, and we know not how: there is something in us that can be without us, and will be after us; though it is strange that it hath no history what it was before us, nor cannot tell how it entered in us. . . . Whilst I study to find how I am a Microcosm, or little World, I find myself something more than the great. There is surely a piece of Divinity in us, something that was before the Elements, and owes no homage unto the Sun. . . .

One General Council is not able to extirpate one single Heresy: it may be cancelled for the present, but revolution of time, and the like aspects from Heaven will restore it, when it will flourish till it be condemned again. For as though there were a Metempsychosis, and the soul of one man passed into another, Opinions do find, after certain Revolutions, men and minds like those that first begat them. To see ourselves again, we need not look for Plato's year: every man is not only himself: there have been many Diogenes, and as many Timons, though but few of that name: men are lived over again; the world is now as it was in Ages past; there was none then, but there hath been some one since that parallels him, and is, as it were, his revived self.[14]

JOHN MILTON (1608–1674)
British Poet

[From his college friend Henry More, Milton acquired a fondness for Plato, and in the poem that follows, "On the Death of a Fair Infant," the Platonic influence seems evident. Milton also "made use of Hermes Trismegistus and the works of the Kabalists."[15]]

Wert thou that just Maid who once before
Forsook the hated earth, O tell me sooth,
And cam'st again to visit us once more?
Or wert thou that sweet smiling Youth? . . .
Or any other of that heavenly brood

Let down in cloudy throne to do the world some good?
Or wert thou of the golden-winged host,
Who, having clad thyself in human weed,
To earth from thy prefixed seat didst post,
And after short abode fly back with speed
As if to show what creatures heaven doth breed;
Thereby to set the hearts of men on fire,
To scorn the sordid world, and unto Heaven aspire?[16]

The Cambridge Platonists

[In the seventeenth century, Cambridge University became the center of a movement that attracted considerable attention. Its leaders were known as the Cambridge Platonists, the most prominent of whom were Henry More, Ralph Cudworth, and John Smith. However, the movement was not confined to Cambridge. Two of its leading supporters, John Norris and Joseph Glanvill, were from Oxford.

Inge relates that in 1630 More took his degree at Christ's College and "began the study of 'the Platonic writers, Marsilius Ficinus, Plotinus himself, Mercurius Trismegistus, and the mystical divines. . . . ' Here he found his own spiritual kin, and with them he lived to the end."[17] Hobbes said that if his own philosophy were not true he knew none that he should sooner adopt than Henry More's of Cambridge. Samuel Johnson esteemed him as "one of our greatest divines and philosophers and no mean poet." More's philosophical works, Coleridge declared, "contain more enlarged and elevated views of the Christian dispensation than I have met with in any other single volume; for More had both philosophical and poetic genius supported by immense erudition."[18]

The Cambridge Platonists, wise in the science of their day and schooled in precise Cartesian thinking, nevertheless rejected the materialism toward which Descartes had directed the awakening Western intellectuality. They rendered the moral inspiration of the Renaissance into an English idiom for future generations. The Neoplatonic revival of the Italian Renaissance was, of course, one major inspiration. Another was the Kabala. Continuing the task begun by Philo Judaeus, the English Platonists endeavored to reconcile the Platonic doctrines with the Hebrew Bible. In fact, Plato was considered to be Moses speaking Attic Greek! More's work on the Kabala appeared in 1653, entitled "A conjectural essay of interpreting the mind of Moses according to a threefold Cabbala," and John Milton became deeply learned in this mystical Jewish lore, which embraces the reincarnation perspective, as we have seen.

Cudworth's encyclopedic book *The True Intellectual System of the Universe* was published in London in 1678. It has been called "a storehouse of learning on the ancient opinions of the nature, origin, pre-existence, transmigration, and future of the soul." Although he dismissed the Platonic doctrines of preexistence and reincarnation as "offensive absurdities," he nevertheless focused attention on these ideas, and a number of his fellow Platonists gave them serious attention. Glanvill, who was chaplain to King Charles II, has already been quoted on reincarnation. Selections from More's writings follow next. Thomas Burnet, another noted divine of this period, impressed by the antiquity and prevalence of reincarnation, called it "fatherless, motherless, and without genealogy."[19]

The appearance of the Cambridge Platonists was particularly opportune as Dean Inge indicates in his Hulsean Lectures at Cambridge published as *The Platonic Tradition in English Thought:*

> It was [Burnet's] deliberate opinion that the corruptions of the English clergy, their avarice, self-indulgence, and neglect of duty, were so notorious, that "if a new set of men had not appeared of another stamp, the Church had quite lost her esteem over the nation." . . . "I can come into no company of late," says a contemporary, "but I find the chief discourse to be about a certain new sect of men called Latitude-men." . . . Edward Fowler, afterwards Bishop of Gloucester, had also "heard them represented as a generation of people that have revived the abominable principles of the old Gnostics."

"No one can read the books of these men," says Inge, "without feeling that there was a real outpouring of the Spirit at Cambridge at this time, which in the future may engage more sympathetic attention than it has done yet."[20]]

HENRY MORE (1614–1687)

British Philosopher

[In the essay and poem that follow Henry More touches on rebirth while mainly considering preexistence, and cites many reincarnationists to support his views.]

If it be good for the souls of men to be at all, the sooner they are, the better . . . Wherefore the pre-existence of souls is a necessary result of the wisdom and goodness of God. . . . The face of Providence in the world seems very much to suit with this opinion, there being not any so natural and easy account to be given of those things that seem the most harsh in the affairs of men, as from this hypothesis: that their souls did once subsist in some other state . . . and of their own natures, they undergo several calamities and asperities of fortune, and sad drudgeries of fate, as a punishment inflicted, or a disease contracted from the several obliquities of their apostasy. Which key is . . . able to unlock that recondite mystery of some particular men's almost fatal averseness from all religion and virtue, their stupidity and dullness and even invincible slowness to these things from their very childhood, and their incorrigible propension to all manner of vice. . . . Which sad scene of things must needs exceedingly cloud and obscure the ways of Divine Providence, and make them utterly unintelligible; unless some light be let in from the present hypothesis. . . .

And as this hypothesis is rational in itself, so has it also gained the suffrage of all philosophers of all ages, of any note, that have held the soul of man incorporeal and immortal. . . . Let us cast our eye, therefore, into what corner of the world we will, that has been famous for wisdom and literature, and the wisest of those nations you shall find the asserters of this opinion. In Egypt, that ancient nurse of all hidden sciences, that this opinion was in vogue amongst the wisest men there, the fragments of Trismegistus do sufficiently witness . . . of which opinion, not only the Gymnosophists, and other wise men of Egypt, were, but also the Brahmans of India, and the Magi of Babylon and Persia. . . . To these you may add the abstruse philosophy of the Jews, which they call their Cabbala, of which the soul's pre-existence makes a considerable part, as all the learned of the Jews do confess. . . .

[You] may add Zoroaster, Pythagoras, Epicharmus, Cebes, Euripides, Plato, Euclid, Philo, Virgil, Marcus Cicero, Plotinus, Iamblichus, Proclus, Boethius, Psellus, and several others, which it would be too long to recite. And if it were fit to add [Church] fathers to philosophers, we might enter into the same list Synesius and Origen; the latter of whom was surely the greatest light and bulwark that ancient Christianity had. . . . But I have not yet ended my catalogue; that admirable physician Johannes Fernelius is also of this persuasion, and . . . discovers those two grand-masters of medicine, Hippocrates and Galen, to be so, too. Cardan, also, that famous philosopher of his age, expressly concludes that the rational soul is both a distinct being from the soul of the world, and that it does pre-exist before it comes into the body; and lastly, Pomponatius, no friend to the soul's immortality, yet cannot but confess that the safest way to hold it is also therewith to acknowledge her pre-existence.

The Immortality of the Soul[21]

> I would sing the pre-existency
> Of Human souls, and live once o'er again
> By recollection and quick memory
> All that is passed since first we all began.
> But all too shallow be my wits to scan
> So deep a point and mind too dull to clear
> So dark a matter. . . .

[The poet addresses the "Sacred Soul of Plotinus dear":]

> Tell what we mortals are. Tell what of old we were.
> A spark or ray of Divinity
> Clouded in earthly fogs, and clad in clay,
> A precious drop sunk from eternity
> Spilt on the ground, or rather slunk away. . . .
> Show fitly how the pre-existing soul
> Enacts and enters bodies here below
> And then entire unhurt can leave this moul[d].
> *A Platonic Song of the Soul*[22]

FRANCISCUS MERCURIUS VAN HELMONT (1614–1699)
Belgian Naturalist and Philosopher

[Van Helmont, in *De Revolutione Animarum,* adduced in two hundred problems all the arguments that may be urged in favor of the return of souls into human bodies according to Kabalistic ideas. The book, published in London in 1684, bears the title *Two Hundred Queries Moderately Propounded Concerning the Doctrine of the Revolution of Human Souls.* In *Reincarnation in World Thought* we stated that Van Helmont's work "together with Baron Knorr von Rosenroth's book mentioned earlier, have the distinction of being the first volumes in Western, or for that matter, Eastern literature specifically devoted to reincarnation." We have since discovered the existence of an earlier work. In the Jung Institute's *Eranos Yearbook* for 1955 a sixty-page article appeared on transmigration as taught in Jewish mysticism. The author, Gershom Scholem, mentions that a tenth-century writer, Kirkisani, in his *Book of the Lights,* affirmed that the Karaic teacher Anan ben David accepted the doctrine in the eighth century. "Anan wrote a book on it, and his followers preserved the doctrine."[23]]

THOMAS VAUGHAN (1622?–1665)
British Hermetist, Neoplatonist, Kabalist, and Alchemist

[Thomas Vaughan, the twin brother of the poet Henry Vaughan, was one of the mystical philosophers Sir Isaac Newton devotedly read. The *Britannica* states that "Sir Isaac spent much time in the study of the works of the alchemists," also that he "diligently studied the works of Jacob Boehme."[24] From Vaughan's *Anthroposophia Theomagica*—or a Discourse on the Nature of Man and His state after Death:[25]]

I look on this life as the progress of an essence royal: the soul but quits her court to see the country. . . . Thus her descent speaks her original. God in love with His own beauty frames a glass, to view it by reflection. But the frailty of the matter excluding eternity, the composure was subject to dissolution. Ignorance gave this release the name of death, but properly it is the soul's birth and a charte‹ that makes for her liberty. She hath several ways to break up house, but her best is without a disease. This is her mystical walk, an exit only to return. . . . The magicians tell me that the soul passes out of one mode and enters another. . . .

The soul of man, while she is in the body, is like a candle shut up in a dark lanthorn, or a fire that is almost stifled for want of air. Spirits—say the Platonics—when they are "in their own country" are like the inhabitants of green fields who live perpetually amongst flowers, in a spicy, odorous air; but here below, "in the circle of generation," they mourn because of darkness and solitude, like people locked up in a pest-house. "Here do they fear, desire and grieve," etc. This makes the soul subject to so many passions, to such a Proteus of humors. Now she flourishes, now she withers—now a smile, now a tear; and when she hath played out her stock, then comes a repetition of the same fancies, till at last she cries out with Seneca: "How long this self-same round?" . . .

Who seeketh to be more than a man, or to know the harmony of the world and be born again?[26]

JOHN DRYDEN (1631–1700)
British Poet

[From John Dryden's "Ode to the Memory of Mrs. Anne Killigrew":]

> If thy pre-existing soul
> Was form'd at first with myriads more,
> It did through all the mighty poets roll
> Who Greek or Latin laurels wore,
> And was that Sappho last, which once it was before.
> If so, then cease thy flight, O heaven-born mind!
> Thou hast no dross to purge from thy rich ore:
> Nor can thy soul a fairer mansion find,
> Than was the beauteous frame she left behind:
> Return to fill or mend the choir of thy celestial kind.

BENEDICT SPINOZA (1632–1677)
Dutch Philosopher

[From Spinoza's celebrated work *Ethics,* Book V, Proposition 23:]

It is impossible for us to remember that we had existence prior to the body, since the body can have no vestige of it, and eternity cannot be defined in terms of time or have any relation to time. But, nevertheless, we have in our experience a perception that we are eternal. For the mind is sensible no less of what it understands than of what it remembers. . . . Although, therefore, we do not remember that we existed before the body, yet we perceive that our mind is eternal, in so far as it involves the body's essence under the category of eternity, and that this its existence cannot be defined by time or interpreted by duration.

LEIBNIZ (1646–1716)

German Philosopher and Mathematician

[Macneile Dixon writes of Leibniz—"the greatest intellectual genius since Aristotle"—that he "appears as a bright prophetic star, forerunner and foreteller of new ways of thought. . . . Nearly three centuries ago, the scientific acumen and prescience of Leibniz enabled him to foresee, and even in a measure anticipate, many conclusions arrived at by the most recent science." Leibniz said that matter is but another name for energy. Empty space is a fiction: Space and time are inseparable. By his own acute and original route he arrived at the modern theory of "the unconscious." "In the view of this most suggestive and remarkable thinker," continues Dixon, "just as a nation is composed of persons, so the universe may best be understood as consisting of an infinite variety of living and active beings, monads, as he called them. . . . 'The world,' said Leibniz, 'is not a machine. Everything in it is force, life, thought, desire.' The monads reflect the universe, each from its own angle, each in its own degree. . . . This great community extends both upwards and downwards from man through the whole creation. The world, in brief . . . is a living society."[27]

In an article honoring Leibniz (*Scientific American*, May 1968), Frederick Kreiling reveals that his philosophic bent kept him wary of fallacies that attracted Descartes and even Newton, and also enabled him to point the way to many of the most recent innovations in mathematics and its practical applications. In his early career "it was the logical and the occult which interested him most; he studied the number diagrams of the 13th century Spanish mystic Ramón Lull, for example."

From the context of the statements that follow, Leibniz does not appear to limit the term "body" to the physical instrument, but includes the inner bodies of men and animals, and believing that these invisible constituents never completely die, he prefers the term "metamorphosis" to "metempsychosis" when referring to reincarnation. Usually, the term metempsychosis is applied to taking on a brand new personality, but according to Leibniz—and we might add Oriental philosophy—this is not correct.

The first extract is not directly on reincarnation, but lays a basis for the reference that follows.]

There is nothing waste, nothing sterile, nothing dead in the universe; no chaos, no confusions, save in appearance. . . . We must not imagine . . . that each soul has a mass or portion of matter appropriated or attached to itself for ever. . . . For all bodies are in a perpetual flux like rivers, and parts are passing in and out of them continually. Thus the soul only changes its body bit by bit and by degrees, so that it is never despoiled of all its organs all together . . . neither are there any entirely separate souls, nor superhuman spirits without bodies.

Monadology[28]

As animals are usually not born completely in conception or generation, so neither do they perish completely in what we call death; for it is reasonable that what does not begin naturally should not come to an end in the order of nature either. Thus, casting off their masks or their rags, they merely return to a more subtle scene, on which, however, they can be as sensible and as well ordered as on the greater one. . . . Thus not only souls but animals also are ingenerable and imperishable; they are only developed, enveloped, re-clad, stripped, transformed; souls never leave the whole of their body, and do not pass from one body to another which is entirely new to them. Thus there is no metempsychosis, but there is metamorphosis.

Principles of Nature[29]

[James Ward in his Gifford Lectures *The Realm of Ends* summarizes Leibniz's views on preexistence and reincarnation:[30]]

According to the pluralistic, as according to the Leibnizian view, all the individuals there are have existed from the first and will continue to exist indefinitely. Birth and death, then, cannot really be what they seem to be. . . . [Leibniz believes] that all souls have pre-existed "always in a sort of organized body," which at the time of generation undergoes a certain trans-formation and augmentation. . . . Death, as the more or less complete disso-lution of the organism, means that the soul in consequence, so far as it is thus deprived of its *locus standi,* is, to use Leibniz's phrase, in the position of a deserter from the general order. Temporarily it is in a like position during sleep; and death for Leibniz was but a longer and profounder sleep: in neither case did he believe that the continuity of the individual's life was completely broken. . . .
Is there some principle of "conservation of value" tending to prevent rational, self-conscious spirits from lapsing back into merely animal souls? This question Leibniz answered with a decided affirmative.[31]

JOSEPH ADDISON (1672–1719)
British Essayist, Poet, and Statesman

["There is not, in my opinion," says Joseph Addison, "a more pleasing consideration than that of the perpetual progress which the soul makes towards the perfection of its nature, without ever arriving at a period in it. To look upon the soul as going on from strength to strength to consider that she is to shine forever with new accessions of glory and brighten to all eternity; that she will be still adding virtue to virtue and knowledge to knowledge, carries in it something wonderfully agreeable to that ambition which is natural to the mind of man."[32] Yet, in the first lines that follow from Addison's play *Cato,* he senses perhaps a fearful reaction in the immature man toward the prospect of a never-ending future. Macneile Dixon once mentioned the incongruity of people hoping for eternal life yet experiencing trepidation at the thought of an hour in their own company! What would they do with eternity! Thus, the *Bhagavad-Gita* speaks of becoming "*fitted* for immortality." Quoting from Scene I of Act V of *Cato:*]

> Eternity—thou pleasing, dreadful thought,
> Through what variety of untried being,
> Through what new scenes and dangers must we pass?
> The wide, th' unbounded prospect lies before me,
> But shadows, clouds, and darkness rest upon it.
> . . . . I shall never die.
> The soul, secure in her existence, smiles
> At the drawn dagger, and defies its point.
> The stars shall fade away, the sun himself
> Grow dim with age, and Nature sink in years;
> But thou shall flourish in immortal youth,
> Unhurt amidst the war of elements,
> The wreck of matter, and the crush of worlds.

EIGHTEENTH-CENTURY ENLIGHTENMENT

The Age of Reason

[The Age of Reason, known as the Eighteenth-Century Enlightenment, was a time of momentous transition in practically every area of Western development. It was precipitated by Isaac Newton's discovery in the previous century of a fundamental universal order in the cosmos, by the rationalism of Descartes, and the empiricism of Bacon and Locke. The Enlightenment philosophers advocated a logical and scientific approach to religious and social issues. All remnants of the Middle Ages—feudalism, reliance on spiritual authority, censorship of thought, religious intolerance—fell under their attack. Among the leaders were Rousseau and Voltaire in France; David Hume and Alexander Pope in England; Kant, Lessing, and Herder in Germany; and Benjamin Franklin and Thomas Paine in America.

Many of these thinkers were Deists, believing that there is a universal religion natural to all men in all times and places. Deity was acknowledged on the evidence of reason and nature and not upon supernatural revelation. As to reincarnation, most of the men just named will have something to say on the subject in the pages to come. From some of the selections it is evident that the Grecian and Roman influence still predominated but in the latter part of the century fresh breezes began to blow in from two other quarters: one from Germany in the form of the philosophical and cultural revolution set in motion by Immanuel Kant, and the other from the Orient. This was the time in which India's religious treasures were being discovered by the West and some of her scriptures appeared in translation. As both movements penetrated deep into the following century, the opening item in our discussion on the nineteenth century will go into all this with more particularity.]

VOLTAIRE (1694–1778)
French Philosopher and Author

[Voltaire has written that "the doctrine of metempsychosis is, above all, neither absurd nor useless. . . . It is not more surprising to be born twice than once; everything in nature is resurrection."[1] Under "Soul," in his *Philosophical Dictionary*, Voltaire speaks of the origin of reincarnation in Western classical times:]

Pherecydes was the first among the Greeks who believed that souls existed from all eternity; and not the first, as has been supposed, who said that the soul survived the body. Ulysses, long before Pherecydes, had seen the souls of heroes in the infernal regions; but that souls were as old as the world was a system which had sprung up in the East, and was brought into the West by Pherecydes. I do not believe that there is among us a single system which is not to be found among the ancients. The materials of all our modern edifices are taken from the wreck of antiquity.[2]

[Under "Original Sin," in the *Philosophical Dictionary*, Voltaire tells of the views of the Socinians who were founded in sixteenth-century Poland by the Italian theologian Faustus Socinus, and adds some thoughts of his own on the soul's origin:]

The Socinians or Unitarians make capital of the doctrine of original sin. They call the acceptance of this doctrine the "original sin" of Christianity. It is an outrage against God, they say. To dare to say that He created all the successive generations of mankind only to subject them to eternal punishment under the pretext that their earliest ancestor ate of a particular fruit in a garden is to accuse Him of the most absurd barbarity. This sacrilegious imputation is even more inexcusable among Christians, since there is no mention of this invention of original sin either in the Pentateuch [the first five books of the Old Testament], or in the Gospels, whether apocryphal or canonical, or in any of the writers called the "first Fathers of the Church."
. . . Souls were either created from all eternity, with the result that they are infinitely older than Adam's sin and have no connection with it, or they are formed at the time of conception, with the result that God must exercise eternal vigilance and create in each instance a new spirit that He will render eternally miserable.[3]

BENJAMIN FRANKLIN (1706–1790)

American Statesman, Scientist, and Philosopher

[Benjamin Franklin's epitaph, written by himself at the age of twenty-two, is called by Carl Van Doren "the most famous of American epitaphs," although it was never used on his tombstone.[4] It appears, slightly modified, in almost a dozen versions, which is not surprising as he often made copies for friends and did not confine himself to the original wording.[5] It reads:]

The Body of B. Franklin,
Printer,
Like the Cover of an Old Book,
Its Contents Torn Out
And
Stripped of its Lettering and Gilding,
Lies Here
Food for Worms,
But the Work shall not be Lost,
For it Will as He Believed
Appear Once More
In a New and more Elegant Edition
Revised and Corrected
By the Author.

[This epitaph reveals how Franklin felt when he was a young man, but how about later on? A letter has been preserved, written by Franklin when he was seventy-nine, that answers this question:]

When I see nothing annihilated and not a drop of water wasted, I cannot suspect the annihilation of souls, or believe that [God] will suffer the daily waste of millions of minds ready made that now exist, and put Himself to the continual trouble of making new ones. Thus, finding myself to exist in the world, I believe I shall, in some shape or other, always exist; and, with all the inconveniences human life is liable to, I shall not object to a new edition of mine, hoping, however, that the *errata* of the last may be corrected.[6]

[Emerson in his *Journals* quotes the eighty-year-old Franklin as writing to a friend:]

I feel as if I was intruding among posterity when I ought to be abed and asleep. I look upon death to be as necessary to the constitution as sleep. We shall rise refreshed in the morning.[7]

HENRY FIELDING (1707–1754)
British Novelist and Playwright

[Henry Fielding's novel A Journey from This World to the Next narrates the tale of one who has just died. En route to heaven, numerous souls are met returning to earth life. In heaven he finds several historically famous characters, including Julian, the ''Apostate,'' and is amazed to see the latter, thinking he surely would have been entitled to the bottomless pit. ''He told me, that several lies had been raised on him in his former capacity, nor was he so bad a man as he had been represented. However, he had been denied [immediate admittance to Elysium], and forced to undergo several subsequent pilgrimages on earth.'' A long list of these incarnations is given with details thereof.[8]]

DAVID HUME (1711–1776)
Scottish Philosopher, Historian, Economist, and Essayist

[Renowned for his skeptical philosophy, Hume was one of the most outspoken of the Enlightenment philosophers who glorified man's cold reasoning powers as his sole tool to gain knowledge. On the Continent he is classified with Bacon and Locke as the three Britons deserving the name of classical philosophers. However, for some Germans, Hume's only title to fame is that one of his propositions stung Kant into formulating the philosophy contained in *The Critique of Pure Reason*. Hume, of course, was no reincarnationist, but he did make the following admission in his essay "The Immortality of the Soul":]

Reasoning from the common course of nature, and without supposing any new interposition of the Supreme Cause, which ought always to be excluded from philosophy; what is incorruptible must also be ungenerable. The soul, therefore, if immortal, existed before our birth: And if the former existence noways concerns us, neither will the later. . . . The Metempsychosis is, therefore, the only system of this kind, that philosophy can hearken to.[9]

FREDERICK THE GREAT (1712–1786)
King of Prussia

[Shortly before his death, Frederick the Great said:]

Well, I feel that soon I shall have done with my earthly life. Now, since I am convinced that nothing existing in nature can be annihilated, so I know for a certainty that the more noble part of me will not cease to live. Though I may not be a king in my future life, so much the better: I shall nevertheless live an active life and, on top of it, earn less ingratitude.[10]

IMMANUEL KANT (1724–1804)
German Philosopher and Metaphysician

[We will defer a consideration of Kant's place in the development of European thought to the opening item for the next century, "Transcendentalism in Europe." Here we will simply quote Schopenhauer's opinion: "The chief jewel in the crown of Frederick the Great [was] Immanuel Kant. Such a man as Kant could not have held a salaried position under any other monarch on the globe at that time and have expressed the things that Kant did."[11]

Kant's first speculations on reincarnation appeared in an early paper entitled "General History of Nature and Theory of the Heavens." There he expressed the opinion that souls start imperfect from the sun, and travel by planet stages farther and farther away to a paradise in the coldest and remotest planet of our system. Our first selection is from that paper, to be followed by extracts from his celebrated work, *Critique of Pure Reason*.]

In view of the endless duration of the immortal soul throughout the infinity of time, which even the grave itself does not interrupt . . . shall the soul remain forever attached to this one point of world-space, our earth? Will it never participate in a closer contemplation of the remaining wonders of creation? Who knows but that the intention is for it to become acquainted at close range, some day, with those far distant globes of the cosmic system and the excellence of their institutions, which from this distance already provoke our curiosity? Perhaps for just such a purpose some globes of the planetary system are in a state of preparation as a new dwelling place for us to occupy after we have completed the period of time allotted for our sojourn here. Who knows but that the satellites coursing around Jupiter will some day shine on us?

General History of Nature[12]

Generation in the human race . . . depends on . . . many accidents . . . on the views and whims of government, nay, even on vice, so that it is difficult to believe in the eternal existence of a being whose life has first begun under circumstances so trivial, and so entirely dependent on our own choice. . . . It would seem as if we could hardly expect so wonderful an effect from causes so insignificant. But, in answer to these objections, we may adduce the transcendental hypothesis, that all life is properly intelligible, and not subject to the changes of time, and that it neither began in birth, nor will end in death. . . . If we could see ourselves and other objects as *they really are,* we should see ourselves in a world of spiritual natures, our community with which neither began at our birth nor will end with the death of the body.

Critique of Pure Reason (Part II: i, iii)

[In *The Realm of Ends* (p. 404fn.), James Ward calls attention to the above passage and states that in Kant's lectures on metaphysics shortly before the publication of the *Critique* he taught the preexistence of the soul. Ward cites Max Heinze's *Vorlesungen Kant's über Metaphysik,* 1894, p. 547, of the reprint from the Transactions of the Royal Society of Saxony.]

G. E. LESSING (1729–1781)
German Dramatist and Critic

[Henry E. Allison writes in *Lessing and the Enlightenment:*

Lessing was one of the seminal minds of the eighteenth century. In addition to being an important innovator in drama, literary criticism, and aesthetic theory, he was one of the most significant religious thinkers of his time. This has long been recognized by German scholars, who have devoted scores of volumes to an analysis of his religious philosophy, but as is unfortunately so often the case, he has been almost completely ignored by the English-speaking world. . . . It was, Kierkegaard tells us, Lessing who first suggested to him the concept of the leap and the famous formula "truth is subjectivity," and it was also, I believe, Lessing who more than anyone else led Kierkegaard to see the paradoxical nature of Christianity's claim to ground an individual's eternal happiness upon a historical event. Lessing, however, was far more than one of the numerous influences on Kierkegaard. He was the founder of a whole new conception of religious truth and one of the most articulate and profound advocates of the doctrine of man's spiritual development.[13]

The opening extract is from *Lessing's Observations Upon Campe's Philosophical Dialogues.*]

Is it after all so certain that my soul has only once inhabited the form of man? Is it after all so unreasonable to suppose that my soul, upon its journey to perfection, should have been forced to wear this fleshly veil more than once? Possibly this migration of the soul through several human bodies was based on a new system of thought. Possibly this new system was merely the oldest of all.[14]

[What follows is the famous conclusion of Lessing's *Education of the Human Race,* and has been called his "religious testament."]

Is this hypothesis [of metempsychosis] ridiculous merely because it is the oldest, because the human intellect adopted it without demur, before men's minds had been distracted and weakened by the sophistry of the schools? . . . On the contrary, the first and earliest opinion in matters of speculation is invariably the most probable, because it was immediately accepted by the sound understanding of mankind. . . . Why should I not return as often as I am capable of acquiring fresh knowledge and further power? Do I achieve so much in one sojourning as to make it not worth my while to return? Never! Or, is it that I forget my former life? Well for me that I forget. The recollection of my former state would enable me to turn my present condition to but poor account. And have I forgotten forever what I must forget for the time being? Or is it that I should lose so much time? Lose time! What need have I for haste? Is not the whole of eternity mine?[15]

GEORG CHRISTOPH LICHTENBERG (1742–1799)

German Physicist, Mathematician, and Satirist

[This distinguished scientist related in "Remarks of the Author About Himself" that at the age of eight he was guided to the idea of metempsychosis by an unsual boy of his acquaintance.[16] In *Selbstscharacteristik* ("Self-Study") he wrote: "I cannot get rid of the thought that I died before I was born. . . . I feel so many things that were I to write them down the world would regard me as a madman. Consequently, I prefer to hold my peace."[17]]

J. G. HERDER (1744–1803)

German Philosopher

[To provide a glimpse of Herder and his time we quote first from Frederick Burkhardt's introduction to the English translation of Herder's classic *Gott:*

> The closing years of the eighteenth century in Germany saw the beginning of a period of intellectual and literary activity which has rarely been equalled in the history of the human mind. It is no exaggeration to say . . . that [Herder] enriched more different fields of knowledge than any man of his time. Literature, education, philosophy, history, theology, philology, jurisprudence and biblical criticism all received fruitful and lasting contributions from his pen.[18]

In the foreword to Burkhardt's translation, Horace Friess comments on Herder's interest in the Orient: "Herder, who so assiduously sought out the spiritual expressions of all persons, would certainly—were he alive today—take interest in the further meeting of oriental and occidental thought. In these very Conversations . . . he introduced some excerpts from eastern literature."[19]

Our selections come from Herder's *Dialogues on Metempsychosis,* translated by the American transcendentalist Frederic Hedge:]

Do you not know great and rare men who cannot have become what they are at once, in a single human existence? Who must often have existed before in order to have attained that purity of feeling, that instinctive impulse for all that is true, beautiful and good—in short, that elevation and natural supremacy over all around them? . . .

Have you never observed that children will sometimes, of a sudden, give utterance to ideas which makes us wonder how they got possession of them, which presuppose a long series of other ideas and secret self-communings, which break forth like a full stream out of the earth, an infallible sign that the stream was not produced in a moment from a few raindrops, but had long been flowing concealed beneath the ground? . . .

Have you never had remembrances of a former state, which you could find no place for in this life? . . . Have you not seen persons, been in places, of which you were ready to swear that you had seen those persons, or had been in those places before? . . . And such are we; we who, from a hundred causes, have sunk so deep and are so wedded to matter, that but few reminiscences of so pure a character remain to us. The nobler class of men who, separated from wine and meat, lived in perfect simplicity, temperate and according to the order of Nature, carried it further, no doubt, than others, as we learn from the example of Pythagoras, of Iarchas, of Apollonius, and others, who remembered distinctly what and how many times they had been in the world before.

If we are blind, or can see but two steps beyond our noses, ought we therefore to deny that others may see a hundred or a thousand degrees farther, even to the bottom of time, into the deep, cool well of the fore-world, and there discern everything plain and bright and clear? . . .

I am not ashamed of my half-brothers, the brutes; on the contrary as far as they are concerned, I am a great advocate of metempsychosis. I believe, for a certainty, that they will ascend to a higher grade of being, and am unable to comprehend how anyone can object to this hypothesis which seems to have the analogy of the whole creation in its favor.[20]

SIR WILLIAM JONES (1746–1794)
British Orientalist and Jurist

[During his short life Sir William Jones became one of the great scholars of England. He was famous in jurisprudence and Oriental languages. While judge of the high court in Calcutta, he founded the Asiatic Society of Bengal, through which, as well as through his publications, he had a great influence on Oriental study and philology in Europe. He translated the Hindu *Laws of Manu;* the *Hitopadasa;* Kalidasa's famous drama *Sakuntala;* and considerable portions of the Vedas. Radhakrishnan quotes this excerpt from a letter of Sir William as an example of a Westerner who viewed with favor the doctrine of rebirth:

> I am no Hindu; but I hold the doctrine of the Hindus concerning a future state to be incomparably more rational, more pious, and more likely to deter men from vice, than the horrid opinions inculcated by Christians on punishments without end.[21]

His translation of *Sakuntala* was rendered into German in 1791 and enthusiastically welcomed by Herder and Goethe. Winternitz quotes this pertinent remark of August Schlegel: "Will the English perhaps claim a monopoly of Indian literature? It would be too late. Cinnamon and cloves they may keep; but these mental treasures are the common property of the educated world."[22]]

JOHANN EHLERT BODE (1747–1826)
German Astronomer

[Like his contemporary Immanuel Kant, the astronomer Johann Ehlert Bode—after whom Bode's Law was named—speculated on the soul's progress among the heavenly bodies. The French science writer Louis Figuier reports in his book *The Tomorrow of Death* that "Bode has written that we start from the coldest planet of our solar system (Uranus), and advance progressively from planet to planet, ever drawing near the Sun. In the Sun will live, in the opinion of this astronomer, the most perfect beings."[23] Bode did not conceive that, in his present bodily constitution, man could dwell in the heart of our system, poetically called "the solar palace" in some Eastern philosophies.]

EASTERN AND TRANSCENDENTAL INFLUENCES IN THE NINETEENTH CENTURY

Transcendentalism in Europe

["During the classical period of German literature metempsychosis attracted such attention that the period may almost be styled the flourishing epoch of the doctrine." Thus writes Alfred Bertholet, professor of theology at the University of Basel.[1] This period had its origin in the transcendental philosophy of Immanuel Kant, whose *Critique of Pure Reason*, published in 1871, opened a new era in metaphysical thought. Carlyle repeats August Schlegel's view that in its influence on the moral culture of Europe, Kant's philosophy was as important as the Reformation itself.[2]

Kant undertook to transfer attention from the objects that engaged the mind to the mind itself. He proposed a revolution in metaphysics comparable to the Copernican revolution in astronomy. Like Copernicus, who found it impossible to explain the movements of the heavenly bodies on the supposition of their turning round the earth, posited the sun as the center, so Kant, perceiving the confusion that resulted from making man a satellite of the external world, resolved to place him in the central position. However, this German philosopher, of partly Scottish heritage, was not concerned only with man in his sensuous, intellectual, and phenomenal aspects, but with his subjective, intuitional, noumenal sides as well.

As explained by Professor E. M. Joad, Kant posited the existence of two selves in man, which he called respectively the empirical self and the transcendental self. The former is but a bundle or series of psychological events. "By a variety of subtle arguments Kant sought to show that this bundle or series of events cannot be all that we mean when we talk of the I. There is also, he held, a continuing self which underlies and links them together, although of this continuing self we are not normally conscious. By virtue of this continuing self we belong, he taught, to the world of reality, and escape from the everyday world of appearance of which the empirical self is a member."[3] That Kant conceived of the possibility that this continuing self could have repeated existences is evident from his statements on reincarnation which we quoted.

Fichte was an enthusiastic interpreter of Kant's teachings, endeavoring to render them intelligible and attractive to minds of ordinary culture. Others whose brilliance added light and ardor to the Kantian revolution were Lessing, Herder, Schleiermacher, Goethe, Schiller, Jean Paul Richter, Friedrich Schlegel, Hegel, and Schopenhauer, all of whom are quoted on reincarnation either in this section or elsewhere in this work.

The transcendental movements in England and America were extensively influenced by these German thinkers.[4] Carlyle undertook the study of German and championed the cause of German philosophy and literature in the English reviews. He also made excellent translations, such as Goethe's *Wilhelm Meister.* Coleridge commenced the study of German when he was twenty-four, and at twenty-six, accompanied by Wordsworth, visited Germany, spending fourteen months there in hard study.

In New England we find Frederic Hedge, a father of American transcendentalism, translating Herder's *Dialogues on Metempsychosis* and other German works. (His own affirmative views on rebirth, along with those of Emerson, Alcott, and Thoreau, will be given later.) It is seldom appreciated today that the very name of the American movement had its source in Kant, as John Deedy makes plain in an article commemorating a famous agricultural experiment by the New England group:

> Transcendentalism took its name from the *Critique of Pure Reason,* Immanuel Kant's 1781 treatise in which he used the term "transcendental" to refer to ideas received by intuition rather than through the experience of the senses. [In the 1830s] the transcendental principle . . . took root in New England through Unitarianism, which was then making its break with Puritan formalisms. The transcendental notion of a God immanent in nature and the individual soul had an instant appeal to Unitarian intellectuals suddenly in revolt against the old concepts of a wrathful God and a depraved human nature.[5]

Among Kant's successors the influence of Oriental thought became more and more pronounced. August Schlegel published the first German translation of the *Bhagavad-Gita,* as well as other Sanskrit works, and paid high tribute to the author of the *Gita:*

> By the Brahmins, reverence of masters is considered the most sacred of duties. Thee therefore, first, most holy prophet, interpreter of the Deity, by whatever name thou wast called among mortals, the author of this poem by whose oracles the mind is rapt with ineffable delight to doctrines lofty, eternal, and divine—thee first, I say, I hail, and shall always worship at thy feet."[6]

In *The Wonder that Was India,* A. L. Basham writes: "From Goethe on-wards most of the great German philosophers knew something of Indian philosophy. Schopenhauer, whose influence on literature and psychology has been so considerable, indeed openly admitted his debt, and his outlook was virtually that of Buddhism. The monisms of Fichte and Hegel might never have taken the forms they did if it had not been for the Anquetil-Duperron translation of the *Upanishads* and the work of other pioneer Indologists."[7]

The revolution in the world of philosophy and literature was accompanied by a like resurgence in the world of music. The great composers were steeped in the literary and philosophical spirit of their day. Bach, who lived some decades before, sensed the social awakening to come and the dreams for a brighter morrow. He wrote: "In the architecture of my music I want to dem-onstrate to the world the architecture of a new and beautiful social common-wealth. . . . The harmony of the stars in the heavens, the yearning for brotherhood in the heart of man. This is the secret of my music." At a scientific conclave in Washington, D.C., celebrating the five hundredth an-niversary of Copernicus's birth, the world-renowned physicist Werner Heisenberg spoke of the relationship between philosophical and scientific discoveries on the one hand and a burst of creative activity in the arts on the other. He remarked that Haydn in his string quartets tried to express the emotions set forth in the innovative writings of Rousseau and Goethe. "And then Mozart, Beethoven, Schubert gathered in Vienna, competing in the solution of this problem."[8]

Beethoven was also to come under the spell of the Orient. He was fond of copying mystical sentences from Eastern literature, and permanently framed on his desk this quotation: "I am that which is, I am all that was, that is, and that shall be."[9] The music of Richard Wagner, as we shall later see, was strongly influenced by Buddhist ideas on reincarnation.

The remainder of this chapter will illustrate how various lines of transcen-dental thinking were transmitted through the writings of eminent authors and leaders of thought in both Europe and America.]

J. W. VON GOETHE (1749–1832)

German Poet

[In an article "Goethe The Botanist," Frank Lipp writes: "As a poet, Johann Wolfgang von Goethe belongs in the select company of Shakespeare, Homer, Dante—immortals all, who used words as if they had just sprung from the womb of language, fresh and radiant and unique; who breathed, each into his own language, a scope and power that it had not had before. But Goethe the scientist, though his contributions were immense, is not so well known."[10] Also not well known is Goethe's serious interest in reincarnation.

The poet once remarked: "Surely I must have lived before the time of the Emperor Hadrian, for everything Roman attracts me with irrepressible force."[11] The Orient also interested him and he "was one of the first to become acquainted with the literature of India."[12] George Santayana in his essay "Goethe's Faust" has gathered this conception of the poet's view of reincarnation: "A deep mind has deep roots in nature,—it will bloom many times over. But what a deep mind carries over into its next incarnation— perhaps in some remote sphere—is not its conventional merits and demerits, its load of remorse, or its sordid memories. These are washed away in its new baptism. What remains is only what was deep in that mind, so deep that new situations may again imply and admit it."[13]

A similar idea is contained in a letter of Goethe to his close friend Charlotte von Stein: "How well it is that men should die, if only to erase their impressions and return clean washed."[14] Yet he must have believed that some memories survive, for in a letter written in 1776 to Christoph Wieland— known as the German Voltaire—Goethe states regarding Frau von Stein: "I cannot explain the significance to me of this woman or her influence over me, except by the theory of metempsychosis. Yes, we were once man and wife. Now our knowledge of ourselves is veiled, and lies in the spirit world. I can find no name for us—the past, the future, the All!"[15]

Frau von Stein apparently shared Goethe's views on rebirth, for in a memorial tribute at Zwickau in Saxony in 1892, on the occasion of the one hundred and fiftieth anniversary of her birth, a speaker said that she "considered life as a school into which the human spirit enters, coming from its heavenly home. Laden with weakness, sin and doubts, after having overcome this difficult ordeal, grown in knowledge and been purified, it enters again through the gates of death, its spiritual home, and continues thus in different forms of existence, which are always renewing themselves."[16]

The first selection given here is from *Faust*, followed by one of Goethe's well-known short poems, and then excerpts are offered from a remarkable conversation between Goethe and Johannes Falk. As to Goethe's *Faust*— which is most unlike Marlowe's and Gounod's, whose heroes are irredeemably damned—the major portion of his work is concerned with the doctor's ultimate redemption through cleansing psychological and mystical experiences resulting in practical deeds of benefit to man.]

> . . . . Two souls contend
> In me and both souls strive for masterdom,
> Which from the other shall the scepter rend.
> The first soul is a lover, clasping close
> To this world tentacles of corporal flame,
> The other seeks to rise with mighty throes
> To those ancestral meadows whence it came.
>
> *Faust (Act I, Scene 2)*

The soul of man is like to water;
From Heaven it cometh
To Heaven it riseth
And then returneth to earth,
Forever alternating.
"Song of the Spirits over the Waters"[17]

[At Wieland's funeral, in 1813, Johannes Falk asked Goethe what Wieland was now doing. In the course of his lengthy reply, Goethe said:]

I am certain that I have been here as I am now a thousand times before, and I hope to return a thousand times. . . . Respecting ourselves, however, it almost seems that our previous sojourns were too commonplace to deserve a second thought in the eyes of nature. . . . I cannot deny that there may be higher natures than our own among the Monads [Souls]. A World-Monad may produce out of the womb of its memories that which will prove prophetic but is actually a dim remembrance of something long expired. Similarly, human genius in a lightning flash of recollection can discover the laws involved in producing the universe, because it was present when those laws were established. . . .

As to the Monad to whom we are indebted for Wieland's appearance on earth, I cannot see what would prevent it from entering into the highest relations with the universe. . . . It would not astonish me if thousands of years hence I should meet him as a World-Monad—a star of the first magnitude. . . . When one reflects upon the eternity of the universe, one can conceive of no other destiny than that the Monads should eventually participate in the bliss of the Gods as joyfully cooperating forces. The work of creation will be entrusted to them. . . . Man is the dialogue between nature and God. On other planets this dialogue will doubtless be of a higher and profounder character. What is lacking is Self-Knowledge. After that the rest will follow.[18]

WILLIAM BLAKE (1757–1827)

British Poet, Artist, and Mystic

[From the frequency with which William Blake is quoted in serious literature today, one may be assured that he is truly a poet for our time. At the beginning of the epoch of political and social revolution, he kept crying out, What deep secrets are you forgetting, in this struggle to be free? What new chains will you forge with this brave, new dispensation?

In her two-volume work *Blake and Tradition*, Kathleen Raine reveals that Blake was one of the early readers of the 1785 Wilkins' edition of the *Bhagavad-Gita*, and that in his poem "Vala, or The Four Zoas" "the teaching of the *Bhagavad-Gita* may have colored [his] vision of the Great Battle, whose dead return again and again to generation." "The three causes of reincarnation given in the sixteenth book of the *Gita*," she points out, "are lust, wrath, and avarice." "Blake's generating specters are similarly characterized. They are 'meer passion and appetite'; they are also 'Cruel and ravening with Enmity and Hatred and War.' "[19] In the same poem Blake says that for such souls "the Pangs of Eternal birth are better than the Pangs of Eternal death." Miss Raine comments:

> Blake's "Pangs of Eternal birth" bring the souls back to the battle again and again; but this, they say, is better than the "Eternal death" which would come about from a refusal to go on with the Great Battle; for with all its suffering, it is an affirmation of life, the process by which the souls are harvested. The anguish of the body is as nothing to the 'Eternal death' of the apathetic soul who refuses to engage in life."[20]

Yeats writes that "it must never be forgotten that whatever Blake borrowed from Swedenborg or Boehme, from mystic or kabalist, he turned to his own purposes, and transferred into a new system, growing like a flower from its own roots . . . and that he stands among the mystics of Europe beside Jacob Boehme and the makers of the *Kabala,* as original as they are and as profound."[21]

To appreciate the selections that follow, a few words from John Beer's volume on Blake may be helpful:

> Blake's humanism . . . rests on the presupposition that all men possess an eternal form which subsists in the interplay between Vision and Desire. Eternal Man exists primarily by those two faculties, which nourish his genius and promote his generosity. But men as we know them have fallen from this estate. As a result, the fruitful dialectic between Vision and Desire is replaced by a warring and fruitless dialectic between Reason and Energy. . . . Blake took over and developed Swedenborg's hint that the Fall was a division *within* man rather than a separation from something outside him. In a Fall which takes place by such division, *all* the powers are correspondingly diminished, withering in their isolation from the synthesizing whole which would allow them to grow together and nourish one another.[22]]

In my brain are studies and chambers filled with books and pictures of old, which I wrote and painted in ages of eternity before my mortal life; and these works are the delight and study of archangels. . . . You, O dear Flaxman, are a sublime archangel, my friend and companion from eternity. I look back into the regions of reminiscence, and behold our ancient days before this earth appeared and its vegetative mortality to my mortal vegetated eyes. I see our houses of eternity which can never be separated, though our mortal vehicles should stand at the remotest corners of heaven from each other.

Letter to John Flaxman, the Sculptor[23]

Tell me where dwell the thoughts forgotten till thou call them forth?
Tell me where dwell the joys of old? and where the ancient loves,
And when they will renew again, and the night of oblivion past,
That I might traverse times and spaces far remote, and bring
Comforts into a present sorrow and a night of pain?
"Visions of the Daughters of Albion"

. . . . [Man] stores his thoughts
As in a store house in his memory. He regulates the forms
Of all beneath and all above . . . he rises to the Sun,
And to the Planets of the Night, and to the stars that gild
The Zodiacs, and the stars that sullen stand to north and south;
He touches the remotest pole, and in the center weeps
That Man should labour and sorrow, and learn and forget, and return
To the dark valley whence he came, and begin his labour anew.
In pain he sighs, in pain he labours in his universe. . . .
And in the cries of birth and in the groans of death his voice
Is heard throughout the Universe; wherever a grass grows,
Or a leaf buds, The Eternal Man is seen, is heard, is felt,
And all his sorrows, till he reassumes his ancient bliss.
"Vala, or The Four Zoas" (Night the Eighth)

THOMAS TAYLOR (1758–1835)

British Classical Scholar

[Thomas Taylor, a friend of William Blake's, is regarded by some as the giant Platonic scholar of all time. Surnamed "The Platonist," he published more than sixty books covering the writings of Plato, Aristotle, and the Neoplatonists, most of these being translated into English for the first time. Alexander Wilder writes of him: "It must be conceded that he was endowed with a superior qualification—that of an intuitive perception of the interior meaning of the subjects which he considered. Others may have known more Greek, but he knew more Plato." Emerson called him "that eminent benefactor of scholars and philosophers,"[24] and he could have added poets, for Kathleen Raine, in speaking of Blake's great debt to the Platonic philosophers and to Taylor's translations thereof, remarks: "Perhaps Taylor's greatest service to the romantic poets (and others since, from Coleridge, Keats, and Shelley to Yeats and AE) was in teaching the use of symbolic discourse as the language of metaphysical thought. Plotinus passes with ease from myth to philosophy and from philosophy to myth, as did Plato himself when he soared into the regions of 'The immortal mind, that hath forsook her mansion in this fleshly nook.'"[25] Quoting from Taylor's introduction to his translation of *The Works of Plato:*]

Let not the reader . . . be surprised at the solitariness of the paths through which I shall attempt to conduct him, or at the novelty of the objects which will present themselves in the journey: for perhaps he may fortunately recollect that he has travelled the same road before, that the scenes were once familiar to him, and that the country through which he is passing is his native land. . . .

As the human soul, according to Plato, ranks among the number of those souls that sometimes follow the mundane divinities [and sometimes do not] hence it possesses a power of descending infinitely into generation, or the sublunary region, and of ascending from generation to real being. . . . It remains, therefore, that every soul must perform periods, both of ascensions from generation, and of descensions into generation; and that this will never fail, through an infinite time. From all this it follows that the soul, while an inhabitant of earth, is in a fallen condition, an apostate from deity, an exile from the orb of light.[26]

FRIEDRICH SCHILLER (1759–1805)

German Poet and Dramatist

[In Friedrich Schiller's poem "The Mystery of Reminiscence," addressed "To Laura," he tries to explain his deep love for her. Were they "brothers in the days of yore, twin-bound both souls, and in the link they bore sigh to be bound once more?" Or "knew we the light of some extinguished sun . . .? Yes, it *is* so!—And thou were bound to me in the long-vanished Eld eternally! . . ."

> Weep for the godlike life we lost afar—
> Weep!—thou and I its scattered fragments are;
> And still the unconquered yearning we retain—
> Sigh to restore the rapture and the reign,
> And grow divine again.[27]

Such ecstatic thinking hardly sounds possible coming from a man trained to be an army surgeon, a career from which Schiller fortunately fled.

When the poet completed his medical and academic studies at the Karlsschule in Stuttgart at twenty-one, his graduating thesis was titled "Concerning the Connection between the Animal and the Spiritual Nature of Man." The examining committee ordered the essay printed despite its chief fault, in their eyes, that the writer so frequently gave rein to his imagination. In Section 27, treating of death, he wrote: "Matter decomposes into its final elements, which now wander through the kingdoms of nature in other forms and conditions. . . . The soul continues to exercise its power of thought and views the universe from other aspects. Of course, one can say, that it has not in the least exhausted this sphere as yet. . . . Can one be sure that this earth is forever lost? Do we not lay aside many a book we do not understand, to take it up again years later when we will understand it better?''']

J. G. FICHTE (1762–1814)
German Philosopher and Metaphysician

[From J. G. Fichte's *The Destination of Man,* translated by Frederic Hedge, one of the founders of the transcendentalist movement in America:]

These two systems, the purely spiritual and the sensuous—which last may consist of an immeasurable series of particular lives—exist in me from the moment in which my active reason is developed, and pursue their parallel course. . . . The former alone gives to the latter meaning, and purpose, and value. I am immortal, imperishable, eternal, so soon as I form the resolution to obey the law of Reason. . . . After an existence of myriad lives [the supersensuous world] cannot be more present than at this moment. Other conditions of my sensuous existence are to come; but these are no more the true life than the present condition. . . . Even because [Nature] puts me to death she must quicken me anew. It can only be my higher life, unfolding itself in her, and that which mortals call death is the visible appearing of a second vivification. . . .

Man is not a product of the world of sense; and the end of his existence can never be attained in that world. His destination lies beyond time and space and all that pertains to sense.[28]

JEAN PAUL RICHTER (1763–1825)
German Author

[Although he wrote other types of literature, Jean Paul was the outstanding novelist of his day and greatly influenced German authors as well as the composer Robert Schumann. The first selection quoted here is called his swan song and bears the subtitle ''On the Immortality of the Soul.'']

The least valid objection to the theory of soul-circulation is that we forget these journeyings. Even during this life and without experiencing a ''change of clothes,'' multifarious conditions vanish from our memories. How then should we expect to remember the different bodies and the still more varied conditions experienced in previous lives? Why not allow a way of thinking to enjoy full light that a Plato, a Pythagoras, and whole nations and eras have not disdained? . . . Let the soul return as often as it wishes. Certainly the earth is rich enough to bestow ever new gifts, new centuries, new countries, new minds, new discoveries and hopes.

Selina[29]

Always employ a language some years in advance of the child (men of genius in their books speak to us from the vantage-ground of centuries) . . . Let the teacher, especially he who is too much in the habit of attributing all learning to teaching, consider that the child already carries half his world, that of mind—the objects, for instance, of moral and metaphysical contemplation—ready formed within him; and hence language, being provided only with physical images, cannot give, but merely illumine, his mental conceptions.

Levana, or the Doctrine of Education[30]

NAPOLEON BONAPARTE (1769–1821)

Emperor of France (Napoleon I)

[Here was a man born in the humblest possible condition of life, rising until he dominated empires and sent kings from their thrones at a single word, a man who, in those strange, abnormal conditions into which he sometimes passed, would cry out to his marshals: "I am Charlemagne. Do you know who I am? I am Charlemagne." Emil Ludwig quotes him as stating: "Tell the Pope that I am keeping my eyes open; tell him that I am Charlemagne, the Sword of the Church, his Emperor, and as such I expect to be treated."[31]

Prince Talleyrand in his *Memoirs* writes thus of a stormy meeting on June 18, 1811, between Bonaparte and several dignitaries of the Church:

> The phrase which follows, and which he repeated every three or four minutes . . . revealed the depth of his thought. "Messieurs," he exclaimed to them, "you wish to treat me as if I were Louis le Débonnaire. Do not confound the son with the father. You see in me Charlemagne. . . . I am Charlemagne, I . . . yes, I am Charlemagne."[32]

Whatever may be the truth of this claim, it does seem interesting that what history calls the Holy Roman Empire began in A.D. 800 with the French king Charlemagne (Charles the Great)—when he was crowned at Saint Peter's by Pope Leo III as "the great and peace-giving Emperor of the Romans"—and after surviving a thousand years ended with Napoleon who dismembered it so thoroughly it never managed to revive. Friedrich Heer tells of this in his history *The Holy Roman Empire:*

> The imperial church, for a thousand years the prop and stay of the Holy Roman Empire [and which in later years often had been at odds with the

Papacy] was broken up for good. . . . In permitting this liquidation . . . the "new Charlemagne" dealt the Holy Roman Empire its death blow. Charles the Great had created the imperial church and laid the foundations of the Holy Roman Empire. The "second Charlemagne" dissolved the imperial church and assumed the style of an emperor. . . . In France, obsequious churchmen "happy to have discovered someone to restore the church's liberty, never tired of comparing Napoleon with Charles the Great". . . . Now the true Charles-emperor had appeared. . . . At his coronation he used insignia allegedly or actually descended from Charles the Great.[33]]

G . W . F . H E G E L (1 7 7 0 – 1 8 3 1)
German Philosopher

[Lately there has been a genuine revival of interest in Hegel's metaphysics as well as in his social and political theories. The book scene is flooded with studies of this great thinker who conceived of the philosopher in the grand manner, and not merely as an underlaborer to the scientist, as Locke and a host of others have. Hegel took seriously Plato's saying that the philosopher is "the spectator of all time and all existence," and attempted to comprehend the entire universe in his system. He believed that the whole of human history is a process through which mankind has been making spiritual and moral progress in its advance toward self-knowledge. History has a plot and the philosopher's task is to discern it. In an article in the *New York Review* (May 29, 1975), "Spreading Hegel's Wings," Anthony Quinton reviews ten of the recent books on Hegel, and remarks: "There are good reasons why Hegel's metaphysics . . . should exert a continuing fascination. . . . Its extraordinary scope, the breadth and variety of its creator's learning, and the integrity of his admittedly baffling intellectual style endow it with a formida-ble quality that demands attention."

The extracts that follow are taken from Hegel's *Philosophy of History:*]

Change while it imports dissolution, involves at the same time the rise of a new life—that while death is the issue of life, life is also the issue of death. This is a grand conception; one which the Oriental thinkers attained, and which is perhaps the highest in their metaphysics. In the idea of Metempsychosis we find it evolved in its relation to individual existence. . . . Spirit—consuming the envelope of its existence—does not merely pass into another envelope, nor rise rejuvenescent from the ashes of its previous form; it comes forth exalted, glorified, a purer spirit. . . .

The principles of the successive phases of Spirit . . . are themselves only steps in the development of one universal Spirit. . . . Nothing in the past is lost for it, for the Idea is ever present; Spirit is immortal; with it there is no past, no future, but an essential *now*. This necessarily implies that the present form of Spirit comprehends within it all earlier steps. . . . The life of the ever present Spirit is a circle of progressive embodiments, which looked at in one aspect still exist beside each other, and only as looked at from another point of view appear as past. The grades which Spirit seems to have left behind it, it still possesses in the depths of its present.[34]

WILLIAM WORDSWORTH (1770–1850)

British Poet

[In a 1927 issue of the London *Spectator* appeared this information: "There did not seem, until recently, to be any definite reference to the belief [of reincarnation] in Wordsworth's poems, for the well-known lines, 'Our birth is but a sleep and a forgetting,' are a statement of the soul's pre-existence, rather than of its repeated returns to earth. But the newly discovered poem in [his sister's] Dorothy Wordsworth's handwriting (the manuscript of which is to be sold at Sotheby's) provides remarkable evidence of the poet's interest in this age-old doctrine."[35] The lines are addressed to an infant, and begin as follows:

> Oh, sweet new-comer to the changeful earth,
> If, as some darkling seers have boldly guessed,
> Thou hadst a being and a human birth,
> And wert erewhile by human parents blessed,
> Long, long before thy present mother pressed
> Thee, helpless stranger, to her fostering breast.

In view of the foregoing, Wordsworth's "Ode to Immortality," extracts from which follow, may be invested with new significance. Walter Pater wrote in *Appreciations, Wordsworth:* "He had pondered deeply . . . on those strange reminiscences and forebodings which seem to make our lives stretch before and behind us. . . . Following the soul backwards and forwards, on these endless ways, his sense of man's dim, potential powers became a pledge to him, indeed, of a future life, but carried him back also to that mysterious notion of an earlier state of existence—the fancy of the Platonists—the old heresy of Origen."[36]

The reincarnationist, believing as he usually does in a lengthy state of spiritual bliss and assimilation between earth lives, would naturally concur in much of the imagery that follows. This celebrated poem turns attention from a fearful preoccupation with the life-to-come to an inspiring consideration of the life-that-was. Most importantly, it offers a fresh, elevated view of childhood in strong contrast with the harsh miserable-sinner outlook of the Fundamentalists. The ode is entitled "Intimations of Immortality from Recollections of Early Childhood."]

Our birth is but a sleep and a forgetting;
The Soul that rises with us, our life's Star,
Hath had elsewhere its setting,
And cometh from afar.
Not in entire forgetfulness
And not in utter nakedness,
But trailing clouds of glory do we come
From God who is our home.
Heaven lies about us in our infancy!

Shades of the prison-house begin to close
Upon the growing Boy;
But He beholds the light, and whence it flows
He sees it in his joy.
The Youth, who daily farther from the east
Must travel, still is Nature's Priest,
And by the vision splendid
Is on his way attended;
At length the Man perceives it die away,
And fade into the light of common day.

Earth fills her lap with pleasures of her own. . . .
The homely Nurse doth all she can
To make her Foster-child, her Inmate Man,
Forget the glories he hath known,
And that imperial palace whence he came . . .
Though nothing can bring back the hour
Of splendour in the grass, of glory in the flower . . .
Yet in my heart of hearts I feel your might.

SIR WALTER SCOTT (1771–1832)

Scottish Novelist and Poet

[The following is from E. D. Walker's *Reincarnation* in which he introduces some selections from Sir Walter Scott in this way:]

Most of us have known the touches of feeling and thought that seem to be reminders of forgotten things. Sir Walter Scott was so impressed by these experiences that they led him to a [consideration of] pre-existence. In his diary was entered this circumstance, February 17, 1828: "I cannot, I am sure, tell if it is worth marking down, that yesterday, at dinner time, I was strangely haunted by what I would call the sense of pre-existence, viz. a confused idea that nothing that passed was said for the first time; that the same topics had been discussed and the same persons had stated the same opinions on them. . . . The sensation was so strong as to resemble what is called a *mirage* in the desert and a calenture on board ship. . . . It was very distressing yesterday, and brought to my mind the fancies of Bishop Berkeley about an ideal world. There was a vile sense of unreality in all I said or did.''[37]

That this was not due to the strain upon his later years is evident from the fact that the same experience is referred to in one of his earliest novels, where this "sense of pre-existence" was first described. In *Guy Mannering,* Henry Bertram questions: "Why is it that some scenes awaken thoughts which belong, as it were, to dreams of early and shadowy recollections, such as old Brahmin moonshine would have ascribed to a state of previous existence. How often do we find ourselves in society which we have never before met, and yet feel impressed with a mysterious and ill-defined consciousness that neither the scene nor the speakers nor the subject are entirely new; nay, feel as if we could anticipate that part of the conversation which has not yet taken place.''[38]

SAMUEL T. COLERIDGE (1772–1834)

British Poet and Critic

[A twenty-five-page article entitled ''Coleridge—Metempsychosis'' appeared in the *Journal of English Literary History* (December 1958), published by Johns Hopkins University. The writer, Irene Chayes, traced the poet's interest in reincarnation to Chevalier Ramsay and Thomas Taylor whose works he was studying when his poem ''On a Homeward Journey upon Hearing of the Birth of a Son'' was written in 1796.]

> Oft o'er my brain does that strange fancy roll
> Which makes the present (while the flash doth last)
> Seem a mere semblance of some unknown past,
> Mixed with such feelings as perplex the soul
> Self-questioned in her sleep; and some have said
> We lived, ere yet this robe of flesh we wore.
> O my sweet baby! when I reach my door,
> If heavy looks should tell me thou art dead,
> (As sometimes, through excess of hope, I fear)
> I think that I should struggle to believe
> Thou wert a spirit, to this nether sphere
> Sentenc'd for some more venial crime to grieve;
> Didst scream, then spring to meet Heaven's quick reprieve
> While we wept idly o'er thy little bier!

FRIEDRICH VON SCHLEGEL (1772–1829)

German Philosopher

[Friedrich von Schlegel, the brother of August von Schlegel, studied Oriental languages in Paris from 1802 to 1804. He apparently was the first to give the impulse to Indological studies in Germany through his book *The Language and Wisdom of the Indians,* which appeared in 1808.[39] *The Philosophy of Life* lectures, from which the last selection quoted here is taken, were translated into English and published in London in 1847.]

Philosophy has primarily to refute two basic errors: firstly, that the human soul can dissolve into nothingness, and secondly, that man, without any effort of his own, is already fully endowed with immortality. . . . Man as he is now is entirely too imperfect, too material, to claim that higher kind of immortality. He will have to enter into other earthly, yet far more refined and transfigured forms and developments before he can directly partake of the eternal glory of the divine world of light. . . .

The idea of metempsychosis, embraced by mysticism, is remarkable in itself for its antiquity. . . . It does not permit the soul to pass to full freedom before it has incarnated in many bodies. Here we view metempsychosis in its most general meaning as continuance of spirit, alternately using organic forms, and not in the sense of . . . an aggravating punishment ever accelerating.

Cologne Lectures (1804–1806)[40]

Inasmuch as the true Indian teaching of metempsychosis, as we now know it correctly from the sources, is too serious and solemn to find much credence and applause in our time, the attempt has been made recently to carry it entirely into the realm of romanticism and to paint the future life in glowing colors as a sort of astronomical excursion from one star to another. . . . Would it not be more advisable, and more appropriate to human intellect, if man would first turn his gaze upon himself and his present dwelling place, the earth, instead of at once disappearing into the starry skies? May not he find that which he seeks so often in the distance far closer at hand?

The Philosophy of Life[41]

CHARLES FOURIER (1772–1837)

French Social Scientist and Reformer

[Charles Fourier is generally regarded as the founder of Socialism. A famous example of a Fourieristic experiment, Brook Farm in the United States, captured the interest of the American Transcendentalists. Emerson, however, found a number of drawbacks in Fourier's ideas, but nevertheless wrote in his article, "Fourierism and the Socialists": "The increasing zeal and numbers of the disciples of Fourier, in America and in Europe, entitle them to an attention which their theory and practical projects will justify and reward. . . . In a day of small, sour, and fierce schemes, one is admonished and cheered by a project of such friendly aims, and of such bold and generous proportion; there is an intellectual courage and strength in it, which is superior and commanding."[42]

Fourier was a reincarnationist, as his various books, including his noted *Theory of Universal Unity,* reveal. In introducing *The Passions of the Human Soul,* the translator, the Reverend John Reynell Morell, states that Fourier believed in an "alternating passage from the visible into the invisible world, and vice versa, [which] commenced with the existence of humanity on this globe, and will continue to the end of time; that is, until the decline of this planet Earth, and the final transmigration of humanity *en masse* unto another planet." In the book itself Fourier states:]

I do not reckon the numerous revivals or incarnations of our souls on the globe as the future life. . . . In fact, at the epochs when it is freed from the human body, it revives instantly in the great soul of the globe, whereof it is part and parcel, and disdains the present life, as at the moment of waking we despise or cherish a dream, according as it has been happy or unhappy. Now the civilized and barbarian state is an ugly dream to 99/100 of souls. . . . After a period passed in the great soul, they go to sleep and are born again upon the globe in a new body. . . . Some exceptional individuals . . . remember their past existences.[43]

ROBERT SOUTHEY (1774–1843)

British Poet and Prose Writer

[A letter by Robert Southey, poet laureate (1813–1843):]

I have a strong and lively faith in a state of continued consciousness from this stage of existence, and that we shall recover the consciousness of some lower stages through which we may previously have passed seems to me not impossible. . . . The system of progressive existence seems, of all others, the most benevolent, and all that we do understand is so wise and so good, and all we do or do not, so perfectly and overwhelmingly wonderful, that the most benevolent system is the most probable.[44]

JOHN LEYDEN (1775–1811)

Scottish Poet and Orientalist

[From an "Ode to Scottish Music":]

> Ah, sure, as Hindoo legends tell,
> When music's tones the bosom swell
> The scenes of former life return,
> Ere sunk beneath the morning star,
> We left our parent climes afar,
> Immured in mortal forms to mourn.

SIR HUMPHRY DAVY (1778–1829)

British Chemist and Physicist

[Sir Humphry Davy, the son of a wood-carver, combined the discipline of a great scientist with the ardor and imagination of a poet. Although renowned for his researches in electrochemistry and other scientific fields, all his life he privately wrote poetry. Coleridge would attend Davy's scientific lectures "to increase his stock of metaphors," and declared that if Davy "had not become the first chemist, he would have been the first poet of his age; he only wanted the art." From Davy's *Consolations in Travel,* Dialogue IV:]

We sometimes, in sleep, lose the beginning and end of a dream, and recollect the middle of it, and one dream has no [seeming] connection with another, and yet we are conscious of an infinite variety of dreams, and there is a strong analogy for believing in an infinity of past existences, which must have had connection. . . . With its present organization, the intellect of man is naturally limited and imperfect; but this depends upon its material machinery; and in a higher organized form, it may be imagined to possess infinitely higher powers. . . . It does not, however, appear improbable to me, that some of the more refined machinery of thought may adhere, even in another state, to the sentient principle; for though the organs of gross sensation, the nerves and brain, are destroyed by death, yet something of the more ethereal nature . . . may be less destructible. And I sometimes imagine, that many of those powers which have been called instinctive belong to the more refined clothing of the spirit; conscience, indeed, seems to have some undefined source, and may bear relations to a former state of being.

PIERRE JEAN DE BÉRANGER (1780–1857)

French Lyric Poet

[Pierre Jean de Béranger was one of France's very popular poets. His poems lent themselves to musical rendering and were sung all over the country.

Goethe and Heinrich Heine were some of the admirers of his work. This
poem is called "La Metempsycose":]

In Philosophic mood, last night, as idly I was lying,
That souls may transmigrate methought there could be no denying:
So, just to know to what I owe propensities so strong,
I drew my soul into a chat—our gossip lasted long.
"A votive offering," she observed, "well might I claim from thee;
For thou in being hadst remained a cipher but for me:
Yet not a virgin soul was I when first in thee enshrined."
Ah! I suspected, little soul, thus much that I should find![45]

ARTHUR SCHOPENHAUER (1788–1860)

German Philosopher

[Schopenhauer apparently was the first to collect and publish references to
reincarnation beliefs from ancient and contemporary times. This he did in
one chapter of his chief work, *The World as Will and Idea,* introducing the
compilation with the words: "We find the doctrine of metempsychosis
springing from the earliest and noblest ages of the human race, always
spread abroad on the earth as the belief of the great majority of mankind."[46]
His interest in the subject appears to date from a sojourn at Weimar in the
winter of 1813–1814, when Goethe's friend Friedrich Maier, an orientalist of
great attainments, introduced Schopenhauer to the literature of Buddhism,
for which he conceived a boundless admiration.

Albert Einstein writes that "Buddhism, as we have learnt from the wonderful writings of Schopenhauer," contains a strong element of "cosmic
religious feeling."

It is very difficult to explain this feeling to anyone who is entirely without it,
especially as there is no anthropomorphic conception of God corresponding to
it. The individual feels the nothingness of human desires and aims and the
sublimity and marvellous order which reveal themselves both in nature and in
the world of thought. He looks upon individual existence as a sort of prison and
wants to experience the universe as a single significant whole.[47]

As is well known, Schopenhauer's theorizing on occasion led him to deep
despair. This has been overemphasized by critics who have not studied his
entire philosophy, although it is true that like the Eastern philosophers he
regarded the external universe as an illusion and thus ceaselessly pain-
producing to those who accepted the dream for reality. One special cause for
his pessimistic outbursts seems to have been his belief that an impassable
gulf existed between the conscious personality and what he called the Will,

and von Hartmann later termed the Unconscious. As the personal consciousness was thought to dissolve completely at death without transferring its
memories or experiences to the Will or the Unconscious, its life was purely
illusory, meaningless to itself, and its struggles and sufferings were forever
unrewarded. Gustave Geley, a noted French medical doctor, makes an interesting analysis of what he calls the missing element in the philosophy of
Schopenhauer and von Hartmann, and asks:

> Why should consciousness be exclusively bound to the temporary
> semblances which make up the universe? Why should not all that falls within its
> domain be registered, assimilated, and preserved by the eternal essence of
> being? What! The divine principle, the will or the unconscious, is to be allowed
> all potentialities except one, and that the most important of all—the power to
> acquire and retain the knowledge of itself? How much more logical it is to
> presume that this real and eternal will which is objectified in transitory and
> fictitious personalities, will keep integrally the remembrances acquired during
> these objectifications.[48]

Of course, as everyone knows now, experiments in hypnotism demonstrate
that every thought and experience, even the most fleeting, is indelibly
preserved in the subconscious mind, technically called the unconscious when
speaking from the standpoint of waking consciousness, but which in reality is
obviously a deeper state of awareness.

From the extracts presented here from Schopenhauer's writings it appears
that he took a more fluidic position than the foregoing criticisms would
suggest. Also it is interesting that a note of optimism resounds through most
of the thoughts expressed. With his disciples this was not usually the case;
they tended to emphasize the harshness and cruel "injustices" of life. According to H. P. Blavatsky, "a firm grasp of the principles of Karmic Law
knocks away the whole basis of the imposing fabric reared by the disciples of
Schopenhauer and Von Hartmann. . . . Objectors to the doctrine of Karma
should recall the fact that it is absolutely *out of the question* to attempt a reply
to the Pessimists on other data."[49]

In the succession of births . . . the persons who now stand in close connection or contact with us will also be born along with us at the next birth,
and will have the same or analogous relations and sentiments towards us as
now, whether these are of a friendly or a hostile description. . . .

What sleep is for the individual, death is for the will. . . . It would not
endure to continue the same actions and sufferings throughout an eternity
without true gain, if memory and individuality remained to it. It flings them
off, and this is lethe; and through this sleep of death it reappears refreshed
and fitted out with another intellect, as a new being—"a new day tempts to
new shores." . . .

These constant new births, then, constitute the succession of the life-dreams of a will which in itself is indestructible. . . . Every new-born being indeed comes fresh and blithe into the new existence, and enjoys it as a free gift: but there is, and can be, nothing freely given. Its fresh existence is paid for by the old age and death of a worn-out existence which has perished, but which contained the indestructible seed out of which this new existence has arisen: they are one being. To show the bridge between the two would certainly be the solution of a great riddle.

The World as Will and Idea[50]

The moral meaning of metempsychosis in all Indian religions is not merely that in a subsequent rebirth we have to atone for every wrong we commit, but also that we must regard every wrong befalling us as thoroughly deserved through our misdeeds in a former existence. . . .

The individuality disappears at death, but we lose nothing thereby for it is only the manifestation of quite a different Being—a Being ignorant of time, and, consequently, knowing neither life nor death. . . . When we die, we throw off our individuality like a worn-out garment, and rejoice because we are about to receive a new and better one. . . .

Were an Asiatic to ask me for a definition of Europe, I should be forced to answer him: It is that part of the world which is haunted by the incredible delusion that man was created out of nothing, and that his present birth is his first entrance into life.

Parerga and Paralipomena[51]

JOHAN LUDVIG HEIBERG (1791–1860)

Danish Author

[From metaphysical considerations we turn to a deeply moving episode from Heiberg's "The Newly Married," a long poem concerning events that transpired during the author's honeymoon. The scene depicts a newlywed couple seeking shelter in the home of a poor widow and her adopted son Fredrik, who as an orphaned child found her in a strange way. The little fellow filled an empty place in her heart, her own son being dead. Fredrik, now grown, falls so passionately in love with the young bride that he secretly schemes to kill the husband on a hunting trip. The mother has a fearful premonition and speaks to Fredrik thus:]

"I have never told you, my son . . . maybe the heart gets rest, when I speak to you of my fate; maybe it becomes easier, when we are two to carry the secret tortures. That son, which was given me in my marriage, oh—you don't know how he died!—he was decapitated and his blood covered the scaffold. Rejected by a young and beautiful maiden, who was deaf and blind to his love, he killed a more lucky lover . . . while hunting."

"That morning, when he was to suffer his horrible doom . . . my son sank to my breast and exclaimed: 'Give me a word, a powerful word, which will comfort me on my last walk alive!' And I . . . . but Fredrik, you frighten me! . . . You stare at me as white as a corpse.''

"Oh mother! stop!—You said: 'When before your saviour you stand say: My God and my Brother! Forgive me for your martyr-wounds; for my anger and for my mother!' ''

"How do you know that?''

"It was I! I am your real son, and now he lives the life anew.''

"Fredrik, has insanity overtaken your mind?''

"No, mother, don't be afraid! But up to now, I walked as one blind, through all these long years. My consciousness awoke in this hour. Now I see my entire self, now I see the basis of my life and at the same time I hope and I tremble. Ah, I feel again my horrible fear, when my head I laid on the block. But still my thought held the comforting words you spoke.

"When the ax fell my consciousness left me. I woke up in strange places; and in my wanderings my eye rested on a man in white garments . . . Maybe he was my Saviour, but ah! I did not know him, so my prayer to him I did not say, though his eyes were so mild looking . . . his hair was shining light. He said: 'Turn around! Your place is not here. On earth you suffered death for your crime; here is no punishment, no penalty. So go back, down to earth to live over again your days.'

"Then I turned back on fearful foot; wandering ever so long. . . . I needed rest and slept a sleep so deep I knew nothing of what happened. But, when I woke up as a child I sensed I was another. Oh, mother, look at me; I need you to console me now. Not another time, that I can promise for certain, shall your son make sad your heart.—She does not answer! . . . What a deep sigh she draws—She is dead!''

PERCY BYSSHE SHELLEY (1792–1822)

British Poet

[In "Epipsychidion" Shelley wrote: "Narrow the heart that loves, the brain that contemplates, the life that wears, the spirit that creates, one object, and one form, and builds thereby a sepulchre for its eternity." Such lines as well as others we will quote did not spring from mere flights of poetic fancy, for Shelley was given to deep pondering on philosophical subjects. In his essay "On a Future State," he asked: "Have we existed before birth? It is difficult to conceive the possibility of this." Could there exist "a principle or substance which escapes the observation of the chemist and anatomist" and preexists our birth? The poet answers:]

It certainly *may* be; though it is sufficiently unphilosophical to allege the possibility of an opinion as a proof of its truth. Does it see, hear, feel, before its combination with those organs on which sensation depends? Does it reason, imagine, apprehend . . . ? If there are no reasons to suppose that we have existed before that period at which our existence apparently commences, then there are no grounds for [the] supposition that we shall continue to exist after our existence has apparently ceased. So far as thought and life is concerned, the same will take place with regard to us, individually considered, after death, as had [taken] place before our birth.[52]

[In Dowden's *Life of Shelley,* the following anecdote of the poet is reported as told by his friend Hogg:]

One morning we had been reading Plato together so diligently that the usual hour of exercise passed away unperceived. We sallied forth hastily to take the air for half an hour before dinner. In the middle of Magdalene Bridge we met a woman with a child in her arms. Shelley was more attentive at that instant to our conduct in a life that was past, or to come, than to a decorous regulation . . . of his behavior. . . . With abrupt dexterity he caught hold of the child. The mother . . . held it fast by its long train.

"Will your baby tell us anything about pre-existence, madam?" he asked in a piercing voice and with a wistful look. The mother made no answer, but perceiving that Shelley's object was not murderous, but altogether harmless, she . . . relaxed her hold. "Will your baby tell us anything about pre-existence, madam?" he repeated, with unabated earnestness. "He cannot speak, sir," said the mother seriously.

"Worse and worse," cried Shelley with an air of deep disappointment. . . . "But surely the babe can speak if he will. . . . He may fancy perhaps that he cannot, but it is only a silly whim. He cannot have forgotten entirely the use of speech in so short a time. The thing is absolutely impossible." . . .

Shelley sighed deeply as we walked on. "How provokingly close are those newborn babes! but it is not the less certain, notwithstanding the cunning attempts to conceal the truth, that all knowledge is reminiscence. The doctrine is far more ancient than the times of Plato, and as old as the venerable allegory that the Muses are the daughters of Memory; not one of the nine was ever said to be the child of Invention."[53]

[In the poem "With a Guitar, to Jane," Shelley casts Ariel from Shakespeare's *Tempest* in the role of a transcendent Self in man—a Self that is crucified when neglected. However, André Maurois, in his biography *Ariel, The Life of Shelley,* obviously identifies that character with Shelley himself. In chapter eighteen, "Second Incarnation of the Goddess," Maurois states, ''so now he contemplated in Jane's an image of the Antigone whom he had surely known and loved in a previous existence.''[54] In the poem, Ariel is offering the lovely Miranda the gift of a guitar:]

> . . . . Take
> This slave of music for the sake
> Of him, who is the slave of thee. . . .
> Poor Ariel sends this silent token
> Of more than ever can be spoken;
> Your guardian spirit, Ariel, who
> From life to life must still pursue
> Your happiness;—for thus alone
> Can Ariel ever find his own. . . .
> When you die, the silent moon,
> In her interlunar swoon,
> Is not sadder in her cell
> Than deserted Ariel;
> When you live again on earth,
> Like an unseen star of birth
> Ariel guides you o'er the sea
> Of life from your nativity. . . .
> This is all remembered not;
> And now, Alas! the poor sprite is
> Imprisoned, for some fault of his
> In a body like a grave.

[In ''Hellas'' (lines 196–210), Shelley expands his concept of reincarnation to embrace worlds and universes:]

> Worlds on worlds are rolling ever
> From creation to decay,
> Like the bubbles on a river,
> Sparkling, bursting, borne away.
> But they are still immortal
> Who, through birth's orient portal
> And death's dark chasm hurrying to and fro,
> Clothe their unceasing flight
> In the brief dust and light
> Gathered around their chariots as they go;
> New shapes they still may weave,
> New gods, new laws receive;
> Bright or dim are they as the robes they last
> On Death's bare ribs had cast.

THOMAS CARLYLE (1795–1881)

Scottish Essayist and Historian

[In our chapter on Myths and Symbols, we quoted from Thomas Carlyle's *Heroes and Hero-Worship* in which he spoke of the Twilight-of-the-Gods myth that depicted the death of the universe followed by its rebirth. He commented: "Curious; this law of mutation, which also is a law written in man's inmost thought, had been deciphered by these old earnest Thinkers in their rude style; and how, though all dies, and even gods die, yet all death is but a phoenix fire-death, and new-birth into the Greater and the Better! It is the fundamental Law of Being for a creature made of Time, living in this Place of Hope. All earnest men have seen into it; may still see into it." In *Sartor Resartus,* now to be quoted, Carlyle used different imagery for rebirth. This most influential of his works met with unqualified disapproval when serialized in *Frazer's Magazine* in 1833 and 1834 and had to await publication in book form in America. In fact it was the enthusiasm of Emerson and the other New England transcendentalists for Carlyle's writings, accompanied by an invitation to lecture in America, that awakened the British public to his value, and he became the most talked of writer of his time.]

Could anything be more miraculous than an actual authentic Ghost? The English Johnson longed, all his life, to see one . . . Foolish Doctor! Did he never, with the mind's eye as well as with the body's look round him into that full tide of human Life he so loved; did he never so much as look into Himself? . . . Are we not Spirits, that are shaped into a body, into an Appearance; and that fade away again into air and invisibility? . . . Nay, if you consider it, what is Man himself, and his whole terrestrial Life, but an Emblem; a Clothing or visible Garment for that divine life of his, cast hither, like a light-particle down from Heaven? . . .

Ghosts! There are nigh a thousand-million walking the Earth openly at noontide; some half-hundred have vanished from it, some half-hundred have arisen in it, ere thy watch ticks once. . . . Death and birth are the vesper and matin bells that summon mankind to sleep and to rise refreshed for new advancement. . . .

The curtains of Yesterday drop down, the curtains of Tomorrow roll up; but Yesterday and Tomorrow both *are.* Pierce through the Time-element, glance into the Eternal. . . . Is the white Tomb of our Loved One . . . but a pale spectral Illusion? Is the lost Friend still mysteriously Here? . . . Know of a truth that only the Time-shadows have perished, or are perishable; that the real Being of whatever was, and whatever is, and whatever will be, *is* even now and forever. This [idea] should it unhappily seem new, thou mayest ponder at thy leisure; for the next twenty years, or the next twenty centuries. . . .[55]

HEINRICH HEINE (1797–1856)

German Lyric Poet and Critic

[In Heinrich Heine's *Book of Ideas* he tells of a vision he had in Venice: "I could not eat, still less could I drink. Hot tears fell into my glass, and in that glass I saw my beloved home, the blue waters of the sacred Ganges; the Himalayas, with their eternal snows."[56] The first selection is from Heine's *Die Nordsee,* or *The North Sea:*]

I know that I am laying myself open to ridicule, but the truth must be told: I am tormented not a little by the disproportion between body and soul . . . and I often ponder on the doctrine of metempsychosis. Who can understand the divine irony which delights in accentuating the manifold contradictions between body and soul? Who can tell what tailor now inherits the soul of a Plato, what dominie is heir to Caesar's spirit? . . . Perchance the soul of Genghis Khan now animates a reviewer who, without knowing it, daily slashes the souls of his faithful Bashirs and Kalmucks in the pages of a critical journal. . . .

But who is able to look down on the ways of mortals from the heights of omniscience of the past? As I walk by night on the seashore, and listen to the song of the waves, all sorts of visions and memories flood my brain. I seem as though I had once looked down from above on the same shifting scene, and, dizzy with terror, had fallen to the earth. I seem as though, with telescopic eyes, I had seen the stars moving through the heavens large as life . . . then, as from millennial depths, there surge up . . . thoughts of primeval wisdom, but all so misty that I know not what they mean.[57]

[From Chapter 17 of Heine's *Die Bader von Lucca* comes this conversation between himself and a friend:]

H.: Regarding my actions in this world, I care little about the existence of heaven or hell; self-respect does not allow me to guide my acts with an eye to heavenly reward or fear of hellish punishment. I pursue the good because it is beautiful and attracts me, and shun the bad because it is ugly and repulsive. All our actions should originate from the spring of unselfish love, whether there be continuation after death or not.

M.: Then, you do not believe in immortality?

H.: I, doubt it? I, whose heart is rooted in the most distant millenniums of the past . . . I, should not believe in immortality?

PIERRE LEROUX (1797–1871)

French Philosopher, Journalist, and Statesman

[Pierre Leroux was co-founder with George Sand of *Revue Independante*. A number of French writers of this period viewed with sympathy the doctrine of many lives. Among those to be quoted shortly are Balzac, George Sand, Victor Hugo, and Flaubert. A writer in the London *Fortnightly Review* discusses Leroux's conception of rebirth as found in his best known work *De l'Humanité:*]

Pierre Leroux shows that, according to Plato and Descartes, the being who lives before you, and that you imagine to have been born yesterday only to die tomorrow, is an eternal being who has already lived . . . It is the principle of Reminiscence of Plato and of innate ideas of Descartes. What then matters it that the various beings coming again into life should have no *formal* recollection of their previous existence? Each of their existences is a link in the chain; but they do not repeat one another, they are not the useless reproduction of a single manifestation. . . . In sleep our ideas, our sensations, our sentiments of the evening before, seem to become incarnate in us, become ourselves by a phenomenon analogous to that of the digestion and assimilation of our bodily food. It is thus that sleep regenerates us, and that we emerge from it the stronger, with a certain oblivion. In death, which is a mightier oblivion, it seems that our life becomes digested and elaborated. Then comes the awakening, or new birth. . . . We are in our potentiality the exact sequel of what we were, still the same being but grown larger.[58]

A. BRONSON ALCOTT (1799–1888)

American Educator and Transcendentalist

[Bronson Alcott, the father of Louisa May Alcott, was among the leading lights of the American transcendental movement that centered first around Concord and Boston, and then spread far and wide, affecting appreciably the American way of life. That Louisa May shared her father's views on reincarnation will become evident when we discuss her separately. Our opening selections are from *The Record of a School* by Elizabeth P. Peabody, a book that contains her eyewitness reports of classes conducted by Alcott while she was his assistant at the famous, but short-lived, Temple School in Boston. In the preface to the third edition (1874), Miss Peabody wrote:

The great interest inspired by Louisa May Alcott's *Little Men* has led to the inquiry if ever there was or could be a school like Plumfield; and she has proposed the re-publication of the *Record of a School,* which was published thirty-eight years ago, and which suggested some of the scenes described in *Little Men.* . . . What I witnessed in his schoolroom threw for me a new light into the profoundest mysteries that have been consecrated by the Christian symbols; and the study of childhood made there I would not exchange for anything else I have experienced in life.

That her feeling was shared by the children at their own level is abundantly evident throughout these remarkable journals. One day, for example, Alcott asked the children whether a conversation on ideas, such as they had just finished, was more interesting than one on steam engines. Many said it was. A little boy exclaimed, "I never knew I had a mind till I came to this school"; and a great many more burst out with the same idea. To quote now from the journals, to be followed by direct quotations from Alcott's own writings:]

January 15 [1835] . . . What is the meaning of the word *recollect?* . . . Are you now collecting or re-collecting the impressions of childhood? Some thought they had begun to re-collect, as well as to collect. Shall I tell you an idea some people have of recollecting, reminiscence, remembrance? Yes, said several of them. Mr. Alcott continued (pointing to the bust of Plato), That man believed that all our feelings and thoughts were the remembrances of another state of existence, before we came into the world in our present bodies. And he (pointing to the cast of Jesus Christ) used to say of himself that he came forth from God; that he had lived before. In the Gospel of St. John there are many passages in which he refers to his pre-existent state. . . .

January 30 . . . What do you mean by *birthday?* . . . Birthday is the day on which the spirit is put into the body, said [one] boy. Did you get that idea in this school? said Mr. Alcott. I never thought of such subjects before I came to this school, said he. . . . One of the boys added, that he had always had an indistinct idea that the soul lived before the body, that there was a transmigration of souls. . . .

February 4 . . . Some expressed the idea that the soul shaped and made the body; others that the body was made, and the soul put into it. Which is right? said one boy. That is more than I can tell, but I incline to the first opinion. You are all nearly right, however; you have the important ideas; birth is not the beginning of the spirit; life is the remembrance or a waking up of spirit. All the life of knowledge is the waking up of what is already within. [The class had been discussing Wordsworth's "Ode to Immortality."]

Record of Mr. Alcott's School[59]

To conceive a child's acquirements as originating in nature, dating from his birth into his body, seems an atheism that only a shallow metaphysical theology could entertain in a time of such marvelous natural knowledge as ours. "I shall never persuade myself," said Synesius, "to believe my soul to be of like age with my body." And yet we are wont to date our birth, as that of the babes we christen, from the body's advent . . . as if time and space could chronicle the periods of the immortal mind.

Concord Days[60]

[In April 1876 Alcott wrote to Walt Whitman and made this brief allusion to the passing of Thoreau who died twelve years earlier:]

My visit to you with Thoreau remains a pleasant memory to me. He has withdrawn for a little while; but I shall cherish the hope of interchanging words with you before we leave the scene of "things."

Letters of A. Bronson Alcott[61]

Life is a current of spiritual forces. In perpetual tides, the stream traverses its vessels to vary its pulsations and perspective of things. . . . Vast systems of sympathies, antedating and extending beyond our mundane experiences, absorb us within their sphere, relating us to other worlds of life and light. . . . Memory sometimes dispels the oblivious slumber, and recovers for the mind recollections of its descent and destiny. Some relics of the ancient consciousness survive, recalling our previous history and experiences.

Tablets[62]

HONORÉ DE BALZAC (1799–1850)

French Novelist

[The selections are from chapter 6 of Balzac's *Seraphita*. In introducing the translation by Katharine Wormeley in the American edition of Balzac's works, George Frederic Parsons writes that the novel had been penned when Balzac was "fresh from mystical and occult studies which had filled his mind to saturation. . . . To Balzac himself, whose versatility and sympathetic range were almost as broad and deep as those of Nature, this final flight of his philosophical and theosophical exposition was painful and laborious." "The toil upon this work," wrote Balzac in 1835, "has been crushing and terrible," yet some critics believed that in beauty and power it surpassed his previous creations.

Parsons relates that in the heroine Seraphita, "we contemplate . . . the culminating product of a long chain of incarnations during which the dominant impulse has been uniformly spiritual. . . . The sixth chapter . . . is chiefly occupied with the beautiful and noble discourse in which the dying mystic unfolds to her companions the secret of 'the Path.' . . . Once more, and now with large insistence, the doctrine of reincarnation is dwelt upon, and referred to as the necessary and sole explanation of human evolution."[63]]

All human beings go through a previous life in the sphere of Instinct, where they are brought to see the worthlessness of earthly treasures, to amass which they gave themselves such untold pains! Who can tell how many times the human being lives in the sphere of Instinct before he is prepared to enter the sphere of Abstractions, where thought expends itself on erring science, where mind wearies at last of human language? For, when Matter is exhausted, Spirit enters. Who knows how many fleshly forms the heir of heaven occupies before he can be brought to understand the value of that silence and solitude whose starry plains are but the vestibule of Spiritual Worlds? He feels his way amid the void, makes trial of nothingness, and then at last his eyes revert upon the Path. Then follow other existences—all to be lived to reach the place where Light effulgent shines. Death is the post-house of the journey.

A lifetime may be needed merely to gain the virtues which annul the errors of man's preceding life. . . . The virtues we acquire, which develop slowly within us, are the invisible links that bind each one of our existences to the others—existences which the spirit alone remembers, for Matter has no memory for spiritual things. Thought alone holds the tradition of the bygone life. The endless legacy of the past to the present is the secret source of human genius. . . .

The final life, the fruition of all other lives, to which the powers of the soul have tended, and whose merits open the Sacred Portals to perfected man, is the life of Prayer. . . . Silence and meditation are the means of following [that] Way. . . . It is thus that the separation takes place between Matter, which so long has wrapped its darkness round you; and Spirit, which was in you from the beginning . . . now brings noon-day to your soul.[64]

VICTOR HUGO (1802–1885)

French Author

[In the research annals of reincarnation literature there are a number of reports of children dying at an early age supposedly being reborn within a few years to the same parents.[65] Victor Hugo's poem, ''The Return,'' from his volume *Contemplations,* is on this theme. Reincarnationists hold that such a rapid return is natural because the quickly departing soul had no time to garner experience requiring a long heavenly state of assimilation. In the poem Hugo affirms that ''mothers who mourn, your cries are not unheard. Divine love notes the fall of even one small bird, and oft returns the fledgling to its mother's nest. The link between cradle and grave is thus expressed.'' In illustration, Hugo relates that a woman had a beloved son, who succumbed to a fatal illness at the age of three. The mother was inconsolable.]

And still her grief would not abate.
At last she bore another child, and great
Was the father's joy; and loud his cry: ''A Son!''
That day, to thus rejoice—he was the only one.
Dejected and wan the mother lay; her soul was numb . . .

Then suddenly she cried with anguish wild,
Her thoughts less on the new than on the absent child. . . .
"My angel in his grave, and I not at his side!"
Speaking through the babe now held in her embrace
She hears again the well-known voice adored:
" 'Tis I,—but do not tell!" He gazes at her face.

GEORGE SAND (1803–1876)

French Author

[George Sand's novel *Consuelo*, from which we quote, was begun in 1842, not long after Chopin's several years' residence with her. The *Britannica* describes the work as "*fantaisies à la Chopin.*"[66]]

"Consuelo," he said to her . . . " I am going to leave you for a time, and then I shall return to earth by means of a new birth. I shall return accursed and despairing if you abandon me now, in my last hour. . . . We are brethren; ere we become lovers, death must once more separate us. But we must be united by the marriage-vow, that I may be reborn calm and strong, and free, like other men, from the memory of past lives which has been my torment and my punishment for so many centuries. Consent to this vow. It will not bind you to me in this life, which I am about to leave, but it will reunite us in eternity. It will be as a seal to help us to recognise one another when the shades of death have effaced the clearness of our memories."[67]

[In a more philosophical vein George Sand once penned these words:]

Cast into this life, as it were, into an alembic, where, after a previous existence which we have forgotten, we are condemned to be remade, renewed, tempered by suffering, by strife, by passion, by doubt, by disease, by death. All these evils we endure for our good, for our purification, and, so to speak, to make us perfect. From age to age, from race to race, we accomplish a tardy progress, tardy but certain, an advance of which, in spite of all the skeptics say, the proofs are manifest. If all the imperfections of our being and all the woes of our estate drive at discouraging and terrifying us, on the other hand, all the more noble faculties, which have been bestowed on us that we might seek after perfection, do make for our salvation and deliver us from fear, misery and even death. Yes, a divine instinct that always grows in light and strength helps us to comprehend that nothing in the whole world wholly dies and that we only vanish from the things that lie about us in our earthly life, to reappear among conditions more favorable to our eternal growth in good.[68]

SIR EDWARD BULWER-LYTTON (1803–1873)
British Novelist

[The works of Sir Edward Bulwer-Lytton contributed to the wave of interest in mystical and occult literature that swept over the West in the latter half of the nineteenth century. Occasional references to reincarnation are found therein. In Godolphin he wrote: "Why cheat ourselves with words so vague as life and death! What is the difference? At most, the entrance in and the departure from one scene in our wide career. How many scenes are left to us! We do but hasten our journey, not close it."[69] In Zanoni, his chief mystical work, he remarked: "A short time, like a day in thy incalculable life, and the form thou dotest on is dust! Others . . . go hand in hand, each with each, unto the tomb; hand in hand they ascend from the worm to new cycles of existence."[70]

The selections that follow are from A Strange Story, which revolves around the possibility of a man losing his soul. The reincarnationist who believes in the awful possibility of such a wasted incarnation is likely to be unimpressed by the oft-repeated argument that the prospect of many lives will encourage procrastination. He also sees in Lytton's novel a solution to the puzzle of how human beings can become monstrous fiends. The teller of the Strange Story is a Dr. Fenwick who has been deeply disturbed by the behavior of an evil acquaintance named Margrave. The doctor had been inclined to doubt the existence of soul, having come under the influence of the then growing school of materialism. Through the agency of a magical potion, he "enters" the brain and inner consciousness of Margrave as it existed during a serious moral crisis three years previously.]

The brain now opened on my sight, with all its labyrinth of cells. I seemed to have the clue to every winding in the maze. I saw therein a moral world, charred and ruined, as, in some fable I have read, the world of the moon is described to be; yet withal it was a brain of magnificent formation. . . . I observed three separate emanations of light; the one a pale red hue, the second a pale azure, the third a silvery spark. The red light . . . undulated from the brain along the arteries, the veins, the nerves. And I murmured to myself, "Is this the principle of animal life?" The azure light equally permeated the frame, crossing and uniting with the red, but in a separate and distinct ray . . . And again I murmured to myself, "Is this the principle of intellectual being, directing or influencing that of animal life; with it, yet not of it?"

But the silvery spark! What was that? Its centre seemed the brain. But I could fix it to no single organ. Nay, wherever I looked through the system, it reflected itself as a star reflects itself upon water . . . so independent of all which agitated and vexed the frame, that I became strangely aware that if the heart stopped in its action, and the red light died out, if the brain were paralyzed, that energetic mind smitten into idiocy . . . still that silver spark would shine the same, indestructible by aught that shattered its tabernacle. . . . "Can that starry spark speak the presence of the soul?" . . . And gazing yet more intently on the spark, I became vaguely aware that it was not the soul, but the halo around the soul, as the star we see in heaven is not the star itself, but its circle of rays. . . .

In the heart of the light, [the soul] reflected back on my own soul its ineffable trouble, humiliation, and sorrow; for those ghastly wrecks of power placed at its sovereign command it was responsible: and, appalled by its own sublime fate of duration, was about to carry into eternity the account of its mission in time. . . . I saw that the mind was storming the soul, in some terrible rebellious war—all of thought, of passion, of desire. . . . I could not comprehend the war, nor guess what it was that the mind demanded the soul to yield. Only the distinction between the two was made intelligible by their antagonism. And I saw that the soul, sorely tempted, looked afar for escape from the subjects it had ever so ill-controlled, and who sought to reduce to their vassal the power which had lost authority as their king. . . . And suddenly the starry spark rose from the ruins and the tumult around it—rose into space and vanished. And where my soul had recognized the presence of soul, there was a void. . . .

As my eyes, in the Vision, followed the azure light, undulating as before . . . I perceived that [its] essence . . . had undergone a change: it had lost that faculty of continuous and concentrated power by which man improves on the works of the past, and weaves schemes to be developed in the future of remote generations; it had lost all sympathy in the past, because it had lost all conception of a future beyond the grave; it had lost conscience, it had lost remorse. . . . If Sir Philip Derval could be believed, Margrave was possessed of powers, derived from fragmentary recollections of a knowledge acquired in a former state of being, which would render his remorseless intelligence infinitely dire. . . . The azure light was even more vivid in certain organs useful to the conservation of existence . . . secretiveness, destructiveness, and the ready perception of things immediate to the wants of the day [but] the mind wanted the *something*, without which men could never found cities, frame laws, bind together, beautify, exalt the elements of this world. . . . The ant, and the bee, and the beaver congregate and construct; but they do not improve. Man improves because the future impels onward that which is not found in the ant, the bee, and the beaver—that which was gone from the being before me. I shrank appalled into myself. . . . "Have I ever then doubted that soul is distinct from mind?"[71]

✳ ✳ ✳
The American Transcendentalists[72]

[In an article, "The Transcendentalists on Reincarnation," printed in *Sunrise* (August 1959), these introductory remarks appeared:

> In 1836 a group of younger Unitarians who dared to believe in the inherent worth of man, the divinity of all Nature and the continuity of the soul's life after death, openly revolted against the "corpse-cold Unitarianism" of their Harvard associates and, spearheaded by Emerson, Hedge and Ripley, formed the Transcendental Club of America. Whereas these ideas so long ago taught in India, Persia and Greece and more currently by Kant and Goethe, Wordsworth, Coleridge and Carlyle, were not at all new, they had for centuries in Europe remained the property of the intellectual elite. Now, germinating in the soil of the New World, they blossomed with extraordinary vigor, taking the form of a practical crusade against every form of tyranny—of soul as well as of body.

In a letter (October 1, 1840), George Ripley—who was to become the founder of Brook Farm—wrote to Unitarian friends:

> There is a class of persons who desire a reform in the prevailing philosophy of the day. These are called Transcendentalists, because they believe in an order of truths which transcends the sphere of the external senses. Their leading idea is the supremacy of mind over matter. Hence they maintain that the truth of religion does not depend on tradition, nor historical facts, but has an unerring witness in the soul. There is a light, they believe, which enlighteneth every man that cometh into the world; there is a faculty in all—the most degraded, the most ignorant, the most obscure—to perceive spiritual truth when distinctly presented; and the ultimate appeal on all moral questions is not to a jury of scholars, a hierarchy of divines, or the prescriptions of a creed, but to the common sense of the human race.[73]

The marked influence of the German transcendentalists on the American movement has been noted. The contribution of ancient Greece is abundantly manifest. The Platonic philosophers, incidentally, were not studied by the transcendentalists in translations but in the original Greek. The English transcendentalists also played a prominent part. Carlyle, Coleridge, and Wordsworth were everywhere read and talked about.

A decisive and far-reaching contribution came from the Orient. Scarce copies of the first English translations of the *Bhagavad-Gita, Upanishads, Vedas,* and *Puranas* found their way into the hands of Emerson, Thoreau, and the others.[74] Thoreau translated from the French a Sanskrit story *The Transmigration of the Seven Brahmins,* and his glowing tribute to the *Gita,* also

Emerson's, may be found under "Hinduism." In the introduction of *The Transmigration of the Seven Brahmins,* Arthur Christy of Columbia University provides details of Thoreau's interest in the East, saying that "the fascination which the Orientals possessed for Thoreau is perfectly evident to the reader who skipped no pages in *Walden* and the *Week.* The sacred scriptures of the East held his attention through all his creative years. . . ."[75] Upon reading the *Gita,* Charles Malloy, a friend of Emerson, said that he found in it "the whole of Emerson's philosophy."[76]

In 1824 the Unitarians in America took a lively interest in the celebrated Hindu leader Ram Mohun Roy, who had "adopted Unitarianism" while retaining his own religion and Buddhism as well. A British-Indian Unitarian Association was formed, and the Reverend Charles H. A. Dall was sent to Calcutta, where he effected an alliance with Roy's Brahmo-Samaj. In *Unitarianism in America,* George Willis Cooke states that "the two potent influences shaping the ancient Puritanism of Salem into Unitarianism were foreign commerce and contact with the Oriental religions."[77]

Arthur Christy's *The Orient in American Transcendentalism* explores this merging of Eastern and Western cultures, and concentrates particularly on the part played by Emerson, Thoreau, and Bronson Alcott.[78] In prefacing the book, Christy quotes Romain Rolland's *Prophets of the New India:* "It would be a matter of deep interest to know exactly how far the American spirit had been impregnated, directly or indirectly, by the infiltration of Hindu thought during the nineteenth century; for there can be no doubt that it has contributed to the strange moral and religious mentality of the modern United States. . . . I do not know whether any historian will be found to occupy himself seriously with the question. It is nevertheless a psychological problem of the first order, intimately connected with the history of our civilization." Christy envisioned his own book "as an attempt to write the first chapter of the general study Romain Rolland suggests."

With the blending in America of four streams of transcendental philosophy—the Greek, German, English, and Oriental—each carrying the theme of reincarnation, it is but natural to find fairly frequent references to rebirth in the writings of the New England group. From the quotations that appear in this section it will be observed how refreshingly original was the viewpoint of these men.]

RALPH WALDO EMERSON (1803–1882)

American Philosopher and Essayist

[The first intimation of Ralph Waldo Emerson's sympathy for the idea of many lives is found in his *Journals* for 1830: "The soul is an emanation of the Divinity, a part of the soul of the world, a ray from the source of light. It comes from without into the human body, as into a temporary abode, it goes out of it anew; it wanders in ethereal regions, it returns to visit . . . it passes into other habitations, for the soul is immortal.''[79] An 1843 journal entry reads: "Life itself is an interim and a transition; this, O Indur, is my one and twenty thousandth form, and already I feel old Life sprouting underneath in the twenty thousand and first, and I know well that he builds no new world but by tearing down the old for materials.''[80]

An earlier entry reveals that a clear distinction existed in Emerson's mind between the supposed rebirth of the external personality and the return of the eternal Self or Soul: "People are uneasy because the philosopher seems to compromise their personal immortality. Mr. Quin thinks that to affirm the eternity of God and not to affirm the reappearance of Mr. Quin, bodily and mentally with all the appearances and recollections of Mr. Quin . . . is to give up the whole ship. But Mr. Quin is a sick God.''[81]

Space cannot be spared to quote from Emerson's letters, but two sentences from one of them are difficult to omit. Writing to Margaret Fuller after a visit to New York, the sage of Concord exclaimed: "What a Bay! what a River! what climate! what men! . . . Me my cabin fits better, yet very likely from a certain poorness of spirit; but in my next transmigration, I think I should choose New York.''[82] We turn now to his essays, concluding with extracts from "Immortality," Emerson's last published essay, and end, as he did, with the quotation from the *Upanishads*.]

It is the secret of the world that all things subsist and do not die, but only retire a little from sight and afterwards return again. . . . Nothing is dead; men feign themselves dead, and endure mock funerals and mournful obituaries, and there they stand looking out of the window, sound and well, in some new strange disguise. Jesus is not dead; he is very well alive; nor John, nor Paul, nor Mahomet, nor Aristotle; at times we believe we have seen them all, and could easily tell the names under which they go.

"Nominalist and Realist"[83]

Where do we find ourselves? In a series of which we do not know the extremes, and believe that it has none. We wake and find ourselves on a stair; there are other stairs below us which we seem to have ascended; there are stairs above us, many a one, which go upward and out of sight. But the Genius which according to the old belief stands at the door by which we enter, and gives us the lethe to drink, that we may tell no tales, mixed the cup too strongly, and we cannot shake off the lethargy now at noonday. Sleep lingers all our lifetime about our eyes.

"Experience"[84]

Every soul is by . . . intrinsic necessity quitting its whole system of things, its friends and home and laws and faith, as the shell-fish crawls out of

its beautiful and stony case, because it no longer admits of its growth, and
slowly forms a new house. . . . We cannot part with our friends. We cannot
let our angels go. We do not see that they only go out that archangels may
come in. We are idolaters of the old. We do not believe in the riches of the
soul, in its proper eternity and omnipresence. . . . We linger in the ruins of
the old tent where once we had bread and shelter and organs, nor believe that
the spirit can feed, cover, and nerve us again. . . . But we sit and weep in
vain. The voice of the Almighty saith, "Up and onward for evermore!"

"Compensation"[85]

[Emerson originated the expression "do your thing." These excerpts appear
to be on that theme:]

Man is that noble endogenous plant which grows, like the palm, from
within outward. . . . The best discovery the discoverer makes for himself. It
has something unreal for his companion until he too has substantiated it. It
seems as if the Deity dressed each soul which he sends into nature in certain
virtues and powers not communicable to other men, and sending it to perform one more turn through the circle of beings, wrote *"Not transferable,"*
and *"Good for this trip only,"* on these garments of the soul. . . . Each is
uneasy until he has produced his private ray into the concave sphere and
beheld his talent also in its last nobility and exaltation.

"Uses of Great Men"[86]

The Arabians say, that Abul Khain, the mystic, and Abu Ali Seena, the
philosopher, conferred together; and, on parting, the philosopher said, "All
that he sees, I know;" and the mystic said, "All that he knows, I see." If one
should ask the reason of this intuition, the solution would lead us into that
property which Plato denoted as Reminiscence, and which is implied by the
Brahmins in the tenet of Transmigration. The soul having been often born,
or, as the Hindoos say, "travelling the path of existence through thousands
of births," having beheld the things which are here, those which are in
heaven and those which are beneath, there is nothing of which she has not
gained the knowledge: no wonder that she is able to recollect, in regard to
any one thing, what formerly she knew.

"Swedenborg; or, the Mystic"[87]

We must infer our destiny from the preparation. We are driven by instinct
to [store] innumerable experiences which are of no visible value, and we may
revolve through many lives before we shall assimilate or exhaust them. Now
there is nothing in nature capricious, or whimsical, or accidental, or unsupported. Nature never moves by jumps, but always in steady and supported
advances. . . . If there is the desire to live, and in larger sphere, with more

knowledge and power, it is because life and knowledge and power are good for us, and we are the natural depositaries of these gifts. The love of life is out of all proportion to the value set on a single day, and seems to indicate . . . a conviction of immense resources and possibilities proper to us, on which we have never drawn. . . .

[Emerson quotes from the *Katha Upanishad:*] "The soul is not born; it does not die; it was not produced from any one. Nor was any produced from it. Unborn, eternal, it is not slain, though the body is slain; subtler than what is subtle, greater than what is great. . . . Thinking the soul is unbodily among bodies, firm among fleeting things, the wise man casts off all grief. The soul cannot be gained by knowledge, not by understanding, not by manifold science. It can be obtained by the soul by which it is desired. It reveals its own truths."

"Immortality"[88]

FREDERIC H. HEDGE (1805–1890)
American Transcendentalist and Unitarian Minister

[The Transcendental Club of America was first known as Hedge's Club or, more formally, The Symposium, in honor of Plato. The public dubbed it the Transcendental Club and the name stuck. Hedge, it will be recalled, was the translator of Herder's "Dialogues on Metempsychosis." We quote from his own work, *Ways of the Spirit, and Other Essays:*]

We reach back with our recollection and find no beginning of existence. Who of us knows anything except by report of the first two years of earthly life? . . . We began to exist for others before we began to exist for ourselves. Our experience is not co-extensive with our being, our memory does not comprehend it. We bear not the root, but the root us.

What is that root? We call it soul. Our soul, we call it; properly speaking, it is not ours, but we are its. It is not a part of us, but we are a part of it. It is not one article in an inventory of articles which together make up our individuality, but the root of that individuality. It is larger than we are, and older than we are,—that is, than our conscious self. The conscious self . . . is not aboriginal, but a product,—as it were, the blossoming of an individuality. . . . And the soul which does so blossom exists before that blossom unfolds. . . . The supposition of pre-existence . . . seems best to match the supposed continued existence of the soul hereafter. . . . The eternal destination which faith ascribes to the soul presupposes an eternal origin. . . . This was the theory of the most learned and acute of the Christian Fathers, (Origen) . . .

A new body and organism I hold to be an essential part of the soul's destination.[89]

HENRY WADSWORTH LONGFELLOW (1807–1882)

American Poet

[Listed in Christy's *The Orient in American Transcendentalism* are fifty-seven books constituting "The Oriental Library of Henry Wadsworth Longfellow." Among them are the 1785 and 1867 editions of Wilkins's translation of the *Bhagavad-Gita.* We quote from the poet's "Rain in Summer":]

> Thus the seer,
> With vision clear,
> Sees forms appear and disappear,
> In the perpetual round of strange,
> Mysterious change
> From birth to death, from death to birth;
> From earth to heaven, from heaven to earth;
> Till glimpses more sublime,
> Of things, unseen before,
> Unto his wondering eyes reveal
> The Universe, as an immeasurable wheel
> Turning forevermore
> In the rapid and rushing river of Time.

JOHN GREENLEAF WHITTIER (1807–1892)

American Poet

[Whittier's interest in Oriental religion and philosophy is reviewed in two articles by Arthur Christy.[90] The stanza that follows from Whittier's poem "The Preacher" is a paraphrase of several verses from chapter 2 of the *Bhagavad-Gita,* the chapter that deals preeminently with the periodic return of the soul.]

> In the Indian fable Arjoon hears
> The scorn of a god rebuke his fears:
> "Spare thy pity!" Krishna saith;
> "Not in thy sword is the power of death!
> All is illusion,—loss but seems;
> Pleasure and pain are only dreams;
> Who deems he slayeth doth not kill;
> Who counts as slain is living still.
>   *"The Preacher"*

The river hemmed with leaving trees
Wound through its meadows green,
A low blue line of mountains showed
The open pines between. . . .

No clue of memory led me on,
But well the ways I knew;
A feeling of familiar things
With every footstep grew. . . .

A presence, strange at once and known,
Walked with me as my guide;
The skirts of some forgotten life
Trailed noiseless at my side.

Was it a dim-remembered dream?
Or glimpse through aeons old?
The secret which the mountains kept
The river never told.

"A Mystery"

CHARLES C. EMERSON (1808–1836)

American Transcendentalist

[The extract that follows appeared in "Notes from the Journal of a Scholar," in *The Dial*.[91] Frothingham identifies the author as Charles Emerson, the brother of Ralph Waldo.[92]]

The reason why Homer is to me like a dewy morning is because I too lived while Troy was, and sailed in the hollow ships of the Grecians to sack the devoted town. The rosy-fingered dawn as it crimsoned the tops of Ida, the broad seashore dotted with tents, the Trojan hosts in their painted armor, and the rushing chariots of Diomede and Idomeneus,—all these I too saw: my ghost animated the frame of some nameless Argive. . . . We forget that we have been drugged with the sleepy bowl of the Present. But when a lively chord in the soul is struck, when the windows for a moment are unbarred, the long and varied past is recovered. We recognize it all. We are no more brief, ignoble creatures, we seize our immortality, and bind together the related parts of our secular being.

JAMES FREEMAN CLARKE (1810–1888)
American Transcendentalist and Unitarian Minister

[James Freeman Clarke was one of the founding members of the Transcendental Club. Toward the close of his career he wrote the two-volume work *Ten Great Religions,* which was widely read and from which our selections come. It was something of an innovation for its time not only because of its contents but because of its name. The majority of religionists still conceived of religion in the singular; one true faith existed, all other beliefs were pagan superstition. One of the chapters is entitled "The Soul and Its Transmigration in All Religions."]

That man has come up to his present state of development by passing through lower forms is the popular doctrine of science today. What is called evolution teaches that we have reached our present state by a very long and gradual ascent from the lowest animal organizations. It is true that the Darwinian theory takes no notice of the evolution of the soul, but only of the body. But it appears to me that a combination of the two views would remove many difficulties which still attach to the theory of natural selection and the survival of the fittest. . . . The modern doctrine of evolution of bodily organisms is not complete, unless we unite with it the idea of a corresponding evolution of the spiritual monad, from which every organic form derives its unity. Evolution has a satisfactory meaning only when we admit that the soul is developed and educated by passing through many bodies. . . . If we are to believe in evolution, let us have the assistance of the soul itself in this development of new species.[93]

[As evident from one of his letters, Charles Darwin, himself, did take note of the possibility of immortality and by inference some form of reincarnation. Many people comfort themselves with the idea that although they themselves will die, their life and good works will live on in others, thereby acquiring a kind of eternality. From the long-range evolutionary viewpoint, Darwin saw the chimerical nature of such hopes, once the continuity of soul-life is proved impossible. In the letter mentioned he speaks of the inevitable destruction of our solar system when "the sun with all the planets will grow too cold for life." "Believing as I do that man in the distant future will be a far more perfect creature than he now is, it is an intolerable thought that he and all other sentient beings are doomed to complete annihilation after such long-continued progress." (It would be as if nothing had really happened here at all!) "To those who fully admit the immortality of the human soul," he adds, "the destruction of our world will not appear so dreadful."[94]]

HENRY DAVID THOREAU (1817–1862)
American Transcendentalist and Author

[Under "The Bhagavad-Gita" in the section on Hinduism, we quoted from Thoreau's *Walden,* in which he reveals that in the morning at Walden Pond he bathes his "intellect in the stupendous and cosmogonal philosophy of the *Bhagavad-Gita* . . . in comparison with which our modern world and its literature seem puny and trivial." In chapter 5 he wrote: "I am conscious of the presence and criticism of a part of me, which, as it were, is not a part of me, but spectator, sharing no experience, but taking note of it and that is no more I than it is you. When the play, it may be the tragedy, of life is over, the spectator goes his way. It was a kind of fiction, a work of the imagination only, so far as he was concerned."

We offer first some excerpts from Thoreau's letters.[95]]

July 8, 1843, to Emerson: And Hawthorne, too, I remember as one with whom I sauntered in old heroic times along the banks of the Scamander amid the ruins of chariots and heroes.

April 3, 1850, to Harrison Blake: I lived in Judea eighteen hundred years ago, but I never knew that there was such a one as Christ among my contemporaries.

February 27, 1853, to Harrison Blake: As the stars looked to me when I was a shepherd in Assyria, they look to me now a New Englander.

[From Thoreau's journals[96]:]

November 12, 1841: Methinks the hawk that soars so loftily and circles so steadily and apparently without effort, has earned this power by faithfully creeping on the ground as a reptile in a former state of existence.

1845–1847: Why should we be startled by death? Life is a constant putting off of the mortal coil—coat, cuticle, flesh and bones, all old clothes.

May 6, 1851: [Quoting from *The Harivansa,* which forms part of the great Hindu epic *The Mahabharata:*] "A being returns to life in consequence of the affection which he has borne for terrestrial things: he finds himself emancipated when he has felt only indifference for them."

June 26, 1851: Visited a menagerie this afternoon. . . . What constitutes the difference between a wild beast and a tame one? How much more human the one than the other! Growling, scratching, roaring, with whatever beauty and gracefulness, still untamable, this royal Bengal tiger or this leopard.

They have the character and the importance of another order of men. The majestic lions, the king of beasts,—he must retain his title. . . . It is unavoidable, the idea of transmigration; not merely a fancy of the poets, but an instinct of the race.

July 16, 1851: As far back as I can remember I have unconsciously referred to the experiences of a previous state of existence.

WALT WHITMAN (1819–1892)

American Poet

[In the leading article in the *Saturday Review* for October 31, 1959, entitled "Walt Whitman's Buried Masterpiece," Malcolm Cowley wrote:

> Whitman believed . . . that there is a distinction between one's mere personality and the deeper Self [and that] by means of metempsychosis and karma we are all involved in a process of spiritual evolution that might be compared to natural evolution. Even the latter process, however, was not regarded by Whitman as strictly natural or material. He believed that animals have a rudimentary sort of soul ("They bring me tokens of myself"), and he hinted or surmised, without directly saying, that rocks, trees, and planets possess an identity, or "eidolon," that persists as they rise to higher states of being. The double process of evolution, natural and spiritual, can be traced for ages into the past, and he believed that it will continue for ages beyond ages. . . . All men are divine and will eventually be gods. . . . The universe was an eternal becoming for Whitman, a process not a structure, and it had to be judged from the standpoint of eternity.

Whitman's "Song of Myself," from which the first selections are taken, constitutes the bulk of the original edition of *Leaves of Grass* (1855), and has been included in all subsequent editions. Emerson wrote Whitman concerning the work: "I find it the most extraordinary piece of wit and wisdom that America has yet contributed. . . . I greet you at the beginning of a great career, which yet must have had a long foreground somewhere, for such a start. I rubbed my eyes a little to see if this sunbeam were no illusion."[97]

The parallels between *Leaves of Grass* and Hindu teachings have been carefully presented in *Whitman in the Light of Vedantic Mysticism* by V. K. Chari.[98] Emerson is known to have remarked to F. B. Sanborn that *Leaves of Grass* was "a mixture of the *Bhagavad-Gita* and the New York *Herald*."[99] However, as stated by Cowley in his article:

> What is extraordinary about this Eastern element is that Whitman, when he was writing the poems of the first edition, seems to have known little or nothing about Indian philosophy.[100] It is more than doubtful that he had even read the

"*Bhagavad-Gita*," one of the few Indian works then available to Americans in translation. He does not refer to it in his notebooks of the early 1850s, where he mentions most of the books he was poring over. A year after the first edition was published, Thoreau went to see him in Brooklyn and told him that "Leaves of Grass" was "wonderfully like the Orientals." Had Whitman read them, he asked. The poet answered. "No, tell me about them." He seems to have taken advantage of Thoreau's reading list, since words from the Sanskrit (notably *Maya* and *Sudra*) appear in some of the poems written after 1858. They do not appear in "Song of Myself," in spite of the recognizably Indian ideas expressed in the poem.

Quoting now from this long poem:]

I wish I could translate the hints about the dead young men and women,
And the hints about old men and mothers, and the offspring taken soon
    out of their laps.
What do you think has become of the young and old men?
And what do you think has become of the women and children?
They are alive and well somewhere,
The smallest sprout shows there is really no death. . . .

I know I am deathless,
I know this orbit of mine cannot be swept by a carpenter's com-
    pass. . . .
And whether I come to my own today or in ten thousand or ten million
    years,
I can cheerfully take it now, or with equal cheerfulness I can wait . . .
I laugh at what you call dissolution,
And I know the amplitude of time. . . .
To be in any form, what is that?
(Round and round we go, all of us, and ever come back thither). . . .
Believing I shall come again upon the earth after five thousand
    years. . . .

The clock indicates the moment—but what does eternity indicate?
We have thus far exhausted trillions of winters and summers,
There are trillions ahead, and trillions ahead of them.
Births have brought us richness and variety,
And other births will bring us richness and variety. . . .
Rise after rise bow the phantoms behind me,
Afar down I see the huge first Nothing, I know I was even there. . . .
Immense have been the preparations for me,
Faithful and friendly the arms that have help'd me.
Cycles ferried my cradle, rowing and rowing like cheerful boat-
    men. . . .

I tramp a perpetual journey, (come listen all!). . . .
Not I, not any one else can travel that road for you,
You must travel it for yourself.
It is not far, it is within reach. . . .
And as to you Life I reckon you are the leavings of many deaths,
(No doubt I have died myself ten thousand times before.) . . .
This day before dawn I ascended a hill and look'd at the crowded
    heaven.
And I said to my spirit, When we become the enfolders of those orbs,
    and the pleasure and knowledge of everything in them, shall we be
    fill'd and satisfied then?
And my spirit said, No, we but level that lift to pass and continue
    beyond.
You are also asking me questions and I hear you,
I answer that I cannot answer, you must find out for yourself.
                                                     "Song of Myself"[101]

I saw the face of the most smear'd and slobbering idiot they had at the
    asylum,
And I knew for my consolation what they knew not,
I knew of the agents that emptied and broke my brother,
The same wait to clear the rubbish from the fallen tenement,
And I shall look again in a score or two of ages,
And I shall meet the real landlord perfect and unharm'd, every inch as
    good as myself. . . .
                                                             "Faces"[102]

Facing west from California's shores,
Inquiring, tireless, seeking what is yet unfound,
I, a child, very old, over waves, towards the house of maternity, the
    land of migrations, look afar,
Look off the shores of my Western sea, the circle almost circled;
For starting westward from Hindustan, from the vales of Kashmere,
From Asia, from the north, from the God, the sage, and the hero,
From the south, from the flowery peninsulas and the spice islands,
Long having wander'd since, round the earth having wander'd,
Now I face home again, very pleas'd and joyous,
(But where is what I started for so long ago?
And why is it yet unfound?)
                            "Facing West from California's Shores"[103]

[In "Song of the Rolling Earth," the poet speaks to weary souls, urging them
to "work on, age after age; nothing is to be lost." "Say on, sayers! sing on,

singers! Delve! mould! pile the words of the earth!'' The work ''may have to wait long, but will certainly come to use.'' And then, ''when the materials are all prepared and ready, the architects shall appear. . . . I swear to you the architects shall appear without fail.''[104] Who are the architects? In Whitman's poem ''To Him That Was Crucified,'' he salutes Christ ''and those who are with you, before and since,'' and has them speak of their ceaseless work:]

We all labor together transmitting the same charge and succession,
We few equals indifferent of lands, indifferent of times,
We, enclosers of all continents, all castes, allowers of all theologies,
Compassionaters, perceivers, rapport of men. . . .
We walk upheld, free, the whole earth over, journeying up and down
    till we make our ineffaceable mark upon time and the diverse eras,
Till we saturate time and eras, that the men and women of races,
    ages to come, may prove brethren and lovers as we are.[105]

[The following selections resume the birth date sequence.]

GIUSEPPE MAZZINI (1805–1872)
Italian Liberator

[The *Columbia Encyclopedia* provides this interesting sketch of Giuseppe Mazzini's career: ''His youth was spent in literary and philosophical studies. He early joined the Carbonari, was imprisoned (1830–1), and went into exile. In Marseilles he founded the secret society Giovine Italia (Young Italy), which led a vigorous campaign for Italian unity. . . . His influence on Italian liberals was tremendous. . . . Mazzini's work was inspired by his great moral strength. His program was not only political, but deeply social, aiming at human redemption on a religious and moral basis, at liberty, and at justice. His literary style is remarkably fine. He wrote on politics, social science, philosophy, and literature.''[106] Quoting from Bolton King's *The Life of Mazzini:*]

[Mazzini] speaks of memory as the consciousness of the soul's progress up from earlier existences; love would be a mockery, if it did not last beyond the grave; the unity of the race implies a link between the living and the dead; science teaches there is no death but only transformation. He held passionately to his faith in immortality. . . . The individual soul, he thought, progresses through a series of reincarnations, each leading it to a more perfect development, and the rapidity of its advance depends on its own purification. And as the individual has his progress through a series of existences, so collective man progresses ever through the human generations.[107]

EDGAR ALLAN POE (1809–1849)
American Author

[In one of Edgar Allan Poe's short stories, "Berenice," he wrote:]

It is mere idleness to say that I had not lived before—that the soul has no previous existence. . . . You deny it?—let us not argue the matter. Convinced myself, I seek not to convince. There is, however, a remembrance of aerial forms—of spiritual and meaning eyes, of sounds, musical yet sad; a remembrance which will not be excluded; a memory like a shadow, vague, variable, indefinite, unsteady; and like a shadow, too, in the impossibility of my getting rid of it while the sunlight of my reason shall exist.[108]

[From Poe's essay "Eureka":]

We walk about, amid the destinies of our world-existence, encompassed by dim but ever present Memories of a Destiny more vast—very distant in the bygone time, and infinitely awful. . . . We live out a Youth peculiarly haunted by such dreams; yet never mistaking them for dreams. As Memories we know them. During our Youth the distinction is too clear to deceive us even for a moment. . . . Existence—self-existence—existence from all Time and to all Eternity—seems, up to the epoch of Manhood, a normal and unquestionable condition:—seems, because it is.[109]

OLIVER WENDELL HOLMES (1809–1894)
American Author

[From "The Chambered Nautilus":]

> This is the ship of pearl, which, poets feign,
> Sails the unshadowed main . . .
> Year after year beheld the silent toil
> That spread his lustrous coil;
> Still, as the spiral grew,
> He left the past year's dwelling for the new,
> Stole with soft step its shining archway through,
> Built up its idle door,
> Stretched in his last-found home, and knew the old no more.

Thanks for the heavenly message brought by thee,
Child of the wandering sea . . .
From thy dead lips a clearer note is born . . .
Through the deep caves of thought I hear a voice that sings—
Build thee more stately mansions, O my soul!
As the swift seasons roll!
Leave thy low-vaulted past!
Let each new temple, nobler than the last,
Shut thee from heaven with a dome more vast,
Till thou at length art free,
Leaving thine outgrown shell by life's unresting sea!

ALFRED LORD TENNYSON (1809–1892)

British Poet

As when with downcast eyes we muse and brood,
And ebb into a former life, or seem
To lapse far back in a confusèd dream
To states of mystical similitude,
If one but speaks or hems or stirs his chair
Ever the wonder waxeth more and more,
So that we say, "All this hath been before,
All this hath been, I know not when or where:"
So, friend, when first I looked upon your face,
Our thoughts gave answer each to each, so true—
Opposed mirrors each reflecting each—
Although I knew not in what time or place,
Methought that I had often met with you,
And either lived in either's heart and speech.

Early Sonnets No. 1

[On the birth of a son:]

Out of the deep, my child, out of the deep,
Where all that was to be, in all that was,
Whirl'd for a million aeons thro' the vast
Waste dawn of multitudinous-eddying light—
Out of the deep, my child, out of the deep,
Thro' all this changing world of changeless law,
And every phase of ever-heightening life,
And nine long months of antenatal gloom . . .
Thou comest . . . A babe in lineament and limb
Perfect, and prophet of the perfect man . . .

Live thou! and of the grain and husk, the grape
And ivy-berry, choose; and still depart
From death to death thro' life and life, and find
Nearer and ever nearer Him, who wrought
Not matter, nor the finite-infinite,
But this main-miracle, that thou art thou,
With power on thine own act and on the world.

De Profundis

This truth within thy mind rehearse,
That in a boundless universe
Is boundless better, boundless worse. . . .

Yet how should I for certain hold,
Because my memory is so cold,
That I first was in human mould? . . .

It may be that no life is found,
Which only to one engine bound
Falls off, but cycles always round.

As old mythologies relate,
Some draught of Lethe might await
The slipping thro' from state to state. . . .

But, if I lapsed from nobler place,
Some legend of a fallen race
Alone might hint of my disgrace. . . .

Or, if thro' lower lives I came—
Tho' all experience past became
Consolidate in mind and frame—

I might forget my weaker lot;
For is not our first year forgot?
The haunts of memory echo not.

The Two Voices

FRANCIS BOWEN (1811–1890)

American Philosopher

[Francis Bowen taught philosophy at Harvard, and was also editor of the *North American Review*. He is chiefly remembered for his *Modern Philosophy from Descartes to Schopenhauer and Hartmann*. We quote from his article "Christian Metempsychosis," which appeared in the *Princeton Review* for May 1881.]

It has been said that no prudent man, if the election were offered to him, would choose to live his present life over again; and as he whom the world calls *prudent* does not usually cherish any lofty aspirations, the saying is probably true. We are all so conscious of the many errors and sins that we have committed that the retrospect is a saddening one; and worldly wisdom would probably whisper, ''It is best to stop here, and not try such a career over again.'' But every one would ardently desire a renewal of his earthly experience if assured that he could enter upon it under better auspices, if he believed that what we call death is not the end of all things even here below, but that the soul is then standing upon the threshold of a new stage of earthly existence, which is to be brighter or darker than the one it is just quitting, according as there is carried forward into it a higher or lower purpose. . . .

We can easily imagine and believe that every person now living is a representation of some one who lived perhaps centuries ago under another name, in another country. . . . He has entered upon a new stage of probation, and in it he has now to learn what the character which he there formed naturally leads to when tried upon a new and perhaps broader theatre. . . .

I know not how it may seem to others, but to me there is something inexpressibly consolatory and inspiring in the thought that the great and good of other days have not finally accomplished their earthly career, have not left us desolate, but that they are still with us. . . . We are unwilling to believe that their beneficent activity was limited to one short life on earth, at the close of which there opened to them an eternity without change, without further trial or action, and seemingly having no other purpose than unlimited enjoyment. . . .

Why should it be thought incredible that the same soul should inhabit in succession an indefinite number of mortal bodies . . . ? Even during this one life our bodies are perpetually changing, though by a process of decay and restoration which is so gradual that it escapes our notice. Every human being thus dwells successively in many bodies, even during one short life.

[The *New York Times* (September 29, 1954) reports that Dr. Paul C. Aebersold, director of the isotopes division of the United States Atomic Energy Commission, stated in the annual report of the Smithsonian Institution: ''Tracer studies show that the atomic turnover in our bodies is quite rapid and complete. . . . In a year approximately 98 percent of the atoms in us now will be replaced by other atoms we take in in our air, food, and drink.'' In fifty-three weeks, then, the turnover will be complete. Thus a man of seventy-five has had at least seventy new brains and bodies, and this naturally raises significant questions for physiology and psychology: Where are the memories of a lifetime stored? How is the sense of individual identity preserved throughout these numerous ''re-embodiments''?]

CHARLES DICKENS (1812–1870)

British Novelist

We have all some experience of a feeling, that comes over us occasionally, of what we are saying and doing having been said and done before, in a remote time—of our having been surrounded, dim ages ago, by the same faces, objects, and circumstances—of our knowing perfectly what will be said next, as if we suddenly remembered it!

David Copperfield[110]

At sunset, when I was walking on alone, while the horses rested, I arrived upon a little scene, which, by one of those singular mental operations of which we are all conscious, seemed perfectly familiar to me, and which I see distinctly now. . . . In the foreground was a group of silent peasant girls, leaning over the parapet of the little bridge [in Ferrara] . . . In the distance a deep bell; the shade of approaching night on everything. If I had been murdered there, in some former life, I could not have seemed to remember the place more thoroughly, or with a more emphatic chilling of the blood; and the real remembrance of it acquired in that minute is so strengthened by the imaginary recollection that I hardly think I could forget it.

"Through Bologna and Ferrara"
Pictures from Italy

ROBERT BROWNING (1812–1889)

British Poet

[In "One Word More" Robert Browning addressed his wife: "I shall never, in the years remaining, paint you pictures, no, nor carve you statues. This of verse alone, one life allows me . . . Other heights in other lives, God willing." Elizabeth Barrett Browning must have shared her husband's reincarnation views for in her "Aurora Leigh" these lines appear: "Let who says 'The soul's a clean white paper,' rather say a palimpsest, a prophet's holograph," which becomes "defiled, erased, and covered" by the writing of a monk; the apocalypse, superimposed by the obscene text of a Longus, and yet we still "may discern perhaps some fair, fine trace of what was written once, some upstroke of an alpha and omega." To quote from some of Browning's poems:]

> At times I almost dream
> I too have spent a life the sages' way,
> And tread once more familiar paths. Perchance
> I perished in an arrogant self-reliance

Ages ago; and in that act, a prayer
For one more chance went up so earnest, so
Instinct with better light let in by death,
That life was blotted out—not so completely
But scattered wrecks enough of it remain,
Dim memories, as now, when seems once more
The goal in sight again. . . .
I go to prove my soul!
I see my way as birds their trackless way.
I shall arrive! what time, what circuit first,
I ask not. . . .
                    "Paracelsus" (Part I)

There's a fancy some lean to and others hate—
That, when this life is ended, begins
New work for the soul in another state,
Where it strives and gets weary, loses and wins:
Where the strong and the weak, this world's congeries,
Repeat in large what they practised in small,
Through life after life in unlimited series;
Only the scale's to be changed, that's all.
                    "Old Pictures in Florence"

RICHARD WAGNER (1813–1883)
German Composer

[Writing to Mathilde Wesendonck in 1855, Richard Wagner advised her to procure the book *Indian Legends* edited by Holtzmann. "All are beautiful," he said, "but if you wish to find out my religion, read *Usinar*. How shamed stands our whole culture by these purest revelations of the noblest humanism in the ancient East!"[111] In 1857 he confided to her that he had "unconsciously become a Buddhist."[112] His first acquaintance with Buddhism, however, dated from his twenties when he lived with his brother-in-law, Hermann Brockhaus, a Sanskrit scholar and teacher. Later, upon taking up Buddhism again, this time stimulated by his enthusiastic study of Schopenhauer, Wagner had a strong compulsion to compose a reincarnation opera, *Die Sieger,* The Victors. Regarding the latter, we quote from an illuminating article, "Buddhism and Wagner," by Granville Pyne, a Wagnerian specialist and chairman of the Wagner Society in England. He introduces his observations with a sentence from Wagner's autobiography:

". . . Bournouff's *Introduction à L'Histoire du Bouddhisme* interested me most among my books [during the winter of 1855–1856], and I found material for a dramatic poem, which has stayed in my mind ever since, though only vaguely sketched."[113] This was *The Victors (Die Sieger)*. . . . Wagner found great underlying beauty in this material and saw the possibility of dealing with reincarnation through the special techniques of music-drama, in which the music could describe the past while the words spoke of the present. He thought that this greatly influenced his subsequent development. *The Victors* continued to haunt his imagination for twenty years, but it never came to fruition. The emotional and metaphysical impulse aroused in Wagner by *The Victors* was discharged in *Tristan and Isolde,* and the rest of this thought on the subject found a natural outlet in his last work, *Parsifal.* . . . One thing is certain: Buddhism laid a hand on the volcanic genius and tempestuous personality of Richard Wagner, whereby his works are different from what they otherwise would have been.[114]

From other sources the following extracts from Wagner's writings have been gathered; the first concerns *Die Sieger.*]

To the mental eye of Buddha the past life of any being he meets is like an open book. . . . The simple story [of *Die Sieger*] assumed significance by having the previous life of the leading characters merge into the present existence by means of an accompanying musical reminiscence. Having immediately realized how to present clearly this double life through simultaneously sounding music, I applied myself to the execution of the poem with particular devotion.

Collected Writings[115]

From all time the minds that have attained . . . to a clear perception, have turned to the minds of the multitude still in bondage . . . and, having compassion on them, have sought a means of communication with them. Foremost among these enlightened spirits have been the founders of religions. . . . Certainly the Indian Prince Buddha spoke the language which most nearly gives expression to that lofty enlightenment. . . . If we are to speak of this highest perception in terms understood by the people it can only be done under the form of pure and primitive Buddhist teaching. Especially important is the doctrine of the transmigration of souls as the basis of a truly human life.

Letter to August Roeckel (1855)[116]

I cannot take my life, for the Will to accomplish the Object of Art would draw me back into life again until I realized that Object, and so I would only be re-entering this circle of tears and misery.

Letter to Hans Bülow (September 27, 1858)[117]

[In a letter to Mathilde Wesendonck—who inspired the composing of *Tristan and Isolde*—Wagner wrote: "In contrast to reincarnation and karma all other views appear petty and narrow."[118] In another letter, written in Paris in August 1860, he said to her:]

A prose translation of the four pieces, *Hollander, Tannhäuser, Lohengrin,* and *Tristan,* is soon to be issued. . . . I have just gone through these translations and in so doing I was obliged to recall clearly to mind all the details of my poems. Yesterday *Lohengrin* touched me very much, and I cannot but hold it to be the most tragic poem of all, since only an immensely wide outlook upon life can provide a reconciliation between Lohengrin and Elsa. Only the profoundly conceived idea of Reincarnation could give me any consolation, since that belief shows how all at last can reach complete redemption. . . . According to the beautiful Buddhist belief, the spotless purity of Lohengrin finds a simple explanation in the fact that he is the continuation of Parsifal, who had to fight for his purity. Even so Elsa in her rebirth would reach to the height of Lohengrin. . . Thus all the terrible tragedy of life is seen to be nothing but the sense of Separateness in Time and Space.[119]

[The excerpt below is from the closing lines of the *Götterdämmerung*. Wagner specifically directed that they be unsung because "the musician cannot help seeing for himself that the verses have to be omitted in the live production inasmuch as their meaning is emphatically expressed in the orchestral music itself.[120] Contrary to Wagner's apparent intention, the stanza is omitted in current librettos. When the composer has Brünhilde, in these last moments of the immolation scene, say that she will return no more to earthly incarnation, he is adhering to the original Scandinavian and Germanic myth we have briefly considered in chapter 4.]

> The home of desire I leave behind
> Illusions forever avoid.
> The open door of return and being
> I close forever.
> Yearning for regions of peace,
> The holy land of choice,
> Released from the path of return,
> So wanders the Wise one forth.

[Our last brief quotations are from Wagner's final and most controversial opera, *Parsifal*. As with all his works, the libretto was written by himself. Although Christian symbology, particularly the Knights of the Grail myth, dominates the work, we learned earlier that his uncompleted Buddhist opera *Die Sieger* found an outlet therein. Certain elements from the story of Buddha's life seem likewise to have been carried over. The well-known episode in which a swan is shot by Buddha's wicked cousin is apparently transposed by

Wagner. The evil magician Klingsor, hurling at Parsifal a spear that remains suspended in the air, is likewise in the old Buddhist tales, where Mara, the tempter, does the same thing.

As to reincarnation and karma, the knight Gurnemanz sings in Act I respecting Kundry, the leading woman character: "Here she lives today— perhaps anew to suffer penance for debts incurred in former life, for which forgiveness still is due." Kundry is told in Act II: "You were Herodias—and what else? Gundryggia there. Kundry here." Herodias, it will be recalled, was the wife of Herod, and according to the Gospels she caused the beheading of John the Baptist. According to the opera, she also mocked Christ on the cross and for centuries was condemned to a tormented existence. "Now I try," says Kundry, "from world to world to find Him again."]

SÖREN KIERKEGAARD (1813–1855)

Danish Religious Philosopher

[In 1842 when Sören Kierkegaard was twenty-nine, he penned these words, which were discovered after his death among his unpublished writings:]

"Write," said the voice, and the prophet answered: "For whom?" The voice said: "For the dead, for those you have loved in antiquity." "Will they read me?" "Yes, for they will come back as posterity."[121]

HERMAN MELVILLE (1819–1891)

American Novelist

[In 1851 Herman Melville's epic-drama *Moby-Dick* appeared. Unfavorably received, the career of a promising author was permanently eclipsed. In 1921 a noted English critic announced that he had been induced to read this forgotten book, and that "having done so, I hereby declare that since letters began there never was such a book, and that the mind of man is not constructed so as to produce such another; that I put its author with Rabelais, Swift, Shakespeare."[122] Some, of course, may not agree with this view, but within a decade Melville was regarded as one of the great writers of all time. Willard Thorp, Holmes professor of *belles lettres* at Princeton, remarks that in Melville's earlier work *Mardi*,

> Melville struggles with a theme that in varying forms would reappear in *Moby-Dick, Pierre, The Confidence Man* and *Billy Budd*. He states it thus in *Pierre:* "Ah, if man were wholly made in heaven, why catch we hell-glimpses? Why in the noblest marble pillar . . . ever should we descry the sinister vein?" In *Moby-Dick* this theme is incarnated in Captain Ahab's vengeful search for the

white whale, who represented for him all the evil in the world [and during one of his ventures had actually snipped off his leg]. If he can strike his harpoon into Moby-Dick, he may be able to destroy him and what he symbolizes. . . . But Ahab's Promethean quest changes to personal vengeance on the sea-beast who has maimed him. He turns from the creative principle of light to the false god of fire whose "right worship is defiance." In the end he and his ship and its crew are destroyed by Moby-Dick. Only Ishmael, the narrator, survives . . . He deserves to survive because he has learned that in this world "there is a wisdom that is woe; but there is a woe that is madness." Let a man not look too long in the face of the unholy fire.[123]

Now for the selections from *Moby-Dick* that bear on reincarnation:]

In the sperm fishery, this is perhaps one of the most remarkable incidents in all the business of whaling: One day the planks stream with freshets of blood and oil; on the sacred quarter-deck enormous masses of the whale's head are profanely piled. . . . But a day or two after, you look about you . . . you would all but swear you trod some silent merchant vessel, with a most scrupulously neat commander. . . . Many is the time, when, after the severest uninterrupted labours . . . continuing straight through for ninety-six hours, [and after which all hands] have finally bestirred themselves to cleanse the ship, and make a spotless dairy room of it . . . the poor fellows . . . are startled by the cry of "There she blows!" and away they fly to fight another whale, and go through the whole weary thing again.

"Oh! my friends, but this is man-killing! Yet this is life. For hardly have we mortals by long toilings extracted from this world's vast bulk its small but valuable sperm; and then, with weary patience, cleansed ourselves from its defilements, and learned to live here in clean tabernacles of the soul; hardly is this done, when—There she blows!—the ghost is spouted up, and away we sail to fight some other world, and go through young life's old routine again. Oh! the metempsychosis! Oh! Pythagoras, that in bright Greece, two thousand years ago, did die, so good, so wise, so mild; I sailed with thee along the Peruvian coast last voyage—and, foolish as I am, taught thee, a green simple boy, how to splice a rope! . . .

The mingled, mingling threads of life are woven by warp and woof: calms crossed by storms, a storm for every calm. . . . [We pass] through infancy's unconscious spell, boyhood's thoughtless faith, adolescence, doubt (the common doom), then scepticism, then disbelief, resting at last in manhood's pondering repose of If. But once gone through, we trace the round again: and are infants, boys, and men, and Ifs eternally. Where lies the final harbour, whence we unmoor no more? In what rapt ether sails the world of which the weariest will never weary? . . .

[Captain Ahab, himself a New England Quaker, addresses three white flames that lightning caused to appear on the ship's masts and which were silently burning like gigantic wax tapers before an altar:] Oh! thou clear spirit of clear fire, whom on these seas I as Persian once did worship, till in the sacramental act so burned by thee, that to this hour I bear the scar; I now know thee, thou clear spirit, and I know that thy right worship is defiance. . . . No fearless fool now fronts thee. I own thy speechless, placeless power; but to the last gasp of my earthquake life will dispute its unconditional, unintegral mastery in me. In the midst of the personified impersonal, a personality stands here. Though but a point at best; Whenceso'er I came; whenceso'er I go, yet while I earthly live, the queenly personality lives in me, and feels her royal rights. . . . Now I do glory, in my genealogy. . . .

[As the point of no return approaches, a more contrite Ahab thinks:] Forty—forty—forty years of continual whaling! forty years of privation, and peril . . . has Ahab forsaken the peaceful land, for forty years to make war on the horrors of the deep! . . . But do I look very old, so very, very old? I feel deadly faint, bowed, and humped, as though I were Adam, staggering beneath the piled centuries since Paradise. . . . What is it, what nameless, inscrutable, unearthly thing is it; what hidden lord and master, and cruel, remorseless emperor commands me; that against all natural lovings and longings, I so keep pushing, and crowding, and jamming myself on all the time; recklessly making me ready to do what in my own proper, natural heart, I durst not so much as dare? . . . Ye see an old man cut down to a stump; leaning on a shivered lance; propped up on a lonely foot. 'Tis Ahab—his body's part; but Ahab's soul's a centipede, that moves upon a hundred legs. . . . Ahab is for ever Ahab, man. This whole act's immutably decreed. 'Twas rehearsed by thee and me a billion years before this ocean rolled.[124]

[In this last speech the captain hides behind the excuse that his life as he lived it was *fated* to be so lived. There is, of course, a difference between saying that the great psychological struggle and battle of life is immutably decreed and saying that our *choice* in that battle is likewise decreed. J. B. Priestley sums up the lesson of Melville's saga in this illuminating way: Moby-Dick "is entirely evil only in the mind of Captain Ahab . . . the mind in its complete self-dependence, in its ruthless opposition to the whale as a force of Nature. . . . The whale is neither good nor evil. It is the mighty Other or Opposite, what we leave when we split totality and claim half as our own before demanding the whole again . . . and the more we separate ourselves from it, challenge it, hunt it and hope to destroy it, the more powerful, menacing, and finally destructive it becomes."[125] D. H. Lawrence, however, saw the more hopeful and positive side of the story. He called it "the Gethsemane of Ahab, before the last fight; the Gethsemane of the human soul seeking the last self-conquest, the last attainment of extended consciousness—infinite consciousness."[126] But the latter is only possible when the individual's stubborn self-will is surrendered in favor of the Universal Will, the supreme Self in each and all.]

GUSTAVE FLAUBERT (1821–1880)
French Novelist

[The extracts here are from a letter that Flaubert wrote in 1866 as published in *The George Sand–Gustave Flaubert Letters*. In her reply Sand did not evince the enthusiasm of her early days for the many-lives viewpoint (as made evident by a previously quoted excerpt), but, as an older woman, indicated a kind of world-weariness with having, as she says, already lived too much. In Flaubert's letter he mistakenly takes it for granted that reincarnation is a new idea to her.]

I don't experience, as you do, this feeling of a life which is beginning, the stupefaction of a newly commenced existence. It seems to me, on the contrary, that I have always lived! And I possess memories which go back to the Pharaohs. I see myself very clearly at different ages of history, practising different professions and in many sorts of fortune. My present personality is the result of my lost personalities. . . . Many things would be explained if we could know our real genealogy. . . . Thus heredity is a just principle which has been badly applied.[127]

FEODOR DOSTOEVSKY (1821–1881)
Russian Novelist

[From *The Brothers Karamazov:*]

"This legend is about Paradise. There was, they say, here on earth a thinker and philosopher. He rejected everything, 'laws, conscience, faith,' and above all, the future life. He died; he expected to go straight to darkness and death and he found a future life before him. He was astounded and indignant. 'This is against my principles!' he said. And he was punished for that . . . he was sentenced to walk a quadrillion kilometres in the dark . . . and when he has finished the quadrillion, the gates of heaven would be opened to him and he'll be forgiven. . . . Well, this man who was condemned to the quadrillion kilometres, stood still, looked round and lay down across the road. 'I won't go, I refuse on principle!' . . . He lay there almost a thousand years and then he got up and went on."

"What an ass!" cried Ivan, laughing nervously. . . . . "Does it make any difference whether he lies there for ever or walks the quadrillion kilometres? It would take a billion years to walk it?''

"Much more than that. . . . But he got there long ago and that's where the story begins."

"What, he got there? But how did he get the billion years to do it?''

"Why, you keep thinking of our present earth! But our present earth may have been repeated a billion times. Why, it's become extinct, been frozen; cracked, broken to bits, disintegrated into its elements, again 'the water above the firmament,' then again a comet, again a sun, again from the sun it becomes earth—and the same sequence may have been repeated endlessly and exactly the same to every detail.''[128]

ERNEST RENAN (1823–1892)

French Historian, Philologist, Critic

[From Ernest Renan's address at the tomb of Ivan Turgenev, delivered October 1, 1883, and included in Turgenev's *Oeuvres Dernières*.]

We cannot let the remains which are about to be returned to his country return without a farewell to the spirit of the genius, whom it was our privilege for many years to know and to love. . . . I will but speak to you of his soul such as it was revealed to me in the beautiful retreat which gave us the opportunity of an illustrious friendship. . . . He was born essentially impersonal. His conscience was . . . the conscience of a people. Before his birth, he had lived thousands of years and infinite successions of dreams concentrated in the depths of his soul. . . .

The silent genius of the collective masses is the source of all great things. But the mass is without voice. It knows but to suffer and to stammer. It needs an interpreter, a prophet to speak for it. . . . The great man is that prophet when he is at the same time a genius and a man of heart. That is why the great man is the least free of men. He can neither do nor say what he wishes. A God speaks in him—ten centuries of sorrows and hopes obsess and command him. . . . Like the universe itself, [Turgenev] recommenced a thousand times the unfinished work.[129]

CONRAD FERDINAND MEYER (1825–1898)

Swiss Poet and Historical Novelist

[From a letter to Friedrich von Wiss, dated August 7, 1880:]

In the last few years I have gone through more than I am ever willing to confess. Truly what sustained me was a thought on reincarnation. I told myself: evidently you did something terrible in a former existence. Said the voice of fate: just for that the fellow shall go to earth and become a Meyer. Now both have to suffer through honestly, before a change for the better may be attained.[130]

From this point on, scientists, psychologists, and philosophers who should properly appear in this chapter have been reserved for chapter 6, "New Horizons in Science, Psychology, and Philosophy." The remainder of the present chapter considers reincarnation in Western literature, and also includes the views of men of action, and pioneers in various fields of Occidental life.

LEO TOLSTOY (1828–1910)
Russian Novelist; Social and Religious Philosopher

[In his late forties, when Leo Tolstoy was celebrated as a novelist, life became meaningless and absurd to him, and thoughts of suicide invaded his consciousness. In *My Confession* he wrote:

> Such was the condition I had come to, at a time when all circumstances of my life were pre-eminently happy ones. . . . Moreover, my mind was neither deranged nor weakened; on the contrary, I enjoyed a mental and physical strength which I have seldom found in men of my class and pursuits: I could keep up with a peasant in mowing, and could continue mental labor for ten hours at a stretch, without any evil consequences.
> The mental state in which I then was seemed to me summed up in the following: my life was a foolish and wicked joke played upon me by I knew not whom. . . . Illness and death would come . . . if not today, then tomorrow, to those whom I loved, to myself, and nothing would remain but stench and worms. All my acts, whatever I did, would sooner or later be forgotten, and I myself be nowhere. Why, then, busy one's self with anything? How could men see this, and live? . . . I felt a horror of what awaited me. . . . I could not patiently await the end . . . and I longed to free myself . . . by a rope or a pistol ball.[131]

How Tolstoy resolved this dilemma is the story of *My Confession,* but as to the problem of self-destruction, he wrote years later in his diary:

> How interesting it would be to write the story of the experiences in this life of a man who killed himself in his previous life; how he now stumbles against the

very demands which had offered themselves before, until he arrives at the
realization that he must fulfil those demands. Remembering the lesson, this man
will be wiser than others.[132]

In 1896 when this was written, reincarnation was not a new idea to Tolstoy,
for thirty years previously in *War and Peace* his heroine Natasha took part in
the following conversation:]

"How quiet you young people are!"

"Yes, we're talking philosophy," said Natasha. . . . "Do you know, I
think . . . that one goes on remembering, and remembering; one remembers
till one recalls what happened before one was in this world."

"That's metempsychosis," said Sonya, who had been good at lessons . . .
"The Egyptians used to believe that our souls had been in animals, and
would go into animals again."

"No, do you know, I don't believe that we were once in animals," said
Natasha . . . "but I know for certain that we were once angels somewhere beyond, and we have been here, and that's why we remember
everything." . . .

"If we had been angels, why should we have fallen lower?" said Nikolay.
"No, that can't be!"

"Not lower . . . who told you we were lower? . . . This is how I know I
have existed before," Natasha replied, with conviction: "The soul is immortal, you know . . . so, if I am to live for ever, I have lived before too, I have
lived for all eternity."

"Yes, but it's hard for us to conceive of eternity," said Dimmler, who had
joined the young people, with a mildly condescending smile, but now talked
as quietly and seriously as they did.

"Why is it hard to conceive of eternity?" said Natasha. "There will be
today, and there will be tomorrow, and there will be forever, and yesterday
has been, and the day before."[133]

[In 1904 Tolstoy completed an arrangement in four volumes of the thoughts
of great men under the title *Krug Tchtenia*—The Circle of Reading—grouped
to provide reading matter for each day of the year. Frequently he headed a
page with a contribution of his own, as was the case for March 12: "The
deeds of the preceding life give the direction to the present life. That is what
the Hindus call Karma." Tolstoy's overall philosophy on reincarnation may
be summed up in this letter published two years before his death:]

You are asking me about the Buddhist idea of "Karma." . . . Now our
whole life, from birth unto death, with all its dreams, is it not in its turn also a

dream, which we take as the real life, the reality of which we do not doubt only because we do not know of the other more real life? . . . The dreams of our present life are the environment in which we work out the impressions, thoughts, feelings of a former life. . . . As we live through thousands of dreams in our present life, so is our present life only one of many thousands of such lives which we enter from the other, more real life . . . and then return after death. Our life is but one of the dreams of that more real life, and so it is endlessly, until the very last one, the very real life,—the life of God. . . . I wish you would understand me; I am not playing, not inventing this: I believe in it, I see it without doubt.[134]

HENRIK IBSEN (1828–1906)
Norwegian Dramatist and Poet

[As already mentioned, the Roman Emperor Julian believed himself a reincarnation of Alexander the Great. The following lines from Henrik Ibsen's tragedy *The Emperor Julian* point up this idea:]

MAXIMUS   Must I remind you how fortune has borne you, as on mighty pinions, through an agitated and perilous life? Who are you, sire? Are you Alexander born again, not, as before in immaturity, but perfectly equipped for the fulfillment of the task?

JULIAN   Maximus!

MAXIMUS   There is One who ever reappears, at certain intervals, in the course of human history. He is like a rider taming a wild horse in the arena. Again and yet again it throws him. A moment, and he is in the saddle again, each time more secure and more expert; but off he has had to go, in all his varying incarnations, until this day. Off he had to go as the god-created man in Eden's grove; off he had to go as the founder of the world-empire; off he must go as the prince of the empire of God. Who knows how often he has wandered among us when none have recognized him? . . .

JULIAN (looking far away)   Oh, unfathomable riddle—![135]

DANTE GABRIEL ROSSETTI (1828–1882)
British Painter and Poet

[Dante Gabriel Rossetti wrote a reincarnation story called "St. Agnes of Intercession," included in his *Collected Works*.[136] The following lines are from his poem "Sudden Light."]

I have been here before,
But when or how I cannot tell;
I know the grass beyond the door,
The sweet keen smell,
The sighing sound, the lights around the shore.
You have been mine before.—
How long ago I may not know:
But just when at that swallow's soar
Your neck turned so,
Some veil did fall,—I knew it all of yore.

EMILY DICKINSON (1830–1886)

American Poet

Afraid? Of whom am I afraid?
Not death; for who is he?
The porter of my father's lodge
As much abasheth me.
Of life? Twere odd I fear a thing
That comprehendeth me
In one or more existences
At Deity's decree.
Of resurrection? Is the east
Afraid to trust the morn?[137]

LOUISA MAY ALCOTT (1832–1888)

American Novelist

[It is perhaps not surprising that Louisa May Alcott, the famous daughter of Bronson Alcott—who lived in the world of Emerson, Thoreau, and the other Concordians—should have written in a letter to a friend:]

I think immortality is the passing of a soul through many lives or experiences, and such as are truly lived, used, and learned, help on to the next, each growing richer, happier and higher, carrying with it only the real memories of what has gone before. . . . I seem to remember former states and feel that in them I have learned some of the lessons that have never since been mine here and in my next step I hope to leave behind many of the trials I have struggled to bear here and begin to find lightened as I go on. This accounts for the genius and great virtue some show here. They have done well in many phases of this great school and bring into our class the virtue or the gifts that make them great or good. We don't remember the lesser things. They slip away as childish trifles, and we carry on only the real experiences.[138]

SAMUEL BUTLER (1835–1902)

British Author and Satirist

[Although reincarnation was evidently accepted by Samuel Butler, the twin doctrine of karma appears to have received little appreciation from this author of *The Way of All Flesh*.]

We commonly know that we are going to die, though we do not know that we are going to be born. But are we sure this is so? We may have had the most gloomy forebodings on this head and forgotten all about them. . . .

I must have it that neither are the good rewarded nor the bad punished in a future state, but every one must start anew quite irrespective of anything they have done here and must try his luck again and go on trying it again and again *ad infinitum*. Some of our lives, then, will be lucky and some unlucky and it will resolve itself into one long eternal life during which we shall change so much that we shall not remember our antecedents very far back (any more than we remember having been embryos) nor foresee our future very much, and during which we shall have our ups and downs *ad infinitum*—effecting a transformation scene at once as soon as circumstances become unbearable.

The Note-Books of Samuel Butler[139]

We have been three lights to one another and now we are two,
For you go far and alone into the darkness;
But the light in you was stronger and clearer than ours . . .
Out, out into the night you go,
So guide you and guard you Heaven and fare you well! . . .

Yet for the great bitterness of this grief
We three, you and he and I,
May pass into the hearts of like true comrades hereafter,
In whom we may weep anew and yet comfort them,
As they too pass out, out, out into the night,
So guide them and guard them Heaven and fare them well!
"In Memoriam, February 14, 1895, To H. R. F."[140]

Not on sad Stygian shore, nor in clear sheen
Of far Elysian plain, shall we meet those
Among the dead whose pupils we have been. . . .
We shall not argue saying " 'Twas thus" or "Thus,"

Our argument's whole drift we shall forget;
Who's right, who's wrong, 'twill be all one to us;
We shall not even know that we have met.
Yet meet we shall, and part, and meet again,
Where dead men meet, on lips of living men.
"The Life After Death"[141]

QUEEN ELISABETH OF AUSTRIA (1837–1898)

German-born Empress of Austria, Wife of Franz Josef

[Constantin Christomanos, Queen Elisabeth of Austria's Greek tutor, who often accompanied her on long walks, wrote in his *Vienna Diary:*]

Speaking of the difference between culture and civilization, she says: "Civilization is reading, culture is the thoughts. . . . Everyone has culture within himself as heritage of all his pre-existences, absorbs it with every breath and in this lies the great unity." . . . Of Dante and other great ones, she says: "They are souls, who, from ages past have come anew to earth to continue their work and to anticipate the development of others still to come."

"Our innermost being," she added, "is more valuable than all titles and honors." "These are colored rags with which we try to cover our nudities. Whatever is of value in us we bring from our previous lives that were spiritual."[142]

EDOUARD SCHURÉ (1841–1929)

French Author

[Although Edouard Schuré was popular as a journalist and music critic, a friend of Wagner, Nietzsche, and many celebrities of the time, he is now chiefly known for his work *The Great Initiates,* an influential volume with writers and artists in France, among them, Gauguin, who will be considered shortly. Published in 1889, the work in French alone has gone through 220 editions, and continues to sell widely. The inspiration to write it came during Schuré's residence in Florence: "In a flash I saw the Light that flows from one mighty founder of religion to another, from the Himalayas to Iran, from Sinai to Tabor, from the Crypts of Egypt to the sanctuary of Eleusis. These Great Initiates, those mighty figures whom we call Rama, Krishna, Hermes, Moses, Orpheus, Pythagoras, Plato, and Jesus, appeared before me in a homogeneous group."[143] A chapter is devoted to each of the *Grands Initiés,* our extract coming from "Pythagoras and the Delphic Mysteries."]

The doctrine of the ascensional life of the soul through series of existences is the common feature of esoteric traditions and the crown of theosophy. I will add that it is of the utmost importance to us. For the man of the present day rejects with equal scorn the abstract and vague immortality of philosophy and the childish heaven of an infant religion. And yet he abhors the dryness and nothingness of materialism. Unconsciously he aspires to the consciousness of an *organic immortality* responding at once to the demands of his reason and the indestructible needs of his soul. . . .

Lives follow without resembling one another, but a pitiless logic links them together. Though each of them has its own law and special destiny, the succession is controlled by a general law, which might be called the repercussion of lives. . . . There is not a word or action which has not its echo in eternity, says a proverb. According to esoteric doctrine, this proverb is literally applied from one life to another.[144]

EDWARD CARPENTER (1844–1929)
British Author

[After leaving Cambridge, Edward Carpenter entered the Anglican ministry where he remained for five years. A visit to the United States in 1877 transformed his life, for here he met and talked with Emerson, Whitman, Lowell, Bryant, and Oliver Wendell Holmes, and was inspired to write.

He later traveled in the Orient and visited India and Ceylon. P. D. Ouspensky writes in *Tertium Organum:* "Edward Carpenter, directly and without any allegories and symbols, formulated the thought that the existing consciousness by which contemporary man lives, is merely the transitory form of another higher consciousness, which *even now* is manifesting in certain men, after appropriate preparation and training. This higher consciousness Edward Carpenter names *cosmic consciousness.*"[145] The Canadian psychiatrist and theosophist R. M. Bucke was later to employ this expression as the title of his influential work on the subject. Some of Carpenter's reincarnation poems are "After Long Ages" and "When a Thousand Years Have Passed." In *The Art of Creation* he suggests how man may some day prove and make conscious use of his previous existences:]

Here in this perennial, immeasurable consciousness sleeping within us we come again to our Celestial City, our Home from which as individuals we proceed, but from which we are never really separated. . . . Every man feels doubtless that his little mortal life is very inadequate, and that to express and give utterance to all that is in him would need many lives, many bodies. . . . The important thing . . . is to see that undoubtedly various orders of consciousness do exist, *actually embedded within us,* and that the words I and Thou do not merely cover our bodily forms and the outlines of our minds as we habitually represent them to ourselves, but cover also immense tracts of intelligence and activity lying behind these and only on occasions coming into consciousness. . . . To command these tracts in such a way as to be able to enter in and make use of them at will, and to bring them into permanent relation with the conscious ego, will I think be the method of advance, and the means by which all these questions of the perduration and reincarnation of the ego, and its real relation with other egos, will at length be solved.[146]

PAUL GAUGUIN (1848–1903)

French Artist

[Under the title "Gauguin's Religion," Thomas Buser writes in the *Art Journal* (Summer 1968): "Gauguin was by no means a creative nor a systematic theologian. Nevertheless his religious belief went beyond the ordinary anticlericalism and apologetics of his time. His Faith was easily more mystical than that prevalent in the Church at the time." "Quite simply, Gauguin seems to have been enamored of theosophy." "The human soul, in Gauguin's theosophy," is "destined to metempsychosis," and fits into a definite framework of evolution. The author apparently bases some of these conclusions on a posthumous work, *Modern Thought and Catholicism,* written by the artist during his final years in Tahiti and from which we now quote. It opens with the query "Whence do we come, what are we, where do we go?"—the title of the large canvas Gauguin finished in 1898.]

The materialists smile when one speaks to them of an embodied or disembodied soul, saying that no one has ever been able to see one of them with a magnifying-glass or the naked eye, forgetting that no one has ever been able to see an atom of air or of matter, however much it may be volatilized. . . .

The soul . . . constitutes the generating center of all its organism, the pivot around which [everything] gravitates. . . . The soul, residing temporarily in a special organism, develops therein its animal faculties . . . and when this special organism breaks up, as the soul survives, it becomes a germ [which is] qualified from metamorphosis to metamorphosis, to ascend to a [universal or] *general life* . . .

The parable of Jacob's ladder extending from earth to heaven, which the angels of God ascend and descend by steps, indeed resembles the ascent and descent by gradations from the lowest to the highest of life, according to the more or less active exercise of their qualities . . . degrading or elevating according to merit or demerit. The idea of metempsychosis, recognized in the Hindu religion, and which Pythagoras, deriving it from the Hindus, taught in

Greece, also reveals how far this conception of *the general life* of animal and human souls dates from the past, for transmigration also had the principle of graduated ascension.

From what has preceded, [it follows that] it is the soul which has formed its organism; that it is the soul which has produced the evolution of living organisms constituting species. . . . God . . . as a symbol of the pure eternal spirit, the *general spirit* of the universe . . . becomes the principle of all harmonies, the end to be attained, presented by Christ, and before him by Buddha. And all men will become Buddhas.[147]

WILLIAM ERNEST HENLEY (1849–1903)
British Poet, Editor, and Playwright

[The first four lines of this poem by William Ernest Henley "To W.A." are sufficiently well known to be included in *Bartlett's Familiar Quotations,* but the important part seldom finds its way into print.]

Or ever the knightly years were gone
With the old world to the grave,
I was a King in Babylon
And you were a Christian Slave.
I saw, I took, I cast you by,
I bent and broke your pride. . . .
And a myriad suns have set and shone
Since then upon the grave
Decreed by the King in Babylon
To her that had been his Slave.
The pride I trampled is now my scathe,
For it tramples me again.
The old resentment lasts like death,
For you love, yet you refrain.
I break my heart on your hard unfaith,
And I break my heart in vain.

AUGUST STRINDBERG (1849–1912)
Swedish Dramatist and Novelist

[From *Zones of the Spirit:*]

The teacher said: "Life is hard to live, and the destinies of men appear very different. . . . It is therefore difficult to know how one should behave in life, what one should believe, what views one should adopt, or to which party one should adhere. This destiny is not the inevitable blind fate of the ancients, but the commission which each one has received, the task he must perform. The Theosophists call it Karma, and believe it is connected with a past which we only dimly remember. . . ."

The pupil asked: "If it is so, why is not one informed of one's Karma from the beginning?"

The teacher answered: "That is pure pity for us. No man could endure life, if he knew what lay before him. Moreover, man must have a certain measure of freedom; without that, he would be only a puppet. Also the wise think that the voyage of discovery we make to discover our destiny is instructive for us. . . ."

Darwinism made it seem probable that men derived their origin from animals. Then came the Theosophists with the opinion that our souls are in process of transmigration from one human body to another. Thence comes this excessive feeling of discomfort, this longing for deliverance, this sensation of constraint, the pain of existence, the sighing of the creature. Those who do not feel this uneasiness, but flourish here, are probably at home here. Their inexplicable sympathy for animals and their disbelief in the immortality of the soul points to a connection with the lower forms of existence of which they are conscious, and which we cannot deny.[148]

LAFCADIO HEARN (1850–1904)

Author, Journalist, Teacher

[Western fascination for Japan's culture and religions traces back to Lafcadio Hearn who through many books and articles built bridges of understanding between that country and the West. Hearn had an unusual history. Born on a Greek island of a Maltese mother and Anglo-Irish father, he spent his early years in Dublin, London, and France, and then lived in the United States for almost two decades as an impoverished journalist. When Harper and Brothers sent him to Japan in 1890 to write something about this little-known island, he adopted the country, became in all ways a Japanese, taught in the universities, and by his own request had a Zen Buddhist funeral. Introducing a recent anthology of Hearn's writings, Kazumitsu Kato relates:

Hearn came to live in Japan permanently at the moment when the government and the upper classes sought quite frenziedly to transform Japan into a Westernized, industrial society. Hearn had little faith in this process and foresaw the evils it would bring. He and a few like-minded friends played an extraordinarily significant role in persuading Japanese officials to preserve parts of Japan's priceless artistic and religious heritage which, under the new dispensation, had been left to rot in abandoned temples and monasteries . . .

In Japan, Hearn's writings, translated into Japanese, remain a vital and important part of Japanese culture. . . . [He] achieve[d] the signal feat of being able to explain their religion successfully both to the West and to the Japanese who came after him.[149]

We have previously quoted Lafcadio Hearn on reincarnation, and add here some passages covering a wide spectrum of topics, thus concluding this chapter on nineteenth-century writers.]

Proof that a reconsideration of the problem of the Ego is everywhere forcing itself upon Occidental minds, may be found not only in the thoughtful prose of the time, but even in its poetry and romance. . . . Creative art, working under larger inspiration, is telling . . . what marvellous deepening of emotional power, may be gained in literature with the recognition of the idea of pre-existence. Even in fiction we learn that we have been living in a hemisphere only, that we have been thinking but half-thoughts, that we need a new faith to join past with future over the great parallel of the present, and so to round out our emotional world into a perfect sphere.

Kokoro[150]

I seemed to understand as never before, how the mystery that is called the Soul of me must have quickened in every form of past existence, and must as certainly continue to behold the sun, for other millions of summers, through eyes of other countless shapes of future being. . . . For thousands of years the East has been teaching that what we think or do in this life really decides—through some inevitable formation of atom-tendencies or polarities—the future place of our substance, and the future state of our sentiency. . . . Acts and thoughts, according to Buddhist doctrines, are creative. . . . What we think or do is never for the moment only, but for measureless time; it signifies some force directed to the shaping of worlds— to the making of future bliss or pain. . . . And when all the stars of the visible Night shall have burnt themselves out, those atoms will doubtless again take part in the orbing of Mind—and will tremble again in thoughts, emotions, memories—in all the joys and pains of lives still to be lived in worlds still to be evolved. . . . The very delusion of delusions is the idea of death as loss.

Kotto[151]

The child is incomparably superior to the average man in seeing the character of things. . . . If I were to ask twenty little children—say, five or six years old—to look at the same tree . . . and to tell me what they think of it, I am sure that many of them would say wonderful things. They would come much nearer to the truth than the average university student, and this just because of their absolute innocence. To the child's imagination every- thing is alive—stones, trees, plants, even household objects. For him everything has a soul. . . . Nor is this the only reason for the superiority of the child's powers of observation. His instinctive knowledge, the knowledge inherited from millions of past lives, is still fresh, not dulled by the weight of the myriad impressions of education, and personal experience.

Talks to Writers[152]

Great music is a psychical storm, agitating to unimaginable depth the mystery of the past within us. Or we might say that it is a prodigious incantation—every different instrument and voice making separate appeal to different billions of prenatal memories. There are tones that call up all ghosts of youth and joy and tenderness; there are tones that evoke all phantom pain of perished passion; there are tones that resurrect all dead sensation of majesty and might and glory—all expired exultations, all forgotten magnanimities. Well may the influence of music seem inexplicable to the man who idly dreams that his life began less than a hundred years ago! But the mystery lightens for whomsoever learns that the substance of Self is older than the sun. . . . To every ripple of melody, to every billow of harmony, there answers within him, out of the Sea of Death and Birth, some eddying immeasurable of ancient pleasure and pain.

In Ghostly Japan[153]

Hopeless . . . any attempt to tell the real pain of seeing my former births. I can say only that no combination of suffering possible to individual being could be likened to such pain—the pain of countless lives interwoven. It seemed as if every nerve of me had been prolonged into some monstrous web of sentiency spun back through a million years. . . . For, as I looked backward, I became double, quadruple, octuple . . . I became hundreds and thousands—and feared with the terror of thousands—and despaired with the anguish of thousands . . . yet knew the pleasure of none. . . .

Then in the moment when sentiency itself seemed bursting into dissolution, one divine touch ended the frightful vision, and brought again to me the simple consciousness of the single present. Oh! how unspeakably delicious that sudden shrinking back out of the multiplicity into unity!—that immense, immeasurable collapse of Self into the blind oblivious numbness of individuality!

"To others also," said the voice of the divine one who had thus saved me—"to others in the like state it has been permitted to see something of their pre-existence. But no one of them ever could endure to look far. Power to see all former births belongs only to those eternally released from the bonds of Self. Such exist outside of illusion—outside of form and name; and pain cannot come nigh them. But to you, remaining in illusion, not even the Buddha could give power to look back more than a little way."

Gleanings in Buddha-Fields[154]

I remember when a boy lying on my back in the grass, gazing into the summer blue above me, and wishing I could melt into it,—become a part of it. . . . Now I think that in those days I was really close to a great truth,—touching it, in fact, without the faintest suspicion of its existence. I mean the truth that the wish *to become* is reasonable in direct ratio to its largeness,—or, in other words, that the more you wish to be, the wiser you are; while the wish *to have* is apt to be foolish in proportion to its largeness. Cosmic law permits us very few of the countless things that we wish to have, but will help us to become all that we can possibly wish to be. . . .

By wanting to be, the monad makes itself the elephant, the eagle, or the man. By wanting to be, the man should become a god. Perhaps on this tiny globe, lighted by only a tenth-rate yellow sun, he will not have time to become a god; but who dare assert that his wish cannot project itself to mightier systems illuminated by vaster suns, and there reshape and invest him with the forms and powers of divinity? Who dare even say that his wish may not expand him beyond the Limits of Form, and make him one with Omnipotence? And Omnipotence, without asking, can have much brighter and bigger playthings than the Moon.

Exotics and Retrospectives[155]

TWENTIETH CENTURY— AGE OF TRANSITION

The literature on reincarnation in the twentieth century has grown to such proportions that we can aim only at offering a choice sampling. Scientists, psychologists, and philosophers who should properly be included in this chapter have been reserved for chapter 6.

CHARLES KELSEY GAINES (1854–1944)

American Educator

[Dr. Charles Kelsey Gaines was professor of Greek philosophy at St. Lawrence University. *Gorgo*,[1] his historical novel of ancient Athens, is precious for its stories of Socrates teaching a child—one of which is given here. We open with a selection from the prologue to *Gorgo*.]

I stopped short; I flung down the book. "It is a lie," I cried bitterly, "a cruel, hateful lie," I almost shouted,—and the whole class stared at me in amazement. A strange outburst was that for the dingy, drowsy Greek room of the little New England college. I was as much surprised as any; I stood confounded at myself. For then it was that I remembered. The passage which I was translating seemed innocent enough—to all the rest. We were reading at sight . . . the Twelfth Oration of Lysias. . . .

"And although he has been the author of all these and still other disasters and disgraces, both old and new, both small and great, some dare to profess themselves his friends; although it was not for the people that Theramenes died, but because of his own villainy" —

Then I choked and stopped. Tears swam in my eyes, and a hot flush scalded my cheeks. . . . "It is a lie," I burst forth. "A cruel, hateful lie. . . . I will not read it—I will not read another line." . . . For the past had opened like a darkness lightning-cleft; all in one moment I felt the injustices of ages, the shame of an aeon of scorn—and they asked me to read against myself the lying record. . . . After that they nicknamed me Theramenes: I was nicknamed after myself, and none suspected. . . .

Forget! I have far too much to remind me. What is this seething democracy in which we live but Athens renewed? In a thousand ways I am reminded— but I forbear. Yet—do you imagine that I alone among living men have walked those ancient streets? Not so: but the rest do not remember.

[From Chapter Seven, "A Walk with Socrates":]

He drew me very close upon his shoulder. "Do you not always know what is right? Think carefully, little one; do you not always know?"

I pondered a long while. "Yes," I answered, "I do know, when I stop to remember; but how do I know?"

"You have said it. You remember."

"But when did I learn?" I cried, in astonishment. . . .

"It is hard to explain," he said. . . . "Do you see those walls? They stretch far; but you saw that they had a beginning, and you know that they have an end. For all things that have a beginning have an end. But that which has no beginning can have no end. Can you think otherwise?"

"But is there anything like that?"

"You know the meaning of what men call 'time,'" he said. "Can you think that it had any beginning? or that it will ever have an end?"

"No; it goes on always. But time—it isn't anything at all," I persisted.

"Well," he said, "you, at least, are something; for you can think and know. But can you remember when first you began to be?"

"No; I cannot remember."

"Perhaps, then, there is something within you that had no beginning. And if that is so, it has had plenty of time to learn. Some think,'' he said, ''that what we call learning is really only remembering. . . . And if there is something within us that was not born and can never die, but is like time itself, can this be anything else than that part of us which thinks and knows, which men call the soul?''

''It must be that,'' I said; ''for they put the rest in the ground or burn it up. I never understood about the soul before.''

''And now,'' said he, ''which part do you think is best worth caring for,— that part which we cast away like a useless garment when it is torn by violence or grows old and worn, or that part which lives always?''

''It is foolish to ask me that; of course it is the part that doesn't die,'' I answered.

''I am glad,'' said he, ''that you think this a foolish question. Yet there are many who do not understand even this; for just as some care only for clothes, some care only for their bodies. And that, perhaps, is why people do not remember all at once, but very slowly and not clearly, just as one would see things through a thick veil, such as the women sometimes wear before men. It is only when this veil, which is our flesh, is woven very light and fine, or when it has grown old and is worn very thin, that we can see anything through it plainly; and even then all that we see looks misty and does not seem real.''

''Yes, but the women can peep over,'' I explained.

''And we, too, doubtless, can peep over sometimes,'' he answered, smiling.

GEORGE BERNARD SHAW (1856–1950)
Irish Playwright, Novelist, and Critic

[From the epilogue to *Saint Joan:*]

JOAN   And now tell me: shall I rise from the dead, and come back to you a living woman? . . . What! Must I burn again? Are none of you ready to receive me? . . . O God that madest this beautiful earth, when will it be ready to receive Thy saints? How long, O lord, how long?

[From *Back to Methuselah,* Part I, ''The Garden of Eden,'' followed by some excerpts from Part II, ''The Twentieth Century'':]

THE SERPENT   The serpent never dies. Some day you shall see me come out of this beautiful skin; a new snake with a new and lovelier skin. That is birth. . . . I made the word ''dead'' to describe my old skin that I cast when I was renewed. I call that renewal being born.

EVE Born is a beautiful word.

THE SERPENT Why not be born again and again as I am, new and beautiful every time?

SAVVY I believe the old people are the new people, reincarnated. I suspect I am Eve. I am very fond of apples, and they always disagree with me.

CONRAD You are Eve in a sense. The Eternal Life persists, only it wears out Its bodies and minds and gets new ones, like new clothes. You are only a new hat and frock on Eve.

FRANKLYN Yes. Bodies and minds ever better fitted to carry out Its eternal pursuit.

LUBIN (with quiet skepticism) What pursuit, may one ask, Mr. Barnabas?

FRANKLYN The pursuit of omnipotence and omniscience. Greater power and greater knowledge: these are what we are all pursuing even at the risk of our lives and the sacrifice of our pleasures. Evolution is that pursuit and nothing else. It is the path to godhead. A man differs from a microbe only in being further on the path.

ARTHUR CONAN DOYLE (1859–1930)

British Novelist

[In *The Adventures of Conan Doyle,*[2] a recent biography of this famous author, he is shown to be more interesting and fascinating than his fictional creation Sherlock Holmes. The biographer, Charles Higham, surprisingly discloses Conan Doyle's passionate interest in the world of the occult, particularly spiritualism. On occasion he also had an interest in theosophy, and when his wife died, he "returned to his peregrinations in Blavatskyland," to use the words of the novelist Paul Theroux.[3] In 1926 Sir Arthur wrote a two-volume *History of Spiritualism,* in which he remarked:]

When the question is asked, "Where were we before we were born?" we have a definite answer in the system of slow development by incarnation, with long intervals of spirit rest between, while otherwise we have no answer, though we must admit that it is inconceivable that we have been born in time for eternity. Existence afterwards seems to postulate existence before.

As to the natural question "Why, then, do we not remember such existences?" we may point out that such remembrance would enormously complicate our present life, and that such existences may well form a cycle which is all clear to us when we come to the end of it, when perhaps we may see a whole rosary of lives threaded upon one personality.

The convergence of so many lines of theosophic and Eastern thought upon this one conclusion, and the explanation which it affords in the supplementary doctrine of Karma of the apparent injustice of any single life, are arguments in its favor, and so perhaps are those vague recognitions and memories which are occasionally too definite to be easily explained as atavistic impressions.[4]

JAMES M. BARRIE (1860–1937)
Scottish Novelist and Dramatist

[James M. Barrie once wrote that ''if we unlock the rooms of the far past we can peer in and see ourselves busily occupied in beginning to become you and me.''[5] In his play *The Admirable Crichton,* an English lord, his lazy, arrogant daughters, and a few others are shipwrecked on a remote island with the family's very proper butler Crichton, who soon transforms the place into an idyllic paradise. By unanimous acclaim he becomes their governor, and the lord and ladies willing servants. A possible explanation for Crichton's extraordinary powers is offered in the third act.]

CRICHTON   He had a chance—that butler—in these two years of becoming a man . . . There have been many failures, but there has been some success . . . That butler seems a far-away figure to me now, and not myself. I hail him, but we scarce know each other. . . . for in my soul he is now abhorrent . . . But if I thought it best for you I'd haul him back. . . .

LADY MARY   You say these things, but you say them like a king. . . .

CRICHTON   A king! Some people hold that the soul but leaves one human tenement for another, and so lives on through all the ages. I have occasionally thought of late that, in some past existence, I may have been a king. It has all come to me so naturally, not as if I had to work it out, but—as—if—I—remembered. . . . It may have been; you hear me, it may have been.

LADY MARY   It may have been. . . . You are the most wonderful man I have ever known, and I am not afraid.[6]

ERNEST THOMPSON SETON (1860–1946)
British-born American Nature Writer and Artist
Founder of Boy Scouts of America

[Ernest Thompson Seton, author of nature books for young people, wrote and exquisitely illustrated some forty volumes during his long life. Creatively active into his late eighties, he was on the eve of a ten-thousand-mile lecture tour when he died at Seton Village in New Mexico. Seton was characterized by *Time* magazine (November 4, 1946) as "a man who, in an age of sweeping mechanization, had loved the natural earth, its seasons and its creatures with rare intensity and an unusual power to communicate his vision to others."

Seton did much for the American Indian, and together with his wife of later years, Julia Seton—an authority on Indian life—wrote the small volume *The Gospel of the Red Man*. Mrs. Seton tells in the foreword of a crucial event in the life of the "Chief," a title by which Seton was known the world over from the time he founded and headed the Boy Scouts of America in 1910. The event occurred five years before he founded that organization.]

In March, 1905, we were in Los Angeles on a lecture tour. The morning after the lecture, we were met at the Van Nuys Hotel by some Eastern friends who, addressing the Chief, said: "We have a message for you. There is a strange woman in the Hills who wishes to see you." Accordingly, we took the tram to the end of the track, then set out on foot to climb what, I think, are now called the Beverly Hills. On the green slope higher up was a small white cottage; in front of this, a woman dressed like a farmer's wife. . . .

She was introduced to us as a Mahatma from India, although born in Iowa. She had left her home as a small child, had spent many years studying under the Great Masters, and was now back on a mission to America. She was a strange-looking person. We could not tell whether she was thirty or a hundred and thirty years old. . . . Her eyes had the faraway veiled look of a mystic. Her talk was commonplace as she served coffee and cakes. We wondered why she had sent the summons. Finally, after an hour, we rose to leave.

Then, suddenly, she turned on the Chief with a total change of look and demeanor. Her eyes blazed as she said, in tones of authority: "Don't you know who you are?" We were all shocked into silence as she continued: "You are a Red Indian Chief, reincarnated to give the message of the Red-man to the White race, so much in need of it. Why don't you get busy? Why don't you set about your job?"

The Chief was moved like one conscience-stricken. He talked not at all on the road back, and the incident was not mentioned for long after. But I know that the strange woman had focussed his thoughts on the mission he had been vaguely working on for some years. He has never since ceased to concentrate on what she had termed "his job."[7]

GUSTAV MAHLER (1860–1911)
German Composer

[Richard Specht, Gustav Mahler's close friend and biographer, relates of his visit to the composer in Hamburg in 1895:]

In the course of the conversation Mahler said very emphatically: "We all return; it is this certainty that gives meaning to life and it does not make the slightest difference whether or not in a later incarnation we remember the former life. What counts is not the individual and his comfort, but the great aspiration to the perfect and the pure which goes on in each incarnation."[8]

[Deryck Cook, the renowned Mahler authority, in his program notes for Mahler's Third Symphony put out by London Records,[9] relates that the symphony was begun in 1895, the very period mentioned above, and that some sort of reincarnation of life through the kingdoms is clearly intimated. The title of the symphony was "The Joyful Knowledge," which came from Nietzsche's book of the same name. (Nietzsche's views on rebirth will receive attention later.) Cook states that "the title was borrowed by Mahler to indicate a new-found optimism, or rather a kind of mystical revelation of the validity and purpose of existence." Mahler is quoted in a letter as stating that he wanted to express in the work an evolutionary development of nature that hides "within itself everything that is frightful, great, and also lovely." "Of course no one ever understands this. It always strikes me as odd that most people when they speak of 'nature,' think only of flowers, little birds, and woodsy smells. No one knows the god Dionysus, the great Pan. There now! You have a sort of programme—that is, a sample of how I make music. Everywhere and always, it is only the voice of nature!" The vast first movement represented "nature in its totality . . . awakened from fathomless silence that it may ring and resound." The subsequent movements portray the stages of life from vegetable and animal life through mankind, back to the omniscient, omnipotent source.]

MAURICE MAETERLINCK (1862–1949)
Belgian Poet, Dramatist, Essayist

Let us return to reincarnation . . . for there never was a more beautiful, a juster, a purer, a more moral, fruitful and consoling, nor to a certain point, a more probable creed than theirs [the theosophists]. It alone, with its doctrine of successive expiations and purifications, accounts for all the physical and intellectual inequalities, all the social iniquities, all the hideous injustices of fate. But the quality of a creed is no evidence of its truth. Even though it is the religion of six hundred millions of mankind, the nearest to the mysterious origins, the only one that is not odious and the least absurd of all, it will have to do what the others have not done, to bring unimpeachable testimony; and what it has given us hitherto is but the first shadow of a proof begun.

On Eternity[10]

We parted, and not a word was spoken, but at one and the same moment had we understood our inexpressible thought. We know now that another love had sprung to life, a love that demands not the words, the little attentions and smiles of ordinary love. We have never met again. Perhaps centuries will elapse before we ever do meet again.

> Much is to learn, much to forget,
> Through worlds I shall traverse not a few

before we shall again find ourselves in the same movement of the soul as on that evening; but we can well afford to wait. . . .

Perhaps [human beings] do not yet know what the word "to love" means. . . . It is a thing that lies a thousand fathoms deeper, where our softest, swiftest, strongest words cannot reach it. At moments we might believe it to be a recollection, furtive but excessively keen, of the great primitive unity. . . . The souls of all our brethren are ever hovering about us, craving for a caress, and only waiting for the signal. But how many beings there are who all their life long have not dared make such a signal! It is the disaster of our entire existence that we live thus away from our soul, and stand in such dread of its slightest movement. Did we but allow it to smile frankly in its silence and its radiance, we should be already living an eternal life.

The Treasure of the Humble[11]

WINCENTY LUTOSLAWSKI (1863–?)

Polish Educator

[The extract below is from Professor Wincenty Lutoslawski's *Pre-existence and Reincarnation*. At Harvard in 1899, William James wrote the preface to Lutoslawski's work *The World of Souls*, a book that also discusses reincarnation. James wrote: "The author of the book to which I write this Preface has shown by that weighty English work, *The Logic of Plato*, that he is an accomplished philosopher in the technical and scholarly sense of that much-abused term. . . . [He] honours philosophy; he even adores it, along its platonising traditions; but he finds little use in its skeptical scruples and inhibitions. He is a genuine transcendentalist, in the Emersonian sense."]

In the nineteenth century the number of those who professed belief in palingenesis increased very considerably all over the world, but in no other country is the unanimity in this respect so complete as in Poland. All the greatest poets of Poland, such as Mickiewicz, Slowacki, Krasinski, Norwid, Wyspianski, mention their past lives as a matter of course, and the greatest masterpiece of Polish literature, the *Spirit-King* of Slowacki, is a mystic autobiography in which the poet narrates his past incarnations. Besides the poets also the famous philosopher Cieszkowski and the mystic Towianski admit palingenesis.[12]

DAVID LLOYD GEORGE (1863–1945)
British Prime Minister (1916–1922)

[In a diary entry for September 3, 1919, Lord Riddell recorded these words of his friend Lloyd George:]

When I was a boy, the thought of Heaven used to frighten me more than the thought of Hell. I pictured Heaven as a place where there would be perpetual Sundays with perpetual services, from which there would be no escape, as the Almighty, assisted by cohorts of angels, would always be on the look-out for those who did not attend. It was a horrible nightmare. The conventional Heaven with its angels perpetually singing, etc., nearly drove me mad in my youth and made me an atheist for ten years. My opinion is that we shall be reincarnated . . . and that hereafter we shall suffer or benefit in accordance with what we have done in this world. For example, the employer who sweats his workpeople will be condemned to be sweated himself. . . .[13]

HENRY FORD (1863–1947)
American Businessman

[The following interview with Henry Ford appeared in the Hearst papers for April 27 and 28, 1938:]

When I was a young man, I, like so many others, was bewildered. I found myself asking the question. . . . "What are we here for?" I found no answer. Without some answer to that question life is empty, useless. Then one day a friend handed me a book.[14]. . . That little book gave me the answer I was seeking. It changed my whole life. From emptiness and uselessness, it changed my outlook upon life to purpose and meaning. I believe that we are here now and will come back again. . . . Of this I am sure . . . that we *are* here for a purpose. And that we go on. Mind and memory—they are the eternals.

[Another interview with Ford is reported by George Sylvester Viereck:]

I adopted the theory of Reincarnation when I was twenty-six. . . . Religion offered nothing to the point. . . . Even work could not give me com-

plete satisfaction. Work is futile if we cannot utilize the experience we collect
in one life in the next. When I discovered Reincarnation it was as if I had
found a universal plan. I realized that there was a chance to work out my
ideas. Time was no longer limited. I was no longer a slave to the hands of the
clock. . . . Genius is experience. Some seem to think that it is a gift or
talent, but it is the fruit of long experience in many lives. Some are older
souls than others, and so they know more. . . .

The discovery of Reincarnation put my mind at ease. . . . If you preserve
a record of this conversation, write it so that it puts men's minds at ease. I
would like to communicate to others the calmness that the long view of life
gives to us.[15]

RUDYARD KIPLING (1865–1936)

British Author

[In chapter 6, we will be quoting from the *Diary and Sundry Observations of
Thomas Edison*. Here we take one sentence: "Rudyard Kipling, in one of his
best stories, had a London bank clerk get a glimpse of a former reincarnation
when he was a Greek galley slave."[16] This is Kipling's "The Finest Story in
the World" and is contained in his volume *Many Inventions*.[17] The hero
envisions writing a book containing the memories of his previous lives and
lifting the veils of future ones, but after falling in love with a lady, the
memory gradually fades, and so the "finest story in the world" was never
written.

The first poem is from "When Earth's Last Picture Is Painted."]

When earth's last picture is painted, and the tubes are twisted and dried,
When the oldest colors are faded, and the youngest critic has died;
We shall rest, and faith, we shall need it—lie down for an aeon or two,
Till the Master of all Good Workmen shall put us to work anew.[18]

[The lines that follow appeared as the opening editorial in the *Wall Street
Journal* (June 10, 1975) under the caption "Epitaph for New York City."
Their source is Kipling's 1919 poem "The Gods of the Copybook Headings." It should be explained that each morning in the schoolroom of old a
maxim or proverb was displayed that the children were obliged to copy into
their notebooks.]

As I pass through my incarnations in every age and race,
I make my proper prostrations to the Gods of the Market-Place.
Peering through reverent fingers I watch them flourish and fall.
And the Gods of the Copybook Headings, I notice, outlast them
   all . . .

They denied that Wishes were Horses; they denied that a Pig had
    Wings.
So we worshipped the Gods of the Market who promised these beauti-
    ful things.

On the first Feminian Sandstones we were promised the Fuller Life
(Which started by loving our neighbor and ended by loving his wife)
Till our women had no more children and the men lost reason and faith,
And the Gods of the Copybook Headings said: "The Wages of Sin is
    Death."

In the Carboniferous Epoch we were promised abundance for all,
By robbing selected Peter to pay for collective Paul;
But, though we had plenty of money, there was nothing our money
    could buy,
And the Gods of the Copybook Headings said: "If you don't work you
    die."

Then the Gods of the Market tumbled, and their smooth-tongued
    wizards withdrew,
And the hearts of the meanest were humbled and began to believe it
    was true
That All is not Gold that Glitters, and Two and Two make Four—
And the Gods of the Copybook Headings limped up to explain it once
    more. . . .[19]

JEAN SIBELIUS (1865–1957)

Finnish Composer

[A friend of Sibelius's family reports to the editors that Jean Sibelius spoke
openly with intimate friends of his conviction in reincarnation, and also of
what appeared to him to be remembrances of previous lives. The former
music critic, and later drama critic, for the *New York Times,* Howard Taub-
man, stated in an article in honor of Sibelius on the occasion of his ninetieth
birthday:]

The interrelationship between life and art is one of Sibelius' chief concerns. . . . Sibelius' identification with the fields, the woods, the sea and the
sky is so profound that it has always permeated his music. . . . As a boy,
Sibelius wandered in the wilderness of his native province of Häme. Birds
always fascinated him. "Millions of years ago, in my previous incarnations,"
he once told Jalas [his son-in-law], "I must have been related to swans or
wild geese, because I can still feel that affinity."[20]

✳ ✳ ✳

Ireland's Literary Renaissance[21]

[In his 1937 biography of George Russell, *A Memoir of AE,* John Eglinton observed: "Probably there has never been in any country a period of literary activity which has not been preceded or accompanied by some stimulation of the religious interest. Anyone in search of this in Ireland at this time may find it if he looks for it. . . . He will find it, unless he disdains to look in that direction, in the ferment caused in the minds of a group of young men by the early activities of the Theosophical Movement in Dublin. The proof is, not only that there was no other religious movement in Ireland at this time, but that Yeats and Russell, who were to be the principal leaders of the Literary Revival, were closely associated with this one."[22] Stephen Gwynn in *Irish Literature and Drama* mentions that these two men "were to dominate the entire literary revival and affect the whole intellectual life of Ireland in their time."[23]

The Theosophical Movement and its extensive literature on reincarnation will receive treatment in chapter 7. Here we merely concern ourselves with the effects of its teachings in Ireland. Ernest Boyd's *Ireland's Literary Renaissance* contains a chapter "The Dublin Mystics," with the subtitle "The Theosophical Movement." He writes:

> The Theosophical Movement provided a literary, artistic and intellectual centre from which radiated influences whose effect was felt even by those who did not belong to it. Further, it formed a rallying-ground for all the keenest of the older and younger intellects, from John O'Leary and George Sigerson, to W. B. Yeats and AE. It brought into contact the most diverse personalities, and definitely widened the scope of the new literature, emphasizing its marked advance on all previous national movements. . . . It was an intellectual melting-pot from which the true and solid elements of nationality emerged strengthened, while the dross was lost.[24]

In addition to Yeats and AE, Boyd mentions the prominent part played in the awakening by Charles Johnston, Charles Weekes, and other writers associated with the Dublin Theosophical Society. The society was founded in 1886 by Johnston, a boyhood friend of Yeats, and AE joined in 1887 at Yeats's instigation. From 1892 to 1897 they published a monthly magazine, *The Irish Theosophist.* William Q. Judge, the Dublin-born American theosophist and close colleague of Madame Blavatsky, was in intimate contact with the Dublin group and was their special hero.[25] James Joyce in *Ulysses* speaks of the group's regard for "Judge, the noblest Roman of them all."[26] AE wrote in 1932: "Judge was the most impressive man I ever met, not by any air of dignity but simply from what he was.''[27] At the time of Judge's death, AE wrote in *The Irish Theosophist* (April 1896) concerning Judge's first meeting with the group in Dublin in 1892:

> I hardly thought what he was while he spoke, but on departing . . . an inner exhaltation lasting for months witnessed his power. . . . Shall I not say the truth I think? Here was a hero out of the remote, antique, giant ages come among us wearing but on the surface the vesture of our little day. We, too, came out of the past, but in forgetfulness; he with memory and power soon regained.

We turn now to a brief consideration of Yeats, to be followed shortly by selections from AE's writings. Then James Stephens and James Joyce will receive attention. As all these writers frequently dwelt on reincarnation themes, their work must be regarded as of some importance in contributing to the present interest in the subject.]

WILLIAM BUTLER YEATS (1865–1939)

Irish Poet and Playwright

[The reviewer of the *Collected Poems of W. B. Yeats* in *Newsweek* suggests that Yeats's perception of rebirth did not come in intuitive flashes, but was the result of study and reflection. The reviewer adds: "Toward the end of his life, Yeats began to find personal strength and a fiery poetic imagery in the realm of the transcendental. . . . His interest in religion was especially confusing to many readers because of the unorthodox, occult terms in which he expressed it. As a youth, he was fascinated by the Russian theosophist Madame Blavatsky, and he went on to explore other avenues of Eastern mysticism."[28]

In *Later Phase in the Development of W. B. Yeats*, Shankar Mokashi-Punekar remarks:

> How much Yeats owes to the popular texts of Theosophy can hardly be missed by an unprejudiced observer. Madame Blavatsky herself uses the term "Principles," to refer to the crypto-natural elements of man. A comparison of the chapter [on the afterdeath states] entitled "On the Kamaloka and Devachan" in her *The Key to Theosophy* with Yeats's "A Soul in Judgment," would convince even a casual reader that Yeats was indeed continuing the same wisdom. . . .[29]

One of Yeats's last poems, "Under Ben Bulben," is dated September 4, 1938, three months before his death. It concludes with his inscribed epitaph and gives directions for his burial. The second stanza reads:]

Many times man lives and dies
Between his two eternities,
That of race and that of soul,
And ancient Ireland knew it all.
Whether man die in his bed
Or the rifle knocks him dead,
A brief parting from those dear
Is the worst man has to fear.
Though grave-diggers' toil is long,
Sharp their spades, their muscles strong,
They but thrust their buried men
Back in the human mind again.[30]

GEORGE W. RUSSELL (1867–1935)

Irish Author, Painter, Editor

[The British scientist Raynor Johnson writes of George Russell in *The Light and the Gate:*

If it is greatness to become the embodiment of spirituality to many others, AE may be counted probably the greatest Irishman of his day. . . . All who met him felt that he was "different"—in some way apart from them, as though he had strayed into this world from an older and wiser one with which he was more familiar. . . . Dr. Monk Gibbon said, "He saw things in their eternal procession."

He had an intense sympathy with man in his outcast state. . . . He [wrote]: "I remember the deep peace which came to me when I had the intuition that Christ, Prometheus, are in every heart, that we all took upon ourselves the burden of the world like the Christ, and were foreseers as Prometheus was, of the agony of the labour he undertook, until the chaos is subdued and wrought in some likeness to the image in the divine imagination."[31] Much of his poetry speaks of man at this age-long task—the outcast from the "Ancestral Self"— the "fallen majesty"—making his slow way back again.[32]

Some authors speak of AE's connection with theosophy and the Dublin Theosophical Society, referred to on a previous page, as no more than a phase of AE's early development that he outgrew. His own actions and words tell a different story. He reorganized the Dublin Theosophical Society under the name the Hermetic Society, a group that subsequently attracted many of the younger Irish poets. He did this in order to focus on the work and teachings of the original founders of the theosophical movement, which the prominent theosophists of the day had been ignoring.

AE actively conducted the Hermetic Society until his departure for London in 1933, two years before his death. He wrote concerning the work of this group: "It waxed and waned and waxed again, and I felt inwardly satisfied that they all more or less passed through a bath of Theosophical ideas. . . . My own writing is trivial, and its only merit is that it was written in a spiritual atmosphere generated by a study of H. P. Blavatsky and the sacred books . . . the *Bhagavad-Gita, Upanishads,* Patanjali, and one or two other scriptures."[33] Captain Patrick Bowen, a close friend of AE, quotes the latter as saying that having bathed in Madame Blavatsky's *Secret Doctrine, The Voice of the Silence,* and *The Key to Theosophy,* "I marvelled what I could have done to merit birth in an age wherein such wisdom was on offer to all who could beg, borrow, or steal a copy of those works."[34] (Selections from *The Secret Doctrine* and *The Key to Theosophy* will be found in chapter 7. Extracts from *The Voice of the Silence*—or The Book of the Golden Precepts— were given in chapter 3 under "Tibetan Buddhism.")

Russell's best-known work, *The Candle of Vision,* apparently had an influence on Jung. This is learned from an editor's footnote to a letter of the psychiatrist to Sir Herbert Read. Jung wrote: "The great problem of our time is that we don't understand what is happening to the world. We are confronted with the darkness of our soul, the unconscious. . . . We have simply got to listen to what the psyche spontaneously says to us. . . . Who is the awe-inspiring guest who knocks at our door portentously?" This guest, the editor comments, may be the same as the fantasy figure of Jung's earliest childhood dream. In the 1920s, he adds, Jung "encountered a parallel figure, 'the pilgrim of eternity,' in *The Candle of Vision* by the Irish poet AE, which impressed him profoundly."[35] Quoting now from that work:]

From long pondering I have come to believe in the eternity of the spirit and that it is an inhabitant of many spheres, for I know not how otherwise I can interpret to myself the myriad images that as memories or imaginations cling to it, following it into the body as birds follow the leader in the migratory flock. . . . To those who cry out against romance I would say, You yourself are romance. You are the lost prince herding obscurely among the swine. The romance of your spirit is the most marvellous of stories. Your wanderings have been greater than those of Ulysses. . . .

Looking back . . . through the vistas of memory I see breaking in upon the images of this world forms of I know not what antiquity. I walk out of strange cities steeped in the jewel glow and gloom of evening, or sail in galleys over the silvery waves of the antique ocean. I reside in tents, or in palace chambers, go abroad in chariots, meditate in cyclopean buildings, am worshipper of the Earth gods upon the mountains, lie tranced in Egyptian crypts, or brush with naked body through the long sunlit grasses of the prairies. Endlessly the procession of varying forms goes back into remote yesterdays of the world. . . . Are they not . . . memories of the spirit incarnated many times?

And if so, again I ask myself is it only on earth there has been this long ancestry of self? For there is another self in me which seemed to know not the world but revealed itself to the listening bodily life in cosmic myths, in remote legends of the Children of Darkness and the Children of Light, and of the revolt against heaven. And another self seemed to bring with it vision or memory of elemental beings, the shining creatures of water and wood, or who break out in opalescent color from the rocks or hold their court beneath the ponderous hills. And there was another self which was akin to the gloomy world of the shades, but recoiled shuddering from them. And there was yet another self which sought out after wisdom, and all these other selves and their wisdom and memories were but tributary to it. . . .

It is only when I turn to the literature of vision and intuition, to the sacred books and to half sacred tradition, to the poets and seers, that I find a grandiose conception of nature in which every spiritual experience is provided for. . . . What little I know finds its place in the universe of their vision. Whether they are Syrian, Greek, Egyptian or Hindu, the writers of the sacred books seem to me as men who had all gazed upon the same august vision and reported of the same divinity.[36]

[AE made his sole visit to the United States in the 1920s, having been invited by Vice-President Henry Wallace, before he became secretary of agriculture. Russell had long worked in Irish agricultural affairs, having edited the *Irish Homestead* for twenty years and later the *Irish Statesman* for another ten. The architect Claude Bragdon in *Merely Players* records his impressions of AE when the latter visited New York. Bragdon met him first at the Poetry Society's dinner in his honor, where each speaker in turn assured everyone that AE was the most loved man in Ireland. Then at a small gathering, after discussing "matters of great moment pertaining to the inner life," Russell told this story which hinted at the origin of his pseudonym AE:]

He said that when he was a boy he was just like other boys . . . except that he seemed to have a more vivid imagination, for he was always telling himself wonderful stories of gods and demi-gods, and miraculous happenings in some Valhalla, and to these characters he assigned names. He had no other idea but that he invented these stories and these names.

But one day while waiting at the desk of the village library for the librarian to bring him a story book, he happened to glance at the open page of a book that was lying there, and his eye encountered the word "Aeon." He declared that his surprise and excitement were so great that he left the library empty-handed and walked about the streets for two hours before he could muster up sufficient calmness and courage to ask the librarian what book it was, and if he might look at it. For the name Aeon was one which he had given to the hero of one of his own stories, a name which he regarded as peculiarly his own . . . and it was upsetting to discover that such was plainly not the case.

The book proved to be a treatise on Gnostic religion and cosmogony and in it, to his utter amazement, he found recorded, in a mass of legendary lore, those very stories which he thought he had invented—even the names of the characters were the same. This forced him to the conclusion that either his imaginings were recovered memories of things learned or experienced in some antecedent life, or that in some inexplicable manner he had tapped, so to speak, the memory of nature.[37]

[AE discussed these possible past-life recalls with the biologist Sir Julian Huxley; their conversation will be reported later. He must have also spoken about them to J. B. Priestley, for when writing in 1950 to a biographer of AE, Priestley remarked that "somebody like AE does make one sympathetic to the belief" in reincarnation.[38]]

JAMES STEPHENS (1882–1950)
Irish Poet and Novelist

[In Hilary Pyle's biography *James Stephens,* she calls his work "the important bridge between the first Irish writers of the Celtic Twilight period and the new, more sophisticated writers."[39] "As early as *Insurrections,*" she states, "Stephens saw that in evolution lies our hope of deliverance," while "in *The Hill of Vision* he examined it in connection with the doctrine of reincarnation, picturing all live things coming to the Source of Life for refreshment before they set out again."[40] In her chapter "The Influence of Blake and of Theosophy," Miss Pyle mentions that in *The Demi-Gods* Stephens attempted an account of the theosophical idea of evolution, and spoke of reincarnation in this way: "While generation succeeds generation a man has to fight the same fight. At the end he wins, and he never has to fight that battle again, and then he is ready for Paradise."[41] Quoting the poem "A Prelude and a Song" from *The Hill of Vision:*]

> Deep Womb of Promise! Back to thee again
> And forth, revivified, all living things
> Do come and go,
> Forever wax and wane into and from thy garden;
> There the flower springs,
> Therein does grow
> The bud of hope, the miracle to come,
> For whose dear advent we are striving, dumb
> And joyless. . . .

Until our back and forth, our life and death
And life again, our going and return
Prepare the way: until our latest breath,
Deep-drawn and agonized, for him shall burn
A path: for him prepare
Laughter and love and singing everywhere,
A morning and a sunrise and a day![42]

JAMES JOYCE (1882–1941)

Irish Author

[Referring first to Stuart Gilbert's well-known work *James Joyce's Ulysses,*
prepared in Paris with Joyce's constant help, we quote from one section
amusingly titled "MET-HIM-PIKE-HOSES":

In the first episode of Mr. Bloom's day ("Calypso") several themes are
stated which will recur frequently throughout *Ulysses,* and it is characteristic of
the Joycean method that one of the most important of these leitmotifs should be
presented in a casual manner and a ludicrous context. Mrs. Bloom has been
reading in bed *Ruby: The Pride of the Ring* . . . She asks her husband what
that word in the book means—"met him pike hoses." He leaned downward
and read near her polished thumbnail. "Metempsychosis?" . . . Mr. Bloom
explains. "Some people believe that we go on living in another body after
death, that we lived before. They call it reincarnation. That we all lived before
on the earth thousands of years ago or on some other planet. They say we have
forgotten it. Some say they remember their past lives." . . .
    The passages [several more of which are quoted] indicate the persistence of
the idea, or, rather, word "metempsychosis," in Mr. Bloom's memory. But it is
not only as one of Mr. Bloom's possessions that the doctrine of reincarnation is
mentioned in Ulysses. Allusions, direct or indirect, to it are frequent, and . . .
[it] is, in fact, one of the directive themes of the work. . . . References to the
eternal recurrence of personalities and things abound in Ulysses and many of
the obscurer passages can be readily understood if this fact be borne in mind.[43]

In this study of *Ulysses,* Gilbert tells of Joyce's contact with theosophy and
the Irish theosophists, and writes in the preface: "When we chanced to be
discussing . . . Mme. Blavatsky's entertaining *Isis Unveiled,* [Joyce] asked
me if I had read any of Sinnett's work. (A. P. Sinnett, a cultured and intelligent man, was a member of Mme. Blavatsky's circle in India, and her biographer.) Naturally I took the hint and procured his [volumes on theosophy]
Esoteric Buddhism and *Growth of the Soul,* well-written books from which
Joyce certainly derived some of his material."
In James Atherton's *The Books of the Wake* he states in the chapter "Other

Sacred Books'' used in Joyce's *Finnegans Wake:* "There are many schools of Buddhism and the first attempt to unite them was made by an American, Colonel H. S. Olcott [president-founder of the Theosophical Society], whose *Buddhist Catechism* was used by Joyce. . . . [Joyce] believed that rebirth was the recompense for death; not . . . the result of ignorance and unsatisfied desire, and the cause of sorrow. It is probably because of their insistence on rebirth that Joyce combines Vishnuism with Buddhism."[44] The American poet Eugene Jolas writes that in *Finnegans Wake* Joyce has "painted the rotations of the wheel of life." "He has made a hero out of Time: incessant creation and return. He rebuilt the city across the ages in Finn's multiple metamorphoses."[45]

Leon Edel, in his book on Joyce, remarks that "all of Joyce, from the sermons on Hell in the *Portrait of the Artist* to the last words of *Finnegans Wake,* echoes of Life, Death and Resurrection; the cycles of history, which from the beginning measure the life of Man, were ever present in his mind . . ."[46] The *Portrait of the Artist* concludes with these words of the hero Stephen Dedalus as he ventures forth into the world to embark upon his career: "I GO TO ENCOUNTER FOR THE MILLIONTH TIME THE REALITY OF EXPERIENCE AND TO FORGE IN THE SMITHY OF MY SOUL, THE UNCREATED CONSCIENCE OF MY RACE. . . ."]

[The following selections resume the birth date sequence.]

ROMAIN ROLLAND (1866–1944)
French Author

[There is apparently no end to the coming to the West of gurus from India, and it is beyond the scope of the present work to attempt to keep track of them. They, of course, have played a part in feeding the fire of interest in rebirth. One of the early movements was the Neo-Vedanta of Ramakrishna and his disciple Swami Vivekananda. Ramakrishna missions were set up in Europe and America and there has since been a more or less continuous flow of Vedantic teachers. Romain Rolland, a Nobel Laureate, and a true-blood representative of European cultural interests and development, explained his own startling conversion to Vedanta in *New Prophets of India,* from which our selection is taken. Rolland was a friend of Freud, and the latter in *Civilization and Its Discontents* describes an experience that was ever present with Rolland, "a feeling which he would like to call a sensation of 'eternity,' a feeling of something limitless, unbounded, something 'oceanic.' It is purely subjective experience, not an article of belief."[47]]

When staff in hand in [earlier] years I scoured the roads of thought, I found
nothing that was strange in any country. All the aspects of mind that I found
or felt were in their origin the same as mine. Outside experience merely
brought me the realization of my own mind, the states of which I had noted
but to which I had no key. Neither Shakespeare nor Beethoven nor Tolstoy
nor Rome, the master that nurtured me, ever revealed anything to me except
the "Open Sesame" of my subterranean city, my Herculaneum, sleeping
under its lava. And I am convinced that it sleeps in the depths of many of
those around us. But they are ignorant of its existence just as I was. Few
venture beyond the first stage of excavation. . . .

I have just rediscovered the key of the lost staircase. . . . The staircase in
the wall, spiral like the coils of a serpent, winds from the subterranean
depths of the Ego to the high terraces crowned by the stars. But nothing that
I saw there was unknown country. I had seen it all before and I knew it
well—but I did not know where I had seen it before. More than once I had
recited from memory, though imperfectly, the lesson of thought learned at
some former time (but from whom? One of my very ancient selves. . . .)
Now [in Hindu teachings] I reread it, every word clear and complete. . . .

I am no dilettante and I do not bring to jaded readers the opportunity to
lose themselves, but rather to find themselves—to find their true selves,
naked and without the mask of falsehood. . . . There is neither East nor
West for the naked soul; such things are merely its trappings. The whole
world is its home.[48]

ARNOLD BENNETT (1867–1931)

British Novelist and Dramatist

[This excerpt from Arnold Bennett's novel *The Glimpse* reminds one of Lafcadio Hearn's vision quoted earlier, and offers insights as to what for some
individuals could be the cyclic processes of spiritual evolution preceding
more advanced stages of awakening.]

And in the ecstatic void the vision of the whole cycle of my existence
began to be revealed to me, rolling itself backward into the unguessed deeps
of the past, so that I might learn. I saw the endless series of my lives,
recurring and recurring. . . . I ceased to be Morrice Loring and became a
legion. These lives flashed up before me one anterior to another, mere moments between the vast periods that separated them. . . . And one life was
not more important to me than another. All were equally indispensable and
disciplinal. . . .

The variety of those imprisonments seemed endless. Some were fevers of desire; others had almost the calmness of a final wisdom. Some were cruel; some were kind. In some the double barriers were so thin that the immortal prisoner shone through them; and men wondered. And in the next the walls might be hopelessly thick again. . . . Undulations in the curve of evolution.[49]

MARY JOHNSTON (1870–1936)
American Novelist

[Mary Johnston, best known for her novel *To Have and to Hold,* includes a number of passages on our theme in *Sweet Rocket.* One is chosen, which for beauty and power seems best.]

There was something that awed in the perception that ran from one to another, that held them in a shift, shimmering band. . . . There fell a sense of having done this times and times and times, a sense of hut and cave, so often, so long, in so many lands, that there was a feel of eternity about it. Rain and the cave and the fire and the inner man still busied with his destiny! . . . "How old—how old! How long have we done this?" The rhythm of the storm, the rhythm of the room, the rhythm of the fire, passed into a vast, still sense of ordered movement. "Of old, and now, and tomorrow—everywhere and all time—until we return above time and place, and division is healed."[50]

PIET MONDRIAN (1872–1944)
Dutch Artist

["Abstract art of one kind or another has changed the face of the modern world," writes Hilton Kramer, art editor of the *New York Times,* in an article commemorating the centennial of one of its principal founders, Wassily Kandinsky.[51] As Kramer and others point out,[52] four of the major pioneers in this field—Mondrian, Kandinsky, Klee, and Malevich—were directly influenced by some form of theosophy. (Reincarnation is at the heart of theosophical philosophy. See chapter 7.) However, a good deal of what occurred later in abstract expressionism and various nonobjective experiments appears to have had little relation to theosophical ideas or ideals.

Kramer in tracing Kandinsky's development discusses the crucial period when the artist studied theosophy, enabling him "to make his revolutionary leap into abstraction. . . . Kandinsky needed a theoretical framework . . . for carrying painting beyond the realm of representation. . . . With a mind

like [his]—at once intellectual and mystical, seeking 'laws' and principles
before commiting itself to practice—the idea must always precede its realization." His "commitment to theosophy guaranteed—to him, at least—that
abstract art would attain a higher spiritual meaning." Kandinsky himself
wrote that spiritual "methods are still alive and in use among nations whom
we, from the height of our knowledge, have been accustomed to regard with
pity and scorn. To such nations belong the people of India . . . Madame
Blavatsky was the first person, after a life of many years in India, to see a
connection between these 'savages' and our 'civilization.' In that moment
rose one of the most important spiritual movements, one which numbers a
great many people today, and has even assumed a material form in the
Theosophical Society."[53]

However, Kandinsky never actually joined the society. It was different
with Mondrian who became a member in Holland in 1909. Frank Elgar in his
book *Mondrian* states that the artist was "deeply concerned with matters of
religion and always actively interested in theosophy."[54] Elgar quotes Martin
James in *Art News,* 1957:

> Mondrian's theosophy was more than a personal quirk. Several artists
> around 1910 sought through it deeper and more universal values, meaning
> behind meaning, new dimensions to understanding. The thought that the an-
> cient seers perceived and imparted a veiled wisdom, that behind the many
> guises of truth there is *one* truth, is partly based on Oriental and Neo-Platonic
> ideas; it easily links with the romantic and symbolist theory of illuminism,
> which gives the artist extraordinary, even occult power of insight into the
> nature of the world, the reality behind appearances—a new content for art.

Another art historian, Robert Welsh, states that by the winter of 1913–1914
Mondrian's "attachment to Theosophy was so well appreciated that, although then living in Paris, he was asked to write an article on the subject
'Art and Theosophy,' for *Theosophia*," the leading organ of the Dutch
movement. Welsh's lengthy article "Mondrian and Theosophy" opens the
large volume *Piet Mondrian Centennial Exhibition* published by the
Guggenheim Museum in New York in 1972. Welsh explains that "the ideas
relevant to the present discussion were proliferated in numerous texts, lectures, and discussions undertaken by Madame Blavatsky and her followers."
"However, for the sake of convenience," he adds, "and because its role as a
source for other quotations often has been overlooked, the monumental, two
volume *Isis Unveiled* of 1877," by Blavatsky, "will provide the exclusive test
upon which our discussion is based," a Dutch translation of *Isis* having been
available to Mondrian. We have space only to touch upon this discussion
here, but selections from *Isis* will be found in chapter 7.

In relating several of Mondrian's paintings to the theosophical view of
evolutionary growth through reincarnation, Welsh points particularly to one

called *Metamorphosis,* and another, the celebrated triptych *Evolution,* and comments:

> Evolution is no less than the basic tenet in the cosmological system predicated by Madame Blavatsky and, as such, replaces the Christian story of Creation as an explanation for how the world functions. This cosmology is analogous to Hindu and other mythologies which stress a perpetual cosmic cycle of creation, death and regeneration. It also has much in common with the Darwinian scientific theory of evolution. Darwin's only essential mistake, in Blavatsky's opinion, was to substitute matter for spirit as the motivating force in the universe. In her own world view, matter, though constituting a necessary vehicle through which the world of spirit was to be approached, clearly stands second in importance to the latter phenomenon. . . .
>
> This conceptual polarity . . . pervades the art theoretical writings of Mondrian, beginning with his letter to Querido of 1909, and is epitomized in his *Sketchbooks* of circa 1912–14. In the latter text he specifically alludes to the Theosophical Doctrine of Evolution as a determining factor in the history of art. In short, Mondrian could not have chosen as the theme of his monumental triptych a doctrine which was more central to Theosophic teaching than this.

Inasmuch as art uses a nonverbal medium for expression, it is obviously unwise to attempt to pin down too closely particular paintings to definite philosophical conceptions. Nevertheless, there appears to be little doubt that the artists already named, as well as Gauguin who was previously quoted, participated in the ferment of ideas set in motion in the last century by the theosophical movement in which reincarnation is a central teaching. A kinship between abstract art and the idea of many lives possibly existed in the thinking of the early founders of nonrepresentational painting, because in both cases forms and appearances are regarded as mayavic, or illusionary, constantly transformed and replaced. Hence the instinctive resort of these artists to symbolic devices and their disdain for copying fixed models. However, in an article on Mondrian, Hilton Kramer points out that:

> Later abstractionists, particularly in America, carried the reduction of visual incident in painting to extremes Mondrian himself never dreamed of, yet his work has never been eclipsed by these later efforts. On the contrary, its stature has increased with the passage of time, and one of the reasons for this, I believe, is precisely the relation that obtains—and is seen to obtain—between his art and its metaphysical foundations. We do not feel, in the presence of a Mondrian, that we are being offered a "merely" esthetic delectation. We feel ourselves in the presence of a larger struggle—indeed, a larger world—in which mind grapples with eternal threats to its fragmentation and dissolution. . . . [Today, in art,] what were once problems of metaphysical debate and social redemption are reduced to problems of style and taste. Inevitably, the requisite tension—the inner drama of a protagonist perfecting not a style but a vision—is missing.[55]

SOMERSET MAUGHAM (1874–1965)

British Novelist and Playwright

[Somerset Maugham speaks of reincarnation in *The Razor's Edge;* his leading character discusses the subject in relation to visions experienced of possible previous lives. In Maugham's autobiography, *The Summing Up,* published six years before that novel, he says he found only one explanation of the problem of evil "that appealed equally to my sensibility and to my imagination. This is the doctrine of the transmigration of souls." Yet he could not accept it. "There is no explanation for evil." He wrote:]

It would be less difficult to bear the evils of one's own life if one could think that they were but the necessary outcome of one's errors in a previous existence, and the effort to do better would be less difficult too when there was the hope that in another existence a greater happiness would reward one. But if one feels one's own woes in a more forcible way than those of others (I cannot feel your toothache, as the philosophers say) it is the woes of others that arouse one's indignation. It is possible to achieve resignation in regard to one's own, but only philosophers obsessed with the perfection of the Absolute can look upon those of others, which seem so often unmerited, with an equal mind. If Karma were true one could look upon them with pity, but with fortitude. Revulsion would be out of place and life would be robbed of the meaninglessness of pain which is pessimism's unanswered argument. I can only regret that I find the doctrine . . . impossible to believe.[56]

SIR WINSTON CHURCHILL (1874–1965)

British Statesman and Historian

[A few days after Sir Winston Churchill's death, foreign correspondent C. L. Sulzberger devoted his column in the *New York Times* (February 1, 1965) to some thoughts on the event:]

Despite his immense gusto for life, in a rather jovial cozy way Churchill never minded contemplating the mystery of death. . . . [One] time he was asked if he believed in an afterlife. After a moment's hesitation he said no, that he thought there was only "some kind of velvety cool blackness," adding then: "Of course, I admit I may be wrong. It is conceivable that I might well be reborn as a Chinese coolie. In such a case I should lodge a protest."

ROBERT FROST (1875–1963)

American Poet

[It is a moving experience to hear Robert Frost, in one of his last re-cordings,[57] recite these concluding lines of his well-known poem "Birches":]

> So was I once myself a swinger of birches.
> And so I dream of going back to be.
> It's when I'm weary of considerations,
> And life is too much like a pathless wood
> Where your face burns and tickles with the cobwebs
> Broken across it, and one eye is weeping
> From a twig's having lashed across it open.
> I'd like to get away from earth awhile
> And then come back to it and begin over.
> May no fate willfully misunderstand me
> And half grant what I wish and snatch me away
> Not to return. Earth's the right place for love:
> I don't know where it's likely to go better.
> I'd like to go by climbing a birch tree,
> And climb black branches up a snow-white trunk
> *Toward* heaven, till the tree could bear no more,
> But dipped its top and set me down again.
> That would be good both going and coming back.
> One could do worse than be a swinger of birches.

RAINER MARIA RILKE (1875–1926)

German Lyric Poet and Writer

[W. H. Auden calls Rainer Maria Rilke almost the first poet since the seven-teenth century to find a fresh solution for the poet's eternal problem of expressing abstract ideas in concrete form. The Princess Marie of Thurn and Taxis wrote in *Recollections of R. M. Rilke* that "deep down he considered Russia his soul-home, convinced that in a former incarnation he lived in Moscow."[58] In his "Sonnets to Orpheus," Rilke yearningly asks: "But when, in which of all our lives do we finally become open and receptive?" Elsewhere, speaking of death and return to earth life, he wrote: "Perhaps one only seeks a homecoming and welcome, pursues it, till the circle rounds, back to that home, feeling with a strange certainty, dreamlike and sad, that he had lost it once before."[59]]

JACK LONDON (1876–1916)
American Novelist

[In James Jones's *From Here to Eternity*, Jack London's novels are extolled, particularly those that attempt to explain reincarnation.[60] One of these, *The Star Rover*—published in London as *The Jacket*—sounds the note of rebirth on almost every page. The story concerns a prisoner in San Quentin who learns to outwit the maddening boredom of solitary confinement and the torture of the straitjacket through a special technique of separating the mind from the body. Thus "liberated" he begins to relive portions of previous incarnations. The novel is actually based on the recorded experience of Ed Morrell, a prisoner of San Quentin, whose autobiography was published as *The Twenty-Fifth Man*. London's interest in reincarnation may derive from a contact with theosophy. In *Martin Eden* he has his hero—after an encounter with a theosophist—reading Madame Blavatsky's *Secret Doctrine*. *Martin Eden* was first published in 1908.[61] Quoting from *The Star Rover:*]

All my life I have had an awareness of other times, and places. I have been aware of other persons in me. . . . I, whose lips had never lisped the word "king," remembered that I had once been the son of a king. More—I remembered that once I had been a slave and a son of a slave, and worn an iron collar round my neck.

I, like any man, am a growth. I did not begin when I was born, nor when I was conceived. I have been growing, developing, through incalculable myriads of millenniums. All these experiences of all these lives, have gone to the making of the soul-stuff or the spirit-stuff that is I. . . . I am all of my past, as every protagonist of the Mendelian law must agree. All my previous selves have their voices, echoes, promptings in me. . . . I am man born of woman. My days are few, but the stuff of me is indestructible. I have been woman born of woman. I have been a woman and borne my children. And I shall be born again. Oh, incalculable times again shall I be born; and yet the stupid dolts about me think that by stretching my neck with a rope they will make me cease.[62]

EDGAR CAYCE (1877–1945)
American Healer and Clairvoyant

[A tremendous interest in reincarnation has been evoked through the reputed healings of Edgar Cayce, who it is claimed had the power, while in self-induced trance, to read the past lives of people and detect karmic causes leading to present troubles. Cayce, a devout Christian, was very disturbed to find himself relating the previous incarnations of patients, and it was only after much study and searching of the scriptures that he reconciled himself to the concept of rebirth.

Cayce's healing career did not begin with these past-life readings. For over twenty years the readings had been purely medical. "In his early years," Cayce "was as startled as the next man to learn he had given medical counsel to an Italian in fluent and flawless Italian. Nor was the complicated medical terminology that rolled off his tongue any more intelligible to him in his waking state than was the fluent Italian."[63] Then one day in October 1923 a man named Arthur Lammers came to see Cayce. An account of the visit is told in Thomas Sugrue's *There Is a River:*

> Lammers . . . asked questions Edgar did not understand—what were the mechanics of the subconscious, what was the difference between spirit and soul, what were the reasons for personality and talent? He mentioned such things as the cabala, the mystery religions of Egypt and Greece, the medieval alchemists, the mystics of Tibet, yoga, Madame Blavatsky and theosophy, the Great White Brotherhood, the Etheric World. Edgar was dazed.
>
> "You ought to find out about these things," Lammers said. . . . There are hundreds of philosophic and thousands of theological systems. Which are right and which are wrong? . . . What is the real nature of the soul and what is the purpose of this experience on earth? Where do we go from here? . . . What were we doing before we came here? Haven't you asked any of those questions?"
>
> "No," Edgar said. He couldn't think of another word to say. He didn't dare tell the truth: that he had always considered such an idea sacrilegious, because God was revealed in the Bible, and to suppose that [Cayce through his readings] could answer the mysteries of the universe would be an open invitation for Satan to speak through him. That was what he had felt. Now, as he heard Lammers speak, he knew the feeling had passed.[64]

When Cayce gave Lammers a reading, the astounding words "He was a monk" came through. From then on the readings often referred to previous lives. Also, Sanskrit terms Cayce never heard of, such as *karma* and *akasa*, became part of his natural vocabulary in trance.

What is especially constructive about Cayce's work is its ethical tone. In one reading, addressed to a man who had written several times for help, this advice was offered:

> Yes, we have the body here; this we have had before. As we find, there have been physical improvements in the body, yet there is much, much to be desired. As already indicated, this is a karmic condition and there must be measures taken by the entity to change its attitude toward things, conditions, and its fellow man. So long as mechanical things were applied for physical correction,

improvements were seen. But when the entity becomes so self-satisfied, so self-centered, as to refuse spiritual things, and does not change its attitude; so long as there is hate, malice, injustice, jealousy; so long as there is anything within at variance with patience, long suffering, brotherly love, kindness, gentleness, there cannot be a healing of the condition of this body. What does the entity want to be healed for? That it may gratify its own physical appetites? That it may add to its own selfishness? Then, if so, it had better remain as it is. . . . Will you accept, will you reject? It is up to you. We are through—unless you make amends.[65]

The foregoing is found in *Many Mansions*. The author, Gina Cerminara, spent several years going through carefully kept records of the more than thirty thousand cases that came under Cayce's influence. Based on the readings, this classification of physical karma is given by Dr. Cerminara, summarized partly in our own words:

The first and most obvious is termed "Boomerang Karma," the most mechanical type of cause and effect. An example is provided. "A college professor who had been born totally blind, heard about Cayce on a radio program. . . . He applied for a physical reading and experienced conspicuous improvement in health and vision by following its instructions. Within three months he had achieved 10 per cent vision in his left eye, which had been considered hopeless by eye specialists. . . . It was in Persia that he had set in motion the spiritual law which resulted in his blindness in the present. He had been a member of a barbaric tribe whose custom was to blind its enemies with red-hot irons, and it had been his office to do the blinding."[66]

A second type of karma is given the name "Organismic," since it involves the misuse of the organism in one life with an appropriate affliction resulting in a later incarnation. A man suffering from digestive weakness since infancy was revealed as having been a glutton in a previous life.

The last, and most intriguing type, is called "Symbolic," and this example is given: A young man had suffered since early childhood with anemia; his father was a physician, but every known treatment was of no avail. A life reading traced his affliction to an incarnation five lifetimes back, in Peru, where the entity had ruthlessly seized control of the country, thereby becoming its ruler. "Much blood was shed," says the reading; "hence anemia in the present." Dr. Cerminara comments: "His own body became the field of slaughter; it became, as it were, the sacrificial altar on which his crime was expiated. This lifelong bodily deficiency constitutes a far more protracted form of educative justice than [Boomerang Karma, or] bloody death on a battlefield could possibly have accomplished. The entity once shed the blood of a people for whom he felt a conqueror's contempt; now he himself is a weakling, by virtue of his own bloodstream deficiency. . . . "[67]]

HERMANN HESSE (1877–1962)

German-Swiss Author

[In reviewing two of Hesse's books issued by a New York publisher (eight more being scheduled for publication), Webster Schott wrote in *Life* (July 16, 1968):

> Like history, literature repeats itself. Youth has discovered Hermann Hesse again. Creator of elegant narratives that transform the inner wars of personality into heroic struggles against the unexamined life, Hesse speaks the soul language of the young. . . . Yet his novels aren't adolescent fare. Their subtleties make work. Their simplicity belies galaxies of knowledge in motion—history, theology, psychology, philosophy. Rilke, T. S. Eliot, Gide, Thomas Mann rightly called Hesse a master. Like a spiritual filter, his fiction purifies and dignifies the quest of civilized man for a purpose in harmony with his nature. . . . His plots unfold like gigantic maps of the soul.

Selections are first offered from Hesse's major work, his last novel *Das Glasperlenspiel,* published in complete form in 1945 and awarded the Nobel Prize in 1946. In the introduction to the Bantam paperback edition—called *Magister Ludi (The Glass Bead Game)*—Theodore Ziolkowski relates how Hesse came to write the book: "The idea that came to him, he wrote to a friend in 1945, was 'Reincarnation as a mode of expression for stability in the midst of flux.' Long before he began writing, he remarks, he had in mind 'an individual but supratemporal life. . . . a man who experiences in a series of rebirths the grand epochs in the history of mankind.' " A *New York Times* reviewer of an earlier translation said that "Hesse plunges into the realm of universal humanity, with all the wide-ranging love of St. Francis, the mysticism of Buddha, the psychological insight of Dostoevsky, the world-embracing striving of Goethe, and the Europeanism of Nietzsche."

Das Glasperlenspiel is an attempt to formulate an ideal design for living, and takes us into a future where a very different order of society from our own exists. Many ingenious methods leading to self-discovery are used in the advanced schools. One important task assigned to pupils is the writing of imaginary autobiographies set in any period of the past the students may choose. As the story explains:]

A remnant of the ancient Asian doctrine of reincarnation and the transmigration of souls survived in this playful, highly flexible form. All teachers and students were familiar with the concept that their present existence might have been preceded by others, in other bodies, at other times, under other conditions. To be sure they did not believe this in any strict sense; there was no element of dogma in the idea. Rather, it was an exercise, a game for the

imaginative faculties, to conceive of oneself in different conditions and sur-
roundings. In writing such Lives students . . . learned to regard their own
persons as masks, as the transitory garb of an entelechy. . . . Incidentally,
there was a rather considerable number of students who not only more or less
believed in the idea of reincarnation, but also in the truth of their own
fictional Lives.[68]

[Three of the lives written by the hero Joseph Knecht are given in an appendix to the main story and are said by Hesse to be perhaps the most important
parts of the book. The last "life," a marvel of evocative scenes and images,
is titled "The Indian Life," and portrays a young man in a forest in India who
bitterly learns the meaning of *maya* or illusion through a wonderful, terrible
dream sent unbeknown to himself by his teacher. Here are his feelings and
experiences as he wakes up, the volume closing with these paragraphs:]

Numbed and paralysed, Dasa stood there. . . . Oh, how rapidly, grue-
somely and profoundly had he been taught Maya! . . . He had had enough
and more than enough of this dreaming, of this demonic patchwork quilt of
events, joys and sufferings. . . . He desired no more wife or child, neither
throne nor victory nor revenge, neither happiness nor cleverness, neither
might nor virtue: he desired nothing but peace, nothing except an end,
wanted nothing except to bring this eternally revolving wheel, this endless
picture-show to a standstill and to extinguish it. . . . But what then? Then
there would be a pause of unconsciousness, slumber or death, and immediately one would be awake once more, would be obliged to let in the stream of
life into one's heart again, and the beautiful, terrifying flood of pictures—
endless and inescapable—would ensue until the next consciousness, until the
next death. . . . Ah, there was no extinction, no end! . . .

Restlessness brought him to his feet again. . . . When he arrived at the hut
the master received him with a remarkable look, a slightly questioning, half
commiserating, half merry look of complicity such as an older boy might give
to a junior upon his returning from a rather tiring and somewhat shameful
adventure, some test of courage that had been allotted to him. . . . This
young man had presumably once in an earlier life been awakened and had
breathed a mouthful of reality, otherwise he would not have come to this spot
and remained so long. Now he seemed to be truly awake and ripe for the
entrance to the long way. It would take many years to teach him the correct
procedure. . . . Nothing more can be told of Dasa's life for from then on-
wards it took a path beyond pictures and stories.[69]

[In Hesse's poem "All Deaths," he tells of passing up the stairways of the
lower kingdoms to the state of man. "I have already died all deaths, and I am
going to die all deaths again. . . . Many times over you will hunt me down

from death to birth on the painful track of the creations, the glorious track of the creations.''[70]

Hesse's *Siddhartha,* of which a beautiful motion picture has been made, has been called the most widely read novel of today's generation. It is the story of a youth, Siddhartha, who meets the Buddha—known in *his* youth as the Prince Siddhartha—but cannot accept the teachings of even this ''greatest of men.'' He must work out his own destiny and solve his own doubts through experience, just as the Buddha himself did. Quoting from a closing scene:]

Often [Siddhartha and the ferryman Vasudeva] sat together in the evening on the tree trunk by the river. They both listened silently to the water, which to them was not just water, but the voice of life, the voice of Being, of perpetual Becoming. . . . The water continually flowed and flowed and yet it was always there; it was always the same and yet every moment it was new. Who could understand, conceive this? . . . The river knows everything; one can learn everything from it. . . .

''Have you also learned [this] secret from the river; that there is no such thing as time? . . . The river is everywhere at the same time, at the source and at the mouth, at the waterfall, at the ferry, at the current, in the ocean and in the mountains, everywhere, and that the present only exists for it, not the shadow of the past, nor the shadow of the future?''

''That is it,'' said Siddhartha, ''and when I learned that, I reviewed my life and it was also a river, and Siddhartha the boy, Siddhartha the mature man and Siddhartha the old man, were only separated by shadows, not through reality. Siddhartha's previous lives were also not in the past, and his death and his return to Brahma are not in the future. Nothing was, nothing will be, everything has reality and presence.'' Siddhartha spoke with delight. This discovery had made him very happy. Was then not all sorrow in time, all self-torment and fear in time? Were not all difficulties and evil in the world conquered as soon as one conquered time?[71]

JOHN MASEFIELD (1878–1967)
British Poet, Dramatist, and Novelist

[In ''The Pioneer Laureate,'' a tribute to John Masefield on his eighty-seventh birthday, his longtime friend J. H. B. Peel commented on the poet's affirmation that ''he is a simple Christian'': ''His creed is not so simple. As the poems reveal, he picks an eclectic path, even to the point of many reincarnated returns.''[72] (Incidentally, Masefield was a close friend of another reincarnationist, W. B. Yeats. A room they shared in London is now a museum.) Peel cites in particular Masefield's well-known poem ''A Creed.'' This was an early poem. Later Masefield must have undergone a period of doubts, for in the 1923 edition of his *Collected Poems* the first lines of stanza one and two were changed to read: "I *held* that when a person dies . . ." and "Such *was* my own belief and trust . . ." However, in the 1935 and all subsequent editions, the original wording was reinstated and in this form the poem is here reprinted:]

I hold that when a person dies
His soul returns again to earth;
Arrayed in some new flesh-disguise,
Another mother gives him birth.
With sturdier limbs and brighter brain
The old soul takes the road again.

Such is my own belief and trust;
This hand, this hand that holds the pen,
Has many a hundred times been dust
And turned, as dust, to dust again;
These eyes of mine have blinked and shone
In Thebes, in Troy, in Babylon. . . .

And I shall know, in angry words,
In gibes, and mocks, and many a tear,
A carrion flock of homing-birds,
The gibes and scorns I uttered here.
The brave word that I failed to speak
Will brand me dastard on the cheek.

And as I wander on the roads
I shall be helped and healed and blessed;
Dear words shall cheer and be as goads
To urge to heights before unguessed.
My road shall be the road I made;
All that I gave shall be repaid.

So shall I fight, so shall I tread,
In this long war beneath the stars;
So shall a glory wreathe my head,
So shall I faint and show the scars.
Until this case, this clogging mould,
Be smithied all to kingly gold.

LORD HUGH DOWDING (1882–1970)

British Air Chief Marshal

[Of Lord Hugh Dowding's triumph over the German Air Force in August and September 1944, which saved Britain from invasion, Winston Churchill said:

''We must regard the generalship here shown as an example of genius in the art of war.''[73] However, the air marshal was not a warrior by nature, and although he shared with General Patton[74] of the American forces a belief in many lives, he was a very different sort of man. In *Lynchgate* he wrote: ''I am personally convinced beyond any shadow of a doubt that reincarnation is a fact.''[75] In a speech on ''Painful Experiments on Animals,'' delivered before the House of Lords (July 18, 1957), Lord Dowding applied his reincarnationist philosophy to the subject:]

I firmly believe that painful experiments on animals are morally wrong, and that it is basically immoral to do evil in order that good may come—even if it were proved that mankind benefits from the suffering inflicted on animals. . . . I cannot leave this subject without some reference to its esoteric side—to the place of the animal kingdom in the scheme of things, to man's responsibility to animals, and to the results of man's failure to meet this responsibility.

As the human race evolves, it becomes ready for fresh revelation, and the defect in most of the world's religions is that they fail to realize this very important fact. The priests are inclined to say ''everything that is necessary for salvation is contained in this Book. It is unnecessary and, indeed impious, to search elsewhere.'' It is I think, this aspect of our childhood's teaching which leads to the idea that animals have no continuing life after physical death. That phrase in the 49th Psalm, ''The beasts that perish,'' has much to answer for, for it is a fact that the beasts do not perish any more than do men. All life is one, and all its manifestations with which we have contact are climbing the ladder of evolution. The animals are our younger brothers and sisters, also on the ladder but a few rungs lower down than we are. It is an important part of our responsibilities to help them in their ascent, and not to retard their development by cruel exploitation of their helplessness.[76]

KAHLIL GIBRAN (1883–1931)
Lebanese-born American Author

[From *The Prophet,* Kahlil Gibran's most popular work:]

Brief were my days among you, and briefer still the words I have spoken. But should my voice fade in your ears, and my love vanish in your memory, then I will come again, and with a richer heart and lips more yielding to the spirit will I speak. Yes, I shall return with the tide, and though death may hide me and the greater silence enfold me, yet again will I seek your understanding. . . . Know, therefore, that from the greater silence I shall return.

. . . Forget not that I shall come back to you. . . . A little while, a moment of rest upon the wind, and another woman shall bear me.[77]

[Barbara Young wrote in her biography of Gibran, *This Man from Lebanon:*]

One evening when we were doing *Sand and Foam*, I piled cushions on the floor and sat upon them instead of occupying my usual chair. Then I had a strange feeling of familiarity about the gesture, and I said, ''I feel as if I've sat like this beside you many times—but I really haven't.'' [Gibran] waited a moment—as he often did before replying. . . . Then he said, ''We have done this a thousand years ago, and shall do it a thousand years hence.''

And during the writing of *Jesus, The Son of Man,* the drama of some incident, now and again, was so overwhelming that I felt, and said, ''It is so real. It seems as if I had been there.'' And his answer came, almost like a cry, ''You were there! And so was I!'' Thus Gibran expressed over and over again, his utter belief in what he called ''the continuity of life.'' The Theosophist . . . and divers other trends of thought and belief, call it reincarnation. He never used the word. It was his profound certainty that the life that is the human spirit has lived and shall live timelessly, that the bonds of love, devotion, and friendship shall bring together these endlessly reborn beings, and that animosity, evil communications, and hatred have the same effect of reassembling groups of entities from one cycle to another. Indifference acts as a separating influence. Those souls who neither love nor hate, but remain entirely self-contained as regards one another, meet but once in the pattern of the ages.[78]

D. H. LAWRENCE (1885–1930)
British Novelist

[Although D. H. Lawrence does not often speak directly of future lives, we learn from William York Tindall's biography that he had a definite leaning toward Eastern religions.[79] Professor Tindall traces the novelist's debt to the Hindu Upanishads through Mme. Blavatsky and theosophy in general, and more particularly to a theosophist, James M. Pryse, a onetime resident of Dublin, who lived in the same household with Yeats, AE, and Charles Johnston. In the chapter ''Susan Unveiled,'' Tindall states that ''in a letter to a friend who was evidently in spiritual distress, Lawrence recommended Mme. Blavatsky's *Isis Unveiled* . . . he especially recommended her *Secret Doctrine*.''[80] ''Mrs. Lawrence informed me that her husband read and delighted in all of Mme. Blavatsky's works. . . . Symbolic clues to the past were never more knowingly followed by the most orthodox Theosophist. The foreword to *Fantasia of the Unconscious,* 1922 . . . might have been written by Mme. Blavatsky herself."[81] To support this statement, Tindall quotes from the foreword:

"I honestly think that the great pagan world of which Egypt and Greece were the last living terms . . . had a vast and perhaps perfect science of its own, a science in terms of life. . . . I believe that this great science . . . was universal, established all over the existing globe. I believe it was esoteric, invested in a large priesthood. Just as mathematics and mechanics and physics are defined and expounded in the same way in the universities of China or Bolivia or London or Moscow today, so, it seems to me, in the great world previous to ours a great science and cosmology were taught esoterically in all countries of the globe, Asia, Polynesia, America, Atlantis and Europe." . . . This is simple theosophy.

Tindall adds that "although Lawrence seems elsewhere to have taken little interest in metempsychosis, *The Plumed Serpent* contains several references to the cyclical development of races and to reincarnation under the law of Karma." This haunting novel of Mexico, considered to be one of Lawrence's best, centers around the prophecy that the great teacher of the Aztecs, Quetzalcoatl or the Plumed Serpent, will return someday and bring about a renaissance of the ancient culture. Tindall, who writes the introduction to a paperback edition, states that "the theme of rebirth is supported by symbols so central and impressive that it would be more accurate to say that theme and narrative serve them. . . . Lawrence makes his feathered snake not only a sign of unity but of those dying and reviving gods he learned about from Frazer. Like Attis, Osiris, and Adonis, Quetzalcoatl has died in order to live." Don Ramón, one of the main characters, exclaims: "The universe is a nest of dragons, with a perfectly unfathomable mystery at the center of it. If I call the mystery the Morning Star, surely it doesn't matter!"[82]

Later when Don Ramón's little Christian-raised son tells him that "there never was any Quetzalcoatl, except idols," the father replies: "Is there any Jesus, except images?" "Yes, papa." "Where?" "In heaven." "Then in heaven there is also Quetzalcoatl. And what is in heaven is capable of coming back to earth."[83]]

T. S. ELIOT (1888–1965)
American-born British Author

[According to Dr. Walter Miller, when T. S. Eliot wrote his famous poem "The Waste Land" and opened a new era in twentieth-century poetry, he had been studying theosophy, and much of the symbolism in the poem reflects that study. Dr. Miller, prolific author and professor of literature at Columbia University, discussed this in his Spring 1976 course at Columbia

University's School of Continuing Education. "The Waste Land" was published in 1922 and composed a year earlier during a period when Eliot was undergoing severe nervous problems.

Eliot's interest in Eastern literature is mentioned by several authors. Philip Headings in his volume *T. S. Eliot* remarks that "the doctrines of the *Bhagavad-Gita*" are "pervasively relevant to Eliot's poems and plays," and that "the philosophical poets whom Eliot admires most" were "Dante, Lucretius, and the writers of the *Bhagavad-Gita.*"[84]

In "The Waste Land" there appear to be a number of allusions to reincarnation. One example is several lines from part 3, "The Fire Sermon," concerning Tiresias, an elderly personage whose story is found in Ovid, and whom Eliot regards as the most important individual in his poem, uniting all the rest: " . . . when the human engine waits like a taxi throbbing waiting, I Tiresias, though blind, throbbing between two lives . . . can see at the violet hour, the evening hour that strives Homeward, and brings the sailor home from sea. . . . "[85] Another possible example is this stanza from part 5, "What the Thunder Said":

> Who is the third who walks always beside you?
> When I count, there are only you and I together
> But when I look ahead up the white road
> There is always another one walking beside you
> Gliding wrapt in a brown mantle, hooded
> I do not know whether a man or a woman
> —But who is that on the other side of you?[86]

Regarding "The Fire Sermon," Eliot states in a note that "the complete text of the Buddha's Fire Sermon (which corresponds in importance to the Sermon on the Mount)" and from which he took several words, "will be found translated in the late Henry Clarke Warren's *Buddhism in Translations* (Harvard Oriental Series). Mr. Warren was one of the great pioneers of Buddhist studies in the Occident."[87] Turning to this short sermon from the *Maha-Vagga,* we find these concluding words of Buddha concerning the victorious disciple: "He becomes divested of passion, and by the absence of passion he becomes free, and when he is free be becomes aware that he is free; and he knows that rebirth is exhausted, that he has lived the holy life, that he has done what is behooved him to do, and that he is no more for this."[88]]

EUGENE O'NEILL (1888–1953)

American Playwright

[The selections here are from Eugene O'Neill's *The Great God Brown.* An unusual feature of this psychological drama is the wearing of masks by the characters when their ordinary selves talk, but when the inner man speaks, the masks are removed.]

ACT I

DION (wearily bitter). I'll take the job. One must do something to pass away the time, while one is waiting—for one's next incarnation. . . .

ACT II

DION (sadly). You've given me strength to die.

CYBEL You may be important, but your life's not. There's millions of it born every second. . . . And it's not sacred—only the you inside it. The rest is earth.

DION "Into thy hands, O Lord," . . . (Suddenly with a look of horror). Nothing! To feel one's life blown out like the flame of a cheap match . . . ! (He claps on his mask and laughs harshly). To fall asleep and know you'll never, never be called to get on the job of existence again! "Swift be thine approaching flight! Come soon-soon!" . . .

CYBEL There, don't be scared. . . . When the time comes, you'll find it's easy. . . .

DION . . . What haunted, haunting ghosts we are! We dimly remember so much it will take us so many million years to forget! . . .

ACT IV

BROWN [is dying]. And when I wake up . . . ?

CYBEL The sun will be rising again. . . . Always spring comes again bearing life! Always again! Always, always forever again!—Spring again!—life again—summer and fall and death and peace again! But always, always, love and conception and birth and pain again—spring bearing the intolerable chalice of life again!—bearing the glorious, blazing crown of life again! . . .

[From the closing lines of the play:] "So long ago! And yet I'm still the same Margaret. It's only our lives that grow old. We *are* where centuries only count as seconds, and after a thousand lives our eyes begin to open."[89]

HERVEY ALLEN (1889–1949)
American Novelist

[In *Anthony Adverse,* Hervey Allen remarks that "the accounts of the good and evil of a lifetime cannot be balanced by explanations, and the books closed. The balance is carried forward into other lives; into actions and reactions until equilibrium results."[90]

To introduce the selection that will follow from Allen's *Bedford Village,*
mention should be made that the deeper students of Masonry have frequently
shown a serious interest in reincarnation[91] and find intimations of it in their
ritual. Thus a high-ranking Mason, William Wilmshurst, writes in *The
Masonic Initiation:*

> The observant Masonic student is made aware by the formula used at
> Lodge-closing, that by some great Warden of life and death each soul is called
> into this objective world to labour upon itself, and is in due course summoned
> from it to rest from its labours and enter into subjective celestial refreshment,
> until once again it is recalled to labour. For each the "day," the opportunity for
> work at self-perfecting, is duly given; for each the "night" cometh when no
> man can work at that task. . . .
>
> The world-old secret teaching upon this subject, common to the whole of the
> East, to Egypt, the Pythagoreans and Platonists, and every College of the
> Mysteries, is to be found summed up as clearly and tersely as one could wish in
> the *Phædo* of Plato, to which the Masonic seeker is referred as one of the most
> instructive of treatises upon the deeper side of the science. It testifies to the
> great rhythm of life and death above spoken of, and demonstrates how the soul
> in the course of its career weaves and wears out many bodies, and is continu-
> ally migrating between objective and subjective conditions, passing from labour
> to refreshment and back again many times in its great task of self-fulfillment
> . . . until such time as its work is completed and it is "made a pillar in the
> House of God and no more goes out"[92] as a journey-man builder into this
> sublunary workshop.[93]

Quoting from *Bedford Village:*]

In North America, especially in the newer settlements, Masonry in sundry
and various ways filled vital and long-felt wants. . . . To many a simple
frontier youth, in particular, the experience of initiation was frequently
overwhelming. . . . For, instead of arriving in some rude loft . . . the new
initiates would now seem to have been translated into the finished cavernlike
abode of some powerful magician or spiritual personage, a being superior to
and aloof from the wild self-planted nature without. . . . Only a missing
password had been needed—and they had at last gained entrance to his very
home.

"At last"—because this place and the spirit that dwelt there must after all
have always been quite close by. . . . In the recesses of their lonely minds
they had sought this dwelling through forests of dream-afflicted nightmare.
Somehow, somewhere it had been lost. Now they had suddenly come upon it—
again! . . . "Why, this was not a garret! No, this was that old place!" They
would be astonished. But that was not what would astonish them most. It
was this: Each would suddenly feel that he had been alive for ages. He would

instantly "remember" that he had often and often seen this familiar place
before.[94]

ROBERT STROUD (1890–1963)
"The Birdman of Alcatraz"

[Robert Stroud, probably the most celebrated prisoner of recent times, died
at the age of seventy-three after fifty-four years of imprisonment, forty-two
years of which were spent in complete isolation—the longest period of solitary confinement experienced by anyone in United States history. Despite
unbelievable hardships and the opposition of prison officials, this man, who
had only a third-grade education, learned mathematics, astronomy, languages,
music, painting, law, gained worldwide recognition as a foremost authority on bird diseases, and devoted many years to planning prison reforms.
Stroud's biography, told by Thomas Gaddis in *Birdman of Alcatraz,* was later
dramatized in the motion picture of that name. Concerning Stroud's early
days in Leavenworth prison, Gaddis relates:]

His hatred of punishment grew with his reading and his pent-up ego swelled
with the view of worlds he could not reach. He became grave and inwardly ardent. He studied and worked deeper into astronomy, seeing, in his
mind's eye, the sky and its heavenly bodies swimming in limitless space.
. . . But now he discovered something truly illimitable, beyond astronomy,
in the spacious metaphysics of the Orient. He stumbled upon theosophy. One
of his letters to his mother revealed that, even as a boy, he had held the
persistent notion that he had lived before. . . . Enthralled by his reading,
Stroud embraced the brotherhood of Karma, thought-transference and reincarnation. . . . "I soon saw the two phases of theosophy," he wrote to his
mother, "the theory and practice of occultism, and the holding of life with
respect to the theory of brotherhood, karma. . . . The second was of the
highest value attainable. I started to live by the second phase."[95]

HENRY MILLER (1891–   )
American Author and Artist

[In an interview with Henry Miller in London in 1961,[96] the famous novelist
discussed his trilogy *The Rosy Crucifixion,* and spoke of the healing power of
psychological suffering: "When a man is crucified, when he dies to himself,
the heart opens up like a flower. Of course you don't die, nobody dies, death
doesn't exist, you only reach a new level of vision, a new realm of consciousness, a new unknown world. Just as you don't know where you came
from, so you don't know where you're going. But that there is something
there, before and after, I firmly believe."

Miller's interest in literature that focuses on reincarnation, karma, and related themes is evident from his volume *Books in My Life*. Among the books listed as those "which influenced me most"—a list largely composed of the great books of the past and present—is H. P. Blavatsky's *The Secret Doctrine*. He also refers to her as one of the touchstones in his life.[97] In a recent interview[98] Miller was explaining what he meant by the experience of "conversion," and recalled a day in Paris in 1934. He was reading, he said, books by Madame Blavatsky, when he came across a photograph of her face. He told the interviewer:

> . . . I was hypnotized by her eyes and I had a complete vision of her as if she were in the room. Now I don't know if that had anything to do with what happened next, but I had a flash, I came to the realization that I was responsible for my whole life, whatever had happened. I used to blame my family, society, my wife . . . and that day I saw so clearly that I had nobody to blame but myself. I put everything on my own shoulders and I felt so relieved. Now I'm free, no one else is responsible.

In the theosophical books Miller had been reading, "responsibility for one's whole life" was justifiable because one had lived previously to that life; otherwise how could a person be accountable for his childhood and youth, which in turn have such marked effects upon later life? Miller said that to come to this realization of responsibility is "a kind of awakening." "I remember a story of how one day the Buddha was walking along and a man came up to him and said: 'Who are you, what are you?' and the Buddha promptly answered 'I am a man who is awake.'" Miller commented: "We're asleep, don't you know, we're sleepwalkers."]

PEARL S. BUCK (1892–1973)

American Author

[In *The Living Reed,* a historical novel about Korea, Pearl Buck writes of Liang, a baby born to Yul-han and his wife Induk:]

At first Yul-han thought of the child only as his son, a part of himself, a third with Induk. As time passed, however, a most strange prescience took hold of [Yul-han's] mind and spirit. . . . He perceived that the child possessed an old soul. It was not to be put in words, this meaning of an old soul. Yul-han, observing the child, saw in his behaviour a reasonableness, a patience, a comprehension, that was totally unchildlike. He did not scream when his food was delayed, as other infants do. Instead, his eyes calm and contemplative, he seemed to understand and was able to wait. These eyes, quietly alive, moved from Yul-han's face to Induk's when they talked, as though he knew what his parents said. . . . He gazed at them with such intelligence, such awareness, that it was as if he spoke their names, not as his parents, but as persons whom he recognized. . . . Yul-han, watching, felt a certain awe, a hesitancy in calling him "my son," as though the claim were presumption. "If I were a Buddhist," he told Induk one day, "I would say that this child is an incarnation of some former great soul."

[Liang meets his uncle Yul-chun for the first time. Yul-chun was a Korean hero known to the people as "The Living Reed."] The child was barely awake but being amiable and benign by nature, he roused himself and smiled at his uncle at first without much concern. Suddenly, however, an inexplicable change took place. The smile left his face, he leaned forward in his mother's arms and gazed most earnestly into his uncle's eyes. He gave a cry of joy, he reached out his arms. . . . while Yul-han and Induk stood transfixed in amazement. [Recalling the event years later, the uncle remarked to Liang:] "You sprang into my arms . . . you knew me from some other life."[99]

J. B. PRIESTLEY (1894–)
British Novelist, Critic, and Playwright

[André Maurois in his article "Tragic Decline of the Humane Ideal" speaks of J. B. Priestley's reincarnation play *I Have Been Here Before:* "The subject of this play was the Eternal Return, the idea that the same events occur over and over again, that men find themselves, after millions of years, in situations which they have previously encountered, and that, each time, they make the same mistakes which cause the same tragedies. But the author of the play . . . admits that certain men, at the moment when they find themselves on the threshold of their drama, remember confusedly their previous misfortunes and find in this memory the strength to thwart destiny by a free action which breaks the fatal chain."

Maurois sees an application of all this to the suicidal wars in which mankind is repeatedly involved, and which are based, he says, on the erroneous belief that "after a period of violence . . . a new golden age will dawn for mankind because a particular class or race has triumphed." "In the name of this false ideal men cut one another's throats, asphyxiate one another, willingly undergo the most horrible torments. . . . Such is the cycle which humanity has already traversed a great many times. May we hope that it will at last say to itself, 'I have been before,' and that it will eventually find the wisdom to renounce self-destruction?"[100] Quoting from the play:]

ORMUND: If I'd any sense I'd use [my revolver to kill myself]. No more questions that can't be answered, twisting like knives in your guts. Sleep, a good sleep, the only good sleep.

DR. GÖRTLER: I am afraid you will be disappointed. It will be a sleep full of
dreams—like this. And the questions will still be there. You cannot blow
them to bits with a pistol.

ORMUND: . . . I suppose you believe that if I take the jump into the dark,
I'll find myself back again on the old treadmill. Well, I don't believe it. I
can find peace.

DR. GÖRTLER: You can't. Peace is not somewhere just waiting for you. . . .
You have to create it. . . . Life is not easy. It provides no short cuts, no
effortless escapes. . . . Life is penetrated through and through by our
feeling, imagination and will. In the end the whole universe must respond
to every real effort we make. We each live a fairy tale created by
ourselves.

ORMUND: What—by going around the same damned dreary circle of existence as you believe?

DR. GÖRTLER: We do not go round a circle. That is an illusion, just as the
circling of the planets and stars is an illusion. We move along a spiral
track. It is not quite the same journey from the cradle to the grave each
time. Sometimes the differences are small. Sometimes they are very important. We must set out each time on the same road but along that road
we have a choice of adventures.[101]

ALDOUS HUXLEY (1894–1963)

British-American Author

[From Aldous Huxley's *The Perennial Philosophy:*]

The eschatologists of the Orient affirm that there are certain posthumous
conditions in which meritorious souls are capable of advancing from a heaven
of happy personal survival to genuine immortality in union with the timeless,
eternal Godhead. And, of course, there is also the possibility (indeed, for
most individuals, the necessity) of returning to some form of embodied life,
in which the advance towards complete beatification, or deliverance through
enlightenment, can be continued. . . .

Orthodox Christian doctrine does not admit the possibility, either in the
posthumous state or in some other embodiment, of any further growth towards the ultimate perfection of a total union with the Godhead. But in the
Hindu and Buddhist versions of the Perennial Philsophy the divine mercy is
matched by the divine patience: both are infinite. For oriental theologians there
is no eternal damnation; there are only purgatories and then an indefinite
series of second chances to go forward towards not only man's, but the whole
creation's final end—total reunion with the Ground of all being. . . .

In the Vedanta cosmology there is . . . something in the nature of a soul that reincarnates in a gross or subtle body, or manifests itself in some incorporeal state. The soul is not the personality of the defunct, but rather the particularized I—consciousness out of which a personality arises. [This conception] is logically self-consistent and can be made to "save the appearances"—in other words, to fit the odd and obscure facts of psychical research.[102]

THOMAS WOLFE (1900–1938)

American Novelist

[From the narrative of Thomas Wolfe's autobiographical novel *Look Homeward, Angel,* it is evident that the title points to the preexistence and immortality of the inner self in man. The title, in fact, strikes an appropriate note for the reincarnation theme with which the story, and our extracts, opens and closes. In the middle selections given here, the hero, Eugene Gant, reminisces as a babe in the crib, and then as a boy during preschool days.]

Each of us is all the sums he has not counted; subtract us into nakedness and night again, and you shall see begin in Crete four thousand years ago the love that ended yesterday in Texas. . . . Each moment is the fruit of forty thousand years. (Chapter 1)

Lying darkly in his crib, washed, powdered, and fed, he thought quietly of many things before he dropped off to sleep. . . . He saw his life down the solemn vista of a forest aisle, and he knew he would always be the sad one: caged in that little round skull, imprisoned in that beating and most secret heart, his life must always walk down lonely passages. . . . He had been sent from one mystery into another: somewhere within or without his consciousness he heard a great bell ringing faintly, as if it sounded undersea, and as he listened, the ghost of memory walked through his mind, and for a moment he felt that he had almost recovered what he had lost. (Chapter 4)

Secure and conscious now in the guarded and sufficient strength of home, he lay with well-lined belly before the roasting vitality of the fire, poring insatiably over great volumes in the bookcase. The books he delighted in most were . . . called *Ridpath's History of the World*. Their numberless pages were illustrated with hundreds of drawings, engravings, wood-cuts: he followed the progression of the centuries pictorially before he could read. . . . The past unrolled to him in separate and enormous visions; he built unending legends upon the pictures of the kings of Egypt, charioted swiftly by soaring horses, and something infinitely old and recollective seemed to awaken in him as he looked upon fabulous monsters, the twined beards and huge beast-bodies of Assyrian kings, the walls of Babylon. (Chapter 6)

[In the closing paragraphs of the volume, Eugene Gant, as a young man, is shown venturing forth into the world:] He stood naked and alone in darkness . . . he stood upon the ramparts of his soul, before the lost land of himself. . . . Lost in the thickets of myself, I will hunt you down until you cease to haunt my eyes with hunger. I heard your foot-falls in the desert, I saw your shadow in old buried cities, I heard your laughter running down a million streets, but I did not find you there. And no leaf hangs for me in the forest; I shall lift no stone upon the hills; I shall find no door in any city. But in the city of myself, upon the continent of my soul, I shall find the forgotten language, the lost world, a door where I may enter.[103]

CHARLES A. LINDBERGH (1902–1974)

American Aviator

[Charles Lindbergh's *The Spirit of St. Louis* is far more than a tale of courage and adventure concerning his historic flight across the Atlantic. (When we read the extracts from this book, we may understand why he chose to call his first story of the flight *We*.) The later work reveals the strange dissociation of states of consciousness that went on within himself as the thirty-four-hour flight proceeded and he waged a superhuman battle to keep awake. (He had not slept during the night and day preceding.) First, a separation was observed to take place between mind and body—aspects of himself he usually regarded as indivisible. Overwhelmed with drowsiness the senses and organs sought sleep though obviously it meant their certain death, but the mind entity standing "apart" held firm. In turn the mind became unable to preserve wakefulness, only to give way to a transcendent power that Lindbergh hardly suspected was within him. Finally, in midocean, the conscious mind fell fast asleep, and this third element, this new "extraordinary mind," which at first he feared to trust, now directed the flight. Here, in brief, is what he says occurred:

The fuselage behind became crowded with ghostly human presences, transparent, riding weightless with him in the plane. No surprise is experienced at their arrival, and without turning his head he sees them all, for his skull has become "one great eye, seeing everywhere at once." They seem able to disappear or show themselves at will, to pass through the walls of the plane as though no walls existed. Sometimes voices from afar off resound in the plane, familiar voices, advising him on his flight, encouraging him, conveying messages unattainable in normal life.

What connection exists between these "spirits" and himself? It is more like a reunion of friends after years of separation, "as though I've known all of them before in some past incarnation." Perhaps they are the products of the experience of ages, dwellers of a realm closed to the men of our world. He feels himself in a transitional state between earthly life and a vaster region beyond, as if caught in the magnetic field between two planets and propelled by forces he cannot control, "representing powers incomparably stronger than I've ever known." Only when his conscious direction of the plane's course seems imperative does he find himself momentarily wakened, to be soon followed by these long, strange interludes of "sleep" with eyes wide open.

Values are changing within his consciousness. For twenty-five years it has been imprisoned in walls of bone, and he had not recognized the endlessness of life, the immortal existence that lies outside. Is he already "dead" and about to join these "phantoms"? Death ceases to be the final end he thought it was. Simultaneously, he lives in the past, the present, and the future. Around him are "old associations, bygone friendships, voices from ancestrally distant times." Yes, he is flying in a plane over the Atlantic, but he is also living in ages long past.[104]]

RUMER GODDEN (1907–   )
British Author

[Rumer Godden's *The River,* as those who read the book or saw Jean Renoir's memorable film will recall, is the story of Harriet, a young girl growing up in India, where Miss Godden herself lived as a child. A work of great delicacy and sensitivity, it portrays the wonder and innocence of childhood against the background of nature and Oriental life. Some selections follow:]

Harriet . . . went back to the house, and on her way she passed Victoria with her doll. "I play so beautifully with my baby," she said to Harriet as Harriet passed. "She was born again yesterday."

"You are always having her born," said Harriet scornfully.

"Why not?" asked Victoria. "You can be born again and again, can't you?"

It was puzzling. Every time Harriet examined somebody's silly remark, it seemed not to be so silly. . . .

Sometimes, in the night, Harriet thought about death. She thought about Father and Mother dying, or Nan, who was really very old, then she would hastily wake Bea to comfort her. When Ram Prasad's wife died, she was carried on a string bed to the river and put on a pyre and burned. Afterwards her ashes were thrown on the water. . . . Harriet . . . had not seen the body, only those ashes, and they did not seem to have anything to do with a person who had lived and walked and talked and eaten food and played with her baby and laughed. . . .

She asked Father what Buddhists did when they died; he took down a

book and read to her about a drop sliding into the crystal sea. . . . She asked
Mother, and Mother pointed out that Harriet knew already that Jesus rose
from the dead; some people, she added, believe that you come back over and
over again, to live another life each time, "A better life," said Mother.

"Goodness, how good you must be in the end," said Harriet.

That was the idea, Mother thought, and if you were not good, she went on
to say, you came back as something lower. . . . Bogey, who did not like to
be labelled good or bad, was bored with the idea. "I should rather have done
with it," said Bogey.

All these thoughts seemed like cracks in the wholeness of Harriet's unconsciousness. It had cracked before, of course, but now she was growing
rapaciously.[105]

J. D. SALINGER (1919–   )

American Author

[J. D. Salinger's short story "Teddy" concerns a phenomenal ten-year-old
American boy who matter-of-factly recalls a previous incarnation in India.
Brought before several panels of skeptical professors, they are soon confounded by his knowledge and clairvoyant powers. Teddy's casual attitude
toward death—even his own foreseen tragic death within the hour—seems
evident from these brief selections:]

[Nicholson is speaking:] "As I understand it . . . you hold pretty firmly
to the Vedantic theory of reincarnation."

"It isn't a theory, it's as much a part—"

"All right," Nicholson said quickly. He smiled, and gently raised the flats
of his hands, in a sort of ironic benediction. "We won't argue that point, for
the moment. Let me finish. . . . From what I gather, you've acquired certain
information through meditation, that's given you some conviction that in
your last incarnation you were a holy man in India, but more or less fell from
Grace—"

"I wasn't a holy man," Teddy said. "I was just a person making very nice
spiritual advancement. . . . I met a lady, and I sort of stopped meditating.
. . . I would have had to take another body and come back to earth again
anyway—I mean I wasn't so spiritually advanced that I could have died, if I
hadn't met that lady, and then gone straight to Brahma and never again have
to come back to earth. But I wouldn't have had to get incarnated in an
American body if I hadn't met that lady. I mean it's very hard to meditate and
live a spiritual life in America. People think you're a freak if you try to.
. . ."

"Is it true, or isn't it, that you informed the whole Leidekker examining
bunch . . . when and where and how they would eventually die? . . ."

"I didn't tell them when they were actually going to die. That's a very false rumor," Teddy said. "I could have, but I knew that in their hearts they really didn't want to know. I mean I knew that even though they teach Religion and Philosophy and all, they're still pretty afraid to die." Teddy sat, or reclined, in silence for a minute. "It's so silly," he said. "All you do is get the heck out of your body when you die. My gosh, everybody's done it thousands of times. Just because they don't remember it doesn't mean they haven't done it. It's so silly." . . .

Nicholson said: "Ever think you might like to do something in research when you grow up? Medical research, or something of that kind? It seems to me, with your mind, you might eventually—" . . .

"That wouldn't interest me very much. Doctors stay too right on the surface. They're always talking about cells and things. . . . I grew my own body. Nobody else did it for me. So if I grew it, I must have known how to grow it. Unconsciously, at least. I may have lost the *conscious* knowledge of how to grow it sometime in the last few hundred thousand years, but the knowledge is still *there*, because—obviously—I've used it. . . . It would take quite a lot of meditation and emptying out to get the whole thing back—I mean the conscious knowledge—but you could do it if you wanted to. If you opened up wide enough."[106]

JAMES JONES (1921–1977)
American Novelist

[From James Jones's *From Here to Eternity:*]

"Some day they will rank Joe Hill right up alongside old John the Baptist. He must have done something great, back a long time ago before he was ever Joe Hill, to have earned a chance at a ticket like that one." When Prewitt asked what he meant, he said, "In one of his previous lives." . . .

Jack Malloy believed in reincarnation, because to his logical mind, it was the only logical explanation. And it was for this same reason that he worshipped the memory of Joseph Hillstrom so. "He was a saint. He had to be one, to have been given the life he was allowed to have."

[Prewitt] remembered one day for no good reason how Jack Malloy had always talked about Jack London all the time, and how he had worshipped him almost as much as Joe Hill. . . . So he started to [read London's books] in earnest. Of them all, he liked *Before Adam* and *The Star Rover* the best because for the first time they gave him a clear picture of what Malloy had meant by reincarnation of souls. He thought he could see now, how there could just as easily be an evolution of souls in different bodies, just like there had been an evolution of bodies in different souls from . . . prehistoric times. . . . It seemed to be logical. . . .[107]

NORMAN MAILER (1923–)
American Author

[From Norman Mailer's volume *Marilyn,* a biography of Marilyn Monroe, which seeks to explain her tragic suicide:]

If we want to comprehend the insane, then we must question the fundamental notion of modern psychiatry—that we have but one life and one death. The concept that no human being has ever existed before or will be reincarnated again is a philosophical rule of thumb which dominates psychiatry; yet all theory built upon this concept has failed—one is tempted to say *systemically*—in every effort to find a consistent method of cure for psychotics. Even the least spectacular processes of reasoning may therefore suggest that to comprehend psychosis, and the psychology of those who are exceptional (like our heroine), it could be time to look upon human behavior as possessed of a double root. While the dominant trunk of our actions has to be influenced by the foreground of our one life here and now and living, the other root may be attached to some karmic virtue or debt some of us (or all of us) acquired by our courage or failure in lives we have already lived. If such theory is certainly supported by no foundation, nonetheless it offers some immediate assistance for comprehending the insane, since it would suggest we are not all conceived in equal happiness or desperation.

Any human who begins life with the debt of owing existence somewhat more than others is thereby more likely to generate an ambition huge enough to swallow old debts. (And be less content with modest success.) Of course, the failure of such ambition must double all desperation. Double-entry bookkeeping on a celestial level! . . . Yet if we are to understand Monroe, and no one has . . . why not assume that [she] may have been born with a desperate imperative formed out of all those previous debts and failures of her whole family of souls. . . . To explain her at all, let us hold to that karmic notion as one more idea to support in our mind while trying to follow the involuted pathways of her life.[108]

RICHARD BACH (1936–)
American Aviator and Author

[*Jonathan Livingston Seagull* has become a legend of our time, and perhaps of future generations, too. Richard Bach expresses discomfort at being considered the real author. I don't write like that, he says. The inspiration to put down the first few pages came one day when a voice out of nowhere said "Jonathan Livingston Seagull." But it took eight years for the conclusion to come through, this time in dream. *Time* magazine, in a cover story on the tiny volume, quotes Bach as saying: ``Jonathan is that brilliant little fire that burns within us all, that lives only for those moments when we reach perfection.''[109]

Jonathan was an isolated outcast because he passionately sought mastery of the art of flying, while the flock lived short, bored, fearful, angry lives haggling for food. ``There's a reason to life!'' he told them. ``We can lift ourselves out of ignorance. . . . We can be free. *We can learn to fly!*'' They would not listen. In his next incarnation, this time in an advanced world that is at first mistaken for heaven, Jonathan meets Chiang, a remarkable gull who initiates him into the occult mysteries of conquering space and time and finding the Eternal Here and Now. Yearning to bring this wonderful wisdom to earth Jon incarnates here again. The scene that follows takes place in the advanced world, and Jon is ``speaking'':]

``Where is everybody, Sullivan?'' he asked silently, quite at home now with the easy telepathy that these gulls used instead of screes and gracks. ``Why aren't there more of us here? Why, where I came from there were . . .''

``. . . thousands and thousands of gulls, I know.'' Sullivan shook his head. ``The only answer I can see, Jonathan, is that you are pretty well a one-in-a-million bird. Most of us came along ever so slowly. We went from one world into another that was almost exactly like it, forgetting right away where we had come from, not caring where we were headed, living for the moment. Do you have any idea how many lives we must have gone through before we even got the first idea that there is more to life than eating, or fighting, or power in the Flock? A thousand lives, Jon, ten thousand! And then another hundred lives until we began to learn that there is such a thing as perfection, and another hundred again to get the idea that our purpose for living is to find that perfection and show it forth. The same rule holds for us now, of course; we choose our next world through what we learn in this one. Learn nothing, and the next world is the same as this one, all the same limitations and lead weights to overcome. . . . But you, Jon, learned so much at one time that you didn't have to go through a thousand lives to reach this one.''[110]

STORIES OF ``REMEMBRANCES'' OF PAST LIVES

[In the annals of reincarnation literature there are many case histories of individuals who seem to remember former lives. In the next chapter the leading scientific investigator in the field, Dr. Ian Stevenson, will be discussing this type of possible recall as well as his methods of research. Dr. Stevenson is now Carlson Professor of Psychiatry at the University of Virginia Medical School, where he was formerly chairman of the department of neurology and psychiatry.

The stories that follow are presented as originally told, the task of analysis being left to the reader. The first account appeared in *The American Magazine* (July 1915), under the title "Was It Reincarnation?" It won first prize in a national contest on "The Most Extraordinary Coincidence I Know Of." The author lived in Minneapolis, Minnesota.]

The value of a coincidence lies in its exactitude. Anyone with inventive genius may weave together a combination of circumstances which would be very remarkable, if true—and such inventions mark "fiction" across the tale. Perhaps the best internal evidence of the truth of this little story is its simplicity. Another matter worth noting is that the diary in which the record was made many years ago and the documentary history in which the note was found are still in existence, and the characters are still living to bear witness—if their word be believed.

And this is the way one of the most absolutely truthful women I ever knew or can hope to know told the story:

"Anne, my little half-sister, younger by fifteen years, was a queer little mite from the beginning. She did not even look like any member of the family we ever heard of, for she was dark almost to swarthiness, while the rest of us all were fair, showing our Scotch-Irish ancestry unmistakably.

"As soon as she could talk in connected sentences, she would tell herself fairy stories, and just for the fun of the thing I would take down her murmurings with my pencil in my old diary. She was my especial charge—my mother being a very busy woman—and I was very proud of her. These weavings of fancy were never of the usual type that children's fairy tales take; for, in addition to the childish imagination, there were bits of knowledge in them that a baby could not possibly have absorbed in any sort of way.

"Another remarkable thing about her was that everything she did she seemed to do through habit, and, in fact, such was her insistence, although she was never able to explain what she meant by it. If you could have seen the roystering air with which she would lift her mug of milk when she was only three and gulp it down at one quaffing, you would have shaken with laughter. This particularly embarrassed my mother and she reproved Anne repeatedly. The baby was a good little soul, and would seem to try to obey, and then in an absent-minded moment would bring on another occasion for mortification. 'I can't help it, Mother,' she would say over and over again, tears in her baby voice, 'I've always done it that way!'

``So many were the small incidents of her 'habits' of speech and thought and her tricks of manner and memory that finally we ceased to think anything about them, and she herself was quite unconscious that she was in any way different from other children.

``One day when she was four years old she became very indignant with Father about some matter and, as she sat curled up on the floor in front of us, announced her intention of going away forever.

`` 'Back to heaven where you came from?' inquired Father with mock seriousness. She shook her head.

`` 'I didn't come from heaven to you,' she asserted with that calm conviction to which we were quite accustomed now. 'I went to the moon first, but—You know about the moon, don't you? It used to have people on it, but it got so hard that we had to go.'

``This planned to be a fairy tale, so I got my pencil and diary.

`` 'So, my father led her on, 'you came from the moon to us, did you?'

`` 'Oh, no,' she told him in casual fashion. 'I have been here lots of times—sometimes I was a man and sometimes I was a woman!'

``She was so serene in her announcement that my father laughed heartily, which enraged the child, for she particularly disliked being ridiculed in any way.

`` 'I was! I was!' she maintained indignantly. 'Once I went to Canada when I was a man! I 'member my name, even.'

`` 'Oh, pooh-pooh,' he scoffed, 'little United States girls can't be men in Canada! What was your name that you 'member so well?'

``She considered a minute. 'It was Lishus Faber,' she ventured, then repeated it with greater assurance, 'that was it—Lishus Faber.' She ran the sounds together so that this was all I could make out of it—and the name so stands in my diary today, 'Lishus Faber.'

`` 'And what did you do for a living, Lishus Faber, in those early days?' My father then treated her with the mock solemnity befitting her assurance and quieting her nervous little body.

`` 'I was a soldier'—she granted the information triumphantly—'and I took the gates!'

``That was all that is recorded there. Over and over again, I remember, we tried to get her to explain what she meant by the odd phrase, but she only repeated her words and grew indignant with us for not understanding. Her imagination stopped at explanations. We were living in a cultured community, but although I repeated the story to inquire about the phrase—as one does tell stories of beloved children—no one could do more than conjecture its meaning.

``Someone encouraged my really going further with the matter, and for a year I studied all the histories of Canada I could lay my hands on for a battle in which somebody 'took the gates.' All to no purpose. Finally I was directed by a librarian to a 'documentary' history, I suppose it is—a funny old volume with the s's all like f's, you know. This was over a year afterward, when I had quite lost hope of running my phrase to earth. It was a quaint old book, interestingly picturesque in many of its tales, but I found one bit that put all the others out of my mind for a time. It was a brief account of the taking of a little walled city by a small company of soldiers, a distinguished feat of some sort, yet of no general importance. A young lieutenant with his small band— the phrase leaped to my eyes—'took the gates' . . . and the name of the young lieutenant was 'Aloysius Le Fèbre.' "

[Going back to the part where the child states that mankind once lived on the moon, this may sound quite fantastic, but theosophists might find it corroborative of their views that the moon was once a living planet and the former home of present humanity.[1] It is now known that the moon rocks brought back by the astronauts are older than any found on earth.]

[This unusual story is told by a British psychiatrist, Dr. Arthur Guirdham, who reveals that the case history of the woman patient under consideration left him no alternative but to accept reincarnation. He met her first in 1961 when he was chief psychiatrist at Bath Hospital, England, where she came to consult him about persistent nightmares. These dreams were accompanied by shrieks. so loud that she and her husband feared they would wake the street. Our source material is a published interview with Dr. Guirdham, and one of his lectures; also his book on the case, *The Cathars and Reincarnation.*[2] In the interview, from which we first quote, he opens by telling the background of his patient:]

She had been suffering for years from dreadful dreams of murder and massacre. . . . I examined the woman for neuroses. She had none, but as the dreams had occurred with such regularity since the age of 12, she was worried about them. She was a perfectly sane, ordinary housewife. There was certainly nothing wrong with her mental faculties.

After a few months, she told me that when she was a girl . . . she had written [the dreams] down. She had also written things that came into her mind, things she couldn't understand about people and names she had never heard of. She gave me the papers and I started to examine them.

[What first amazed him, Dr. Guirdham says, was the verses of songs she had written as a schoolgirl. They were in medieval French, a subject she had never taken at school, as he later checked.]

I sent a report of her story to Professor Père Nellie of Toulouse University and asked his opinion. He wrote back immediately that this was an accurate account of the Cathars, or Cathari, a group of [people of] Puritan philosophy in Toulouse in the 13th Century. [See ``Reincarnation in the Dark Ages`` in chapter 3.]

She [also] told me of the massacre of the Cathars. She told in horrid detail of being burned at the stake. . . . I was astounded. I had never thought of reincarnation, never believed in it or disbelieved. . . . She also said that in her previous life she was kept prisoner in a certain church crypt. Experts said it had never been used for this purpose. Then further research showed that so many religious prisoners were taken on one occasion, that there was no room for all of them in regular prisons. Some had been kept in that very crypt. . . .

In 1967 I decided to visit the south of France and investigate. I read the manuscripts of the 13th Century. Those old manuscripts—available only to scholars who have special permission—showed she was accurate. She gave me names and descriptions of people, places and events, all of which turned out to be accurate to the last detail. There was no way she could have known about them. Even of the songs she wrote as a child, we found four in the archives. They were correct word for word. . . .

I started this as a clinical exercise, and I have proved that what a 20th-Century person told me about a 13th-Century religion—without any knowledge of it—was correct in every detail.[3]

[In the *Cathars and Reincarnation,* Dr. Guirdham accumulates much evidence of the girl's knowledge of thirteenth-century practices. She had made correct drawings of old French coins, jewelry worn, and the layout of buildings. She was able to place accurately in their family and social relationships, people who were by no means historical characters, who do not appear in the textbooks, but who were ultimately traced by going back to the records of the Inquisition. These minor characters ``are still traceable owing to the ant-like industry of the Inquisitors and their clerks.`` As to her burning, the patient transcribed for Dr. Guirdham this dream written in shorthand many years previously:]

The pain was maddening. You should pray to God when you're dying, if you can pray when you're in agony. In my dream I didn't pray to God. . . . I didn't know when you were burnt to death you'd bleed. I thought the blood would all dry up in the terrible heat. But I was bleeding heavily. The blood was dripping and hissing in the flames. I wished I had enough blood to put the flames out. The worst part was my eyes. I hate the thought of going blind.

. . . In this dream I was going blind. I tried to close my eyelids but I couldn't. They must have been burnt off, and now those flames were going to pluck my eyes out with their evil fingers. . . .

The flames weren't so cruel after all. They began to feel cold. Icy cold. It occurred to me that I wasn't burning to death but freezing to death. I was numb with the cold and suddenly I started to laugh. I had fooled those people who thought they could burn me. I am a witch. I had magicked the fire and turned it into ice.[4]

[In Dr. Guirdham's lecture "Reincarnation and the Practice of Medicine," he adds some further details:]

Twenty-five years ago, as a student, a school girl at the age of 13, she was insisting that Cathar priests did not always wear black. You'll find the statement that they did in any book on the subject written in any language until 1965. She was very worried, because she always thought that I might not believe her when she said that her friend in the 13th century wore dark blue. It now transpires that at one sitting of the Inquisition (the Inquisition of Jacques Fournier, who was bishop at Palmiers), it came out ten times in one session that Cathar priests sometimes wore dark blue or dark green. But that fact had been lying in the archives in Latin for long enough, and was only accessible to the public in 1965 when Duvernoy edited the record of the said Inquisitors that was published at Toulouse in 1966. But this woman knew this in 1944 as a school girl.

Again she could describe rituals . . . in a house, a kind of convent. . . . Professor Nelli, the greatest living authority on the Troubadours—who definitely are spiritually connected with the Cathars—wrote to me and said, "This is almost exactly Cathar ritual, making allowance for local deviations." He also added later that he could tell me where the place was, the convent of Montreal. By way of future advice he added that, in case of doubt one should "go by the patient." Professor Nelli is a most meticulous and skeptical assessor of evidence.

When I first wrote to Professor Duvernoy at Toulouse, he said, "Get in touch with me about anything you want, I am astonished at your detailed knowledge of Catharism." I couldn't say, "I've got this by copying down the dreams of a woman of thirty-six or seven which she had when she was a Grammar School girl of thirteen." He's found out since, but he's all the more keen to supply me with the evidence. . . .

If the professors at Toulouse are amazed at the accuracy with which an English girl can produce details of Catharism known to few, that is good enough for me. . . . All I have done in this matter was to listen to the story, act as an amateur historian, and to verify from many sources the details she had noted. I believe this to be a unique and entirely valid experience.[5]

[In the early days of his motion picture career, Melvyn Douglas related this true story:]

Robin Hull was a little fellow, just five years old. He talked well for his age, for the most part. But often . . . his mother noticed him uttering strange sounds. . . . They were, she decided, an unintelligible abracadabra left over from his infancy. However, as time went on and Robin came to speak more and more fluently, she really thought it odd that he should continue uttering these same strange sounds. . . . ``I really don't understand it,'' she told her dinner guests one evening. ``Robin really says these sounds as if they had definite meaning to him. Moreover, he repeats many of them so frequently that I have come to recognize them.''

One of the Hull guests was a woman interested in reincarnation. ``Would you let me come and sit with you in the nursery one afternoon . . . just on the chance Robin might talk this way?'' she asked. ``I'd be glad to,'' Mrs. Hull told her. So the next afternoon found the two women in the nursery with Master Hull. He was extremely obliging. He said dozens of strange sounding words. His mother's guest was fascinated. ``I'm sure he is saying real words,'' she said. ``Words which would mean something to someone . . . if we could only find the right someone. . . . Please let me bring a professor I know . . . He is familiar with a number of the Asiatic languages.'' Mrs. Hull agreed to have the professor come, although now she admits that she wished she hadn't mentioned anything about Robin's curious jargon. She didn't relish a lot of people with strange beliefs trooping into his nursery and proceeding to read their own meaning into everything he said.

A week later her friend came with the professor. . . . Robin . . . talked as usual. He very evidently wasn't at all self-conscious about these strange sounds he made. . . . Finally after more than an hour had passed, they left the nursery. The professor turned to Mrs. Hull. ``The words Robin keeps saying are from a language and dialect used in northern Tibet,'' he told her. ``There's no doubt about many of them. Others I do not recognize at all. . . . Was he, by any remote chance, there as a baby? Have you or your husband, or any of your family, or any of your husband's family ever been there?'' To all these questions Alice Hull shook her head.

Then the professor called Robin. . . . ``Where did you learn the words you say?'' ``In school,'' Robin told him. ``But, Robin dear,'' interrupted his mother, ``you've never been to school.'' ``When I went to school—before,'' said Robin, his little brow furrowed. ``Do you remember what the school

looked like?" the professor asked. . . . For a long minute Robin was
thoughtful. Then he said, "Yes, I remember. It was in the mountains. But
they weren't the kind of mountains we went to in the summer,
mamma. . . ."

"Was this school you went to made of wood or of stone . . . ?" "It was
stone," said Robin. "And tell me, what were the teachers like? Were they
ladies or men?" "They were men," Robin showed no hesitancy on this
score. "But they didn't dress like you and my daddy. They had skirts. With a
sash around their waist that looked like a rope. . . ." And Robin gave a
detailed description of the school.

[The professor was so impressed with everything the boy said, he undertook the long journey—long in those days—to Asia and northern Tibet in
search of the school. Fortunately, the latter area is close to China, and not so
difficult of access as eastern Tibet. Eventually the Hulls received this letter
from him:]

"I have found the school about which Robin told us. It is in the Kuen-lun
mountains, rocky and arid, and, of course, not at all like the mountains
where Robin now spends his summers. And it tallies with Robin's description in every detail. So do the lamas (priests) who teach there."[6]

[The experience just related is technically called by parapsychologists as an
example of xenoglossy—the ability to speak an identifiable foreign language
that has not been learned by ordinary means. The two forms of xenoglossy,
recitative and responsive, will be explained in the "Ian Stevenson" section.

The editors know of one case in this category that was orally related by a
prominent New York physician, Dr. Marshall W. McDuffie, who died in the
1930s. To the mystification of Dr. McDuffie and his wife Wilhelmina, their
twin baby boys were found to be conversing among themselves in some
unknown vernacular. The children were eventually taken to the foreign language department at Columbia University, but none of the professors present
could identify their speech. However, a professor of ancient languages happened to pass by and was amazed to discover that the babies were speaking
Aramaic, a language current at the time of Christ!

Two cases of xenoglossy were reported in a German newspaper,
Rheinischer Merkur (May 31, 1947), published in Koblenz:]

We have recently been informed that a Sicilian peasant, not used to drinking, was regaled by friends with heavy wine, until he sank into a deep sleep;
when he awoke, to the astonishment of his family he addressed his surround-

ing friends with completely strange words, which turned out to be old Greek. The peasant is absolutely uneducated and never spoke or understood Greek, still less the classical language of the old Hellenes. It posed quite a riddle to his friends and to the professors who were called and recognized the words as genuine. So the only explanation left was the belief in transmigration of the soul. . . .

Not only here with us, but also abroad in the whole world, things happen, of which our school learning never even dreams about. . . . A similar case is described in a message from India. In the town of Ihansi, a small girl fell out of a third story window. She did not suffer any bodily harm, but suddenly started to talk in several languages, which turned out to be old Indian dialects which had not been used for very many years and had died out.

[In 1974 appeared Edward Ryall's *Second Time Around*, published in London. The American edition was titled *Born Twice—Total Recall of a Seventeenth-Century Life*.[7] This is one of the cases that Dr. Stevenson spent several years researching. In his introduction to the volume he tabulates some of his findings, and reserves for the appendix more detailed results of his investigations.

In *Born Twice*, Edward Ryall chronicles his life as John Fletcher, a yeoman farmer born in 1645 in the countryside of Polden Hills, Somerset, England. He participated in the Monmouth Rebellion, and the Battle of Sedgemoor, had a sadly ending love affair with Melanie, took part in the hiding of Joseph Alleine and the rescue of Susannah Fuller from the bully Adrian Toombes, and had a near-fatal accident in the mill of Moorlinch. He was killed in 1685 by a cavalryman in the army of King James II. Fletcher had volunteered to take part in the abortive insurrection against the king by the Duke of Monmouth.

In 1902, 217 years later, Edward Ryall was born. One lovely summer evening when he was eight years old, standing in a quiet country garden with his father, he looked up at the dark night sky and saw a shooting star. His father pointed it out as Halley's Comet. The lad imprudently remarked that he had seen it before and was sternly reprimanded. Because of the antagonism of his family, Ryall told no one of his memories for many years. Eventually he confided some of them to his wife. At the age of sixty, he at last felt free to speak out.

In its wealth of detail, *Born Twice* goes far beyond other reports of distant memories. Dr. Stevenson found that Ryall's account of seventeenth-century life in England was astonishingly complete and accurate, including many obscure details that only rare studies of the period would mention. Consequently, the paramount question before Stevenson was: Did Ryall ever read this material? Was his affirmation true that he never read any specialized book dealing with the events of the seventeenth century? In addition to Stevenson's intensive historical research, he interviewed Ryall in England, and thereafter carried on a voluminous correspondence. He writes:

> Throughout this exchange Edward Ryall has . . . shown a remarkable consistency in what he has written about his memories. Sometimes he has caught me in lapses of memory about what he had written earlier in reply to some query from me. I have never sought to trick him, or for that matter, any other subject whose case I have investigated. For exposing the occasional liars I have met I have mainly relied on their betraying themselves through inconsistencies in their accounts at different times or through the development into visibility of obvious motives for personal profit from whatever they were saying. Edward Ryall has . . . never displayed the least sign of a mercenary attitude towards [his experiences].

Stevenson remarks that "the existence of numerous novels supposedly based on memories of previous lives—whose authors evidently wish to reach all markets—increases the danger that the present book will be assigned to their group."

> The authors of such books often claim that their basic plots and characters derive from true memories of real previous lives and they justify the use of a novel form as providing the only format in which they can get their story before the public. Once committed to this corruption the temptations for heightening interest by small and larger embellishments soon transform such a work from what might have been a description of psychical experiences through the stage of a historical novel, to that of pure fiction. . . .
>
> Having no illusions about the difficulty of attaining truth, I am convinced that the search for it is very badly served by mixing what we have found of it with fantasy. In the composition of the present work, Edward Ryall had no need of my advice because he was determined to report his memories as accurately as he could without any conscious additions from his imagination or other extraneous sources. I nevertheless gave him my counsel on this point, which was never to add to his book, so far as he could prevent himself, anything that he was not sure derived from his memories of the previous life of John Fletcher that he says he remembers. I know he has tried to do this and I think he has succeeded.

Regarding his own memories, Ryall writes: "My memories of the seventeenth century are as much an integral part of my mind as are my recollections of this present life. They are present in my waking consciousness and are not the product of any effort at profound recall, except when I wish to clear up a point which has become vague or doubtful.'' After the clash with his father over Halley's Comet, "I refrained from speaking of my memories although they grew more vivid and interesting. I can remember that for a period of time I seemed to be transported, at varying intervals and quite without any effort on my part, to other scenes in which I met strange people. They seemed to be sombre and hard-working, in fact, they were *always* at work, and although I could observe their movements and comprehend their speech, yet not one of them seemed to notice my presence.'' "This rather upset me,'' he said, ``for I felt that I belonged to them and with them, rather than to those around me in this life.'' "This stage passed, and was followed by the unfolding of more certain memories, as I know them still, in which I was in another life, another era, as an active participant, able to communicate with those around me, and to identify the people and places of those far-off days.'' "In my style of thinking or writing of my other life . . . I think and write in the first person, as though my two lives are one continuous entity, and that I, Edward Ryall, am still John Fletcher.''

In the epilogue Ryall shares with his readers a momentous experience—a dramatic impingement of the past upon the present. It occurred in February 1945 during World War II when after the retreat of the Germans from certain parts of Italy, Ryall was in charge of a line-laying party at Marina de Pisa. Despite his four years war experience he became careless about watching the ground for mines and booby traps while stringing his copper wires on the trees overhead. In introducing what happened, Ryall says: "Here let me say that I have never had the slightest inclination to dabble in the occult in any way. I have no ideas, or knowledge, concerning its many ramifications. I have led such a busy, hard-working life that I have not given such matters more than a passing thought. How much greater, then, was the impression which the following incident made upon me, especially so in that it seemed to confirm some of the memories of a previous life which are an integral part of my make-up.''

> Suddenly I was halted in my tracks by what seemed to be an actual physical force holding me back and a voice, in the accent and idiom of West Country speech, spoke into my ear. The soft, slow sweet tones of my dear wife of long ago, unmistakable and moving, distinctly bade me: "Take heed, dear John! O not again, dear heart, not again!''
> My heart seemed literally to bound within me. I stood rooted to the spot, in a cold sweat. When I was able to pull myself together, I looked very carefully at the ground ahead, and there, only three or four paces ahead on my line of march, were the stakes of a line of picket mines, with the trip wire concealed by layers of leaves. But a few feet more, and I should have been hurled into an even more sudden and violent end than that with which I met in the seventeenth century.

We cannot go into all of Dr. Stevenson's findings. They include verifying Ryall's statements as to the time of the appearance of Halley's Comet three years before his death as Fletcher; the dates and days of the week for events described; the names of local clergymen and other notables of the section; numerous customs peculiar to the period; various coins then in circulation; agricultural, commercial, and domestic objects used; and the words and expressions current among persons living in that area and period. In fact, so many expressions that are presently obsolete are used by Ryall in his narrative that a five-page glossary had to be included to explain their meaning.

Ryall writes that one of the most vivid of his memories is "the brilliant display of the Northern Lights on the night before the battle" of Sedgemoor. "This baffled Dr. Stevenson for a time." "Finally, however, he wrote to say that he had come upon an American edition of Macaulay's *History of England* published in New York, in 1849, which mentioned this phenomenon, the author quoting among his sources some lines from the contemporary poet Dryden, who had himself witnessed the display."

Evaluating the case as a whole, Dr. Stevenson suggests that because of their unusual wealth of detail, Edward Ryall's memories "may command the respect of historians of Restoration England—in the next century if not in this one," for he reveals many intimate details of life in that period that the historians of the time apparently did not think necessary to mention. "It follows also," says Stevenson, "that if anyone agrees with me that Edward Ryall has lived before and remembers doing so, his case has contributed not a little to the slowly accumulating evidence of reincarnation." The psychiatrist concludes his introduction to *Born Twice* with these comments:

> Edward Ryall's case, like others of its type that I consider genuine, conveys something of which we all stand in need—hope. I happen to be a person who does not think the times we live in worse than any other. But if they are, then I would attribute the fact not to our widespread materialism as regards physical objects, but to the equally widespread and much more doleful materialism concerning our own natures. I do not think that such materialism creates selfishness and despair, but it certainly encourages them.
>
> The idea of a second time round suggests both hope and an incentive to better conduct. Edward Ryall reproaches John Fletcher somewhat for the folly of getting himself killed in the prime of life and at an age when he had undiminished affections and unfinished responsibilities. How many others would have shown more wisdom than he when pulled between loyalty to a dear friend and attachment to family? Only Edward Ryall should pass judgment on John Fletcher. But Edward Ryall has also had a chance to improve on John Fletcher's management of his dilemmas and if John Fletcher has become Edward Ryall in a new body, therein lies hope for the rest of us.

Dr. Stevenson adds that "unfortunately, hope has no inherent connection with truth." "Falsehood and delusions have nourished it as much as truth has. I would not endorse any doctrine as true only because it was hopeful, but if a belief, such as that of reincarnation, may be both true and hopeful, it would seem foolish not to examine the evidence that we have for it. Edward Ryall has contributed to this evidence and he deserves many readers and their gratitude.'']

[The next three cases of supposed remembrances were among the first reported by Dr. Stevenson, and appeared with others in his published essay ``The Evidence for Survival from Claimed Memories of Former Incarnations.''[8] The lengthy case histories he has subsequently analyzed and published take so much space to retell, these simpler ones have been chosen instead. However, in the section on Dr. Stevenson in this volume, a presentation of an intriguing case of xenoglossy to which he devotes an entire volume is recounted.]

The Case of Eduardo Esplugus-Cabrera. A four year old boy who lived in Havana told his parents about a home and different parents he claimed to have had in a previous life. His statements taken together gave the following items of information:

> When I lived at 69 Rue Campanario, my father's name was Pierro Seco, and my mother's Amparo. I recollect that I had two little brothers with whom I used to play, and whose names were Mercedes and Jean. The last time that I went out of this house was Sunday, 28th February, 1903, and my mother then cried a great deal while I was leaving the house. This other mother of mine had a very clear complexion and black hair. She used to make hats. I was then thirteen and I bought drugs at the American chemist's because they were cheaper than the other shops. I left my little bicycle in the room below when I came back from my walk. I was not called Eduardo as I am now, but Pancho.

The parents were sure the boy had never been to the house he named. To test the matter they made a long detour to reach the street where the house was, this house being quite unfamiliar to them and, so they firmly believed, should have been to the boy also. On arrival at the street, the boy immediately recognized the house as the one about which he had been talking. They encouraged the boy to enter the house, but he found it occupied by strangers whom he did not recognize. The parents then made further inquiries about the previous occupants of the house and uncovered the following facts.

Number 69 Rue Campanario was occupied until a short time after the month of February, 1903, by Antonio Seco who had by then (1907) left Havana. Señor Seco had a wife called Amparo and three sons called Mercedes, Jean and Pancho. Pancho had died in the month of February, 1903, just prior to the departure of the Seco family. Near the house in question was a druggist's shop corresponding to the boy's statements.

Of the eight statements made by the boy which it was possible to verify, seven correctly matched the facts and one (his father's Christian name) did not.[9]

Case of Robert. A six year old Belgian boy insisted that a portrait of his Uncle Albert (who had been killed in the First World War in 1915) was a portrait of himself. This boy was especially devoted to his paternal grandmother in contrast to her other grandchildren who largely ignored her. He was happy and healthy when with her, sullen and disobedient when with his own parents. Albert, the boy's uncle and claimed previous incarnation, had been the marked favorite of the grandmother and had meant far more to her than her other son, the father of Robert. When Robert was three and first saw a swimming pool, he ran along the diving board and dived in. Albert had been a fine diver. When a visitor pointed a moving picture camera at Robert and turned the handle with a clicking noise, he protested, saying, "Don't! Don't! They killed me that way the last time!" Albert had been killed by machine gun fire while trying to destroy a German emplacement. Robert, his grandmother reported, had used to her pet names Albert had used, and told her of likes and dislikes which Albert and she had privately shared.[10]

The Case of Alexandrina Samona. On March 15th, 1910, Alexandrina Samona, five year old daughter of Dr. and Mrs. Carmelo Samona, of Palermo, Sicily, died of meningitis to the great grief of her parents. Three days later, Mrs. Samona had a dream in which Alexandrina seemed to appear to her and say, "Mother, do not cry any more. I have not left you for good; I shall come back again little, like this." In the dream the child gestured with her hand to indicate a small baby. The same dream recurred three days later. . . .

A pregnancy . . . seemed improbable because of a previous operation on Mrs. Samona which was thought to have reduced or abolished her fertility. However, within a year Mrs. Samona [gave] birth to twin girls. One of these proved to bear an extraordinary physical resemblance to the first Alexandrina and was given the same name. Alexandrina II resembled Alexandrina I not only in appearance but also in disposition and likes and dislikes. The two Alexandrinas shared the following similarities of physical form and function: left-handedness (none of the other children of the Samonas were left-handed); hyperaemia of the left eye; slight seborrhea of the right ear; and slight facial asymmetry. With regard to the similarities between the two Alexandrinas Dr. Samona stated:

I can affirm in the most positive manner that in every way, except for the hair
and eyes, which are actually a little lighter than those of the first Alexandrina at
the same age, the resemblance continues to be perfect. But even more than on
the physical side, the psychological similarity developing in the child gives the
case in question further and greater interest. Alexandrina is indifferent to dolls
and prefers to play with children of her own age, a preference which was
equally noticeable with the other Alexandrina. Like her, too, she is always
anxious that her little hands should be clean and insists on having them washed
if they are in the least degree dirty. Like her predecessor again, she shows a
singular repugnance for cheese and will not touch soup if it has the least taste of
cheese in it. . . . When she has a chance of opening the chest of drawers in the
bedroom it is a great amusement to her to pull out the stockings and to play with
them. This was also a passion of the other Alexandrina.

Dr. Samona cited other examples of small but characteristic traits of behavior which the two Alexandrinas shared. . . .

When Alexandrina II was eight, her parents told her they planned to take
her to visit Monreale and see the sights there. At this Alexandrina II inter-
jected: "But, Mother, I know Monreale, I have seen it already." Mrs.
Samona told the child she had never been to Monreale, but the child replied:
"Oh, yes, I went there. Do you not recollect that there was a great church
with a very large statue of a man with his arms held open, on the roof? And
don't you remember that we went there with a lady who had horns and that
we met with some little red priests in the town?"

At this Mrs. Samona recollected that the last time she went to Monreale
she had gone there with Alexandrina I some months before her death. They
had taken with them a lady friend who had come to Palermo for a medical
consultation as she suffered from disfiguring excrescences on her forehead.
As they were going into the church, the Samonas' party had met a group of
young Greek priests with blue robes decorated with red ornamentation.

As the child apparently recalled incidents and not merely scenes at Monreale, she could not have derived the statements from a picture or photograph of the place. Mrs. Samona only with difficulty recalled the episode
when Alexandrina II mentioned it, and so it is unlikely that she had previously told Alexandrina II about it. It is not, however, impossible for her to
have done this and subsequently forgotten both the episode and its narration
to Alexandrina II.[11]

[The following story appeared in *Coronet* for July 1952, under the title
" 'Blind Tom': Mystery of Music." Webb B. Garrison is the author.]

Most Georgia farmers of a century ago were very particular about their
annual crop of slaves. . . . And Perry H. Oliver, of Muscogee County, was

no exception. But spring, 1850, brought him keen disappointment. . . . The baby [of one of his slaves, was born] stone blind. Later, Oliver sold the mother at a slave auction to Gen. James Bethune of Columbus, Georgia. Then he pulled the blind youngster from hiding. "Here," he chuckled, "I forgot to tell you she has a boy. I'm throwing him in free."

Bethune took the baby back to his plantation and named him Thomas Greene Bethune. . . . Sounds fascinated the sightless boy. He would sit for hours listening to the harsh grating of a corn sheller, or stand under the eaves absorbed in the dripping of rain. When the boy was four, Bethune bought a piano for his daughters. The girls soon noticed that the face of the little slave lighted whenever they played the instrument.

One night after the family had retired, Bethune heard music coming from the drawing room. He went down to investigate. The room was pitch dark, yet the melody continued. . . . The light of his candle disclosed Blind Tom playing with rapt attention. Recognizing the boy's unusual talent, his master gave him free access to the piano and decided to engage a professional teacher in Columbus. But after hearing him play, the musician refused to take him as a pupil. "That boy," he declared, "already knows more about music than I will ever know."

[At the age of seven] Tom made his debut on the concert stage in Columbus, and the audience applauded wildly. By the time he was fifteen, Blind Tom was a veteran of many concerts [both in the United States and abroad]. He was playing Beethoven, Mendelssohn, Bach, Chopin . . . and many others. He knew at least 5,000 compositions by heart. The sightless youth could hear a composition played once, then repeat it without error. In 1860, he played in Washington, D.C. Skeptics tested him with two new compositions, one 13 pages in length and the other 20. Tom listened quietly, played both without effort. On another occasion, he heard Beethoven's *Third Concerto* for the first time, then played the solo part. . . .

This wizard of the keyboard was not only blind; he had a low-grade mentality. . . . His vocabulary was limited to a few hundred words. . . . He died in Hoboken in 1908, a grotesque but world-famous prodigy whose powers are as much a mystery today as during his fantastic public career.

[Some other interesting facts about the blind musician have been given in an article in *Etude* (August 1940), one being that right from the start he used both the black and white keys of the piano. As the keys are not a natural arrangement, but an ingenious device invented by man, it is hard to understand how a blind child of four could operate them without some prior acquaintance with the piano and a period of training in its use.]

[In April 1927 an article appeared in the *Los Angeles Examiner* signed by C. H. W., telling of a New England child who had a frightful waking vision of two big yellow cats eating up a person named ``Marcella.`` In daily life the little girl knew of no one by that name, nor had she ever seen a lion in her present short life. The report continues:]

The circumstance had about passed from active memory when it occurred again, and . . . kept recurring, although with diminishing frequency and violence, all through her childhood. It was a subject about which she was very sensitive and would not talk nor permit anyone else to do so.

She grew up and married, and her husband was sent by our Government upon some diplomatic mission to Rome. One day she was a member of a dinner party at which sat a lady, a stranger to her, whose face was so familiar that it attracted her eyes again and again. Upon leaving the dinner table this stranger came up to her and asked her to walk out into the garden . . . and when beyond the hearing of the rest of the party she turned to our little New England girl, saying: ``Don't you remember me? I was Marcella and you saw me torn to pieces by the lions in the arena. I felt positive I should meet you in this incarnation.``

[``You Have Lived Before`` is the title of an article by the Irish author Shaw Desmond, which appeared in condensed form in *World Digest* (October 1940). ``After a quarter of a century's study`` of reincarnation, he finds ``that there is behind it a wealth of evidence which appears unshakable,`` and attempts to support this statement by recounting a persistent vision of his life as a Roman gladiator—a vision that offered the theme for his novel *Echo*. Besides this personal testimony, he gives the similar ``recollections`` of others. The most striking one, we give here. It presumably concerns a man of the author's acquaintance.]

Mr. Leroy Beaumont, as I will call him, though that is not his real name, from childhood had a horrible dream which returned vividly at intervals. In this dream he is an officer in strange pagan dress and equipment commanding troops at a walled camp by a broad river. In the dream he enters a house on the river bank where, after killing a spearman on guard, he finds a beautiful woman, whom he drives brutally back to the camp, where she dies of a broken heart. But always before her death in the dream, she curses him, telling him that one day *``he would wear his uniform as a mockery and would beg to her for food.``*

I was in New York at the time of ``Ben Hur.`` To the filming of this great pageant of Roman times came Beaumont, out-of-work, glad, starving as he was, to get a job as "super." On being handed his costume, he was horror-stricken to note that helmet and shield, kilt and sandals, sword and tunic were identical with those of his nightmare dream.

Returning to England, he was compelled to tramp the roads for work, sinking lower and lower. Walking from Gravesend to Chatham and going down Frindsbury Hill and walking along the river to Rochester, he was astonished to find that he knew every hill and also the site of the "camp," although he had never visited those places before. Knocking at one door, a fine blonde woman [appeared before him, and] he asked her for some food. She gasped, stared at him, and then, with eyes full of hate and horror, told him to "Go away!" He also stared—for he was looking at the woman of his dreams.

✳

[Few today recall General Homer Lea (1876–1912), the American cripple who with Dr. Sun Yat Sen overthrew the Manchu Dynasty of China, setting in motion the wheels of a new Asiatic era. As a small boy he had a dream that left an unforgettable impression. In it appeared strange men and strange sounds. At the age of ten, the dream reappeared. This time he knew the men to be Chinese soldiers. The dream came for the third time at sixteen; and this time he knew the sounds for Chinese war trumpets. It returned a fourth time, years later, just before his departure for China.

After leaving college he turned his entire attention to military strategy. In some way he gained ascendancy over the Chinese youth of San Francisco and Los Angeles, organized them, cut off the queues—the mark of servitude to the Manchu Dynasty—and began shipping them to China. Shortly afterward he followed. Then began the first unsuccessful rebellion. Lea came back with a price on his head, in all Oriental usage a disgraced man, yet Kang Yu Wei, ex-premier of China, and Liang Ki Chew, an imperial prince, attached themselves to him like servitors. His military record caused him at various times to be consulted by Lord Roberts, commander-in-chief of the British army, and Kaiser Wilhelm. The latter had a special carriage built to enable Lea to see army maneuvers.

Lea came to know Dr. Sun Yat Sen and together they plotted and carried out the uprising which made a republic—in name—of China. He died soon after, having played jackstraws with the destinies of more human beings than Napoleon probably ever realized were in the world. Like Napoleon, he considered himself a "man of destiny"; and like Napoleon, speculated upon his own peculiarities as derived from other lives of the past. A Buddhist monk, reading his palm, grew pale and pronounced the hand that of a king—or so they say.[12]]

✳

[Rather than offering a ``memory`` of a former existence, the next episode from the life of a sixteen-year-old boy may possibly explain how—in the case of one dying at an early age through sickness or ``accident``—a new body can be obtained within a short time. This ``inside`` account was given in the *Sunday Express,* May 26, 1935. W. Martin of Liverpool is reported as saying:]

In 1911, at the age of sixteen, I was staying about twelve miles away from my own home when a high wall was blown down by a sudden gust of wind as I was passing. A huge coping stone hit me on top of the head. It then seemed as if I could see myself lying on the ground, huddled up, with one corner of the stone resting on my head and quite a number of people rushing toward me. I watched them move the stone and someone took off his coat and put it under my head, and I heard all their comments: ``Fetch a doctor.`` ``His neck is broken.`` ``Skull smashed.``

One of the bystanders asked if anyone knew where I lived, and on being told I was lodging just around the corner, he instructed them to carry me there. All this time it appeared as though I were disembodied from the form lying on the ground and suspended in midair in the center of the group, and I could hear everything that was being said.

As they started to carry me it was remarked that it would come as a blow to my people, and I was immediately conscious of a desire to be with my mother. Instantly I was at home and father and mother were just sitting down to their midday meal. On my entrance mother sat bolt upright in her chair and said, ``Bert, something has happened to our boy.``

There followed an argument, but my mother refused to be pacified and said that if she caught the 2:00 p.m. train she could be with me before 3:00 p.m. She had hardly left the room when there came a knock at the front door. It was a porter from the railway station with a telegram saying I was badly hurt.

Then suddenly I was again transported—this time it seemed to be against my wish—to a bedroom, where a woman whom I recognized was in bed, and two other women were quietly bustling around, and a doctor was leaning over the bed. Then the doctor had a baby in his hands. At once I became aware of an almost irresistible impulse to press my face through the back of the baby's head so that my face would come out at the same place as the child's.

The doctor said, ``It looks as though we have lost them both,`` and again I felt the urge to take the baby's place to show him he was wrong, but the thought of my mother crying turned my thoughts in her direction, when straight-away I was in a railway carriage with her and my father.

I was still with them when they arrived at my lodgings and were shown to the room where I had been put to bed. Mother sat beside the bed and I longed to comfort her, and the realization came that I ought to do the same thing I had felt impelled to do in the case of the baby and climb into the body on the

bed. At last I succeeded, and the effort caused the real me to sit up in bed
fully conscious. Mother made me lie down again, but I said I was all right,
and remarked it was odd she knew something was wrong before the porter
had brought the telegram.

Both she and Dad were amazed at my knowledge. Their astonishment was
further increased when I repeated almost word for word some of the conversation they had had at home and in the train. I said I had been close to birth
as well as death, and told them that Mrs. Wilson, who lived close to us at
home, had had a baby that day, but it was dead because I would not get into
its body. We subsequently learned that Mrs. Wilson died on the same day at
2:05 p.m. after delivering a stillborn girl.

[David Spangler, a renowned figure in the small community movement, had a
somewhat comparable experience. In *The Magic of Findhorn,* Paul Hawken
quotes him as saying:[13]

> I was having psychic experiences when I was a baby, before I could read. I
> can remember having experiences then of a dual consciousness. I was observ-
> ing a very large ship sinking; lifeboats were coming away from it. I had a strong
> sense of having to try to do something. I was aware of the fear and the panic. It
> was nighttime, and the lights of the ship were going out, boats were pulling
> away, and the ship went down.
>
> I had this very strong impulse to seek help and remember clearly opening my
> eyes and seeing a crib, being completely disoriented, not knowing who or where
> I was, what I was doing in the crib or how old I was. I still thought that I was an
> adult, and I tried to speak. I wanted to tell the people in the room who must
> have been my parents that the ship had sunk, but the only thing that came out
> was a squeal and squeak, and within a few moments the adult sense was gone,
> and I remember nothing after that. I was very small. These experiences con-
> tinued throughout my childhood.

When he was seven he had an experience that changed his entire life. "It
was a sense of total identification with everything in the Universe. David
Spangler ceased to exist; an entirely different consciousness took over. In
that moment I knew who I was. I had a sense of the eternality of my existence . . . There was no limit to my identity . . ." The experience had a
tremendous impact. "I didn't talk about it, but it completely altered my
frame of reference. It was an experience of waking up. I couldn't translate it
into my seven-year-old consciousness easily. And from that point on, I have
had a sense of being in two different dimensions simultaneously, of being in
this one and in another one."

As David grew older he realized that "man is the ultimate answer to all his
problems; he always has been and always will be." "Man's consciousness

through the ages, from the moment when he first awakened as an individual and began to compare himself with his environment, has sought to become identified with the Divine processes flowing within himself so that he could be free . . .'' The present age, as it gives rise to a New Age, will be ''a time when man comes home again to his spirit.'' A higher type of consciousness will then unfold in him and he will become ''king of his own life.'']

[The teller of the following tale, the last we will recount, needs no introduction to those who read the concluding item under Christianity. He is the Reverend Leslie Weatherhead, former president of the Methodist Conference of Great Britain, and until his retirement in 1960 was minister of London's historic City Temple for three decades. In his 1957 talk ''The Case for Reincarnation,''[14] he reported:]

Captain and Mrs. Battista, Italians, had a little daughter born in Rome, whom they called Blanche. To help look after this child they employed a French-speaking Swiss ''Nannie'' called Marie. Marie taught her little charge to sing in French a lullaby song. Blanche grew very fond of this song and it was sung to her repeatedly. Unfortunately Blanche died and Marie returned to Switzerland. Captain Battista writes, ''The cradle song which would have recalled to us only too painful memories of our deceased child, ceased absolutely to be heard in the house . . . all recollection of [it] completely escaped from our minds.''

Three years after the death of Blanche, the mother, Signora Battista, became pregnant, and in the fourth month of the pregnancy she had a strange waking-dream. She insists that she was wide awake when Blanche appeared to her and said, in her old familiar voice, ''Mother, I am coming back.'' The vision then melted away. Captain Battista was skeptical, but when the new baby was born in February, 1906, he acquiesced in her being also given the name Blanche. The new Blanche resembled the old in every possible way.

Nine years after the death of the first Blanche, when the second was about six years of age, an extraordinary thing happened. I will use Captain Battista's own words: ''While I was with my wife in my study which adjoins our bedroom, we heard, both of us, like a distant echo, the famous cradle song, and the voice came from the bedroom where we had left our little daughter Blanche fast asleep . . . we found the child sitting up on the bed and singing with an excellent French accent the cradle song which neither of us had certainly ever taught her. My wife . . . asked her what it was she was singing, and the child, with the utmost promptitude, answered that she was singing a French song. . . . ''

" 'Who, pray, taught you this pretty song?' I asked her. 'Nobody; I know it out of my own head,' answered the child. . . . " The Captain ends with a sentence which, short of calling him a liar, it is hard to set on one side. "The reader may draw any conclusion he likes from this faithful narrative of facts to which I bear my personal witness. For myself, the conclusion I draw from them is that the dead return. . . . It looks as though, in certain circumstances, the dead are permitted to visit the world again in another body."

New Horizons in Science, Psychology, and Philosophy

![bird] THE WORLD OF SCIENTISTS

It would be curious if we should find science and philosophy taking up again the old theory of metempsychosis, remodeling it to suit our present modes of religious and scientific thought, and launching it again on the wide ocean of human belief. But stranger things have happened in the history of human opinion.

JAMES FREEMAN CLARKE

A new scientific truth does not triumph by convincing its opponents and making them see the light, but rather because its opponents eventually die and a new generation grows up that is familiar with it.

MAX PLANCK

THOMAS H. HUXLEY (1825–1895)
British Scientist, Humanist, and Educator

[In the foreword to *T. H. Huxley*, a biography (1959) by Cyril Bibby, Julian Huxley wrote: "It is right and proper that T. H. Huxley should be commemorated in this centenary of the birth of the modern theory of evolution; for if Darwin was its prime creator, Huxley was its greatest Protagonist."

417

"Huxley was much more than Darwin's bulldog," Sir Julian adds. While "I have always looked up to my grandfather with a blend of awe and admiration . . . I had thought mainly of his scientific abilities, his sheer intellectual brilliance, and his prophetic morality." But from reading Dr. Bibby's volume, "I have gained a new insight . . . and am more than ever amazed by the range of his interests, his capacities and his achievements. It shows him as an outstanding figure in nineteenth century thought, and one who left a permanent mark on the world's scientific and educational structure."[1] In a letter to Sir John Simon, Thomas Huxley remarked that "the cosmos remains always beautiful and profoundly interesting in every corner—and if I had as many lives as a cat I would leave no corner unexplored."[2]

Huxley coined the word "agnostic," because "the chief thing I was sure of was that I did not know a great many things that the—ists and—ites about me professed to be familiar with."[3] When Charles Kingsley's *Water Babies* appeared with its "one true, orthodox, rational, philosophical, logical, irrefragable, realistic, inductive, deductive, seductive, productive, salutary" doctrine "that your soul makes your body, just as a snail makes his shell," Huxley assured its author that he was as ready to believe that doctrine as its converse, because it was impossible to obtain any evidence as to the truth of either.[4]

Huxley studied theology to such effect that he could often confute the theologians in his disputes with them. It is not surprising, then, that he looked into such subjects as reincarnation.]

In the doctrine of transmigration, whatever its origin, Brahmanical and Buddhist speculation found, ready to hand, the means of constructing a plausible vindication of the ways of the Cosmos to man. . . . Yet this plea of justification is not less plausible than others; and none but very hasty thinkers will reject it on the ground of inherent absurdity. Like the doctrine of evolution itself, that of transmigration has its roots in the world of reality; and it may claim such support as the great argument from analogy is capable of supplying.

Evolution and Ethics and Other Essays[5]

I understand the main tenet of Materialism to be that there is nothing in the universe but matter and force. . . . *Kraft und Stoff*—force and matter—are paraded as the Alpha and Omega of existence. . . . Whosoever does not hold it is condemned by the more zealous of the persuasion to the Inferno appointed for fools or hypocrites. But all this I heartily disbelieve. . . . There is a third thing in the universe, to wit, consciousness, which . . . I can not see to be matter or force, or any conceivable modification of either. . . .

The student of nature, who starts from the axiom of the universality of the law of causation, can not refuse to admit an eternal existence; if he admits the conservation of energy, he can not deny the possibility of an eternal energy; if he admits the existence of immaterial phenomena in the form of consciousness, he must admit the possibility, at any rate, of *an eternal series of such phenomena.* (Italics added.) . . .

Looking at the matter from the most rigidly scientific point of view, the assumption that, amidst the myriads of worlds scattered through endless space, there can be no intelligence, as much greater than man's as his is greater than a blackbeetle's, no being endowed with powers of influencing the course of nature as much greater than his, as his is greater than a snail's, seems to me not merely baseless, but impertinent. Without stepping beyond the analogy of that which is known, it is easy to people the cosmos with entities, in ascending scale until we reach something practically indistinguishable from omnipotence, omnipresence, and omniscience.

Essays upon Some Controverted Questions[6]

THOMAS EDISON (1847–1931)

American Inventor

[As Thomas Edison was an early and lifelong member of the Theosophical Society,[7] it is not surprising that during his last illness when reporters inquired if he believed in survival after death, he replied: "The only survival I can conceive is to start a new earth cycle again."[8] On his eightieth birthday he was asked: "Do you believe man has a soul?" He answered that man as a unit of life "is composed of swarms of billions of highly charged entities which live in the cells. I believe that when a man dies, this swarm deserts the body, and goes out into space, but keeps on and enters another cycle of life and is immortal."[9] In *The Diary and Sundry Observations of Thomas Alva Edison,* the inventor provides these further thoughts:]

I cannot believe for a moment that life in the first instance originated on this insignificant little ball which we call the earth . . . The particles which combined to evolve living creatures on this planet of ours probably came from some other body elsewhere in the universe. . . . The more we learn the more we realize that there is life in things which we used to regard as inanimate, as lifeless. . . .

I don't believe for a moment that one life makes another life. Take our own bodies. I believe they are composed of myriads and myriads of infinitesimally small individuals, each in itself a unit of life, and that these units work in squads—or swarms, as I prefer to call them—and that these infinitesimally small units live forever. When we "die" these swarms of units, like a swarm of bees, so to speak, betake themselves elsewhere, and go on functioning in some other form or environment.[10]

LUTHER BURBANK (1849–1926)

American Horticulturist

[From *Our Beloved Infidel,* the biography of Luther Burbank, by Frederick Clampett:]

In no phase of his religious belief is Luther Burbank less understood and more inaccurately reported than that pertaining to the subject of personal immortality. . . . In the long procession of distinguished scientists and scholars . . . who traveled the well-worn path to the door of Luther Burbank's cottage were many Hindu leaders and disciples of the Vedanta philosophy of India. So close was the bond between their philosophy of life and that of Burbank that a hospitable welcome always awaited them. . . . It may safely be affirmed that the inspiring motive of his desire to master the Vedantic theory of reincarnation had no connection with a yearning after personal immortality . . . [Rather] he was deeply interested in the claim that reincarnation was based on evolution, and in the sequel to that claim that reincarnation was founded on the law of cause and effect. . . . His own hesitation [at first] in affirming a belief in the preexistence of soul . . . was the logical outcome of a life trained to slow methods in the field of science. If his life-work had placed restraint upon his judgment in things mortal, how much more in things immortal? . . . Often had he seen life portrayed, he professed to me, as did Walt Whitman in his *Leaves of Grass,* when he said: "As to you, Life, I reckon you are the leavings of many deaths; no doubt I have died myself ten thousand times before."[11]

GUSTAF STRÖMBERG (1882–1962)

Swedish-American Astronomer and Physicist

[Albert Einstein wrote concerning Dr. Gustaf Strömberg's book *The Soul of the Universe:* "What impressed me particularly was the successful attempt to pick out of the bewildering variety of researches that which is of essential value, and to present it in such a way that the concept of Oneness of all knowledge can for the first time be stated with definite intent." According to Strömberg, "the study is based mainly on facts from physics, biology, and physiology. The facts are well known to students, the new things lie in the emphasis, the viewpoints, and the interpretations." Here we present the conclusions on immortality and reincarnation, taken from chapter 11, entitled "The Soul."[12]]

There is no doubt about the existence of the human soul if we define it properly. The human soul is in the first place the ego of the human being, a perceiving, feeling, willing, thinking and remembering entity. It is, for instance, not a set of memories, but the possessor of a particular group of memories, most of which never rise to the level of consciousness. . . . The soul is something which gives unity to the mental complex of a man. That such a unity should be recognized and given a name was felt very early in the history of mankind. Although the "observation" of this unity is not made with the aid of our sense organs, it must, nevertheless, be regarded as valid; in fact, this observation is more direct than ordinary sense observations which only give us shadow pictures of the external world. We have become so accustomed to this unity within ourselves that it takes a mental effort to describe it in proper terms and to realize its significance. . . .

Our memories are indelibly "engraved" in our brain field, that is, the electrical field which determines the structure and functions of our brain. By analogy we conclude that our brain field, and the "memory genie" associated with it, contract in unchanged form [at death] and disappear from the physical world, that is, the world of matter, radiation and force fields. Where does the brain field go to? Presumably it goes back to the same world from which it originally came. Since it no longer has any size, or at least any definable size, its properties can not be described in the language used in the science of physics. In other words, it disappears into a non-physical world. . . .

The realization of this "principle of conservation of mental categories" led to the theory of the nature and origin of mental qualities described earlier in this book. This theory has an important relationship to Plato's idea of a *recollection* by our soul of conditions in the world from which it originally came. The conclusion at which we arrive is that in the non-physical world to which we return at death, there is the space and time of our perception, but not the metrical space and time of physics. . . . There are therefore good reasons for making the following important assertion: *A soul is indestructible and immortal. It carries an indelible record of all its activities.* . . .

Some souls have had a few years of development on earth, while others are completely blank; they are nothing but potentialities. The opportunities for development differ tremendously among different souls. If we assume that the earthly development has a *meaning*, an ulterior purpose, our inherent sense of justice tells us that it would be unfair for the different souls as individual entities to have such unequal opportunities, even if we do not consider the apparent waste involved in the unsuccessful emergence of so many undeveloped souls. Furthermore, the earthly development of most human souls is far from inspiring. The lack of opportunity from which the majority of people suffer while on earth leads to the hypothesis of a development after death. This development probably takes place in a "form" which can not be described in terms based on the present mental characteristics of the human race. Perhaps it may take the form of a new earthly or planetary incarnation, or in the permanent or temporary submergence of our souls in the realm beyond space and time.

Opinions differ whether human souls can be reincarnated on the earth or not. In 1936 a very interesting case was thoroughly investigated and reported by the governmental authorities in India. A girl (Shanti Devi from Delhi) could accurately describe her previous life (at Muttra, five hundred miles from Delhi) which ended about a year before her "second birth." She gave the name of her husband and child and described her home and life history. The investigating commission brought her to her former relatives, who verified all her statements. Among the people of India reincarnations are regarded as commonplace; the astonishing thing for them in this case was the great number of facts the girl remembered. This and similar cases can be regarded as additional evidence for the theory of the indestructibility of memory. . . .

Many questions could be asked, but our observations tell us very little. We must have recourse to intuitions, although naturally great caution must be exercised. It is difficult to estimate [their] value . . . because in general they can not be subjected to unequivocal tests. But having realized the existence of a world beyond space and time where ideas have their origin we see them in a new light.[13]

[In a later work, *The Searchers,* Dr. Strömberg speaks more affirmatively as to rebirth. The selections that follow are mainly from the introduction and epilogue of this dialogue story. Where there are parentheses enclosing remarks, it is the characters who are speaking.]

Our real selves, our souls, belong before our birth, during our organic life and after our death to the non-physical world. . . . All the memories of our last and our previous lives can be reviewed [there] in full details in an instant, since there are no atoms which in the physical world block and slow down all our mental activities. . . . (The atoms form a screen or veil that makes it possible for us to concentrate on the immediate requirements of our earthly life. When this veil disappears at death, our memories from this and perhaps from earlier lives crowd in upon us without hindrance, tormenting us or blessing us). . . . The memories of the cruel acts we have committed against men and animals follow us through eternity. The victims of a tyrant are all there, and the memories of their suffering haunt their oppressor. The torment he suffers will probably produce a strong urge in his mind to make a new "emersion" into the physical world, partly in order to escape temporarily from the pangs of his conscience and partly to make an attempt to improve his record. . . .

The question whether or not the world is what it looks like has been asked by thinking men since time immemorial. . . . Most men of the present time are *realists* who claim that the world is what it appears to be to their sense organs, and they are interested in action and not in speculation about ultimate things. . . . There are also men of another type who regard the material objects of the realist as fleeting phenomena in their own minds. Plato was perhaps the first to give these ideas a systematic form. His philosophy was characterized by a certain contempt for a knowledge directly derived from our senses. The real world is not a world of matter, but a world of ideas. Our mind is able to discover and to study the world behind that of our sense perceptions, because our soul, that is, the personality behind our mind, is born with a true knowledge of fundamental realities. This knowledge is in a subconscious form, but by intellectual efforts, stimulated and aided by observations, we can bring it up to the level of consciousness. Then, and only then, do we know something about the real nature of the world and about the meaning of our own lives. . . .

(I am convinced that we live in eternity now, but like an unborn child we are in deep sleep. Occasionally we have lucid moments when we realize that the world is not what it looks like. When we really wake up we may find eternity dimly spread out in front of us and our past clearly distinguishable behind us.)[14]

HERMANN WEYL (1883–1955)

German Mathematician

[Dr. Hermann Weyl is well known for his work in relativity theory, quantum mechanics, differential equations, and the philosophy of mathematics. The brief extract that follows is from *The Open World,* Dr. Weyl's lectures on the metaphysical implications of science, and concerns the much-debated subject of free will versus fate or determinism. Heisenberg's generally accepted principle of uncertainty posited that at the atomic level one can predict the motion of say a mass of electrons, but it is impossible to predict what an individual electron will do. Does the same apply to man?]

Physics has never given support to that truly consistent determinism which maintains the unconditioned necessity of everything which happens. . . . Kant's solution of the dilemma [regarding free will and determinism] can only be carried through honestly if one believes in the existence of the individual from eternity to eternity, in the form of a Leibniz monad, say, or by metempsychosis as the Indians and Schopenhauer believe. Nevertheless, it is of sufficient importance that physics has always admitted a loophole in the necessity of Nature.[15]

JULIAN HUXLEY (1887–1975)

British Biologist

[As might be expected from an open-minded scientist, Sir Julian Huxley had changed his mind a number of times regarding the nature of man. One of his latest thoughts—which seems to remove him from the ranks of the materialists—will be found in the next item on Joseph Wood Krutch. The following was written over forty years ago:]

Egg and sperms carry the destiny of the generations. The egg realizes one chance combination out of an infinity of possibilities; and it is confronted with millions of pairs of sperms, each one actually different in the combination of cards which it holds. Then comes the final moment in the drama—the marriage of egg and sperm to produce the beginning of a large individual. . . . Here too, it seems to be entirely a matter of chance which particular union of all the millions of possible unions shall be consummated. One might have produced a genius, another a moron . . . and so on. . . . With a realization of all that this implies, we can banish from human thought a host of fears and superstitions. No basis now remains for any doctrine of metempsychosis.[16]

[That chance operates in these matters is, of course, a theory that has yet to be proved. An alternative possibility is that the laws of magnetic affinity are at work. The problem regarding heredity and reincarnation has been given one possible answer by Professor Ducasse (see chapter I), and James Ward will give relevant comment later. The latter uses an analogy to show how "disembodied souls could steer their way back to a suitable rebirth": "An atom liberated from its molecular bonds is described as manifesting an unwonted activity, technically known as 'the nascent state'; but still it does not recombine indifferently with the first free atom that it encounters, but only with one for which it has an 'affinity.' And 'there seems to be nothing more strange or paradoxical in the suggestion that each person enters into connection with the body that is most fitted to be connected with him.' " Dr. Ward adds that "a liberated spirit" returning to incarnation "ought to be credited with vastly more *savoir vivre* than a liberated atom"!]

[In Julian Huxley's contribution to a book of essays called *Where Are the Dead?* he no longer speaks of reincarnation as a superstitious belief, but offers a rather materialistic theory as to how it could work:]

There is nothing against a permanently surviving spirit-individuality being in some way given off at death, as a definite wireless message is given off by a sending apparatus working in a particular way. But it must be remembered that the wireless message only becomes a message again when it comes in contact with a new, material structure—the receiver. So with our possible spirit-emanation. It . . . would never think or feel unless again 'embodied' in some way. Our personalities are so based on body that it is really impossible to think of survival which would be in any true sense *personal* without a body of sorts. . . . I can think of *something* being given off which would bear the same relation to men and women as a wireless message to the transmitting apparatus; but in that case 'the dead' would, so far as one can see, be nothing but disturbances of different patterns wandering through the universe until . . . they . . . came back to actuality of consciousness by making contact with something which could work as a receiving apparatus for mind.[17]

[Regarding the foregoing theory that between incarnations "the dead" are without a body to operate through, Hindu philosophy would disagree, as it posits a series of ever-finer sheaths that "envelop" the conscious entity, each sheath corresponding to its appropriate plane or state of manifestation. One of the supposed powers of the soul is the power to clothe itself in the substance of whatever plane it may be operating on. As the physical plane is a very gross one, there are held to be many intervening stages of finer and finer substances between it and the formless state of universal spirit. These inner "bodies" are enumerated and described in chapter 7.[18] (See also references in the Index under "Bodies, Inner.")]

[We conclude with a report of a conversation that took place years ago between Constance Sitwell and George Russell (AE) respecting the latter's remembrances of former lives. Mrs. Sitwell tells the story:]

One evening it was about the intuitions he had had of his own incarnations that he talked. "They tell me that my recollections and visions are ancestral memories—a mere phrase. I talked to Julian Huxley about it once. You tell me, I said, that a man cannot transmit musical knowledge, or a language he has mastered, or a craft, to his children? No, he said, you may transmit a tendency, but everything has to be learnt afresh. And yet you tell me, I said, that when I get a glimpse of strange cities and buildings I have never seen, vivid and alive in every detail, the figures in the streets, the sharp shadows, it has nothing to do with me, but is a memory of some hypothetical ancestor of mine who may have gone on the Crusades? Huxley didn't know what to say. He told me he had sat up all night once trying to find a flaw in one of my arguments, and had to give up!"[19]

JOSEPH WOOD KRUTCH (1893–1970)

American Naturalist, Educator, Essayist, Critic

[It comes as no surprise to encounter passing but suggestive references to the possibility of rebirth in Joseph Wood Krutch's writing. He was one who had truly absorbed the philosophic tone of Thoreau and Emerson, and seemed to have a special affinity for Wordsworth—and to these men the idea of reincarnation was wholly natural. Speaking in *The Desert Year* of his first associations with the austere yet inspiring desert, Krutch wrote: "For three successive years following my first experience I returned with the companion of my Connecticut winters to the same general region, pulled irresistibly across the twenty-five hundred miles between my own home and this world which would have been alien had it not almost seemed that I had known and loved it in some previous existence."[20]

As a naturalist, Krutch often had provocative things to say about the evolutionary processes, noting that more and more Darwinists are dissatisfied with Darwinian evolutionary theory as the answer to the development of form and intelligence. The probability of a preexisting and postexisting intelligence in evolution seems implicit in this passage from Krutch's autobiography, *More Lives Than One:*]

"The soul" is indeed a vague conception and the reality of the thing to which it refers cannot be demonstrated. But consciousness is the most self-evident of all facts. . . . The physiologists are very fond of comparing the network of our cerebral nerves with a telephone system but they overlook the significant fact that a telephone system does not function *until someone talks over it*. The brain does not create thought (Sir Julian Huxley has recently pointed out this fact); it is an instrument which thought finds useful. Biologists have sometimes referred to the origin of life as "an improbable chemical accident." But is not the assumption of an "improbable chemical accident" which results ultimately in something capable of discussing the nature of "improbable chemical accidents" a staggering one? Is it not indeed preposterous? Is it not far easier to believe that thought in some potential form must be as primary as matter itself?[21]

[Krutch's ideas have been supported by a number of neurologists, to mention a few: Sir Charles Sherrington, father of neurophysiology and a Nobel laureate; his successor W. Grey Walter, a leading authority on brain waves; and Sir Francis Walshe.[22] Sir John Eccles, another Nobel recipient, has similar views. On the basis of half a century's experience in exploring the brain, he is convinced, *Newsweek* reports, that the brain and mind are separate and distinct. "If we are essentially automatons, then all moral judgments are phony." How could Lieutenant Calley be blamed for anything he did? he asks. "We should not pretend that consciousness is not a mystery. I can explain my body and my brain, but there's something more . . . What makes me a unique being?"[23]

Recently the internationally distinguished Canadian neurosurgeon Wilder Penfield recorded in book form the results of his long experience in this field. He writes in *The Mystery of the Mind:*

> The neurophysiologist's initial undertaking should be to try to explain the behavior of this being [Man] on the basis of neuronal mechanisms alone. . . . The challenge that comes to every neurophysiologist is to explain in terms of brain mechanisms all that men have come to consider the work of the mind, if he can. And this he must undertake freely, without philosophical or religious bias.

But what if, after a lifetime of work along these lines, he should find that this effort fails? Then, Dr. Penfield says: "If he does not succeed in his explanation, using proven facts and reasonable hypotheses, the time should come, as it has to me, to consider other possible explanations." Recently, "a remarkable body of material has come into my hands and I have stumbled on exciting discoveries," which justify the theory that instead of one element in man there are two elements.

Even before this, he had made some parallel discoveries through brain surgery. Such surgery is perhaps unique in causing no pain, and can therefore be carried on with the patient in full consciousness. Dr. Penfield's famous experiment—widely applauded by the behaviorist psychologists—was that by using an electrode over the exposed portion of the brain he could cause particular memories to come before the patient's eye. He emphasizes, however, that the patient knows that it is the *doctor* who is triggering these recollections, even though the patient cannot see him doing so. Furthermore, and most importantly, Dr. Penfield now discloses that while the presentation of a memory can be caused by an outside stimulus, *not so with a human decision.* "There is no place in the cerebral cortex where electrical stimulation will cause a patient to believe or decide."

As to the new "remarkable body of material," mentioned, we cannot take space to describe or summarize it, but simply offer Dr. Penfield's conclusions. Their relevance to our subject is simply that they support the basic theory of the reincarnationist that there *are* two elements in man, and that one of these has a sustaining continuity.]

For my own part, after years of striving to explain the mind on the basis of the brain-action alone, I have come to the conclusion that it is simpler (and far easier to be logical) if one adopts the hypothesis that our being does consist of two fundamental elements. . . . To expect the highest brain-

mechanism or any set of reflexes, however complicated, to carry out what the mind does, and thus perform all the functions of the mind, is quite absurd.
. . .

Because it seems to me certain that it will always be quite impossible to explain the mind on the basis of neuronal action within the brain, and because it seems to me that the mind develops and matures independently throughout an individual's life as though it were a continuing element, and because a computer (which the brain is) must be programmed and operated by an agency capable of independent understanding, I am forced to choose the proposition that our being is to be explained on the basis of two fundamental elements. This, to my mind, offers the greatest likelihood of leading us to the final understanding toward which so many stalwart scientists strive.
. . .

[The brain as a computer] is a thing without the capacity to make completely new decisions, without the capacity to form new memory records, and a thing without that indefinable attribute, a sense of humor. [It] is incapable of thrilling to the beauty of a sunset or of experiencing contentment, happiness, love, compassion. These, like all awarenesses, are functions of the mind. . . . The mind is aware of what is going on. . . . It understands. It acts as though endowed with an energy of its own. It can make decisions and put them into effect by calling on various brain mechanisms. . . . [According to the dualistic hypothesis] the mind must be viewed as a basic element in itself. . . . It has a *continuing existence*. . . . When it no longer has its special connection to the brain [as during deep sleep], it exists in the silent intervals and takes over control when the highest brain mechanism does go into action.[24]

J. B. RHINE (1895–   )

American Parapsychologist

[Dr. J. B. Rhine hardly needs an introduction, as he is an internationally known psychic researcher, was director for many years of the parapsychology laboratory at Duke University and then headed the Institute for Parapsychology. The extracts that follow are from an article in the *American Weekly* (April 8, 1956) "Did You Live Before?" in which Dr. Rhine, at the request of the editors, discussed the famous case of Bridey Murphy. When granting permission to use his article, Dr. Rhine made some minor changes. Over a million copies were sold of Morey Bernstein's *The Search for Bridey Murphy*,[25] the book having been published in more than thirty countries. (For a follow-up survey of the facts in this provocative case, see "How the Case of the Search for Bridey Murphy Stands Today" in Professor C. J. Ducasse's *A Critical Examination of the Belief in a Life After Death*.)[26]]

In brief, *Bridey Murphy* is the story of Ruth Simmons, a young housewife living in Pueblo, Colorado. . . . One evening in 1952 she agreed to be the subject of a hypnotism experiment. The hypnotist was a young businessman, Morey Bernstein. At first he led her back through what we commonly call age-regression. . . . Eventually she remembered the toys she loved when she was only one year old. There was nothing unusual about this, but in a second session the hypnotist suggested, "Your mind will be going back . . . back until you find yourself in some other scene, in some other place, in some other time. You will be able to talk to me about it and answer my questions."

The gist of her response was that she was a little Irish girl named Bridey Murphy, who lived in Cork with her mother Kathleen, her barrister father Duncan, and one brother. . . . The year was 1806. She told how, at fifteen, she attended Mrs. Strayne's school in Cork "studying to be a lady," and how she later married Brian MacCarthy and went to live in Belfast. As the sessions continued, all recorded on tape, the life story carried on through the years, up to Bridey's death at the age of sixty-six. She claimed that, after bodily death, Bridey existed in the spirit world for forty years, then was reborn in Iowa, in 1923, to take up her life as Ruth—the present Ruth Simmons.

Checking later with the Irish Consulate, the British Information Service, the New York Public Library and other sources, Mr. Bernstein learned that a number of Bridey's statements were consistent with historical fact. If Ruth, who never had visited Ireland, had no normal way of knowing these things, didn't this raise the question: Does reincarnation really occur? . . .

In the first place nobody knows, and there is no way of finding out, that the hypnotized girl did not already have all the verified facts somewhere in her memory. . . . What had she read or otherwise absorbed that could have been woven into the tale of Bridey? . . . It also is possible that this young woman could have gained her knowledge through telepathy or clairvoyance, two forms of what we call extrasensory perception (ESP). . . . [Also] for a careful study of so important a matter as reincarnation, it would be necessary to know what went on in the conversations that took place with the girl awake, between sessions, as well as when hypnotized. . . .

If we are to consider the question seriously, and try to find some proof of reincarnation, leading a person back through hypnotic regression—as was done in this case—is the wrong road to take. Science should first attempt to discover whether there is a spirit personality which can exist apart from its body. . . .

Let us make our explorations as carefully as possible and go as cautiously into interpretations and applications as the gravity of the issues deserves. Let us get to the facts about men as we do about atoms. As we anxiously scan the skies for the new menace science has brought out of the hidden resources of nature, it is timely, is it not, for the scientist to peer over the edge of his

physical foundations and ask: What, if anything, may follow the final ob-
literating blast?

RAYNOR C. JOHNSON (1901–   )

British Physicist

[In his various works Dr. Raynor C. Johnson has sought to integrate science
and religion. In his widely read volume *The Imprisoned Splendor,* the chapter
"Pre-Existence, Reincarnation and Karma" receives this introduction:]

It is probably true to say that a number of my readers have already reacted
to the title of this chapter with some measure of emotional interest or aversion. Some people seem curiously and almost instinctively interested in these
topics, others, frequently religious-minded people, feel antagonistic, as
though some strange pagan faith was subtly menacing their cherished beliefs.
The average thoughtful Western man has in general given little consideration
to these matters, although his reticence does not always match his knowledge. In any attempt to formulate a philosophy of life and endeavor to see
meaning in our pilgrimage, these ancient beliefs cannot be lightly set aside.
It is our duty to weigh them carefully, and without prejudice, in order to see
if they illuminate for us tracts of experience which would otherwise remain
dark and mysterious. . . .

The idea of reincarnation presents no logical difficulties, whatever be the
emotional reaction to it. What the soul has done once by the process of
incarnation in a physical body, it can presumably do again. (By the term
"soul" we mean that individualized aspect of the Self, including . . . the
Intuitive self—and Higher Mind, all of which are regarded as immortal.) We
should of course bear in mind that what is meant by the phrase "have lived
before" is not that the physical form Raynor Johnson has lived on earth
previously, but rather Raynor Johnson is only a particular and temporary
expression of an underlying immortal soul which has adopted previous and
quite possibly different appearances.[27]

[In *A Religious Outlook for Modern Man,* Dr. Johnson writes that "the only
satisfactory solution of man's dilemma is to be found in his discovery of the
enormous resources of his inner self." "This," he says, "is no easy quest or
achievement, but it is a possible one, and the most satisfying one. In this way
he may ride out the storms of this modern age with inner serenity, in the
assurance that come what may, there is nothing really to fear."[28] Later in the
volume he discusses some of these resources in relation to the puzzling cases
of child prodigies.]

In scientific work it is often the exceptional happening which offers us clues to wider understanding. . . . We are told that Sir William Hamilton at the age of five, could answer a difficult mathematical question and would then "run off cheerfully to play with his little toy cart." If we are prepared to recognise the possibility of previous lives, then we might have a basis for explaining these things as a rare example of overflow of previously attained ability into a succeeding life. The permanent soul which stores the wisdom, goodness, artistic sensitivity, interest, and skills of the past, surely influences in some degree the new personality which it is sending forth into the world.

Normally, we should expect some of these interests or capacities to awaken as the child develops. Some may remain wholly latent, for a soul may desire to broaden its experience rather than to intensify certain aspects of it. Plato has a theory that the kind of knowledge which comes easily is "old" knowledge, in the sense that we have laid foundations for it in prior lives, while the learning in which at first we find little interest or which presents difficulty, is probably being met for the first time. On this view, the child prodigy would be the reincarnation of a soul of very specialised development. It is sometimes found that the genius fades out at an early age, as though the soul, as soon as it was able to do so, threw up other fields of interest and withdrew the exceptional one, for the sake of a wider and more balanced development.[29]

JOHN A. WHEELER (1911–)

American Physicist

[An interview with Dr. John A. Wheeler and three other scientists is reported in the *Intellectual Digest* for June 1973, under the title "The Princeton Galaxy." In large letters the caption heading the article reads: "Four Princeton scientists fire a starburst of ideas about ends, beginnings, transformations and reincarnations: 'cycle after cycle, not only of man but of the universe itself.'" The interviewer, Florence Helitzer, opened with these words:

> The language of modern physics is alluring. Such words as "birth," "death" and "rebirth" and phrases like "cycles of creation and destruction" constantly recur. These words have been encountered before in other contexts: in myth and fairy tale, in oriental religion and in the Bible, in literature and in philosophy. . . . In an attempt to find a bridge between past culture and current physics, now reaching into an immense universe, questions drawn from religion, mysticism and philosophy were put to four eminent cosmologists who teach and do research at Princeton University.

Our focus will be on Dr. Wheeler whose theories regarding the "black holes" in space, as a possible result of gravitational collapse, have received widespread attention. Wheeler was a colleague of Niels Bohr and one of the first scientists to concentrate on nuclear fission. The interviewer said to him: "The end of the world is anticipated by the existence of the black hole, a star having undergone gravitational collapse. This phenomenon is an invisible omen of our future, you've said, because gravitational collapse is the ultimate destiny of the universe. But you have also suggested that this end will become a new beginning—that something else, something new and different, will be reborn from the ashes." Dr. Wheeler replied:

> I am thinking of the oriental concepts of reincarnation and of cycle after cycle, not only of man, but of the universe itself. I would be the last person to know how to analyze this kind of idea in a sensible way.

He could not, in addition, see how "individuality" could survive the process of universal collapse. Later, however, he suggested that there may be more than a physical dimension to man:

> No theory of physics that deals only with physics will ever explain physics. I believe that as we go on trying to understand the universe, we are at the same time trying to understand man. Today I think we are beginning to suspect that man is not a tiny cog that doesn't really make much difference to the running of the huge machine but rather that there is a much more intimate tie between man and the universe than we heretofore suspected. Only as we recognize that tie will we be able to make headway into some of the most difficult issues that confront us. Nobody thinking about it from this point of view can fail to ask himself whether the particles and their properties are not somehow related to making man possible. Man, the start of the analysis, man, the end of the analysis—because the physical world is in some deep sense tied to the human being.

One of the other scientists interviewed, Jeremiah Ostriker, who recently won the American Astronomical Society's Warner Prize, stated: "There are a lot of similarities between the mystic's view of the world and Einstein's. I don't know whether it's coincidental that currently the best cosmology is a 'big bang' cosmology and that the best potential rival is a cyclic one, which is more like the Eastern view. I am intrigued. I suspect that I could learn a lot just from thinking and talking about it." Dr. Wheeler added: "One has to be very humble in the face of people who have dealt with these eternal issues over so many generations."]

IAN STEVENSON (1918–)

Canadian-born American Psychiatrist and Parapsychologist

[Schopenhauer once gave this criterion for the demonstration of truth. Truth, he said, always explains and unifies. He used an analogy: "When we have to deal with an inscription whose alphabetical characters are unknown, we make successive trials until we reach a combination that gives intelligible words and coherent sentences. No doubt then remains that the decipherment is correct. . . . In the same way the reading of the world-cipher should carry its own proof."[30] If this criterion were sufficient, and it were applied to the theory of rebirth, how would that theory stand up? Would we have "understandable words and coherent sentences" in explaining the universe and its innumerable mysteries? Whatever our answer, as far as most scientists are concerned they can only be satisfied with empirical facts, and where reincarnation is concerned they want unquestionable proof as to when, where, and with whom, an individual living today supposedly preexisted. One such scientist is Dr. Ian Stevenson.

Stevenson is regarded by a number of his peers in the scientific community as the world's leading authority on the subject of life after death, and, in particular, reincarnation as one possible means of survival. He first came to public attention in 1960 when his "Evidences for Survival from Claimed Memories of Former Incarnations" was the prize-winning essay in the American Society for Psychical Research contest in honor of William James, one of its early presidents. Stevenson was then chairman of the department or neurology and psychiatry at the University of Virginia School of Medicine, but later stepped down from this position to free himself from administrative details that hampered his reincarnation research, which at a moment's notice could take him to distant parts of the world. He is now Carlson Professor of Psychiatry at the university, and also heads the small division of parapsychology there. Before writing the essay for the S.P.R. contest he had studied hundreds of instances in which children or adults seemed to remember a past life, presenting a select few "in the evaluation of which reincarnation becomes a very serious contender as the most plausible explanation of the empirical facts." With one exception, the claimed memories on which Dr. Stevenson bases his conclusions arose naturally and spontaneously in normal states of consciousness.

A portion of Dr. Stevenson's essay follows:]

The writer of a review of this kind has the privilege and perhaps the obligation of saying how he personally interprets the data. I will say, therefore, that I think reincarnation the most plausible hypothesis for understanding the cases of this series. This is not to say that I think they prove reincarnation either singly or together. Indeed, I am quite sure they do not. But for each of the alternative hypotheses I find objections or shortcomings which make them for me unsuitable explanations of all the cases, although they may apply to some. . . .

A large number of cases in which the recall of true memories is a plausible hypothesis should make that hypothesis worthy of attention. I think the number of cases in the present collection confers that respectability on the hypothesis, even though many of these cases may have particular aspects which make some other hypothesis more plausible in such cases. Expectations can harmfully influence perceptions. If we proceed in an investigation with the expectation of confirming a particular hypothesis, we may think we discover more evidence for it than we do. But the reverse type of misperception can also occur with equal harm. If we reject offhand, as most Westerners are inclined to do, the hypothesis of reincarnation, we may exclude from our investigations those conditions which could permit further relevant data to emerge.

The evidence I have assembled and reviewed here does not warrant any firm conclusion about reincarnation. But it does justify, I believe, a much more extensive and more sympathetic study of this hypothesis than it has hitherto received in the West. Further investigation of apparent memories of former incarnations may well establish reincarnation as the most probable explanation of these experiences. Along this line we may in the end obtain more convincing evidence of human survival of phsyical death than from other kinds of evidence. In mediumistic communications we have the problem of proving that someone clearly dead still lives. In evaluating apparent memories of former incarnations, the problem consists in judging whether someone clearly living once died. This may prove the easier task and, if pursued with sufficient zeal and success, may contribute decisively to the question of survival.[31]

[Three of the cases as presented by Dr. Stevenson in this study may be found at the end of chapter 5 under "Stories of 'Remembrances' of Past Lives." Also in that section is a report of Edward Ryall's *Twice Born,* a unique case in the annals of reincarnation literature that was thoroughly researched by Dr. Stevenson. In retelling that story we included Stevenson's findings.]

[*Twenty Cases Suggestive of Reincarnation* is a 354-page book by Dr. Stevenson, published in 1966, and which has now become a classic in the field. Stevenson had traveled to Europe, the Near East, Asia, South America, Alaska, and other parts of the United States to conduct cn-the-spot investigations of reported cases. "This is not a fantastic, but a thoroughly factual book," writes one reviewer, "and possibly an important milestone in the exploration of a staggering idea."[32]

Reviewing some of Dr. Stevenson's findings in *Look* (October 20, 1970), Eugene Kinkead quoted Dr. Gertrude Schmeidler, a professor of psychology at City College in New York, as saying that "Stevenson is a most careful and conscientious person of great intellectual ability and high professional standards. He has a most painstaking approach to collection and analysis of raw data." Dr. Albert Stunkard, chairman of the department of psychiatry at the University of Pennsylvania in Philadelphia, said: "Stevenson's present work . . . seems queer to many conventional scientists. It is certainly controversial. But he is the most critical man I know of working in that sphere, and perhaps the most thoughtful, with a knack for building into his research appropriate investigative controls." The article reports that Stevenson became interested in reincarnation because of a "growing feeling of dissatisfaction that available knowledge of heredity and environmental influences, considered either alone or together, often didn't account for personality as we see it."

In an interview Stevenson explained that "in studying cases of reincarnation I have to use the methods of the historian, lawyer and psychiatrist. I gather testimony from as many witnesses as possible. It is not uncommon for me to interview 25 people in regard to one case of reincarnation. And I have frequently gone back to interview the same people several years later. . . . I have first to eliminate the possibility of fraud. Then I have to rule out the possibility that the subject years ago, through word of mouth, through a newspaper account, or something of that sort, got details of the stranger they now claim to have been in a previous life. . . . Finally I must investigate the possibility that the subject may possess information he could have obtained by extrasensory means, telepathy for example." He remarked, however, that "extrasensory perception cannot account for the fact that the subject has skills and talents not learned—such as the ability to speak a foreign language without having had the opportunity to learn it in this present life."[33] Nor could it account for strange birthmarks that seemed to have a peculiar relationship to the "prior" personality, as in one instance where a boy, among twenty-six items "remembered," claimed his throat had been slit by robbers, and in the present life was born with a scar around his neck. Many of the cases involved individuals who "remembered" over twenty-five items from their previous life which were subsequently verified. As almost all the reports concerned persons who in their supposed last existence died at an early age and "reincarnated" in a few years, the previous relatives were still alive to confirm claimed memories. Quoting now from *Twenty Cases:*]

So far, most of the best evidence bearing on reincarnation has come from spontaneous cases. Relevant material does not often arise in the laboratory under circumstances where we can exert even moderate control. Some of the earliest and most thorough investigators of the evidence for reincarnation

used hypnosis to regress subjects back in time to supposed "previous lives."
. . . The "personalities" usually evoked during hypnotically-induced re-
gressions to a "previous life" seem to comprise a mixture of . . . the subject's current personality, his expectations of what he thinks the hypnotist
wants, his fantasies of what he thinks his previous life ought to have been,
and also perhaps elements derived paranormally. . . .

In the international census of cases suggestive of reincarnation which I
have undertaken, I now have nearly six hundred cases listed. Of these my
colleagues and I have personally investigated about a third. . . . The twenty
cases presented in this volume provide a representative sample of the cases I
have investigated at first hand. . . . I believe . . . that the evidence favoring
reincarnation as a hypothesis for the cases of this type has increased since I
published my review in 1960.[34]

[A more up-to-date figure of the number of cases as well as other pertinent
information is provided by Professor J. G. Pratt in the volume *The Psychic
Realm: What Can You Believe?* (Dr. Pratt worked with J. B. Rhine at Duke
University for a quarter of a century, has several books on parapsychology to
his credit, and has written over a hundred scientific papers for various journals.) In the chapter "Memories of Another Life," which deals with Stevenson's research, Dr. Pratt reports that "as of July 1974 the files on reincarnation cases in the University of Virginia Division of Parapsychology contained
a total of 1,339 distinct instances of persons claiming such memories that had
been reported directly to the investigator or to his associates in the field or
reported through correspondence."[35]

It is commonly supposed that such cases are found usually in Eastern
countries where reincarnation is generally accepted. However, Dr. Pratt
states that of the 1,339 cases on file, "the United States has the most, with
324 cases (not counting American Indian and Eskimo), and the next five
countries in descending order are Burma (139 cases), India (135), Turkey
(114), and Great Britain (111)." "These figures should not be taken, however, as giving the relative density of cases in the various countries, since the
conditions that influence whether or not existing cases will be reported to the
investigator vary widely from one part of the world to another." In the West,
where reincarnation is not generally accepted, there is a tendency to ignore,
suppress, or indulgently smile at statements of children who wish to talk
about the time previous to birth. Quoting from *The Psychic Realm:* "Such
statements usually are not taken very seriously. A friend says she has been
told that when she was about three she frequently made such comments as,
'When I was old—when I was eighty, before I was born . . .' She had no
recollection of this, and since her mildly puzzled parents never pressed their
little girl for an explanation, whatever memories she may have had were

never explored.''[36] But in India, too, according to Stevenson, there are reasons for suppression, one deriving from a superstitious fear that children remembering previous lives will die young.

As already indicated, Stevenson carefully considers the possibility as to whether "remembrances" are derived paranormally. On this point Dr. Pratt writes:

> The ESP interpretation of the cases encounters a number of difficulties. The children with memories about an earlier life do not, as a rule, show any signs of being generally gifted with ESP ability. If their "memories" are really only disguised ESP, why should it be exhibited in such a specialized, narrow way? These children would, in any event, have to be credited with super-psi in order to acquire such a large number of correct details about the life, relatives, and circumstances of a particular dead person. ESP, even of this special and peculiar kind, could not account for the existence of special skills without practice, and the birthmark evidence is clearly beyond the scope of ESP.

Discussing the latter evidence, Pratt remarks that a "special feature of Dr. Stevenson's work, which greatly strengthens the rebirth hypothesis," lies in this very area.

> Among the memories given by the children in these cases are those covering the circumstances of a violent death that ended their previous life. They describe, for example, being shot in particular parts of their body, and these remembered wounds correspond in location to the scarlike birthmarks on the body of the child. Dr. Stevenson has in several instances been able, after the previous family has been identified and located, to find the medical records covering the death of the previous personality and has confirmed that the location of the wounds did indeed correspond with the child's memories as well as with the locations of the birthmarks.]

[In 1974 a revised and enlarged edition of *Twenty Cases Suggestive of Reincarnation* was published, this time by the University Press of Virginia, and in the preface Stevenson explains the reason for its appearance: "This book was originally published . . . as Volume 26 of the Proceedings of the American Society for Psychical Research. It was and still is addressed primarily to scientists of any discipline who may find the contents of interest and value. But a larger public has manifested a growing interest in the work and to meet this demand a new edition has been prepared. . . . As regards the interpretation of the cases, I have little to add to what I said earlier . . . What I can add will be best reserved for . . . a new book of case reports in preparation."

This new book turned out to be a series of volumes under the title *Cases of the Reincarnation Type*. Volume one was published in 1975 by the University Press of Virginia, and the remaining volumes are awaiting publication.

In 1974 the same publisher brought out another Stevenson volume called

Xenoglossy, which received considerable attention in the press before publication, and to this work we now turn.[37]

Xenoglossy is a word invented by an early parapsychologist referring to the ability to speak an identified language not learned by the speaker in any normal way. Stevenson believes the case he reports to be one of his strongest in this field. "I spent a lot of time on that," he said. (Sixteen years, to be exact!) "I think I finally have a dossier that would have been acceptable to J. Edgar Hoover."

These remarks occurred in an interview with Dr. Stevenson concerning his reincarnation researches, reported by Alton Slagle in a five-article syndicated series published in 1974.[38] The case just mentioned is called an example of responsive xenoglossy rather than recitative xenoglossy. In the latter case an individual merely repeats, as by rote, words of a foreign language. In responsive xenoglossy—which is quite rare—the person can converse and answer questions in the language. To conserve space, we use the résumé published in the just-mentioned series:]

Lydia Johnson was not looking for a previous life when she agreed to help her husband with his experiments in hypnotism. She proved an excellent subject, capable of slipping easily into a deep trance. Dr. Harold Johnson (not their real names) was a respected Philadelphia physician. He had taken up hypnotism two years earlier, thinking it might help in treating some of his patients. Now, as his experiments with his wife progressed, he decided to try hypnotic regression, taking her back in time.

Suddenly, she flinched, as if struck, and screamed. She grabbed her head. He ended the session immediately, but his wife had a headache that could not be explained. Twice Johnson repeated the session. The result was the same. On awakening from the trance, Lydia each time said she had visualized a scene with water, and with old people seemingly being forced into it to drown. She had felt herself being pulled down, and then the blow—the scream—and the headache.

Johnson called in another hypnotist, a Dr. John Murray (also a pseudonym). Murray repeated the regression . . . but before the pain could strike again, he instructed her: "You are 10 years younger than that." Then it happened. She began to talk. Not sentences, just words, an occasional phrase. Part was in broken English, part in a foreign language unfamiliar to anyone present. But her voice. It was deep, masculine, earthy. Then from the mouth of the pretty, 37-year-old housewife, the chilling words: "I am a man." The name? "Jensen Jacoby." She pronounced it YEN-sen YAH-ko-bee.

She began, in halting English punctuated by foreign words, to describe a past life. In this, and sessions that followed, she told in that low, guttural voice, of living in a tiny village in Sweden some three centuries ago. The sessions were tape recorded, and careful notes were kept. Swedish linguists were called in to translate Jensen's statements. In the later sessions he spoke amost exclusively in Swedish, a language totally strange to Lydia.

"What do you do for a living?" he was asked.

"En Bonde (a farmer)," he answered.

"Where do you live?"

"I huset (in the house)."

"Var ligger huset? (Where is the house located?)"

"I Hansen (in Hansen)."

Jensen showed a simple personality harmonious with the peasant life he described. He showed little knowledge of anything beyond his own village and a trading center he visited. . . . He raised cows, horses, goats, chickens, ate goat's cheese, bread, milk, salmon and poppy seed cakes made by his wife, Latvia. . . . He had built his own stone house, and he and Latvia had no children. He was one of three sons; his mother was Norwegian and had run away from home.

Objects were brought in, and Lydia was asked to open her eyes and identify them. As Jensen, she did—a model of a 17th-Century Swedish ship, which she correctly called "skuta," a wooden container used for measuring grain, a bow and arrow, and poppy seeds. She did not recognize or know how to use modern tools, such as pliers. . . .

After the eighth session, Lydia was resting while her husband and others discussed the mystery in another room. Suddenly, unexpectedly and without hypnosis, Jensen reappeared. He had to be forced back, dismissed by the hypnotists. Fearing permanent possession of his wife's personality by this stranger, Johnson ended the experiments. No further attempt was made to communicate with Jensen.

[Although in the case of Lydia Johnson hypnosis was used, Stevenson is still of the opinion that where a child talks spontaneously it is of more value. Quoting from the newspaper series:]

Stevenson has used hypnotism in a few cases, but admits "I haven't succeeded in a single case" in obtaining through his experiments verifiable information on what seemed to be a previous life. "I think most domestic experiments in this area are worthless. People don't understand what they're getting into, and they're usually just tapping their own subconscious minds. Then they come up with fiction and novels. Occasionally, they may get into trouble. There have been some cases of people becoming so absorbed with these alleged spirits that they haven't been able to get rid of them. They've become sort of preoccupied. There have been one or two cases of people becoming psychotic."

[In summation, it should be mentioned that Dr. Stevenson frequently emphasizes that his research has thus far brought to light *evidences* suggestive of reincarnation and not final proofs. When asked in the foregoing interview whether he himself believes in reincarnation, he replied: "I don't want to put it that way, because I don't think my belief is of importance. What I do believe is that of the cases that we now know, reincarnation—at least for me—is the best explanation that we've been able to come up with. . . . There is an impressive body of evidence, and I think it's getting stronger all the time. I think a rational man, if he wants, can believe in reincarnation on the basis of evidence."]

PSYCHOLOGISTS
AND DOCTORS OF THE MIND

WILLIAM JAMES (1842–1910)
American Psychologist and Philosopher

[At Harvard in 1893 William James delivered his famous Ingersoll lecture, *Human Immortality,* in which he denied that the findings of physiological psychology had rendered the idea of immortality without scientific justification. These findings, he said, rest on the view that the brain functions only in a productive capacity in relation to thought. He pointed out that the brain could as easily transmit ideas that have an origin elsewhere. He argued that "when finally a brain stops acting altogether, or decays, that special stream of consciousness which it subserved will vanish entirely from this natural world. But the sphere of being that supplied the consciousness would still be intact; and in that more real world with which, even whilst here, it was continuous, the consciousness might, in ways unknown to us, continue still."[1] In his preface to the second edition, James enlarged upon these views and spoke of reincarnation:]

So many critics have made one and the same objection to the doorway to immortality which my lecture claims to be left open by the "transmission theory" of cerebral action, that I feel tempted, as the book is again going to press, to add a word of explanation. If our finite personality here below, the objectors say, be due to the transmission through the brain of portions of a pre-existing larger consciousness, all that can remain after the brain expires is the larger consciousness itself as such. . . . But this, the critics continue, is the pantheistic idea of immortality, survival, namely, in the soul of the world, not the Christian idea on immortality, which means survival in strictly personal form. . . .

The plain truth is that one may conceive *the mental world behind the veil in as individualistic a form as one pleases, without any detriment to the general scheme by which the brain is represented as a transmissive organ.* If the extreme individualistic view were taken, one's finite mundane consciousness would be an extract from one's larger, truer personality, the latter having even now some sort of reality behind the scenes. And in transmitting it . . . one's brain would also leave effects upon the part remaining behind the veil; for when a thing is torn, both fragments feel the operation.

And just as (to use a very coarse figure) the stubs remain in a checkbook whenever a check is used, to register the transaction, so these impressions on the transcendent self might constitute so many vouchers of the finite experiences of which the brain had been the mediator; and ultimately they might form that collection within the larger self of memories of our earthly passage.
. . .

It is true that all this would seem to have affinities rather with pre-existence and with possible reincarnations than with the Christian notion of immortality. But my concern in the lecture was not to discuss immortality in general. It was confined to showing it to be *not incompatible* with the brain-function theory of our present mundane consciousness. I hold that it is so compatible, and compatible moreover in fully individualized form. The reader would be in accord with everything that the text of my lecture intended to say, were he to assert that every memory and affection of his present life is to be preserved, and that he shall never in *sæcula sæculorum* cease to be able to say to himself: "I am the same personal being who in old times upon the earth had those experiences."[2]

[To his Gifford lectures, *The Varieties of Religious Experience,* James added a postscript, drawing attention to the Buddhist idea of karma, which, of course, is closely connected with reincarnation in Buddha's philosophy:]

I am ignorant of Buddhism and speak under correction, and merely in order the better to describe my general point of view; but as I apprehend the Buddhist doctrine of Karma, I agree in principle with that. All supernaturalists admit that facts are under the judgment of higher law. . . . I state the matter thus bluntly, because the current of thought in academic circles runs against me, and I feel like a man who must set his back against an open door quickly if he does not wish to see it closed and locked. In spite of its being so shocking to the reigning intellectual tastes, I believe that a candid consideration of piecemeal supernaturalism and a complete discussion of all its metaphysical bearings will show it to be the hypothesis by which the largest number of legitimate requirements are met. That of course would be a program for other books than this; what I now say sufficiently indicates to the philosophic reader the place where I belong.[3]

SIGMUND FREUD (1856–1939)
Austrian Psychiatrist and Psychoanalyst

[These selections from Freud's article "Thoughts for the Times on War and Death," written in the World War I era, do not exactly fit under the title of the present chapter, and some will find them pointing to a possibly *receding* horizon rather than a new one, but nevertheless the thoughts expressed may prove useful by way of contrast.]

To anyone who listened to us [in the West] we were prepared to maintain that death was the necessary outcome of life. . . . In reality, however, we . . . showed an unmistakable tendency to put death on one side, to eliminate it from life. . . . The complement to this cultural and conventional attitude towards death is provided by our complete collapse when death has struck down someone whom we love. . . . But this attitude . . . towards death has a powerful effect on our lives. Life is impoverished . . . when the highest stake in the game of living, life itself, may not be risked. . . . We dare not contemplate a great many undertakings which are dangerous. . . .

It is an inevitable result of all this that we should seek in the world of fiction, in literature and in the theatre compensation for what has been lost in life. . . . In the realm of fiction we find the plurality of lives which we need. We die with the hero . . . yet we survive him and are ready to die again just as safely with another hero. . . .

When primeval man saw someone who belonged to him die . . . then, in his pain, he was forced to learn that one can die, too, and his whole being revolted against the admission. . . . So he devised a compromise; he conceded the fact of his own death . . . but denied it the significance of annihilation. . . . His persisting memory of the dead became the basis for assuming other forms of existence and gave him the conception of a life continuing after apparent death.

These subsequent existences were at first no more than appendages to the existence which death had brought to a close—shadowy, empty of content, and valued at little. . . . After this it was no more than consistent to extend life backwards into the past, to form the notion of earlier existences, of the transmigration of souls and of reincarnation, all with the purpose of depriving death of its meaning as the termination of life. . . . It was only later that religions succeeded in representing [the] after-life as the more desirable, the truly valid one. . . .

. . . at bottom no one believes in his own death, which amounts to saying: in the unconscious every one of us is convinced of his immortality.[4]

[While this great psychiatrist speaks with positive assurance as to how primeval man thought, he could hardly have any scientific data to go on, considering that anthropologists now find that man is over three and a half million years old! Any speculations on the subject usually reflect the investigator's personal views as to the nature of man and his destiny. Regarding the early races, it seems obvious that the only possible clues as to the way they thought about immortality and rebirth are to be found in the myths, symbols, and traditions that have been transmitted from remote ages. (See chapters 2 and 4.)

Freud hopefully tries to quell modern man's fear of dying. But where does this fear come from? It apparently was not natural to the early races, for many surviving remnants, such as the American Indian and the Eskimo, manifested perfect calm in the face of death—before their cultures were interfered with by the white man. When discussing rebirth earlier, Julius Caesar pointed to the remarkable fearlessness of the Celts of Gaul. Other examples are given in the chapter "Reincarnation among the Early Races." (See particularly the comments of Margaret Mead and others about the Balinese.)

Freud's theories about man underwent some changes as he continued his investigations, and we will be quoting shortly from Dr. Herbert Fingarette's *The Self in Transformation,* which draws on Freud's later ideas and reveals how they could support such concepts as karma and rebirth when more fully worked out. Fingarette's volume has been called "a high-powered microscope," bringing "profound illumination into psychoanalysis" and should be regarded as "required reading for all psychiatrists, psychoanalysts, and clinical psychologists of any school of persuasion."[5]

In a conversation with Ludwig Binswanger, Freud startled his friend and colleague by admitting that "mankind has always known that it possesses spirit; I had to show it that there are also instincts." Several years later, when Binswanger delivered an address commemorating Freud's eightieth birthday, the latter wrote him: "I've always lived only in the *parterre* [pit] and basement of the building. You claim that with a change of viewpoint one is able to see an upper story which houses such distinguished guests as religion, art, etc. . . . If I had another lifetime of work before me, I have no doubt that I could find room for these noble guests in my little subterranean house."[6]]

GUSTAVE GELEY (1868–1924)

French Psychologist, Physician, and Medical Researcher

[It was previously shown that Aristotle as a young man accepted preexistence and reincarnation, but later largely rejected such ideas for the reason that the soul had no remembrance of previous lives. Thus far a wide spectrum of views has been presented on this subject, and now, based on the discoveries of modern psychology, Dr. Gustave Geley adds some suggestive observations, which we take from his book *From the Unconscious to the Conscious*.

In addition to his medical research activities, Geley was director of the Institut Métapsychique International, having been selected for the post by Charles Richet, Camille Flammarion, and other French scientists. Among the propositions that his volume seeks to establish are: "(1) That which is 'essential' in the universe is eternal and indestructible; permanent through all the transitory appearances of things. (2) That which is essential in the universe passes, by evolution, from the unconscious to the conscious. (3) Individual consciousness is an integral part of that which is essential in the universe, and itself indestructible and eternal, it evolves from unconsciousness to consciousness."]

Starting without preconceived ideas, and proceeding to the study of subconscious psychology without heed to the formulae and dogmas of classical teaching, we experience a great surprise. The subconscious appears as the very essence of individual psychology. That which is most important in the individual psychism is subconscious. The foundation of the Self, its characteristic qualities, are subconscious. All the innate capacities are subconscious; likewise the higher faculties—intuition, talents, genius, artistic or creative inspiration. . . . The greater part of [these faculties] escape from the will . . . and show their existence only by bringing to light intermittent and apparently spontaneous results. This subconscious psychic activity, powerful in itself, is reinforced by a still more potent and infallible memory which leaves the feeble and limited conscious memory far behind. . . . No remembrance, no vital or psychological experience is lost. . . .

All conscious acquisitions are assimilated and transmuted into faculties. This is noticeable in the course of existence. . . . Psychological progress can be the result only of this transmutation of knowledge into faculties. And this transmutation is subconscious. It does not take place among the unstable and ephemeral cerebral molecules; it necessitates a deep-seated and continuous elaboration in the essential and permanent part of the being; that is, in his subconscious dynamo-psychism. Thus the perpetual disintegration of the conscious personality is of small importance. The permanent subconscious individuality retains the indelible remembrance of all the states of consciousness which have built it up. From these states of consciousness which it has assimilated it constructs new capacities. . . .

Since then in the course of our existence we find the origin of a part only of the contents of subconsciousness, it is at least permissible to seek the remainder in anterior experiences. . . . If in place of a single existence, we include a series of successive existences, the acquisition of consciousness by the primitive unconsciousness can readily be understood. . . . It is thus that the living being passes little by little from unconsciousness to consciousness. Against this inference of rebirth, no objections of a scientific kind can be raised. We may seek in vain for a single one in the whole stock of knowledge. Forgetfulness of previous existences has but slight importance for modern science. Remembrance plays but a secondary part in normal psychology; forgetfulness is habitual and is the rule. . . .

On the other hand, above this cerebral memory is the subconscious memory—the infallible memory of the true and complete individuality, [which] is indestructible as the being itself. In this essential memory there are engraved permanently all the events of the present life, and all the remembrances and conscious acquisitions of the vast series of antecedent lives.

In the light of the . . . propositions just stated, individual evolution can be understood and all naturalistic and philosophical problems relating to the individual can be resolved. No doubt from the metaphysical point of view the concept gives a large range to hypothesis, but from the psychological standpoint, there is no enigma on which it does not shed light.[7]

CARL G. JUNG (1875–1961)

Swiss Psychiatrist and Psychologist

[Not long before he died, Carl Jung said that "the old question posed by the Gnostics, 'Whence comes evil?' has been given no answer by the Christian world. . . . Today we are compelled to meet that question; but we stand empty-handed, bewildered, and perplexed. . . . As the result of the political situation and the frightful, not to say diabolic triumphs of science, we are shaken by secret shudders and dark forebodings; but we know no way out, and a very few persons indeed draw the conclusion that this time the issue is the long-since-forgotten soul of man."

These words appeared in Jung's impressive and influential posthumous autobiography, *Memories, Dreams, Reflections.*[8] In the chapter "On Life after Death," he said that hitherto he had "never written expressly about a life after death" but now would like to state his ideas. "Perhaps one has to be close to death to acquire the necessary freedom to talk about it." He reveals that for most of his life he had pondered this problem and that all his works "are fundamentally nothing but attempts, ever renewed, to give an answer to the question of the interplay between the 'here' and the 'hereafter.' "[9] Many years earlier he had written in a commentary on an old Chinese text:

Death is psychologically just as important as birth, and . . . an integral part of life. It is not the psychologist who must be questioned as to what happens finally to the detached consciousness. Whatever theoretical position he as-

sumed, he would hopelessly overstep the boundaries of his scientific compe-
tence. He can only point out that the views of our text with respect to the
timelessness of the detached consciousness, are in harmony with the religious
thought of all times and with that of the overwhelming majority of mankind. He
can say, further, that anyone who does not think this way would stand outside
the human order, and would, therefore, be suffering from a disturbance in his
psychic equilibrium. As physician then, I make the greatest effort to fortify, so
far as I have the power, a belief in immortality, especially in my older patients
to whom such questions come menacingly near.[10]

Of similar interest are Jung's remarks to his friend Miguel Serrano. After
presenting evidence to suggest that the mind could act independently of the
brain, he said: "There are other phenomena which can support this hypothesis. You know, of course, that a small child has no clearly defined sense of
the Ego. . . . Nevertheless, it has been proven that small children have
dreams in which the Ego is clearly defined, just as it is in mature people."
"In these dreams," he went on, "the child has a clear sense of the *persona*,"
but if, "from a physiological point of view, the child has no Ego, what is it in
the child which produces these dreams, dreams which, I may add, affect him
for the rest of his life? And another question: If the physical Ego disappears
at death, does that other Ego also disappear, that other which had sent him
dreams as a child?"[11]

The first indication we seem to have of Jung's interest in reincarnation
comes from a lecture entitled "Concerning Rebirth" that he delivered at the
Eranos Meeting of 1939, and which he revised in 1950. He opens with a
consideration of metempsychosis and reincarnation, and defines reincarnation in these words:

This concept of rebirth necessarily implies the continuity of personality. Here
the human personality is regarded as continuous and accessible to memory, so
that, when one is incarnated or born, one is able, at least potentially, to remember that one has lived through previous existences and that these existences were one's own, i.e., that they had the same ego-form as the present life.
As a rule, reincarnation means rebirth in a human body.

The lecture also considers other types of rebirth such as resurrection, and
rebirth within one life. Commenting on rebirth in all its forms, Jung said:

The mere fact that people talk about rebirth, and that there is such a concept
at all, means that a store of psychic experiences described by that term must
actually exist. . . . I am of the opinion that the psyche is the most tremendous
fact of human life. . . . Rebirth is not a process that we can in any way
observe. We can neither measure nor weigh nor photograph it. It is entirely
beyond sense perception.

Jung concludes that "rebirth is an affirmation that must be counted among the primordial affirmations of mankind. These primordial affirmations are based on what I call archetypes. . . . There must be psychic events underlying these affirmations which it is the business of psychology to discuss—without entering into all the metaphysical and philosophical assumptions regarding their significance."[12]

In *Memories, Dreams, Reflections,* Jung relates that he had listened attentively to the Indian teaching of reincarnation and searched the world of his own experience for authentic signs to justify this idea, since he required empirical evidence before he could accept it. Nothing convincing could be found until, in his final years, he had a series of dreams which seemed to illustrate the process of reincarnation in a deceased person of his acquaintance. Thereafter he viewed the problem of rebirth in another light, though without declaring a settled opinion.[13] However, the following passages from *Memories, Dreams, Reflections* reveal how frequently and naturally he thought in terms of many lives:]

My life as I lived it had often seemed to me like a story that has no beginning and no end. I had the feeling that I was a historical fragment, an excerpt for which the preceding and succeeding text was missing. . . . I could well imagine that I might have lived in former centuries and there encountered questions I was not yet able to answer; that I had to be born again because I had not fulfilled the task that was given to me. When I die, my deeds will follow along with me—that is how I imagine it. I will bring with me what I have done. In the meantime it is important to insure that I do not stand at the end with empty hands. . . .

The meaning of my existence is that life has addressed a question to me. Or, conversely, I myself am a question which is addressed to the world, and I must communicate my answer, for otherwise I am dependent upon the world's answer. That is a suprapersonal life task, which I accomplish only by effort and with difficulty. . . . My way of posing the question as well as my answer may be unsatisfactory. That being so, someone who has my karma—or I myself—would have to be reborn in order to give a more complete answer. It might happen that I would not be reborn again so long as the world needed no such answer, and that I would be entitled to several hundred years of peace until someone was once more needed who took an interest in these matters and could profitably tackle the task anew. I imagine that for a while a period of rest could ensue, until the stint I had done in my lifetime needed to be taken up again. . . .

It seems probable to me that in the hereafter . . . there exist certain limitations, but that the souls of the dead only gradually find out where the limits of the liberated state lie. Somewhere "out there" there must be a determinant, a necessity conditioning the world, which seeks to put an end to the after-death state. This creative determinant—so I imagine it—must decide what souls will plunge again into birth. Certain souls, I imagine, feel the state of three-dimensional existence to be more blissful than that of Eternity. But perhaps that depends upon how much of completeness or incompleteness they have taken across with them from their human existence. . . .

In my case it must have been primarily a passionate urge toward understanding which brought about my birth. For that is the strongest element in my nature. This insatiable drive toward understanding has, as it were, created a consciousness in order to know what is and what happens, and in order to piece together mythic conceptions from the slender hints of the unknowable.[14]

[Another passage from this same volume seems particularly appropriate to quote. Jung had been describing one of his dreams, which he deciphered in these words: "I am projected by the magic lantern as C. G. Jung. But who manipulates the apparatus?"]

I had dreamed once before of the problem of the self and the ego. In that earlier dream I was on a hiking trip. I was walking along a little road through a hilly landscape [and] came to a small wayside chapel. The door was ajar, and I went in. . . . On the floor in front of the altar, facing me, sat a yogi—in lotus posture, in deep meditation. When I looked at him more closely, I realized that he had my face. I started in profound fright, and awoke with the thought: "Aha, so he is the one who is meditating me. He has a dream, and I am it." I knew that when he awakened, I would no longer be.

I had this dream after my illness in 1944. It is a parable: My self retires into meditation and meditates my earthly form. To put it another way: it assumes human shape in order to enter three-dimensional existence, as if someone were putting on a diver's suit in order to dive into the sea. When it renounces existence in the hereafter, the self assumes a religious posture, as the chapel in the dream shows. In earthly form it can pass through the experiences of the three-dimensional world, and by greater awareness take a further step toward realization. The figure of the yogi, then, would more or less represent my unconscious prenatal wholeness . . . Like the magic lantern, the yogi's meditation "projects" my empirical reality.[15]

[In 1944 Jung had a serious heart attack. During the period of unconsciousness he experienced these remarkable visions:]

The images were so tremendous that I myself concluded that I was close to death. My nurse afterward told me, "It was as if you were surrounded by a bright glow." That was a phenomenon she had sometimes observed in the dying. . . .

It seems to me that I was high up in space. Far below I saw the globe of the earth, bathed in a gloriously blue light. I saw the deep blue sea and the continents. Far below my feet lay Ceylon, and in the distance ahead of me the subcontinent of India. . . . Far away to the left lay a broad expanse— the reddish-yellow desert of Arabia. . . . I could also see the snow-covered Himalayas, but in that direction it was foggy and cloudy. . . . I knew that I was on the point of departing from the earth. Later I discovered how high in space one would have to be to have so extensive a view—approximately a thousand miles! The sight of the earth from this height was the most glorious thing I had ever seen. . . .

I had the feeling that everything was being sloughed away; everything I aimed at or wished for or thought, the whole phantasmagoria of earthly existence, fell away or was stripped from me—an extremely painful process. Nevertheless something remained; it was as if I now carried along with me everything I had ever experienced or done . . . I might also say: it was with me, and I was it . . . I consisted of my own history, and I felt with great certainty: this is what I am. . . . I [believed] I would at last understand— this too was a certainty—what historical nexus I or my life fitted into. I would know what had been before me, why I had come into being, and where my life was flowing. . . . My life seemed to have been snipped out of a long chain of events, and many questions had remained unanswered. Why had it taken this course? Why had I brought [into earth life] these particular assumptions with me? What had I made of them? What will follow? I felt sure that I would receive an answer to all these questions . . .

While I was thinking over these matters, something happened that caught my attention. From below, from the direction of Europe, an image floated up. It was my doctor, Dr. H.—or, rather, his likeness—framed by a golden chain or a golden laurel wreath. I knew at once: "Aha, this is my doctor, of course, the one who has been treating me. But now he is coming in his primal form. . . . In life he was . . . the temporal embodiment of the primal form, which has existed from the beginning. Now he is appearing in that primal form."

Presumably I too was in my primal form, though this was something I did not observe but simply took for granted. As he stood before me, a mute exchange of thought took place between us. Dr. H. had been delegated by the earth to deliver a message to me, to tell me that there was a protest against my going away. I had no right to leave the earth and must return. The moment I heard that, the vision ceased. . . .

I was profoundly disappointed, for now . . . the painful process of defoliation had been in vain. . . . Disappointed, I thought, "Now I must return to the 'box system' again." For it seemed to me as if behind the horizon of the cosmos a three-dimensional world had been artificially built up, in which each person sat by himself in a little box. And now I should have to convince myself all over again that this was important! Life and the whole world struck me as a prison, and it bothered me beyond measure that I should again be finding all that quite in order. I had been so glad to shed it all, and now it had come about that I—along with everyone else—would again be hung up in a box by a thread. . . .

It was only after the illness [during which he had experienced several other visions] that I understood how important it is to affirm one's own destiny. In this way we forge an ego that does not break down when incomprehensible things happen; an ego that endures, that endures the truth, and that is capable of coping with the world and with fate. . . . Nothing is [then] disturbed—neither inwardly nor outwardly, for one's own continuity has withstood the current of life and of time.[16]

The Dead Who Have Returned to Life

[A possible corroboration of certain aspects of Jung's experiences may be found in a rare heart arrest case where Victor Solow—a fifty-six-year-old New York film maker, normally skeptical in religious matters—died for twenty-three minutes. After drastic attempts to revive him failed, the team of doctors were certain he had irreversibly died. Then one last desperate try accomplished the "impossible." Here is what Solow said happened when he was "over there."]

For me, the moment of transition from life to death—what else can one call it?—was easy. There was no time for fear, pain or thought. . . . I was moving at high speed toward a net of great luminosity. The strands and knots where the luminous lines intersected were vibrating with a tremendous cold energy. The grid appeared as a barrier that would prevent further travel. I did not want to move through the grid. For a brief moment my speed appeared to slow down. Then I was in the grid. The instant I made contact with it, the vibrant luminosity increased to a blinding intensity which drained, absorbed and transformed me at the same time. There was no pain. The sensation was neither pleasant nor unpleasant but completely consuming. The nature of everything had changed. Words only vaguely approximate the experience from this instant on.

The grid was like a transformer, an energy converter transporting me through form and into formlessness, beyond time and space. Now I was not in a place, nor even in a dimension, but rather in a condition of being. This new "I" was not the I which I knew, but rather a distilled essence of it, yet something vaguely familiar, something I had always known buried under a superstructure of personal fears, hopes, wants and needs. This "I" had no connection to ego. It was final, unchangeable, indivisible, indestructible pure spirit. While completely unique and individual as a fingerprint, "I" was, at the same time, part of some infinite, harmonious and ordered whole. I had been there before. . . .

[When life returned to the body] a hard time followed. I could not connect with the world around me. . . . It seemed that by chance I had been given this human body and it was difficult to wear. . . . Was I really here now, or was it an illusion? Was that other condition of being I had just experienced the reality, or was *that* the illusion? I would lie there and observe my body with suspicion and amazement. It seemed to be doing things of its own volition and I was a visitor within. How strange to see my hand reach out for something. Eating, drinking, watching people had a dream-like slow-motion quality as if seen through a veil. . . . On the sixth day there was a sudden change. When I woke up, the world around me no longer seemed so peculiar. Something in me had decided to complete the return trip. . . .

A recurrent nostalgia remains for that other reality, that condition of indescribable stillness and quiet where the "I" is part of a harmonious whole. The memory softens the old drives for possession, approval and success. . . . I am glad I am here and now. But I know that this marvelous place of sun and wind, flowers, children and lovers, this murderous place of evil, ugliness and pain, is only one of many realities through which I must travel to distant and unknown destinations.[17]

[As to actual death, recent scientific studies have disclosed that it is usually peaceful and blissful, despite the suffering and fear that may precede it, and as to the very last moments, Thomas Powers writes in "Learning to Die" (*Harper's,* June 1971): "Some doctors have found evidence that the experience of patients still conscious has an element of the mystical. The doctors are quick to say that they are not talking about God and religion and parapsychological cultism. . . . In a secular age, as practitioners of a science which tends toward mechanism, doctors reluctantly speak of 'soul' or 'spirit.' But, in the safety of anonymity, they return again and again to the puzzle of what it is that 'dies' when the body ceases to function."

Of those also reluctant to speak publicly of what happens at death and perhaps after was Dr. Elisabeth Kübler-Ross, the Swiss-born psychiatrist who, after the appearance of her 1969 volume *On Death and Dying,* became internationally recognized as an eminent authority on the psychiatric aspects of terminal illness. In an interview reported in *People* (November 24, 1975), she has now made the startling disclosure that beyond a shadow of a doubt there is a life after death. When granting permission to quote here the following extracts from the interview, Dr. Ross took the trouble to make a number of corrections in her remarks as reported in *People:*]

Initially I was afraid other scientists would say, "Oh, Ross has seen too many dying patients. She's slipped." But while I was answering questions after a speech last January, a woman whose small son had been declared dead and then revived, asked if there was something beyond death. I forgot the 1,000 others there and said, "I know for a fact that there is life after death." . . .

About seven years ago, a patient who had been declared dead despite heroic resuscitation efforts spontaneously came alive three-and-a-half hours later. She shared with me how she felt: she had floated out of her physical body and watched herself being worked on. She described in minute detail the resuscitation team—who was there, who wanted to give up, who wanted to continue, who told a joke to relieve the tension. This gave me my first clue. . . . Since then I have investigated similar cases from Australia to California, involving patients from age 2 to 96—I have hundreds of very clear-cut cases from all over the world, both religious and nonreligious people. One had been "dead" 12½ hours. All experienced the same thing.

They virtually shed their physical bodies, as a butterfly comes out of a cocoon. They describe a feeling of peace, often beautiful, indescribable peace, no pain, no anxiety. And they were perfect—completely whole. A young man whose leg was cut off in an automobile accident floated above the crash scene and observed the rescue effort, and recalls his leg being intact.[18] They were so content that they resented, sometimes bitterly, the attempts to bring them back to life because they were coming back to a dreadful existence—cancerous bodies, amputated limbs. Not one of them was afraid to die again. . . .

After the transition [following death] you achieve a higher understanding which includes a review of your own life. You evaluate all your actions, words and thoughts; you are fully aware also of the effects of your deeds and thoughts on others. It is not God who condemns you, you condemn yourself.

[My investigative] work involves friends from many fields of science—even some physicians. Whenever I find myself needing tools or information, I have many physicists, some super neurologists, people in electronics—all serious scientists and professionals who are impressed with what we know and who are working on our project. This cross-verification is important for the skeptic mind. . . . I will be able to give hard numbers and much more data when we publish my findings. [But] the headlines really bother me—PSYCHIATRIST DISCOVERS LIFE AFTER DEATH! How can I discover something people have known for 2,000 years!

[In a report by Paul Bannister, "Top Scientists Now Convinced There Is Life after Death," the president of the American Psychiatric Association, Dr. Robert Gibson, is quoted as saying: "I know Dr. Ross, and I cannot find words to fully express my tremendous admiration for her contributions to our understanding of the final stages of life. Her research in death and dying is remarkable. It will have enduring value for decades to come."[19]

Dr. Ross is not unique in her findings. Under the title "New Studies of the Dying Process Provide Impetus for Scientific Inquiries on the Question of Life after Death," Kenneth Briggs writes in the *New York Times* (April 20, 1976) that "interest in the field appears to be on the increase, judging from the number of conferences and papers on the subject." "One factor in the growing interest," he says, "is the availability of greater numbers of subjects because of advances in resuscitative techniques." Through this means "the question of whether there is life after death, long the province of theologians, psychics and ordinary speculators," has now "become a subject of investigation among members of the scientific community." In the process of investigation, researchers have "come upon some theological questions of concern to religious thinkers." "For example, is the transition from life to an afterlife to be understood as an extension of natural life"—which reincarnationists tend to believe—"or does it depend on a special divine act?"

The first major work to be published in this new field—and one which also raises the question of reincarnation—is *Life after Life* by Raymond A. Moody, Jr.[20] Dr. Moody taught philosophy for several years, then became an M.D., and now is a resident in psychiatry. During this latter period he studied the phenomena of survival of bodily death, lecturing to various nursing and medical groups. He was unaware, however, that similar research was being conducted by other doctors, and it was only with the prepublication copy of *Life after Life* that he was brought together with Dr. Kübler-Ross, whose research not only paralleled his own, but *duplicated* his findings. She introduced the Bantam paperback edition of *Life after Life*, which soon became a best seller, being serialized in various magazines and newspapers.

In his chapter "The Experience of Dying," Dr. Moody writes: "Despite the wide variation in the circumstances surrounding close calls with death and in the types of persons undergoing them, it remains true that there is a striking similarity among the accounts of the experiences themselves. In fact, the similarities among various reports are so great that one can easily pick out about fifteen separate elements which recur again and again in the mass of narratives that I have collected. On the basis of these points of likeness, let me now construct a brief, theoretically "ideal" or "complete" experience which embodies all of the common elements, in the order in which it is typical for them to occur." (The italics are Dr. Moody's.)

"A man is dying and, as he reaches the point of greatest physical distress, he hears himself pronounced dead by his doctor. He begins to hear an uncomforta-

*ble noise, a loud ringing or buzzing, and at the same time feels himself moving
very rapidly through a long dark tunnel. After this, he suddenly finds himself
outside of his own physical body, but still in the immediate physical environment, and he sees his own body from a distance, as though he is a spectator. He
watches the resuscitation attempt from this unusual vantage point and is in a
state of emotional upheaval.*

*"After a while, he collects himself and becomes more accustomed to his odd
condition. He notices that he still has a 'body,' but one of a very different nature
and with very different powers from the physical body he has left behind. Soon
other things begin to happen. Others come to meet and to help him. He glimpses
the spirits of relatives and friends who have already died, and a loving, warm
spirit of a kind he has never encountered before—a being of light—appears
before him. This being asks him a question, nonverbally, to make him evaluate
his life and helps him along by showing him a panoramic, instantaneous
playback of the major events of his life. At some point he finds himself approaching some sort of barrier or border, apparently representing the limit
between earthly life and the next life. Yet, he finds that he must go back to the
earth, that the time for his death has not yet come. At this point he resists, for by
now he is taken up with his experiences in the afterlife and does not want to
return. He is overwhelmed by intense feelings of joy, love, and peace. Despite
his attitude, though, he somehow reunites with his physical body and lives."*

In his chapter "The Being of Light," Dr. Moody explains further:

What is perhaps the most incredible common element in the accounts I have
studied, and is certainly the element which has the most profound effect upon
the individual, is the encounter with a very bright light. Typically, at its first
appearance this light is dim, but it rapidly gets brighter until it reaches an unearthly brilliance. . . . Despite the light's unusual manifestation, however,
not one person has expressed any doubt whatsoever that it was a being, a being
of light. Not only that, it is a personal being. It has a very definite personality.
The love and the warmth which emanate from this being to the dying person
are utterly beyond words, and he feels completely surrounded by it and taken up
in it, completely at ease and accepted in the presence of this being. . . .

Interestingly, while the above description of the being of light is utterly invariable, the identification of the being varies from individual to individual and
seems to be largely a function of the religious background, training, or beliefs
of the person involved. Thus, most of those who are Christians in training or
belief identify the light as Christ and sometimes draw Biblical parallels in support of the interpretation. A Jewish man and woman identified the light as an
"angel."

In some Eastern philosophies, the "being of light" is viewed as man's
own Higher Self. In Hinduism it is given various names, one being
Manasa Taijasi. In Sanskrit, *Taijasi* means "the radiant," while *Manasa*

is defined as the Higher Mind, or Ego, that which reincarnates from life to life.[21] At death it is said to appear before the dying person in the manner described by Dr. Moody, and then, after various purgatorial conditions are experienced by the departed, this radiant being raises him to the heavenly condition, where he is re-united with his true Self.

Dr. Moody states that after the resuscitation experience, the individual tries to tell others, but he has trouble doing so. "In the first place, he can find no human words adequate to describe these unearthly episodes. He also finds that others scoff, so he stops telling other people. Still, the experience affects his life profoundly, especially his views about death and its relationship to life."[22]

Elsewhere in the volume, Dr. Moody writes: "Many people have made remarks to the effect that, 'There are just no words to express what I am trying to say,' or 'They just don't make adjectives and superlatives to describe this.' One woman put this to me very succinctly when she said: 'Now, there is a real problem for me as I'm trying to tell you this, because all the words I know are three-dimensional. As I was going through this, I kept thinking, "Well, when I was taking geometry, they always told me there were only three dimensions, and I always just accepted that. But they were wrong. There are more." And, of course, our world—the one we're living in now—*is* three-dimensional, but the next one definitely isn't. And that's why it's so hard to tell you this. . . . I can't really give you a complete picture.' "[23]

In answering the question "What bearing, if any, do the experiences which you have studied have on the possibility of reincarnation?" the doctor replied that the cases he investigated neither proved nor disproved the theory. "If reincarnation does occur, it seems likely that an interlude in some other realm would occur between the time of separation from the old and the entry into the new one. Accordingly, the technique of interviewing people who come back from close calls with death would not be the proper mode for studying reincarnation. . . . Other methods can be and have been tried in investigating reincarnation. . . . The case of Bridey Murphy is the most famous, but there are many others, some even more impressive and well-documented, which are not as widely known. . . . It is also worth noting that *The Tibetan Book of the Dead,* which so accurately recounts the stages of near-death encounters, says that reincarnation does occur at some later point, after the events which have been related by my subjects." Dr. Moody adds that "readers who wish to pursue this question further are referred to the excellent study, *Twenty Cases Suggestive of Reincarnation,* by Ian Stevenson, M.D."—a book also listed in Dr. Moody's short bibliography of eight books.[24] (See our review of *Twenty Cases* in the section devoted to Dr. Stevenson's research.)]

ERIK H. ERIKSON (1902–   )

American Psychoanalyst and Author

[Dr. Erik H. Erikson is a leading figure in the field of psychoanalysis and human development. In *Gandhi's Truth,* which won the Pulitzer Prize and the 1970 National Book Award, he gave attention to the origins of militant nonviolence in India. The selections from this book are concerned with the Hindu view of rebirth, and conclude with his own surprising convictions.]

What we would ascribe to the beginnings of the life cycle the Hindu view projects into previous lives which determine the coordinates of a person's rebirth in this one: not only *where* a child was to be reborn *(desha)* and *when (kala),* but also his *innate trends (gunas)* and therefore the efforts *(shrama)* which can be expected of one thus endowed and growing up in his caste at his period of history. He may emerge, then, in the caste of the Brahmans and learn to be literate, or in that of Kshatrias and learn how to fight and to rule, among the Vaisyas and handle goods or hold lands, or among the Sudras to toil in the sweat of his brow. Or, indeed, he may miss all of these honored occupations and go through this life doomed to touch what others will avoid and, therefore, be untouchable himself. But the Untouchable, too, has unlimited chances ahead of him.

We in the West are proudly overcoming all ideas of predestination. But we would still insist that child training can do no more than underscore what is given—that is, in an epigenetic development fixed by evolution. And we can certainly sense in any seminar—clinical or historical—how we continue to project ideas of doom and predetermination either on hereditary or constitutional givens, on early experience and irreversible trauma, or on cultural and economic deprivation—that is, on a past, as dim as it is fateful. And let us face it: "deep down" nobody in his right mind *can* visualize his own existence without assuming that he has always lived and will live hereafter; and the religious world-views of old only endowed this psychological [feeling] with images and ideas which could be shared, transmitted, and ritualized.[25]

GINA CERMINARA

American Psychologist

[In *The World Within,* Dr. Gina Cerminara tells about a Hindu boy who in a school essay on his favorite animal, the cat, said: "The cat has four legs one in each corner. He also has nine lives, which he does not use in Europe because of Christianity." This, she adds, "like many other commentaries from children . . . is curiously significant." Later forms of Christian teaching *have* "made it difficult," she says, "for anyone to make use of more than one lifetime."[26] Dr. Cerminara has worked hard to widen the Western conception of immortality, particularly through her books on the Edgar Cayce readings. Her *Many Mansions* has evoked serious and widespread interest in reincarnation and Cayce, and has been translated into various European languages, Icelandic, Japanese, and Ceylonese. She disclosed in an interview in *The American Theosophist* (February 1977) that her background was theosophical: her grandmother and father were theosophists. It was only natural, she said, that after several years of studying thousands of readings at the Cayce headquarters that she found they resonated with her theosophical education. From *Many Mansions:*]

If it could be demonstrated scientifically that man is not merely a body, but also a soul inhabiting a body; and that, further, this soul existed before birth and will continue to exist after death, the discovery would transform psychological science. It would be as if a shaft had been dropped from surface levels of soil to deep-lying strata of the earth. . . . First of all, such an added dimension of time would enlarge man's understanding of personality traits. Psychologists have for some time been making close statistical and clinical studies of the qualities that compose personality. These studies are monuments to the ingenuity of man's mind; they have had many practical applications in personnel work, vocational guidance, and clinical psychology—and yet they represent what would seem to be only the narrow foreground of man.

Acceptance of the reincarnation principle throws a floodlight of illumination on the unnoticed background. The landscape so illumined has a strange and beautiful fascination of its own, but its principal importance is that within it can be discerned the slow, winding paths by which traits and capacities and attitudes of the present were achieved. . . . Psychiatrists concur in the view that the major life attitudes of the psyche arise from the unconscious. The reincarnation principle merely expands the scope of the unconscious to include the dynamics of past-life experience.[27]

[Relating these ideas to karma, as taught in Buddhism, Dr. Cerminara writes in *The World Within:*]

A passage in the Buddhist scriptures shows us an interesting fragment of conversation between Ananda, one of Buddha's disciples, and Buddha on the subject of karma. "How deep is this causal law!" Ananda exclaims. "How deep it seems! . . ." And Buddha answered, saying, "Say not so Ananda, say not so. Deep indeed is this causal law, and deep it appears to be. But it is by not knowing, by not understanding, by not penetrating this doctrine that the world of men has become entangled like a ball of twine, unable to pass beyond the Way of Woe and the ceaseless round of rebirth." Buddha seems completely persuaded of the fact that *ignorance* of karma and reincarnation can be a hindrance to spiritual progress, and conversely that *knowledge* of them can be immeasurably helpful.

Not that a noble and beautiful and fruitful life cannot be lived without this knowledge. Countless men and women of many religious faiths have lived great and even saintly lives in complete ignorance of, or disbelief in, reincarnation. And yet it seems likely, to the present writer at least, that at a certain stage of evolution, a knowledge of reincarnation is indispensable for full comprehension of oneself and of life in general. The final redemption of self could hardly be made without a conscious dredging of the past and conscious transmutation of it. Perhaps we have reached a stage of our history where this knowledge is necessary to us—otherwise it would not be appearing in so many places.[28]

[Another passage from *The World Within* suggests the bearing of this outlook on the field of race relations, and might also apply to religious antagonisms and conflicts:]

It becomes clear that anyone who accepts the idea of reincarnation cannot, with impunity, despise at wholesale any alien race or nation; for if he does so, he thereby runs the risk of despising his own past or future self. It must constantly be remembered, in the matter of race as in everything else, that man *is* a soul, and *has* a body, which he uses. . . . A proper understanding of this relationship of soul to body is . . . the first intellectual step towards a tolerance that shall be thorough and scientific rather than superficial and sentimental. When one recognizes that the body is merely the transitory expression and vehicle of the soul, one must of necessity see that to despise a man for his race, nationality, or color, is as absurd and unreasonable as to despise an actor for the costume he is wearing.

The longer one reflects upon the matter, in fact, the more does one's sense of separativeness and self-importance tend to dissolve. For if my soul has incarnated in black bodies and white, in red bodies and brown bodies and yellow; if each of these peoples has at one time or another been the creator of great civilizations equal to, comparable to, or even superior to our own, in the great moving kaleidoscope of history; if I participated in those colors and those civilizations, whether as an inferior or a superior member, whether as peasant or prince, whether as moron or as mastermind—how then can I remain smugly convinced of the unique importance and superiority of the race or nation to which I happen to belong in the present?[29]

IRA PROGOFF (1921–   )

American Psychologist

[Dr. Ira Progoff is author of the widely read book *The Death and Rebirth of Psychology*. In his later volume, *The Symbolic and the Real*, he explains why Plato's Meno has a profound meaning for modern man:]

Socrates undertook to prove that a slave boy who had never been taught mathematics could have a knowledge of certain mathematical facts drawn forth from him by a skillful teacher. To do this, Socrates questioned the boy carefully, evoking from him by the processes of thought which he stirred in him, new insights of which the boy had not before been aware. From this Socrates deduced that teaching is not a matter of something being placed in one person by another, but is a question of eliciting something that is already present, although only implicitly and latently, at hidden depths of the individual's mind.

On the face of it, this demonstration accords very well with the style of modern thinking. The modern mind is quite prepared to understand what Socrates was doing and to agree with him in principle that the process of education at its best is a drawing forth of capacities of knowledge that are present but undeveloped in the individual. . . . But Socrates had quite another view of what was to be inferred from his demonstration with the untutored slave boy. To him the facility with which he was able to draw new insights out of the boy was proof that the boy had known these things all along, but that he had not been aware of them. He had forgotten that he knew them. . . . To Socrates it was self-evident that the boy's capacity was the result of an experience he had had in a previous lifetime. What has been called Socrates' "favorite doctrine" was at the base of this. It was a doctrine with a very ancient lineage, the belief that the immortality of the individual soul is expressed in many incarnations at different points in history. . . .

The great task, then, as Socrates envisioned the problem of gaining knowledge, is to remember the things that one has known in earlier lifetimes. It seems clear in this connection that Socrates was interested primarily not in recalling the personal events of previous existences, but in recalling the underlying capacities of knowledge which had been accumulated in the course of its past lives by the person (or specifically by his "soul" as Socrates conceived of the soul). He would not see much point, for example, in attempting to identify the names and places of persons in whose form an individual had lived during previous incarnations; neither did he care to remember daily events, nor to recall emotional, personal encounters. These would have a subjectivity and pettiness that would place them beyond the pale of his primary concerns.

He would be interested, however, in establishing a connection and a new relationship with the qualities of cognition which had been developed in past experiences, such as one's relationship with mathematics, or with medicine, or with poetry. Such qualities of experience, representing underlying capacities of knowledge, would be of great relevance because they would provide access to larger awareness for the person in his present life. . . . Socrates' goal as a goad was to stir men up so that the traces of knowledge garnered through the timeless journey of the soul could come alive again . . . in order that it might serve as an inward source of truth.

We can see at this point a striking similarity between the calling of Socrates and the trend of work emerging in modern depth psychology. Both proceed on the hypothesis that the resources of wisdom are hidden in the depths of the human being, and that they are best able to unfold in meaning when they are stirred to full expression. . . . Both modern psychology and the Socratic way are instances of men's disciplined attempts to reach toward reality in modes of thought that fit the tone and temper of their times. Beyond their differences in style lies a quality of integrity that unites them; and from this unity we may eventually be able to draw the model of a psychological and spiritual perspective that will answer our modern need.[30]

HERBERT FINGARETTE (1921–   )

American Philosopher and Psychologist

[These selections are from Dr. Herbert Fingarette's *The Self in Transformation,* considered a major contribution to psychoanalytic thought. Assuming the truth of a number of Freud's formulations, the author points to where they may lead when more fully worked out. And, as Benjamin Nelson points out in a foreword to the Harper Torchbook edition, "Fingarette escapes the logical and spiritual blunders which have regrettably dogged orthodox Freudianism from the time the earthshaking insights of psychoanalysis were prematurely encased in rigid molds."

Our brief samplings are chiefly from the seventy-page chapter "Karma and the Inner World." Interestingly, Fingarette is not concerned with "proving" reincarnation and karma, but rather in assessing their self-transforming capacity. In doing this he finds significant parallels between the insights achieved by Freud and those of the ancient psychologists of the East. "I am not psychologizing reincarnation," he says. "I want to present it as a reality, not a metaphor. . . . I am trying to preserve it whole."

Dr. Louis De Rosis, reviewing the book in *The Library Journal,* states: "The volume is a high-powered microscope used by a brilliant philosopher to bring profound illumination into psychoanalysis—not only to its basic theoretical underpinnings but to its relationships in the whole scheme of man's being. This is truly required reading for all psychiatrists, psychoanalysts, and clinical psychologists of any school or persuasion. It should also have more than passing meaning for the informed layman.'']

The doctrine of karma, whether we accept it or not, poses profound questions about the structure, transformation, and transcendence of the Self. It raises in new ways general questions of ontology. We may be parochial and dismiss the doctrine, especially its theses on reincarnation, as obvious superstition. Or we may recall that it was not any self-evident spiritual superficiality but the historical accident of official Christian opposition which stamped it out as an important Greek and Roman doctrine, a doctrine profoundly meaningful to a Plato, as well as to the masses. Perhaps more significant, it has remained, from the first millennium B.C. until the present, an almost universal belief in the East, even among most of the highly trained and Western-educated contemporary thinkers. . . .

Certainly we can avoid some irrelevant psychological hurdles if it be stressed at once that, in our discussion of karma and reincarnation, we will not have jumped into an antiscientific position, nor will we be treating reincarnation as ''pseudo'' or as ''super'' science. The real issues are philosophical. They have nothing to do with amassing reports of *wunderkinder,* Indian yogis, or the periodic newspaper sensationalisms exploiting fakes or unfortunates claiming inexplicable knowledge of past events. These ''marvels'' are as philosophically uninteresting to us as it turns out that they are to the great prophets of karma. . . .

The assumption in this chapter is that joining a fresh examination of karmic doctrine to an examination of certain aspects of psychoanalytic therapy will throw a new light on therapy, on the meaning of the karmic doctrine, and on certain of our major philosophical and cultural commitments. The task of the reader in such a discussion is to see what the evidence and the argument say rather than to read into the words the Westerner's stock interpretation of ''esoteric'' doctrines.

The Judaeo-Christian apprehends life on earth as a unique cosmic event, a coming out of nothing, a staking of all on the one chance, and, finally, a reaping of eternal reward or punishment. The Far Eastern image is of a multitude of interconnected lives, a slow and arduous struggle toward spiritual enlightenment. The physicalistic image is of a cosmically meaningless life, beginning and ending in nothingness. . . .

In the West, we tend to think of heaven and hell as analogues to our penological practices: the punishment is physical discomfort and psychic isolation (prison) regardless of the specific nature of the criminal act. The karmic law is much closer to the old Greek notion of cosmic justice, or to the notion of ''poetic justice.'' The punishment exactly fits the crime. But poetic justice must operate within a life, if not this one, then another one. It cannot

be realized if life terminates in an essentially static heaven or hell. . . .
Karmic law is not the edict of an All-Powerful Disciplinarian, not an expression of will accompanied by the threat of sanctions. It purports to be factual
description: Somehow or other, things do eventually "balance out" in the
moral realm; each moral action produces, eventually, its quite specific moral
reaction. And our constant strivings are constantly producing new "karma"
as well as bringing past karma to fruition; the weary round of births and
deaths is perpetuated.

In the course of spiritual progress toward freedom from the round of births
and rebirths one eventually achieves the power of remembering past lives.
One then sees their connection with the present life. The ordinary person can
neither remember nor understand: "And what happened to you in your
mother's womb, all that you have quite forgotten."[31] The greater the spiritual
progress, the greater the ability and the easier the task. Knowledge of one's
former lives is [in Buddhism] one of the "five kinds of superknowledge."[32] In
achieving this "superknowledge," one is concurrently achieving liberation
from the karmic bonds. As in psychoanalysis, this knowledge is not the goal,
but it is a distinctive ingredient in the achievement of freedom. Spiritual
knowledge and spiritual freedom are born as one. . . .

[Dr. Fingarette compares the effect on feelings of responsibility of the
idea of many lives, or "selves," extending over long periods of time, with
that of the psychoanalytic view of multiple selves experienced within the
span of one life:]

We become responsible agents when we can face the moral continuity of
the familiar, conscious self with other strange, "alien" psychic entities—our
"other selves." We should perhaps speak of an "identity" with other selves
rather than a "continuity." For we must accept responsibility for the "acts"
of those other selves, we must see these acts as *ours*. As Freud said of our
dream lives, they are not only in me but act "from out of me as well."

Yet identity is, in another way, too strong a term. . . . The psychoanalytic
quest for autonomy reveals the Self in greater depth; it reveals it as a *community* of selves. The genuinely startling thing in this quest is not simply the
discovery that these other, archaic selves exist, nor even that they have an
impact in the present. What startles is the detailed analysis of the peculiarly
close, subtle, and complex texture of the threads which weave these other
selves and the adult conscious self into a single great pattern.

It is a special, startling kind of intimacy with which we deal. It calls for me
to recognize that I suffer, whether I will or no, for the deeds of those other
selves. It is an intimacy which, when encountered, makes it self-evident that
I must assume responsibility for the acts and thoughts of those other persons

as if they were I. Finally and paradoxically, in the morally clear vision which thus occurs, there emerges, as in a montage, a new Self, a Self free of bondage to the old deeds of the old selves. For it is a Self which sees and therefore sees through the old illusions which passed for reality. . . . The self moving through the rich flux of experience is now not blinded and hobbled by the old superimposed and stereotyped fantasies which formed a tightly and dynamically interrelated community of selves generating its own repetitive destiny. . . .[33]

The karmic notion is that the old self acts, and the later selves, though they did not commit the acts, legitimately inherit their fruits as those fruits ripen in the course of time. This is an occurrence which need not involve generations or epochs; it may be from moment to moment or day to day: Coomaraswamy summarizes and emphasizes that "it is constantly overlooked that the majority of references [in Hindu scripture] to . . . repeated birth and repeated death refer to this present life. . . ." And he refers to the concept of *punar bhava* ("becoming") as meaning that "man dies and is reborn daily and hourly in this present life."[34]

I am interested . . . in the karmic doctrine as . . . an expression of the genuine dialogue of spirit. . . . The doctrine's spiritual function . . . is that of providing a conceptual and action framework within which a person may explore and reorganize the psychomoral community of selves which constitute the person. . . .

Siwek has expressed the view that the doctrine of reincarnation is morally enervating: for not only are we assured of an indefinite number of lives in which to rectify our ways, but the widespread desire to keep on living on earth is a powerful motive to "sin" *in order* to assure rebirth. This view is understandable as "external," a result of seeing the words of the doctrine rather than its meaning as it functions in the appropriate context. . . . The doctrine of reincarnation does not receive its spiritual impulse and quality from theoretical discussion. I have tried to set the stage for detailed analysis by suggesting that karmic insight emerges in the situation of one who is driven by anxiety and suffering, who seeks self-awareness, and who is grappling in a highly personal and direct way with the fragmented, enslaving lives which he has lived, is living, and hopes to escape. For one who is not urgently concerned with suffering and illusion, who does not feel despair and the need for illumination, the doctrine of reincarnation is indeed a devilish snare. . . . We cannot toy with the idea of reincarnation as an intellectual or cultural curiosity having a certain piquant and quaint validity and still discover its power and its worth. . . . One earns a vision by living it, not merely thinking about it.[35]

THE PHILOSOPHER
LOOKS AT REBIRTH

FRIEDRICH NIETZSCHE (1844–1900)

German Philosopher and Poet

[In his essay "Cosmopolitan View of Nietzsche," the noted Indian author Coomaraswamy called the impact of this widely influential philosopher "the awakening of the conscience of Europe."[1] Friedrich Nietzsche himself said: "My life-task is to prepare for humanity a moment of supreme self-consciousness, a Great Noontide when it will gaze both backwards and forwards, when it will emerge from the tyranny of accident and the priesthood, and for the first time pose the question of the Why and Wherefore of humanity as a whole."[2]

The first selections quoted here are from *Thus Spake Zarathustra*. His Zarathustra, of course, is a poetic invention and should not be identified with the Iranian teacher, although from childhood Nietzsche appears to have had a close affinity for that sage. The philosophy of the Superman, expounded in *Zarathustra*, was unfortunately linked for many decades with German nationalist policies. As is now well known, this came about because Nietzsche's sister perverted his message to justify and dignify Nazism, and thereby helped change the course of European history. "I know my fate," he wrote in 1888, "my name will be connected with the remembrance of something monstrous, a crisis, the like of which has never before occurred on earth." Professor H. F. Peters, who quotes this in his biography *Zarathustra's Sister*, also reports Nietzsche as saying: "People like my sister must be irreconcilable enemies of my thoughts and my philosophy."[3]

In the extract that follows, Coomaraswamy reveals that the philosophy of the Superman has an ancient heritage. (In the light of earlier chapters, we know it was viewed, as Nietzsche will be shown to view it, against the background of many lives.)

> Of special significance is the beautiful doctrine of the Superman—so like the Chinese concept of the Superior Man, and the Indian Maha Purusha, Bodhisattva and Jivamukta. . . . The doctrine of the Superman, whose virtue stands "beyond good and evil," who is at once the flower and the leader and savior of men, has been put forward again and again in the world's history.

In Nietzsche's autobiography *Ecce Homo,* he wrote regarding *Zarathustra:* "The fundamental idea of my work—namely, the Eternal Recurrence of all things—this highest of all possible formulae for a Yea-saying philosophy, first occurred to me in August 1881. I made a note of the thought on a sheet of paper, with the postscript: 6,000 feet beyond men and time! That day I happened to be wandering through the woods alongside of the lake of Silvaplana, and I halted beside a huge pyramidal and towering rock. . . . It was then that the thought struck me."[4] In his "Explanatory Notes to 'Thus Spake Zarathustra,'" Nietzsche further affirms: "The doctrine of the Eternal Recurrence is the turning point of history. . . . The moment in which I begot recurrence is immortal, for the sake of that moment alone I will endure recurrence. . . . We must desire to perish in order to arise afresh,—from one day to the other. Wander through a hundred souls,—let that be thy life and thy fate! And then finally: desire to go through the whole process once more!"[5] The poem overflows with this spirit:]

Everything goeth, everything returneth; eternally rolleth the wheel of existence. Everything dieth, everything blossometh forth again; eternally runneth on the year of existence.

Everything breaketh, everything is integrated anew; eternally buildeth itself the same house of existence. All things separate, all things again greet one another; eternally true to itself remaineth the ring of existence. . . .

Behold, we know what thou teachest: that all things eternally return, and ourselves with them, and that we have already existed times without number, and all things with us. . . .

A long twilight limped on before me, a fatally weary, fatally intoxicated sadness, which spake with yawning mouth.

"Eternally he returneth, the man of whom thou art weary, the small man"—so yawned my sadness. . . . "Ah, man returneth eternally! The small man returneth eternally!"

Naked had I once seen both of them, the greatest man and the smallest man: all too like one another—all too human, even the greatest man!

All too small, even the greatest man!—that was my disgust at man! And the eternal return of the smallest man!—that was my disgust at all existence! . . .[6]

[The greatest man, of course, is not yet a Superman, and in the section "The Seven Seals," Nietzsche offers a more jubilant conception of eternity, each of the seven stanzas ending with these lines:]

Oh, how could I not be ardent for Eternity and for the marriage-ring of rings—the ring of the return?

Never yet have I found the woman by whom I should like to have children, unless it be this woman whom I love: for I love thee, O Eternity!

For I love thee, O Eternity![7]

[The next selections are from Nietzsche's notes entitled "Eternal Recurrence." The translator, Anthony Ludovici, states in his preface: "The notes concerning the Eternal Recurrence are said by Mrs. Foerster-Nietzsche to have been the first that Nietzsche ever wrote on the subject of his great doctrine. This being so, they must have been composed toward the autumn of the year 1881. . . . Until the end, he regarded it as the inspiration which had led to his chief work, *Thus Spake Zarathustra*."[8]]

In every one of these cycles of human life there will be one hour where for the first time one man, and then many, will perceive the mighty thought of the eternal recurrence of all things:—and for mankind this is always the hour of Noon. . . . From the moment when this thought begins to prevail all colours will change their hue and a new history will begin. . . . Let us guard against teaching such a doctrine as if it were a suddenly discovered religion! It must percolate through slowly, and whole generations must build on it and become fruitful through it,—in order that it may grow into a large tree which will shelter all posterity. . . .

This doctrine is lenient towards those who do not believe in it. It speaks of no hells and it contains no threats. He who does not believe in it has but a fleeting life in his consciousness. . . . The political mania at which I smile just as merrily as my contemporaries smile at the religious mania of former times is above all Materialism, a belief in the world, and in the repudiation of a "Beyond," of a "back-world." . . .

My doctrine is: Live so that thou mayest desire to live again,—that is thy duty,—for in any case thou wilt live again! . . . The question which thou wilt have to answer before every deed that thou doest: "Is this such a deed as I am prepared to perform an incalculable number of times?" is the best ballast. . . . Let us stamp the impress of eternity upon our lives! This thought contains more than all the religions which taught us to condemn this life as a thing ephemeral, which bade us squint upwards to another and indefinite existence.—We must not strive after distant and unknown states of bliss and blessings and acts of grace, but must live so that we would fain live again and live for ever so, to all eternity!—Our duty is present with us every instant. . . . We must implant the love of life, the love of every man's own life in every conceivable way! . . . *This* life is thy eternal life![9]

BERNARD BOSANQUET (1848–1923)

British Philosopher and Writer

[From Bernard Bosanquet's Gifford Lectures, 1912, published as *Value and Destiny of the Individual:*]

[Metempsychosis has been] of enormous influence in the history of philosophy and religion. . . . It is, I am convinced, the form which Plato preferred to give to his working conception of human survival, and, in shapes largely borrowed and spiritualized from Oriental tradition, it is exceedingly popular today. Dr. McTaggart's advocacy of it on strict philosophical grounds is familiar to students. . . . In the doctrine of metempsychosis . . . the bare subject or ego, the naked form of personality, the soul-thing is supposed to persist; but no content of the personality goes with it. We are offered chains of personalities linked together by impersonal transitions. We need only point out in passing the difficulty, which Aristotle put his finger on, in the conception of an identical soul animating wholly different bodies in succession. . . .[10]

Advocates of [metempsychosis] point to the fact that character and the principles of knowledge can persist in the soul through intervals of oblivion and unconsciousness, wholly apart from specific memories of the incidents of their acquisition. Why, it is asked, should they not persist from life to life, as they persist from day to day, and from youth to age, unimpaired by intervals of unconsciousness and by the loss of particular memories? Such a conception affords, to minds of any elevation, a motive for self-improvement which for them is all the stronger that it is wholly divorced from ideas of a personal self-satisfaction in a future world. . . .

[As to the theological theory of creationism] I may draw attention here to a difficulty which Mr. Bradley mentions, nearly following Plato, *Republic* 611 A. "A constant supply of new souls, none of which ever perished, would obviously land us in an insoluble difficulty" (the universe being held incapable of increase).[11] It would follow that some souls must perish, or be used over again as in metempsychosis.[12]

The Cambridge Reincarnationists

[The next three philosophers—James Ward, G. Lowes Dickinson, and John McTaggart—were all actively associated with Cambridge University. Their efforts to revive the idea of reincarnation seem reminiscent of the work of the seventeenth-century Cambridge Platonists.]

JAMES WARD (1843–1925)
British Philosopher and Psychologist

[James Ward was professor of mental philosophy at Cambridge from 1897 to 1925. He was also interested in science and received doctorates in that field from both Cambridge and Oxford. The following is from his Gifford lectures for 1907–1910, published as *The Realm of Ends:*]

I make bold to deny, that the theory of pre-existence [and reincarnation] "creates new difficulties." It involves "a ramifying network" of assumptions unquestionably; but if it "is certainly not capable of positive disproof," the objector is bound to show that the result of the whole is worthless. Till then, summarily to reject it involves the still more extravagant assumption that we have exhausted all possibilities and that what may be only our lack of knowledge of its empirical conditions is tantamount to a proof of its impossibility. As Kant, whose words I have adopted, has said, this arrogance of negation does not eliminate in the least the practical value of such hypotheses. The appeal to ignorance no doubt cuts both ways: it does not allow us to treat hypotheses as knowledge, but on the other hand it does not destroy their working utility if, consistently with what we do know, they enable us even tentatively to reach a completer and more satisfactory *Weltanschauung*.

As regards this particular hypothesis of pre-existence and a plurality of lives, its complexity is no advantage certainly; but even so the disadvantage is reduced in proportion as the separate assumptions are analogous with actual experience and consilient with each other. After all it should give the scornful objector pause, to think how many of the vital processes, about which we have definite knowledge, involve an elaborate adjustment of multifarious details that would be utterly incredible but for its familiarity. Is it then unreasonable to expect still more marvelous conjunctions in the wider dimensions of the world beyond the grave? And is it not also possible—just because of such wider dimensions—that what to us seems complicated or impossible is really as simple as say movement into a third dimension, which yet a being confined to two might fail to understand? . . .

The objection to transmigration or metempsychosis [on the grounds of personal discontinuity between lives] has been met by assuming that the personal discontinuity is only temporary, and that the successive lives of a given subject may be eventually connected through continuous but latent memories that are revived after death or when all the soul's *Wanderjahre* are over. So, for example, Professor Campbell Fraser thinks. Compare his *Theism*, Vol. II, p. 249. And still more definitely Renouvier, *Le Personnalisme*, 1903, p. 220. A similar view was held by Max Drossbach, J. Reynaud and many others. . . .

Between one active life and another there may well be . . . an intermediate state of mental rumination, and reflection, as many theologians have assumed. This state, it has been said, "is not a domain of deeds and works, for the external conditions for these are wanting . . . it is the domain of inwardness, of silent consideration and pondering, a domain of recollection *(Erinnerung)* in the full sense of the word."[13] Such a self-purgatory of all souls seems a worthier idea than the one-sided expiatory purgatory of the Romish Church, which has so little moral efficacy that it may be curtailed by extraneous ceremonial. We can perhaps suppose that this process [of rumination] may be a preparation for a new life, provided . . . the change in character is notwithstanding still somehow retained. . . .

But even so, if this series [of rebirths] is to have any real continuity or meaning, if it is to be not merely a series but a progression, then at every return to life, either Providence must determine, or the naturient soul must itself select, its appropriate reincarnation. Otherwise, if disembodied souls are to be blown about by the winds of circumstance like other seeds, we should only have a repetition of that outrageous fortune which the doctrine of transmigration was supposed to redress. . . .

This difficulty in turn has been met by the further and bolder assumption, that disembodied souls do in fact steer their own way back to a suitable rebirth. An atom liberated from its molecular bonds is described as manifesting an unwonted activity, technically known as "the nascent state"; but still it does not recombine indifferently with the first free atom that it encounters, but only with one for which it has an "affinity." And "there seems to be nothing more strange or paradoxical in the suggestion that each person enters into connection with the body that is most fitted to be connected with him."[14] . . . A liberated spirit ought to be credited with vastly more *savoir vivre* than a liberated atom. Further it must be allowed that this suggestion is quite in keeping with the conservation of values, which men like Lotze and Höffding regard as axiomatic—at any rate experience often verifies, and never certainly belies it. Finally it minimises the objection to personal continuity that is often based on the facts of heredity.[15]

G. LOWES DICKINSON (1862–1932)
British Humanist and Philosopher

[From G. Lowes Dickinson's Ingersoll Lecture on immortality at Harvard University in 1909 entitled "Is Immortality Desirable?":]

The scientific denial of immortality is based upon the admitted fact of the connection between mind and brain, when it is assumed that death of the brain must involve death of that, whatever it be, which has been called soul. This may indeed be true, but it is not necessarily or obviously true; it does not follow logically from the fact of the connection. . . . The soul, as Plato thought, may be capable of existing without the body, though it be imprisoned in it as in a tomb. It looks out, we might suppose, through the window of the senses; and its vision is obscured or distorted by every imperfection of the glass. "If a man is shut up in a house," Dr. McTaggart has remarked, "the transparency of the windows is an essential condition of his seeing the sky. But," he wittily adds, "it would not be prudent to infer that if he walked out of the house he could not see the sky, because there was no longer any glass through which he might see it." . . . That the soul therefore dies with the brain is an inference, and quite possibly a mistaken one. If to some minds it seems inevitable, that may be as much due to a defect of their imagination as to a superiority of their judgment. . . .

It may be held that life, as we know it, is so desirable that though it would not be a good thing to prolong it indefinitely, it would be a good thing to repeat it over and over again. That we may treat this notion fairly, I will ask you to suppose that in none of these repetitions is there any memory of the previous cycles, for every one, I expect, would agree that the repetition of a life, every episode of which is remembered to have occurred before is a prospect of appalling tediousness. Supposing, however, that memory were extinguished at each death, we have a position that may be worth examining. It is, as many of you will remember, the position of that remarkable man of genius, Nietzsche, and if only for that reason, deserves a moment's consideration. . . . [He said:] "Oh! How could I fail to be eager for eternity, and for the marriage ring of rings, the ring of recurrence? For I love thee, O eternity!"[16]

Do we, too, love this eternity? The answer seems plain. So far as a man judges any life, his own or another's, to be valuable, here and now, in and for itself, apart from any consideration of immortality, he will reasonably desire that it should be repeated as often as possible, rather than occur once and never again; for the positive value he finds in it will be reproduced in each repetition. On the other hand, so far as he finds any life in itself not to be valuable, or that its value depends upon some other kind of immortality, the prospect held out by Nietzsche will leave him cold or fill him with dismay. . . . But at this point it may really be more modest to say "I," to tell you simply how I feel, and to ask you whether you feel the same.

I find, then, that, to me, in my present experience, the thing that at bottom matters most is the sense I have of something in me making for more life and better. All my pain is at last a feeling of the frustration of this; all my happiness a feeling of its satisfaction. I do not know what that is; I am not prepared to give a coherent account of it; I ought not, very likely, to call it "it," and to imply the category of substance. I will abandon, if necessary, under criticism, any particular terms in which I may try to describe it; I will abandon anything except Itself. For it is real. It governs all my experience, and determines all my judgments of value. If pleasure hampers it, I do not desire pleasure; if pain furthers it, I do desire pain. And what I feel in myself, I infer in others. If I may be allowed to use that ambiguous and question-begging word "soul," then I agree with the poet Browning that "little else is worth study save the development of soul." This is to me the bottom fact of experience. And no one can go any further with me in my argument who does not find in my words an indication, however imperfect, of something which he knows, in his own life, to be real.

What, then, is it that this which I call the "soul" seeks? It seeks what is good; but it does not know what is the ultimate Good. As a seventeenth-century writer has well put it: "We love we know not what, and therefore everything allures us. As iron at a distance is drawn by the loadstone, there being some invisible communication between them, so is there in us a world of Love to somewhat, though we know not what in the world that should be. There are invisible ways of conveyance by which some great thing doth touch our souls, and by which we tend to it. Do you not feel yourself drawn by the expectation and desire of some great thing?"[17]

This "great thing" it is our business to find out by expereince. We do find many good things, but there are always other and better beyond. That is why it is hazardous to fix one's ideal, and say finally, "This or that would be heaven." For we may find, as the voyagers did in Browning's "Paracelsus," that the real heaven lies always beyond; beyond each Good we may attain here; but also, which is my present point, beyond death. The whole strength of the case for immortality, as a thing to be desired, lies in the fact that no one in this life attains his ideal. The soul, even of the best and most fortunate of us, does not achieve the Good of which she feels herself to be capable and in which alone she can rest. The potentiality is not fully realized. I do not infer from this that life has no value if the Beyond is cut off. . . . But what I do maintain is that life here would have infinitely more value if we knew that beyond death we should pursue, and ultimately to a successful issue, the elusive idea of which we are always in quest.[18]

[Dickinson's interest in reincarnation may be traced to 1884 when he was twenty-two. The famous British author E. M. Forster was a protégé of Dickinson, and in Forster's biography of his mentor, the following excerpt from an 1884 Dickinson letter is quoted:

Never again will I regret that I've spent years over Greek. I'm sitting at "Plato's feet" at present, and have really never experienced such "ecstasy" in the literal sense; why, I can't tell you, but so it is. I seem to have got a new light for reading him, and it seems all clear and quite necessarily and incontrovertibly true. And moreover in the "Phaedrus" is much palpable "Esoteric Buddhism": do read it again, if you haven't lately, and there you will find the indestructibility of life, and the successive incarnations, and the one great consciousness.[19]

"Esoteric Buddhism" refers to a book on theosophy of that title by A. P. Sinnett, formerly editor of the *Pioneer* of Allahabad, the official organ of the

British government in India. *Esoteric Buddhism* was published in 1883 and created quite a stir in intellectual circles in England.

In 1884 Madame Blavatsky and Colonel H. S. Olcott—president of the Theosophical Society—visited England for many months. Forster mentions that Dickinson heard Olcott speak and was immensely impressed with Mohini Chatterjee, a Brahmin theosophist in the theosophical party. Dickinson's letters at this time were full of references to Mohini. When finally the young man had courage to beg for an audience, the Brahmin approved Dickinson's idea to study Plato, a study that was to pervade much of his life and writings thenceforth. Incidentally, another of Chatterjee's admirers was Yeats who wrote a reincarnation poem in his honor.[20] Mohini advises in the poem how a thought of one's numerous lives could quell the sensual passions of youth.

Forster in his biography often mentions John McTaggart, one of Dickinson's closest friends, and next to be considered.]

JOHN ELLIS McTAGGART (1866–1925)
British Philosopher

[By the time he was twenty-five, John McTaggart had been called the most distinguished dialectician and metaphysician since Hegel. In 1897 he became lecturer in the Moral Sciences at Trinity College, Cambridge. C. D. Broad, who succeeded him at Cambridge, declared that his system was the work of genius, which places its author "in the front rank of the great historical philosophers," and one that "may quite fairly be compared with the *Enneads* of Plotinus, the *Ethics* of Spinoza, and the *Encyclopaedia* of Hegel."[21]

The selections that follow are from McTaggart's small volume *Human Immortality and Pre-Existence,* which originally was part of his large work *Some Dogmas of Religion* published in 1906. In these volumes he says that "if we succeed in proving immortality, it will be by means of considerations which would also prove pre-existence. I do not see how existence in future time could be shown to be necessary in the case of any being whose existence in past time is admitted not to be necessary. If the universe got on without me a hundred years ago, what reason could be given for denying that it might get on without me a hundred years hence?"]

Even the best men are not, when they die, in such a state of intellectual and moral perfection as would fit them to enter heaven immediately. . . . This is generally recognized, and one of two alternatives is commonly adopted to meet it. The first is that some tremendous improvement—an improvement out of all proportion to any which can ever be observed in life—takes place at the moment of death. . . . The other and more probable alternative is that the process of gradual improvement can go on in each of us after the death of our present bodies. . . .

Now it might be said that our chief ground for hoping for a progressive improvement after death would be destroyed if memory periodically ceased [when we are reborn]. Death, it might be argued, would not only remove us from the field of our activity, but would deprive us of all memory of what we had done, and therefore whatever was gained in one life would be lost at death. We could no more hope for a permanent improvement than a man on the treadmill can hope to end higher than he started. . . .

We must ask, therefore, what elements of value are carried on by memory from the present to the future. And then we must consider whether they can be carried on *without* memory.

I think I shall be in agreement with most people when I say that memory is chiefly of value in our lives in three ways. In the first place, it may make us wiser. The events which we have seen, and the conclusions at which we have arrived, may be preserved in memory, and so add to our present knowledge. In the second place, it may make us more virtuous. The memory of a temptation, whether it has been resisted or successful, may under various circumstances help us in resisting present temptation. In the third place, it may tell us that people with whom we are now related are the people whom we have loved in the past, and this may enter as an element into our present love of them. . . . If the past could help the present in a like manner *without* the aid of memory, the absence of memory need not destroy the chance of an improvement spreading over many lives.

Let us consider wisdom first. Can we be wiser by reason of something which we have forgotten? Unquestionably we can. Wisdom is not merely, or chiefly, amassed facts, or even recorded judgments. It depends primarily on a mind qualified to deal with facts, and to form judgments. Now the acquisition of knowledge and experience, if wisely conducted, may strengthen the mind. Of that we have sufficient evidence in this life. And so a man who dies after acquiring knowledge—and all men acquire some—might enter his new life, deprived indeed of his knowledge, but not deprived of the increased strength and delicacy of mind which he had gained in acquiring the knowledge. And, if so, he will be wiser in the second life because of what has happened in the first. Of course he loses something in losing the actual knowledge. . . . And is not even this loss really a gain? For the mere accumulation of knowledge, if memory never ceased, would soon become overwhelming, and worse than useless. . . .

With virtue the point is perhaps clearer. For the memory of moral experiences is of no value to virtue except in so far as it helps to form the moral character, and if this is done, the loss of the memory would be no loss to virtue. Now we cannot doubt that a character may remain determined by an event which has been forgotten. I have forgotten the greater number of the good and evil acts which I have done in my present life. And yet each must have left a trace on my character. And so a man may carry over into his next life the dispositions and tendencies which he has gained by the moral contests of this life. . . .

There remains love. The problem here is more important, if, as I believe, it is in love, and in nothing else, that we find not only the supreme value of life, but also the supreme reality of life, and, indeed, of the universe. . . . Much has been forgotten in any friendship which has lasted for several years within the limits of a single life—many confidences, many services, many hours of happiness and sorrow. But they have not passed away without leaving their mark on the present. They contribute, though they are forgotten, to the present love which is not forgotten. In the same way, if the whole memory of the love of a life is swept away at death, its value is not lost if the same love is stronger in a new life because of what passed before. . . .

The chance of a love recurring in any future life, must depend primarily on the conditions which determine where and how the lovers are born in the future life. For if memory does not survive death, it will be impossible for love to occur in any life in which people do not meet. If the conditions which determine the circumstances of our birth, and through them our juxtapositions throughout life, were themselves determined by chance, or by some merely mechanical external necessity, the probability of meeting our friends in another life would be too small to be regarded. . . . If immortality is to give us an assurance or a hope of progressive improvement, it can only be if we have reason to believe that the interests of spirit are so predominant a force in the universe that they will find, in the long run, satisfaction in the universe. And, in this case, the constitution of the universe would be such that, whether with or without memory, love would have its way.[22]

[On the latter point McTaggart wrote to a woman in New Zealand: "I can't help thinking it probable that people who meet once will meet often on the way up. That they should meet at all seems to show that they must be connected with the same part of the pattern of things, and if so they would probably often be working together. Very fanciful, no doubt, but more probable than thinking that it goes by chance, like sand grains in a heap, which is what one thinks in these scientific days, unless one thinks for oneself."[23]]

[An appropriate introduction to the final selections from McTaggart is a passage from *Human Immortality and Pre-Existence:*

The most effective way of proving that the doctrine of pre-existence is bound up with the doctrine of immortality would be to prove directly that the nature of man was such that it involved a life both before and after the present life. But . . . such a demonstration, if it is possible at all, as I believe it to be, would be far beyond the scope of this book, since it would involve a determination of

some of the most fundamental characteristics of reality. . . . In the nine years
which have passed since I first wrote these pages, I have become more firmly
convinced that the nature of reality can be shown to be such as to justify a
belief both in immortality and in pre-existence. I hope at some future time to
publish my grounds for this conviction, as part of a treatise on the general
question of the fundamental nature of reality.[24]

Dr. McTaggart fulfilled this hope in his two-volume work *The Nature of
Existence*. Dr. Broad writes: "If subtle analysis, rigid reasoning and constructive fertility, applied with tireless patience to the hardest and deepest
problems of metaphysics, and expressed in language which always en-
lightens the intellect and sometimes touches the emotions, be a title to philosophical immortality, then McTaggart has fully earned his place among the
immortals by *The Nature of Existence*."[25] As one reads what will follow,
it becomes apparent how far removed the author was from the plane of
wishful thinking. In this relation, we first quote from G. Lowes Dickinson's
biography of McTaggart:

He believed that the world of appearance was moving, on the whole,
towards the world of Reality, and that all souls would in the end arrive
there. It was a very long, and might be a very terrible, journey . . . and
McTaggart himself anticipated very bad times for himself. He would say,
as he observed the inhabitants of a slum, that he himself might be thus in
some other life; and at times he would console himself for the fact that,
while he was so happy [and] his friends were not, by the reflection that his
turn for a bad time might come later. . . . As he never lost touch with his
old friends, so he never ceased to make new ones. Neither class, nor age,
nor occupation could keep him apart from congenial souls. He went through
life knitting up relations which he believed to have originated in former
existences. . . .[26]]

Let us turn from the effect of the loss of memory to the more general
question of the effect of a plurality of lives. If there is such a plurality
extending over a long future, our prospects after leaving our present bodies
have possibilities of evil much greater than those generally admitted by
theories of immortality which reject . . . the possibility of an endless hell.
Such theories hold, in some cases, that we shall pass immediately at death to
a state of complete and endless beatitude. . . .

We have, however, no right, on the view which we have taken, to share
this optimism as to the immediate temporal future. The temporal future will
consist of a greater number of successive lives. It is true that, in the long run,
the later will be better than the earlier. But the rate of improvement may
be very slow—so slow that it might be imperceptible for centuries—and it
may be broken by periods of oscillation in which a man was actually in a
worse condition than he had been previously. With regard to knowledge, to

virtue, and to love, we have no ground for supposing that improvement will not be very slow, and that it will not be broken by intervals of deterioration. And with regard to happiness, there is no form of suffering which history records to have happened in the past, which may not lie in the path of any one of us in the future. . . . The universe has evil in it—that is beyond doubt. . . . All that we can say is that this evil, however great it may be, is only passing. . . . The very greatness of the evil which we endure gives us some slight anticipation of the greatness of the good which outweighs it infinitely. . . .

The prospect of many such lives as ours has [also] a bright as well as a dark aspect. . . . Such life as ours now, in which sin jostles with virtue, and doubt with confidence, and hatred with love, cannot satisfy us, but it can teach us a great deal—far more than can be learned between a single birth and a single death. Not only because the time is so short, but because there are so many things which are incompatible within a single life. No man can learn fully in one life the lessons of unbroken health and of bodily sickness, of riches and of poverty, of study and action, of comradeship and isolation, of defiance and of obedience, of virtue and of vice. And yet they are all so good to learn. Is it not worth much to be able to hope that what we have missed in one life may come to us in another?

And though the way is long, it can be no more wearisome than a single life. For with death we leave behind us memory and old age, and fatigue. We may die old but we shall be born young. And death acquires a deeper and more gracious significance when we regard it as part of the continually recurring rhythm of progress—as inevitable, as natural, and as benevolent as sleep.[27]

MOHANDAS K. GANDHI (1869–1948)

Indian Social Philosopher, Apostle of Nonviolence

[Extracts from Gandhi's letters to Madeleine Slade, a British admiral's daughter who renounced position and comfort to follow Gandhi:]

The more I observe and study things, the more convinced I become that sorrow over separation and death is perhaps the greatest delusion. To realize that it is a delusion is to become free. There is no death, no separation of the substance. And yet the tragedy of it is that though we love friends for the substance we recognize in them, we deplore the destruction of the insubstantial that covers the substance for the time being. Whereas real friendship should be used to reach the whole through the fragment. You seem to have got the truth for the moment. Let it abide forever. . . .

What you say about rebirth is sound. It is nature's kindness that we do not remember past births. Where is the good either of knowing in detail the numberless births we have gone through? Life would be a burden if we carried such a tremendous load of memories. A wise man deliberately forgets many things, even as a lawyer forgets the cases and their details as soon as they are disposed of. Yes, "death is but a sleep and a forgetting." . . .

[Your] Mother is slowly going. It will be well if the end comes soon. It is better to leave a body one has outgrown. To wish to see the dearest ones as long as possible in the flesh is a selfish desire and it comes out of weakness or want of faith in the survival of the soul after the dissolution of the body. The form ever changes, ever perishes, the informing spirit neither changes nor perishes. True love consists in transferring itself from the body to the dweller within and then necessarily realizing the oneness of all life inhabiting numberless bodies.[28]

[Gandhi's long-range view of many lives apparently gave him the courage, in the midst of many failures, to pursue ceaselessly the goals he envisioned. Here are thoughts carrying this suggestion:]

If for mastering the physical sciences you have to devote a whole lifetime, how many lifetimes may be needed for mastering the greatest spiritual force that mankind has known?[29] For if this is the only permanent thing in life, if this is the only thing that counts, then whatever effort you bestow on mastering it is well spent.[30]

Having flung aside the sword, there is nothing except the cup of love which I can offer to those who oppose me. It is by offering that cup that I expect to draw them close to me. I cannot think of permanent enmity between man and man, and believing as I do in the theory of rebirth, I live in the hope that if not in this birth, in some other birth I shall be able to hug all humanity in friendly embrace.[31]

S. RADHAKRISHNAN (1888–1975)

Oriental Philosopher, President of India (1962–1967)

[Charles Moore in 1957 called Dr. Radhakrishnan "a versatile genius, universally recognized and acclaimed for his remarkable ability as teacher, lecturer, scholar, and administrator, as philosopher, statesman, and India's cultural ambassador throughout the East and the West." Not only has "his absolute tolerance brought him recognition . . . as the greatest living interpreter of Indian philosophy, religion, and culture, but also as an original and creative thinker of the first order."[32]

Radhakrishnan became the first Indian to hold a chair at Oxford University, where he was appointed Spalding Professor of Eastern Religions and Ethics. His translations and interpretations of classic Hindu texts have been widely read in the United States and Europe, contributing to the kind of understanding that was one of his principal goals. His major two-volume *Indian Philosophy* made it possible for that philosophy to be included for formal study in universities throughout the world.

His *Eastern Religions and Western Thought* has been quoted a number of times in the present anthology. At a lecture opening the Center for the Study of World Religion at Harvard Divinity School in 1961, Dr. Radhakrishnan said: "It is one of the major tragedies of the world that the great religions, instead of uniting mankind in mutual understanding and goodwill, divide mankind by their dogmatic claims and prejudices." Eastern and Western religions, he declared, can borrow from each other as "two sides of the same mold."

Dr. Moore remarks that "according to Radhakrishnan, mâyâ has not meant to Indian philosophers . . . that the world is illusion. The world of everyday events and things is not ultimate reality, to be sure, but neither is it unreality. He defended the reality of the empirical world; it finds its basis in the Absolute. The Absolute is the source of its many transformations. . . . In this way he . . . paves the way for much greater understanding of India's greatest heights of thought and for a possible meeting of the minds of East and West."[33]

Furthermore, he was convinced that the true aim of liberation from the round of rebirths should not be "escape from the world of space and time but to be enlightened, wherever we may be. It is to live in this world knowing that it is divinely informed. . . . For those who are no longer bound to the wheel of *samsara,* life on earth is centered in the bliss of eternity. Their life is joy and where joy is, there is creation. They have no other country here below except the world itself. They owe their loyalty and love to the whole of humanity."[34]

From *An Idealist View of Life,* written when Radhakrishnan taught at Oxford, we select the following:]

The way to realisation is a slow one. Hindu and Buddhist thought, the Orphic mysteries, Plato and some forms of early Christianity maintain that it takes a long time for realising the holy longing after the lost heaven. . . . The Hindu holds that the goal of spiritual perfection is the crown of a long patient effort. Man grows by countless lives into his divine self-existence. Every life, every act, is a step which we may take either backward or forward. By one's thought, will and action one determines what one is yet to be. According to Plato, the wise man turns away from the world of the senses, and keeps his inward and spiritual eye ever directed to the world of the eternal idea, and if only the pursuit is maintained, the individual becomes freed from the bonds of sensualism. . . .

Our feet are set on the path of the higher life, though they wander uncertainly and the path is not seen clearly. There may be the attraction of the ideal but no assent of the whole nature to it. The utter self-giving which alone can achieve the end is not easy. But no effort is wasted. We are still far from realising the implications of the spiritual dignity of man in matters of conduct, individual and social. It requires an agelong effort carried on from life to life and from plane to plane. . . . If only we can support this higher life, the long labour of the cosmic process will receive its crowning justification and the evolution of centuries unfold its profound significance. . . .

The world process reaches its consummation when every man knows himself to be the immortal spirit. . . . Till this goal is reached, each saved individual is the centre of the universal consciousness. . . . To be saved is not to be moved from the world. Salvation is not escape from life. The individual works in the cosmic process no longer as an obscure and limited ego, but as a centre of the divine or universal consciousness embracing and transforming into harmony all individual manifestations. It is to live in the world with one's inward being profoundly modified. The soul takes possession of itself and cannot be shaken from its tranquillity by the attractions and attacks of the world.

The spiritual illumination does not make the individual life impossible. If the saved individuals escape literally from the cosmic process, the world would be forever unredeemed. It would be condemned to remain for all time the scene of unending strife and darkness. . . . Mahayana Buddhism declares that Buddha standing on the threshold of nirvana took the vow never to make the irrevocable crossing so long as there was a single undelivered being on earth. *The Bhagavata Purana* [a Hindu scripture] records the following prayer: "I desire not the supreme state with all its eight perfections nor the release from rebirth; may I assume the sorrow of all creatures who suffer and enter into them so that they may be made free from grief." . . . This respect for the individual as individual is not the discovery of modern democracy.[35]

CHRISTMAS HUMPHREYS (1901–)
British Author and Buddhist Philosopher

[Christmas Humphreys, the author of a wide variety of books on Buddhism, became in 1924, at the age of twenty-three, president-founder of the Buddhist Society in London—the oldest, largest, and most active Buddhist center in the West, its magazine *The Middle Way* also enjoying preeminence among Buddhist periodicals. All schools of Buddhism have apparently found welcome over the years at the London headquarters, and it was owing largely to Humphreys' influence that the Zen works of D. T. Suzuki were published, which brought into being the widespread Zen movement of recent times. Alan Watts became interested in Buddhism through the society, and for a period was co-editor of *The Middle Way*. Humphreys is still president of the society, and strangely enough, has carried on a distinguished career as a lawyer and advocate side by side with his Buddhist activities. On the occasion of the fiftieth anniversary of his contact with Buddhism, Humphreys gave a talk on how he became attracted to that philosophy:

> At the age of sixteen I was an enthusiastic Christian. . . . I had a brother four years older who in 1917 was killed at Ypres, and the bottom of my world fell out. I was filled, beyond my personal grief, with a furious sense of injustice. . . . There was no more sense in the world as there was no more happiness. I began to read widely in the field of comparative religion.

In 1918 he came upon Coomaraswamy's *Buddha and the Gospel of Buddhism*, and he said to himself "That is true, and it seems that I am a Buddhist!" His "real explosion of awareness," he says, came through understanding the ideas of karma and rebirth. "The first doctrine that seemed to me obvious was Rebirth." But "I was not re-learning this 'Buddhism'; I was remembering it. I knew it, almost without troubling to re-read the book, and in a short time I was writing and giving talks on Buddhism." Yet he was not completely satisfied with Buddhism as it is usually taught in the world. Yes, he had found a path to travel. "I saw the road but why is it there?"

> Where was the map, or a section of it, of which I could see the beginning and a vision of its end? For even the next step can be dull when the very direction of the Way remains unknown . . . Mrs. Rhys Davids said, "Buddhism is the long road between our imperfections now and the perfection which is latent in each human mind." But I wanted that Plan.

"I remember stopping in the street in Cambridge and demanding loudly, 'It won't do, dammit, it won't do! Who am I and what am I, revolving on this speck of mud in this particular universe?'"

> I found my Plan, in a commentary on what are called the Stanzas of Dzyan, a very old Tibetan scripture, in a book called *The Secret Doctrine*, by H. P. Blavatsky. This for the first time gave me what seemed to me then, and seems to me now, a clear exposition in outline of the coming into being of the universe and its ceasing to be, and within this the genesis and meaning of man. Here was a map of becoming . . .[36]

He also saw that it was unnecessary for him to give up secular life and become a Buddhist monk. Subsequently he heard of the phrase "wearing the Yellow Robe internally," used by William Q. Judge—one of the founders of the Theosophical Society—to indicate that "which all can try to do."

At first the Buddhist Society was a branch of the London Theosophical

Society. "In 1926 by common consent of all Members . . . we left the Theosophical Society, on the ground that in our view its activities were then encrusted with peripheral organizations to the exclusion of the great teaching given to Madame Blavatsky by her masters in Tibet."[37]

In Humphreys' many books—including the best-selling Pelican paperback *Buddhism*—karma and reincarnation are given preferred treatment as ideas of indispensable value to humanity in its progress "on the Way." Our selections are from his small volume *Karma and Rebirth,* which has been in print since 1943 in the "Wisdom of the East" series, published by John Murray. In the introduction the author states that the book is "a humble attempt to reconsider the subject in the light of such 'authorities' as are available," mainly the scriptures of the Hindus and Buddhists. "When to these are added, by way of commentary, the writings of H. P. Blavatsky, who was herself trained in Tibetan monasteries, there is available a triple 'authority' which, taken as a whole provides the basis for an all-embracing Law which guides and governs the evolution of mankind." "Yet the ultimate authority for any doctrine is not in the written nor in the spoken word, but rather in its own sweet reasonableness, and in the fact that it is ratified by the intuition and seems to 'work out' in the day's experience."]

Many persons on being first introduced to karma demand the precise details of its working, and failing to receive them refuse to accept the Law. It is useful to ask them in reply if they know the nature of electricity. If they are truthful they answer, No. To which one may reply, Nor does one know the nature of Karma but, like our knowledge of electricity, we know just a little how it works. The rest is a matter of research and experience. . . .

Life is One, and all its forms are interrelated. It follows that every act [and thought] by any form of life, from the highest to the lowest, must react on every other form. The power of thought is terrifying, for thoughts are truly things, and once created have an independent existence of their own. The length and strength of [their] life depends on the intensity and clarity of the thinker's mind, but good or bad, each thought is a power, a living power for good or evil respectively. As such it affects not only the thinker, ennobling or debasing his mind for future thinking, but it affects all other life in the Universe. . . . Acting from the highest levels in his being, man is the creative and controlling force in the Universe; acting from the lowest he is the worst enemy both of himself and the One Life. . . . "Life becomes what it does." There, in five words, is the essence of the Law. . . . Hence Maeterlinck's famous saying, "Let us always remember that nothing befalls us that is not of the nature of ourselves." . . .

All good acts acquire merit for the actor in that at some future date, in this life or a later one, the cause will bear its due effect. This is a fact, but it is a low, unworthy motive for the doing of good deeds. As the Chinese Taoist,

Chuang-Tzu, proclaimed, "Rewards and punishments are the lowest form of education." The reason is that behind such motive is the spur either of fear or else of low desire for the pleasure which the noble deed is believed to bring. This limitation of thought may serve, like blinkers, to keep the thinker to a simple ethical code, but will not produce enlightenment. . . . None the less, the doctrine of merit is a useful application of the Law of Karma to the daily round, for whatever the motive, the habit of good deeds will purify the mind, and prepare it for greater widening of its scope. A better motive for right living is a wider appreciation of the Law and its relation to the Universe as a whole [and] the desire to assist all life towards enlightenment. . . .

Conscience is a Karmic memory. The Essence of Mind is deathless, and its ray, the consciousness *(vinnana)* which moves from life to life, is a storehouse of immensely complex memory. Even though the brain, which is new in each life, has forgotten the lessons of past experience, the inner mind remembers, and when temptation murmurs again of the pleasures of a certain low desire, the voice of memory replies, "But what of the cost in suffering, the price that you paid?"

Do we deserve all that happens to us, or are there occasional "accidents" in which we suffer without justice? An immediate answer would be that if so, there must equally be unmerited happiness, for which in due course we must compensate. . . . The key to the problem is time, one of the necessary illusions of manifestation. It would be impossible, at least to our conception, to guide an incoming "soul" to a body and set of circumstances which exactly accord with its needs and deserts, and all that did not do so, pleasant or unpleasant, would presumably be the subject of later adjustment by the all-embracing and utterly just Law. . . .

As a gentleman pays his debts, so a Karmically educated gentleman invites the bill and pays it willingly. Here, however, a curious minor law asserts itself. It seems to be that he who deliberately takes himself in hand, and sets about the task of his own self-development, calls down on himself a larger share of "suspended" Karma than otherwise he would have had to endure [at that particular moment of time]. The price of entry on the Path with open eyes, it seems, is an immediate testing, self-demanded; and many a student, finding the reward of incipient effort to be, not as he hoped a sense of spiritual well-being but a host of trials and obstacles, gives up the attempt, and joins once more the army of drifters who, with no higher goal than personal happiness, form the bulk of mankind. Those who survive these apparent testings find themselves at the entrance to a Path whose end is self-enlightenment, and on this Path, "the first step is to live to benefit mankind." . . .

Sooner or later each incarnation comes to an end. The mask begins to perish and the actor, laden with new experience . . . longs for a period of

rest wherein to digest the lessons of that life. And so the body dies. . . .
[Quoting from a Buddhist funeral service:] "When the day's work is ended,
night brings the benison of sleep. So death is the ending of a larger day, and in
the night that follows every man finds rest, until of his own volition he
returns to fresh endeavor and to labors new. So has it been with this our
brother, so will it be for all of us, until the illusion of a separated self is finally
transcended, and in the death of self we reach Enlightenment."[38]

OTHER PHILOSOPHERS

[This section would hardly be complete without recalling the writers who
appear in the introductory essays in chapter 1: W. Macneile Dixon, Huston
Smith, and C. J. Ducasse. Dixon taught at the University of Glasgow. Additional passages from his Gifford lectures appear in the closing pages of this
volume. Huston Smith has been teaching philosophy for many years at Massachusetts Institute of Technology. His writings and lecture tours have done
much to link Eastern and Western thought. Ducasse, a former president of
the American Philosophical Association, taught for over thirty years at
Brown University, and also lectured at the universities of California, Chicago,
Columbia, Cornell, and Michigan. Probably no author and teacher in
America did more than Dr. Ducasse in interesting students and professional
colleagues in reincarnation.]

7

The Theosophical Movement and the Reincarnation Renaissance

Although all sorts of miraculous tales had come to Europe two thousand years [ago] from the fabled land of India, with its wise men. . . . yet no real knowledge of Indian philosophy and philosophical practices can be said to have existed until, thanks to the efforts of the Frenchman, Anquetil du Perron, the Upanishads were transmitted to the West. A general . . . knowledge was first made possible by Max Müller, of Oxford, and the Sacred Books of the East edited by him. To begin with, this knowledge remained the preserve of Sanskrit scholars and philosophers. But it was not so very long before the theosophical movement inaugurated by Madame Blavatsky possessed itself of the Eastern traditions and promulgated them among the general public.

C. G. JUNG
Psychology and Religion: West and East

Theosophy is a religious philosophy with definite mystical concerns that can be traced to the ancient world but is of catalytic significance in religious thought in the 19th and 20th centuries. . . . The movement has been a catalytic force in the 20th century revival of Buddhism and Hinduism, and a pioneering agency in the promotion of greater Western acquaintance with Eastern thought. In the United States it has influenced a whole series of religious movements . . . In the estimation of some scholars, no other single organization has done more to popularize Asian religions and philosophical ideas in the West.

Encyclopaedia Britannica
(Britannica Three, 1974)

[From our consideration of Western thought prior to the 1870s, it became evident that many leading minds in the world of religion, science, philosophy, art, and literature had something stimulating to say on the subject of reincarnation. As to the masses, however, the teaching was practically unknown from the time of the bloody crusade against the widespread Christian Gnostic Cathari movement of the Middle Ages until the last quarter of the nineteenth century. (See the "Early Christian" section of chapter 5.) Thus shortly before the advent of the theosophical movement, Edward Tylor, the father of anthropology, could write in his noted work *Primitive Culture:*

> We have traced the theory of metempsychosis in stage after stage of the world's civilization, scattered among the native races of America and Africa, established in the Asiatic nations . . . rising and falling in classic and medieval Europe, and lingering at last in the modern world as an intellectual crotchet, of little account but to the ethnographer who notes it down as an item of evidence for his continuity of culture.

What holds sway in nineteenth-century religion, he says, is faith in an everlasting heaven, which provides "an answer to the perplexed problem of the allotment of happiness and misery in the present world, by the expectation of another world to set this right."[1] What brought about an awakening to an alternative view is the theme of this chapter.

Thus far the reader has made frequent contact with theosophical ideas, for he could not help observing in chapter 5 and elsewhere in this volume that a surprising number of the well-known writers of recent eras, as well as individuals in other fields, were either members of the Theosophical Society or had a more or less intimate acquaintance with the literature of theosophy and its principal exponent, H. P. Blavatsky. Among writers there were D. H. Lawrence, T. S. Eliot, Henry Miller, Conan Doyle, Jack London, Maeterlinck, Sir Edwin Arnold, and the leaders of Ireland's literary revival, Yeats, George Russell, James Stephens, and James Joyce. Among inventors there was Thomas Edison, and among religious philosophers were Nicolas Berdyaev, Richard Wilhelm, Christmas Humphreys, and D. T. Suzuki. Among artists, Gauguin, Mondrian, Kandinsky, Malevich, and Paul Klee. In the present chapter Gandhi and H. G. Wells will be added to the list, as well as two social historians, Lewis Mumford and Theodore Roszak, together with several distinguished scientists: Einstein, Gustaf Strömberg, Camille Flammarion, and Sir William Crookes.

It may not be strange that all these individuals should be included in a volume on rebirth, and in relation to theosophy, considering that the reincarnation renaissance the Western world is presently experiencing had its inception with the theosophists of the last century.

While it is difficult to obtain accurate up-to-date figures of reincarnation belief in the West as a whole, statistics are available as to the percentages of

Protestants and Catholics who now accept rebirth. The following percentages to be found in the February 1969 twelve-nation Gallup Poll's "Special Report on Religion" seem particularly revealing because neither Protestanism nor Catholicism teaches the doctrine of many lives: Austria 20%, Canada 26%, France 23%, Great Britain 18%, Greece 22%, the Netherlands 10%, Norway 14%, Sweden 12%, United States 26%, West Germany 25%.[2] However startling these figures may be, the percentages would enormously increase if the census were addressed to the youth of today. Our task, then, is to trace the early beginnings of this phenomenal change in Western thinking.]

THE THEOSOPHICAL MOVEMENT AND ITS FOUNDERS

[The theosophical movement originated in New York City in 1875 and soon became worldwide, with active centers in the major cities of Europe, North America, and India. In addition to Helena Petrovna Blavatsky—a Russian noblewoman who had studied in India and Tibet—the chief founders were Henry S. Olcott and William Q. Judge. Olcott had been an agriculturist, a Civil War colonel, and latterly a lawyer and journalist. When Abraham Lincoln died, Olcott was one of a three-man commission appointed by the government to investigate the assassination. Judge was a young Irish-American lawyer, who was later to play an important role in the movement, particularly in America.

In an editorial in the *New York Herald* (May 10, 1891)—two days after H. P. Blavatsky's death—this evaluative appreciation of her work appeared:

> No one in the present generation, it may be said, has done more toward reopening the long sealed treasures of Eastern thought, wisdom, and philosophy. No one certainly has done so much toward elucidating that profound wisdom-religion wrought out by the ever-cogitating Orient, and bringing into the light those ancient literary works whose scope and depth have so astonished the Western world, brought up in the insular belief that the East had produced only crudities and puerilities in the domain of speculative thought. Her own knowledge of Oriental philosophy and esotericism was comprehensive. No candid mind can doubt this after reading her two principal works. Her steps often led, indeed, where only a few initiates could follow, but the tone and tendency of all her writings were healthful, bracing, and stimulating. . . .
>
> The work of Madame Blavatsky has already borne fruit, and is destined, apparently, to produce still more marked and salutary effects in the future.

Careful observers of the time long since discerned that the tone of current thought in many directions was being affected by it. A broader humanity, a more liberal speculation, a disposition to investigate ancient philosophies from a higher point of view, have no indirect association with the teachings referred to. Thus Madame Blavatsky has made her mark upon the time.

Strangely enough, the theosophical movement, though Western in origin, brought about a revival of interest in reincarnation in the Orient as well as the Occident.[3] The influence of the missionaries and of materialistic science had caused many Hindus to lose faith in their religious heritage, and the educated Indian youths in particular were fast becoming atheists. We will have occasion to go into all this a little later, but here we merely illustrate by quoting from Gandhi. In his *Autobiography* he reveals that the Hindu "bible," *The Bhagavad-Gita,* which was to exert such a profound influence on his personal and public life, and which, as we have seen, treats frequently of rebirth, was not even read by him until as a young man he lived in England. He writes:

> Towards the end of my second year in England I came across two Theosophists, brothers. . . . They talked to me about the *Gita.* . . . They invited me to read the original with them. I felt ashamed, as I had read the divine poem neither in Sanskrit nor in Gujarati. . . . I began reading the *Gita* with them. . . . They also took me on one occasion to the Blavatsky Lodge and introduced me to Madame Blavatsky and Mrs. Besant. . . . I recall having read, at the brothers' instance, Madame Blavatsky's *Key to Theosophy.* This book stimulated in me the desire to read books on Hinduism, and disabused me of the notion fostered by the missionaries that Hinduism was rife with superstition. . . .
>
> [Later in South Africa] I came in close contact with almost every theosophist [at the Johannesburg Theosophical Society]. I had religious discussions with them every day. There used to be readings from theosophical books, and sometimes I had occasion to address their meetings.[4]

Gandhi mentions in his *Autobiography* that Allan O. Hume,[5] a British theosophist, was founder in 1885 of the Indian National Congress,[6] which did a good deal toward lifting the spirits of the conquered nation. Gandhi told his biographer Louis Fischer that "in the beginning the leading Congressmen were theosophists." "Theosophy," he explained, "is the teaching of Madame Blavatsky." "It is Hinduism at its best." Twice he emphasized: "Theosophy is the brotherhood of man."[7]

In appreciation for what the theosophical movement has done in various ways in India, the Indian government issued a special stamp in 1975 to commemorate the movement's one hundredth birthday. The seal as well as the motto of the society—"There Is No Religion Higher Than Truth"—were reproduced on the stamp.

While Gandhi spoke of theosophy as "Hinduism at its best," we learned earlier that the renowned Zen Buddhist teacher D. T. Suzuki identified it with pure Mahayana Buddhism. However, H. P. Blavatsky herself emphasized that theosophy and the theosophical movement are not confined to Eastern religions and sciences. Much of her writings are devoted to explaining the Christian symbols and the esoteric aspects of Christianity. And as to Jesus, she called him "one of the grandest and most clearly-defined figures on the panorama of human history," one who "instead of growing paler will become with every century more pronounced and clearly defined."[8]

The most important of our aims, she writes, "is to revive the work of Ammonius Saccas," the founder of the Neoplatonic school of seventeen centuries ago. The work of that school, she states, was "to reconcile all religions, sects and nations under a common system of ethics, based on eternal verities."[9] Hence the Neoplatonists were known as the *eclectic* theosophical school, the word theosophy, meaning godlike wisdom, being first used by them. The aim of Ammonius was to induce Gentiles, Christians, Jews, and other peoples "to lay aside their contentions and strifes, remembering only that they were all in possession of the same truth under various vestments. . . . "[10]

Regarding modern theosophy, H. P. Blavatsky said that it is neither a religion, a science, nor a philosophy, but as a definite body of teaching endeavors to synthesize these three ways of looking at life.

The theosophical movement had and has three officially declared objects. The first is "to form the nucleus of a Universal Brotherhood of Humanity, without distinction of race, creed, sex, caste or color." The second, which in the early days was "to promote the study of Aryan and other Eastern literatures, religions and sciences," became expanded a little later to read: "the comparative study of ancient and modern religions, philosophies, and sciences . . . " The third is "to investigate unexplained laws of nature and the psychical powers of man."[11] Today, of course, such goals sound quite acceptable, but in the Victorian age they were innovative.

Speaking of the high moral goals embodied in the constitution and rules of the Theosophical Society, Madame Blavatsky confessed that "none of them are enforced. They express the ideal of our organization,—but the practical application of such things we are compelled to leave to the discretion of the Fellows themselves."

> Unfortunately, the state of men's minds in the present century is such that, unless we allow these clauses to remain, so to speak, obsolete, no man or woman would dare to risk joining the Theosophical Society. This is precisely why I feel forced to lay such a stress on the difference between true Theosophy and its hard-struggling and well-intentioned, but still unworthy vehicle, the Theosophical Society.[12]

Regarding the three objects of the society, the study of reincarnation and karma fell within the scope of the second and third, while the practical application of these twin doctrines helped fulfill the first. "Karma and reincarnation," wrote Madame Blavatsky, "are in reality the A B C" of theosophy.[13] They lead to the deeper study of her works. However, their acceptance was not a requirement for membership, freedom of thought being a cardinal principle of theosophical education. In the *Key to Theosophy* she wrote that a true system of education "should produce the most vigorous and liberal mind, strictly trained in logical and accurate thought, and not in blind faith." People should be "taught self-reliance, love for all men, altruism, mutual charity, and more than anything else, to think and reason for themselves."[14]

In that same work she answers an inquirer who wishes to know if the Theosophical Society is a political organization. "Certainly not," she replied. "As a society it takes absolutely no part in any national or party politics," although individual members are free to work for social and political improvements wherever they live. However, "to seek to achieve political reforms, before we have effected a reform in *human nature*," she said, "is like putting new wine into old bottles. . . . No lasting political reform can ever be achieved with the same selfish men at the head of affairs as of old."[15]

Elsewhere she indicated that for the theorists "who view man as a mere physical problem," and are thus unable to recognize "the inner, greater, higher self," there can be no solution to social problems. "Race hatreds and sectarian and social antipathies are insurmountable if attacked from the outside," and consequently "no amount of argument based upon exoteric considerations of social morals or expediency, can turn the hearts of the rulers of nations away from selfish war and schemes of conquest." But as all beings are in essence identical, they are potentially "open to influences which center upon the human 'heart,' and appeal to the human intuition"; and as there can be but one truth—"the soul and life of all creeds," as distinguished from their sectarian differences—"it is possible to effect a reciprocal alliance for the research of and dissemination of that basic Truth."[16]

In the nineteenth century an undertaking with the objectives we have been describing necessarily involved criticism of the orthodox dogmas—religious, scientific, and social—that were dividing rather than uniting humanity. It involved focusing attention on ideas like reincarnation and karma, which had been deleted or obscured in Western religions (see chapter 3). All critics of orthodoxy find enemies, and H. P. Blavatsky was no exception. The editorial from the *New York Herald,* just quoted, mentioned that "few women in our time have been more persistently misrepresented, slandered, and defamed." Probably the worst ever said about her was elaborately compiled by Professor Elliott Coues of the Smithsonian Institution in Washington, D.C.,

and published in the New York *Sun,* the paper owned and edited by the
distinguished editor Charles Dana, his paper being one of the most influential
and widely circulated of the day. This savagely calumniating material, under
the title "Blavatsky Unveiled," filled seven columns of small type—a veritable arsenal for subsequent biographical defamers of H.P.B. But what most
of her later "biographers" neglect to explain, while repeating the old stories,
is that she promptly sued for libel, and that the *Sun's* lawyers finally had to
admit in pretrial hearings that none of the charges could be proved. However, most of H.P.B.'s critics today are ignorant of this fact, and innocently
retell the old stories as unquestionable happenings.

As we shall see, Theodore Roszak does this very thing in *Unfinished
Animal,* a book which speaks at length of the revolutionary conception of
evolution presented by H.P.B. in *The Secret Doctrine.* Under the heading
"Madame Blavatsky's Secret Doctrine," he writes:

> Helena Petrovna Blavatsky . . . has had a bad press ever since she appeared
> . . . in 1875 as organizer of the Theosophical Society. . . . One of the great
> liberated ladies of her day—she could not help but draw withering, critical fire
> by her every act and word, especially when she presumed to challenge the most
> entrenched intellectual orthodoxies of the age. Still today people who have
> never read a line she wrote remain adamantly convinced she was a fraud and a
> crank.

The result has been, says Roszak, that "Theosophy, one of the most adventurous and intriguing bodies of nineteenth-century thought," has not received the attention it deserves.

After repeating as true certain innuendos circulated by H.P.B.'s antagonists, he remarks, "In any case, it is not HPB's controversial reputation
or personal angularities that concern us here, but rather her ideas." At issue
is "the quality of her thinking," and, he adds, "in this regard she is surely
among the most original and perceptive minds of her time. . . . Above all,
she is among the modern world's trailblazing psychologists of the visionary
mind."

It seems clear from Mr. Roszak's quotations from *Isis Unveiled* and his
comments thereon that he regards H.P.B. as having exercised a fundamentally emancipating influence on the Western mind through the conception of
evolution as moral and spiritual, as well as physical. Her books reveal, he
says, "the first philosophy of psychic and spiritual evolution to appear in the
modern West." She traces "from the universal ether to the incarnate human
spirit one uninterrupted series of entities. . . . This immersion of spirit is for
the purpose of vastly enriching our consciousness. . . . By our collective
evolutionary course, and by innumerable personal incarnations, we make our
way through all the realms of being: mineral, plant, animal, human, divine.
And it is by virtue of this hard-won 'harvest of experience' that each human
being becomes a microcosm of the universe."[17]

Recently, one of the frequently repeated accusations against H.P.B. received wide publicity in *Newsweek* (November 24, 1975). In a featured article on the centennial of the theosophical movement, the magazine charged that she had "at least one illegitimate child." But in the *Sun* libel case, her lawyers produced sworn testimony of two gynecologists that she never had any children, and was physiologically incapable of having a legitimate to say nothing of an illegitimate child!

H.P.B. died before the case could be terminated, and this under the New York State libel laws automatically ended the suit. Although now under no legal obligation, the *Sun* was sufficiently honorable to do what is one of the rarest things a newspaper will do—make a voluntary editorial retraction. But it took them over a year after her death to take this step:

> We print on another page an article in which WILLIAM Q. JUDGE deals with the romantic and extraordinary career of the late Madame HELENA P. BLAVATSKY. We take occasion to observe that on July 20, 1890, we were misled into admitting into the Sun's columns an article by Dr. E. F. COUES of Washington, in which allegations were made against Madame BLAVATSKY's character, and also against her followers, which appear to have been without solid foundation. Mr. JUDGE's article disposes of all questions relating to Madame BLAVATSKY as presented by Dr. COUES, and we desire to say that his allegations respecting the Theosophical Society and Mr. JUDGE personally are not sustained by evidence, and should not have been printed. (September 26, 1892.)[18]

From Mr. Judge's long article, a few brief paragraphs have been selected, one of which relates to reincarnation. He opens thus: "A woman who for some reason or another, has kept the world—first her little child world and afterward two hemispheres—talking of her, disputing about her, defending or assailing her character and motives, joining her enterprise or opposing it might and main, and in her death being as much telegraphed about between two continents as an emperor, must have been a remarkable person. . . ."

> She was connected with the rulers of Russia. Speaking in 1881, her uncle, Gen. Fadeef, joint Councillor of State of Russia, said that, as daughter of Col. Peter Hahn, she was granddaughter of Gen. Alexis Hahn von Rotternstern Hahn of old Mecklenburg stock, settled in Russia, and on her mother's side daughter of Helene Fadeef and granddaughter of Princess Helena Dolgorouky. Her maternal ancestors were of the oldest families in Russia and direct descendants of the Prince or Grand Duke Rurik, the first ruler of Russia. Several ladies of the family belonged to the imperial house, becoming Czarinas by marriage. One of them, a Dolgorouky, married the grandfather of Peter the Great, and another was betrothed to Czar Peter II. . . . In Paris I met three princes of Russia and one well-known General, who told of her youth and the wonderful things related about her then. . . .

After describing her childhood and worldwide travels as a young woman, W. Q. Judge states that "it was in the United States that she really began the work that has made her name well known in Europe, Asia, and America. . . . There certainly was no selfish object in this, nor any desire to raise money. She was in receipt of funds from sources in Russia and other places until they were cut off by reason of her becoming an American citizen. . . . Venal writers . . . have said she strove to get money from so-called dupes, but all her intimate friends know that over and over again she has refused money; that always she has had friends who would give her all they had if she would take it, but she never took any nor asked [for] it."

> The aim and object of her life were to strike off the shackles forged by priestcraft for the mind of man. She wished all men to know that they are God in fact, and that as men they must bear the burden of their own sins, for no one else can do it. Hence she brought forward to the West the old Eastern doctrines of karma and reincarnation. Under the first, the law of justice, she said each must answer for himself, and under the second make answer on the earth where all his acts were done.
>
> She also desired that science should be brought back to the true ground where life and intelligence are admitted to be within and acting on and through every atom in the universe. Hence her object was to make religion scientific and science religious, so that the dogmatism of each might disappear. . . . The theory of man's origin, powers and destiny brought forward by her, drawn from ancient Indian sources, places us upon a higher pedestal than that given by either religion or science, for it gives to each the possibility of developing the godlike powers within and of at last becoming a co-worker with nature.[19]

In a leading publication in the United States, *The North American Review,* H. P. Blavatsky wrote a long article entitled "Recent Progress in Theosophy." Included were some remarks as to why theosophy entered the arena of thought when it did, and as those reasons naturally relate to why it was believed propitious to introduce the theory of reincarnation to people in the West, we quote them here: "Since it is undeniable that . . . materialistic bias has been rapidly culminating under university influence during the past half century, it is too evident that the creation of the Theosophical Society at the time when it arose was most timely, and a step toward the defense of *true* science and *true* religion against a sciolism that was becoming more and more arrogant."

> The theosophical movement was a necessity of the age, and it has spread under its own inherent impulsion, and owes nothing to adventitious methods. From the first it has had neither money, endowment, nor social or governmental patronage to count upon. It appealed to certain human instincts and aspira-

tions, and held a certain lofty ideal of perfectibility, with which the vested extraneous interests of society conflicted, and against which these were foredoomed to battle. Its strongest allies were the human yearnings for light upon the problem of life, and for a nobler conception of the origin, destiny, and potentialities of the human being.

. . . theosophy has aimed at uniting all broad religious people for research into the actual basis of religion and scientific proofs of the existence and permanence of the higher Self. Accepting thankfully the results of scientific study and exposure of theological error, and adopting the methods and maxims of science, its advocates try to save from the wreck of cults the precious admixture of truth to be found in each. Discarding the theory of miracle and supernaturalism, they endeavor to trace out the kinship of the whole family of world-faiths to each other, and their common reconciliation with science.[20]

Regarding "the ideal of perfectibility," theosophy teaches that to reach the highest degree possible in our world, many incarnations are required. That those who have achieved it are humanity's great teachers, beings like Jesus, Buddha, and Krishna, who as members of a fraternity of highly evolved souls ceaselessly help mankind to the degree its karma and evolutionary development permit. There is a "well-known belief in the East," says H. P. Blavatsky, "that every additional Buddha or Saint is a new soldier in the army of those who work for the liberation or salvation of mankind." Particularly in northern Buddhist countries that teach the doctrine of *Nirmanakayas*—those who renounce Nirvana in order "to invisibly assist mankind and lead it finally to *Paranirvana*"—"every new *Bodhisattva,* or initiated great Adept" becomes a member of this fraternity.[21] At crucial periods of human history these beings are said to incarnate publicly among men, adapting their wisdom to the needs of the peoples to whom they come. Succeeding generations gradually substitute dogmas and rituals for the living spirit of truth, and consequently the teachings in their purity must be presented again.

While the Russian theosophist spoke of theosophy as one such restatement, she herself assumed no grand titles, claiming no higher status than a pupil under the tutelage of some of the wise men of the East. And respecting her own previous incarnations, she preserved an absolute silence. At the time of her death, William Stewart Ross, a well-known author and agnostic of the day, editor of *The Agnostic Journal,* emphasized her humble qualities:

In spite of her tremendous attainments and unrivaled talent, she had not a vestige of pedantic assumption, and had the simple heart of a child. . . . Her followers are gnostic on grave issues of teleology on which I am only agnostic. . . . To me Madame Blavatsky is dead, and another shadow has fallen athwart my life. . . . Theosophy or no Theosophy, the most extraordinary woman of our century, or of any century, has passed away. . . . "Impostor" indeed! She was almost the only mortal I have ever met who was *not* an impostor. . . . and one of the very few who ever understood me.[22]

This last comment probably refers to the much-publicized Hodgson report published in 1885 by the Society for Psychical Research in London, which concluded that Madame Blavatsky "has achieved a title to permanent remembrance as one of the most accomplished, ingenious, and interesting impostors in history." Richard Hodgson, a young man in his twenties, had gone to India to investigate her. He ruled out motives arising from vanity, religious mania, or the desire for pecuniary gain. How then account for her tremendous labors for theosophy? She was an undercover agent for the Russians! (England and Russia were fierce antagonists during this period.) The suspicion of her being a Russian spy, however, was nothing new. When she went to India to start the Theosophical Society there, her every movement, for many months, was under the surveillance of the British intelligence service. Incidentally, her books were proscribed in Czarist Russia during her life, as they are today in Communist Russia.

When eighty-three years after the issuance of the Hodgson report, *Time* magazine repeated the espionage and other charges—as most biographies and encyclopedias do—the Honorable Secretary for the London Society for Psychical Research wrote to the editor of *Time* on July 25, 1968:

We would like to make a correction to the article on Religion published in the issue of "Time" dated July 19, 1968. In this feature, under Theosophy, it is stated in connection with Madame Blavatsky: "Controversial wherever she went, she was accused of fraud, forgery, and even of spying for the Czar." We would point out that, as stated in all copies of the Proceedings of this Society, "Responsibility for both the facts and the reasonings in papers published in the Proceedings rests entirely with the authors." Comments on Madame Blavatsky were contained in a report by Richard Hodgson in Part IX of Proceedings dated December 1885 and any accusations therein contained are the responsibility of the author and not this organization.[23]

Returning to the theosophical teaching of the existence of a fraternity of perfected souls as the product of evolutionary growth through numerous reincarnations, it is interesting to learn that H.P.B.—as her pupils called her—expressed regret, two years before her death, for having introduced the subject to Western attention. In *The Key to Theosophy* she wrote:

Every bogus swindling Society, for commercial purposes, now claims to be guided and directed by "Masters," often supposed to be far higher than ours! . . . Thousands of men have been held back from the path of truth and light through the discredit and evil report which such shams, swindles, and frauds have brought upon the whole subject.

The author "would rather people should seriously think that the only Mahatmaland is the grey matter of her brain, and that, in short, she has evolved them out of the depths of her own inner consciousness, than that their names and grand ideal should be so infamously desecrated as they are at present. . . . It is only her unwillingness to pose in her own sight as a crow parading in peacock's feathers that compels her to this day to insist upon the truth" as to the source of her knowledge.[24]

From numerous accounts of the early days of the movement, H.P.B., as a result of her training in the East, was able to perform, at will, a rare order of psychic phenomena. H. G. Wells remarked once that he had always wondered at the phenomena produced by "Mahomet, the Yogi, and Madame Blavatsky." "Here," he said, "we plumb some profounder law—deeper than the ordinary laws of nature."[25] P. D. Ouspensky wrote in a letter regarding volume I of Olcott's diary (which describes many of the unusual phenomena H.P.B. produced): "I read it first the year Olcott died, 1907. I always consider it the strangest book in the universe, because in spite of all that people can say I always feel that Olcott did not lie, and this is the most remarkable."[26]

In an article, "What of Phenomena," written in 1888, H.P.B. explained why such experiments were carried on and why they were later stopped. As her explanation bears on the possibility of the existence of an enduring Self in man, some pertinent passages are presented:

"Occult phenomena" . . . failed to produce the desired effect . . . It was supposed that intelligent people, especially men of science, would, at least, have recognized the existence of a new and deeply interesting field of inquiry and research when they witnessed physical effects produced at will, for which they were not able to account. It was supposed that theologians would have welcomed the proof, of which they stand so sadly in need in these agnostic days, that the soul and the spirit are not mere creations of their fancy . . . but entities quite as real as the body, and much more important. These expectations were not realized. The phenomena were misunderstood and misrepresented, both as regards their nature and their purpose. . . .

That the phenomena did excite curiosity in the minds of those who witnessed them, is certainly true, but it was, unfortunately, for the most part of an idle kind. The greater number of the witnesses developed an insatiable appetite for phenomena for their own sake, without any thought of studying the philosophy or the science of whose truth and power the phenomena were merely trivial and, so to say, accidental illustrations. . . . Except in a few isolated and honorable instances, never [were they] received in any other character than as would-be miracles, or as works of the Devil, or as vulgar tricks, or as amusing gape-seed, or as the performances of those dangerous "spooks" that masquerade in seance rooms, and feed on the vital energies of mediums and sitters. . . .

An occultist can produce phenomena, but he cannot supply the world with brains, nor with the intelligence and good faith necessary to understand and appreciate them. Therefore, it is hardly to be wondered at, that *word* came to abandon phenomena and let the ideas of Theosophy stand on their own intrinsic merits.[27]

However catalytic in power, theosophy never became a faddish mass movement.[28] It sent no missionaries abroad; it did not proselyte or indoctrinate. Such methods are regarded contrary to the spirit of theosophical education. William Q. Judge once remarked: ''No one was ever converted to Theosophy. Each one who *really* comes into it does so because it is only 'an extension of previous beliefs.' '' ''This,'' he added, ''will show you that Karma is a true thing. For no idea we get is any more than an extension of previous ones. That is, they are cause and effect in endless succession. . . . Through Brotherhood we receive the knowledge of others, which we consider until (if it fits us) it is ours.''[29]

Judge lectured throughout the United States. In the larger cities it was not unusual to have fifteen hundred to two thousand people in attendance. His small book *The Ocean of Theosophy*[30] is considered by many to be the best epitome of Madame Blavatsky's *Secret Doctrine,* and is in constant demand. In his writings and lectures, rebirth and karma were always given primary attention. In 1893 at the Chicago World's Fair where the World Parliament of Religions was held—an unprecedented event in world history—he was chairman of the Theosophical Congress, which turned out to be the most successful event of the parliament. At the three-day Theosophical Congress, two distinguished Oriental delegates, H. Dharmapala from the Buddhist world and Professor Chakravarti from the Hindu—both theosophists— lectured, and Annie Besant came over from England. The main events attracted wide coverage in the world press.

So many of the public jammed the Theosophical Congress, the managers of the parliament accorded it two unplanned weekend meetings before the general parliament itself. Although four thousand could be seated at the final meeting, hundreds stood in the aisles and by the walls. In two of Mrs. Besant's lectures she highlighted karma and rebirth in relation to social problems, and several other speakers gave prominence to these ideas. Mr. Judge delivered before the main parliament a lengthy presentation on ''the lost chord of Christianity,'' as he often called reincarnation. The next night, also before the parliament, he discussed rebirth from the viewpoint of the universal law of cycles. His speech, however, was abruptly interrupted by one of the parliament managers—a Presbyterian minister—who explained to the crowd that as there was no one at the Presbyterian meeting, it was believed that many members had wandered into the present hall by mistake owing to a confusion in the notifications; so would they please leave immediately. Not a person in that vast audience stirred![31]

H.P.B. died two years before the World Parliament of Religions convened. Over the years a number of theosophists have claimed to be her successor, but Judge never considered himself as such, nor would allow anyone else to place the mantle on him. "Of course somebody will be elected president of the European Theosophical Societies," he told reporters, "but that is only a mundane matter. In the spiritual sense nobody can succeed her."[32] How he viewed his mentor is candidly told in a memorial tribute:

> In 1874, in the City of New York, I first met H. P. Blavatsky in this life. By her request, sent through Colonel H. S. Olcott, the call was made in her rooms in Irving Place . . . It was her eye that attracted me, the eye of one whom I must have known in lives long passed away. She looked at me in recognition at that first hour, and never since has that look changed. Not as a questioner of philosophies did I come before her, not as one groping in the dark for lights that schools and fanciful theories had obscured, but as one who, wandering many periods through the corridors of life, was seeking the friends who could show where the designs for the work had been hidden. And true to the call she responded, revealing the plans once again, and speaking no words to explain, simply pointed them out and went on with the task.
>
> It was as if but the evening before we had parted, leaving yet to be done some detail of a task taken up with one common end; it was teacher and pupil, elder brother and younger, both bent on the one single end, but she with the power and the knowledge that belong but to lions and sages. So, friends, from the first I felt safe. Others I know have looked with suspicion on an appearance they could not fathom, and though it is true they adduce many proofs which, hugged to the breast, would damn sages and gods, yet it is only through blindness they failed to see the lion's glance, the diamond heart of H.P.B.[33]

Since H.P.B.'s death, the interest in her writings has increased, particularly among scholars and scientists, as we will see when we take up her monumental work *The Secret Doctrine*. In November 1975, in commemoration of the one hundredth anniversary of the founding of the theosophical movement, a six-day world congress of theosophists convened in New York. Two organizations using the name the Theosophical Society exist today, one with international headquarters in Adyar, Madras; the other in Pasadena, California. An independent, nonorganizational association, the United Lodge of Theosophists, with centers in many parts of the world, was formed in 1909 by Robert Crosbie and others in Los Angeles where its parent lodge is located. The original theosophy of Blavatsky and Judge is its chief concern, and its publishing company, The Theosophy Company, keeps the writings of these two continually in print in unaltered form.

From this introductory glimpse into the general trend of theosophical thinking and activities, we will endeavor to penetrate deeper by presenting selections from H. P. Blavatsky's two major works, an interview with her, and other pertinent material, our purpose being to uncover the ideas that originally set in motion the reincarnation renaissance of modern times. Some attention will also be paid to the results achieved in various countries.

Quotations from the Russian theosophist's translation *The Voice of the Silence* will be found under "Tibetan Buddhism." Ouspensky gives a number of extracts from this translation in his *Tertium Organum,* calling it one of the outstanding books in theosophical literature and one of "real mystical sentiment." In his work he writes: "*What we have needed for a long time is synthesis.* The word *synthesis* was emblazoned on the banner of the contemporary theosophical movement started by H. P. Blavatsky." He believed, however, that later theosophists failed to carry forward this aim.[34]

In the limited space remaining it is hardly possible to take up the writings of twentieth-century theosophists, and we list just a few of the many students of theosophy that branched off on their own: Rudolf Steiner, who headed the German section of the Theosophical Society, which he joined in 1902. In 1912, a year before he left, he formed the Anthroposophical Society based on his own metaphysical researches. Krishnamurti, a Hindu child, was adopted by Annie Besant and groomed to be a world messiah. Upon reaching manhood he courageously disavowed the title, and has since worked independently with a large international following. Charles Fillmore, who became a founder of the popular Unity School of Christianity, turned his conception of theosophy into a saccharine teaching adapted to healing and self-help practices.

A witness to the various splinter-off developments of the theosophical movement, George Russell, has written that he "never found in those who came after H.P.B. and Judge the same knowledge, wisdom and inner light."[35]]

THE TEACHING AND PROGRAM THAT SPARKED THE REVIVAL

Even members of the Theosophical Society have often wondered why H. P. Blavatsky and others well known in the Society lay so much stress on doctrines like Karma and Reincarnation. It is not alone because these doctrines are easily apprehended and beneficent to individuals, not only because they furnish, as they necessarily do, a solid foundation for ethics, or all human conduct, but

*because they are the very keynotes of the higher evolution of man. Without
Karma and Reincarnation evolution is but a fragment; a process whose beginnings are unknown, and whose outcome cannot be discerned; a glimpse of what
might be; a hope of what should be. But in the light of Karma and Reincarnation
evolution becomes the logic of what* MUST *be. The links in the chain of being are
all filled in, and the circles of reason and of life are complete. Karma gives the
eternal law of action, and Reincarnation furnishes the boundless field for its
display. Thousands of persons can understand these two principles, apply them
as a basis of conduct, and weave them into the fabric of their lives, who may not
be able to grasp the complete synthesis of that endless evolution of which these
doctrines form so important a part.*

WILLIAM Q. JUDGE
"The Synthesis of Occult Science"

"Isis Unveiled"

[H. P. Blavatsky's first work, *Isis Unveiled,* was published in New York in
1877, and comprised two volumes totaling twelve hundred pages of fine
print, volume one entitled Science, volume two Theology. When one reads
the reviews[36] it can be appreciated why the first thousand copies were sold in
nine days:

> A marvellous book both in matter and manner of treatment. Some idea may be
> formed of the rarity and extent of its contents when the index alone comprises
> fifty pages, and we venture nothing in saying that such an index of subjects was
> never before compiled by any human being.—*Daily Graphic*

> It must be acknowledged that she is a remarkable woman, who has read more,
> seen more, and thought more than most wise men. Her work . . . demands the
> earnest attention of thinkers.—*Boston Evening Transcript*

> An extremely readable and exhaustive essay upon the paramount importance
> of re-establishing the Hermetic philosophy in a world which blindly believes
> that it has outgrown it.—*New York World*

> One who reads the book carefully through, ought to know everything of the
> marvellous and mystical, except perhaps, the passwords. . . . It is one of the
> remarkable productions of the century.—*New York Herald*

The preface to volume one opens with these words: "The work now submitted to public judgment is the fruit of a somewhat intimate acquaintance
with Eastern adepts and study of their science. It is offered to such as are

willing to accept truth wherever it may be found, and to defend it, even looking popular prejudice straight in the face. It is an attempt to aid the student to detect the vital principles which underlie the philosophical systems of old. . . . It is meant to do even justice, and to speak the truth alike without malice or prejudice. But it shows neither mercy for enthroned error, nor reverence for usurped authority. It demands for a spoliated past, that credit for its achievements which has been too long withheld. . . . Toward no form of worship, no religious faith, no scientific hypothesis has its criticism been directed in any other spirit. Men and parties, sects and schools are but the mere ephemera of the world's day. TRUTH, high-seated upon its rock of adamant, is alone eternal and supreme.'' In the preface to volume two the author writes:

> Were it possible, we would keep this work out of the hands of many Christians whom its perusal would not benefit, and for whom it was not written. We allude to those whose faith in their respective churches is pure and sincere, and those whose sinless lives reflect the glorious example of that Prophet of Nazareth, by whose mouth the spirit of truth spake loudly to humanity. . . . These have ennobled Christianity, but would have shed the same lustre upon any other faith they might have professed. . . . They are to be found at this day, in pulpit and pew, in palace and cottage; but the increasing materialism, worldliness and hypocrisy are fast diminishing their proportionate number. Their charity, and simple, child-like faith in the infallibility of their Bible, their dogmas, and their clergy, bring into full activity all the virtues that are implanted in our common nature . . . We have always avoided debate with them, lest we might be guilty of the cruelty of hurting their feelings; nor would we rob a single layman of his blind confidence, if it alone made possible for him holy living and serene dying. . . .

''An analysis of religious beliefs in general,'' the author continues, ''this volume is in particular directed against theological Christianity, the chief opponent [in those days] of free thought. It contains not one word against the pure teachings of Jesus, but unsparingly denounces their debasement into pernicious ecclesiastical systems that are ruinous to man's faith in his immortality and his God and subversive of all moral restraint.''

While reincarnation is clearly taught in *Isis,* the author does not feature it as she does in subsequent works, but contents herself with merely paving the way in an anti-reincarnationist society for a more sympathetic appreciation of this ancient tenet. Such end is also indirectly accomplished through the frequent discussion of Hinduism and Buddhism. In taking up the *Bhagavad-Gita,* for example, she writes: ''The grandest mysteries of the Brahmanical religion are embraced within this magnificent poem.''[37] As we have seen, the philosophy of rebirth pervades this sacred Hindu text.

Some critics have said that when *Isis* was written, Madame Blavatsky did not accept reincarnation,[38] but our selections will easily show otherwise. It is true that previous to *Isis* she did not write or speak *publicly* on rebirth. In a letter concerning the early days of the theosophical movement in New York, W. Q. Judge wrote: "H.P.B. told me personally many times of the real doctrine of reincarnation, enforced by the case of the death of my own child, so I know what she thought and believed."[39] Even in her childhood, reincarnation was apparently not a foreign idea. Vera de Jelihovsky, H.P.B.'s sister, and a well-known Russian author of the time, tells, in her reminiscences, of the marvelous reincarnation tales the little Helena used to spin out to her spellbound playmates. Madame Jelihovsky asks: "Where had she heard of reincarnation, or who could have taught her anything of the superstitious mysteries of metempsychosis in a Christian family?"[40]

In her theosophical writings, H.P.B. was cautious to sort out what she considered to be real evidence for rebirth and imagined evidence. In *Isis Unveiled,* for example, discounting as evidence for rebirth what reincarnationists often cite in its favor, she writes: "The well-known fact—one corroborated by the personal experience of nine persons out of ten—that we often recognize as familiar to us, scenes, and landscapes, and conversations, which we see or hear for the first time, and sometimes in countries never visited before. . . . is no proof of reincarnation." What then could be the basis for such "recognition"? Modern psychology usually attributes it to *déjà vu,* or double cerebration. Her explanation in cases in which reincarnation is not a factor is that "a man who knows that he has never visited in body, nor seen the landscape and person that he recognizes, may well assert that still has he seen and knows them, for the acquaintance was formed" *during sleep.* She then explains how this may be possible.[41]

In the selections from *Isis* that follow, it will be observed that the author prefers the term metempsychosis to reincarnation. She found the latter word unsatisfactory at that period because of its association with the immature ideas of the French school of spiritists founded by Allen Kardec, who introduced the word in the 1860s. In *The Key to Theosophy,* H.P.B. remarks that when *Isis* was written "reincarnation was not believed in by any Spiritualists, either English or American. . . . The Reincarnationists of the Allen Kardec School believe in an arbitrary and immediate reincarnation. With them, the dead father can incarnate in his own unborn daughter, and so on. They have neither Devachan, Karma, nor any philosophy that would warrant or prove the necessity of consecutive rebirths."[42]

A few references are here brought together which—after laying the basis of immortality—go into metempsychosis at both the individual and cosmic levels.]

When, years ago, we first travelled over the East, exploring the penetralia of its deserted sanctuaries, two saddening and ever-recurring questions oppressed our thoughts. [One was:] Who ever saw the IMMORTAL SPIRIT of man, so as to be able to assure himself of man's immortality? It was while most anxious to solve these perplexing problems that we came into contact with certain men, endowed with such mysterious powers and such profound knowledge that we may truly designate them as the sages of the Orient. To their instructions we lent a ready ear. They showed us that by combining science with religion, the existence of [the] immortality of man's spirit may be demonstrated like a problem of Euclid. For the first time we received the assurance that the Oriental philosophy has room for no other faith than an absolute and immovable faith in the omnipotence of man's own immortal self. We were taught that this omnipotence comes from the kinship of man's spirit with the Universal Soul. . . . [They said:] Prove the soul of man by its wondrous powers. . . .

A flower blossoms; then withers and dies. It leaves a fragrance behind, which, long after its delicate petals are but a little dust, still lingers in the air. . . . Let a note be struck on an instrument, and the faintest sound produces an eternal echo. A disturbance is created on the invisible waves of the shoreless ocean of space, and the vibration is never wholly lost. . . . And man, we are asked to believe, man, the living, thinking, reasoning entity, the indwelling deity of our nature's crowning masterpiece, will evacuate his casket and be no more! Would the principle of continuity which exists even for the so-called *inorganic* matter, for a floating atom, be denied to the spirit, whose attributes are consciousness, memory, mind, LOVE! Really, the very idea is preposterous. . . .

The doctrine of *Metempsychosis* has been abundantly ridiculed by men of science and rejected by theologians, yet if it had been properly understood in its application to the indestructibility of matter and the immortality of spirit, it would have been perceived that it is a sublime conception. . . . There was not a philosopher of any notoriety who did not hold to this doctrine of metempsychosis, as taught by the Brahmans, Buddhists, and later by the Pythagoreans. Origen and Clemens Alexandrinus, Synesius and Chalcidius, all believed in it; and the Gnostics, who are unhesitatingly proclaimed by history as a body of the most refined, learned, and enlightened men, were all believers in metempsychosis. . . . If the Pythagorean metempsychosis should be thoroughly explained and compared with the modern theory of evolution it would be found to supply every "missing link" in the chain of the latter. But who of our scientists would consent to lose his precious time over the vagaries of the ancients?

The esoteric doctrine teaches, like Buddhism and Brahmanism, and even the *Kabala,* that the one infinite and unknown Essence exists from all eternity, and in regular and harmonious successions is either passive or active. In the poetical phraseology of [the Hindu lawgiver] Manu these conditions are called the "day" and the "night" of Brahmâ. The latter is either "awake" or "asleep." . . . Upon inaugurating an active period an expansion of this Divine essence, *from within outwardly,* occurs in obedience to eternal and immutable law, and the phenomenal or visible universe is the ultimate result of the long chain of cosmical forces thus progressively set in motion. In like manner, when the passive condition is resumed, a contraction of the Divine essence takes place, and the previous work of creation is gradually and progressively undone. The visible universe becomes disintegrated, its material dispersed; and "darkness," solitary and alone, broods once more over the face of the "deep." To use a metaphor which will convey the idea still more clearly, an outbreathing of the "unknown essence" produces the world; and an inhalation causes it to disappear. *This process has been going on from all eternity, and our present universe is but one of an infinite series which had no beginning and will have no end.*

Is it enough for man to know that he exists? Is it enough to be formed a human being to enable him to deserve the appellation of MAN? It is our decided impression and conviction, that to become a genuine spiritual entity, which that designation implies, man must first *create* himself anew, so to speak—*i.e.,* thoroughly eliminate from his mind and spirit, not only the dominating influence of selfishness and other impurity, but also the infection of superstition and prejudice. . . .

As the watch passes from hand to hand and room to room in a factory, one part being added here, and another there, until the delicate machine is perfected, according to the design conceived in the mind of the master before the work was begun; so, according to ancient philosophy, the first divine conception of man takes shape little by little, in the several departments of the universal workshop, and the perfect human being finally appears on our scene.

This philosophy teaches that nature never leaves her work unfinished; if baffled at the first attempt, she tries again. When she evolves a human embryo, the intention is that a man shall be perfected—physically, intellectually, and spiritually. His body is to grow mature, wear out, and die; his mind unfold, ripen, and be harmoniously balanced; his divine spirit illuminate and blend easily with the *inner* man. No human being completes its grand cycle, or the "circle of necessity," until all these are accomplished. . . . As the laggards in a race struggle and plod in their first quarter while the victor darts past the goal, so, in the race [toward conscious] immortality, some souls outspeed all the rest and reach the end, while their myriad competitors are toiling under the load of matter, close to the starting point. Some unfortunates fall out entirely, and lose all chance of the prize; some retrace their steps and begin again. . . .

Thus, like the revolutions of a wheel, there is a regular succession of death and birth, the moral cause of which is the cleaving to existing objects, while the instrumental cause is *karma* (the power which controls the universe, prompting it to activity), merit and demerit.

[The author now contrasts the doctrine of karma and rebirth with the orthodox Christian teaching of forgiveness of sins, or vicarious atonement:]

Of all the original manuscripts that have been translated from the various languages in which Buddhism is expounded, the most extraordinary and interesting are Buddha's *Dhammapada,* or Path of Virtue, translated from the Pali by [Max Müller], and the *Wheel of the Law* . . . translated by Henry Alabaster. . . . "The Buddhists hold that nothing which is contradicted by sound reason can be a true doctrine of Buddha." . . . The Buddhists do not believe in any pardon for their sins, except after an adequate punishment for each evil deed, and a proportionate compensation to the parties injured. . . . The *Wheel of the Law* has the following: "Buddhists believe that every act, word, or thought has its consequence, which will appear sooner or later in the present or in the future state. Evil acts will produce evil consequences, good acts will produce good consequences. . . ."

This is strict and impartial justice. This is the idea of a Supreme Power which cannot fail, and therefore, can have neither wrath nor mercy, but leaves every cause, great or small, to work out its inevitable effects. [Jesus said:] "With what measure you mete, it shall be measured to you again"[43] [and this] neither by expression nor implication points to any hope of future mercy or salvation by proxy. [However, in the church,] Christians are promised that if they only believe in the "precious blood of Christ," this blood offered by Him for the expiation of the sins of the whole of mankind, will atone for every mortal sin. [Do the Gospels] affirm that Jesus gave himself as a voluntary sacrifice? On the contrary, there is not a word to sustain the idea. They make it clear that he would rather have lived to continue what he considered his mission, and that *he died because he could not help it, and only when betrayed.* . . . We have his own despairing words, "NOT MY WILL, but thine, be done!" (Luke xxii, 42, 43.)

How strangely illogical is this doctrine of the Atonement. We propose to discuss it . . . from the Buddhist standpoint, and show . . . that it has proved one of the most pernicious and demoralizing of doctrines. . . . the cause of three-fourths of the crimes of so-called Christians. . . . The clergy say: no matter how enormous our crimes against the laws of God and of man, we have but to believe in the self-sacrifice of Jesus for the salvation of mankind, and His blood will wash out every stain. God's mercy is boundless and unfathomable. It is impossible to conceive of a human sin so damnable that the price paid in advance for the redemption of the sinner would not wipe it out if a thousandfold worse. And, furthermore, it is never too late to repent. Though the offender wait until the last minute of the last hour of the last day of his mortal life, before his blanched lips utter the confession of faith, he may go to Paradise . . . These are the assumptions of the Church.

But if we step outside the little circle of creed and consider the universe as a whole balanced by the exquisite adjustment of parts, how all sound logic, how the faintest glimmering sense of Justice revolts against this Vicarious Atonement! If the criminal sinned only against himself, and wronged no one but himself; if by sincere repentance he could cause the obliteration of past events, not only from the memory of man, but also from that imperishable record, which no deity—not even the Supremest of the Supreme—can cause to disappear, then this dogma might not be incomprehensible. . . .

Can the *results* of a crime be obliterated even though the crime itself should be pardoned? The effects of a cause are never limited to the boundaries of the cause, nor can the results of crime be confined to the offender and his victim. Every good as well as evil action has its effects, as palpably as the stone flung into a calm water. The simile is trite, but it is the best ever conceived, so let us use it. The eddying circles are greater and swifter, as the disturbing object is greater or smaller, but the smallest pebble, nay, the tiniest speck, makes its ripples. And this disturbance is not alone visible and on the surface. Below, unseen, in every direction—outward and downward—drop pushes drop until the sides and bottom are touched by the force. More, the air above the water is agitated, and this disturbance passes, as the physicists tell us, from stratum to stratum out into space forever and ever; an impulse has been given to matter, and that is never lost, can never be recalled!

So with crime, and so with its opposite. The action may be instantaneous, the effects are eternal. When, after the stone is once flung into the pond, we can recall it to the hand, roll back the ripples, obliterate the force expended, restore the etheric waves to their previous state of non-being, and wipe out every trace of the act of throwing the missile, so that Time's record shall not show it ever happened, then, *then* we may patiently hear Christians argue for the efficacy of this Atonement.

The Chicago *Times* recently printed the hangman's record of the first half of the present year (1877)—a long and ghastly record of murders and hangings. Nearly every one of these murderers received religious consolation, and many announced that they had received God's forgiveness through the blood of Jesus, and were going that day to Heaven! . . . [They] slew their victims, in most cases, without giving them time to repent, or call on Jesus to wash them clean with his blood. [The victims] perhaps, died sinful, and, of course,—consistently with theological logic—met the reward of their greater or lesser offenses. But the murderer . . . pronounces the charmed words of conversion, and goes to the scaffold a redeemed child of Jesus! Except for the murder, he would not have been prayed with, redeemed, pardoned. Clearly this man did well to murder, for thus he gained eternal happiness? And how about the victim, and his or her family, relatives, dependants, social relations—has Justice no recompense for them? Must they suffer in this world and the next, while he who wronged them sits beside the "holy thief" of Calvary and is forever blessed? On this question the clergy keep a prudent silence.

A rationalist and a skeptic says: "I have questioned at the very doors of their temples several hundreds of Buddhists, and not found one but strove, fasted, and gave himself up to every kind of austerity, to perfect himself and acquire immortality; not to attain final annihilation". . . . As well as this author we have questioned Buddhists and Brahmanists and studied their philosophy. *Apavarg* has wholly a different meaning from annihilation. It is but to become more and more like [the deific essence] of whom he is one of the refulgent sparks, that is the aspiration of every Hindu philosopher and the hope of the most ignorant is *never to yield up his distinct individuality*. . . . The same with the doctrine of metempsychosis, so distorted by European scholars. . . .

Indeed, it is more than difficult to avoid sharing this doctrine of periodical incarnations. Has not the world witnessed, at rare intervals, the advent of such grand characters as [Krishna, Buddha, and Jesus]? . . . No orthodox Brahmans and Buddhists would deny the Christian incarnation; only, they understand it in their own philosophical way . . . The very corner-stone of their religious system is periodical incarnations of the Deity. Whenever humanity is about merging into materialism and moral degradation, a Supreme Spirit incarnates himself in his creature selected for the purpose. . . . The early Christian Church, all imbued with Asiatic philosophy, evidently shared the same belief—otherwise *it would have neither erected into an article of faith the second advent, nor . . . invented the fable of Anti-Christ as a precaution against possible future incarnations* [of other saviors]. Neither could they have imagined [as they did] that Melchisedek was an avatar of Christ. They had only to turn to the *Bhagavad-Gita* to find Christna [Krishna] saying to Arjuna: "He who follows me is saved by wisdom and even by works. . . . *As often as virtue declines in the world, I make myself manifest to save it.*" . . .

Kapila, Orpheus, Pythagoras, Plato, Basilides, Marcian, Ammonius, and Plotinus founded schools and sowed the germs of many a noble thought, and disappearing left behind them the refulgence of demi-gods. But the three personalities of Krishna, Gautama, and Jesus appeared like true gods each in his epoch, and bequeathed to humanity three religions built on the imperishable rock of ages. . . . Purify the three systems of the dross of human dogmas, the pure essence remaining will be found identical. . . .

In the ancient philosophy there was no missing link to be supplied by what Tyndall calls an "educated imagination"; no hiatus to be filled with volumes of materialistic speculations . . . Our "ignorant" ancestors traced the law of evolution throughout the whole universe. . . . So from the universal ether to the incarnate human spirit, they traced one uninterrupted series of entities. These evolutions were from the world of spirit into the world of gross matter; and through that back again to the source of all things. The "descent of species" was to them a descent from the spirit, primal source of all.[44]

H.P.B. and Olcott in India

[Early in 1879, two years after *Isis* was published, H. P. Blavatsky and Colonel Olcott removed to India to establish the work of the Theosophical Society there. According to the noted Buddhist scholar Edward Conze they arrived at a crucial psychological moment in Eastern affairs. And as we shall see, they came at a time when the survival of reincarnation philosophy was in serious jeopardy in much of the East. Here is what Conze says in his *Buddhism: Its Essence and Development,* a work that Mircea Eliade—head of the religious history department at the Chicago University Divinity School and a religious philosopher of note—praises as "perhaps the best book on the subject [of Buddhism] published so far in a European language."

> The year 1875 marks an event of great importance. Madame Blavatsky and Colonel Olcott founded [in New York] the "Theosophical Society." Its activities accelerated the influx of knowledge about Asiatic religions, and restored self-confidence in the wavering minds of the Asiatics themselves. At that period, European civilization, a blend of science and commerce, of Christianity and militarism, seemed immensely strong. The latent dynamite of national war and class war was perceived by only a few. A growing number of educated men in India and Ceylon felt, as the Japanese did about the same time, that they had no alternative but to adopt the Western system with all that it entails. The Christian missionaries looked forward to speedy mass conversions.

"But then the tide turned, rather suddenly and unexpectedly," said Conze. "A few members of the dominant race, white men and women from Russia, America and England, Theosophists, appeared among the Hindus and Ceylonese to proclaim their admiration for the ancient wisdom of the East. Madame Blavatsky spoke about Buddhism in terms of the highest praise, Colonel Olcott wrote a 'Buddhist Catechism,'[45] and A. P. Sinnett published a very successful book in which all kinds of mysterious, but fascinating ideas were presented as 'Esoteric Buddhism.' . . . By its timely intervention, the Theosophical Society has done a great service to the Buddhist cause."[46]

While residing in India, as international president of the Theosophical Society, Olcott visited Ceylon on many occasions, and rendered considerable assistance to the people there. An article in the *New York Herald Tribune* (February 18, 1962), written by Martin G. Berck of the United Nations, tells of this:

> Throughout the Island of Ceylon, from the ancient capital of Anuradhapura to the venerated peak of Shri Pada, polished brass lamps were lit yesterday as Buddhists paused to do religious honor to an American. . . . With such homage, Ceylonese Buddhists marked the death on February 17, 1907, of Col. Henry Steel Olcott, whom they regard as a key and sainted figure in the renaissance of their religion and their national culture.

In 1968, Ceylon—or Sri Lanka as it is now called—issued a special stamp commemorating Olcott's work in promoting education and Buddhism there. Only two Buddhist schools existed in Ceylon in 1880 when H. P. Blavatsky and Olcott visited; all the rest were missionary or church operated schools that had almost extinguished Buddhism in Ceylon. By 1900, largely through Olcott's efforts, the Buddhist schools numbered two hundred (*The Middle Way*, May 1973, p. 44). In addition to Olcott's picture, the stamp depicts the Buddhist flag he designed. Madame Blavatsky explained that hitherto the Buddhists "had no such symbol as the cross affords to the Christians, and consequently have lacked that essential sign of their common relation to each other." The flag was but one of many examples, she said, of the fraternal force the theosophical movement was trying to evoke among all peoples.[47]

Olcott had been so successful in reviving Buddhism in Ceylon, and also in Burma, that in 1888 a national committee of Japanese Buddhist priests invited him to do the same for Japan, and sent a representative to India to escort him to their country. In an address to the theosophists, the delegate pleaded that Olcott should "put courage in the hearts of our young men, to prove to the graduates of our colleges and universities and to those who have been sent to America and Europe for education, that Western science is not infallible, and not a substitute but the natural sister of religion." Under the joint auspices of the nine main Japanese Buddhist sects, Olcott made a four-month lecture tour of the entire island. It stimulated such interest that it became a national event. On a subsequent visit, the Emperor of Japan was in one of the audiences.

From the foregoing, it is obvious that the survival of the teaching of reincarnation had been at stake in Buddhism during these critical times. But what about in Hinduism? In India, theosophy not only reinforced and strengthened the Hindu's ancestral belief in rebirth, but its teaching concerning a brotherhood of Masters of Wisdom restored the conviction that humanity is not alone and unaided in its struggles; that India's great Rishis and Sages were still working with mankind, and at cyclic intervals reincarnated openly among men. The Brahmins had been dolefully insisting that during the present Kali Yuga—a spiritually dark age lasting some 400,000 years—the Rishis and Mahatmas had retired to distant spheres and would return only in the ensuing Satya Yuga—the golden age of purity.

In an address on the occasion of the third anniversary of the Bengal theosophical society (June 27, 1885), at which some seven hundred were present, Colonel Olcott spoke of some of the transformations India had been undergoing since the arrival of the theosophists:

> What was the condition of Hinduism ten years ago was a matter too fresh in everybody's recollection to be in doubt. . . . The Shastras neglected, the ancient Tols of the Brahman gurus closed, the precious books mouldering upon the shelves for want of buyers . . . And, to complete the picture of national desolation, the crowded Pantheon of Hindu Theology became a mere quarry of old stone images, lifeless, meaningless, jeered at by even the callowest youths of the modern schools and colleges. This was the condition of India and Indian public opinion when the Theosophical movement began.
>
> Is it so now? Look through the land, examine the native newspapers and other literature of the day, and answer. From every side come the signs of an Aryan revival. The old books find buyers, and new editions are being demanded; Sanskrit schools are reopening. . . . There is the beginning of a conviction in the Hindu mind that their forefathers were wise and good, and their motherland the "cradle of arts and creeds."[48]

It is only natural that the revival of Hinduism and Buddhism in the East had important repercussions in the West, and paved the way for an ever-growing interest in Eastern philosophy and religion among people of ordinary culture not merely the scholarly and erudite. This was fostered by the frequent reports in the newspapers in Europe and America of the activities of the theosophists in the Orient. Obviously, if Hinduism and Buddhism had been replaced in the East by sectarian forms of Christianity, or by atheistic philosophies, the present wide-scale study of oriental teachings would never have taken place.

Numerous branches of the Theosophical Society were formed all over India, and most importantly H.P.B. founded the magazine *The Theosophist,* described on its title page as "a monthly journal devoted to oriental philosophy, art, literature and occultism." The magazine enjoyed an international circulation, and, in addition to articles from her pen, opened its pages to contributions from India's leading pundits. In this setting she found it timely to provide more profound and detailed information on reincarnation than had appeared in *Isis*. And as to historical aspects of the teaching, her opening article "What is Theosophy?" mentions that "in a series of articles entitled 'The World's Great Theosophists,' we intend showing that from Pythagoras, who got his wisdom in India, down to our best known modern philosophers and theosophists . . . many believed and yet believe in metempsychosis or reincarnation of the soul. . . ."

This latter intention, however, was not realized until the volume *Reincarnation, A Study of Forgotten Truth*, by the theosophist E. D. Walker, was published in 1888 by Houghton Mifflin in Boston and Lovell in New York. Walker's preliminary researches first appeared in *The Path* magazine, founded and edited in New York by W. Q. Judge. In book form it became for seventy years the major work in this field of historical research and underwent numerous editions. In the 1904 reprint by a new publisher, it was stated: "The advent of the Theosophical Society has caused the ennobling doctrine of 'Reincarnation' to become a household topic among all classes in the Western world. . . . and the present edition is in response to the demand created by the wide circulation of this work."]

❊ ❊ ❊
H.P.B. in London

[Early in 1885 H.P.B. left India for good and lived largely in retirement in various places in Europe, working day and night on her forthcoming book *The Secret Doctrine*. In 1887 she settled permanently in London where she founded the magazine *Lucifer*. For this magazine she wrote her most challenging commentaries on modern civilization, at the same time indicating the light shed by theosophy on modern problems. The title page bears this quotation from Yonge: "Lucifer is no profane or satanic title. It is the Latin Luciferus, the light-bringer, the morning star. . . . the pure pale herald of daylight." In the opening pages she explains that the word, deriving from *lux, lucis,* "light," and *ferre,* "to bring," "is typical of the divine spirit which sacrificed itself for humanity."

Shortly after *Lucifer* was started, some of the more ardent students of theosophy—most of them young people—formed an additional London group that was called the Blavatsky Lodge despite H.P.B.'s vehement protests regarding the name. This soon became the center of theosophical activities in Britain and the Continent, and many highly educated men and women of note became members. They had numerous scientific and philosophical questions to ask when *The Secret Doctrine* was published late in 1888, and urged her to answer them at the Blavatsky Lodge meetings. Her answers are recorded in the volume *Transactions of the Blavatsky Lodge*.[49] Yeats attended the meetings and after one of them remarked: "To me she's still an interrogation mark, but wonderful in every way. Yet when she's gone the fellow who opens the door will think he can take her place."[50] (The leading parts played by Yeats, George Russell, and other Irish theosophists in Ireland's literary renaissance have been considered in chapter 5. The movement in Ireland, however, was to have a pervasive influence far beyond literary circles or national boundaries.)

Among those attending the Blavatsky Lodge meetings were some interested chiefly in psychology, and H.P.B. on occasion replied to their questions in the pages of *Lucifer*. Her most notable article in this area is "Psychic and Noëtic Action," in which she examines the shortcomings of the then prevailing "physiological psychology," and contrasts the latter with the psychology of modern and ancient theosophy. "Noëtic" is an adjective of *Nous*, which H.P.B. defines in her *Theosophical Glossary* as "a Platonic term for the Higher Mind or Soul." "It means Spirit as distinct from animal Soul—*psyche*." It is the "divine consciousness or mind in man." The Greeks, she said, borrowed the word from the Egyptian *Nout*.[51]

In the 1930s, much of the material in "Psychic and Noëtic Action" was reviewed in an article called "What Is the Soul?" by the British philosopher and agnostic C. E. M. Joad, who, until his death in 1953, was widely known for his lucid analyses of modern culture and philosophy. He wrote:

> Madame Blavatsky . . . postulates two souls or selves which are broadly defined as follows. The first is body-dependent, that is to say, the events in it are determined by prior events taking place in the body; it is known as the "Lower Self," or as "psychic activity." "It manifests itself, through our organic system" and "from its lowest to its highest manifestations, it is nothing but motion."
>
> The second self, known as the "Higher Self" [which], instead of being a mere bundle of psychological events, like the first self . . . is a unity, or rather, it is a unifying principle. It has no special organ as its counterpart in the body—for how can there be a specific organ to determine the motions of that which unifies all organs? . . . It is not, therefore, located in the brain . . . Its activity, described as "Noëtic" as opposed to the "psychic" activity of the first self, derives from the "Universal Mind." . . . Finally, the Higher Self is identical and continuing in and through different lives. It is the permanent element which runs like a thread through the different existences which are strung like beads along its length.

Professor Joad then gives examples of how "the distinction between the two selves is applied by Madame Blavatsky, with great ingenuity, to counter some of the difficulties raised for any spiritualized philosophy by scientific materialism.'' In concluding the article—written in 1937—he remarks: "It is impossible not to feel the greatest respect for Madame Blavatsky's writings on this subject, respect and, if the word may be permitted, admiration. Writing when she did, she anticipated many ideas which, familiar today, were in the highest degree novel fifty years ago.''[52]

In "Psychic and Noëtic Action," H.P.B. reveals that in each incarnation there is a bridging element between the higher and lower self, which from one point of view is a projection of the higher, immortal Self, and from another, its reflection in a more material medium. Its all-important function will be made plain in the extracts that follow from her article, but first she explains that "the metaphysics of occult physiology and psychology postulate within mortal man an immortal entity, 'divine Mind,' or *Nous,* whose pale and too often distorted reflection is that which we call 'Mind' and intellect in man— virtually an entity apart from the former during the period of every incarnation.'' "The rational, but earthly or physical intellect of man" is "incased in, and bound by, matter." The Higher Mind is "that which reincarnates periodically . . . while its reflected 'Double,' changing with every new incarnation and personality, is, therefore, conscious but for a life-period."

> The latter "principle" is the Lower Self, or that, which manifesting through our *organic* system, acting on this plane of illusion, imagines itself the *Ego Sum,* and thus falls into what Buddhist philosophy brands as the "heresy of separateness." The former, we term INDIVIDUALITY, the latter *Personality.* . . .
>
> The "Higher Ego" cannot act directly on the body, as its consciousness belongs to quite another plane and planes of ideation; the "lower" *Self* does: and its action and behavior depend on its free will and choice as to whether it will gravitate more towards its parent . . . or the "animal" which it informs, the man of flesh. The "Higher Ego," as part of the essence of the UNIVERSAL MIND,[53] is unconditionally omniscient on its own plane, and only potentially so in our terrestrial sphere, as it has to act solely through its *alter ego*—the Personal Self. . . . It is a part of the mission of [this incarnated aspect of the Higher Ego], to get gradually rid of the blind, deceptive element which, though it makes of it an active spiritual entity on this plane, still brings it into so close contact with matter as to entirely becloud its divine nature and stultify its intuitions. . . . The *Personal Ego,* becoming at one with its divine parent, shares in the immortality of the latter.

"Psychic and Noëtic Action" was published in two installments, and ended with these words: "Thrice blessed he who has learned to discern the Noëtic from the Psychic action of the 'Double-Faced' God in him, and who knows the potency of his own Spirit—or 'Soul Dynamics.' ''[54]]

✳ ✳ ✳
"The Secret Doctrine"

[After hearing mentioned so frequently the title of H. P. Blavatsky's chief
work *The Secret Doctrine*, it is only natural for the reader to wonder what
these volumes are all about. We will give substantial quotations from the
text, but first present some preliminary considerations, and begin with a
letter written in 1935 by George Russell to the Irish author Sean O'Faolain:

> You dismiss H. P. Blavatsky rather too easily as "hocus pocus." Nobody
> ever affected the thought of so many able men and women by "hocus pocus."
> The real source of her influence is to be found in *The Secret Doctrine*, a book on
> the religions of the world suggesting or disclosing an underlying unity between
> all great religions. It was a book which Maeterlinck said contained the most
> grandiose cosmogony in the world, and if you read it merely as a romantic
> compilation, it is one of the most exciting and stimulating books written for the
> last hundred years. It is paying a poor compliment to men like Yeats, Maeter-
> linck, and others, to men like Sir William Crookes, the greatest chemist of
> modern times, who was a member of her society, to Carter Blake, F.R.S., the
> anthropologist, and the scholars and scientists in many countries who read H. P.
> Blavatsky's books, to assume that they were attracted by "hocus pocus."
>
> If you are ever in the National Library, Kildare Street, and have a couple of
> hours to spare, you might dip into "The Proem" to *The Secret Doctrine*, and
> you will understand the secret of the influence of that extraordinary woman on
> her contemporaries. . . . You should not be misled by popular catch-words
> . . . but try to find out the real secret of H. P. Blavatsky's influence, which still
> persists strong as ever, as I have found over here [in London] among many
> intellectuals and well-known writers.[55]

In addition to those mentioned, other noted scientists associated with the
various theosophical societies have been Thomas Edison and Gustaf Strömberg (both of whom were quoted earlier), and the French astronomer
Camille Flammarion.[55a] The leading scientist in reincarnation research,
Dr. Ian Stevenson, had a theosophical background—both his parents were
theosophists. Incidentally, Albert Einstein is said to have always had
The Secret Doctrine on his desk.[56]

What has fascinated the scientists who have studied the work is that the
author anticipated so many discoveries in their own fields. When the physicists and chemists of her day were convinced that the atom was the ultimate
building block of the universe, she affirmed the infinite divisibility of the
atom. When anthropologists were grudgingly allowing man an antiquity of

only several hundred thousand years, she spoke, as present researchers do, in terms of millions. She considered as fact such later scientific discoveries as the identity of substance and energy; the transmutation of elements; the illusory nature of matter—that matter is not what we see; that space is not empty, there being no vacuity anywhere; that life is possible on other planets and worlds; that the moon was not torn from the earth but was older than the earth. (Scientists were recently astounded to discover that the moon rocks brought back by the astronauts were older than any to be found on the earth!)

Another source of wonderment has been her accurate prophecies of future developments in science, psychology, religion, and world affairs. Lewis Mumford, discussing Jung's *Memories, Dreams, and Reflections* (*The New Yorker,* May 23, 1964), mentioned the psychiatrist's prevision of World War I, and commented: "This dream, uncanny in retrospect because it was soon verified by events, may be placed in the same category as Madame Blavatsky's much earlier and even more realistic vision of the destruction of whole cities by nuclear blasts."

Another prophecy of H.P.B.'s was quite specific as to dates of fulfillment. In *The Secret Doctrine* she wrote:

> The exact extent, depth, breadth, and length of the mysteries of Nature are to be found only in Eastern esoteric sciences. So vast and so profound are these that hardly a few, a very few of the highest Initiates—those *whose very existence is known but to a small number of Adepts*—are capable of assimilating the knowledge. Yet it is all there, and one by one facts and processes in Nature's workshops are permitted to find their way into the exact Sciences, while mysterious help is given to rare individuals in unravelling its arcana. It is at the close of great Cycles, in connection with racial development, that such events generally take place. We are at the very close of the cycle of 5,000 years of the present Aryan Kaliyuga; and between this time [1888] and 1897 there will be a large rent made in the Veil of Nature, and materialistic science will receive a death-blow.[57]

Did anything momentous occur in science during that period? In 1895 Roentgen discovered by accident the X-ray; in 1896 Zeeman was able to polarize light in a magnetic field. In that year Madame Curie discovered radioactivity. In 1897 Lorentz made the preliminary discovery of the electron, and later that year Thomson confirmed its actuality. The import of these discoveries was discussed by Dr. Karl Compton, former president of the Massachusetts Institute of Technology, in his address as retiring president of the American Association for the Advancement of Science:

> The history of science abounds with instances where a new concept or discovery has led to tremendous advances into vast new fields . . . whose very

existence has hitherto been unsuspected. . . . But to my notion, no such instance has been so dramatic as the discovery of the electron, the tiniest thing in the universe, which within one generation has transformed a stagnant science of physics, a descriptive science of chemistry and a sterile science of astronomy into dynamically developing sciences fraught with intellectual adventure, inter-relating interpretations and practical values. . . .

In science, as in human affairs, great events do not occur without a background of development. The electron has an ancestry which can be traced back through the centuries. Its immediate progenitors were the electromagnetic theory of light, spectroscopy, and the leakage of electricity through gases. First cousins were X-rays and radioactivity and quantum theory, for, out of a background of long investigation and of bewildering and apparently unrelated phenomena, there burst upon the scientific world the X-ray in 1895, radioactivity in 1896, and the electron in 1897. . . . That only the pioneers of the scientific world were prepared for these discoveries, however, is witnessed by the fact that a standard textbook of chemistry widely used in my student days in 1904 stated that, "atoms are the indivisible constituents of molecules."[58]

When *The Secret Doctrine* was published, the general view in chemistry and physics was—as expressed by Büchner—"to accept infinite divisibility is absurd and amounts to doubting the very existence of matter." The author of *The Secret Doctrine* answered: "The atom *is* elastic, ergo the atom is divisible, and must consist of particles, or of sub-atoms. . . . It is on the doctrine of the illusive nature of matter, and the infinite divisibility of the atom, that the whole science of Occultism is built. It opens limitless horizons to *substance* informed by the divine breath of its soul in every possible state of tenuity."[59] According to the theosophists, it is because matter at every stage of concretion, or refinement, *can be* dispersed, and then reaggregated by its ensouling essence, that both death and rebirth are possible for all centers of life, be they worlds, gods, men, atoms, or even quarks—the latest supposed constituent of the atom, believed by some physicists to be far smaller than protons and electrons. Regarding the latter theory, the leading theoretical physicist since Einstein, Werner Heisenberg, comments:

Even if quarks could be found, for all we know they could again be divided into two quarks and one antiquark, etc., and thus they would not be more elementary than a proton. . . . We will have to abandon the philosophy of Democritos and the concept of fundamental elementary particles. We should accept instead the concept of fundamental symmetries, which is a concept out of the philosophy of Plato.[60]

Regarding all of H. P. Blavatsky's writings, and especially *The Secret Doctrine,* she made it quite plain, as stated in the preface to that work:

These truths are in no sense put forward as a *revelation;* nor does the author claim the position of a revealer of mystic lore, now made public for the first time in the world's history. For what is contained in this work is to be found scattered throughout thousands of volumes embodying the scriptures of the great Asiatic and early European religions, hidden under glyph and symbol, and hitherto left unnoticed because of this veil. What is now attempted is to gather the oldest tenets together and to make of them one harmonious and unbroken whole. The sole advantage which the writer has over her predecessors, is that she need not resort to personal speculations and theories. For this work is a partial statement of what she herself has been taught by more advanced students, supplemented, in a few details only, by the results of her own study and observation. . . .

It is perhaps desirable to state unequivocally that the teachings . . . contained in these volumes, belong neither to the Hindu, the Zoroastrian, the Chaldean, nor the Egyptian religion, neither to Buddhism, Islam, Judaism nor Christianity exclusively. The Secret Doctrine is the essence of all these. Sprung from it in their origins, the various religious schemes are now made to merge back into their original element, out of which every mystery and dogma has grown, developed, and become materialized.

The writer . . . is fully prepared to take all the responsibility for what is contained in this work, and even to face the charge of having invented the whole of it. That it has many shortcomings she is fully aware; all that she claims for it is that, romantic as it may seem to many, its logical coherence and consistency entitle this new Genesis to rank, at any rate, on a level with the "working hypotheses" so freely accepted by modern science. Further, it claims consideration, not by reason of any appeal to dogmatic authority, but because it closely adheres to Nature, and follows the laws of uniformity and analogy.

The expression "the secret doctrine," puzzling to many, refers to the hidden kernel of truth claimed to exist behind and within the husk of the popular exoteric religions. The great teachers of mankind are shown by H.P.B. to have taught two doctrines: one suited to the comprehension of the masses, the other to their initiated disciples. It will be recalled that Jesus on several occasions declared that to the multitudes he taught parables, but to his apostles he revealed the mysteries of the kingdom of heaven.[61] Such secrecy apparently arises from dire necessity: Occult knowledge and power are highly dangerous in the hands of the selfish and ambitious, while with the masses are soon materialized and profaned.

In the introduction to *The Secret Doctrine* (p. xxiii), the author speaks of a number of esoteric schools, "the seat of which is beyond the Himalayas, and whose ramifications may be found in China, Japan, India, Tibet, and even in Syria, besides South America." It is noteworthy that Tibet is regarded only as a branch, not the main center, as some imagine theosophists to believe.

The Secret Doctrine bears the subtitle "The Synthesis of Science, Religion, and Philosophy." Volume one of this two-volume work is called Cosmogenesis and describes the reincarnation of worlds—more particularly the rebirth and reawakening of our own universe after its long pralayic rest. The second volume, Anthropogenesis, discusses the evolution of the human form; the lighting up of mind by the incarnation of human monads from prior worlds; the subsequent evolution and reincarnation of the early races of men up to the present period; the future development projected for those races if the original grand design is carried out. W. Q. Judge writes:

> Nowhere else in English literature is the Law of Evolution given such sweep and swing. It reminds one of the ceaseless undertone of the deep sea, and seems to view our Earth in all its changes "from the birth of time to the crack of doom." It follows man in his triple evolution, physical, mental, and spiritual, throughout the perfect circle of his boundless life. Darwinism had reached its limits and a rebound. Man is indeed evolved from lower forms. But *which* man? the physical? the psychical? the intellectual? or the spiritual? The Secret Doctrine points where the lines of evolution and involution meet; where matter and spirit clasp hands; and where the rising animal stands face to face with the fallen god; for *all natures* meet and mingle in man.[62]

All this can hardly be portrayed in a few extracts from *The Secret Doctrine*. Here we offer some selections on other phases of reincarnation, and on the scientific proofs on which the work is said to rest. But first, and most importantly, the basic root concepts underlying the work as a whole are taken from the Proem to volume one. These alone place the theosophical view of rebirth in proper context.]

Before the reader proceeds . . . it is absolutely necessary that he should be made acquainted with the few fundamental conceptions which underlie and pervade the entire system of thought to which his attention is invited. These basic ideas are few in number, and on their clear apprehension depends the understanding of all that follows. . . . The Secret Doctrine establishes three fundamental propositions:

(*a*) An Omnipresent, Eternal, Boundless, and Immutable PRINCIPLE on which all speculation is impossible, since it transcends the power of human conception and could only be dwarfed by any human expression or similitude. . . . To render these ideas clearer to the general reader, let him set out with the postulate that there is one absolute Reality which antecedes all manifested, conditioned, being. This Infinite and Eternal Cause . . . is the rootless root of "all that was, is, or ever shall be." It is of course devoid of all attributes and is essentially without any relation to manifested, finite Being. It is "Be-ness" rather than Being (in Sanskrit, *Sat*), and is beyond all thought or speculation.

This "Be-ness" is symbolized in the Secret Doctrine under two aspects.

On the one hand, absolute abstract Space, representing bare subjectivity
. . . On the other, absolute Abstract Motion representing Unconditioned
Consciousness. Even our Western thinkers have shown that Consciousness
is inconceivable to us apart from change, and motion best symbolizes
change, its essential characteristic. . . . Thus, then, the first fundamental
axiom of the Secret Doctrine is this metaphysical ONE ABSOLUTE—BE-NESS.
. . . It may, however, assist the student if a few further explanations are
given here.

Herbert Spencer has of late so far modified his Agnosticism, as to assert
that the nature of the "First Cause,"[63] which the Occultist more logically
derives from the "Causeless Cause," the "Eternal," and the "Unknowable," may be essentially the same as that of the Consciousness which wells
up within us: in short, that the impersonal reality pervading the Kosmos is
the pure noumenon of thought.

Parabrahm (the One Reality, the Absolute) is the field of Absolute Consciousness. . . . But once that we pass in thought from this (to us) Absolute
Negation, duality supervenes in the contrast of Spirit (or consciousness) and
Matter, Subject and Object. Spirit (or Consciousness) and Matter are, however, to be regarded not as independent realities, but as the two facets or
aspects of the Absolute. . . .

Hence it will be apparent that the contrast of these two aspects of the
Absolute is essential to the existence of the "Manifested Universe." Apart
from Cosmic Substance, Cosmic Ideation [or Spirit] could not manifest as
individual consciousness, since it is only through a vehicle of matter that
consciousness wells up as "I am I," a physical basis being necessary to focus
a ray of the Universal Mind at a certain stage of complexity. Again, apart
from Cosmic Ideation, Cosmic Substance would remain an empty abstraction, and no emergence of consciousness could ensue. . . . Thus from
Spirit, or Cosmic Ideation, comes our consciousness; from Cosmic Substance the several vehicles in which that consciousness is individualised and
attains to self—or reflective—consciousness. . . .

(b) The Eternity of the Universe *in toto* as a boundless plane; periodically
"the playground of numberless Universes incessantly manifesting and disappearing," called "the manifesting stars," and the "sparks of Eternity."
"The Eternity of the Pilgrim" is like a wink of the Eye of Self-Existence.
("Pilgrim" is the appellation given to our *Monad* . . . during its cycle of
incarnations. It is the only immortal and eternal principle in us, being an
indivisible part of the integral whole—the Universal Spirit, from which it
emanates, and into which it is absorbed at the end of the cycle. . . .)

This second assertion of the Secret Doctrine is the absolute universality of
the law of periodicity, of flux and reflux, ebb and flow, which physical science has observed and recorded in all departments of nature. An alternation

such as that of Day and Night, Life and Death, Sleeping and Waking, is a fact so common, so perfectly universal and without exception, that it is easy to comprehend that in it we see one of the absolutely fundamental laws of the universe.

(c) The fundamental identity of all Souls with the Universal Over-Soul, the latter being itself an aspect of the Unknown Root; and the obligatory pilgrimage for every Soul—a spark of the former—through the Cycle of Incarnation (or "Necessity") in accordance with Cyclic and Karmic law, during the whole term. In other words, no . . . divine Soul can have an independent (conscious) existence before the spark which issued from the pure Essence of the . . . OVER-SOUL, has (a) passed through every elemental form of the phenomenal world of that Manvantara, and (b) acquired individuality, first by natural impulse, and then by self-induced and self-devised efforts (checked by its Karma), thus ascending through all the degrees of intelligence, from the lowest to the highest Manas [or Mind], from mineral and plant, up to the holiest archangel (Dhyani-Buddha). The pivotal doctrine of the Esoteric philosophy admits no privileges or special gifts in man, save those won by his own Ego through personal effort and merit throughout a long series of metempsychoses and reincarnations. . . .

Such are the basic conceptions on which the Secret Doctrine rests. . . . Once that the reader has gained a clear comprehension of them and realised the light which they throw on every problem of life, they will need no further justification in his eyes, because their truth will be to him as evident as the sun in heaven.

To the superficial observer, [Nature] is no better than an immense slaughterhouse wherein butchers become victims, and victims executioners in their turn. It is quite natural that the pessimistically inclined profane, once convinced of Nature's numerous shortcomings and failures, and especially of her autophagous propensities, should imagine this to be the best evidence that there is no deity *in abscondito* within Nature, nor anything divine in her. Nor is it less natural that the materialist and the physicist should imagine that everything is due to blind force and chance, and to the survival of the *strongest,* even more often than of the fittest.

But the Occultists, who regard physical nature as a bundle of most varied illusions on the plane of deceptive perceptions; who recognise in every pain and suffering but the necessary pangs of incessant procreation; a series of stages toward an ever-growing perfectibility, which is visible in the silent influence of never-erring Karma, or *abstract* nature—the Occultists, we say, view the great Mother otherwise. Woe to those who live without suffering.

Stagnation and death is the future of all that vegetates without a change. And how can there be any change for the better without proportionate suffering during the preceding stage? Is it not those only who have learnt the deceptive value of earthly hopes and the illusive allurements of external nature who are destined to solve the great problems of life, pain, and death? . . . The reincarnationists and believers in Karma alone dimly perceive that the whole secret of Life is in the unbroken series of its manifestations. . . .

Those who believe in *Karma* have to believe in *destiny,* which, from birth to death, every man is weaving thread by thread around himself, as a spider does his cobweb. . . . This LAW, whether Conscious or Unconscious—predestines nothing and no one. . . . Karma creates nothing, nor does it design. It is man who plans and creates causes, and Karmic law adjusts the effects; which adjustment is not an act but universal harmony, tending ever to resume its original position, like a bough, which, bent down too forcibly, rebounds with corresponding vigor. If it happens to dislocate the arm that tried to bend it out of its natural position, shall we say that it is the bough which broke our arm, or that our own folly has brought us to grief?

Karma has never sought to destroy intellectual and individual liberty. . . . It has not involved its decrees in darkness purposely to perplex man, nor shall it punish him who dares to scrutinize its mysteries. On the contrary, he who unveils through study and meditation its intricate paths, and throws light on those dark ways, in the windings of which so many men perish owing to their ignorance of the labyrinth of life, is working for the good of his fellow-men. . . .

Believers in Karma cannot be regarded as Atheists or materialists—still less as fatalists. . . . Karma is a highly philosophical truth, a most divine noble expression of the primitive intuition of man concerning Deity. It is a doctrine which explains the origin of Evil, and ennobles our conceptions of what divine immutable Justice ought to be, instead of degrading the unknown and unknowable Deity by making it the whimsical, cruel tyrant, which we call Providence. . . .

An Occultist or a philosopher will not speak of the goodness or cruelty of Providence; but, identifying it with Karma-Nemesis, he will teach that nevertheless it guards the good and watches over them in this, as in future lives; and that it punishes the evil-doer—aye, even to his seventh rebirth. So long, in short, as the effect of his having thrown into perturbation even the smallest atom in the Infinite World of Harmony, has not been finally re-adjusted. For the only decree of Karma—an eternal and immutable decree—is absolute Harmony in the world of matter as it is in the world of Spirit. It is not, therefore, Karma that rewards or punishes, but it is we, who reward or punish ourselves according to whether we work with, through and along with nature, abiding by the laws on which that Harmony depends, or—break them. . . .

[Connected with the workings of karma are] the invisible tablets of the Astral Light,[64] "the great picture-gallery of eternity"—a faithful record of every act, and even thought of man . . . As said in *"Isis,"* this divine and unseen canvas is the BOOK OF LIFE. . . . The Eternal Record is no fantastic dream, for we meet with the same records in the world of gross matter. "A shadow never falls upon a wall without leaving thereupon a permanent trace which might be made visible by resorting to proper processes," says Dr. Draper. . . . "Upon the walls of our most private apartments," [he continues,] "where we think the eye of intrusion is altogether shut out, and our retirement can never be profaned, there exist the vestiges of our acts, silhouettes of whatever we have done."[65] Drs. Jevons and Babbage believe that every thought, displacing the particles of the brain and setting them in motion, scatters them throughout the Universe, and they think that "each particle of the existing matter must be a register of all that has happened." *(Principles of Science,* Vol. II, p. 455.) Thus the ancient doctrine has begun to acquire rights of citizenship in the speculations of the scientific world.

Nor would the ways of Karma be inscrutable were men to work in union and harmony, instead of disunion and strife. . . . Were no man to hurt his brother, Karma-Nemesis would have neither cause to work for, nor weapons to act through. It is the constant presence in our midst of every element of strife and opposition, and the division of races, nations, tribes, societies and individuals into Cains and Abels, wolves and lambs, that is the chief cause of the "ways of Providence." We cut these numerous windings in our destinies daily with our own hands, while we imagine that we are pursuing a track on the royal high road of respectability and duty, and then complain of those ways being so intricate and dark. We stand bewildered before the mystery of our own making, and the riddles of life that we *will not* solve, and then accuse the great Sphinx of devouring us. But verily there is not an accident in our lives, not a misshapen day, or a misfortune, that could not be traced back to our own doings in this or in another life. . . .

Knowledge of Karma gives the conviction that if—"virtue in distress, and vice in triumph makes atheists of mankind," (Dryden), it is only because that mankind has ever shut its eyes to the great truth that man is himself his own saviour as his own destroyer. That he need not accuse Heaven and the gods, Fates and Providence, of the apparent injustice that reigns in the midst of humanity. But let him rather remember and repeat that bit of Grecian wisdom, which warns man to forbear accusing *That* which—

> Just, though mysterious, leads us on unerring
> Through ways unmark'd from guilt to punishment

—which are now the ways and the high road on which move onward the great European nations. The Western Aryans had, every nation and tribe, like their Eastern brethren of the Fifth Race, their Golden and their Iron ages, their period of comparative irresponsibility, or the Satya age of purity, while now, several of them have reached their Iron Age, the Kali Yuga, an age BLACK WITH HORRORS. . . . The only palliative to the evils of life is union and harmony—a Brotherhood IN ACTU, and *altruism* not simply in name. . . .

It is a law of occult dynamics that "a given amount of energy expended on the spiritual or astral plane, is productive of far greater results than the same amount expended on the physical objective plane of existence." [Thus] the suppression of one single bad cause will suppress not one, but a variety of bad effects. And if a Brotherhood or even a number of Brotherhoods may not be able to prevent nations [in the future] from occasionally cutting each other's throats—still unity in thought and action, and philosophical research into the mysteries of being, will always prevent some . . . from creating additional causes in a world already so full of woe and evil. . . . This state will last . . . until we begin acting from *within,* instead of ever following impulses from *without.* . . . The closer the union between the mortal reflection MAN, and his [inner Divine Self], the less dangerous the external conditions and subsequent reincarnations.

Intimately, or rather indissolubly, connected with Karma, then, is the law of rebirth, or of the reincarnation of the same spiritual individuality in a long, almost interminable, series of personalities. The latter are like the various costumes and characters played by the same actor, with each of which that actor identifies himself and is identified by the public, for the space of a few hours. The *inner,* or real man, who personates those characters, knows the whole time that he is Hamlet for the brief space of a few acts, which represent, however, on the plane of human illusion the whole life of Hamlet. And he knows that he was, the night before, King Lear, the transformation in his turn of the Othello of a still earlier preceding night; but the outer, visible character is supposed to be ignorant of the fact.

In actual life that ignorance is, unfortunately, but too real. Nevertheless, the *permanent* individuality is fully aware of the fact, though, through the atrophy of the "spiritual" eye in the physical body, that knowledge is unable to impress itself on the consciousness of the false [or illusionary] personality. . . . "That which is part of our souls is eternal," says Thackeray . . . and though "the book and volume" of the *physical* brain may forget events within the scope of one terrestrial life, the bulk of collective recollections can never desert the divine soul within us. Its whispers may be too soft, the sound of its words too far off the plane perceived by our physical senses; yet the shadow of events *that were,* just as much as the shadow of the events *that are to come,* is within its perceptive powers, and is ever present before its mind's eye.

[Nirvana is discussed in the next extracts from *The Secret Doctrine.* At the time they were written, Westerners were still under the illusion that the Orientals viewed Nirvana as annihilation. Dr. Paul Tillich in his Ingersoll Lecture on Immortality at Harvard evinced a more appreciative understanding but nevertheless was unable to accept what he believed to be the Eastern view because of one difficulty:

> The Nirvana as a symbol of eternal life indicates the life of absolute fullness, not the death of absolute nothingness. The life of Nirvana is beyond all distinction of subject and object; it is everything because it is nothing definite. . . . But in order to reach this, many reincarnations are necessary. They are continuations of temporal existence and consist of punishment and suffering. Only the end of temporal existence brings full participation in eternal life. In it individualization is transcended by participation. A full recession to the ''Ground'' has taken place. But we may ask critically, how can the One be abundance if there is no differentiation within it?[66]

How *The Secret Doctrine* meets this difficulty we shall shortly see. But first some correlative statements from Blavatsky's writings may prove helpful: In *The Key to Theosophy,* in response to the teaching that Spirit loses ''its separated individuality at the moment of its complete re-union with the *Universal Spirit,''* an inquirer comments: ''If we lose even our individuality, then it becomes simply annihilation.'' The author replies:

> I say it *does not,* since I speak of *separate,* not of universal individuality. The latter becomes as a part transformed into the whole; the *dewdrop* is not evaporated, but becomes the sea. Is physical man *annihilated,* when from a foetus he becomes an old man? What kind of Satanic pride must be ours if we place our infinitesimally small consciousness and individuality higher than the universal and infinite consciousness![67]

However, to answer more particularly Dr. Tillich's objection, of ''How can the One be abundance if there is no differentiation within it?'' we quote some further statements of H.P.B. At the day of illumination, she says, ''every Ego has to remember all the cycles of his past incarnations *for Manvantaras. . . .* It sees the stream of its past incarnations by a certain divine light. It sees all humanity at once, but still there is ever, as it were, a stream which is always the 'I.' ''[68] Thus between Manvantaras, while entities are in the Nirvanic or Paranirvanic state, there can never be a complete recession to the Ground. If this happened, each new universe or Manvantara would have to start from scratch, with no fruitage or prior experience to draw upon. In her *Transactions of the Blavatsky Lodge,* H.P.B. says of Nirvana: ''Then everything becomes one, all individualities are merged into one, yet each knowing itself, a mysterious teaching indeed. But then, that which to us now is non-consciousness or the unconscious, will then be absolute consciousness.''[69] *The Secret Doctrine* explains further:]

Sooner or later, all that now seemingly exists, will be in reality and actually in the state of [Paranirvana]. But there is a great difference between *conscious* and *unconscious* ''being.'' The condition of [Paranirvana] without Paramartha, the Self-analysing consciousness . . . is no bliss, but simply extinction (for Seven Eternities). Thus, an iron ball placed under the scorching rays of the sun will get heated through, but will not feel or appreciate the warmth, while a man will. It is only ''with a mind clear and undarkened by personality, and an assimilation of the merit of manifold existences devoted to being in its collectivity (the whole living and sentient Universe),'' that one gets rid of personal existence, merging into, becoming one with, the Absolute, and continuing in full possession of Paramartha (Self-consciousness). . . .[70]

To see in Nirvana annihilation amounts to saying of a man plunged in a sound *dreamless* sleep . . . that he, too, is annihilated. . . . Re-absorption is by no means such a ''dreamless sleep,'' but, on the contrary, *absolute* existence, an unconditioned unity, or a state, to describe which human language is absolutely and hopelessly inadequate. . . . The human mind cannot in its present stage of development . . . reach this plane of thought. It totters here, on the brink of incomprehensible Absoluteness and Eternity. . . .

Nor is the individuality . . . lost, because re-absorbed. For, however limitless—from a human standpoint—the paranirvanic state, it has yet a limit in Eternity. Once reached, the same monad will re-emerge therefrom, as a still higher being, on a far higher plane, to recommence its cycle of perfected activity. . . . Some Vedantins might say: ''This is not so; the Nirvanee can never return''; which is true during the Manvantara he belongs to, and erroneous where Eternity is concerned. For it is said in the Sacred Slokas: *''The thread of radiance which is imperishable and dissolves only in Nirvana, re-emerges from it in its integrity on the day when the Great Law calls all things back into action.''* In each of us that golden thread of continuous life— periodically broken into active and passive cycles of sensuous existence on Earth, and super-sensuous in Devachan—IS from the beginning of our appearance upon this [or any] earth. It is the *Sutratma,* the luminous thread of immortal, *impersonal* monadship, on which [the spiritual essence] of all our earthly lives . . . are strung as so many beads—according to the beautiful expression of Vedantic philosophy. . . .

[The two volumes of *The Secret Doctrine* have each a large section called "Science and the Secret Doctrine Contrasted"—totaling some 350 pages. It is here that the author gathers together available scientific evidence to support the propositions presented in the work. In our next extracts she discusses the relationship between modern and occult science, and also indicates the nature of the proofs upon which, in the final analysis, *The Secret Doctrine* is supposed to rest.]

There can be no possible conflict between the teachings of occult and so-called exact Science, where the conclusions of the latter are grounded on a substratum of unassailable fact. It is only when its more ardent exponents, over-stepping the limits of observed phenomena in order to penetrate into the arcana of Being, attempt to wrench the formation of Kosmos and its *living* Forces from Spirit, and attribute all to blind matter, that the Occultists claim the right to dispute and call in question their theories. Science cannot, owing to the very nature of things, unveil the mystery of the universe around us. Science can, it is true, collect, classify, and generalize upon phenomena; but the occultist, arguing from admitted metaphysical data, declares that the daring explorer, who would probe the inmost secrets of Nature, must transcend the narrow limitations of sense, and transfer his consciousness into the region of noumena and the sphere of primal causes. To effect this he must develop faculties which are absolutely dormant—save in a few rare and exceptional cases—in the constitution of our Race. . . .

It is useless to say that the system [of occult science] is no fancy of one or several isolated individuals. That it is the uninterrupted record covering thousands of generations of Seers whose respective experiences were made to test and to verify the traditions passed orally by one early race to another, of the teachings of higher and exalted beings, who watched over the childhood of Humanity. That for long ages, the "Wise Men" of [our present race], of the stock saved and rescued from the last cataclysm and shifting of continents, had passed their lives *in learning, not teaching.* How did they do so? It is answered: by checking, testing, and verifying in every department of nature the traditions of old by the independent visions of great adepts; *i.e.,* men who have developed and perfected their physical, mental, psychic, and spiritual organisations to the utmost possible degree. No vision of one adept was accepted till it was checked and confirmed by the visions—so obtained as to stand as independent evidence—of other adepts, and by centuries of experiences. . . . The flashing gaze of those seers has penetrated into the very kernel of matter, and recorded the soul of things there, where an ordinary profane, however learned, would have perceived but the external work of form. But modern science believes not in the "soul of things," and hence will reject the whole system of ancient cosmogony. . . . [It believes] that the Universe and all in it has been gradually built up by blind forces inherent in matter. . . .

Suppose that an Occultist were to claim that the first grand organ of a cathedral had come originally into being in the following manner. First, there was a progressive and gradual elaboration in Space of an organizable material, which resulted in the production of a state of matter named *organic* PROTEIN. Then, under the influence of incident forces, those states having been thrown into a phase of unstable equilibrium, they slowly and majestically evolved into and resulted in new combinations of carved and polished wood, of brass pins and staples, of leather and ivory, wind-pipes and bellows. After which, having adapted all its parts into one harmonious and symmetrical machine, the organ suddenly pealed forth Mozart's *Requiem*. This was followed by a Sonata of Beethoven, etc., *ad infinitum;* its keys playing of themselves and the wind blowing into the pipes by its own inherent force and fancy. . . . . . . What would Science say to such a theory? Yet, it is precisely in such wise that the materialistic savants tell us that the Universe was formed, with its millions of beings, and man, its spiritual crown.

[If it were possible to ask H.P.B.'s permission to use the following selections from *The Secret Doctrine*, we wonder whether she would grant it. The subject matter, in her eyes, would probably be regarded as very sacred, and to isolate the material from its context might lead to serious misunderstandings. We trust this will not be the case. The subject first discussed concerns the teachers of infant humanity. In the early days of the human race, H.P.B. says, while it was still in its purity, a Great Being appeared among men, and after him a group of semi-divine, semi-human beings.]

"Set apart" in Archaic *genesis* for certain purposes, they are those in whom are said to have incarnated the highest Dhyanis, "Munis and Rishis from previous Manvantaras"—*to form the nursery for future human adepts,* on this earth and during the present cycle. . . . The "BEING" just referred to, which has to remain nameless, is the *Tree.* . . . "the ever-living-human Banyan". . . . from which, in subsequent ages, all the great *historically* known Sages and Hierophants, such as the Rishi Kapila, Hermes, Enoch, Orpheus, etc., etc. have branched off. As objective *man,* he is the mysterious . . . yet ever present Personage about whom legends are rife in the East . . . It is he who changes form, yet remains ever the same. And it is he again who holds spiritual sway over the *initiated* Adepts throughout the whole world.

He is, as said, the "Nameless One" who has so many names, and yet whose names and whose very nature are unknown [to ordinary man]. He is *the* "Initiator," called the "GREAT SACRIFICE." For, sitting at the threshold of LIGHT, he looks into it from within the circle of Darkness, which he will not cross; nor will he quit his post till the last day of this life-cycle. Why does the solitary Watcher remain at his self-chosen post? Why does he sit by the fountain of primeval Wisdom, of which he drinks no longer, as he has naught to learn which he does not know—aye, neither on this Earth, nor in its heaven? Because the lonely, sore-footed pilgrims on their way back to their *home* are never sure to the last moment of not losing their way in this limitless desert of illusion and matter called Earth-Life. Because he would fain show the way to that region of freedom and light, from which he is a voluntary exile himself, to every prisoner who has succeeded in liberating himself from the bonds of flesh and illusion. . . .

It is under the direct, silent guidance of this MAHA—(great)—GURU that all the other less divine Teachers and instructors of mankind became, from the first awakening of human consciousness, the guides of early Humanity. It is through these "sons of God" that infant humanity got its first notions of all the arts and sciences, as well as of spiritual knowledge; and it is they who have laid the first foundation-stone of those ancient civilizations that puzzle so sorely our modern generation of students and scholars. Let those who doubt this statement explain the mystery of the extraordinary knowledge possessed by the ancients—alleged to have developed from lower and animal-like savages . . . on any other equally reasonable grounds. . . . No man descended from a Palaeolithic cave-dweller could ever evolve such a science unaided, even in millenniums of thought and intellectual evolution. . . .

The mysteries of Heaven and Earth, revealed to the [early] Race by their celestial teachers in the days of its purity, became a great focus of light, the rays from which became necessarily weakened as they were diffused and shed upon an uncongenial, because too material soil. With the masses they degenerated into Sorcery, taking later on the shape of exoteric religions, of idolatry full of superstitions, and man-, or hero-worship. Alone a handful of . . . men—in whom the spark of divine Wisdom burnt bright, and only strengthened in its intensity as it got dimmer and dimmer with every age in those who turned it to bad purposes—remained the elect custodians of the Mysteries . . . [These beings have] *sacrificed themselves for the sins of the world and the instruction of the ignorant. . . . Though unseen, they are ever present. When people say of one of them, "He is dead"; behold, he is alive and under another form. These are the Head, the Heart, the Soul, and the Seed of undying knowledge. . . .*

When mortals shall have become sufficiently spiritualised. . . . men will *know* then, that there never yet was a great World-reformer, whose name has passed into our generation, who *(a)* was not a direct emanation of the LOGOS (under whatever name known to us), *i.e.,* an *essential* incarnation of one of "the seven," of the "divine Spirit who is sevenfold"; and *(b)* who had not appeared before, during the past Cycles. They will recognise, then, the cause which produces in history and chronology certain riddles of the ages; the reason why, for instance, it is impossible *for them* to assign any reliable date to Zoroaster, who is found multiplied by twelve and fourteen in the *Dabistan;* why the Rishis and Manus are so mixed up in their numbers and individ-ualities; why Krishna and Buddha speak of themselves as *re-incarnations,* *i.e.,* Krishna is identified with the Rishi Narayana, and Gautama gives a series of his previous births; and why the former, especially, being "the *very supreme* Brahmâ," is yet called *Amsamsavatara*—"a part of a part" only of the Supreme on Earth. Finally, why Osiris is a great God, and at the same time a "prince on Earth," who reappears in Thoth-Hermes, and why Jesus (in Hebrew, Joshua) of Nazareth is recognised, cabalistically, in Joshua, the Son of Nun, as well as in other personages.

The esoteric doctrine explains it by saying that each of these (as many others) had first appeared on earth as one of the seven powers of the LOGOS, individualized as a God or "Angel" (messenger); then, mixed with matter, they had re-appeared in turn as great sages and instructors who . . . after having instructed the [early] races, had ruled during the Divine Dynasties, and had finally sacrificed themselves, to be reborn under various circum-stances for the good of mankind, and for its salvation at certain critical periods; until in their last incarnations they had become truly only "the parts of a part" on earth, though *de facto* the One Supreme in Nature. . . .

How profoundly true are the words of H. T. Buckle, in his admirable *History of Civilization* (Vol. I, p. 256):

> Owing to circumstances still unknown (Karmic provision, H.P.B.) there ap-pear from time to time great thinkers, who, devoting their lives to a single purpose, are able to anticipate the progress of mankind, and to produce a religion or a philosophy by which important effects are eventually brought about. But if we look into history we shall clearly see that, although the origin of a new opinion may be thus due to a single man, the result which the new opinion produces will depend on the condition of the people among whom it is propagated. If either a religion or a philosophy is too much in advance of a nation it can do no present service but must bide its time until the minds of men are ripe for its reception. . . . Every science, every creed has had its martyrs. *According to the ordinary course of affairs, a few generations pass away, and then there comes a period when these very truths are looked upon as com-monplace facts, and a little later there comes another period in which they are declared to be necessary, and even the dullest intellect wonders how they could ever have been denied.*

It is barely possible that the minds of the present generations are not quite ripe for the reception of Occult truths. [The latter] will remain non-existent to the materialists of our age, in the same way as America was a non-existent myth for Europeans during the early part of the mediaeval ages, whereas Scandinavians and Norwegians had actually reached and settled in that very old "New World" several centuries before. But, as a Columbus was born to re-discover, and to force the Old World to believe in Antipodal countries, so will there be born scientists who will discover the marvels now claimed by Occultists to exist. . . .

[As to the future evolution of humanity,] it is the mankind of the New World . . . whose mission and Karma it is, to sow the seeds for a forthcoming, grander, and far more glorious Race than any of those we know of at present. . . . Pure Anglo-Saxons hardly three hundred years ago, the Americans of the United States have already become a nation apart, and, owing to a strong admixture of various nationalities and inter-marriage, almost a race *sui generis*, not only mentally, but also physically. . . . The exultant pulse will beat high in the heart of the race now in the American zone,[71] but there will be no more Americans when the Sixth [of the Seven Great Root Races] commences, no more, in fact, than Europeans; for they will now become *a new race, and many new nations*. . . . The Cycles of Matter will be succeeded by Cycles of Spirituality and a fully developed mind. On the law of parallel history and races, the majority of the future mankind will be composed of glorious Adepts . . . while . . . the failures of nature [will] vanish from the human family without even leaving a trace behind. Such is the course of Nature under the sway of KARMIC LAW. . . . The whole order of nature evinces a progressive march towards *a higher life*.[72]

❉ ❉ ❉
"Karmic Visions"

[Among certain psychics who believe in reincarnation, there is apparently a strong temptation to say with assurance "who was who" in a previous life, but it was only on the rarest occasions that H. P. Blavatsky gave intimations of this kind. One such occurs in her famous reincarnation story "Karmic Visions," written under a pseudonym. It tells of the rebirth of Clovis, the treacherous, war-loving ruler of the fifth-century Franks, who founded the Frankish kingdom, making Paris his capital. He is supposedly reborn as a monarch in nineteenth-century Germany, and although unnamed in the story, he is obviously the ill-fated and much-loved Frederick III (father of Kaiser Wilhelm of World War I "fame"). After a brief reign of ninety-nine days, Frederick died of cancer of the throat in June 1888, the very month

"Karmic Visions" was published. Queen Victoria visited him during his illness, for her eldest daughter was Frederick's queen.

On the European scene there had been no major wars for several decades—an unusual period of peace, which was to continue for another twenty-five years. Thus, European observers were encouraged to predict for humanity a millennium of peace, prosperity, and scientific progress. It is in this setting that "Karmic Visions" foretells the onslaught of World War I, and also the subsequent time when armies will have weapons to destroy millions instantaneously, as they can today.

"Karmic Visions" has been reprinted in complete form in *Occult Tales of H. P. Blavatsky and William Q. Judge*,[73] and also in a booklet containing several of her articles, where it is thus introduced:

> We can hardly pause to admire H.P.B.'s exquisite prose, in view of the dread implications of this awesome "soul-biography" for many of the nations of the present. The purpose of such searing drama can only be to contribute to a vast change of heart, to help initiate the thinking and acting that will, at long last, release from impotence those who are already filled with the final resolve of the tortured "Soul-Ego" of "Karmic Visions."[74]

The story opens in a war camp of Clovis—now a convert to Christianity. A pagan seeress is brought in as captive. Clovis savagely plunges his sword into her throat when she fearlessly makes this prophecy: "Clovis, thou shalt be reborn among thy present enemies, and suffer the tortures thou hast inflicted upon thy victims. All the combined power and glory thou hast deprived them of shall be thine in prospect, yet thou shalt never reach it!"

Next we find Clovis reborn as Frederick, and our opening selections come from the happy period of his youth and manhood, to be followed by glimpses of him while battling his fatal disease—the tracheotomy operation having left him permanently speechless. At this period he was only heir to the throne. His father had been king of Prussia, but after the Franco-Prussian War, and owing to Bismarck's nationalistic policies, was now the first emperor of a combined Germany.]

Among millions of other Souls, a Soul-Ego is reborn: for weal or for woe, who knoweth! Captive in its new human Form, it grows with it, and together they become, at last, conscious of their existence. Happy are the years of their blooming youth, unclouded with want or sorrow. Neither knows aught of the Past nor of the Future. For them all is the joyful Present: for the Soul-Ego is unaware that it had ever lived in other human tabernacles, it knows not that it shall be again reborn, and it takes no thought of the morrow.

Son of a Prince, born to rule himself one day his father's kingdom; surrounded from his cradle by reverence and honors; deserving of the universal respect and sure of the love of all—what could the Soul-Ego desire more from the Form it dwelt in? And so the Soul-Ego goes on enjoying existence in its tower of strength, gazing quietly at the panorama of life ever changing before its two windows—the two kind blue eyes of a loving and good man.

One day an arrogant and boisterous enemy threatens the father's kingdom, and the savage instincts of the warrior of old awaken in the Soul-Ego. It leaves its dreamland amid the blossoms of life and causes its Ego of clay to draw the soldier's blade, assuring him it is in defence of his country. They make a footstool of the fallen enemy and transform their sire's little kingdom into a great empire. Satisfied they could achieve no more for the present, they return to seclusion and to the dreamland of their sweet home.

But an evil day comes to all in the drama of being. It waits through the life of king and of beggar. It leaves traces on the history of every mortal born from woman, and it can neither be scared away, entreated, nor propitiated. Health is a dewdrop that falls from the heavens to vivify the blossoms on earth only during the morn of life, its spring and summer. It has but a short duration and returns from whence it came—the invisible realms.

> How oft 'neath the bud that is brightest and fairest,
> The seeds of the canker in embryo lurk!
> How oft at the root of the flower that is rarest—
> Secure in its ambush the worm is at work.

The running sand which moves downward in the glass, wherein the hours of human life are numbered, runs swifter. The worm has gnawed the blossom of health through its heart. The strong body is found stretched one day on the thorny bed of pain. The Soul-Ego beams no longer. It sits still and looks sadly out of what has become its dungeon windows, on the world which is now rapidly being shrouded for it in the funeral palls of suffering.

Even in sleep the Soul-Ego finds no rest. Hot and feverish its body tosses about in restless agony. For it, the time of happy dreams is now a vanished shadow, a long bygone recollection. Through the mental agony of the soul, there lies a transformed man. Through the physical agony of the frame, there flutters in it a fully awakened Soul. The veil of illusion has fallen off from the cold idols of the world, and the vanities and emptiness of fame and wealth stand bare, often hideous, before its eyes. [He cries aloud:] "Why, oh why, thou mocking Nemesis, hast thou thus purified and enlightened, among all the sovereigns of this earth, him, whom thou hast made helpless, speechless and powerless?"

The thoughts of the Soul fall like dark shadows on the cogitative faculties of the fast disorganizing body, haunting the thinker daily, nightly, hourly. What he now sees is a throng of bayonets clashing against each other in a mist of smoke and blood; thousands of mangled corpses covering the ground, torn and cut to shreds by the murderous weapons devised by science and civilization, blessed to success by the servants of his God.

A hideous dream detaches itself from a group of passing visions, and alights heavily on his aching chest. The nightmare shows him men, expiring on the battlefield with a curse on those who led them to their destruction. Every pang in his own wasting body brings to him in dream the recollection of pangs still worse, of pangs suffered through and for him. He sees and *feels* the torture of the fallen millions, who die after long hours of terrible mental and physical agony. He sees the old mothers who have lost the light of their souls; families, the hand that fed them. He beholds widowed young wives thrown on the wide, cold world, and beggared orphans wailing in the streets by the thousands. He finds the young daughters of his bravest old soldiers exchanging their mourning garments for the gaudy frippery of prostitution, and the Soul-Ego shudders in the sleeping Form. His heart is rent by the groans of the famished; his eyes blinded by the smoke of burning hamlets, of homes destroyed, of towns and cities in smouldering ruins.

And in his terrible dream, he remembers that moment of insanity in his soldier's life, when standing over a heap of the dead and the dying, waving in his right hand a naked sword red to its hilt with smoking blood, and in his left, the colors rent from the hand of the warrior expiring at his feet, he had sent in a stentorian voice praises to the throne of the Almighty, thanksgiving for the victory just obtained!

"What have they brought thee or to thy fatherland, those bloody victories!" whispers the Soul in him. "A population clad in iron armor," it replies. What is thy future Kingdom, now? A legion of war-puppets, a great wild beast in their collectivity. A beast that, like the sea yonder, slumbers gloomily now, but to fall with the more fury on the first enemy that is indicated to it. Indicated, by whom? It is as though a heartless, proud Fiend, assuming sudden authority, incarnate Ambition and Power, had clutched with iron hand the minds of a whole country.

The whole world is hushed in breathless expectation. Not a wife or mother, but is haunted in her dreams by the black and ominous storm-cloud that overhangs the whole of Europe. The cloud is approaching. It comes nearer and nearer. Oh woe and horror! I foresee once more for earth the suffering I have already witnessed. I read the fatal destiny upon the brow of the flower of Europe's youth! But if I live and have the power, never, oh never shall my country take part in it again!

And now the hand of Fate is upon the couch of pain. The hour for the fulfilment of nature's law has struck at last. The old Sire is no more; the younger man is henceforth a monarch. Voiceless and helpless, he is nevertheless a potentate, the autocratic master of millions of subjects. Cruel Fate has erected a throne for him over an open grave, and beckons him to glory and to power. Devoured by suffering, he finds himself suddenly crowned. The wasted Form is snatched from its warm nest amid the palm groves and the roses; it is whirled from balmy south to the frozen north, whither he speeds to reign and—speeds to die. In the moving palace [of the train] the luxurious vehicle is full of exotic plants. Its swinging monotonous motion lulls the worn-out occupant to sleep. The Soul-Ego takes its flight into Dreamland.

It travels through aeons of time, and lives, and feels, and breathes under the most contrasted forms and personages. It is now a giant, a Yotun who battles fearlessly against a host of monstrous animals, and puts them to flight with a single wave of its mighty hand. Then it sees itself in Helheim, the Kingdom of the Dead, where a Black-Elf reveals to him a series of [his] lives and their mysterious concatenation. "Why does man suffer?" enquires the Soul-Ego. "Because he would become one," is the mocking answer. Forthwith, the Soul-Ego stands in the presence of the holy goddess, Saga. She sings to it of the valorous deeds of the Germanic heroes, of their virtues and their vices. She shows the soul the mighty warriors fallen by the hands of many of its past Forms. It sees itself under the personages of maidens, and of women, of young and old men, and of children. Thus "Death" becomes but a meaningless word for it, a vain sound.

"What is my Past?" enquires the Soul-Ego of Urd, the eldest of the Norn sisters. "Why do I suffer?"

A long parchment is unrolled in her hand, and reveals a long series of mortal beings, in each of whom the Soul-Ego recognises one of its dwellings. When it comes to the last but one, it sees a blood-stained hand doing endless deeds of cruelty and treachery, and it shudders. Guileless victims arise around it, and cry to Orlog for vengeance.

"What is my immediate Present?" asks the dismayed Soul of Werdandi, the second sister.

"The decree of Orlog is on thyself!" is the answer. "But Orlog does not pronounce them blindly, as foolish mortals have it."

"What is my Future?" asks the Soul-Ego despairingly of Skuld, the third Norn sister. "Is it to be forever with tears, and bereaved of Hope?"

No answer is received. But the Dreamer feels whirled through space. The Soul-Ego finds himself as strong and as healthy as he ever was. Yes, it is no longer the tall, noble Form with which he is familiar, but the body of somebody else, of whom he as yet knows nothing. [As Skuld tells him, he lives then in a new era, long after] the instantaneous destruction by pneumo-dyno-vril of the last 2,000,000 of soldiers in the field in the Western portion of the globe.

All around seems strangely changed. Ambition, grasping greediness or envy—miscalled *Patriotism*—exist no longer. Cruel selfishness has made room for just altruism, and cold indifference to the wants of the millions no longer finds favor in the sight of the favored few. Useless luxury, sham pretences—social and religious—all has disappeared. No more wars are possible, for the armies are abolished. Soldiers have turned into diligent, hard-working tillers of the ground, and the whole globe echoes his song in rapturous joy. Kingdoms and countries around him live like brothers. The great, the glorious hour has come at last! That which he hardly dared to hope and think about in the stillness of his long, suffering nights, is now realized. The great curse is taken off, and the world stands absolved and redeemed in its regeneration!

He makes a strong effort and—is himself again. Prompted by the Soul-Ego to REMEMBER and ACT in conformity, he lifts his arms to Heaven and swears in the face of all nature to preserve peace to the end of his days—in his own country, at least.

A distant beating of drums and long cries of what he fancies in his dream are the rapturous thanksgivings, for the pledge just taken. An abrupt shock, loud clatter, and, as the eyes open, the Soul-Ego looks through them in amazement. The heavy gaze meets the respectful and solemn face of the physician offering the usual draught. The train stops. He rises from his couch weaker and wearier than ever, to see around him [honoring the new monarch] endless lines of troops armed with a new and yet more murderous weapon of destruction—ready for the battlefield.

❈ ❈ ❈

An Interview with H.P.B.

[The following are extracts from an interview with H. P. Blavatsky in London in 1887. The interviewer, Charles Johnston, was founder of the Dublin theosophical society of which Yeats and a number of other Irish writers became members. Johnston, who later worked in India, is particularly noted for his translations from the *Upanishads* and similar Hindu scriptures. Around the turn of the century he moved to New York where he taught Sanskrit at Columbia University. He also carried on various theosophical activities.

In describing H.P.B., he said: "There was something in her personality, her bearing, the light and power of her eyes, which spoke of a wider and deeper life. . . . That was the greatest thing about her, and it was always there; this sense of a bigger world, of deeper powers, of unseen might. . . . When the last word is said, she was greater than any of her works, more full of living power than even her marvellous writings. . . . Most perfect work of all, her will carried with it a sense of conviction of immortality. Her mere presence testified to the vigor of the soul."

At the close of the interview there is a discussion on hypnotism and we will quote therefrom because it bears on the present widespread use of that power in attempting to regress individuals back to previous incarnations. While H.P.B. speaks here in general terms of hypnotism, in her writings and particularly the article "Black Magic in Science,"[75] she goes more deeply into the subject.

Among the questions Johnston asked was: How do theosophical teachings benefit humanity?]

H.P.B.   "How does it benefit you to know the laws of life? Does it not help you to escape sickness and death? Well, there is a soul-sickness, and a soul-death. Only the true teaching of Life can cure them. The dogmatic churches, with their hell and damnation, their metal heaven and their fire and brimstone, have made it almost impossible for thinking people to believe in the immortality of the soul. And if they do not believe in a life after death, then they have no life after death. That is the law."

C.J.   "How can what people believe possibly affect them? Either it is or it isn't, whatever they may believe."

H.P.B.   "Their belief affects them in this way. Their life after death is made by their aspirations and spiritual development unfolding in the spiritual world. According to the growth of each, so is his life after death. It is the complement of his life here. All unsatisfied spiritual longings, all desires for higher life, all aspirations and dreams of noble things, come to flower in the spiritual life, and the soul has its day, for life on earth is its night. But if you have no aspirations, no higher longings, no beliefs in any life after death, then there is nothing for your spiritual life to be made up of, your soul is a blank. . . . You reincarnate immediately, almost without an interval, and without regaining consciousness in the other world. . . ."

C.J.   "What else do you teach, as Theosophists?"

H.P.B.   "We teach something very old, and yet which needs to be taught. We teach universal brotherhood."

C.J.   "Don't let us get vague and general. Tell me exactly what you mean by that."

H.P.B.   "Let me take a concrete case. . . . Take the English. . . . How badly they treat my poor Hindus!"

C.J.   "I have always understood that they had done a good deal for India in a material way."

H.P.B.   "What is the use of material benefits, if you are despised and tramped down morally all the time? If your ideals of national honor and glory are crushed in the mud, and you are made to feel all the time that you are an inferior race—a lower order of mortals—pigs, the English call them, and sincerely believe it. Well, just the reverse of that would be universal brotherhood. . . . No amount of material benefit can compensate for hurting their souls and crushing out their ideals.

"Besides there is another side of all that, which we as Theosophists always point out. There are really no 'inferior races,' for all are one in our common humanity; and as we have all had incarnations in each of these races, we ought to be more brotherly to them.

"They are our wards, entrusted to us; and what do we do? We invade their lands, and shoot them down in sight of their own homes; we outrage their women, and rob their goods, and then with smooth-faced hypocrisy we turn round and say we are doing it for their good. . . . But there is a just law, 'the false tongue dooms its lie; the spoiler robs to render.' 'Ye shall not come forth, until ye have paid the uttermost farthing.' "

C.J.   "So that is what the adepts sent you forth to teach?"

H.P.B.   "Yes, that and other things—things which are very important, and will soon be far more important. There is the danger of black magic, into which all the world, and especially America, is rushing as fast as it can go.[76] Only a wide knowledge of the real psychic and spiritual nature of man can save humanity from grave dangers."

C.J.   "Witch-stories in this so-called nineteenth century, in this enlightened age?" . . . .

H.P.B.   "Yes, Sir! Witch-tales in this enlightened age! And mark my words! You will have such witch-tales as the Middle Ages never dreamt of. Whole nations will drift insensibly into black magic,[77] with good intentions, no doubt, but paving the road to hell none the less for that! . . . Do you not see the tremendous evils that lie concealed in hypnotism? . . . Hypnotism and suggestion are great and dangerous powers, for the very reason that the victim never knows when he is being subjected to them; his will is stolen from him. . . . These things may be begun with good motives, and for right purposes. But I am an old woman, and have seen much of human life in many countries. And I wish with all my heart I could believe that these powers would be used only for good! Whoever lets himself or herself be hypnotized, by anyone, good or bad, is opening a door which he will be powerless to shut; and he cannot tell who will be the next to enter! If you could foresee what I foresee, you would begin heart and soul to spread the teaching of universal brotherhood. It is the only safeguard!"

C.J.   "How is it going to guard people against hypnotism?"

H.P.B.   "By purifying the hearts of people who would misuse it. And universal brotherhood rests upon the common soul. It is because there is

one [universal] soul common to all men, that brotherhood, or even common understanding is possible. Bring men to rest on that, and they will be
safe. There is a divine power in every man which is to rule his life, and
which no one can influence for evil, not even the greatest magician. Let
men bring their lives under its guidance, and they have nothing to fear
from man or devil. And now, my dear, it is getting late, and I am getting
sleepy. So I must bid you goodnight!"

And the Old Lady dismissed me with that grand air of hers which never left
her, because it was a part of herself. She was the most perfect aristocrat I
have ever known.[78]

❈ ❈ ❈

Sevenfold Nature of Man

[In our discussion thus far we have saved for special treatment the chief
teaching brought forward in theosophy as a philosophical and scientific basis
for understanding the reincarnation processes; the afterdeath experience;
how karma is carried over into subsequent births; why people in general do
not remember former lives; how that memory may be regained; and a host of
other practical problems connected with our subject. This teaching is technically known as the sevenfold constitution of man, or man's seven principles.
An illuminating presentation thereof is to be found in *The Ocean of Theosophy*
by William Q. Judge, who devotes a number of chapters to the doctrine, and
from which we will quote.

In the preface to the 1915 edition, Robert Crosbie wrote that since this
volume was originally issued in 1893 "thousands of books dealing with
Theosophy have been published by more or less prominent students of
Theosophy, but unfortunately for the public, none of these show the knowledge, grasp and range which is so evident in the present volume." It "is
found by students of *The Secret Doctrine* to be a true abridgement of that
great work and a wonderful aid in its comprehension." H.P.B.'s own evaluative appreciation of Mr. Judge is made clear in these extracts from three of
her letters, the first paragraph having been written at the time of the 1888
national convention of American theosophists in Chicago:

> *My Dearest Brother and Co-Founder of the Theosophical Society:* In address-
> ing to you this letter, which I request you to read to the convention summoned
> for April 22d, I must first present my hearty congratulations and most cordial
> good wishes to the assembled Delegates and good Fellows of our Society,
> and to yourself—the heart and soul of that body in America. We were several
> to call it to life in 1875. Since then *you have remained alone* to preserve

that life through good and evil report. It is to you chiefly, if not entirely, that the Theosophical Society owes its existence in 1888. . . .

H.P.B. would give . . . the whole esoteric brood [of theosophical students] in the U.S.A. for one W.Q.J., *who is part of herself for several aeons.*

The day W.Q.J. resigns, H.P.B. will be virtually dead for the Americans. W.Q.J. is the Antaskarana [bridge] between the two [Minds], the American thought and the Indian—or rather the trans-Himalayan Esoteric Knowledge.[79]

And now for the selections from Judge's *Ocean of Theosophy:*]

Respecting the nature of man there are two ideas current in the religious circles of Christendom. One is the teaching and the other the common acceptation of it; the first is not secret, to be sure, in the Church, but it is so seldom dwelt upon in the hearing of the laity as to be almost arcane for the ordinary person. Nearly everyone says he has a soul and a body, and there it ends. What the soul is and whether it is the real person or whether it has any powers of its own, are not inquired into, the preachers usually confining themselves to its salvation or damnation. And by thus talking of it as something different from oneself, the people have acquired an underlying notion that they are not souls because the soul may be lost by them. From this has come about a tendency to materialism causing men to pay more attention to the body than to the soul. But when the true teaching is known it will be seen that the care of the soul, which is the Self, is a vital matter requiring attention every day, and not to be deferred without grievous injury resulting to the whole man, both soul and body.

The Christian teaching, supported by St. Paul, is that man is composed of body, soul, and spirit. This is the threefold constitution of man, believed by the theologians but kept in the background because its examination might result in the readoption of views once orthodox but now heretical. For when we thus place soul between spirit and body, we come very close to the necessity for looking into the question of the soul's responsibility—since mere body can have no responsibility. And in order to make the soul responsible for the acts performed, we must assume that it has powers and functions. This threefold scheme of the nature of man contains in fact, the Theosophical teaching of his sevenfold constitution, because the four other divisions missing from the category can be found in the powers and functions of body and soul.

The universe evolves from the unknown on seven planes or in seven ways or methods in all worlds, and this sevenfold differentiation causes all the worlds of the universe and the beings thereon to have a septenary constitution. As was taught of old, the little worlds and the great are copies of the whole, and the minutest insect as well as the most highly developed being are *replicas* in little or in great of the vast inclusive original.

Mr. A. P. Sinnett, Editor of the *Pioneer* of Allahabad, the official organ of the Government of [British] India, first outlined in [the nineteenth century, the septenary] nature of man in his book *Esoteric Buddhism,* which was made up from information conveyed to him by H. P. Blavatsky directly from the Great Lodge of Initiates to which reference has been made. And in thus placing the old doctrines before western civilization he conferred a great benefit on his generation. His classification was:

1. The Body, or *Rupa.*
2. Vitality, or *Prana-Jiva.*
3. Astral Body, or *Linga-Sarira.*
4. Animal Soul, or *Kama-Rupa.*
5. Human Soul, or *Manas* [the mind and thinker]
6. Spiritual Soul, or *Buddhi.*
7. Spirit, or *Atma.*

The words in italics are equivalents in the Sanskrit language adopted by him for the English terms. This classification at once gives an idea of what man is, very different from the vague description in the words, "body and soul," and also boldly challenges the materialistic conception that mind is the product of brain, a portion of the body.

[In considering these seven principles, H. P. Blavatsky explains: "Do not imagine that because man is called septenary, he is a compound of seven entities; or of skins to be peeled off like the skins of an onion. The 'principles,' as already said are simply *aspects* and states of *consciousness.* There is but one *real* man, enduring through the cycle of life and immortal in essence, if not in form, and this is *Manas,* the Mind-man or embodied Consciousness. The objection made by the materialists, who deny the possibility of mind and consciousness acting without matter is worthless in our case. We do not deny the soundness of their argument; but we simply ask our opponents, 'Are you acquainted *with all the states of matter,* you who knew hitherto but of three?'"[80]]

Considering [the seven principles] in another manner, we would say that the lower man is a composite being, but in his real nature is a unity, or immortal being, comprising a trinity of Spirit, Discernment, and Mind which requires four lower mortal instruments or vehicles through which to work in matter and obtain experience from Nature. This trinity is that called *Atma-Buddhi-Manas* in Sanskrit, difficult terms to render in English. *Atma* is Spirit, *Buddhi* is the highest power of intellection, that which discerns and judges, and *Manas* is Mind. This threefold collection is the real man.

The four lower instruments or vehicles are shown in this table:

The Passions and Desires
Life Principle
Astral Body
Physical Body

The astral body is the guiding model for the physical one. The matter of which it is composed is electrical and magnetic in its essence. Where we find a man who still feels the leg which the surgeon has cut off, or perceives the fingers that were amputated, then the astral member has not been interfered with, and hence the man feels as if it were still on his person.

The author of *Esoteric Buddhism* gave the name *Kama rupa* to the fourth principle of man's constitution. The reason was that the word *Kama* in the Sanskrit language means "desire," and as the idea intended to be conveyed was that the fourth principle was the "body or mass of desires and passions," Mr. Sinnett added the Sanskrit word for body or form, which is *Rupa*.

The passions and desires are not produced by the body, but, on the contrary, the body is caused to be by the former. It is desire and passion which caused us to be born, and will bring us to birth again and again in some body on this earth or another globe. It is by passion and desire we are made to evolve through the mansions of death called lives on earth. It was by the arising of desire in the unknown first cause, the one absolute existence, that the whole collection of worlds was manifested, and by means of the influence of desire in the now manifested world is the latter kept in existence.

This fourth principle is the balance principle of the whole seven. It stands in the middle, and from it the ways go up or down. It is the basis of action and the mover of the will. As the old Hermetists say: "Behind will stands desire." For whether we wish to do well or ill we have to first arouse within us the desire for either course. The good man who at last becomes even a sage had at one time in his many lives to arouse the desire for the company of holy men and to keep his desire for progress alive in order to continue on his way. Even a Buddha or a Jesus had first to make a vow, which is a desire, in some life, that he would save the world or some part of it, and to persevere with the desire alive in his heart through countless lives. And equally so, on the other hand, the bad man life after life took unto himself low, selfish, wicked desires, thus debasing instead of purifying this principle.

But who or what is it that reincarnates? It is not the body, for that dies and disintegrates; and but few of us would like to be chained forever to such bodies as we now have, admitted to be infected with disease. It is not the astral body, for, as shown, that also has its term and must go to pieces after the physical has gone. Nor is it the passions and desires. They, to be sure, have a very long term, because they have the power to reproduce themselves in each life so long as we do not eradicate them. And reincarnation provides for that, since we are given by it many opportunities of slowly one by one, killing off the desires and passions which mar the heavenly picture of the spiritual man.

The inner Ego, who reincarnates, taking on body after body, storing up the impressions of life after life, gaining experience and adding it to the divine Ego, suffering and enjoying through an immense period of years, is the fifth principle—*Manas*. This is the permanent individuality which gives to every man the feeling of being himself and not some other; that which through all the changes of the days and nights from youth to the end of life makes us feel one identity through all the period; it bridges the gap made by sleep; in like manner it bridges the gap made by the sleep of death. It is this, and not our brain, that lifts us above the animal.

Let us recapitulate: The *Real Man* is the trinity of *Atma-Buddhi-Manas,* or Spirit and Mind, and he uses certain agents and instruments to get in touch with nature in order to know himself. These instruments and agents are found in the lower Four—or the Quaternary—each principle in which category is of itself an instrument for the particular experience belonging to its own field, the body being the lowest, least important, and most transitory of the whole series. The Higher Triad, *Manas, Buddhi,* and *Atma*[81] are the immortal part of us; they in fact, and no other are we. This should be firmly grasped by the mind, for upon its clear understanding depends the comprehension of the entire doctrine. What stands in the way of the modern western man's seeing this clearly is the long training we have all had in materialistic science and materializing religion, both of which have made the mere physical body too prominent. The one has taught of matter alone and the other has preached the resurrection of the body, a doctrine against common sense, fact, logic, and testimony.

[The lower, mortal quaternary, just described, is also loosely called by theosophists the personality—the mask self. And H.P.B. was once asked: "Do you really teach, as you are accused of doing by some Spiritualists and French Spiritists, the annihilation of every personality?" She replied: "We do not. . . . The *entire* annihilation of the *personal* consciousness" is "an exceptional and rare case, I think. The general and almost invariable rule is the merging of the personal into the individual or immortal consciousness of the Ego, a transformation or a divine transfiguration, and the entire annihilation only of the lower *quaternary*."[82] The personal consciousness had originally been infused into the quaternary at birth, as a projection from its parent, the Higher Self, and can only be lost if it utterly misuses its life on earth, and has no spiritual harvest to return to the Parent, for assimilation into the higher consciousness during the long heavenly afterdeath condition.

However, to the rule that the quaternary is entirely disintegrated soon after death, and hence cannot reincarnate, there are apparently some exceptions. An intriguing passage in *Isis Unveiled* provides several examples. In such cases the astral monad, or the essential elements of the personality, are reused instead of dispersing after death. Here is the passage:

> Reincarnation of the "astral monad" . . . is not a rule in nature; it is an exception, like the teratological phenomenon of a two-headed infant. It is preceded by a violation of the laws of harmony of nature, and happens only when the latter, seeking to restore its disturbed equilibrium, violently throws back into earth life the astral monad which has been tossed out of the circle of necessity by crime or accident. Thus, in cases of abortion, of infants dying before a certain age, and of congenital and incurable idiocy, nature's original design to produce a perfect human being, has been interrupted. Therefore . . . the immortal spirit and astral monad of the individual—the latter having been set apart to animate a frame and the former to shed its divine light on the corporeal organization—must try a second time to carry out the purpose of the creative intelligence.[83]

In the light of the foregoing there could be an explanation of certain puzzling phenomena uncovered in the reincarnation researches of Dr. Ian Stevenson discussed in chapter 6. One such is the reproduction of scar marks from one body to its "reincarnated" successor. The "astral monad theory" could also explain why the children Stevenson investigated remembered so many incidents from their claimed previous life. In normal cases of rebirth, the indwelling entity is furnished with a *new* astral and physical brain, and in most cases this prevents or impedes the influx of clear memories of previous lives. Judge writes in *The Ocean of Theosophy:*

> By living according to the dictates of the soul the brain may at last be made porous to the soul's recollections; if the contrary sort of a life is led, then more and more will clouds obscure that reminiscence. But as the brain had no part in the life last lived, it is in general unable to remember. And this is a wise law, for we should be very miserable if the deeds and scenes of our former lives were not hidden from our view until by discipline we become able to bear a knowledge of them.

The next extracts from *The Ocean of Theosophy* add another dimension to the problem of human reincarnational development:]

Although reincarnation is the law of nature, the complete trinity of *Atma-Buddhi-Manas* does not yet fully incarnate in this race. They use and occupy the body by means of the entrance of *Manas,* the lowest of the three, and the other two shine upon it from above, constituting the God in Heaven.[84] This was symbolized in the old Jewish teaching about the Heavenly Man who stands with his head in heaven and his feet in hell. That is, the head *Atma* and *Buddhi* are yet in heaven, and the feet, *Manas,* walk in hell, which is the body and physical life. For that reason man is not yet fully conscious, and reincarnations are needed to at last complete the incarnation of the whole trinity in the body. When that has been accomplished the race will have become as gods. . . . It was so grand a thing in the case of any single person, such as Jesus or Buddha, as to be looked upon as a divine incarnation.

It is because the trinity is not yet incarnate in the race that life has so many mysteries, some of which are showing themselves from day to day in all the various experiments made on and in man. The physician knows not what life is nor why the body moves as it does, because the spiritual portion is yet enshrouded in the clouds of heaven; the scientist is wandering in the dark, confounded and confused by all that hypnotism and other strange things bring before him, because the conscious man is out of sight on the very top of the divine mountain, thus compelling the learned to speak of the "subconscious mind," the "latent personality," and the like; and the priest can give us no light at all because he denies man's godlike nature, and reduces all to the level of original sin. But this old truth solves the riddle and paints God and Nature in harmonious colors.

Let us now consider the states of man after the death of the body and before birth, having looked over the whole field of evolution of things and beings in a general way. This brings up at once the questions: Is there any heaven or hell, and what are they? Are they states or places? We must go back to the subject of the fourth principle of the constitution of man, that called *Kama* in Sanskrit and desire or passion in English. Bearing in mind what was said about that principle, and also the teaching in respect to the astral body and the Astral Light, it will be easier to understand what is taught about the two states, *ante* and *post mortem.*

In chronological order we go into *kama loka*—or the plane of desire—first on the demise of the body, and then the higher principles, the real man, fall into the state of *devachan.*[85] After dealing with *kama loka* it will be more easy to study the question of *devachan.* The breath leaves the body and we say the man is dead, but that is only the beginning of death; it proceeds on other planes. When the frame is cold and eyes closed, all the forces of the body and mind rush through the brain, and by a series of pictures the whole life just ended is imprinted indelibly on the inner man not only in a general outline but down to the smallest detail of even the most minute and fleeting impression. At this moment, though every indication leads the physician to pronounce for death, the real man is busy in the brain, and not until his work there is ended is the person gone.[86] When this solemn work is over the astral body detaches itself from the physical, and, life energy having departed the remaining five principles are in the plane of *kama loka*.

Kama loka—or the plane of desire—is the astral region penetrating and surrounding the earth. In it the ruling force is desire devoid of and divorced from intelligence. Beyond any doubt it is the origin of the Christian theory of purgatory. But if the person was pure minded and of high aspirations, the separation of the principles on that plane is soon completed, permitting the higher triad to go into *devachan*. It is the slag-pit, as it were, of the great furnace of life, where nature provides for the sloughing off of elements which have no place in *devachan*.

During mortal life the desires and passions are guided by the mind and soul; after death they work without guidance from the former master. They are a portion of the *skandhas*—well known in eastern philosophy—which are the aggregates that make up the man. The body includes one set of the *skandhas,* the astral man another, the *kama* principle is another set, and still others pertain to other parts. In *kama* are the really active and important ones which control rebirths and lead to all the varieties of life and circumstance upon each rebirth. They are being made from day to day under the law that every thought combines instantly with one of the elemental forces of nature, becoming to that extent an entity which will endure in accordance with the strength of the thought as it leaves the brain, and all of these are inseparably connected with the being who evolved them. There is no way of escaping; all we can do is to have thoughts of good quality, for the highest of the Masters themselves are not exempt from this law, but they "people their current in space" with entities powerful for good alone.

Now in *kama loka* this mass of desire and thought exists very definitely until the conclusion of its disintegration, and then the remainder consists of the essence of these *skandhas,* connected, of course, with the being that evolved and had them. They can no more be done away with than we can blot out the universe. Hence they are said to remain until the being comes out of *devachan,* and then at once by the law of attraction they are drawn to the being, who from them as germ or basis builds up a new set of *skandhas* for the new life.

We have now approached *devachan*. After a certain time in *kama loka* the being falls into a state of unconsciousness which precedes the change into the next state. It is like the birth into life, preluded by a term of darkness and heavy sleep. It then wakes to the joys of *devachan*.

In the ancient books it is said that this state lasts "for years of infinite number," or "for a period proportionate to the merit of the being"; and when the mental forces peculiar to the state are exhausted, "the being is drawn down again to be reborn in the world of mortals." *Devachan* is therefore an interlude between births in the world. The law of karma which forces us all to enter the world, being ceaseless in its operation and also universal in scope, acts also on the being in *devachan,* for only by the force or operation of Karma are we taken out of *devachan.* It is something like the pressure of atmosphere which, being continuous and uniform, will push out or crush that which is subject to it unless there be a compensating quantity of atmosphere to counteract the pressure. In the present case the karma of the being is the atmosphere always pressing the being on or out from state to state; the counteracting quantity of atmosphere is the force of the being's own life-thoughts and aspirations which prevent his coming out of *devachan* until that force is exhausted, but which being spent has no more power to hold back the decree of our self-made mortal destiny.

The necessity for this state after death is one of the necessities of evolution growing out of the nature of mind and soul. The very nature of *Manas* requires a devachanic state as soon as the body is lost, and it is simply the effect of loosening the bonds placed upon the mind by its physical and astral encasement. In life we can but to a fractional extent act out the thoughts we have each moment; and still less can we exhaust the psychic energies engendered by each day's aspirations and dreams. The energy thus engendered is not lost or annihilated, but is stored in *Manas,* but the body, brain, and astral body permit no full development of the force. Hence, held latent until death, it bursts then from the weakened bonds and plunges *Manas,* the thinker, into the expansion, use, and development of the thought-force set up in life.

The impossibility of escaping this necessary state lies in man's ignorance of his own powers and faculties. From this ignorance delusion arises, and *Manas* not being wholly free is carried by its own force into the thinking of *devachan.* But while ignorance is the cause for going into this state the whole process is remedial, restful, and beneficial. For if the average man returned at once to another body in the same civilization he had just quitted, his soul would be completely tired out and deprived of the needed opportunity for the development of the higher part of his nature.

Everything is as real then to the being as this world seems to be to us. . . . Its state may be compared to that of the poet or artist who, rapt in ecstacy of composition or arrangement of color, cares not for and knows not of either time or objects of the world. If the person has led a colorless life the *devachan* will be colorless; if a rich life, then it will be rich in variety and effect.

[H. P. Blavatsky once wrote: "Immense growths of knowledge itself are possible in Devachan, for the spiritual entity which has begun the 'pursuit' of such knowledge during life. Nothing can happen to a spirit in Devachan, the keynote of which has not been struck during life. . . ."[87] Theosophists therefore speak of the afterdeath states as purely effect states where no new causes are engendered—similar in this way to the subjective nightly dream experiences.]

Devachan is then neither meaningless nor useless. In it we are rested; that part of us which could not bloom under the chilling skies of earth-life bursts forth into flower and goes back with us to earth-life stronger and more a part of our nature than before.

But it is sometimes asked, what of those we have left behind? Do we see them there? We do not see them there in fact, but we make to ourselves their images as full, complete and objective as in life, and devoid of all that we then thought was a blemish. We live with them and see them grow great and good instead of mean or bad. The mother who has left a drunken son behind finds him before her in *devachan* a sober, good man, and likewise through all possible cases, parent, child, husband, and wife have their loved ones there perfect and full of knowledge. This is for the benefit of the soul. You may call it a delusion if you will, but the illusion is necessary to happiness just as it often is in life. And as it is the mind that makes the illusion, it is no cheat. Certainly the idea of a heaven built over the verge of hell where you must know, if any brains or memory are left to you under the modern orthodox scheme, that your erring friends and relatives are suffering eternal torture, will bear no comparison with the doctrine of *devachan*.

The [next] question to consider is whether we here can reach those in *devachan* or do they come here. It is possible for the real man—called the spirit by some—to communicate with us immediately after death for a few brief moments, but, those passed, the soul has no more to do with earth until reincarnated. But entities in *devachan* are not wholly devoid of power to help those left on earth. Love, the master of life, if real, pure, and deep, will sometimes cause the happy Ego in *devachan* to affect those left on earth for their good, not only in the moral field but also in that of material circumstance. This is possible under a law of the occult universe which cannot be explained now with profit, but the fact may be stated. It has been given out before this by H. P. Blavatsky.

[What she stated was this: "We are with those whom we have lost in material form, and far, far nearer to them now, than when they were alive. And it is not only in the fancy of the *Devachanee,* as some may imagine, but in reality. For pure divine love is not merely the blossom of a human heart, but has its roots in eternity. . . . Love beyond the grave, illusion though you may call it, has a magic . . . potency which reacts on the living. A mother's *Ego* filled with love for the imaginary children it sees near itself [in *devachan*], living a life of happiness, as real to *it* as when on earth—that love will always be felt by the children in flesh. It will manifest in their dreams, and often in various events—in *providential* protections and escapes, for love is a strong shield, and is not limited by space or time. . . . And Karma brings sooner or later all those who loved each other with such a spiritual affection to incarnate once more in the same family group."[88] *The Ocean of Theosophy* continues:]

We cannot [consciously] reach those in *devachan* nor affect them unless we are Adepts. The Mahatma, a being who has developed all his powers and is free from illusion, can go into the devachanic state and then communicate with the Egos there. Such is one of their functions. They deal with certain entities in *devachan* for the purpose of getting them out of the state so as to return to earth for the benefit of the race. The Egos they thus deal with are those whose nature is great and deep but who are not wise enough to be able to overcome the natural illusions of *devachan*. Sometimes also the hypersensitive and pure medium goes into this state and then holds communication with the Egos there, but it is rare, and certainly will not take place with the general run of mediums who trade for money.

The whole period allotted by the soul's forces being ended in *devachan,* the magnetic threads which bind it to earth begin to assert their power. The Self wakes from the dream, it is borne swiftly off to a new body, and then, just before birth, it sees for a moment all the causes that led it to *devachan* and back to the life it is about to begin, and knowing it to be all just, to be the result of its own past life, it repines not but takes up the cross again—and another soul has come back to earth.

Everything done in a former body has consequences which in the new birth the Ego must enjoy or suffer, for, as St. Paul said: "Brethren, be not deceived. God is not mocked, for whatsoever a man soweth that shall he also reap." [Or, as the Buddha said:] "My brothers! each man's life the outcome of his former living is; the bygone wrongs bring forth sorrows and woes. The bygone right breeds bliss. . . . This is the doctrine of Karma."[89]

Karma is not a being but a law, the universal law of harmony which unerringly restores all disturbance to equilibrium. In this the theory conflicts with the ordinary materialistic conception about God as a thinking entity, extraneous to the Cosmos, who has to pull down, destroy, or punish that which he created. This has either caused thousands to live in fear of God, in compliance with his assumed commands, with the selfish object of obtaining reward and securing escape from his wrath, or has plunged them into darkness which comes from a denial of all spiritual life. The poor, who see no refuge or hope, cry aloud to a God who makes no reply, and then envy springs up in them when they consider the comforts and opportunities of the rich. They see the rich profligates, the wealthy fools, enjoying themselves unpunished. Turning to the teacher of religion, they meet the reply to their questioning of the justice which will permit such misery to those who did nothing requiring them to be born with no means, no opportunities for education, no capacity to overcome social, racial, or circumstantial obstacles, "It is the will of God." Parents produce beloved offspring who are cut off by death at an untimely hour, just when all promised well. They too have no answer to the question "Why am I thus afflicted?" but the same unreasonable reference to an inaccessible God whose arbitrary will causes their misery. Thus in every walk of life, loss, injury, persecution, deprivation of opportunity, nature's own forces working to destroy the happiness of man, death, reverses, disappointment continually beset good and evil men alike. But nowhere is there any answer or relief save in the ancient truth that each man is the maker and fashioner of his own destiny, the only one who sets in motion the causes for his own happiness and misery. In one life he sows and in the next he reaps. Thus on and forever, the law of Karma leads him. Karma is a beneficent law wholly merciful, relentlessly just, for true mercy is not favor but impartial justice.

[At this point the question naturally arises as to how the incoming entity, returning from *devachan,* receives the fruition of its past karma. How can there be assurance that he will receive no more nor no less than his exact due? What are the mechanics involved? Mr. Judge first enunciates the general laws at work and then provides an illustration of their working in a particular case.]

As a cause set up by one man has a distinct relation to him as a center from which it came, so each one experiences the results of his own acts. The effect is in the cause, and Karma produces the manifestation of it in the body, brain, and mind furnished by reincarnation.

No act is performed without a thought at its root either at the time of performance or as leading to it. These thoughts are lodged in that part of man which we have called *Manas*—the mind, and there remain as subtle but powerful links with magnetic threads that enmesh the solar system, and through which various effects are brought out. The theory put forward in earlier pages that the whole system to which this globe belongs is alive, conscious on every plane, though only in man showing self-consciousness, comes into play here to explain how the thought under the act in this life may cause result in this or the next birth. The modern experiments in hypnotism show that the slightest impression, no matter how far back in the history of the person, may be waked up to life, thus proving it is not lost but only latent.

Take for instance the case of a child born humpbacked and very short, the head sunk between the shoulders, the arms long and legs curtailed. Why is this? His karma for thoughts and acts in a prior life. He reviled, persecuted, or otherwise injured a deformed person so persistently or violently as to imprint in his own immortal mind the deformed picture of his victim. For in proportion to the intensity of his thought will be the intensity and depth of the picture. It is exactly similar to the exposure of the sensitive photographic plate, whereby, just as the exposure is long or short, the impression in the plate is weak or deep. So this thinker and actor—the Ego—coming again to rebirth carries with him this picture, and if the family to which he is attracted for birth has similar physical tendencies in its stream, the mental picture causes the newly-forming astral body to assume a deformed shape by electrical and magnetic osmosis through the mother of the child. And as all beings on earth are indissolubly joined together, the misshapen child is the karma of the parents also, an exact consequence for similar acts and thoughts on their part in other lives. Here is an exactitude of justice which no other theory will furnish.

But as we often see a deformed human being—continuing the instance merely for the purpose of illustration—having a happy disposition, an excellent intellect, sound judgment, and every good moral quality, this very instance leads us to the conclusion that karma must be of several different kinds in every individual case, and also evidently operates in more than one department of our being, with the possibility of being pleasant in effect for one portion of our nature and unpleasant for another.

No spot or being in the universe is exempt from the operation of karma, but all are under its sway, punished for error by it yet beneficently led on, through discipline, rest, and reward, to the distant heights of perfection.

Reincarnation does not mean that we go into animal forms after death, as is believed by some Eastern peoples. "Once a man always a man" is the saying in the Great Lodge [of Masters]. But it would not be too much punishment for some men were it possible to condemn them to rebirth in brute bodies; however, nature does not go by sentiment but by law, and we, not being able to see all, cannot say that the brutal man is brute all through his nature. And evolution having brought *Manas* the Thinker and Immortal Person on to this plane, cannot send him back to the brute which has not *Manas*.

By looking into two explanations for the literal acceptation by some people in the East of those laws of Manu which seem to teach the transmigration into brutes, insects, and so on, we can see how the true student of this doctrine will not fall into the same error.

The first is that various verses and books teaching such transmigration have to do with the actual method of reincarnation, that is, with the explanation of the actual physical processes which have to be undergone by the Ego in passing from the unembodied to the embodied state, and also with the roads, ways, or means of descent from the invisible to the visible plane. This has not yet been plainly explained in Theosophical books, because on the one hand it is a delicate matter, and on the other the details would not as yet be received even by Theosophists with credence, although one day they will be. And as these details are not of the greatest importance they are not now expounded.

The second explanation is, that inasmuch as nature intends us to use the matter which comes into our body and astral body for the purpose, among others, of benefiting the matter by the impress it gets from association with the human Ego, if we use it so as to give it only a brutal impression it must fly back to the animal kingdom to be absorbed there instead of being refined and kept on the human plane. And as all the matter which the human Ego gathered to it retains the stamp or photographic impression of the human being, the matter transmigrates to the lower level when given an animal impress by the Ego. This actual fact in the great chemical laboratory of nature could easily be misconstrued by the ignorant.

But the present-day students know that once *Manas* the Thinker has arrived on the scene he does not return to baser forms; first, because he does not wish to, and second, because he cannot. For just as the blood in the body is prevented by valves from rushing back and engorging the heart, so in this greater system of universal circulation the door is shut behind the Thinker and prevents his retrocession. Reincarnation as a doctrine applying to the real man does not teach transmigration into kingdoms of nature below the human.

[On the foregoing subject H. P. Blavatsky has written: ''Nature, propelled by Karma, never recedes, but strives ever forward in her work on the physical plane; that she may lodge a human soul in the body of a man, morally ten times lower than any animal, but she will not reverse the order of her kingdoms; and while leading the irrational monad of a beast of a higher order into the human form at the first hour of a Manvantara, she will not guide that Ego, once it has become a man, even of the lowest kind, back into the animal species—not during that cycle (or Kalpa) at any rate.''[90]

Regarding this last point, Judge has written of the rare exception to ''once a man always a man'': ''But of course there is the exception of the case where men live bad lives persistently for ages.''[91] Such become failures for that Manvantara, and in the next planetary evolution in a new world must wind their way upward through the lower kingdoms to the man stage again.]

[In the next selection from *The Ocean of Theosophy*, W. Q. Judge takes up the intriguing subject of the origin of mind and self-consciousness in primitive man—a persistent enigma to the anthropologist.]

Between science and Theosophy there is a wide gulf, for the present un-bridged, on the question of the origin of man and the differentiation of species. The teachers of religion in the West offer on this subject a theory dogmatically buttressed by an assumed revelation as impossible as the one put forward by scientific men. And yet the religious expounders are nearer than science to the truth, and in the tales of Cain, Seth and Noah is vaguely shadowed the real story of the other races of men, Adam being but the representative of one single race. Adam is called the first man, but the record in which the story is found shows that other races of men must have existed on the earth before Cain could have founded a city. The Bible, then, does not support the single pair theory. The people who received Cain and gave him a wife were some of those human races which had appeared simultaneously with the one headed by Adam.

The ultimate origin or beginning of man is not to be discovered, although we may know when and from where the men of this globe came.[92] Man never was not. If not on this globe, then on some other, he ever was, and will ever be in existence somewhere in the Cosmos. Ever perfecting and reaching up to the image of the Heavenly Man,[93] he is always becoming.

As man came to this globe from another planet, though of course then a being of very great power before being completely enmeshed in matter, so the lower kingdoms came likewise in germ and type from other planets, and carry on their evolution step by step upward by the aid of man, who is, in all periods of manifestation, at the front of the wave of life. The Egos in these lower kingdoms could not finish their evolution in the preceding globe-chain before its dissolution, and coming to this they go forward age after age, gradually approaching nearer the man stage.

The course of evolution developed the lower principles and produced at last the form of man with a brain of better and deeper capacity than that of any other animal. But this man in form was not man in mind, and needed the fifth principle, the thinking, perceiving one, to differentiate him from the animal kingdom and to confer the power of becoming self-conscious. Going back for a moment to the time when the races were devoid of mind, the question arises, "who gave the mind, where did it come from, and what is it?" It is the link between the Spirit of God above and the personal below; it was given to the mindless monads by others who had gone all through this process ages upon ages before in other worlds and systems of worlds, and it therefore came from other evolutionary periods which were carried out and completed long before the solar system had begun. This is the theory, strange and unacceptable today, but which must be stated if we are to tell the truth about theosophy; and this is only handing on what others have said before.

The manner in which this light of mind was given to the Mindless Men can be understood from the illustration of one candle lighting many. Given one lighted candle and numerous unlighted ones, it follows that from one light the others may also be set aflame. So in the case of *Manas,* or Mind. It is the candle of flame. The mindless men having four elementary principles of Body, Astral Body, Life and Desire [with the higher triad of Spirit-Soul-Mind latent] are the unlighted candles that cannot light themselves. The Sons of Wisdom, who are the Elder Brothers of every family of men on any globe, have the light, derived by them from others who reach back, and yet farther back, in endless procession with no beginning nor end. They set fire to the combined lower principles and the Monad, thus lighting up Manas in the new men and preparing another great race for final initiation. The lighting up of the fire of *Manas* is symbolized in all great religions and in Freemasonry. In the east one priest appears holding a candle lighted at the altar, and thousands of others light their candles from this one.

[The last selections from *The Ocean of Theosophy* focus more explicitly on why reincarnations are needed, and, as these extracts are in the nature of a summary, provide perhaps a good way to conclude our consideration of this text.]

Viewing life and its probable object, with all the varied experience possible for man, one must be forced to the conclusion that a single life is not enough for carrying out all that is intended by Nature to say nothing of what man himself desires to do. The scale of variety of experience is enormous. There is a vast range of powers latent in man which we see may be developed if opportunity be given. Knowledge infinite in scope and diversity lies before us, and especially in these days when special investigation is the rule. We perceive that we have high aspirations with no time to reach up to their measure, while the great troop of passions and desires, selfish motives and ambitions, war with us and among themselves, pursuing us even to the door of death. All these have to be conquered, used, subdued. One life is not enough for all this. To say that we have but one life here with such possibilities put before us and impossible of development is to make the universe and life a huge and cruel joke.

A human life is [around] seventy years, and out of that a large part is spent in sleep and another part in childhood. Thus in one life it is perfectly impossible to attain to the merest fraction of what Nature evidently has in view. We see many truths vaguely which a life gives us no time to grasp, and especially is this so when men have to make such a struggle to live at all. Our faculties are small or dwarfed or weak; we perceive other powers latent in us that cannot possibly be brought out in such a small space of time; and we have much more than a suspicion that the extent of the field of truth is vastly greater than the narrow circle we are confined to. It is not reasonable to suppose that either God or nature projects us into a body simply to fill us with bitterness because we can have no other opportunity here, but rather we must conclude that a series of incarnations has led to the present condition, and that the process of coming here again and again must go on for the purpose of affording us the opportunity needed.

What then is the universe for, and for what final purpose is man the immortal thinker here in evolution? The aim for present man is his initiation into complete knowledge, and for the other kingdoms below him that they may be raised up gradually from stage to stage to be in time initiated also. It is all for the experience and emancipation of the soul, for the purpose of raising [the whole of life] up to the stature, nature, and dignity of conscious god-hood. The great aim is to reach [complete] self-consciousness.

As Mind is being evolved more and more as we proceed in our course along the line of the race development, there can be perceived underneath in all countries the beginning of the transition from the animal man possessed of the germ of real mind to the man of mind complete. All around [is] the evidence that the race mind is changing by enlargement, that the old days of dogmatism are gone and the "Age of Inquiry" has come, that the inquiries will grow louder year by year and the answers be required to satisfy the mind as it grows more and more, until at last, all dogmatism being ended, the race will be ready to face all problems, each man for himself, all working for the good of the whole, and that the end will be the perfecting of those who struggle to overcome the brute [and are] governed by the God within.[94]

❋ ❋ ❋
"The Key to Theosophy"

[We close chapter 7 with a brief look into H. P. Blavatsky's *Key to Theosophy,* a volume published in 1889, and which is in the form of a conversation between an "enquirer" and a "theosophist." In addition to chapters on deity, the theosophical mahatmas, reincarnation, the postmortem states, and the sevenfold nature of man—which in the previous item we have gone into at length—the work considers the practical problems of modern education, and how theosophy can be applied in daily life. In the preface the author writes: "The purpose of this book is exactly expressed in its title . . . It is not a complete or exhaustive textbook of Theosophy, but only a key to unlock the door that leads to the deeper study." It traces the broad outlines of theosophy "and explains its fundamental principles; meeting, at the same time, the various objections raised by the average Western enquirer, and endeavoring to present unfamiliar concepts in a form as simple and in language as clear as possible." "That it should succeed in making Theosophy intelligible without mental effort on the part of the reader, would be too much to expect. . . . To the mentally lazy or obtuse, Theosophy must remain a riddle; for in the world mental as in the world spiritual each man must progress by his own efforts."]

ENQ.   I have heard you say that the identity of our physical origin is proved by science, that of our spiritual origin by [theosophy]. Yet we do not find Darwinists exhibiting great fraternal affection.

THEO.   Just so. That is what shows the deficiency of the materialistic systems. The identity of our physical origin makes no appeal to our higher and deeper feelings. Matter, deprived of its soul and spirit, or its divine essence, cannot speak to the human heart. But the identity of the soul and spirit, of real, immortal man, as Theosophy teaches us, once proven and deep-rooted in our hearts, would lead us far on the road of real charity and brotherly goodwill.

ENQ.   Do you expect that your doctrines could ever take hold of the uneducated masses, when they are so abstruse and difficult that well-educated people can hardly understand them?

THEO.   You forget one thing, which is that your much-boasted modern education is precisely that which makes it difficult for you to understand Theosophy. Your mind is so full of intellectual subtleties and preconceptions that your natural intuition and perception of the truth cannot act. It does not require metaphysics or education to make a man understand the broad truths of Karma and Reincarnation. Look at the millions of poor and uneducated Buddhists and Hindus, to whom Karma and Reincarnation are solid realities, simply because their minds have never been cramped and distorted by being forced into an unnatural groove. They have never had the innate human sense of justice perverted in them by being told to believe that their sins would be forgiven because another man had been put to death for their sakes. And the Buddhists, note well, live up to their beliefs without a murmur against Karma, or what they regard as a just punishment; whereas the Christian populace neither lives up to its moral ideal, nor accepts its lot contentedly. Hence murmuring and dissatisfaction, and the intensity of the struggle for existence in Western lands.

ENQ.   But this contentedness, which you praise so much, would do away with all motive for exertion and bring progress to a standstill.

THEO.   And we, Theosophists, say that your vaunted progress and civilization are no better than a host of will-o'-the-wisps, flickering over a marsh which exhales a poisonous and deadly miasma. This, because we see selfishness, crime, immorality, and all the evils imaginable, pouncing upon unfortunate mankind from this Pandora's box which you call an age of progress, and increasing *pari-passu* with the growth of your material civilization. At such a price, better the inertia and inactivity of Buddhist countries, which have arisen only as a consequence of ages of political slavery.

ENQ.   Then is all this metaphysics and mysticism with which you occupy yourself so much, of no importance?

THEO.   To the masses, who need only practical guidance and support, they are not of much consequence; but for the educated, the natural leaders of the masses, those whose modes of thought and action will sooner or later be adopted by those masses, they are of the greatest importance. It is only by means of the philosophy that an intelligent and educated man can avoid the intellectual suicide of believing on blind faith; and it is only by assimilating the strict continuity and logical coherence of the Eastern, if not esoteric, doctrines that he can realize their truth. Conviction breeds enthusiasm [and] Emerson most truly remarks that "every great and commanding movement in the annals of the world is the triumph of enthusiasm." And what is more calculated to produce such a feeling than a philosophy so grand, so consistent, so logical, and so all-embracing as our Eastern Doctrines?

ENQ.   Do you hope to impart this enthusiasm one day, to the masses?

THEO.   Why not? since history tells us that the masses adopted Buddhism with enthusiasm, while, as said before, the practical effect upon them of this philosophy of ethics is still shown by the smallness of the percentage of crime amongst Buddhist populations as compared with every other religion.[95] The chief point is, to uproot that most fertile source of all crime and immorality—the belief that it is possible for them to escape the consequences of their own actions. Once teach [people] that greatest of all laws, *Karma* and *Reincarnation,* and besides feeling in themselves the true dignity of human nature, they will turn from evil and eschew it as they would a physical danger. [Here, then,] are the four links of the golden chain which should bind humanity into one family, one universal brotherhood: Universal Unity and Causation; Human Solidarity; the Law of Karma; Reincarnation.[96]

A Final Gathering of East and West

Prove all things; hold fast that which is good.

SAINT PAUL
I Thessalonians 5:21

THE BUDDHA: Better than the life of a hundred years of the man who perceiveth not the deathless state is the short life of a single day of the man who senses the deathless state. Him I call a true Teacher who knows the mystery of death and rebirth of all beings, who is happy within himself and enlightened.

—*The Dhammapada*

JESUS OF NAZARETH: "Whom do men say that I the Son of man am?" And the disciples answered: "Some say that thou art Elijah, and others Jeremiah, or one of the prophets." "Verily I say unto you, Among them that are born of women there hath not risen a greater than John the Baptist. And if you will receive it, this is Elijah who was destined to come. He that hath ears to hear, let him hear."

—*Matthew* 16:13–14; 11:11, 14–15

SRI KRISHNA: The wise in heart mourn not for those that live, nor those that die. Never the spirit was born; the spirit shall cease to be never. Never was time it was not. End and Beginning are dreams! Death hath not touched it at all, dead though the house of it seems! Nay, as when one layeth his worn-out robes away, and, taking new ones, sayeth, "These will I wear today!" so putteth by the spirit lightly its garb of flesh, and passeth to inherit a residence afresh.

—*The Bhagavad-Gita (Tr. Sir Edwin Arnold)*

556

HERMES TRISMEGISTUS: The Soul passes from form to form; and the mansions of her pilgrimage are manifold. Thou puttest off thy bodies as raiment; and as vesture dost thou fold them up. Thou art from old, O Soul of man, yea, thou art from everlasting.

—Egyptian Hermetic Fragments

CHUANG-TZU (Taoist Philosopher): There was a beginning. There was a beginning before that beginning. There was a beginning previous to that beginning. Death and life are not far apart. When I look for their origin, it goes back into infinity; when I look for their end, it proceeds without termination. Life is the follower of death, and death is the predecessor of life. What we can point to are the faggots that have been consumed; but the fire is transmitted elsewhere.

—Books of Chuang-Tzu

PLATO: O youth or young man, who fancy that you are neglected by the Gods, know that if you become worse you shall go to the worse souls, or if better to the better, and in every succession of life and death you will do and suffer what like may fitly suffer at the hands of like. This is the justice of heaven, which neither you nor any other unfortunate will ever glory in escaping. Take heed thereof, for it will be sure to take heed of you. If you say—I am small and will creep into the depths of the earth, or I am high and will fly up to heaven, you are not so small or so high that you shall not pay the fitting penalty. And thinkest thou, bold man, that thou needest not to know this?—he who knows it not can never form any true idea of the happiness or unhappiness of life or hold any rational discourse respecting either.

—Laws (Book X)

RABBI SIMEON BEN JOCHAI: All souls are subject to the trials of reincarnation. They know not how they are being at all times judged, both before coming into this world and when they leave it. They do not know how many transformations and mysterious trials they must undergo. The souls must re-enter the absolute substance whence they have emerged. But to accomplish this end they must develop all the perfections, the germ of which is planted in them; and if they have not fulfilled this condition during one life, they must commence another, a third, and so forth.

—The Zohar or *Kabalistic Book of Light*

RUMI (Islam's Poet of the Koran): There have been thousands of changes in form. Look always to the form in the present; for, if you think of the forms in the past, you will separate yourself from your true Self. These are all states of the permanent which you have seen by dying. Why then do you turn your face from death? Die happily and look forward to taking up a new and better form. Like the sun, only when you set in the West can you rise again with brilliance in the East.

—Mathnawi

GIORDANO BRUNO: I have held and hold souls to be immortal. Speaking as a Catholic, they do not pass from body to body, but go to Paradise, Purgatory, or Hell. But I have reasoned deeply, and, speaking as a philosopher, since the soul is not found without body and yet is not body, it may be in one body or in another, and pass from body to body. From Spirit, the Life of the Universe, proceeds the life and soul of everything that has soul and life.

—"Bruno's Trial before the Inquisition"

BALZAC: Who knows how many fleshly forms the heir of heaven occupies before he can be brought to understand the value of that silence and solitude whose starry plains are but the vestibule of Spiritual Worlds? A lifetime may be needed merely to gain the virtues which annul the errors of man's preceding life. The virtues we acquire, which develop slowly within us, are the invisible links that bind each one of our existences to the others—existences which the spirit alone remembers, for Matter has no memory for spiritual things. The endless legacy of the past to the present is the secret source of human genius.

—Seraphita

HENRIK IBSEN: There is One who ever reappears, at certain intervals, in the course of human history. He is like a rider taming a wild horse in the arena. Again and yet again it throws him. A moment, and he is in the saddle again, each time more secure and more expert; but off he has had to go, in all his varying incarnations, until this day. Who knows how often he has wandered among us when none have recognized him?

—The Emperor Julian

RALPH WALDO EMERSON: It is the secret of the world that all things subsist and do not die, but only retire a little from sight and afterwards return again. Nothing is dead; men feign themselves dead, and endure mock funerals and mournful obituaries, and there they stand looking out of the window, sound and well, in some new strange disguise. Jesus is not dead; he is very well alive: nor John, nor Paul, nor Mahomet, nor Aristotle; at times we believe we have seen them all, and could easily tell the names under which they go.

—"Nominalist and Realist"

HENRY DAVID THOREAU: As far back as I can remember I have unconsciously referred to the experiences of a previous state of existence. * * * I lived in Judea eighteen hundred years ago, but I never knew that there was such a one as Christ among my contemporaries. As the stars looked to me when I was a shepherd in Assyria, they look to me now a New-Englander.

—Letters and Journals

WALT WHITMAN: I know I am deathless. No doubt I have died myself ten thousand times before. I laugh at what you call dissolution, and I know the amplitude of time. This day before dawn I ascended a hill and looked at the crowded heaven. And I said to my spirit, When we become the enfolders of those orbs, and the pleasure and knowledge of everything in them, shall we be filled and satisfied then? And my spirit said, No, we but level that lift to pass and continue beyond.

—Leaves of Grass

BENJAMIN FRANKLIN: Finding myself to exist in the world, I believe I shall in some shape or other always exist; and, with all the inconveniences human life is liable to, I shall not object to a new edition of mine, hoping, however, that the *errata* of the last may be corrected.

—Letters

GOETHE: I am certain that I have been here as I am now a thousand times before, and I hope to return a thousand times. When one reflects upon the eternity of the universe, one can conceive of no other destiny than that the Monads or Souls should eventually participate in the bliss of the Gods as joyfully cooperating forces. The work of creation will be entrusted to them. Man is the dialogue between nature and God. On other planets this dialogue will doubtless be of a higher and profounder character.

—"Conversation with Johannes Falk"

THOMAS HUXLEY: In the doctrine of transmigration, whatever its origin, Brahmanical and Buddhist speculation found, ready to hand, the means of constructing a plausible vindication of the ways of the Cosmos to man. None but very hasty thinkers will reject it on the ground of inherent absurdity. Like the doctrine of evolution itself, that of transmigration has its roots in the world of reality.

—Evolution and Ethics

ALBERT SCHWEITZER: By reason of the idea of reincarnation Indian thought can be reconciled to the fact that so many people in their minds and actions are still so engrossed in the world. If we assume that we have but one existence, there arises the insoluble problem of what becomes of the spiritual ego which has lost all contact with the Eternal. Those who hold the doctrine of reincarnation are faced by no such problem. For them that non-spiritual attitude only means that those men and women have not yet attained to the purified form of existence in which they are capable of knowing the truth and translating it into action. So the idea of reincarnation contains a most comforting explanation of reality by means of which Indian thought surmounts difficulties which baffle the thinkers of Europe.

—Indian Thought and Its Development

CARL JUNG: My life as I lived it had often seemed to me like a story-that has no beginning and no end. I had the feeling that I was a historical fragment, an excerpt for which the preceding and succeeding text was missing. I could well imagine that I might have lived in former centuries and there encountered questions I was not yet able to answer; that I had to be born again because I had not fulfilled the task that was given to me. When I die, my deeds will follow along with me—that is how I imagine it. I will bring with me what I have done. In the meantime it is important to insure that I do not stand at the end with empty hands.

—Memories, Dreams, Reflections

WILLIAM BUTLER YEATS: Many times man lives and dies. Whether man die in his bed or the rifle knocks him dead, a brief parting from those dear is the worst man has to fear. Though grave-diggers' toil is long, sharp their blades, their muscles strong, they but thrust their buried men back in the human mind again.

—"Under Ben Bulben"

TOLSTOY: How interesting it would be to write the story of the experiences in this life of a man who killed himself in his previous life; how he now stumbles against the very demands which had offered themselves before, until he arrives at the realization that he must fulfil those demands. * * * The deeds of the preceding life give direction to the present life. This is what the Hindus call Karma.

—Diary and other writings

MATTHEW ARNOLD: And then we shall unwillingly return back to this meadow of calamity, this uncongenial place, this human life; and in our individual human state go through the sad probation all again, to see if we will poise our life at last, to see if we will now at last be true to our only true, deep-buried selves, being one with which we are one with the whole world; or whether we will once more fall away into some bondage of the flesh or mind, some slough of sense, or some fantastic maze forged by the imperious lonely thinking-power.

—"Empedocles on Etna"

NIETZSCHE: My doctrine is: Live so that thou mayest desire to live again—that is thy duty—for in any case thou wilt live again! This doctrine is lenient towards those who do not believe in it. It speaks of no hells and it contains no threats. He who does not believe in it has but a fleeting life in his consciousness. Let us guard against teaching such a doctrine as if it were a suddenly discovered religion! It must percolate through slowly, and whole generations must build on it and become fruitful through it—in order that it may grow into a large tree which will shelter all posterity.

—"Eternal Recurrence"

REVEREND LESLIE WEATHERHEAD: The intelligent Christian asks not only that life should be just, but that it shall make sense. Does the idea of reincarnation help here? If I fail to pass those examinations in life which can only be taken while I dwell in a physical body, shall I not have to come back and take them again? If every birth in the world is the birth of a new soul, I don't see how progress can ever be consummated. Each has to begin at scratch. Each child is born a selfish little animal, not able in character to begin where the most saintly parent left off. How can a world progress in inner things—which are the most important—if the birth of every new generation fills the world with unregenerate souls full of original sin? There can never be a perfect world unless gradually those born into it can take advantage of lessons learned in earlier lives instead of starting at scratch.

—The Case for Reincarnation

GANDHI: If for mastering the physical sciences you have to devote a whole lifetime, how many lifetimes may be needed for mastering the greatest spiritual force that mankind has known? [Ahimsa—harmlessness, universal compassion.] * * * Having flung aside the sword, there is nothing except the cup of love which I can offer to those who oppose me. It is by offering that cup that I expect to draw them close to me. I cannot think of permanent enmity between man and man, and believing as I do in the theory of rebirth, I live in the hope that if not in this birth, in some other birth, I shall be able to hug all humanity in friendly embrace.

—from Indian periodicals

BOOK OF THE GOLDEN PRECEPTS (Tibetan Buddhist Scripture): Soar beyond illusions. Search the eternal and the changeless SELF, mistrusting fancy's false suggestions. The unwary Soul that fails to grapple with the mocking demon of illusion will return to earth the slave of Mara. The Self of Matter and the SELF of Spirit can never meet. One of the twain must disappear; there is no place for both.

"In order to become the knower of [the Universal] SELF, thou hast first of SELF to be the knower." Then thou canst repose between the wings of the GREAT BIRD, which is not born, nor dies throughout eternal ages. Bestride the Bird of Life if thou would'st know. Give up thy life if thou would'st live.

All is impermanent in man except the pure bright essence of Alaya—the Universal SELF. Man is its crystal ray; a beam of light immaculate within, a form of clay material upon the lower surface. Thy shadows [or bodies] live and vanish, that which in thee shall live forever, that which in thee KNOWS, for it is knowledge, is not of fleeting life; it is the Man that was, that is, and will be, for whom the hour shall never strike.

—The Voice of the Silence

What a handful of dust is man to think such thoughts! Or is he, perchance, a prince in misfortune, whose speech at times betrays his birth? I like to think that, if men are machines, they are machines of a celestial pattern, which can rise above themselves, and, to the amazement of the watching gods, acquit themselves as men. I like to think that this singular race of indomitable, philosophizing, poetical beings, resolute to carry the banner of Becoming to unimaginable heights, may be as interesting to the gods as they to us, and that they will stoop to admit these creatures of promise into their divine society.

Our lives are part of the universe and will last as long, but we must wait for the secrets of the history to come. And before we can attain to that final harmony between the universe and ourselves, to which we look forward as the consummation of existence, how much we have to learn about both! Nor can any boundary be set, any "Thus far and no farther" to the expansion of the mind. And in respect of our true natures, of what in truth we are and are capable of becoming, to what heights in knowledge, wisdom, power, the soul can climb, of all this science and philosophy have so far hardly yet spoken.

In our present life we have acquired at the most the alphabet of this knowledge; and as for the universe, of the modes of existence and happiness of what it permits, of its possibilities as an abode for progressive beings like ourselves, we know less than nothing, and no single life could teach us what they may be. Nor can any reason be advanced why we should not in the end become its masters, mold it to our hearts' desires, and make of it a home, the natural and happy estate of the immortal spirits to whom it indefeasibly belongs.

W. MACNEILE DIXON
(Gifford Lectures)

Notes

PREFACE

1. "A Game of Cosmic Roulette," *The New York Times,* November 8, 1971.
2. *More Lives Than One*. New York: William Sloane, 1962, pp. 322–23.
3. New York; Viking, 1974, pp. 47, 49, 51–52.
4. *Ajoblanco,* September 1974.
5. Quoted in the *New York Herald-Tribune,* February 27, 1944.
6. Letter to Dr. Rhine, April 1, 1948. *C. G. Jung Letters,* Princeton University Press, 1973, I, p. 495.
7. New York: William Sloane, 1947, p. 11.
8. *Time,* March 4, 1974, p. 66.

1. THE MYSTERY UNFOLDED

1. *The New York Times,* June 13, 1972, obituary of Edmund Wilson.
2. London: Edward Arnold, 1937 and 1957; New York: St. Martin's Press; Oxford University Press, 1958, Galaxy paperback. Our material is taken largely from the last chapter, "The Verdict."
3. *Yale Review,* Spring 1945.
4. As is now becoming known, Eastern religions also include the ideal of compassionate choice by the advanced soul to return to birth to assist suffering mankind (eds.).
5. On such points, Dr. Williams remarks that "the discussion lies in an area, in which there are no scientific data on which to build arguments—unless we accept as such the data presented by psychic research" (eds.).
6. Springfield, Illinois: Charles C. Thomas, 1961, chapters 20–26.
7. J. B. Pratt, *The Religious Consciousness.* New York: Macmillan, 1943, p. 225.

8. Abraham A. Newman *et al.*, *In Search of God and Immortality*. Garvin lectures, 1949–1960. Boston: Beacon Press, 1961, pp. 142–44.

9. La Salle, Illinois: Open Court, 1951, chapter 21.

10. W. R. Alger, *A Critical History of the Doctrine of a Future Life*. Boston: Roberts Brothers, 1886, p. 475. For half a century Reverend Alger's scholarly volume was the standard work on immortality in Christian circles (eds.).

11. Lafcadio Hearn, *Gleanings in Buddha Fields*. Boston: Houghton Mifflin, 1900, chapter X.

12. McTaggart, *Some Dogmas of Religion*. London: Edward Arnold, 1906, p. 125.

13. Corliss Lamont, *The Illusion of Immortality*. New York: Philosophical Library, 1959, p. 22; Leibniz, *Philosophische Schriften*, ed. Gerhardt, IV, 300.

14. New York: Harper & Row, 1958, chapter II, "Hinduism." Mentor paperback, 1959.

15. Edwin Arnold, *The Light of Asia*, Book the Eighth.

2. LANGUAGE OF MYTH AND SYMBOL

1. *The Wisdom of the Serpent*, Joseph L. Henderson and Maud Oakes. New York: George Braziller, 1963, p. xi. Dr. Henderson, whom we will be quoting a number of times in this chapter, is an American psychiatrist, who during the later years of Jung's life was one of his close colleagues.

2. New York: Harper & Row, 1971, p. 136.

3. *Hamlet's Mill: An Essay on Myth and the Frame of Time*. Boston: Gambit, 1969, pp. 4–6, 310.

4. New York: Knopf, 1976, pp. 25–26.

5. Ibid., p. 181.

6. *American College Dictionary*. New York: Random House, 1957.

7. *Encyclopaedia Britannica*, 11th edition.

8. E. V. H. Kenealy, *The Book of God: The Apocalypse of Adam-Oannes*. London, n.d., pp. 175–76.

9. Ibid.

10. E. D. Walker, *Reincarnation: A Study of Forgotten Truth*. Boston: Houghton Mifflin, 1888, p. 259.

11. E. A. Wallis Budge, *The Book of the Dead: The Papyrus of Ani*. London: 1913, I, pp. 287, 309; II, p. 353fn. Our reproduction of the Benu comes from the Papyrus of Nu. Budge's *Book of the Dead*, Chicago, 1901, II, p. 268.

12. Ibid., II, p. 620.

13. G. W. F. Hegel, *The Philosophy of History*, translator, J. Sibree. New York: Dover, 1956, p. 73.

14. New York: Phinney, Blakeman, 1860, p. 32.

15. London: Edward Arnold, 1914, pp. 161, 229 (paperback reprint: Harper Torchbook, New York, Harper & Row).

16. Hastings's *Encyclopaedia of Religion and Ethics*, XII, p. 432, article, "Transmigration in Greek Religion."

17. *The Platonic Tradition in English Religious Thought*. London: Longmans, Green, 1926, p. 11.

18. G. R. S. Mead, *Orpheus*. London: 1965, p. 192.

19. Chapter 18.
20. "Paracelsus," Part I.
21. *The Masks of God: Oriental Mythology.* New York: Viking, 1962, pp. 3, 137.
22. *The Path* (New York), January 1888, p. 295.
23. *American College Dictionary,* under "Psyche."
24. See index under Leibniz.
25. *Psychoanalysis and Religion.* Yale University Press, 1950, p. 6.
26. Op. cit., pp. 36–37.
27. Ibid., p. 36.
28. Matthew 10:16.
29. *The Masks of God: Oriental Mythology.* New York: Viking, 1962, pp. 3–4.
30. New York: Pantheon, 1954, pp. 86–89.
31. Ibid., pp. 87–88.
32. Ibid., pp. 98–99.
33. New York: Frederick Ungar, 1957, pp. 285–87.
34. Op. cit., pp. 10, 78, 82.
35. July 17, 1965.
36. *The Three Pillars of Zen,* editor, Philip Kapleau. New York: Harper & Row, 1969, p. xii of introduction by Huston Smith.
37. New York: Doubleday, 1964, pp. 106–8.
38. January 6, March 25, April 19, May 20, December 25. Saint Clement of Alexandria set it at November 17 (*Encyclopaedia Britannica,* 1959, article, "Christmas").
39. See under "Thomas Huxley" in chapter 6.
40. Erich von Däniken, *Chariots of the Gods?* New York: Putnam, 1970. Became an international best seller, and was widely featured on television in a documentary, "In Search of Ancient Astronauts."
41. Translator, Thomas Taylor, and included in his *Select Works of Plotinus* (London, 1817), but omitted in the 1912 reprint edited by G. R. S. Mead.
42. Los Angeles: Theosophy Co., pp. 3, 6–7, 8, 9–11.
43. Edwin Arnold, *The Light of Asia,* book first.
44. The expression "a new order of ages" comes from the reverse side of the Great Seal of the United States, where also the words appear "the Heavens approve," together with a drawing of a pyramid, whose capstone, significantly enough, has yet to be completed. The seal is reproduced on the one-dollar bill.
45. *On Heroes, Hero-Worship, and the Heroic in History.* Philadelphia: Henry Altemus, 1893, pp. 55–56 (lecture 1).

3.   THE RELIGIOUS VIEW—EAST AND WEST

HINDU

1. W. Q. Judge, *Echoes from the Orient.* New York: Aryan Press, 1890, pp. 35–36.
2. *Journal of Henry D. Thoreau.* Boston: Houghton Mifflin, 1949, II, pp. 3–4.
3. Moriz Winternitz, *History of Indian Literature.* University of Calcutta, 1927, I, p. 6.
4. Nicol Macnicol, *Hindu Scriptures.* London: 1938, p. xiv.

NOTES

5. A. Schweitzer, *Indian Thought and Its Development*. Boston: Beacon, 1957, p. 47.
6. New York: Harper & Row, 1953, pp. 43–44.
7. X.85.19.
8. V. 46.1.
9. I.164.30; see also I.164.38.
10. V. Raghavan, *The Indian Heritage*. Bangalore: Indian Institute of World Culture, 1963, p. 8.
11. Quoted in R. F. Goudey's *Reincarnation: A Universal Truth*. Los Angeles: Aloha Press, 1928, p. 105.
12. *Six Systems of Indian Philosophy*. New York and London: Longmans, Green, 1899, p. 41.
13. H. P. Blavatsky, *The Secret Doctrine*. London: 1888, I, p. xxx. Reprinted, Los Angeles: Theosophy Co., 1964.
14. V. Raghavan, op. cit., p. xxi.
15. A. A. Macdonell, *A History of Sanskrit Literature*. New York: Appleton, 1929, p. I.
16. Quoted in *The Secret Doctrine*, op cit., I, p. 26.
17. S. Radhakrishnan, *The Principal Upanishads*. New York: Harper, 1953, pp. 18–19.
18. Oxford, 1879, I, pp. lxv, lxvii.
19. Ibid., I, p. lxi.
20. Los Angeles: Cunningham Press, 1951.
21. This Self is the Atman. The idea of "self" in Hindu philosophy can be confusing unless it is realized that, depending on the context, it is used in at least four ways: the lowest is the personal, mortal self. Then there is the ever-evolving reincarnating ego, or soul, which in turn becomes a Divine Self when owing to ceaseless efforts toward spiritual union it is more or less merged in the Atman, the changeless, eternal, universal SELF. Beyond all this is the Absolute, the boundless, impersonal, attributeless, secondless Reality, in which all beings and galaxies are said to have their ultimate source. Johnston translates this as spirit, a rather difficult word in English as it can mean so many things! The Hindus call it Parabrahm, meaning beyond Brahma (eds.).
22. *Time*, November 8, 1948.
23. *Journals of Ralph Waldo Emerson*. Cambridge, Massachusetts: Houghton Mifflin, 1912, VII, pp. 510–11.
24. *The Nation*, May 10, 1910, p. 481.
25. *The Orient in American Transcendentalism*. New York: Columbia University Press, 1932, p. 23.
26. N. V. Guberti, *Materials for Russian Bibliography*. Moscow: 1878, II, pp. 309–13.
27. *Selected Writings of Ralph Waldo Emerson*, editor, Brooks Atkinson. New York: Modern Library, p. 660.
28. *Young India*, August 6, 1925.
29. See index for Gandhi on Reincarnation.
30. *The Five Brothers*. New York: John Day, 1948, p. xii.
31. Matthew 11:12.

32. "As I Ponder'd in Silence," *Leaves of Grass*. New York: Modern Library, p. 4.
33. *The New Yorker,* May 17, 1976, p. 50.
34. That Krishna represents the Atman, the Highest Self in us, is made manifest throughout the dialogue. In chapter 10 he states: "I am the Self seated in the hearts of all beings." However, in some of the extracts he is obviously speaking of himself as a great teacher and avatar (eds.).
35. Mahadev Desai, *The Gita According to Gandhi*. Ahmedabad: Navajivan Publishing House, 1946, pp. 128, 136. See also pp. 10–12.
36. New York: Harper & Row, n.d.
37. This analogy apparently is not to be taken too literally. Enlightened Hindus do not think of the soul or spirit as *encased* in the body. Its nature is held to be far too transcendent to vibrate in unison with gross physical matter. Hence they speak of a gradation of finer and more rarefied sheaths, or "bodies," within man, which when activated bring him *en rapport* with the immortal Self, a ray or emanation of the Universal Self (eds.).
38. This does not mean that there is an individual soul in every animate and inanimate object. Only in self-conscious man does the soul essence become individualized. Respecting the kingdoms below man, it is held that the intelligence at work therein and the cohesive power sustaining forms could not manifest without the substratum of universal soul force holding all together and impelling life to evolve into higher and higher forms of expression (eds.).
39. Raja Yoga, the "Great" Yoga, which purports to reveal how man's lower self may be united with his divine immortal Self. Hatha or body Yoga, a far lower practice, recommends physical and psychic disciplines—postures, breathing exercises, staring at a spot on the wall, etc.—to gain personal ends (eds.).
40. William Q. Judge. Los Angeles: Theosophy Co., pp. 5–7, 9, 11–13, 22–23, 30–31, 39–40, 41–43, 48–51, 93, 97–98, 103–4, 107, 124–25, 131–32. Judge's companion work, *Notes on the Bhagavad-Gita*, from the same publisher, is a particularly illuminating and inspiring discussion of the psychological aspects of this dialogue.
41. The translators explain: "When, at the end of a time-cycle, or *kalpa*, the universe is dissolved, it passes into a phase of potentiality, a seed-state, and thus awaits its next creation" (Appendix I).
42. Translators, Prabhavananda and Isherwood. New York: Harper, 1944, chapter 8.
43. A peculiarity of the mango fruit is that from the inside nut there are thousands of fine fibers spreading out from it through the yellow pulp around, and when the fruit is eaten there is great difficulty in distinguishing the pulp from the fiber. And so—using this analogy—it is difficult for the embodied entity to identify and "separate" the eternal, ever-invisible Self that permeates and sustains all forms, from the illusionary, material bodies that are transient and perishable (eds.).
44. *Sacred Books of the East,* editor, F. Max Müller, VIII (translator, K. T. Telang), pp. 230–31, 241–42, 248–49, 253, 268, 391–94.
45. Eva Martin, *The Ring of Return*. London: Philip Allan, 1927, pp. 47–48.
46. Translator, Georg Bühler, *Sacred Books of the East*, editor, F. Max Müller, XXV, pp. 166, 211–212, 501.

47. *The Eternal Verities*. Los Angeles: Theosophy Co., pp. 120–22.
48. Edinburgh: Orpheus Pub., 1921, pp. 11–19, 33, 35–38, 211–12, 238, 251.
49. *The Living Torch*, an edition of George Russell's writings edited by Monk Gibbon. London: Macmillan, 1937, p. 329.
50. London: Longmans, Green, 1894, p. 165.
51. Ernest Wood, *Vedanta Dictionary*. New York: Philosophical Library, 1964, p. 149.
52. Ibid., pp. 171–73.
53. This sentence is from the Mohini M. Chatterji translation of sloka 534 (eds.).
54. Translator, Charles Johnston. London: John Watkins, 1964, pp. 18–19, 32, 59, 67–68, 84.
55. Translator, J. Holyroyd Reece. New York: Harcourt, Brace, 1925, I, pp. 250–52.

BUDDHIST

1. Foreword to *The Dhammapada*, edited by the Cunningham Press (Alhambra, California), 1955.
2. Boston: Houghton Mifflin, 1900, pp. 208–10.
3. *Buddhist Scriptures*, translator, Edward Conze. Penguin Classics, 1959, pp. 19–20.
4. *The Religions of Man* op. cit., p. 113.
5. *Majjhima-Nikaya* 63; H. C. Warren, *Buddhism in Translations*. Harvard Oriental Series, editor, C. R. Lanman, 1909, p. 122.
6. The aggregates of the perishable personality: form, feelings, perceptions, impulses, and personal consciousness (eds.).
7. George Grimm, *The Doctrine of the Buddha*. Berlin: Akademie-Verlag, 1958, p. 5. This revised Berlin edition is in English, translated by Bhikku Silacara.
8. *Chips from a German Workshop*. New York: Scribner's, 1881, I, pp. 216–17.
9. Mark 4:11. See also Matthew 13:10–16.
10. London: *The Middle Way*, November 1957.
11. "Things he will not have taught." From *A Volume of Indian and Iranian Studies*, presented to Sir E. Denison Ross, 1940.
12. A story in the Pali Canon seems to confirm this. To quote again from George Grimm's work (p. 7): ". . . in the *Mahavagga* I, 14, a work of the *Vinaya-Pitaka* . . . we are told how thirty Brahmin youths ask the Buddha whether he has seen a woman who ran away from them after she robbed one of them. The Buddha solemnly replies by asking them: 'What is better, young men, to look for the woman or to look for your own self?' . . . they abandon everything and accept him as their teacher. . . . We must always clearly bear in mind that the Buddha taught in ancient India which was imbued with a profoundly metaphysical spirit. 'Here religions, outwardly most different, join hands *in the incessant demand to despise as perishable everything earthly, and to keep one's eyes firmly on the imperishable. . . .*' " (eds.).
13. *The Middle Way*, November 1968, pp. 125–26.
14. The Buddha states in the *Undana* (VIII iii), one of the oldest works in the Pali Pitakas: "Monks, there is a not-born, a not-become, a not-made, a not-compounded. Monks, if that unborn, not-become, not-made, not compounded

were not, there would be apparent no escape from this here that is born, become, made, compounded." (*The Minor Anthologies of the Pali Canon,* translator, F. L. Woodward. London: Oxford University Press, 1948, p. 98). Incidentally, Buddha is often accused of being an atheist. Certainly he did not accept an anthropomorphic, personal God, but in the foregoing and elsewhere plainly intimates an absolute, formless, homogeneous, eternal source to all life. A good volume that is devoted to overthrowing the atheism charge is *The God of Buddha* by Jamshed Fozdar (New York: Asia Publishing House, 1973) (eds.).

15. *The Middle Way,* article, "Fifty Years," August 1969, p. 51.

16. Francis Story, "The Case for Rebirth," Kandy, Ceylon: Buddhist Publication Society, 1959, pp. 9–11, 13.

17. Alan Watts, *Psychotherapy, East and West.* New York: Mentor (New American Library), 1963, p. 49.

18. Eduard von Hartmann, *Das Religiose Bewusstsein,* p. 344. Quoted by Carl du Prel in *The Philosophy of Mysticism,* London, 1889, II, p. 253.

19. London: Macmillan, 1905, pp. 291, 294–95.

20. Boston: Estes & Lauriat, 1885, pp. 67–68fn.

21. D. T. Suzuki, *Mysticism: Christian and Buddhist.* New York: Harper & Row, 1957, p. 122.

22. Edward Conze, *Buddhism: Its Essence and Development.* New York: Philosophical Library, 1951, pp. 24–25 (paperback: Harper Torchbook).

23. *The Field of Zen.* London: Buddhist Society, 1969, p. 58.

24. D. T. Suzuki, "Self the Unattainable." (Kyoto) *The Eastern Buddhist* (New Series), October 1970, p. 3.

25. Ibid., pp. 2, 5, 7. See also Suzuki's article "What Is the 'I'?" in *The Eastern Buddhist* (New Series), May 1971 (eds.).

26. *The Field of Zen,* op. cit., p. 51.

27. D. T. Suzuki, quoted in Christmas Humphreys's *A Western Approach to Zen.* London: Allen & Unwin, 1971, pp. 36–37.

28. D. T. Suzuki, "What Is Shin Buddhism?" *The Eastern Buddhist* (New Series), October 1972, p. 5.

29. *Essays in Zen Buddhism,* First Series. London: Luzac, 1927, p. 45.

30. *A Source Book in Indian Philosophy,* editors, Radhakrishnan and Moore. Princeton University Press, 1957, p. 636.

31. Second Supplement. Article, "Edwin Arnold," Oxford University Press.

32. *The International Review,* October, 1879.

33. See also Arthur Christy, *The Orient in American Transcendentalism,* op. cit., pp. 248–58.

34. William Peiris, *Edwin Arnold.* Kandy, Ceylon: Buddhist Publishing Society, 1870, pp. 66–67.

35. Edward Conze, *Buddhism: Its Essence and Development.* New York: Harper & Row, 1959, p. 212. Harper Torchbook.

36. Quoted in *Lucifer* (London), April 1888, III, p. 147.

37. *The Eastern Buddhist* (New Series), May 1972.

38. Paperback editions: London: Routledge & Kegan Paul, 1972. Wheaton, Illinois: Quest Books, 1969.

39. Asoka was no sectarian. His edicts affirm that he ''honors men of all faiths.'' ''If a man extols his own faith and disparages another . . . he seriously injures his own . . . Through concord men may learn and respect the conception of Dharma accepted by others.'' (*The Edicts of Asoka,* editors and translators, N. A. Nikam and Richard McKeon. University of Chicago Press, 1958, pp. 51–52.)

40. C. Humphreys, *Buddhism.* Penguin, 1962, p. 46.

41. Ibid., p. 206.

42. Alhambra, California, 1955.

43. Of the 423 slokas comprising *The Dhammapada* the last 41 are addressed to the Brahmins. In Buddha's time they enforced degrading caste practices such as untouchability, and arrogated to themselves a position that by character and behavior they did not deserve. In these verses the Buddha upholds the ancient Hindu ideal of what a member of the Brahmin caste should be. ''Not by matted locks, not by lineage, not by caste does one become a Brahamana. By his truth and righteousness man becomes a Brahamana. He is blessed'' (393).

44. W. Y. Evans-Wentz, *The Christian Doctrine of Rebirth.* Colombo, Ceylon: Maha-Bodhi Press, 1921, opening quotation. Another translation, in abbreviated form, appears in *Dialogues of the Buddha (Digha-Nikaya).* London: Pali Text Society, 1971, III, p. 222, translators, T. W. and C. A. F. Rhys Davids.

45. *Jataka Tales,* selected and retold by Ethel Beswick. London: John Murray, 1956.

46. This is based on the Indian theory of the periodic destruction and renovation of the universe, each of which takes countless years to accomplish (translator).

47. *Dialogues of the Buddha,* translator, T. W. Rhys Davids. *Sacred Books of the Buddhists,* editor, F. Max Müller. London: Henry Froude, 1899, II, p. 90.

48. *Buddhist Stories,* translator, F. L. Woodward. Madras: Theosophical Publishing House, 1925, pp. 64–68.

49. Buddha usually addressed those who lived in small, closely knit societies or groups. His words may not have been meant to apply to each casual contact made in a modern city teeming with millions of people. Conze's translation of this sentence is used. He identifies it as from the *Samyutta Nikaya* ii 189–90 (E. Conze, *Buddhist Meditation.* London: Allen & Unwin, 1956, p. 123) (eds.).

50. *The Path of Purity,* translator, Pe Maung Tin. London: Pali Text Society, 1971, p. 351.

51. Edward Conze, *Buddhist Wisdom Books.* London: Allen & Unwin, 1958, pp. 50, 54, 62, 63.

52. Chapters XV and XVI. Quoted in *Honen the Buddhist Saint* by Coates and Ishizuka (Chion-in, Kyoto, 1925, p. 98).

53. New York: New American Library, 1955, p. 134.

54. Quoted in *The Teachings of the Compassionate Buddha,* op. cit., pp. 141–42, 149, 153–54. Taken from W. E. Soothill's abridged translation, *The Lotus of the Wonderful Law,* Oxford, 1930.

55. *The Chinese Mind,* editor, Charles A. Moore. University of Hawaii, 1967, pp. 290, 292–93.

56. *A Western Approach to Zen.* London: Allen & Unwin, 1971, p. 76.

57. *The Platform Scripture*, translator, Wing-tsit Chan. New York: St. John's University, 1963, pp. 3, 20.

58. *The Sutra of Hui Neng*, translator, Wong Moul-Lam, editor, Christmas Humphreys. London: Buddhist Society, 1966, pp. 13–14.

59. Dwight Goddard, *A Buddhist Bible*. Thetford, Vermont: Dwight Goddard, 1932, p. 547fn.

60. C. Humphreys, *A Western Approach to Zen*. London: Allen & Unwin, 1971, p. 71.

61. A kalpa is an enormous period of time (eds.).

62. In Hui Neng's day, as well as before and since, some teachers of meditation instructed their pupils to watch their minds and secure tranquillity by the cessation of all thought. Ignorant persons went further and became completely passive. This frequently led to irresponsible mediumship or even insanity (eds.).

63. Pp. 13, 19, 22–23, 30, 32, 41, 62, 87, 104, 107, 108, 121, 123–24, 131–32.

64. *Japan—An Attempts at Interpretation*. New York: Macmillan, 1904, p. 208.

65. *The Rosicrucians, Their Rites and Mysteries*. London: 1887, I, p. 122.

66. Ruth Fuller Sazaki, *Zen—A Religion*. New York: First Zen Institute of America, 1958.

67. *The World of Zen*, editor, Nancy Wilson Ross. New York: Random House, 1960, p. 29.

68. *Japan's Religions*, a one-volume reprint of some of Hearn's writings, edited by Kazumitsu Kato. New York: University Books, 1966, pp. 118–19.

69. Op. cit., pp. 206, 209–10, 212–14, 216.

70. Translator, Eda O'Shiel. London: Rider, 1960, pp. 8, 15–18, 45.

71. Philip Kapleau, *The Three Pillars of Zen*. Boston: Beacon Press, 1967, pp. 155–56, 160–61, 163–64, 171, 177.

72. Quoted in D. T. Suzuki, *The Field of Zen*, editor, C. Humphreys. London: Buddhist Society, 1969, p. xiii.

73. C. Humphreys, *Basic Buddhism*. London: Buddhist Society, n.d., p. 4. Actually, Suzuki's first major works were on Indian Mahayana, written around the turn of the century during an eleven-year residence in the United States, but had a very limited circulation. Although Suzuki is associated in the public mind only with Zen, he was intensely interested in the original Indian Mahayana. He saw no essential difference between them. See Edward Conze's introduction to *On Indian Mahayana Buddhism*, already cited (eds.).

74. L. White, *Frontiers of Knowledge in the Study of Man*. New York: Harper & Row, 1956, pp. 304–5.

75. *The Middle Way*, February 1971, p. 150.

76. Edward Conze, *On Indian Mahayana Buddhism*, p. 1.

77. New York: Harper & Row, 1960, pp. vii, 77–78, 80.

78. London: Buddhist Society, 1947, pp. 27–30.

79. Quoted in *Theosophy* (Los Angeles), December 1970, p. 52.

80. Marco Pallis, *Peaks and Lamas*. New York: Knopf, 1949.

81. New York: Dutton, 1954, pp. 291, 293.

82. Wheaton, Illinois: Theosophical Publishing House, 1972, pp. 10–11.

83. *Tibet, Past and Present*. Oxford University Press, 1968, p. 205.
84. The Bardo stage, or the stage between death and rebirth, is a critical stage wherein one can either attain liberation easily or fall back into Samsaric existence (translator).
85. Translator, Garma C. C. Chang. New Hyde Park, New York: University Books, 1962, I, pp. 16, 33, 80, 102, 301, 304.
86. *Lines of Experience*, translated from the *Lam. rim. bsdus. don*. Dharamsala, India: Library of Tibetan Works and Archives, 1973, pp. 8–13.
87. *Asian Review*, April 1961. Also in booklet form published by the Tibet Society, London, 1961.
88. *Tibetan Messenger*, Winter 1973, p. 6. Published in English in Utrecht, The Netherlands.
89. London: Chatto & Windus, 1957.
90. *Meditation: The Inward Art*. Philadelphia: Lippincott, 1963, pp. 166–67.
91. New York: McGraw-Hill, 1962, pp. 50–51, 236–37.
92. New York: Longmans, Green, 1925, p. 421.
93. *The Middle Way*, August 1965, p. 90.
94. London: John Watkins, 1928.
95. *The Eastern Buddhist* (old series), editor, D. T. Suzuki, vol. 5, p. 377.
96. *The Middle Way*, November 1963.
97. Letter of Christmas Humphreys to one of the editors, dated April 10, 1974.
98. H. P. Blavatsky, *The Voice of the Silence*. Los Angeles: Theosophy Co., pp. 1fn, 3fn, 9, 14–5, 26–7, 29–30, 34, 40, 43–4, 45–6, 49, 53–4, 56, 63, 71, 78–9.

TAOIST

1. Jacket cover of Wing-tsit Chan's translation of *The Platform Sutra of Hui Neng*. Op. cit.
2. *Information Please Almanac*. New York: Simon & Schuster, 1967, p. 445.
3. Huston Smith, *The Religions of Man*, op. cit., p. 176.
4. *The Sayings of Lao-tze*, translator, Lionel Giles. London: John Murray, 1909, Introduction.
5. *Chuang Tzu, Taoist Philosopher and Chinese Mystic*, translator, Herbert A. Giles. London: Allen & Unwin, 1926, pp. 110, 121. Article, "Lao Tzu and the Taoists." *Theosophy* (Los Angeles), November 1926, p. 20.
6. Translator, Lionel Giles. Giles's complete translation is included in *Selections from the Upanishads, and The Tao Te King*. Los Angeles: Cunningham Press, 1951, pp. 89–90, 93–94, 98, 101, 110–11, 139.
7. New York: New Directions, 1965.
8. *The Texts of Taoism*, translator, James Legge. New York: Dover, 1962, Part I, pp. 187, 188, 201–2, 238, 382–83; Part II, pp. 10, 59, 61, 130.
9. New York: Viking Press, 1962, p. 427.
10. Quoted by Dr. Campbell as coming from Arthur Waley's *The Way and Its Power*, pp. 54–55.
11. *The Self in Transformation*. New York: Basic Books, 1963, p. 222. [*Chuang Tsu, Taoist Philosopher and Chinese Mystic*, translator, H. A. Giles, op. cit., p. 47, (eds).]

12. Translator H. A. Giles. London: John Murray, 1955, p. 83.
13. Ibid., p. 33.

EGYPTIAN

1. *A Peculiar Treasure*. New York: Doubleday, 1960, pp. 50, 283, 360.
2. *Hands on the Past* (Pioneer Archaeologists Tell Their Own Story), editor, C. W. Ceram. New York: Knopf, 1966, pp. 162–70.
3. J. Gardner Wilkinson, *The Manners and Customs of the Ancient Egyptians*. London: 1878, III, p. 462.
4. W. M. Flinders Petrie, *Personal Religion in Egypt before Christianity*. London and New York: 1909, pp. 43, 47.
5. *Hastings' Encyclopaedia of Religion and Ethics*, XII, p. 431.
6. New York: Philosophical Library, 1949, pp. 210–11.
7. London: Kegan Paul, Trench, Trübner, 1900, p. 265.
8. New York: *The Theosophical Forum*, March 1894.
9. Los Angeles: Theosophy Co., reprint of original 1892 edition, p. 277.
10. James Bonwick's work appeared in 1878, and was reprinted in 1956 by Falcon's Wing Press (Indian Hills, Colorado), pp. 82–83.
11. As an example here is the Gayatri, a hymn from the *Rig-Veda,* which Brahmins repeat mentally each morning and evening during their devotions: "Unveil, O Thou who givest sustenance to the Universe, from whom all proceed, to whom all must return, that face of the True Sun now hidden by a vase of golden light, that we may see the truth and do our whole duty on our journey to thy sacred seat" ("A Commentary on the Gayatri." New York: *The Path*, January 1893, p. 301). We would hardly accuse Christians and Jews of sun worship, yet in Catholicism there is frequent mention of the Sun-Christ, while in the Old Testament is the prophecy that the "Sun of righteousness" will "arise with healing in his wings" (Malachi 4:2).
12. *The Book of the Dead,* translator, E. A. Wallis Budge. Chicago and London: 1901, I, pp. 16, 145, 211; III, pp. 598, 623.
13. J. B. Priestley, *Man and Time*. New York: Doubleday, 1964, pp. 147–48.
14. S. Radhakrishnan, *Eastern Religions and Western Thought*. Oxford University Press, 1942, p. 190.
15. Saint Augustine wrote: "That which is called the Christian religion existed among the ancients, and never did not exist, from the beginning of the human race until Christ came in the flesh, at which time the true religion which already existed began to be called Christianity" (*Epis. Retrac.,* Lib. I, xiii. 3) (eds.).
16. London 1906 (reprinted 1964). I, pp. 44–46.
17. Ibid., pp. 33–34.
18. *Corpus Hermeticum* X (XI), pp. 7, 19. Eva Martin, *The Ring of Return* (London: Philip Allan, 1927). p. 34. American edition, *Reincarnation, The Ring of Return* (New York: University Books, 1963). G. R. S. Mead, *The Thrice-Greatest Hermes,* II, pp. 145, 153.
19. Translators, Anna Kingsford and Edward Maitland. Madras: 1885, pp. 25, 30–31, 34. In the Hermetic translation of Mead, Part III above is included under "The Sermon of Isis to Horus" (Mead, op. cit., III, p. 189).

PERSIAN

1. De Abstinentia iv, p. 16. *Porphyry on Abstinence from Animal Food,* translator, Thomas Taylor, editor, Esme Wynne-Tyson. New York and London, 1965, pp. 166–67.
2. *The Dabistan,* which we will shortly be considering, mentions a number of Zarathustras.
3. *God in History,* I, Book iii, Chapter vi, p. 276.
4. Khurshed S. Dabu, "Doctrine of Rebirth in Zoroastrianism." Madras: *Theosophist,* November 1966.
5. *The Vendidad,* fargard XIII, paragraph 50–51. *Theosophist,* September 1896, p. 749; *Sacred Books of the East,* editor, Max Müller. Oxford: 1880, IV, pp. 163–64.
6. *Gatha Spenta-Mainyu* (Yasna 49.11). Iruch J. S. Taraporewalla, *The Divine Songs of Zarathustra.* Bombay: 1951, p. 727.
7. Gatha 51–6. Bhagavad Das, *The Essential Unity of All Religions.* Wheaton, Illinois: Quest Books, 1966, p. 173.
8. *The Desatir,* or *The Sacred Writings of the Ancient Persian Prophets,* translator, Mulla Firuz bin Kaus. Bombay: 1818, pp. 7–9. Reprinted in 1975 by Wizard's Bookshelf, Minneapolis, Minnesota.
9. London: 1843, introduction to volume I.
10. Robert C. Cowen, "Ruin Peeks into Past of Britain." *Christian Science Monitor,* October 14, 1954.
11. S. Radhakrishnan, *Eastern Religions and Western Thought.* New York: Oxford University Press, 1940, p. 121.
12. *After Life in Roman Paganism.* New York: Dover, 1959, p. 178.
13. London: 1864, p. 47.
14. Chicago: 1910, p. iv.
15. Ibid., pp. v–vii.
16. Isaac de Beausobré, *Histoire Critique de Manichée et du Manichéisme.* Amsterdam: 1734–1739, I, pp. 245–47; II, pp. 295–299.
17. Ibid., II, p. 298.
18. *Primitive Culture.* London: 1871, chapter 12. Reprinted as *Religion in Primitive Culture.* New York: Harper Torchbook, 1958, pp. 100–101.
19. *Encyclopaedia Britannica,* 1959 edition, article, "Manichaeism."
20. Ibid.

JEWISH

1. New York: Bouton, 1877, II, p. 526. Reprint, Los Angeles: Theosophy Co., 1968.
2. New York: Putnam, 1939, p. 3.
3. *The Works of Flavius Josephus,* translator, William Wiston. Philadelphia: J. Grigg, 1835, II, p. 316. (*The Jewish War,* Book 3, Chap. 8, no. 5.)
4. Ibid., p. 251. (*The Jewish War,* Book 2, Chap. 8, no. 14.)
5. Ibid., p. 40. (*The Antiquities of the Jews,* Book 18, Chap. 1, nos. 2–4.)
6. Regensburg: 1840, III, p. 27.
7. *The Works of Flavius Josephus,* p. 250. (*The Jewish War,* Book 2, Chap. 8, nos. 10–11.)

8. Editor, James Hasting. New York: Scribner's, 1955, vol. 12, pp. 435–40.
9. New York: Scribner's, 1967, pp. 141, 143–45.
10. Oxford University Press, 1917, p. 677fn.
11. "To dust," according to the *Revised Standard Version of the Bible*. New York: Thomas Nelson, 1952.
12. *Metempsychosis*. Cambridge: Harvard University Press, 1914, p. 54.
13. London: Trübner's Oriental Series, 1880, p. 318.
14. Lewis W. Spitz, *The Religious Renaissance of the German Humanists*. Harvard University Press, 1963, p. 67.
15. London: G. Bell, 1913, p. 165.
16. Denis Saurat, *Milton, Man and Thinker*. New York: Dial Press, 1925, Chapter, "The Zohar and the Kabbalah." Saurat, *Blake and Modern Thought*. New York: MacVeagh, 1929.
17. Isaac Myer, *Qabbalah*. Philadelphia, 1888, p. 171. New York: Weiser, 1970.
18. Ibid., p. 221.
19. Op. cit., pp. 323–26.
20. Hinduism has also perpetuated this arrogant error regarding the inferiority of woman, although in Vedic times women were the equal of men, as was also the case in Egypt.
21. Quoted in E. D. Walker's *Reincarnation, A Study of Forgotten Truth*, op. cit., p. 212. Another translation is in Isaac Myer's *Qabbalah*, p. 413. (*The Zohar* ii. 99[b], *Sab-ah D'Mishpatim*, Brody edition, Cremona edition, ii, fol. 45a, col. 177–78.)
22. *Aryan Path* (Bombay), April 1935.
23. Quoted in *The Path* (New York) February 1894, p. 359.
24. Article, "Souls, Transmigration of" (*gilgul hanefesh*).
25. S. Ansky, *The Dybbuk*, translator, H. Alsberg and W. Katzin. New York: Boni & Liveright, 1926, pp. 71–72, 78–79, 81–82, 101.

EARLY CHRISTIAN

1. *Epis. Retrac.*, Lib. I, xiii, 3.
2. The word "again" may be significant. Does it imply that in a former time Jesus had also "risen from the dead"? (eds.).
3. In *The New English Bible*, Oxford University Press and Cambridge University Press, 1961, this reads: "John is the destined Elijah, if you will but accept it."
4. *Princeton Review*, May 1881.
5. *Contra Celsum*, vi, 78. Quoted in S. Radhakrishnan's *Eastern Religions and Western Thought*, op. cit., p. 343.
6. See opening section of the "Later Christian" section of this chapter.
7. "In this age," according to *The New English Bible*, Oxford University Press and Cambridge Univeristy Press, 1961.
8. Sir Edwin Arnold, *The Light of Asia*, Book the Eighth.
9. E. D. Walker, op. cit., p. 225.
10. Beausobré, op. cit., II, p. 493.
11. 1959 edition.
12. *Ante-Nicene Christian Library*, editors, Alexander Roberts and James Donaldson. Edinburgh: Clark, 1867, II, pp. 92–93.

13. Ibid., IV, p. 22.
14. *Patrologiae-Graeca*, IX, p. 706.
15. E. D. Walker, op. cit., p. 232.
16. W. R. Inge, *The Philosophy of Plotinus*. London: Longmans, Green, 1948, II, p. 17.
17. The bracketed insertions are those of the translator.
18. *Ante-Nicene Christian Library*, XV, pp. 496–97.
19. *Phaedo* (81) and (107).
20. *Republic*, X (615).
21. *Aeneid*, VI (758).
22. Chapter 6.
23. Annie Besant, *Reincarnation*. Adyar, Madras: Theosophical Publishing House, 1948, pp. 83–85.
24. 1959 edition.
25. Eleventh edition.
26. W. R. Inge, *The Philosophy of Plotinus*. London: Longmans, Green, 1948, II, pp. 17, 19.
27. *A Select Library of the Nicene and Post-Nicene Fathers of the Christian Church*, Second Series, editors, Philip Schaff and Henry Wace. New York: Scribner's, 1900, III, p. 508.
28. Article, "Metempsychosis," 1913 edition.
29. Beausobré, op. cit., II, p. 492.
30. *Metempsychosis*. Cambridge, Massachusetts: Harvard University Press, 1914, p. 50.
31. *Encyclopaedia Britannica*, 1959 edition, article, "Origen."
32. See *Christian Platonists of Alexandria* by the Reverend Charles Bigg. Oxford University Press, 1886.
33. *Origen and Greek Patristic Theology*. New York: 1901, p. 215.
34. W. R. Inge, *The Platonic Tradition in English Religious Thought*. London: Longmans, Green, 1926, p. 100.
35. *Encyclopaedia Britannica*, 1959 edition, article "Origen."
36. *The Holy Fire*. New York: Harper and Row, 1957, p. 49.
37. *Ante-Nicene Christian Library*, X, p. 432.
38. Book III, Chap. 5, No. 4. *Ante-Nicene Christian Library*, X, pp. 256–58.
39. *A Select Library of the Nicene and Post-Nicene Fathers of the Christian Church*, Second Series, VI, Letter CXXIV, Part 15, p. 244.
40. Ibid., Second Series, VII, pp. 453–54.
41. W. R. Inge, *The Platonic Tradition in English Religious Thought*, p. 28.
42. New York: Macmillan, 1958, pp. 212–15, 217.
43. New York: Appleton, 1874, pp. 62, 64.
44. Book I. Translator, Edward B. Pusey, *Harvard Classics*. New York: P. F. Collier, 1909, VII, p. 9.
45. Eva Martin, op. cit., p. 80.
46. Book XII, chapter 15, no. 24. *A Select Library of the Nicene and Post-Nicene Fathers*, First Series, III, p. 164.
47. The Platonists and their successors did not believe that the soul returned immediately after death. As mentioned earlier Plato spoke of a thousand-year cycle between incarnations (eds.).

48. Book X, chapter 30. *A Select Library of the Nicene and Post-Nicene Fathers,* First Series, II, p. 200.
49. Walker, op. cit., p. 236.
50. Beausobré, op. cit., II, p. 493.
51. Eva Martin, op. cit., pp. 79–80.
52. Beausobré, op. cit., II, p. 493.
53. *Library of Christian Classics,* Philadelphia: Westminster Press, IV, editor, William Telfer, pp. 282, 289, 446.
54. *Ante-Nicene Christian Library,* V, pp. 245–50.
55. Ibid., XXI, pp. 184–85.
56. *The Octavius,* translator, J. H. Freese. New York: Macmillan, 1918, p. 89.
57. See citations in *Reincarnation in World Thought,* editors, J. Head and S. L. Cranston. New York: Julian Press, 1961, p. 108.
58. Simon's reincarnation views are indicated in the *Encyclopaedia of Religion and Ethics,* editor, James Hasting, XI, p. 517; XII, p. 437.
59. Edward Gibbon, *The History of the Decline and Fall of the Roman Empire.* London: John Murray, 1854, II, p. 163.
60. S. Radhakrishnan, *Eastern Religions and Western Thought,* op. cit., p. 200.
61. London: John Watkins, 1918.
62. *Psychology and Alchemy.* New York: Pantheon, 1953, p. 35.
63. *VII Sermones ad Mortuos.* London: John Watkins, 1967.
64. *Aion, Researches into the Phenomenology of the Self.* New York: Pantheon, 1959, pp. 190, 196, 222.
65. The Church Fathers Saint Clement and Origen both testified to an esoteric lining to Christianity. See W. R. Inge, *The Philosophy of Plotinus,* London: Longmans, Green, 1948, II, p. 17. Origen's *Contra Celsum,* I, vii, included in the *Ante-Nicene Christian Library,* editors, Alexander Roberts and James Donaldson. Edinburgh: Clark, 1867, X, pp. 403–4.
66. London: John Murray, 1882. Article, "Gnosticism," II, p. 679.
67. Ibid., Article, "Irenaeus," III, p. 269.
68. Eusebius, *Hist. Eccles.,* iv, 7.
69. *Encyclopaedia Britannica,* 1959 edition, article, "Gnosticism."
70. New York: University Books, 1960, p. 142.
71. London: John M. Watkins, revised edition, 1921, p. xlv.
72. Pp. 293, 315, 320, 322–23.
73. H. Charles Puech, Professor at the Collège de France, *Les nouveaux écrits gnostiques découverts en Haute-Egypte.*
74. An ancient Gnostic sect still surviving in southern Mesopotamia (eds.).
75. See under "Islam" in this chapter.
76. 1913 edition IV, pp. 308–9; XI, p. 311.
77. There has never been a papal encyclical explicitly against reincarnation. See Mentor Religious Classic, *The Papal Encyclicals in Their Historic Context,* by Anne Fremantle.
78. *The Columbia Encyclopedia,* 1956, 2nd edition, "Orthodox Eastern Church."
79. *The Catholic Encylopaedia,* 1913 edition, IV, p. 309.
80. *The Cambridge Medieval History.* Cambridge: 1911–1932, II, p. 47.
81. XI, p. 311. The section on Origen was written by Father Ferdinand Prat, S. J., member of the Biblical Commission, Collège Saint Michel, Brussels.

82. Op. cit., p. 178.

83. New York: Viking, 1964, p. 418.

84. *Encyclopaedia Britannica*, 9th edition, XIII, p. 796.

85. The anathemas in their entirety have been reprinted in *Reincarnation, An East-West Anthology*, editors, J. Head and S. L. Cranston. New York: Julian Press, 1961, pp. 321–25; taken from *A Select Library of Nicene and Post-Nicene Fathers*, Second Series, XIV, pp. 318–20.

86. Editor, F. L. Cross. Oxford University Press, 1957, "Metempsychosis."

87. James M. Robinson, *The Nag Hammadi Codices*. Claremont, California: Institute for Antiquity and Christianity, 1974.

88. New York: Harper, 1888, I, p. 89. Reprinted (1955) in the Scholars Classic Series published by Russell & Russell, New York.

89. *Encyclopaedia Britannica* (1959), "Manichaeism."

90. *Encyclopaedia Britannica*, 9th edition, "Waldeneses."

91. J. V. Görres, *Die Christliche Mystik*. Regensburg: 1840, III, p. 31.

92. London: Watts, 1948, p. 2.

93. *Webster's New International Dictionary*, 2nd. edition, "Cathari."

94. Pp. 15 and 26.

95. Op. cit., I, pp. 52, 61.

96. *Encyclopaedia Britannica*, 11th edition, "Cathars."

97. Op. cit., p. 9.

98. Op. cit., I, p. 89.

99. *Massacre at Montésequr: A History of the Albigensian Crusade*. New York: Pantheon, 1961, p. 35.

100. Op. cit., I, p. 67; II, p. 110.

101. Lecture, "Reincarnation and the Practice of Medicine," delivered on March 25, 1969, before the College of Psychic Science, London. (Dr. Guirdham is a psychiatrist and was chief psychiatrist of Bath Hospital, England.)

102. London: Spearman, 1970, p. 29.

103. As to the massacre of the Albigenses, Dr. William Alva Gifford gives this background in *The Story of the Faith:* "The Albigenses were protected by the powerful Count Raymond of Toulouse, and had enjoyed religious freedom so long that the local clergy feared to discipline them. Pope Innocent III discerned in their individualism a menace to the Catholic Church. The essence of heresy is that one chooses doctrine for oneself. Innocent therefore summoned the faithful of Europe to a crusade against the Albigenses. Men came from everywhere. Simon de Montfort, Earl of Leicester, gave leadership. The Albigenses were crushed; Count Raymond submitted; and out of the crusade arose the Holy Tribunal of the Inquisition, whose sole business was to deal with heresy" (op. cit., pp. 282–83). Not only was the civilization of the Albigenses destroyed but entire populations (men, women, and children) put to the sword by soldiers and armed clerics, mostly from northern France. At the taking of Béziers (July 22, 1209), the Abbot Arnold, being asked how the heretics were to be distinguished from the faithful, replied: "Slay all; God will know his own" (*Encyclopaedia Britannica*, 9th edition, "Albigenses").

104. M'Clintock and Strong's *Cyclopaedia of Biblical, Theological and Ecclesiastical Literature*, "Transmigration."

105. University of California Press, 1967.

ISLAMIC

1. Gul. de Rubruquis, *Rec. des Voy. Soc., de Géographie de Paris*, IV, p. 356. Cited by E. B. Tylor in *Religion in Primitive Culture*. New York: Harper Torchbook, 1958, p. 101fn.
2. Pamphlet no. 2 in the Buddhist Chronicle Series. Ceylon: Maha Bodhi Press, 1921.
3. *Theosophy in Pakistan* (Karachi), October–December 1965.
4. The Imam is one of a succession of religious leaders believed by the Shiites to be divinely inspired. "The Imam is supposed to be a reincarnation of a divinity formerly manifest in Mahomet," according to the *New Oxford Dictionary*, "Reincarnation" (eds.).
5. G. F. Moore, *Metempsychosis*, op. cit., pp. 52–54.
6. London: 1902.
7. Nadarbeg K. Mirza, *Reincarnation and Islam*. Madras: 1927.
8. *The Sayings of Mohammed*. Quoted in *Reincarnation and Islam*, pp. 4–5.
9. *Theosophy in Pakistan*, October–December 1964; January–March 1965.
10. Ibid., October–December 1965.
11. *The Gnostics and Their Remains*. London: 1864, p. 185.
12. New York: Doubleday, 1964, pp. 242–43.
13. Translators, Shea and Troyer, London: 1843, III, pp. 149–50. For later information on *The Dabistan* and its author, see A. V. Williams Jackson's introduction to the abridged edition published in the Universal Classics Library, editor, A. P. C. Griffin, Washington, D.C., 1901.
14. Op. cit.
15. Madras, 1927, pp. 57–58.
16. Pp. 115–16.
17. R. A. Nicholson, *Rumi, Poet and Mystic*. London: Allen & Unwin, 1950, p. 103.
18. Translator, M. H. Abdi. *Theosophy in Pakistan*, January–March 1965, p. 13.
19. Mizra, *Reincarnation and Islam*, pp. 55–56.
20. Ibid.
21. Theodore Besterman, *Collected Papers on the Paranormal*. New York: Garrett, 1968, pp. 8–9, 11.

LATER CHRISTIAN

1. See subsections "The Middle Ages" and "Renaissance and Reformation."
2. New York: 1878, p. 476.
3. Editors, Head and Cranston. New York: Julian Press, 1961, Parts 1 and 2.
4. 1959 edition, article, "Pre-existence."
5. J. M. E. McTaggart, *The Nature of Existence*. Cambridge University Press, 1927, II, p. 383fn.
6. Cited in the item for Franklin in chapter 5.
7. Martin, op. cit., p. 217.
8. London: SCM Press, 1961, p. 137.
9. Loran Hurnscot, A Prison, A Paradise. New York: Viking, 1959, p. 263.
10. *The Problem of Pain*. London: Geoffrey Bles, 1941, p. 112.
11. *The Middle Way* (London), August 1974, p. 53. Adapted from *The Book of Kindred Sayings (Samyutta-Nikaya)*, translator, Mrs. Rhys Davis. London: Pali Text Society, 1971, Part I, pp. 125–26.

12. London, 1662, pp. 51–52, 99, 101–3. Republished with annotations by Dr. Henry More in 1682.

13. Boston: Roberts Bros., 1874, p. 241.

14. Milan: Fratelli Bocca, 1911.

15. The Catholic theologian Baron Friedrich von Hügel also speaks of the archbishop's "acceptance of a doctrine of successive earthly lives for human souls." See *Essays and Addresses on the Philosophy of Religion*. New York: Dutton, 1921, p. 232.

16. W. Lutoslawski, *Pre-Existence and Reincarnation*. London: Allen & Unwin, 1928, pp. 28–29.

17. It includes a bibliography comprising 4,894 books relating to the nature, origin, and destiny of the soul, compiled by Ezra Abbot, librarian of Harvard University. The complete work has been reprinted in the 1970s by Greenwood (Westport, Connecticut) in a two-volume edition (eds.).

18. New York: 1878, pp. 736, 739.

19. Quoted in *Reincarnation as a Phenomenon of Metamorphosis* by Guenther Wachsmuth. New York: Anthroposophic Press, 1937, p. 7.

20. Richard Wilhelm, "Reincarnation." *The Theosophical Path* (Point Loma, California), January 1924, pp. 37–45. Translation printed in said periodical with the permission of Dr. Wilhelm.

21. Paris: YMCA Press, n.d.

22. Boston: Beacon Press, 1952, pp. 222–23.

23. September 25, 1965.

24. "The Second Maurice Elliott Memorial Lecture," November 30, 1961. London: Churches' Fellowship for Psychical Study, pp. 8–9.

25. *Toronto Daily Star*, October 16, 1965.

26. Available from the publisher, M. C. Peto, 4 Oakene, Burgh Heath, Surrey, England.

27. London: Hodder & Stoughton, 1965; Nashville, Tennessee: Abingdon-Cokesbury Press, 1965.

4. REINCARNATION AMONG THE EARLY RACES

1. Quoted in the broadcast lecture "The Author of 'The Golden Bough,' " delivered over BBC by the Reverend Victor White, and published in *The Listener*, January 21, 1954, p. 137.

2. Lord Raglan, *The Temple and the House*. London and New York: 1964, pp. 3–4.

3. *The Belief in Immortality and the Worship of the Dead*, I, p. 29.

4. "Varities of Belief in Reincarnation." *The Hibbert Journal*, April 1957.

5. *The Canadian Theosophist*, January–February 1962.

6. London: Lutterworth, 1947, p. 103.

7. *Woman's Mysteries of a Primitive Culture*. London: Cassell, 1915, pp. 39–40.

8. Ibid., pp. 4–5.

9. New York: Grove Press, 1961, p. 190.

10. "Belief in Rebirth among the Natives of Africa." Theodore Besterman, *Collected Papers on the Paranormal*. New York: Garrett, 1968, pp. 22–59, particularly map, p. 23.

11. *Religion in Primitive Culture*, 1958, edition, p. 103.

12. *Indian Philosophy*. London: Allen & Unwin, 1929, I, p. 251.
13. Quoted in Bhagavan Das's *The Essential Unity of All Religions*. Wheaton, Illinois: Quest Books, 1966, pp. 193–96. Taken from P. G. Bowen's article, "The Ancient Wisdom in Africa," *The Theosophist* (Madras), August 1927.
14. London: Macmillan, 1904, p. 145.
15. *The Belief in Immortality and the Worship of the Dead*, I, p. 127. Later research supports the presumption raised by Frazer. See *Ancient Religions*, editor, Vergilius Ferm. New York: Philosophical Library, 1950, pp. 283–84.
16. Cited in Schmidt's *Doctrine of Descent and Darwinism*, pp. 300–301.
17. Melbourne, 1863, 2nd edition, p. 57.
18. *Theosophy* (Los Angeles). September 1946, pp. 437–38.
19. February 4, 1946.
20. New York: William Morrow, 1949, pp. 389–90.
21. *The New York Times*, October 28, 1973.
22. Chase S. Osborn, *Schoolcraft—Longfellow—Hiawatha*. Lancaster, Pennsylvania: Jacques Cattell Press, 1942.
23. New York: Harper, 1839, I, pp. 172–73.
24. Philadelphia: David McKay, 1896, pp. 220–23.
25. *The New York Times*, June 19, 1966.
26. Pp. 295.
27. *Autobiography of a Winnebago Indian*. New York: Dover, 1963, p. 72 and fn.
28. Boston: Houghton Mifflin, 1911, p. 167.
29. *The Hudson Dispatch* (Jersey City, New Jersey), January 20, 1968. Column of Robert Adams, "Once Upon a Time."
30. Los Angeles: Willing Publishing Co., 1948, p. 24.
31. E. D. Walker, *Reincarnation, A Study of Forgotten Truth*, revised edition. New Hyde Park, New York: University Books, 1965, pp. 335–36. (Note: Other selections from Walker's work are from the 1888 edition, which was reprinted numerous times.)
32. Ian Stevenson, *Twenty Cases Suggestive of Reincarnation*. Charlottesville, Virginia: University Press of Virginia, 1974, pp. 216–17, 219–23.
33. Most of the tribes mentioned in this paragraph are listed in the works cited in the introduction to the present chapter.
34. In a recent volume this observation is confirmed. *Mythology of All Races*, editor, John A. MacCulloch. New York: Cooper Square, 1964. (Vol. 10, *North American Mythology*, p. 10.)
35. *Red Book* (Chicago), March 1946.
36. *Collected Works of the Right Hon. F. Max Müller*. London: Longmans, Green, 1919, XIII, p. 110 *(India, What Can It Teach Us?)*
37. William Q. Judge, *The Ocean of Theosophy*. Los Angeles: Theosophy Co., pp. 81–82, 84–85.
38. Editor, James Hasting, XII, p. 440.
39. New York: W. W. Norton, 1930, p. 23.
40. IV, *de Rebus Gallicia*, p. 3.
41. H. R. Ellis, *The Road to Hel*. Cambridge University Press, 1943, pp. 138–39.
42. London: T. Fisher Unwin, 1901, pp. 95–96.
43. Oxford University Press, 1911, p. 358.

44. "The Celtic Doctrine of Rebirth," Alfred Nutt, *The Voyage of Bran*, editor, Kuno Meyer. London: 1895–1897, II (eds.).
45. New York: Pantheon, 1960, pp. 8–9.
46. Pp. 251, 254–55, revised edition.
47. Kenmore, Ireland: Kenmore Publications Office, 1877, pp. 53–55.

5. THE WESTERN TRADITION

GREEK AND ROMAN HERITAGE

1. *The New Yorker*, November 22, 1947, article on Einstein by Nicolo Tucci; Einstein, *The World As I See It*. (New York: Philosophical Library, 1949, p. 28.)
2. *Manas* (Los Angeles), January 21, 1959, p. 7.
3. London: 1884, p. xliv.
4. C. A. Lobeck, *Aglaophamus*, Köningsburg: 1829, p. 723.
5. Edward Zeller, *History of Greek Philosophy*. London: Longmans, Green, 1880, pp. 67, 69, 71–72.
6. London: Harper, 1909, pp. 79–81.
7. London: John Watkins, 1965, p. 21.
8. Diogenes Laertius, *The Lives and Opinions of Eminent Philosophers*, translator, C. D. Yonge. London: 1853, pp. 339–40.
9. Iamblichus, *Life of Pythagoras*, translator, Thomas Taylor. London: Watkins, 1965, p. 31.
10. *Christopher Marlowe*, editor, Havelock Ellis. London: T. Fisher Unwin, 1893, pp. 227–28.
11. *Harvard Classics*. New York: P. F. Collier, 1909, III, p. 289.
12. 9th edition, article, "Metempsychosis."
13. Thomas Stanley, *History of Philosophy*. London: 1687, p. 570.
14. Verses LII and LIII, included in André Dacier's *The Life of Pythagoras*. London: 1707.
15. Quoted in G. R. S. Mead's preface to *The Select Works of Plotinus*, translator, Thomas Taylor. London: Rider, 1912, pp. xxix–xxx.
16. *De Anima*, Book I, Chap. 3. *Introduction to Aristotle*, editor, Richard McKeon. New York: Modern Library, 1947, p. 160.
17. New York: Harper 1881, article, "Transmigration."
18. *The Gnosis or Ancient Wisdom in the Christian Scriptures*. London: Allen & Unwin, 1937, p. 93.
19. Ibid., p. 97. Neither Socrates nor Aristotle were initiated into the Mysteries (eds.).
20. Princeton University Press, 1961, pp. 284–85.
21. *De Diis et Mundo*, p. iv.
22. New York: 1875, p. 117.
23. *De Esu Carn.*, Or. 1. 7, 240, T. xiii. Quoted in *Orpheus* by G. R. S. Mead. London: John Watkins, 1965, p. 193.
24. Harvard University Press, 1951, pp. 233, 237.
25. *The Odes of Pindar*, including the Principal Fragments. London: Heinemann, 1915, p. 589. Two slight changes have been made in this translation of John Sandys as a result of comparison with other translations.

26. Quoted in *The Splendour That Was Egypt* by Margaret A. Murray, New York: Philosophical Library, 1949, p. 210.
27. G. S. Kirk and J. E. Raven, *The Presocratic Philosophers*. Cambridge University Press, 1957, pp. 351–52.
28. *The Fragments of Empedocles*, translator, William Ellery Leonard. Chicago: Open Court, 1908.
29. New York: Doubleday Anchor Book, 1954, pp. 124–26.
30. "Plato, or the Philosopher." *The Selected Writings of Ralph Waldo Emerson*, editor Brooks Atkinson. New York: Modern Library, 1940, pp. 471–72.
31. *Encyclopaedia Britannica*, 11th edition, article, "Metempsychosis."
32. *Dialogues of Plato*, New York: Random House, 1937, I, pp. 360–61, 366.
33. April 1958, pp. 160, 164.
34. Translator, Josiah Wright.
35. *Manas* (Los Angeles), January 22, 1975, p. 7.
36. J. A. Stewart, *The Myths of Plato*. London: Macmillan, 1905, pp. 170–72.
37. *De Anima*, III. 5, 430ª 23; *Metaphysics*, A 9, 993ª I.
38. Oxford University Press, 1948, pp. 50–52.
39. See also Index under "Memory of Past Lives."
40. *A Collection of Several Philosophical Writings of Dr. Henry More*. London: 1712, Book II, pp. 116–17.
41. Yale University Press, 1922. Reprint, New York: Dover, 1959, pp. 7–10, 12–13, 17, 20–22, 26–28, 30–32, 40.
42. *Ante-Nicene Christian Library*, op. cit., VI, p. 56.
43. F. W. Bussell, *Marcus Aurelius and the Later Stoics*. Edinburgh: 1910, p. 145.
44. Quoted in G. R. S. Mead's *Orpheus*, op. cit., p. 189.
45. Translator, E. S. Shuckburgh. *Harvard Classics*. New York: P. F. Collier, 1909, IX, pp. 72–74.
46. *Gallic War*, translator, William A. MacDevitt, Book VI, p. 14.
47. *The Pharsalia*, I, pp. 449–56.
48. Book II, p. vi.
49. Henri Bergson, *The Philosophy of Poetry: The Genius of Lucretius*, editor and translator, Wade Baskin. New York: Philosophical Library, 1959, pp. 1–2.
50. Ibid., pp. 82–83.
51. Book 3. Except for the last seven lines, the translator is William Ellery Leonard. As to the final lines, the translator is unknown.
52. Banesh Hoffman, *Albert Einstein, Creator and Rebel*. New York: Viking, 1972, p. 254.
53. Boston: Ginn & Co., 1939, pp. 359–60.
54. *Poetical Works of John Dryden*. London: 1886, IV, pp. 292–93.
55. Daniel M. Tredwell, *A Sketch of the Life of Apollonius of Tyana*. New York: 1886, p. 47.
56. Ibid., p. 57.
57. Ibid., p. 327.
58. Philostratus's *Life of Apollonius of Tyana*. Translator, F. C. Conybeare. London: William Heinemann, 1912, I, Book 3, Chaps. 19, 22, 23, 36.
59. London: Macmillan, 1925, p. 520.
60. *Eastern Religions and Western Thought*, op. cit., p. 203.

61. Eva Martin, op. cit., p. 72. Another translation, *Plutarch's Morals,* editor, William W. Goodwin. New York: Atheneum, 1870, V, pp. 286–87, 289.
62. Cambridge University Press, 1918, p. 209.
63. *Encyclopaedia Britannica,* 1959 edition, article, "Neoplatonism."
64. *Neoplatonism.* New York: Scribner's, 1972.
65. *Encyclopaedia Britannica,* 1959 edition, article, "Plotinus."
66. New York: Mentor, 1964, pp. vii, 13–14.
67. See under "Augustine" in Index.
68. Op. cit., p. 41.
69. *The Philosophy of Plotinus.* London: Longmans, Green, 1948, pp. xiii–xiv.
70. London: George Redway, 1896, p. 26.
71. *Plotinus: Psychic and Physical Treatises.* London: Philip Lee Warner, 1921, II, pp. 28–30, 33–34, 39.
72. *Five Books of Plotinus.* London: 1794, pp. 268–69, 273–74, 280, 282–85.
73. Porphyry, *On Abstinence from Animal Food,* translator, Thomas Taylor. New York: Barnes & Noble, 1965, introduction.
74. Article, "Viande" in Voltaire's *Philosophical Dictionary.*
75. *Porphyry, On Abstinence from Animal Food,* p. 143.
76. New York: Metaphysical Pub., 1911, pp. 122, 175, 259–60.
77. See Index under "Fielding."
78. See Index under "Ibsen."
79. Marcellinus Ammianus' History, Book xxv.
80. *The Neo-Platonists.* Cambridge University Press, 2nd edition, 1918, p. 304.
81. Loran Hurnscot, '*A Prison, A Paradise.* New York: Viking, 1959, p. 268.
82. London: 1823, pp. 187–88.
83. Oxford University Press, 1963, pp. 25, 181.
84. Ibid., pp. 304–5.

THE MIDDLE AGES

1. New York: Pantheon, 1949, pp. 198fn., 239, 241–42.
2. Lewis Spence, *Magic Arts in Celtic Britain.* London: Rider, n.d., p. 128.
3. Eva Martin, op. cit., pp. 110–11.
4. London: J. M. Dent, 1909.
5. *New York Herald Tribune,* June 8, 1958.
6. *The Reader's Encyclopaedia,* editor, William Rose Benét. New York: Crowell, 1948, p. 50.
7. Harold Bayley, op. cit., pp. 60–62.
8. G. Butler, *The Leadership of the Strange Cult of Love.* Bristol: 1910, p. 17.
9. Bayley, op. cit., p. 61.
10. New York: 1878, pp. 41, 46.
11. *Magicians, Seers, and Mystics.* New York: Dutton, 1932, pp. 49–50. Published in England as *The Return of the Magi.*
12. London: John Murray, 1926.

RENAISSANCE AND REFORMATION

1. *The Platonic Tradition in English Religious Thought.* London: Longmans, Green, 1926, pp. 21–22.
2. Ibid., p. 22.

3. Ibid., p. 28.
4. Op. cit., p. 56.
5. *Frontiers of Knowledge in the Study of Man.* New York: Harper, 1956, pp. 304–5.
6. This is one of Pico's *Conclusiones Kabalisticae,* drawn by him from Zoharic works, and published by Archangelus de Burgo Novo in *Apologia pro Defensione Doctrinae Cabalae,* 1564. See *The Works of Thomas Vaughan,* editor, A. E. Waite, London: 1919, 6fn.
7. *Encyclopaedia Britannica,* 11th edition, Vol. XI, p. 573.
8. Eva Martin, op. cit., p. 107.
9. New York: Putnam, 1916, pp. 104–5.
10. "Finger Posts of the Middle Ages," *Theosophy* (Los Angeles), March 1944, pp. 206–9.
11. London: Longmans, Green, 1926, pp. 28, 36–37.
12. New York: Macmillan, 1903.
13. *Zahm Zemen,* V.
14. Francis Barham, *The Life and Times of John Reuchlin, or Capnio, the Father of the German Reformation.* London: 1843.
15. Harvard University Press, 1963, p. 71.
16. Ibid., p. 67.
17. *Encyclopaedia Britannica,* 9th edition, article, "John Reuchlin."
18. *The Platonic Tradition in English Religious Thought,* op. cit., pp. 23–24.
19. Petrarch (1304–1374) is considered the first great representative of Renaissance humanism. Revolting against late-medieval scholasticism, and replacing it with unbounded zeal for the study of classical antiquity, he regarded Plato as the greatest of all philosophers. See Paul O. Kristeller, *Eight Philosophers of the Italian Renaissance.* California: Stanford University Press, 1964, p. 9 (eds.).
20. *The Mysteries of Antiquity.* New York: 1878, pp. 48–49, 51–52, 70.
21. Kenneth Mackenzie, London: 1877, pp. 613–14.
22. C. G. Jung's *Collected Works.* New York: Pantheon, XII, *Psychology and Alchemy;* XIII, *Alchemical Studies;* XIV, *Mysterium Coniunctionis.*
23. *The Integration of Personality.* New York: Farrar & Rinehart, 1939, pp. 28, 238.
24. London: 5th revised edition, n.d., p. 214.
25. Chicago University Press, 1964.
26. *Leonardo da Vinci's Note-Books,* translator and compiler, Edward McCurdy. New York: Empire State Book Co., 1935, p. 50.
27. Ibid., pp. 47, 48.
28. *Life* magazine, March 3, 1967. Upon inquiry as to the source of this line, the editors replied: "The quote from Leonardo which headed our article was taken from one of the manuscripts which has just been found—the larger one known as Madrid MS—on folio 6 recto. The entire quote is as follows: 'Read me, O Reader, if you find delight in me, because seldom shall I come back into this world; and you know that the power of such profession is found in just a few who want to recompose similar things afresh. And come, men, to see the miracles which through such studies one can reveal in Nature.' The manuscript was probably written mainly between 1497 and 1503."
29. London: Kegan Paul, 2nd revised edition, n.d., pp. 278–79.
30. G. R. S. Mead, *The Hymn of the Robe of Glory.* London: 1908.

31. I Corinthians 15:35–54.
32. Henry Bett, *Johannes Scotus Erigena*. New York: Russell & Russell, 1964, p. 56.
33. *That Unknown Country*, editor, C. A. Nichols. Springfield, Massachusetts: 1891, p. 47.
34. *Giordano Bruno: Philosopher and Martyr*. Two addresses, the first by Daniel G. Brinton. Philadelphia: McKay, 1890, pp. 13–14.
35. London: Macmillan, 1903, pp. 159–60, 312.
36. Op. cit., p. 21.
37. I. Frith, *Life of Giordano Bruno*. Boston: 1887, p. 123.
38. New York: MD Publications, 1958, p. 143.
39. Ibid., p. 142.
40. *Giordano Bruno, His Life and Thought*. New York: Schuman, 1950, pp. 49, 50, 91. (A volume in The Life of Science Library.)
41. Ibid., p. 91.
42. Translator, Arthur D. Imerti. New Brunswick, New Jersey: Rutgers University Press, 1963, pp. 77, 94–95, 102, 114, 126, 144, 192.
43. Frith, op. cit., p. 262fn.
44. William Boulting, *Giordano Bruno, His Life, Thought, and Martyrdom*. London: Kegan Paul, 1914, pp. 163–64.
45. Frith, pp. 278–79.
46. *The World As I See It*, translator, Alan Harris. New York: Philosophical Library,
47. Ingersoll is quoted on rebirth in *Reincarnation in World Thought*, p. 329.

AGE OF SHAKESPEARE

1. Josephine Waters, "Spenser's Garden of Adonis." Menasha, Wisconsin: Modern Language Association Publications, March 1932, XLVII, pp. 46–80.
2. Editors, Edwin Greenlaw, et al. Baltimore: Johns Hopkins Press, 1932–1938.
3. Form or appearance.
4. Book III, Canto VI, Stanzas 30–33.
5. *Hamlet*, Act I, Scene 2.
6. Ibid., Act III, Scene 1.
7. *King Lear*, Act V, Scene 3.
8. *Macbeth*, Act V, Scene 5.
9. *King Henry VI*, Part I, Act II, Scene 3.
10. *Hamlet*, Act II, Scene 2.
11. London: Chatto & Windus, 1961, pp. 181–82, 195.
12. *The Sonnets of M. A. Buonarroti and T. Campanella*, translator, John Addington Symonds. London: 1878, p. 177.
13. *The Complete Poetry and Selected Prose of John Donne*. New York: Modern Library, 1941, pp. 216–18.
14. *Harvard Classics*. New York: P. F. Collier, 1909, III, pp. 257, 289, 326.
15. Denis Saurat, *Literature and Occult Tradition*. New York: Dial Press, 1930, p. 44.
16. *Complete Poetry and Selected Prose of John Milton*. New York: Modern Library, p. 5.
17. W. R. Inge, *The Platonic Tradition in English Religious Thought*, op. cit., p. 55.

18. E. D. Walker, op. cit., p. 179.
19. Beausobré, op. cit., II, p. 491.
20. Op. cit., pp. 45–46, 65.
21. *A Collection of Several Philosophical Writings of Dr. Henry More,* 4th revised edition. London: 1712, Book II, Chapter 12, pp. 114–16.
22. Henry More, *Philosophical Poems.* Cambridge: 1647, pp. 225, 256, 261.
23. "Seelenwanderung und Sympathie der Seelen in der Judischen Mystik," by Gershom Scholem. *Eranos Jahrbuch* (Rhein Verlag, Basel), XXIV, p. 58. The Karaites rejected Rabbinism and Talmudism, basing their tenets on interpretation of the scriptures. They were founded in Bagdad about A.D. 765 by Anan ben David, were formerly widespread, but in the early parts of the twentieth century numbered only some twelve thousand adherents, chiefly in southern Russia.
24. Eleventh edition, XIX, p. 59.
25. *The Works of Thomas Vaughan,* editors, A. E. Waite. London: 1919, pp. 5–6, 46–47, 50.
26. In this sentence, Vaughan, of course, speaks of spiritual rebirth.
27. *The Human Situation,* op. cit., pp. 315–16.
28. Translator, Mary Morris, *Leibniz: Philosophical Writings.* London: J. M. Dent, 1934, p. 16.
29. Ibid., p. 25.
30. Cambridge University Press, 1911, pp. 204–5, 212–13.
31. Lettre à Arnauld, *Philosophische Schriften,* Gerhardt's edition, II, p. 99f.
32. Walker, op. cit., pp. 322–23.

EIGHTEENTH-CENTURY ENLIGHTENMENT

1. Quoted in Emil Bock's *Widerholt Erdenleben.* Stuttgart: 1952, p. 31: "La doctrine de la metempsychose surtout n'est ni absurde ni inutile. . . . Il n'est pas plus surprenant de naître deux fois qu'un. Tout est résurrection dans la nature."
2. Save for the last sentence, quoted in Orlando J. Smith's *Eternalism.* Boston: Houghton Mifflin, 1902, p. 301. Another translation: Voltaire's Philosophical Dictionary, Sec. X, under "Soul." *Works of Voltaire,* St. Hubert Edition, 1901, VII, pp. 309–10.
3. Editor and translator, Wade Baskin. New York: Philosophical Library, 1961.
4. *Benjamin Franklin.* New York: Viking, 1952, p. 123.
5. *The Papers of Benjamin Franklin,* editor, Leonard W. Labaree. New Haven, Connecticut: Yale University Press, I, p. 310; article, "B. Franklin's Epitaph," L. H. Butterfield. *New Colophon,* 1950, III, pp. 9–30.
6. Letter to George Whatley, May 23, 1785. *The Works of Benjamin Franklin,* editor, Jared Sparks. Boston: 1856, X, p. 174.
7. *The Journals of Ralph Waldo Emerson.* Boston: Houghton Mifflin, 1909, I, p. 320.
8. *The Works of Henry Fielding,* editor, James P. Browne. London: 1871, IV.
9. David Hume, *Essays, Moral, Political and Literary.* London: 1875, II, pp. 400, 404.

10. *Friedericus Rex, Aussprüche und Gedanken.* Compiler, R. Rehlen. No. 1094.
11. Quoted in *Little Journeys to the Homes of Great Philosophers* by Elbert Hubbard. East Aurora, New York: Roycrofters, 1904, XV, p. 19.
12. *Allgemeine Naturgeschichte und Theorie des Himmels.* Koenigsberg and Leipzig: 1755, pp. 198–99 (Part III, Appendix, "Conclusion").
13. Ann Arbor, Michigan: University of Michigan Press, 1966, p. vii.
14. D. Alfred Bertholet, *Transmigration of Souls.* London and New York: Harper, 1909, pp. 105–8.
15. Ibid.
16. *Vermischte Schriften* (Miscellaneous Writings), I, p. 9.
17. Ibid., II, pp. 16–17.
18. *God, Some Conversations,* translator, F. Burkhardt. New York: Veritas Press, 1940, p. 3.
19. Ibid., pp. viii–ix.
20. Frederic H. Hedge, *Prose Writers of Germany.* Philadelphia: 1852, pp. 248–250–51, 257.
21. *The Brahma Sutra,* translator, S. Radhakrishnan. New York: Harper & Row, 1960, p. 206. The letter was taken from *Asiatic Jones* by J. A. Arberry, London, 1946, p. 37.
22. M. Winternitz, *History of Indian Literature.* University of Calcutta, 1927, I, p. 22.
23. Boston: 1888, p. 310.

EASTERN AND TRANSCENDENTAL INFLUENCES IN THE NINETEENTH CENTURY

1. *The Transmigration of Souls,* op. cit., p. 103.
2. O. B. Frothingham, *Transcendentalism in New England.* New York: Putnam, 1876, p. 52.
3. C. E. M. Joad, "What Is the Soul?" *The Aryan Path* (Bombay), May 1937, pp. 200–201.
4. Frothingham, chapters 1–3.
5. "Fruitlands: Memorial to Transcendentalism." *The New York Times,* August 12, 1973.
6. *The Path* (New York), February 1888, pp. 325–26.
7. London: 1954, p. 487.
8. Walter Sullivan, science editor, *The New York Times,* April 29, 1973.
9. J. W. N. Sullivan, *Beethoven, His Spiritual Development.* New York: Knopf, 1927, pp. 212–13.
10. *Garden Journal,* February 1975 (New York Botanical Gardens).
11. K. O. Schmidt, *Die Wiederverkörperung der Seele,* p. 43, n.d.
12. Denis Saurat, *Literature and Occult Tradition.* New York: Dial Press, 1930, p. 44.
13. George Santayana, *Three Philosophical Poets.* Harvard University Press, 1910. (New York: Doubleday Anchor Books, p. 155.)
14. Bertholet, op. cit., p. 104.
15. Ibid.
16. *Lucifer* (London), January 1894, p. 428.

17. *The Works of J. W. von Goethe,* editor, Nathan Haskell Dole. New York: 1902, volume "Poetical Works," p. 192.
18. *Memoirs of Johannes Falk.* Leipzig: 1832. Reprinted in *Goethe-Bibliothek,* Berlin: 1911.
19. The A. W. Mellon Lectures in the Fine Arts, 1962. Princeton University Press, 1968, I, pp. 252, 351.
20. Pp. 352–53.
21. *Poems of William Blake,* editor, William Butler Yeats. New York: Modern Library, p. xxvii.
22. *Blake's Humanism.* Manchester University Press (New York: Barnes & Noble): 1968, pp. 19–20, 23.
23. William Scoones's *English Letters,* 1880, p. 361.
24. *The Dial,* April 1844.
25. Op. cit., I, p. 249.
26. London: 1804, I, pp. iv, lxii–lxiii.
27. *The Works of Friedrich Schiller,* editor, Nathan Haskell Dole. New York: Bigelow, Brown, 1902, volume *Poems,* pp. 9–10.
28. F. H. Hedge, *Prose Writers of Germany,* Philadelphia: 1852, pp. 398, 401, 404.
29. *Jean Paul's Werke.* Berlin and Stuttgart: Paul Nerrlich, n.d., I, p. lxvii.
30. Boston: 1863, p. 348.
31. Emil Ludwig, *Napoleon.* New York: Boni & Liveright, 1926, p. 245.
32. Paris and Boston: Napoleon Society, 1895, II, p. 77.
33. Friedrich Heer, *The Holy Roman Empire,* translator, Janet Sondheimer. New York: Praeger, 1968, p. 276.
34. Translator, J. Sibree. New York: Colonial Press, 1900, pp. 72–73, 78–79.
35. December 10, 1927, p. 1,041.
36. London: 1904, pp. 53–54.
37. Lockhart's *Life of Scott.* First edition, VII, p. 114.
38. Walker, op. cit., pp. 36–37.
39. Radhakrishnan, *Eastern Religions and Western Thought,* op. cit., p. 247.
40. *Kölner Vorlesungen,* editor, von Windischmann. Bonn: 1837, pp. 202–3, 205–6.
41. *Philosophie des Lebens.* Vienna Lectures, 1827, Lecture VI, p. 193. The translation is a new one.
42. *The Dial,* July 1842.
43. London: 1851, I, pp. 220–21.
44. E. D. Walker, op. cit., p. 94.
45. See complete poem in Walker's *Reincarnation,* pp. 173–74.
46. Translators, R. B. Haldane and J. Kemp. London: Kegan Paul, 1906, III, pp. 302–6.
47. *The World as I See It.* New York: Philosophical Library, 1949, p. 26.
48. *From the Unconscious to the Conscious.* New York: Harper, 1920, p. 198.
49. H. P. Blavatsky, *The Secret Doctrine.* Los Angeles: Theosophy Co., 1964, II, p. 304fn.
50. Op. cit., III, pp. 299–300.
51. II, Chapters 10, 15, and 16.
52. *The Complete Works of Percy Bysshe Shelley.* New York: Scribner's, 1929, VI, p. 208.

53. London: 1886, I, p. 81.
54. New York: Frederick Ungar, n.d., p. 146.
55. Book I, Chapter 11; Book III, Chapters 7 and 8. (1888 edition. London: Walter Scott, pp. 64, 223, 236, 238–39.)
56. *Ideen oder das Buch Le Grand.* Included in Heine's *Travel-Pictures,* translator, Francis Storr. London: George Bell, 1907, Book III, p. 120.
57. *Travel-Pictures,* Book II, pp. 94–95.
58. Vol. 17, p. 330 (1872).
59. Boston: Robert Bros., 1874, pp. 104, 132–33, 147–48.
60. Boston: Roberts Bros., 1872, p. 83.
61. Editor, Richard L. Herrnstadt. Ames, Iowa: Iowa State University Press, 1969, p. 669.
62. Boston: Roberts Bros., 1879, pp. 201–3.
63. *Balzac, La Comédie Humaine.* Boston: Pratt, 1904, XXXIX, pp. viii, ix, xxvii, lxxv–lxxvi.
64. Ibid., pp. 175–76, 178–80.
65. One case is reported by Dr. Ian Stevenson in the section "Stories of 'Remembrances' of Past Lives."
66. 1959 edition.
67. Martin, op. cit., pp. 147–49.
68. *Lucifer* (London), April 1889, p. 93.
69. Book II, chapter 25.
70. Book V, chapter 9.
71. *The Works of Edward Bulwer-Lytton.* New York: P. F. Collier, 1901, X, pp. 185–90, 271.
72. To bring together all the American transcendentalists, we temporarily suspend presenting selections in exact birth-year sequence of their authors.
73. O. Frothingham, *George Ripley.* Boston: 1882, pp. 84–85.
74. J. P. Rao Rayapati gives a detailed picture of the gradual involvement of the transcendentalists with Hindu literature in his *Early American Interest in Vedanta.* New York: Asia Publishing House, 1973, pp. 93–106.
75. New York: William Rudge, 1932.
76. F. I. Carpenter, *Emerson and Asia.* Cambridge, Massachusetts: 1930, p. 106.
77. Boston: 1902, p. 72.
78. New York: Columbia University Press, 1932.
79. *Journals of Ralph Waldo Emerson.* Boston: Houghton Mifflin, 1901, II, p. 341.
80. Ibid., VI, pp. 419–20.
81. *The Journals of Ralph Waldo Emerson,* editor, Robert N. Linscott. New York: Modern Library, 1960, p. 190.
82. Ralph L. Rusk, *The Life of Ralph Waldo Emerson.* New York: Scribner's, 1949, p. 289.
83. *The Selected Writings of Ralph Waldo Emerson,* editor, Brooks Atkinson, New York: Modern Library, 1950, p. 445.
84. Ibid., p. 342.
85. Ibid., pp. 187–88.
86. *Emerson's Complete Works.* Boston: Houghton Mifflin, 1886, IV, pp. 12, 32, 35.

87. Ibid., 1886, IV, pp. 93–94.
88. Ibid., 1887, VIII, pp. 319–20, 333.
89. Boston: 1877, chapter 14.
90. *The Aryan Path* (Bombay) June 1933 and May 1934.
91. I, p. 14.
92. O. B. Frothingham, *Transcendentalism in New England,* op. cit., pp. 222–23.
93. Boston: Houghton Mifflin, 1887, II, pp. ix, 190.
94. *The Life and Letters of Charles Darwin,* editor, Francis Darwin. New York: Appleton, 1887, I, p. 282.
95. *The Writings of Henry David Thoreau.* Cambridge, Massachusetts: Houghton Mifflin, 1894, XI, pp. 110, 215, 253.
96. Ibid., 1892, VII, p. 255; *The Journal of Henry D. Thoreau.* Boston: Houghton Mifflin, 1949, I, p. 419; II, pp. 190–91, 271, 306.
97. *Walt Whitman's Leaves of Grass,* the first (1855) edition, editor, Malcolm Cowley. New York: Viking, 1959, p. ix. *The Saturday Review* article was taken from Cowley's introduction to this edition.
98. University of Nebraska Press, 1964.
99. William S. Kennedy, *Reminiscences of Walt Whitman.* London: 1896, p. 173.
100. On this point see also *Early American Interest in Vedanta* by J. P. Rao Rayapati. New York: Asia Publishing House, 1973, pp. 12–15, 104–5 (eds.).
101. *Leaves of Grass.* Book 3, Parts 6, 20, 27, 43–44, 46, 49. (Modern Library edition, pp. 47, 64, 66–67, 68–69, 72.)
102. *Leaves of Grass.* New York: Modern Library, p. 364.
103. Ibid., pp. 90–91.
104. Ibid., pp. 183–84.
105. Ibid., p. 303.
106. 2nd edition.
107. New York: Dutton, 1911, chapter 13.
108. *The Works of the Late Edgar Allan Poe.* New York: 1859, I, p. 43.
109. Ibid., II, pp. 117, 212.
110. Chapter 39.
111. Carl F. Glasenap, *The Life of Richard Wagner,* translator, William Ashton Ellis. London: Kegal Paul, 1900–1906, V, p. 254.
112. S. Radhakrishnan, *Eastern Religions and Western Thought,* op. cit., p. 248.
113. Richard Wagner, *My Life.* London: Constable, reissued 1963, p. 638.
114. *The Aryan Path* (Bombay), September 1966, pp. 417–18.
115. Kapp edition, VI, p. 278.
116. *Richard Wagner's Letters to August Roeckel,* translator, Eleanor C. Sellar. London: 1897, pp. 137–38. *Richard Wagner an August Röckel,* Leipzig: 1912, p. 60.
117. *Richard Wagner Briefe an Hans von Bülow.* Jena: 1916, p. 107.
118. Georg Neidhart, *Werden Wir Wieden Geboren.* Munich, n.d., p. 59.
119. *Richard Wagner an Mathilde Wesendonck Lagebuchblätter und Briefe 1853–1871.* Leipzig: 1922, p. 285 (letter 106a).
120. Richard Wagner, *Gesammelte Schriften und Dichtungen (Collected Writings and Poetry),* Leipzig: 1872, edited by Wagner, VI, pp. 362–63.
121. Emil Bock, op. cit., p. 126.

122. Max Eastman, "The Man Who Wrote *Moby Dick*," *Reader's Digest*, March 1965, p. 192.
123. Britannica, 1959 edition, article, "Herman Melville," vol. 15, p. 231B.
124. Chapters 98, 114, 119, 132, and 134.
125. D. H. Lawrence, *Studies in Classic American Literature*. New York: Viking, 1961, pp. 158–59.
126. J. B. Priestley, *Literature and Western Man*. New York: Harper & Row, 1960, p. 238.
127. Translator, Aimee L. McKenzie. New York: Boni & Liveright, 1921, p. 16.
128. Translator, Constance Garnett. Part IV, Book XI, Chapter 9.
129. Paris: 1885, pp. 298, 302.
130. Briefe, I, p. 95.
131. New York: Thomas Crowell, 1887, pp. 28–30, 35.
132. *Diary of Leo Nickolaevich Tolstoy*, editor, V. G. Chertkov. Moscow: 1906, I, p. 17 (entry for February 13, 1896).
133. Translator, Constance Garnett. New York: Carlton House, pp. 490–91 (Part VII, Chapter 10).
134. Moscow: Magazine, *The Voice of Universal Love*, 1908, No. 40, p. 634. Reprinted in Russian in the Russian magazine *White Lotus*, editor, Militza E. Yurieva Cowling. Santa Barbara, California, No. 4, 1960, pp. 20–21.
135. Act IV, Scene I. *Collected Works of Henrik Ibsen*, editor, William Archer. New York: Scribner's, 1911, p. 393.
136. I, p. 399.
137. *The Poems of Emily Dickinson*. Boston: Little, Brown, 1930, p. 167.
138. *Sunrise*. (Pasadena, California), August 1959, p. 333.
139. Editor, Henry Festing Jones. New York: Dutton, 1917, pp. 16, 362.
140. Ibid., p. 394.
141. Ibid., p. 397.
142. *Tagebuchblätter Wien*, 1899, pp. 81, 97, 227.
143. *The Great Initiates*, translator, Gloria Rasberry. West Nyack, New York: St. George Books, 1961, p. 17.
144. Translator, Fred Rothwell. Philadelphia: David McKay, 1925, II, pp. 109–10, 132–33.
145. Rochester, New York: Manas Press, 1920, p. 317.
146. London: Allen & Unwin, 1916 (3rd edition), pp. 202–3, 206–7.
147. Translator, Frank Lester Pleadwell. Privately printed, 1927. The original manuscript and the translation are now in the possession of the St. Louis Art Museum, St. Louis, Missouri.
148. New York: Putnam, 1913, pp. 50, 145.
149. Lafcadio Hearn, *Japan's Religions*. New Hyde Park, New York: University Books, 1966, pp. xiii–xiv.
150. Boston: Houghton Mifflin, 1896, Chapter 12.
151. London and New York: Macmillan, 1902, pp. 175–76, 182–84.
152. Editor, John Erskine. New York: Dodd, Mead, 1920, pp. 45–46.
153. Boston: Little, Brown, 1899, pp. 239–40.
154. Boston: Houghton Mifflin, 1900, pp. 291–93.
155. Boston: Little, Brown, 1898, pp. 177–78.

TWENTIETH CENTURY—AGE OF TRANSITION

1. Boston: Lothrop, 1903.
2. Charles Higham, *The Adventures of Conan Doyle, The Life of the Creator of Sherlock Holmes.* New York: W. W. Norton, 1976.
3. Theroux reviewed the biography in the *New York Times Book Review,* November 7, 1976.
4. London: Cassell, 1926, II, p. 180.
5. *Journal of the American Podiatry Association,* April 1968.
6. *The Plays of J. M. Barrie.* New York: Scribner's, 1956, pp. 223–24.
7. Los Angeles: Willing Publishing Co., 1948. Seton's books are available at Seton Village, Santa Fe, New Mexico.
8. Richard Specht, *Gustav Mahler.* Berlin: Schuster & Loeffler, 1913, p. 39.
9. Record CSA 2223. Conductor Georg Solti.
10. Translator, Alexander Teixeira de Mattos. New York: Dodd, Mead, 1913, pp. 169–70.
11. Translator, Alfred Sutro and A. B. Walkley. New York: Dodd, Mead, pp. 160, 162–64.
12. London: Allen & Unwin, 1928, p. 24.
13. *Lord Riddell's Intimate Diary of the Peace Conference and After.* London: Victor Gollancz, 1933, pp. 122–23.
14. *A Short View of Great Questions,* by Orlando J. Smith. It marshals the philosophical arguments for reincarnation (eds.).
15. *San Francisco Examiner,* August 28, 1928.
16. New York: Philosophical Library, 1948, p. 215.
17. Boston: Houghton Mifflin, 1891.
18. *Collected Verse of Rudyard Kipling.* New York: Doubleday, 1907, p. 131.
19. *Rudyard Kipling's Verse.* London: Hodder & Stoughton, 1927.
20. *The New York Times,* December 4, 1955.
21. To bring together all the Irish writers belonging to this period, we temporarily suspend presenting selections in the exact birth-year sequence of their authors.
22. London: Macmillan, 1937, p. 1.
23. Quoted on the cover of Francis Merchant's *AE: An Irish Promethean.* Columbia, South Carolina: Benedict College Press, 1954.
24. New York: Knopf, 1922.
25. P. G. Bowen, "AE and Theosophy," *Aryan Path* (Bombay), December 1935, p. 724.
26. New York: Modern Library, 1961, p. 185.
27. Eglinton, *A Memoir of AE,* p. 13.
28. April 9, 1956.
29. Dharwar, India: Karnatak University, 1966, p. 157.
30. *The Collected Poems of W. B. Yeats.* New York: Macmillan, 1960, p. 341.
31. *Song and Its Fountains,* p. 90.
32. London: Hodder & Stoughton, 1964, pp. 15, 40.
33. P. G. Bowen, "AE and Theosophy," op. cit., pp. 722–26.
34. Ibid., p. 723.
35. C. G. Jung Letters. Princeton University Press, 1975, II, p. 590 and fn.

36. London: Macmillan, 1931, pp. 144–47, 149. Reprinted, New York: University Books, 1965.

37. New York: Knopf, 1929, pp. 173–75.

38. Francis Merchant, *AE: An Irish Promethean*, op. cit., p. 240.

39. New York: Barnes & Noble, 1965, p. x.

40. Ibid., p. 42.

41. Ibid., p. 70.

42. Dublin: Maunsel & Co., 1912.

43. New York: Knopf (Vintage paperback), 1952, pp. 33–34, 36. Also Penguin paperback, 1963.

44. New York: Viking, 1960.

45. *We Moderns,* 1920–1940 anniversary catalog of the Gotham Book Mart, New York City in which well-known authors commented on fellow authors of the day.

46. Leon Edel, *The Last Journey.* New York: Gotham Book Mart, 1947, p. 42.

47. Quoted in "Are We a Nation of Mystics?" by A. M. Greeley and W. C. McCready. *The New York Times Magazine,* January 26, 1975, p. 12.

48. Translator, E. F. Malcolm-Smith. New York: Albert and Charles Boni, 1930, pp. xxii–xxiv.

49. New York: Appleton, 1909, pp. 219–21.

50. New York: Harper, 1920, p. 176.

51. *The New York Times Magazine,* December 18, 1966.

52. *Reincarnation in World Thought,* op. cit., pp. 353–54.

53. Wassily Kandinsky, *Concerning the Spiritual in Art.* New York: Wittenborn, Schultz, 1947, p. 32.

54. New York: Praeger, 1968, pp. 87, 88–89.

55. "Mondrian: He Perfected Not a Style but a Vision," *The New York Times,* February 24, 1974.

56. New York: Doubleday, 1938, pp. 264, 285.

57. "Robert Frost Reads His Poetry." Caedmon Records, TC 1060.

58. *Erinnerungen an Rainer Maria Rilke,* p. 83.

59. *Briefe und Tagebücher 1899–1902,* p. 8.

60. See Index under Jones.

61. New York: Macmillan, 1957, pp. 50–51, 98.

62. New York: Macmillan, 1919, pp. 1–2, 252–54.

63. Noel Langley, *Edgar Cayce on Reincarnation.* New York: Paperback Library, 1967, pp. 41–42.

64. New York: Henry Holt, 1942, pp. 234–35.

65. Gina Cerminara, *Many Mansions.* New York: William Sloane, 1950, pp. 88–89. (Also a Signet paperback.)

66. Ibid., pp. 50–51.

67. Ibid., pp. 53–54.

68. Translators, Richard and Clara Winston. New York: Bantam, 1970, p. 100.

69. *Magister Ludi,* translator, Mervyn Savill. New York: Frederick Ungar, 1957, pp. 500–502.

70. *Poems by Hermann Hesse,* translator, James Wright. New York: Farrar, Straus and Giroux, 1970, p. 79.

71. New York: New Directions, 1951, pp. 104, 108–11.

72. London *Daily Telegraph* (Supplement), May 28, 1965.
73. *Daily News* (New York), February 16, 1970.
74. In 1944, during World War II, Patton wrote a poem "Through a Glass Darkly": "So as through a glass and darkly the age-long strife I see, where I fought in many guises, many names—but always me. . . . So forever in the future, shall I battle as of yore, dying to be born a fighter but to die again once more." Quoted in Fred Ayer, Jr.'s, *Before the Colors Fade, Portrait of a Soldier, George S. Patton, Jr.* Boston: Houghton Mifflin, 1964, pp. 96–97.
75. London: Rider, 1945.
76. London: pamphlet of Antivivisection Society, n.d.
77. New York: Knopf, 1951, pp. 83–84, 94–95.
78. New York: Knopf, 1945, pp. 93–94.
79. *D. H. Lawrence and Susan His Cow.* New York: Columbia University Press, 1939.
80. *The Letters of D. H. Lawrence,* editor, Aldous Huxley, p. 476.
81. Ibid.
82. D. H. Lawrence, *The Plumed Serpent.* New York: Vintage, 1959, p. xi.
83. Ibid., p. 295.
84. University of Illinois (Twayne Pub., New York), 1964, pp. 35, 75.
85. *T. S. Eliot, Selected Poems.* New York: Harcourt, Brace & World (Harbrace Paperbound Library), p. 59.
86. Ibid., p. 65.
87. Ibid., p. 72.
88. Harvard University, 1909. Harvard Oriental Series, editor, Charles Rockwell Lanman, III, pp. 351–53.
89. New York: Modern Library, 1959, pp. 333, 337, 343, 374, 377.
90. New York: Holt, Rinehart, 1933, p. 1,055.
91. *Reincarnation in World Thought,* op. cit., pp. 166–67, 235–36.
92. Revelation 3:12.
93. London: John Watkins, 1927, pp. 123–24.
94. New York: Rinehart, 1944, p. 140.
95. New York: Signet paperback, pp. 28–29.
96. *The Paris Review,* Summer-Fall 1962.
97. New York: New Directions paperback, 1969, p. 150 and appendix.
98. *Rolling Stone,* February 27, 1975.
99. New York: John Day, 1963, pp. 305–6, 322–23, 473.
100. *The New York Times,* June 19, 1938.
101. London: William Heinemann, 1937, pp. 98–101.
102. New York: Harper, 1945, pp. 213–15.
103. New York: Scribner's, 1952, pp. 1, 36–37, 63, 662.
104. New York: Scribner's, 1956, pp. 352–53, 361–62, 375, 378, 387, 389–91.
105. New York: Viking, 1946, pp. 41, 49–50.
106. J. D. Salinger, *Nine Stories.* New York: Signet paperback, 1954.
107. New York: Scribner's, 1951, pp. 647–48, 723.
108. New York: Grosset & Dunlap, 1973, pp. 22–23.
109. November 13, 1972, p. 60.
110. New York: Macmillan, 1970, pp. 53–54.

STORIES OF ``REMEMBRANCES`` OF PAST LIVES

1. H. P. Blavatsky, *The Secret Doctrine*, 1888 edition, reprinted by Theosophy Co. (Los Angeles) 1964, I, pp. 149, 154–55, 171–73, 179–81; II, p. 64.
2. London: Spearman, 1970.
3. *National Enquirer*, December 28, 1969.
4. Op. cit., pp. 88–89.
5. Lecture, March 25, 1969, before the College of Psychic Science, London.
6. *Modern Screen*, April 1932.
7. New York: Harper & Row. The selections are from pp. 10, 14–15, 28–30, 33, 165–68, 175–76.
8. April and July 1960 issues of *Journal of the American Society for Psychical Research*. Reprinted in booklet form by M. C. Peto, Burgh Heath, Tadworth, Surrey, England, from which our selections come.
9. Ibid., pp. 18–19.
10. Ibid., p. 20.
11. Ibid., pp. 20–21.
12. Harry Carr, a noted columnist and personal acquaintance of Lea, made known these facts in an article in the *Los Angeles Times*, November 15, 1931.
13. New York: Harper & Row, 1975, pp. 179–80, 194–95.
14. Op. cit.

6. NEW HORIZONS IN SCIENCE, PSYCHOLOGY, AND PHILOSOPHY

THE WORLD OF SCIENTISTS

1. American edition, New York: Horizon Press, 1960.
2. Ibid., p. 1.
3. Ibid., p. 60.
4. Ibid., p. 62.
5. New York: Appleton, 1894, pp. 60–61.
6. New York: Appleton, 1892, pp. 27, 171, 178.
7. Article, "The Cycle Moveth," *Lucifer* (London), March 1890, p. 8; article "The Mysterious Madame Blavatsky," by Kurt Vonnegut, Jr., *McCall's*, March 1970, p. 142.
8. Charles E. Luntz, *The Challenge of Reincarnation*. St. Louis: Luntz Publications, 1957, p. 39.
9. R. F. Goudey, *Reincarnation: A Universal Truth*. Los Angeles: Aloah Press, 1928, pp. 120–21.
10. New York: Philosophical Library, 1948, pp. 235–36.
11. *Our Beloved Infidel*. New York: Macmillan, 1926, pp. 107, 117–19.
12. A paperback reprint of the work was issued in 1965 by the Educational Research Institute in North Hollywood, California.
13. New York: David McKay, 1940.
14. New York, David McKay, 1948, pp. ix, 198–99, 237–38.
15. Yale University Press, 1932, pp. 45–46.
16. *What Dare I Think?* New York: Harper, 1931, pp. 82–83.
17. Quoted in *The Middle Way* (London), August 1969, p. 71.
18. Pp. 539–41.

19. John Eglinton, *A Memoir of AE*. London: Macmillan, 1937, pp. 272–73.

20. New York: William Sloane, 1952, p. 7.

21. New York: William Sloane, 1962, pp. 322–23.

22. Each of these men is quoted in *Reincarnation, An East-West Anthology*, editors, Head and Cranston. New York: Julian Press, 1961, pp. 313–15.

23. June 21, 1971.

24. *The Mystery of the Mind: A Study of the Physiology of Consciousness*. Princeton University Press, 1975, pp. 5, 47, 62, 73, 75–77, 79–81.

25. New York: Doubleday, 1956.

26. Springfield, Illinois: C. C. Thomas, 1961. See also 1965 edition of Bernstein's book, pp. 241–77.

27. New York: Harper & Row, 1953, Chapter 18.

28. London: Hodder and Stoughton, 1963, introduction.

29. Ibid., pp. 178–80.

30. Quoted in Gustave Geley's *From the Unconscious to the Conscious*. New York: Harper, 1920, p. 324.

31. *Journal of the American Society for Psychical Research* (New York), April and July 1960. Published in booklet form by M. C. Peto, 4 Oakene, Burgh Heath, Tadworth, Surrey, England.

32. *The Ottawa Citizen*, October 1, 1966.

33. *National Enquirer*, December 17, 1967.

34. New York: American Society for Psychical Research, 1966, pp. 1–3, 351.

35. Naomi A. Hintze and J. Gaither Pratt, *The Psychic Realm: What Can You Believe?* New York: Random House, 1975. (Dr. Pratt's contribution to each chapter is an analysis of the phenomena related by Mrs. Hintze in the earlier part of the chapter.)

36. P. 243 (reported by Naomi Hintze).

37. British edition, Bristol: John Wright & Sons, 1974.

38. Our selections are taken from the series as it appeared in the New York *Daily News*, August 4 through August 8, 1974.

PSYCHOLOGISTS AND DOCTORS OF THE MIND

1. *The Will to Believe, and Human Immortality*. New York: Dover, 1956, pp. 17–18.

2. Ibid., pp. v–ix.

3. New York: Longmans, Green, 1925, pp. 522–23.

4. *Standard Edition of the Complete Psychological Works of Sigmund Freud*. London: Hogarth Press, 1957, XIV, pp. 289–95.

5. See Index under "Fingarette."

6. *Being-in-the-World*. Selected papers of Ludwig Binswanger, translated and edited by Jacob Needleman. New York: Basic Books, 1963, pp. 4, 183.

7. Translator, Stanley de Brath. New York: Harper, 1920, pp. 122–23, 225–26, 299.

8. New York: Pantheon, 1963, pp. 332–33.

9. Ibid., p. 299.

10. *The Secret of the Golden Flower* (A Chinese Book of Life), translator, Richard Wilhelm, with commentary by C. G. Jung. London: Kegan Paul, 1938, p. 124.

11. Miguel Serrano, *C. G. Jung and Hermann Hesse, A Record of Two Friendships*. New York: Schocken Books, 1966, p. 100.

12. *Collected Works*. New York: Pantheon, 1959, Vol. 9, Part I, *Archetypes and the Collective Unconscious,* pp. 113, 116–17.

13. Op. cit., p. 319.

14. Ibid., pp. 291, 318–19, 321–24.

15. Ibid., pp. 323–24.

16. Ibid., pp. 289–91, 297.

17. "I Died at 10:52 A.M." *Reader's Digest,* October 1974, pp. 178–82.

18. In another interview Dr. Ross said that this young man "gave me details of the accident scene that he couldn't possibly have physically seen—because he was trapped in his car." One such as " 'seeing' his amputated leg lying in the roadway." The doctor adds that "another patient who 'died' on the operating table" said she "watched the operation being conducted on her body . . . Though she'd been under total anesthesia, the woman later described a surgical error that needed correcting—and recounted to the surgeon large portions of his conversation during the time she was 'dead'." *National Enquirer,* June 15, 1976, p. 37.

19. Ibid.

20. Covington, Georgia: Mockingbird Books, 1975. Bantam paperback, 1976.

21. H. P. Blavatsky, *The Theosophical Glossary.* Los Angeles, Theosophy Company, 1973, under "Manas," "Manas Taijasi," and "Taijasi."

22. Pp. 21–23, 58–59 of Bantam edition.

23. Ibid., p. 26.

24. Ibid., pp. 141–42, 187.

25. New York: Norton, 1969, pp. 35–36.

26. New York: William Sloane, 1957, p. 3.

27. New York: William Sloane, 1950, pp. 102–3, 105. Also Signet paperback.

28. New York: William Sloane, 1957, pp. 199–200.

29. Ibid., pp. 136–37.

30. New York: Julian Press, 1963, pp. 48–53.

31. *Saddharmapundarika,* V, p. 70, in *Buddhist Texts,* E. Conze, New York: Philosophical Library, 1954, p. 125.

32. Ibid., V, 71, p. 125.

33. As we have seen, Hindu philosophy holds that at the root of these multiple selves is the Atman, the Higher Self—the witness and spectator, the Real I. "All things hang on me as precious gems upon a string" *(The Bhagavad-Gita)* (eds.).

34. A. K. Coomaraswamy, "Eastern Religions and Western Thought," *The Review of Religion,* 6 (1942), p. 137.

35. New York: Basic Books, 1963; Harper Torchbook, 1965. Pp. 105, 171–72, 178–82, 218, 231, 234, 236.

THE PHILOSOPHER LOOKS AT REBIRTH

1. Ananda Coomaraswamy, *The Dance of Siva.* New York: Sunwise Turn, Inc., 1924, p. 121

2. *The Philosophy of Nietzsche* (a collection of his writings). New York: Modern Library, 1954, p. 887.

3. New York: Crown Publishers, Inc., 1977, pp. viii, 76, 106. Dr. Peters provides

strong evidence that Nietzsche detested anti-Semitism and believed that
"all this talk about a pure German race was nonsense, utter nonsense.
Elisabeth was betraying him and his philosophy by embracing it" (p. 74).
Having consulted material never before available, Dr. Peters exposes the
whole extent of her forgeries and Machiavellian manipulations, and reveals
the enormous influence she exerted as high priestess of the "Nietzsche"
cult on the literary and political life of Germany from the time of Bismarck
to Hitler.

4. *The Philosophy of Nietzsche*, p. xxiv; another translation is given in this same
volume on p. 892.

5. *The Complete Works of Friedrich Nietzsche*, editor, Oscar Levy. New York:
Russell & Russell, 1964, XVI, notes 41, 60, 62.

6. *The Philosophy of Nietzsche*, pp. 244–48.

7. Ibid., pp. 256–60.

8. *Complete Works*, XVI, pp. 237–56.

9. Ibid., pp. 251–52, 254–56.

10. See Chapter 5 under "Aristotle" (eds.).

11. *Appearance*, 2nd edition, p. 502.

12. London: Macmillan, 1913, pp. 267–68.

13. Martensen, *Die Christliche Dogmatik*, 1856, section 275.

14. McTaggart, *Some Dogmas of Religion*, 1906, p. 126.

15. Cambridge University Press, 1911, pp. 402–5.

16. *Thus Spake Zarathustra*, translated by A. Tille.

17. Thomas Traherne, *Centuries of Meditation*, p. 3.

18. G. Lowes Dickinson, *Religion and Immortality*. Cambridge, Massachusetts:
Houghton Mifflin, 1911.

19. E. M. Forster, *Goldsworthy Lowes Dickinson*. London: Edward Arnold, 1934,
pp. 42–43. (New York: Harcourt Brace.)

20. "Mohini Chatterjee," *Collected Poems of W. B. Yeats*. New York: Macmillan,
1960, pp. 242–43.

21. *Proceedings of the British Academy*, 1927.

22. London: Edward Arnold, 1915, pp. 74, 81–82, 105–13.

23. G. Lowes Dickinson, *J. McT. E. McTaggart*. Cambridge: 1931, p. 37.

24. *Human Immortality and Pre-Existence*, pp. 73, 119.

25. G. Lowes Dickinson, *J. McT. E. McTaggart*, p. 128.

26. Ibid., pp. 4, 85–86.

27. *The Nature of Existence*. Cambridge University Press, 1927, II, pp. 396–97, 479.
Reissued in 1968 by Scholarly Press, Grosse Pointe, Michigan.

28. *Gandhi's Letters to a Disciple*. New York: Harper, 1950, pp. 31, 87, 89.

29. *Ahimsa:* harmlessness, nonviolence, universal compassion (eds.).

30. *Harijan*, March 1936.

31. *Young India*, April 2, 1931, p. 54.

32. *A Source Book of Indian Philosophy*, editors, S. Radhakrishnan and Charles
Moore. Princeton University Press, 1957, pp. 610–11.

33. Ibid.

34. *The Sacred Writings of the Sikhs*, translator, Trilochan Singh, et al. New York:
Macmillan, 1960. Introduction by S. Radhakrishnan.

35. London: Allen & Unwin, 1929, Chapter 3. Reprinted in *A Source Book in Indian Philosophy*, op. cit., pp. 634–36.

36. C. Humphreys, "Fifty Years." *The Middle Way*, August 1969, pp. 50–56.

37. C. Humphreys, "A Brief History of The Buddhist Society." *The Middle Way* (Golden Jubilee issue), November 1974, p. 9.

38. London: John Murray, 1943, pps. 34–37, 39–41, 55–56, 64, 69, 78–79, 102.

7. THE THEOSOPHICAL MOVEMENT AND THE REINCARNATION RENAISSANCE

1. 2nd. edition, 1873. Reprinted as *Religion in Primitive Culture*. New York: Harper & Row, 1958, pp. 88, 102–3. (Harper Torchbook.)

2. The Gallup Poll also indicated that large numbers of people instead of saying "I don't believe in reincarnation," merely had no opinion as to whether it was true or not. In the Netherlands, where the number of believers was only 10%, 35% had no opinion; in Great Britain 30%; in the United States 16%, and in Norway 29%.

3. H. P. Blavatsky labored in the United States for six years, and then removed to India, where the Theosophical Society set up headquarters. For an engrossing survey of the results achieved by the theosophists in India and neighboring Buddhist countries, see Blavatsky's article "Our Three Objects" in the September 1889 issue of *Lucifer*, the magazine she founded in London during her last years. The article also appears in the pamphlet "Theosophy and H.P.B.," one of a series published by the Theosophy Company in Los Angeles, containing her important editorials and articles.

4. *Gandhi's Autobiography: The Story of My Experiments with Truth*. Washington, D.C. Public Affairs Press, 1948, pp. 90–91, 321. (Beacon Press, Boston, paperback.)

5. P. 278. See also index under "Hume" in H. P. Blavatsky's *Collected Writings*, editor, de Zirkoff. Wheaton, Illinois: Theosophical Publishing House, 1968, III.

6. Louis Fischer, *The Life of Mahatma Gandhi*. New York: Harper, 1950, pp. 131–32.

7. Ibid., p. 437.

8. *Isis Unveiled*, II, p. 150, op. cit.

9. H. P. Blavatsky, "What Are the Theosophists?" *The Theosophist* (Bombay, India), October, 1879.

10. H. P. Blavatsky, *The Key to Theosophy*. Reprint of original 1889 edition, Theosophy Co. (Los Angeles), pp. 3, 5.

11. Ibid., appendix, p. 308.

12. Ibid., p. 250.

13. H. P. Blavatsky, "Thoughts on Karma and Reincarnation." *Lucifer*, April 1889, p. 94.

14. Op. cit., p. 270.

15. Pp. 231–32.

16. H. P. Blavatsky, "Our Three Objects." Cited in footnote 3 of this chapter.

17. New York: Harper & Row, 1975, pp. 117, 118, 121, 124.

18. Detailed studies of the "*Sun* Libel Case" and other aspects of theosophical history appear in *The Theosophical Movement 1875–1925* (New York: Dutton, 1925) and *The Theosophical Movement 1875–1950* (Los Angeles, California 91801: Cunningham Press, 1951). The latter is also available from Theosophy Co., Los Angeles, California 90007.
19. Reprinted in booklet "H. P. Blavatsky" by W. Q. Judge. Los Angeles: Theosophy Co., pp. 27–36.
20. August 1890. Reprinted in booklet, "Theosophy and the Theosophical Movement," articles by H. P. Blavatsky. Los Angeles: Theosophy Co., pp. 23–36.
21. *The Voice of the Silence,* op. cit., p. 69fn.
22. *Agnostic Journal and Eclectic Review,* May 16, 1891. Reprinted in *Lucifer,* June 1891, pp. 311–16, under the title "How an Agnostic Saw Her." Ross often wrote under the pen name of Saladin, as was the case in this memorial tribute.
23. Quoted in *Theosophy* (Los Angeles), October 1968, p. 384. See also H. P. Blavatsky's *Key to Theosophy,* pp. 273–76, 296–98. In the just-cited histories of the theosophical movement, the background of the Hodgson report—which involved the Christian missionaries in India, who plotted to oust the theosophists from that country—is discussed on pages 59–93 of the Dutton edition and pages 82–105 of the Cunningham Press edition. A close-up analysis of the gross inaccuracies in the Hodgson report will be found in Adlai E. Waterman's *Obituary: The Hodgson Report on Madame Blavatsky* (Adyar, Madras: Theosophical Publishing House, 1963).
24. Op. cit., pp. 297–98, 299, 301.
25. "Man Who Could Work Miracles," *Twenty-Eight Science Fiction Stories of H. G. Wells.* New York: Dover, 1942, p. 701.
26. Frances Steloff, "In Touch with Genius." *Journal of Modern Literature* (Temple University, Philadelphia), April 1975, p. 778.
27. *Lucifer* (London). February 1888, pp. 504–6. Reprinted with her other articles in booklet, "Theosophy and H.P.B." Los Angeles: Theosophy Co.
28. Nevertheless, it did have a wide appeal. In 1895 the number of branches in the United States totaled 102. (See list in *The Path,* May 1895, pp. 69–72.) In Europe and India combined there were an additional hundred lodges.
29. Letters of W. Q. Judge, *Letters That Have Helped Me.* Los Angeles: Theosophy Co., p. 20.
30. Los Angeles: Theosophy Co. Substantial selections from *The Ocean of Theosophy* appear later.
31. George F. Wright, "Incidents of T.S. Congress." *Path,* November 1893, pp. 239–45. Stenographic transcriptions of the talks were printed in a 195-page *Report of the Proceedings of the Theosophical Congress,* held on September 15, 16, 17, and published in 1893 by the American Section Headquarters T.S. in New York City.
32. Editorial in the *New York Daily Tribune,* May 9, 1891, reporting on an interview with W. Q. Judge, regarding the future effect of H. P. Blavatsky's death upon the Theosophical Society.
33. *Lucifer,* June 1891, p. 290.
34. P. G. Ouspensky, *Tertium Organum.* Rochester, New York: Manas Press, 1920, pp. 279, 300–301, 316.

35. *Aryan Path* (Bombay), December 1935, p. 722.
36. Ten reviews are quoted in *Lucifer*, May 1891, p. 242fn.
37. *Isis Unveiled*, II, p. 563.
38. *Isis Unveiled*. Los Angeles: Theosophy Co., 1968, publisher's preface, pp. iii–iv.
39. Letters of W. Q. Judge, published by the compilers as *Letters That Have Helped Me*. Los Angeles: Theosophy Co., 1946, p. 119.
40. Quoted in A. P. Sinnett's *Incidents in the Life of Madame Blavatsky*. New York: Bouton, 1886, pp. 39–40.
41. *Isis Unveiled*, I, pp. 179–80, op. cit.
42. *Key to Theosophy*, p. 191.
43. Matthew vii, 2.
44. Los Angeles: Theosophy Co., 1968 (reprint of original edition), I, pp. vi, 8–9, 12, 39, 114, 285, 345–46; II, pp. 264–65, 533–36, 540–45. The same pagination applies to the revised edition in the *Collected Writings of H. P. Blavatsky*, edited by Boris de Zirkoff, and which contains much background historical material on the writing of *Isis*. (Wheaton, Illinois: Theosophical Publishing House, 1972.)
45. This work has gone through forty editions, has been translated into twenty languages, and is still in print.
46. New York: Harper & Row, 1959, p. 211 (Harper Torchbook).
47. Article, "Our Three Objects," *Lucifer*, September 1889.
48. *The Theosophist* (Madras), August 1885, p. 279; condensed from the *Indian Mirror*.
49. Los Angeles: Theosophy Co.
50. Edmund Russell, "As I Knew Her." *Herald of the Star* (London), May-June 1916.
51. Los Angeles: Theosophy Co., p. 234.
52. *The Aryan Path* (Bombay), May 1937, pp. 201–3.
53. In a footnote in *The Secret Doctrine*, in which the author is explaining the concept of "Divine Thought," she writes: "It is hardly necessary to remind the reader once more that the term 'Divine Thought,' like that of 'Universal Mind,' must not be regarded as even vaguely shadowing forth an intellectual process akin to that exhibited by man. The 'Unconscious,' according to von Hartmann, arrived at the vast creative or rather Evolutionary Plan, 'by a clairvoyant wisdom superior to all consciousness,' which in the Vedantic language would mean absolute Wisdom. Only those who realise how far Intuition soars above the tardy processes of ratiocinative thought can form the faintest conception of that absolute Wisdom which transcends the ideas of Time and Space" (I, 1fn.) (eds.).
54. *Lucifer*, October and November 1890. Reprinted in booklet, *Theosophical Psychology*, as one of four articles by H. P. Blavatsky. Los Angeles: Theosophy Co., pp. 22–23, 27.
55. John Eglinton, *A Memoir of AE*. London: Macmillan, 1937, pp. 164–65. Eglinton by profession was a medical doctor, but as a writer he was Ireland's leading essayist.
55ᵃ. Nicolas Camille Flammarion (1842–1925). Article "The Mysterious Madame Blavatsky," by Kurt Vonnegut, Jr., *McCall's*, March, 1970, p. 142.

56. *The Journal of San Diego History* (San Diego Historical Society), Summer 1974, p. 16. In checking the source of this information we learned that a niece of Einstein, when in India during the 1960s, paid a special visit to the headquarters of the Theosophical Society at Adyar, Madras. She explained that she knew nothing of theosophy or the society, but *had* to see the place because her uncle always had a copy of Madame Blavatsky's *Secret Doctrine* on his desk! The individual to whom the niece spoke was Eunice Layton, a world traveled theosophical lecturer who happened to be at the reception desk when the visitor arrived. (As Dr. Strömberg was a good friend of Einstein, it may be that the latter acquired *The Secret Doctrine* through him. It will be recalled that in our item in chapter 6 on Strömberg we quoted Einstein's praise of this Swedish scientist's volume *The Soul of the Universe.* Strömberg was connected with the old Point Loma theosophical society in San Diego, California.)

57. I, pp. 611–12.

58. *Science,* January 8, 1937.

59. I, pp. 519–20.

60. *Science,* March 19, 1976.

61. Mark 4:11, 33–34; Matthew 13:35.

62. "The Synthesis of Occult Science." *The Path,* May 1892, p. 45. Reprinted in booklet, *Occult Philosophy,* articles by W. Q. Judge. Los Angeles, Theosophy Co.

63. The "first" presupposes necessarily something that is the "first brought forth," "the first in time, space, and rank"—and therefore finite and conditioned. The "first" *cannot be the absolute,* for it is a manifestation. Therefore, Eastern occultism calls the Abstract All the "Causeless One Cause," the "Rootless Root," and limits the "First Cause" to the *Logos,* in the sense that Plato gives to this term. (H.P.B.)

64. "The invisible region that surrounds [and interpenetrates] our globe, as it does every other, and corresponding . . . to the Astral Double in man. A subtle Essence visible only to a clairvoyant eye, and the lowest but one . . . of the Seven Akasic or Kosmic principles. . . . The designation *astral* is ancient, and was used by some of the Neoplatonists" (H. P. Blavatsky, *Theosophical Glossary.* Los Angeles: Theosophy Co., 1973, under "Astral Light").

65. *Conflict between Religion and Science*—Draper, pp. 132, 133.

66. "Symbols of Eternal Life." *Harvard Divinity Bulletin,* April 1962.

67. Op. cit., p. 219.

68. Quoted in *The Friendly Philosopher* by Robert Crosbie. Los Angeles: Theosophy Co., 1945, p. 98.

69. Los Angeles: Theosophy Co., p. 148.

70. Answering an inquirer, H. P. B. wrote in *The Theosophist* (January 1886): I do not "believe in an individual, segregated spirit in me, as a something apart from the whole. . . . [Yet] I maintain as an occultist, on the authority of the Secret Doctrine, that though merged entirely into Parabrahm, man's spirit while not individual *per se,* yet preserves its distinct individuality in Paranirvana, owing to the accumulation in it of the aggregates, or *skandhas* that have survived after each death, from the highest faculties of the Manas [or Mind]. The most

spiritual, i.e. the highest and divinest aspirations of every personality . . . become part and parcel of the Monad [and are] preserved to the end of
the great cycle *(Maha-Manvantara)* when each Ego enters Paranirvana, or is
merged in Parabrahm. To our talpatic, or mole-like comprehension the human
spirit is then lost in the One Spirit, as the drop of water thrown into the sea can
no longer be traced out and recovered. But *de facto* it is not so in the world of
immaterial thought. . . . That such Parabrahmic and Paranirvanic 'spirits,'
or units, have and must preserve their divine (not human) individualities, is
shown in the fact that, however long the 'night of Brahma' or even the Universal Pralaya . . . yet, when it ends, the same individual Divine Monad resumes
its majestic path of evolution . . . and brings with it all the essence of compound spiritualities from its previous countless rebirths" (eds.).

71. The magnetic pull that has drawn and continues to draw so many millions to the
shores of North America—from Europe and the Middle East, and now from
Asia—is inexplicable to many sociologists. The pioneers that first came to this
country were not lured by the promise of riches and an easy life; their toil often
bordered on martyrdom. Utilitarian reasons are simply not sufficient to explain
the phenomenon, or the great American Dream. Recently Khoshwant Singh,
editor of the *Illustrated Weekly of India* (Bombay), wrote in a guest editorial in
the New York *Daily News* (December 8, 1975): "Although making derogatory
remarks about Americans has long been fashionable, no one has yet explained
the fact that, of all the countries in the world, the most sought-after by the
politically or racially persecuted, by the poor, the frustrated, and the ambitious,
by specialists in every branch of medicine, science, and technology—is the
United States of America" (eds.).

72. H. P. Blavatsky, *The Secret Doctrine*. Los Angeles: Theosophy Co. (photographic reprint of original 1888 edition), I, pp. 13–17, 20, 48fn, 53–54, 104,
207–8, 238, 266, 272–73, 277, 297–98, 477–78, 639, 643–45; II, pp. 80, 281–82,
304–6, 348, 358–59, 424, 444–46, 475, 513.

73. The main title is *The Tell-Tale Picture Gallery*. Bombay: International Book
House. Available at Theosophy Co., Los Angeles.

74. "Cycles and Human Destiny." Los Angeles: Theosophy Co.

75. *Lucifer*, June 1890. Reprinted in a booklet of her articles, " 'Magic' in Modern
Science." (Los Angeles: Theosophy Co.)

76. From the 1960s onwards books on witchcraft and sorcery have been selling at a
furious pace. Even high-school students are avidly studying these subjects and
carrying on experiments (eds.).

77. As is now known—and there are a number of books on the subject—Hitler and his
leading Nazis studied black magic and used the knowledge in carrying out the
policies of the Third Reich (eds.).

78. H. P. Blavatsky, *Collected Writings*, editor, de Zirkoff. Adyar, Madras, India:
Theosophical Publishing House, 1960, VIII, pp. 402, 404–9.

79. Quoted in "Biographical Notes" at the conclusion of the volume of W. Q. Judge's
letters, entitled by its compilers *Letters That Have Helped Me*, op. cit.,
pp. 276–78. See also pp. 279–83 for other letters of H.P.B.'s on the status of
Mr. Judge, as well as letters 1 and 5 in the booklet "Five Messages from

H. P. Blavatsky to the American Theosophists in Convention Assembled" (Los Angeles: Theosophy Co.). Letter 5, dated April 15, 1891, was written 23 days before her death on May 8th, and is entirely devoted to the work of Mr. Judge in America, because, as she states "he has proved in a thousand ways his entire loyalty to the best interests of Theosophy and the Society." "Mutual admiration," she adds, "should play no part in a theosophical convention, but honor should be given where honor is due."

80. *Key to Theosophy*, p. 100.

81. *Atma* is not regarded as an *individual* principle, but rather the universal, changeless, Self. It is the "Unborn, Unoriginated, Uncreated, Unformed," of which we have seen the Buddha spoke, as did his Hindu predecessors. It is the Christos of the Gnostics, and other early Christians, according to H.P.B. (*The Secret Doctrine*, II, p. 231fn.). In *The Key to Theosophy*, she describes the Higher Triad in this way: "I. *Atma*, the '*Higher Self*,' is neither your Spirit nor mine, but like sunlight shines on all. It is the universally diffused '*divine principle*' . . . II. *Buddhi* (the spiritual soul) is only its vehicle. Neither each separately, nor the two collectively, are of any more use to the body of man, than sunlight and its beams are for a mass of granite buried in the earth, *unless the divine Duad is assimilated by, and reflected in, some consciousness*. . . . This consciousness or mind is, III. *Manas* . . . the real Individuality . . . which having originally incarnated in the *senseless* human form . . . made of that human-like form *a real man*. It is that Ego, that 'Causal Body,' which overshadows every personality Karma forces it to incarnate into . . . the evanescent masks which hide the true Individual through the long series of rebirths" (Pp. 135–36).

82. *The Key to Theosophy*, pp. 93–94.

83. *Isis Unveiled*, I, p. 351.

84. The term "heaven" is used by theosophists as a state of consciousness, not as a place "up there" (eds.).

85. Devachan is a Tibetan word meaning the state of the gods or devas—a heavenly condition. "Deva" is of Sanskrit origin and literally means the shining one, from the root *div*, to shine (eds.).

86. In a series of lectures delivered at the University of California (Los Angeles) by Dr. Demetrio Sodi-Pullares, a heart specialist, he said: "Human hearts continue to be alive, electrically, *for seven hours* after the patient is declared by doctors to be dead. . . . Cardiograms prove that . . . the heart continues to send out electric currents for several hours" (Los Angeles *Times*, August 6, 1953). It may be significant that rigor mortis sets in only at the eighth hour (eds.).

87. *The Theosophist* (Adyar, Madras), May 1883, p. 202.

88. *The Key to Theosophy*, op. cit., p. 150.

89. *The Light of Asia*, by Edwin Arnold. Book eighth.

90. Quoted in *The Heart Doctrine* (a collection of articles by W. Q. Judge). Los Angeles and Bombay: The Theosophy Co., 1951, p. 127.

91. *Path*, March 1891, p. 383.

92. Theosophy does not teach that man originally arrived here by mechanical means

such as rocket ships. The arrival is said to be by means of incarnation in the forms that have been evolved here. The details on this may be found in *The Secret Doctrine* (eds.).

93. The expression Heavenly Man is one that the Hebrew Kabalists use when referring to Adam Kadmon, the archetypal man, the ideal pattern and model existent in the spiritual world (eds.).

94. W. Q. Judge *The Ocean of Theosophy*. Los Angeles: Theosophy Co., chapters 1, 4–15.

95. Even a hundred years ago, and after centuries of foreign domination in India, the British census of 1881 revealed the rate of criminality in that country as only 1 in 3,787 Buddhists, and 1 in 1,361 Hindus, as against 1 in 274 Europeans residing there (eds.).

96. Op. cit., pp. 43, 233, 245–46.

Acknowledgments

The editors express deep appreciation to the associates, friends, and research assistants, who helped in the preparation of this volume and its predecessors; and to those who translated excerpts from books and periodicals that have not hitherto been published in English. Grateful thanks are also extended to the following authors, publishers, and/or copyright holders for granting permission to quote from the works indicated:

Abingdon-Cokesbury Press, Nashville, Tenn. *The Christian Agnostic* by Leslie Weatherhead.

Allen & Unwin, Ltd., London. *The Art of Creation* by Edward Carpenter; *Pre-Existence and Reincarnation* by W. Lutoslawski; *Thus Spake Zarathustra* by Friedrich Nietzsche, trans. Thomas Common: *The Hibbert Journal*, "Varieties of Belief in Reincarnation" by E. G. Parrinder; *An Idealist View of Life* by S. Radhakrishnan; *Rumi, Poet and Mystic*, trans. R. A. Nicholson; *Buddhist Wisdom Books* by Edward Conze (confirmed by Harper & Row, New York).

American Society for Psychical Research, Inc., New York, and Ian Stevenson. "The Evidence for Survival from Claimed Memories of Former Incarnations," and *Twenty Cases Suggestive of Reincarnation*, by Ian Stevenson.

Edward Arnold (Publishers) Ltd., London. *From Religion to Philosophy* by Francis M. Cornford; *The Human Situation* by W. Macneile Dixon; *Human Immortality and Pre-Existence* by J. E. McTaggart.

The Aryan Path, Bombay, India. Extracts from a number of articles.

Beacon Press, Boston. *Indian Thought and Its Development* by Albert Schweitzer; *Socrates, the Man and His Thought* by A. E. Taylor.

Blaisdell Publishing Company, a division of Ginn and Company, Waltham, Mass. *Classic Myths in English Literature and Art* by Charles Mills Gayley.

Bollingen Foundation, Inc. and Pantheon Books. *The Hero with a Thousand Faces* by Joseph Campbell; *The Myth of the Eternal Return* by Mircea Eliade; *Collected Works of C. G. Jung*, Vol. 9, Pt. I, *The Archetypes and the Collective Unconscious*; Vol. II, *Psychology and Religion: West and East*.

Albert & Charles Boni, Inc., New York. *Prophets of the New India* by Romain Rolland.

Ellen Bosanquet. *Value and Destiny of the Individual* by Bernard Bosanquet.

George Braziller, Inc., New York. *The Wisdom of the Serpent* by Joseph L. Henderson and Maud Oakes.

The Buddhist Society, London. *The Essence of Buddhism* by D. T. Suzuki; *The Sutra of Hui Neng*, trans. Wong Moulam; and extracts from four articles in *The Middle Way*.

Cambridge University Press. *Examination of McTaggart's Philosophy* by C. D. Broad; *The Road to Hel* by H. R. Ellis; *The Nature of Existence* by J. E. McTaggart; *Realm of Ends* by James Ward; *The Neoplatonists* by Thomas Whittaker.

Chatto & Windus, London. *Shakespeare and Platonic Beauty* by John Vyvan.

Cunningham Press, Alhambra, California. *The Dhammapada; Selections from the Upanishads and the Tao Te King*.

Diogenes, Chicago University Press. "The Gnostic Manuscripts of Upper Egypt" by Eva Meyerovitch. Permission granted by successor publisher, Revue International des Sciences Humaines, Paris.

E. P. Dutton & Co., New York. *Seven Years in Tibet* by Heinrich Harrer; *The Life of Mazzini* by Bolton King; *Leibniz' Philosophical Writings,* trans. Mary Morris; Lucretius' *The Nature of Things,* trans. W. E. Leonard.

Faber & Faber, London, and Alfred A. Knopf, New York. *James Joyce's Ulysses* by Stuart Gilbert.

Sigmund Freud Copyrights Ltd., Mr. James Strachey, and The Hogarth Press Ltd. *The Complete Psychological Works of Sigmund Freud,* Vol. 14, "Thoughts for the Times on War and Death."

Garrett Publications, New York. *Collected Papers on the Paranormal* by Theodore Besterman.

Victor Gollancz, Ltd., London. *Lord Riddell's Intimate Diary of the Peace Conference and After* (confirmed by Harcourt, Brace & World, New York).

Solomon R. Guggenheim Foundation, New York, and Professor Robert Welsh. Article "Mondrian and Theosophy" by Robert Welsh, in *Piet Mondrian Centennial Exhibition.*

Dr. Arthur Guirdham. Lecture "Reincarnation and the Practice of Medicine"; *The Cathars and Reincarnation* by Arthur Guirdham (confirmed by Neville Spearman, Ltd., London).

Harcourt, Brace, Jovanovich, Inc., New York. "The Waste Land" in *Collected Poems 1909–1962* by T. S. Eliot. Copyright 1936 by Harcourt, Brace, Jovanovich, copyright 1964 by T. S. Eliot; *Travel Diary of a Philosopher* by Hermann Keyserling.

Harvard Divinity Bulletin, Cambridge, Massachusetts. "Symbols of Eternal Life" by Paul Tillich.

Harvard University Press, Cambridge, Massachusetts. *The Dawn of Philosophy* by George Misch; *Metempsychosis* by G. F. Moore; *The Odes of Pindar,* trans. Sir John Sandys.

William Heinemann Ltd., London. *I Have Been Here Before* by J. B. Priestley, reprinted by permission of A. D. Peters & Co.

Hodder & Stoughton Limited, London. *The Light and the Gate,* and *A Religious Outlook for Modern Man,* by Raynor C. Johnson.

Holt, Rinehart and Winston, New York. *Anthony Adverse* and *Bedford Village* by Hervey Allen; *The Forgotten Language* by Erich Fromm; *Complete Poems of Robert Frost.* Copyright, 1916, 1947 by Holt, Rinehart and Winston, Inc., Copyright, 1944, by Robert Frost; *Magister Ludi* by Hermann Hesse, trans. Richard and Clara Winston; *Magister Ludi* by Hermann Hesse, trans. Mervyn Savill, published by Frederick Ungar, New York, copyright by Holt, Rinehart and Winston; *There Is a River* by Thomas Sugrue, copyright 1942 by Holt, Rinehart and Winston.

Horizon Press, New York. *T. H. Huxley* by Cyril Bibby, copyright 1959.

Houghton Mifflin Company, Boston. *The Soul of the Indian* by Charles Eastman; *Religion and Immortality* by G. Lowes Dickinson.

Hutchinson Publishing Group Limited. *The Japanese Cult of Tranquility* by Karlfried von Durkheim.

Julian Press, New York. *The Symbolic and the Real* by Ira Progoff.

Philip Kapleau. *The Three Pillars of Zen* by Philip Kapleau.

Alfred A. Knopf, Inc., New York. *The Uses of Enchantment* by Bruno Bettelheim; *Ireland's Literary Renaissance* by Ernest Boyd; *Merely Players* by Claude Bragdon; *The Prophet* by Kahlil Gibran, copyright 1923 by Kahlil Gibran, renewal copyright 1951 by Administrators C.T.A. of Kahlil Gibran Estate and Mary G. Gibran.

Liveright Publishing Corporation, New York. *The Dybbuk* by S. Ansky, trans. Henry G. Alsberg and Winifred Katzin.

Longmans, Green, London. *The Philosophy of Plotinus,* and *The Platonic Tradition in English Religious Thought* by W. R. Inge.

David McKay, New York. *The Searchers* and *The Soul of the Universe* by Gustaf Strömberg.

Macmillan & Co., Ltd., London. *Northern Tribes of Central Australia* by Spencer and Gillen.

Dr. W. H. Magee (John Eglinton). *A Memoir of AE* by John Eglinton.

MD Publications, New York. *Centaur, Essays on the History of Medical Ideas* by Félix Martí-Ibáñez.

Mockingbird Books, Inc., Covington, Georgia. *Life After Life* by Raymond Moody, Jr.

John Murray, London. *Jataka Tales,* retold by Ethel Beswick; *Musings of a Chinese Mystic,* ed. Lionel Giles; *Karma and Rebirth* by Christmas Humphreys.

National Enquirer, Lantana, Florida. Article, "Woman Claims She Was Burned at the Stake 700 Years Ago."

New Directions, New York. *Siddhartha* by Hermann Hesse, trans. Hilda Rosner. Copyright, 1951, by New Directions.

New York Times Magazine, "Tragic Decline of the Humane Ideal" by André Maurois.

The News, New York. Extracts from series of articles on reincarnation by Alton Slagle (August 4–August 8, 1974).

Open Court Publishing Company, La Salle, Illinois. *Nature, Mind, and Death* by C. J. Ducasse (confirmed by Dr. Ducasse); "The Religion of the Spirit and the World's Need," by S. Radhakrishnan, from *The Philosophy of Sarvepalli Radhakrishnan.*

Oxford University Press. *Tibet, Past and Present* by Charles Bell; *Aristotle: Fundamentals of the History of His Development* by Werner Jaeger; *Elements of Proclus,* trans. E. R. Dodds; *The Lotus of the Wonderful Law,* trans. W. E. Soothill; *Some Sayings of the Buddha,* trans. F. L. Woodward.

Pali Text Society, London. *The Path of Purity,* trans. Pe Maung Tin.

People Magazine, New York. Interview with Dr. Elisabeth Kübler-Ross, November 24, 1975. Permission granted by Dr. Ross.

Philosophical Library, New York. *The Philosophy of Poetry* by Henri Bergson; *Diary and Sundry Observations of Thomas Alva Edison; The Splendour That Was Egypt* by Margaret A. Murray.

Thomas Powers, article, "Learning to Die," *Harper's,* June 1971.

G. P. Putnam's Sons, New York. *The Nazarene* by Sholem Asch. Copyright, 1939, by Sholem Asch; *The Century of the Renaissance in France* by Louis Batiffol; *Zones of the Spirit* by August Strindberg. Copyright, 1913, by G. P. Putnam's Sons; *Goethe* by Emil Ludwig. Copyright, 1928, by G. P. Putnam's Sons; *Life of Apollonius of Tyana* by Philostratus, trans. F. C. Conybeare.

Dr. J. B. Rhine. "Did You Live Before? from *The American Weekly.*

Routledge & Kegan Paul Ltd., London. *Giordano Bruno, His Life, Thought and Martyrdom* by William Boulting; *The Life of Paracelsus* by Franz Hartmann; *The World as Will and Idea* by Arthur Schopenhauer, trans. Haldane and Kemp; *The Secret of the Golden Flower* by Richard Wilhelm.

Russell & Russell, New York. "Eternal Recurrence," from Vol. 16 of the *Complete Works of Friedrich Nietzsche*.

St. Louis Art Museum, Missouri. *Modern Thought and Catholicism* by Paul Gauguin, trans. Frank Lester Pleadwell.

Saturday Review, New York. "Walt Whitman's Buried Masterpiece" by Malcolm Cowley.

SCM Press, London. *Teenage Religion* by Harold Loukes.

Julia M. Seton. *The Gospel of the Red Man* by Ernest Thompson Seton and Julia M. Seton.

G. Bernard Shaw, The Public Trustee of, and The Society of Authors, London. *Saint Joan*, and *Back to Methuselah* by G. Bernard Shaw.

Irving Shepard, Jack London Ranch, Glen Ellen, California. *The Star Rover* by Jack London.

Sunrise, Pasadena, California. "The Transcendentalists on Reincarnation."

Theosophical Publishing House, Adyar, Madras. *Reincarnation in Islam* by N. K. Mirza; *Buddhist Stories*, trans. F. L. Woodward.

Theosophical Publishing House, Wheaton, Illinois. *The Opening of the Wisdom-Eye* by the Dalai Lama.

Theosophy Company, 245 West 33rd Street, Los Angeles, California 90007. *The Key to Theosophy, Isis Unveiled, The Secret Doctrine, The Voice of the Silence*, by H. P. Blavatsky; *The Ocean of Theosophy* by W. Q. Judge; *The Bhagavad-Gita*, trans. W. Q. Judge; *The Eternal Verities*.

Theosophy in Pakistan. Series, "Reincarnation, Islamic Conceptions," by M. H. Abdi.

University Books, New York. *The Candle of Vision* by George W. Russell.

University of Michigan Press, Ann Arbor, Michigan. *Lessing and the Enlightenment* by Henry E. Allison.

Vedanta Society of Southern California. *The Bhagavad-Gita*, trans. Prabhavananda and Isherwood.

The Viking Press, New York. *The Masks of God: Oriental Mythology* by Joseph Campbell; *The River* by Rumer Godden; *A Prison, a Paradise* by Loren Hurnscot; *The Lives of a Cell* by Lewis Thomas.

John M. Watkins, London. *Fragments of a Faith Forgotten* and *The Thrice Great Hermes*, by G. R. S. Mead; *Pistis Sophia*, trans. G. R. S. Mead; *The Masonic Initiation* by W. L. Wilmshurst.

Leslie D. Weatherhead, and M. C. Peto, England. "The Case for Reincarnation," by Leslie D. Weatherhead.

The Yale Review, New Haven, Connecticut. "Belief in a Future Life" by J. Paul Williams.

Yale University Press, New Haven Connecticut. *After Life in Roman Paganism* by Franz Cumont.

Index

The main subject headings used in the Index will be found listed on the last page of this book. Where there are many page references for an individual or a topic, the main entry—if there is one—will be listed first, and the remaining entries in numerical order.

Headings in Index

The main subject headings used in the Index in relation to reincarnation are listed here for ready reference and to facilitate research.